THE NEW JEWISH
ENCYCLOPEDIA

THE NEW ENCYCLO

EDITED BY

IN ASSOCIATION WITH

WITH A FOREWORD BY

ART EDITOR

CONSULTING EDITORS

WITH ORIGINAL PHOTOGRAPHS BY

JEWISH PEDIA ✦

DAVID BRIDGER PH.D.

SAMUEL WOLK RABBI, J.S.D.

HIS EXCELLENCY ABBA EBAN

STEPHEN KAYSER PH.D.

HAROLD HAYES & ABRAHAM ROTHBERG PH.D.

ANN ZANE SHANKS & MARVIN KONER

BEHRMAN HOUSE, INC. PUBLISHERS, NEW YORK

FOREWORD

ABBA EBAN: THE JEWISH HERITAGE

Thirty-five hundred years ago a small people in a corner of the East Mediterranean evolved ideas of startling depth and originality which have stirred the minds of men in all succeeding generations. From the moment that the Hebrew nation comes within its view, history is face to face with a people of intensive genius touched by a lofty vision of human destiny. The influence of Judaism on the life and thought of mankind bears no relation to the numbers of its adherents or to their achievement in any domain of temporal power. In these terms the Jewish people has always been small and weak. Its vocation has rather been to develop and preserve an intense vitality of spirit. Religion, philosophy, literature, science, political systems and moral ideas have all been profoundly agitated by the currents of the Jewish mind.

The universal scope of this influence becomes the more remarkable when we reflect how little was ever done to force it on other peoples. Judaism was never carried across oceans and continents by conquering potentates bent on converting the "infidel" to an exclusive concept of truth. It was the faith of a single close-knit people which was content to diffuse its values by example, rather than by active proselytism. Jewish ideas were first to be expressed and vindicated within the life of the nation which gave them birth. Thereafter they were offered to humanity— not imposed upon it.

It is thus not surprising that the contemporary world had little premonition of the place which the Hebrew nation would come to occupy in subsequent history. Of all the peoples in the Mediterranean region and its eastern hinterland Israel seemed the least likely to leave an enduring mark. The empires of Egypt and Babylon, Assyria and Persia, Greece and Rome were all endowed at their zenith with a mystery and splendor beyond the emulation of the struggling pastoral kingdom in the Judean hills. One after the other they overshadowed Israel in territory and population, in military strength, in economic power and in the sophistication and refinement of their arts. The surviving literature of these empires reveals no great preoccupation with the strange, aloof and obdurately individualistic neighbor which seemed to live on the outer margin of contemporary issues and events. Whatever we know of Hebrew origins is derived from the testimony which the Jewish people has recorded about itself.

In this record we see it progressing from one insight to another, scrutinizing its own experience in an ardent quest for the meaning and purpose of life. And at every turn of its fate we find it asking the great and searching question about man and his place in the scheme of nature. "When I look at Thy heavens, the work of Thy fingers, the moon and stars which Thou hast established—what is man that Thou art mindful of him, and the son of man that Thou dost care for him? Yet Thou hast made him little less than God and dost crown him with glory and honor."

In such words and in other rhapsodic outbursts of reverent wonder the Jews gave their chief legacy to humanism—the doctrine of man's immense and incomparable dignity.

Any western man writing about Hebrew ideas is himself an integral part of what he is trying to describe. Concepts of Jewish origin are so organic to modern thought that they are often taken as axiomatic, and their revolutionary character is lost from view. Yet the dominant feature of Hebraism is its distinctiveness. It is true that Judaism was not born in a vacuum. Assiduous scholarship can trace influences or parallels in Egyptian, Sumerian, Hittite and Canaanite culture. But when all these are sifted and weighed, the inescapable impression of Judaism is one of departure and revolt, not of continuity. In the history of ideas Judaism draws a line dividing the past from the future in a sharp and radical transformation.

Jewish history portrays the experience of a people in a continuous narrative of over three thousand years. The experience in antiquity is well documented and preserved, articulate and coherent in every stage, and drawing substantive confirmation from the recent discoveries of archeology. It is primarily a literary heritage. There is scarcely any direct impact of ancient Israel on cultural patterns through creativity in sculpture, painting, architecture or other plastic forms. The influence is in two domains. First, there is a moral law within a unique view of history. Second, there is a body of splendid and passionate writing revered over the centuries by more people than have ever come under the spell of any other literature.

The revolt of Judaism against current ideas can be marked in three realms of experience. First comes the doctrine of moral choice. The pre-Jewish civilizations were gripped by religions of fatalism and resignation. Not even Aristotle could rise above the concept of human life as tied to a wheel revolving in its own fixed orbit and coming back to a starting point in darkness and chaos. By identifying their gods with nature these faiths condemned their deities to a law of cyclical repetition which denies any possibility of substantive progress. Only when involved in Greek thought, as in the *Book of Ecclesiastes*, does the Hebrew mind allow this pessimism. "What has been is what will be; and what has been done is what will be done; and there is nothing new under the sun. . . . That which is crooked cannot be put straight." But the true and more dominant theme of Judaism is man's mastery of his world through the divinely given capacity to "*choose the good and reject the evil.*" Clothed with this choice the human being becomes endowed with a new power and dignity setting him apart from the rest of nature.

The moral choice does not operate only in the realm of individual conscience. It has a social implication as well. The societies which preceded the Jewish kingdoms were dominated by permissible exploitation. Man was helpless against the adverse forces of nature and his own innate cruelty and egotism. Against the doctrine of social resignation there arose the Hebrew ideal of social justice. "*Thou shalt love thy neighbor as thyself.*" From this notion of solidarity in human relations came the concept of a moral law applicable to societies as well as to individuals. The Mosaic precepts became the predecessor of all legal systems in history which have ever surrounded the individual with safeguards of compassion and law. The woman, the child, the slave, the old and infirm, even the young man called to arms on the morrow of his marriage, are the objects of tender legislative foresight.

Spreading out into its third circle of influence the Hebrew ideal attacked the prevailing concept of war as a natural state of the universe— a part of man's essential nature. Twenty-five centuries ago the Hebrew prophet proclaimed the doctrine of universal peace. "*Nation shall not lift up the sword against nation, neither shall they learn war any more.*"

These were the triple foundations of the Hebrew ideal: individual morality, social justice, universal peace. Believing themselves to be the responsible custodians of these ideals the Jews maintained their integrity and union even in conditions of dispersion and exile. Their moral teaching was part of a forward-looking view of history, of which the most vivid expression was the messianic idea. Other peoples have dreamed of a golden age in which the conflict between security and freedom is transcended. But all pre-Jewish civilizations placed their golden age in the past, at the beginning of history. Judaism alone saw the era of perfection as lying in the future, at the "end of days," so that all history appeared to unfold in progress toward ascending goals. This belief in the positive direction of human history was stubbornly upheld even though the national experience would have justified a more somber view. Collective and individual suffering attends the Hebrew people at every stage. With its lands devastated, its Temple destroyed, its people dispersed and its faith savagely persecuted, ancient Israel ends its national career. The long night of exile closes in around it. In the ensuing centuries many torments lie ahead; and these are destined to reach a climax of hideous agony in the massacre of European Jewry in the twentieth century. But throughout the generations the heritage of Jewish thought wins one victory after another. Judaism nourishes the great rivers of Christianity and Islam while keeping its own native waters perenially fresh. And shining forth above all triumphs is the victory first of survival, and then of renewal. Nineteen centuries after what had seemed to be the final eclipse of nationhood the Jewish people, reunited with the land and language of its original inheritance, enters upon a new birth of life and freedom.

The gift of Judaism to history lies in the power and depth of its ideas. But these, in their turn, are incarnate in the body of an earthly people. The transmission of the Hebrew legacy works not through abstract disputation but through the illustrative effect of national history. For centuries the culture of nations has been dominated by a gallery of Hebrew persons and events. Moses the lawgiver; Joshua the conqueror; Saul, David, Solomon, the monarchs of Israel's brief temporal glory; Amos the prophet of social justice; Isaiah the preacher of universal peace; Jeremiah, at once the goad and comforter of his people; Ezekiel in distant Babylon brooding on the mysteries of regeneration; Nehemiah the warrior priest; the Maccabees and Bar Kokhba, poignant in hopeless revolt— all these have been the theme of art and story, music and writing in countless lands and generations. Jesus and Paul spring from the deepest soil of Jewish history; and the Church is born out of Israel's loins.

The flight of Hebrew slaves across the Red Sea in search of freedom inspired and consoled all subsequent movements of liberation in the eighteenth and nineteenth centuries. The Exodus is the original prototype of national revolt. In the Middle Ages Judaism affects the human scene through its daughters Christianity and Islam. But the parent, too, lives on within its original and authentic scheme of life, the great nonconformist of all the ages. There are by now two streams of cultural influence. The one flows in specifically Jewish channels through the Rabbinic tradition, the Spanish-Hebrew literature, and the Yiddish and

Modern Hebrew movements of modern times. The other is the stream of indirect influence through the impact of Jewish ideas and Jewish minds on general civilization.

It is, of course, easier to place Maimonides and Judah Ha-Levi, Saadiah Gaon and Bialik within the Jewish heritage than to attribute Einstein and Freud to a Jewish culture. But there is surely something Hebraic in the concentration of Jewish minds in every age on the fundamental questions of purpose and order in the pattern of nature and the life of men. The preponderance of Jews in movements of political liberalism and in nuclear physics cannot be entirely divorced from attitudes of mind at work for centuries in pursuit of social progress, or in quest of the unifying explanation of material phenomena. Some writers have professed to see a contradiction between the particularist and the universal element in Judaism. In his *A Study of History*, British historian Arnold Toynbee is dogmatically certain that it is impossible to fulfill a universal mission while conserving a separate ethos within an exclusive family group. "Judaism cannot fulfill its destiny of becoming a universal religion unless and until the Jews renounce the national form of their distinctive communal identity for the sake of fulfilling their universal religious mission." Whether such a thing can or "cannot" be done—this is precisely what Judaism has in fact achieved. A robust sense of national identity has not prevented this people from sending the repercussions of its influence far and wide into the ocean of universal history. It is probable that a surrender of its "distinctive communal identity" would have involved the eclipse of its cherished values and of its universal mission.

A moral heritage operates far beyond the confines of formal religion. The history of political ideas is heavily crowded with Hebrew memories and associations. Egalitarian ideals reached Europe and America through educational processes based on the Bible. Milton Konvitz, a modern American writer, has accurately said: "It may be possible to arrive at the philosophy of equality within the framework of secular thought, as in the systems of John Dewey and Bertrand Russell and in socialist Marxism. Within the framework of a religious system, however, it is probably impossible to arrive at the philosophy of equality in the absence of a belief in ethical monotheism."

A similar impact of Jewish ideas and forms can be traced in literary development. English and European writers have regarded ancient Hebrew literature both as a source of moral philosophy and as a literary model ranking in esthetic harmony with the Greek and Roman classics.

FOREWORD

The sum of the matter is that millions of men in many lands and generations have been deeply influenced by the Hebrew legacy even when
they have thought themselves to be outside it, or in conflict with it.

Perhaps the most significant thing about the Jewish heritage today is the
presence of an heir to receive it. The corporate survival of the Jewish
community depends on the development of Israel and of free diaspora
groups in America and Europe. Jewish thought is bound to be influenced
by the traumatic experience of the Nazi holocaust. Never in history has
any people borne the memory of six million kinsmen including a million
children methodically herded together, stripped, shorn of hair, crowded
into gas chambers for mass asphyxiation, deprived of gold tooth-fillings,
burnt in crematoria and scattered as dust to the winds of heaven—all
without the slightest sense of purpose or advantage except the satisfaction
of a perverse Germanic lust. Insofar as the object of these horrors was to
extinguish the Jewish heritage, this purpose at least has been frustrated.
Jewish history in this generation is dominated by a fantastic transition
from tragedy to consolation—from the European slaughter-house to the
position of a sovereign State established within the international family.

It is too early to write modern Israel's cultural history. To many
writers and thinkers Israel represents the modernist element in Middle-
Eastern life, striving for progress through technology and science. But no
less potent an influence in the life of the new republic is its sense of continuous association with the traditions of Israel's past. The revival of the
Hebrew language in daily speech, the spectacular results of archeology
in Israel's first decade, the central place of the Bible in the educational
process, and the tendency to refer moral problems to traditional Hebrew
ethics are all symptoms of a desire for the continuity of a heritage.

In Israel today a school of nuclear physics is established a few miles
away from where newly discovered Biblical scrolls are maintained as a
national treasure. This is the symbol of a people's intellectual journey
across four thousand years—from ancient prophecy to modern science,
from the imperishable memories of the past to the inscrutable mysteries
of the future. The only people whose continuous historic memory com-
prehends the full cycle of human thought is reunited with the land and
language in which its most potent creativity was achieved.

Thus, the heritage is not exhausted. It is preserved by history's grace in
conditions favorable to further replenishment in generations still to come.

Rehovoth, Israel, 1962

PREFACE

THE NEW JEWISH ENCYCLOPEDIA hopes to help to extend and make available Jewish knowledge to Jews. It is designed to be an instrument of education and a source of inspiration on the Jewish past and present so that they point toward a future. The facts of Jewish religion, history, ethics, literature and national life are included in a practical and comprehensive digest. If the word *Marrano* is now a historical curiosity, is it altogether irrelevant to modern American suburbia? In a day of totalitarianisms, has Judas Maccabeus' courage and love of liberty gone out of fashion? How shall Hillel's "Golden Rule" be compared with Christianity's, and how do the differences illuminate the confrontation of Jewish and Christian philosophy in our time?

THE NEW JEWISH ENCYCLOPEDIA is a single-volume, handy guide for all those who would like to have the basic and precise information about Judaism ready at hand. This ENCYCLOPEDIA is not intended to substitute for a many-volumed Jewish Encyclopedia. But it will serve as a spur to the young and to the student to delve still further into the riches of Jewish lore and tradition as it teaches them the fundamentals; for their elders and teachers, it will recall things they once knew and would like to be reacquainted with, or to pursue further. Students, teachers, parents and the ordinary man will find that THE NEW JEWISH ENCYCLOPEDIA is a mine of information for speeches, reports, articles, and the simple pleasures of enriched conversation and thought.

Style and presentation are made to conform to the need for a concise encyclopedia which would distill the wealth of information and concentrate on the major Jewish national, political, economic and cultural contributions. Technical terms are reduced to a minimum; transliteration is simplified; and everywhere explanation is delivered with an eye for simplicity of expression and clarity of thought.

In addition, hundreds of illustrations and pictures say more than words alone could. They give the faces of those Jews whose greatness have left their mark; they show the remains and buildings of what once was secular grandeur; and they depict the profound dignity of Jewish ceremony, ritual and belief which have continued to embody spiritual grandeur. From ancient synagogues and Kiddush Cups to modern Menorahs and "Eternal Lights," they make more real and vivid the men and materials out of which the Jewish heritage has been woven.

PREFACE

What is a Jew? That question every Jew must be able to answer if he is to survive and retain his humanity. Only insofar as a man knows what he is does he become and remain human; and only insofar as a Jew knows what he does does he become and remain a Jew. What is a Jew? A Jew is truly part of all that he and his people have been and done, felt and thought. A Jew is a man who has maintained the roots of his nationality, religion and culture by knowing what his fathers, grandfathers and great-grandfathers have dreamed and believed, and drawn sustenance from it. In our time, when the burdens of "identity" and the prevalence of "anxiety" have been a heavy burden to all men, and particularly severe for Jews, they make the extension and availability of Jewish knowledge especially valuable for us.

When you open this book, to read or browse or consult, you touch that knowledge and that heritage; you feel its quality; and you know more of what Jews and Jewishness are made.

A NOTE ON TRANSLATION AND TRANSLITERATION

A Jewish encyclopedia intended for an English-speaking audience must deal with many problems of translation and transliteration from several foreign languages, Yiddish and Hebrew in particular. Dates, abbreviations, and the forms of proper and place names also pose similar thorny and frequently controversial problems. The editors of THE NEW JEWISH ENCYCLOPEDIA have tried to meet these problems in terms of the latest scholarship and contemporary custom, while still paying due regard to traditional and hallowed usage.

Consequently, all Biblical proper and place names, translations, and references are from the usual translations of the Bible. The abbreviations most frequently used are the customary b.c.e., which stands for Before Common Era, and c.e., which stands for Common Era, referring respectively to the times before and after the year 1. In general, ancient geographical place names have been given modern, anglicized forms so that they would be familiar to and easily located by the modern reader.

For the guidance of our readers, we include below two charts. The first is a key to the system we have used in transliterations from Hebrew into English, and the second is the key to the English pronunciation of the transliterated Hebrew terms, which are, in the main, given according to a modified form of the Sephardi pronunciation as used in Israel today.

Chart One: KEY TO TRANSLITERATIONS FROM HEBREW INTO ENGLISH

CONSONANTS				VOWELS (written above, below and in center of letters)	
א	not sounded	ל	l	ָ	a
ב	b	מ	m	ַ	a
ב	v	נ	n	ֵּ	e
ג	g	ס	s	ֶ	e
ד	d	ע	not sounded	ִ	i
ה	h*	פ	p	ֹ	o
ו	v (when not a vowel)	פ	f, ph	וּ	u
ז	z	צ	tz	ֻ	u
ח	ḥ	ק	k	ְ	e
ט	t	ר	r	ֲ	a
י	y (when not part of a vowel)	שׁ	sh	ֱ	e
כ	k	שׂ	s	ֳ	o
כ	kh	ת,ת	t		

*at the end of a word, Hé is not sounded, but we have nevertheless transliterated it into English as h—as, for instance, in Menorah—to differentiate it from Aleph and Ayin, which are also silent at the end of a word.

Chart Two: KEY TO PRONUNCIATION OF TRANSLITERATED HEBREW TERMS

CONSONANTS		VOWELS	
ch	appearing in a limited number of proper names and Biblical terms, is pronounced like its German equivalent.	a	pronounced like a in "father."
		ah	as a above.
ḥ	as ch above.	e	pronounced like e in "get."
kh	as ch above.	eh	as e above.
g	followed by any vowel is pronounced like g in "good."	i	pronounced like i in "big" or like ee in "feet."
gh	as g above.	o	pronounced like o in "most" or like o in "honey."
ph	pronounced like f.	u	pronounced like oo in "boot" or like u in "put."

ACKNOWLEDGMENTS

It is impossible to express our gratitude to all those who contributed to THE NEW JEWISH ENCYCLOPEDIA. A work of this scope and size is necessarily the result of many hands, though willing and working in a single spirit.

But for that small group who helped the editors bear the essential burden of the book, though they bear none of the responsibilities for its shortcomings, we would like to state our thanks publicly. We are profoundly indebted to Samuel Grand, whose advice and taste in analyzing texts and selecting illustrations, reinforced both processes with his scholarly advice and impeccable taste. Our thanks, too, to Morrison Bial whose wide-ranging scholarship and forceful criticism were a whiplash to facts and style alike. To Arthur Kahn, whose review of the material helped to give it greater depth and accuracy, and to Merrill Martin, whose fine sense of esthetics and proportion helped to fix the text on questions of taste, we owe a debt which no mere acknowledgment can repay. In Emanuel Green, who put his knowledge of Biblical and Rabbinical lore at our disposal, we had at hand a continuing source of inspiration and repository of erudition. To Harmon Ephron, whose understanding of the Jewish spirit is both ample and acute, is due a general acknowledgment for having read the manuscript and for having made numerous and valuable emendations and suggestions, particularly with respect to how the spirit of Judaism is embodied in the flesh of Israel's history and people.

Because the visual material is so important an aspect of THE NEW JEWISH ENCYCLOPEDIA and so powerful an adjunct to the text, we are especially grateful to four people who improved its range and eloquence. To Tim Gidal, who made available to us his extensive photographic collection and breadth of knowledge, we are deeply beholden. Frank J. Darmstaedter gave us unstintingly of his time and labor, and opened to us the vast treasures of The Jewish Museum. For enriching the ENCYCLOPEDIA with the original photographs used as alphabetical dividers, we would like to express our gratitude to Ann Zane Shanks, whose artistry and sensitivity illuminated with vividness and color the many facets of Jewish life; and to Marvin Koner, whose skill gave added vigor to everything that came within the compass of his camera's lens.

Though many organizations made their files available to us, we are especially in the debt of the Israel Office of Information, the Joint Distribution Committee, the Yiddish Scientific Institute (YIVO), and the Zionist Archives and Library, which we would like to single out for their kindness and cooperation in giving us free and ready access to their abundant archives.

PICTURE CREDITS

AFL-CIO NEWS: *p. 171.*

ALLEGRO, JOHN M.: *p. 222.*

AMALGAMATED CLOTHING WORKERS OF AMERICA: *p. 11* (bottom).

AMERICAN FRIENDS OF THE HEBREW UNIVERSITY: *pp. 41, 64, 218* (top), *270, 283.*

AMERICA-ISRAEL CULTURAL FOUNDATION: *pp. 22* (top right), *22* (bottom right), *113, 178, 402, 483, 525.*

AMERICAN JEWISH ARCHIVES: *p. 12.*

AMERICAN JEWISH COMMITTEE: *pp. 13, 307* (right).

AMERICAN JEWISH HISTORICAL SOCIETY: *pp. 286, 291, 485.*

AMERICAN ORT FEDERATION: *p. 362.*

AMERICAN ZIONIST COUNCIL, Department of Education and Culture: *pp. 136* (top), *262* (right), *279.*

BARDIN, MAURICE: *pp. 36, 37.*

BICKNELL, W. H. W.: *p. 73* (bottom, etching).

BRANDEIS UNIVERSITY: *pp. 62, 63.*

BRANDON, E.: *p. 99.*

BUFFALO AND ERIE COUNTY HISTORICAL SOCIETY: *p. 20.*

COLUMBIANA LIBRARY: *pp. 392, 438.*

CULVER PICTURES, INC.: *pp. 131, 495* (bottom).

DOUBLEDAY AND CO., INC.: *p. 153.*

ENGELBRECHT, MARTIN: *p. 462.*

FORWARD, JEWISH DAILY: *pp. 69, 190, 290, 506, 537.*

FRENCH EMBASSY PRESS AND INFORMATION DIVISION: *pp. 59, 151* (bottom).

FREUD, ERNST L.—*courtesy of* Basic Books, Inc.: *p. 155.*

FRIEDENBERG, DANIEL M.: *p. 142.*

GANS, JACOB KOPPEL: *p. 371* (embroidery).

GIDAL, TIM: *pp. 5, 9, 26, 29, 39* (right), *42, 48* (top), *54, 58, 93, 108* (top), *114, 115, 116, 132, 135, 158, 165, 179, 181, 186, 191, 196, 198, 199, 203, 204, 206, 212, 232, 254, 298, 300, 309, 312, 314* (top), *332, 336, 354, 367, 368* (top), *368* (bottom), *377, 382, 383, 420, 425, 426, 443, 456, 470, 476, 488* (top), *496* (top), *500, 511, 526, 530, 539.*

GREENWALD, HAZEL—*courtesy of* Hadassah: *pp. 44* (top), *180, 211.*

HARRIS AND EWING: *p. 514.*

HART, SOLOMON A.: *p. 452.*

HEBREW UNION COLLEGE–JEWISH INSTITUTE OF RELIGION: *pp. 39* (left), *272* (right), *444, 496* (bottom), *516, 519.*

Hebrew Union College Museum: *pp. 79* (bottom left), *84* (top left), *361.*

HEBREW UNIVERSITY, JERUSALEM: *pp. 197, 236.*

INTERNATIONAL LADIES' GARMENT WORKERS' UNION (Harry Rubenstein, photographer): *pp. 220, 352.*

ISRAEL GOVERNMENT TOURIST OFFICE: *pp. 23* (top), *24* (top left), *24* (top right), *75, 111, 228, 234, 248, 422, 465* (top), *481.*

ISRAEL OFFICE OF INFORMATION: *pp. 19, 23* (bottom), *43, 46, 52, 68, 73* (top), *74, 107, 108* (bottom), *144, 145, 148, 149, 160, 168, 189, 208* (bottom right), *226, 271, 308, 345, 379, 398, 419, 437, 447, 451, 458, 463, 487.*

JARVIS, J. W.: *p. 355.*

JEWISH MUSEUM (Frank J. Darmstaedter, photographer): *pp. 27* (top), *56, 79* (bottom right), *80* (left), *80* (right), *81* (bottom), *82* (top), *82* (bottom), *83, 84* (top right), *84* (bottom), *87, 89, 91, 129, 243, 264, 267, 310, 314* (bottom), *315, 327, 339* (top), *339* (bottom), *353, 355, 378, 384* (top), *385, 397, 452, 475, 495* (top).

Harry G. Friedman Collection: *pp. 79* (top), *81* (top), *205, 281, 299, 302* (bottom), *318, 328, 346* (left), *371, 372, 393, 431, 462, 465* (bottom left), *482, 488* (bottom).

Oscar Gruss Collection: *pp. 98, 417.*

Morris Morgenstern Foundation: *pp. 350, 351.*

Michael M. Zagayski Collection: *p. 183.*

JEWISH NATIONAL FUND: *pp. 53, 170, 174, 188, 242, 266, 292, 304, 316, 389.*

JEWISH THEOLOGICAL SEMINARY OF AMERICA: *pp. 147* (right), *262* (left), *273* (left), *433.*

Jewish Theological Seminary Library: *pp. 163, 195, 265, 302* (top), *347, 399.*

PICTURE CREDITS

JOINT DISTRIBUTION COMMITTEE: *pp. 35, 102, 103, 123, 182, 246, 247, 252, 330, 436, 455, 466, 477.*

KAUFMANN, ISIDOR—*courtesy of* Dr. Edward Kaufmann: *pp. 51, 417.*

KELLER, G.: *p. 147* (left, copper engraving).

KEREN HA-YESOD, JERUSALEM: *p. 479.*

KONER, MARVIN: *pp. 214–215, 296–297, 334–335, 414–415, 508–509.*

KRAFT, STEPHEN: *pp. xiii, 10.*

LAYNARD, FRANÇOIS: *p. 200.*

MAIMON, MOISEL LEIBOVICH—*courtesy of* Manufacturers Hanover Trust Co.: *p. 306.*

MAYER, MAURICE: *p. 361.*

M^cGRAW-HILL BOOK CO.: *p. 272* (left).

MOSAD BIALIK, ISRAEL: *pp. 22* (top left), *136–137* (bottom), *251.*

NATIONAL FOUNDATION: *p. 423.*

NEW YORK TIMES: *p. 360.*

OPPENHEIM, MORITZ DANIEL: *p. 98.*

PEIXOTTO, GEORGE DE MADURE: *p. 327.*

PICART, BERNARD: *pp. 212, 377.*

SCHATZ, BORIS: *p. 431.*

SHANKS, ANN ZANE: *pp. 1, 32–33, 66–67, 104–105, 120–121, 140–141, 150, 156–157, 176–177, 230–231, 256–257, 276–277, 358–359, 364–365, 394–395, 472–473, 490–491, 502–503, 522–523, 532–533.*

SHEARITH ISRAEL [CONG.], NEW YORK: *p. 468.*

SOCIETY OF FRIENDS OF TOURO SYNAGOGUE, National Historic Shrine, Inc.: *pp. 348, 349.*

STATE OF ISRAEL BONDS, Development Corporation of Israel: *p. 61.*

STEIN, FRED: *p. 126.*

STIEGLITZ, ALFRED—*courtesy of* The Museum of Modern Art, New York, and Georgia O'Keeffe, Stieglitz Estate: *p. 494.*

SULLY, T.: *p. 173.*

TEL AVIV MUNICIPAL ARCHIVES: *pp. 225, 478.*

UNION OF AMERICAN HEBREW CONGREGATIONS, Audio-Visual Aids Dept.: *p. 412.*

UNIVERSITY OF CHICAGO, Oriental Institute: *pp. 11* (top), *22* (bottom left), *36, 37, 218* (bottom), *374, 421, 459.*

WIDE WORLD PHOTOS: *p. 321.*

WOLPERT, LUDWIG: *pp. 267, 346* (right).

YALE UNIVERSITY: *pp. 119, 128.*

YESHIVA UNIVERSITY: *pp. 45, 527.*

YIDDISH SCIENTIFIC INSTITUTE (YIVO): *pp. 16, 17, 38, 44* (bottom), *94, 95, 100, 118, 172, 193, 208* (top left), *219, 268, 274, 284, 294, 313, 341* (top), *341* (bottom left), *341* (bottom right), *342* (top), *342* (bottom), *343* (top), *343* (bottom), *384* (bottom), *387, 388, 407, 408, 409, 410, 434, 435, 448, 505.*

ZIONIST ARCHIVES AND LIBRARY: *pp. 6, 27* (bottom), *117, 239, 241, 273* (right), *288, 329, 356, 401, 428, 457, 534, 538, 540.*

THE NEW JEWISH
ENCYCLOPEDIA

ARON HA-KODESH

And thou shalt put into the ark the testimony which

I shall give thee.

EXODUS

AARON

Son of Amram and Jochebed of the tribe of Levi. He was spokesman for his brother Moses when they requested Pharaoh to free the Israelites from Egypt. Standing before Pharaoh, he performed the miracle of turning his staff into a serpent. The same staff later blossomed with almonds overnight and was kept in the Ark of the Covenant. Aaron was appointed the first priest of the Children of Israel, and the founder of the priestly family (*Kohen*); the other two divisions of the Jewish people are *Levi* and *Israel*. In tradition Aaron is known as peacemaker, particularly in family disputes.

AB see AV.

ABARBANEL see Abravanel.

ABEL see Cain and Abel.

ABRAHAM

First of the three Hebrew Patriarchs, and founder of the Jewish people. His two sons, who play a prominent role in the Bible story, are Isaac by his wife Sarah, and Ishmael, by Hagar. The Bible tells us that God directed Abraham to leave his native Ur of the Chaldees and settle in Canaan, land that was promised to him and his descendants. Tradition attributes to Abraham these characteristics: He was hospitable, as shown by the way he received the visiting three angels who foretold the birth of Isaac; he was God-fearing, as demonstrated by his readiness to sacrifice his son at the command of God; he was a peace-maker, shown by the way he settled the quarrels between his shepherds and those of Lot; he had a sense of righteousness, as exemplified by his plea to God for the saving of Sodom and Gomorrah. Circumcision was commanded to Abraham for himself, his descendants and all who would join the Jewish people, and is known as the Covenant of Abraham. Converts often take the name of Abraham.

ABRAMOWITCH, SHOLOM JACOB see Mendele Mocher Seforim.

ABRAVANEL, DON ISAAC (1437–1508)

Statesman, commentator of the Bible, and mystic. Renowned in Jewish history for his work in behalf of his people, when the expulsion of the Jews from Spain was decreed by the rulers Ferdinand and Isabella in 1492. He was formerly treasurer of Portugal, and in Spain he was put in charge of governmental revenues. Using the power of his office, he offered the Spanish rulers large amounts of money to prevent the expulsion of the Jews, but they refused it because of the intervention of Torquemada, Grand Inquisitor of Spain. Although the king and queen wanted to exempt him from the order of expulsion, Abravanel joined the emigrants. At first he settled in Naples and finally in Venice, where he was given high governmental functions. In spite of his many wanderings, he devoted much time to writing important commentaries on the Scriptures. He also wrote books on mysticism and philosophy.

ACADEMIES, BABYLONIAN

Up to the period of the completion of the *Mishnah* the Palestinian academies had religious jurisdiction over the Jews in Babylonia. At the beginning of the third century the first important Babylonian academy was established in Nehardea. Soon after, a new academy was founded at Sura. When the city of Nehardea was destroyed, a new academy was founded in Pumbedita. There was a succession of great teachers in these academies. About 375 c.e., the task of editing the Talmud was undertaken under the leadership of R. Ashi and was completed about 500 c.e. This date also marks the completion of the period of the Talmudic scholars named "Amoraim," who were succeeded by those called "Saboraim." 150 years later marked the beginning of the period of the "Geonim," the most famous of whom was Saadiah, the Gaon of Sura. The Academy of Sura closed in 946 c.e., while the Academy of Pumbedita lasted another century. The Babylonian academies were known by the name of *Metivta* (Aramaic for "session"). The academies were financially supported by payments received for official decisions on submitted legal questions, and from taxes and contributions from Jewish communities in and outside of Babylonia. See *Babylonia*.

ACADEMIES, PALESTINIAN

Important academies existed in Palestine even before the destruction of the Temple by the Romans. The great schools led by Hillel and Shammai were preceded by the Academy of Shemaiah and Avtalion. After the fall of Jerusalem (70 c.e.), R. Johanan ben Zakkai established himself at the school of Yavneh which became the center of Jewish learning and the seat of the Great Sanhedrin, which formerly met at Jerusalem. A number of laws were adopted to meet conditions following the loss of political independence; certain books of the Bible were canonized and the three daily prayers were regularized. The leading scholars of these academies were called *Tannaim*, the greatest of whom was Akiva. During the period following the revolt of Bar Kokhba, the Academy of Yavneh was removed to Usha in Galilee, later to Bet-Shearim, and still later it was established in Sepphoris. It was there that Rabbi Judah edited the Mishnah, which became the most important text of study in the academies of both Palestine and Babylonia. The center of learning was later moved to Tiberias where the period of great discussions on the texts of the Mishnah began. These legal discussions by the "Amoraim" (expounders) formed the basis for the compilation of the Palestinian Talmud which was completed about 400 c.e. Tiberias continued to be the seat of learning for many years. The last academy was established in the ninth century at Jerusalem. At the end of the 11th century, during the time of the Crusades, Palestinian academies ceased to exist.

ACOSTA, URIEL (ca. 1590–1647)

Philosopher and bitter critic of the rabbinical system of Jewish law and tradition. He was born in Portugal to parents who were secret Jews (Marranos), and was reared in the Catholic faith. In 1615 Acosta, accompanied by his family, went to Holland and settled in Amsterdam, where he embraced the Jewish faith. However, his ideas about Judaism did not agree with the existing Jewish traditional practices and with the interpretations of the Jewish Law by the rabbis, and he began openly to denounce the "Oral Law" (Torah shebe-al Peh). As a result, he was excommunicated by the leaders of the Jewish community. He then published a book in which he denied the immortality of the soul. This offended the rabbinical authorities even more, and for fifteen years Acosta lived in isolation from the Jewish community. Acosta then publicly retracted his denunciations of Jewish beliefs and traditions, and asked for forgiveness. This was granted to him, but soon after he decided to resume his open denunciations of tradition. He was once more placed under the *Ḥerem* ("Great Ban"), and when he again asked to be readmitted to the Jewish community he had to make a public confession of his sin and undergo the traditional flogging. As a result of this experience he shot himself. The life and career of Acosta inspired the writing of the drama "Uriel Acosta" by Gutzkow, and he has also been the hero in many other writings and works of art.

ADAM AND EVE

According to Genesis, the first book of the Bible, God created Adam, the first man, as the ultimate in the creation of the world. He created him "of the dust of the ground" ("Adamah"), hence the given name "Adam." After placing him in the "Garden of Eden," God created Eve, (Hebrew: Ḥavvah, life-bearer) the first woman, from Adam's rib. As a result of the sin of eating the forbidden fruit of the "Tree of Knowledge," Adam and Eve were banished from the Garden of Eden. Later Eve gave birth to several children, among them Cain and Abel.

ADAR

The sixth month of the Hebrew year, corresponding to late February and early March, and consisting of 29 days. The festival of Purim falls on the 14th day of this month. In a Jewish leap-year an extra month is added after the month of Adar, and is called "Adar Sheni" (Second Adar or Ve-Adar). In this case the first Adar would have 30 days and the second Adar 29 days, and Purim is celebrated in the second Adar.

ADDITIONAL SERVICE see Musaf.

ADLER, ALFRED (1870–1937)

A Viennese psychiatrist. He was one of Freud's first followers, but later broke with him to advance his own theories of "individual psychology." He believed feelings of inferiority to be the basis of most psychic disorders, holding that these disorders stem from conditions of repressed power and assertion. In New York City there are, at present, two Adler institutions dedicated to the advancement of his work.

ADLER, CYRUS (1863–1940)

American Jewish leader, educator and scholar. He occupied the presidency of the American Jewish Educational Society, Dropsie College, the American Jewish Committee, and The Jewish Theological Seminary of America. He edited the "Jewish Quarterly Review," was co-editor of the "American Jewish Yearbook," and chairman of the Jewish Publication Society. He was active as leader of the American Jewish Joint Distribution Committee, and co-chairman of the Jewish Agency for Palestine.

ADLER, JACOB (1855–1926)

Yiddish actor. Starting his theatrical career in Russia, and performing in England, he emigrated to New York in 1888, and became the leading Yiddish actor and head of a family of well-known actors of the Yiddish stage.

ADLOYADA

Elaborate Purim carnival celebrated in the city of Tel Aviv, Israel. The name is a three-word combination of a Talmudic phrase "Ad Lo Yada" meaning "Until he did not know." The implication is that it is considered a "Mitzvah" (religious duty) for every Jew to celebrate the festival of Purim by dancing, singing, merry-making, dining and drinking, "until he didn't know Haman from Mordecai . . ." The elaborate manner in which the Adloyada is celebrated has made it a popular cultural and entertainment event in modern Israel, as well as a welcome attraction for tourists. The festivities last for three days. See *Purim*.

ADON OLAM

Opening two Hebrew words of a familiar hymn, presenting in poetic form the relationship between God, the world, and man. It is recited or chanted as part of many services. It is believed to have been written in the 12th century by an unknown author, and has been attributed to a wide variety of poets.

AFIKOMAN

The "dessert," that is, that part of the *Matzah* which is the middle one of the three Matzot at the *Seder* table, and which is eaten at the end of the Passover Seder meal. It is "hidden" by the head of the house at the beginning of the Seder and the finder, usually the youngest at the dinner table, is rewarded for finding it.

AFTERNOON SERVICE see Minḥah.

AGGADAH see Haggadah.

AGUDAT (Agudas) ISRAEL

World organization of orthodox Jewry, established in Poland, 1912. The organization branched out in all leading Jewish communities in Europe as well as in the United States. Agudat Israel places the Torah in the center of Jewish life and attempts to advance Judaism and to organize Jewish life in accordance with the spirit and practices of the Jewish Law. It supports and maintains institutions of orthodox Jewish learning, and operates women's, children's and youth divisions.

Yosef Zvi Dushinsky (center), rabbi and member of the Moatzot Gedole Ha-Torah (supreme rabbinical council) of Agudat Israel, and leader of its Palestinian branch, was a religious educator of note.

5

AHAB

King who ruled from 875 to 853 b.c.e. in the northern Kingdom of Israel. He fought his major battles with the Syrians. In spite of his military leadership and successful efforts to encourage foreign trade, he is remembered as one of the unpopular kings of Israel, largely because of his wife Jezebel. She was responsible for the spreading of the Baal worship in Israel, and for the murder of Naboth in order to take possession of his beautiful vineyard. The prophet Elijah fought bitterly against the wicked and heathen queen and her weak husband.

Aḥad Ha-Am (in Hebrew "one of the people"), the Hebrew essayist and philosophical writer.

AHAD HA-AM (1856–1927)

Pen name of Asher Ginzberg, foremost Russian-born Hebrew philosophical writer and advocate of "Cultural Zionism," as opposed to "Political Zionism." He used the Hebrew periodical "Ha-Shiloaḥ," which he edited, as a platform for criticism of the idea of establishing a Jewish State in Palestine, as championed by the followers of Herzl. He argued that before any attempt was made to establish a Jewish State, the Hebrew cultural survival and development of the Jewish people should first be secured. He therefore believed that the Jewish homeland in Palestine should first become a "spiritual center" designed to influence Jewish communities all over the world and offer them spiritual strength and cultural unity. In 1922 he settled in Tel Aviv. His numerous essays, appearing in several volumes, express his philosophy of Judaism and offer guiding principles for the solution of a great variety of vital Jewish national problems.

AHARONIM see Codes.

AHASUERUS

Persian king who, according to the *Book of Esther*, ruled "from India to Ethiopia." He married a Jewess, Esther, whom he made queen of Persia to replace Vashti, who was removed from her station because of her disobedience. Mordecai, Esther's cousin, uncovered a plot against the king's life. Haman, the wicked vizier, persuaded the king to kill the Jews of Persia. Esther's intervention saved the people, and she and Mordecai thereupon established the feast of Purim in thanksgiving. See *Esther, Book of; Purim.*

AHIJAH

Prophet who urged Jeroboam to revolt against King Solomon, and foretold the breaking up of the Jewish kingdom.

AKDAMUT

A poem written in Aramaic and chanted with a special melody before the reading of the Torah, on the first day of *Shavuot.* It is believed to have been written by Meir ben Isaac Neharai about the middle of the

11th century, in Germany. The poem describes the glory of the Lord, and praises the religious devotion of the Jews and the future reward of the faithful.

AKEDAH

A Hebrew term meaning "binding," referring to Abraham's binding of his son Isaac on an altar on Mt. Moriah as an intended sacrifice in obedience to God's command. Among the reasons given by tradition for the blowing of the ram's horn (Shofar) during the High Holy Days is that this may serve as a reminder of the ram sacrificed in place of Isaac.

AKIVA BEN JOSEPH (c. 50–c. 132)

One of the greatest of the *Tannaim*, (Teachers of the Mishnah) and religious martyr, who inspired Bar Kokhba's revolt against the Romans. His rise to high scholarship and leadership has a romantic background. Akiva, an illiterate shepherd, encouraged by his beautiful and loyal wife Rachel, began the study of Torah at the age of forty, and became the most prominent Tanna and Jewish leader of his time. He personally intervened in Rome in behalf of his suffering people, and as the Roman rule stiffened, he urged Bar Kokhba and other Jewish patriots to rebel against the oppressors. In his interpretation of the Jewish law he advocated democratic procedures, urging that decisions be rendered in accordance with the views held by the majority of leading scholars, and not on the basis of personal authority. Akiva was also instrumental in the canonization of some books of the Hebrew Bible. In the memory of the Jewish people he is held in high esteem and veneration. In the last moments of his life, when tortured by the Roman executioner, he recited the "Shema" calmly, without showing any sign of physical pain. When asked whether he was a magician, he replied:

"I am no magician, but I rejoice at the opportunity now given me to love my God with all my life," and with the word (God is) "One" he breathed his last.

ALAV HA-SHALOM

Hebrew phrase, also pronounced "Olev Hasholem," meaning "peace be unto him," and used when mentioning the name of a deceased man; for a woman one says "Aleha ha-Shalom."

ALENU

First Hebrew word of the closing prayer of the daily liturgy meaning, "It is incumbent upon us." "Alenu" is one of the oldest prayers, and is known to have been recited by Abba Areka, the great Babylonian *Amora* of the 3rd century. Its essential theme is the ultimate turning of all mankind to the true God. It holds a significant place in the liturgy of the High Holy days and is said to have been composed originally for those days.

ALEPH (א)

The first letter of the Hebrew alphabet. It is presumed to represent the head of an ox. In Greek it became Alpha, and together with the second letter *BET* forms the word alphabet, comparable to the a b c designation of the English alphabet. In Hebrew the alphabet is sometimes called "Aleph-Bais."

The numerical value of *Aleph* is one; when followed by an apostrophe its value is 1000.

ALEPH ZADIK ALEPH

Also known as "A.Z.A." A section of the B'nai B'rith Youth Organization, founded in 1923. In 1960 it had a membership of about 15,500 in 600 chapters throughout the United States and Canada. It advocates "a program of cultural, religious, and interfaith community service, as well as social and athletic activities" for Jewish youth. See *B'nai B'rith*.

ALEXANDER THE GREAT (356–323 b.c.e.)

Illustrious conqueror of the East, who showed a favorable attitude toward the Jews, whose country he took without much opposition. His conquest of Judea led to the introduction of Hellenism (Greek Culture), which had far reaching influence on the development of Judaism. Many Jews took the name Alexander, and it is considered a Jewish name.

ALEXANDRIA

Ancient Mediterranean city in Egypt, founded by Alexander the Great in 332 b.c.e. For many centuries it was the leading Jewish community in the diaspora. The Jewish settlers in Alexandria resided in an important quarter of the city, where they erected a most elaborate and beautiful synagogue. For many years the Jews enjoyed special privileges and occupied prominent positions in the economic, military and cultural life of the Greek and Roman empires. Despite the Hellenistic culture to which they were exposed, and by which they were influenced, the Jews of Alexandria remained loyal to Hebrew traditions and never severed their relations with the Palestinian Jewish community. During the Judean revolt against Rome, many Alexandrian Jews joined the fighting armies of Bar Kokhba. Jewish scholars in Alexandria translated the Hebrew Bible into Greek, which translation is known as the "Septuagint." Modern Alexandria had an extensive Jewish population, but as a result of the Sinai campaign in 1956, most of the Jews migrated. See *Philo*.

ALGERIA

North African French colony. It is believed that Italian Jews settled in Algeria about 2,000 years ago, under Roman rule.

New Jewish settlements were added when Algeria came under Arab rule in the 7th century. More Jews settled there as a result of the massacres (1391) and expulsion from Spain (1492). Under Turkish rule, which began in the 16th century, the Jewish community in Algeria developed under favorable conditions. After 1830, when Algeria became a French colony, the condition of the Jews further improved, and in 1870 they were accorded citizenship rights. As a result of World War II, the Jewish community suffered severely. After 1948 about 10,000 Jews left the country and found refuge in Israel. In 1960 the Jewish population of Algeria was about 130,000, about 30,000 of whom were in Algiers.

AL ḤET

Hebrew name of a special prayer, a confession of sins, recited as part of the ritual of the Day of Atonement. It enumerates several lists of sins, each starting with the words "For the sin we have committed before Thee." At the end of each list of transgressions there is a petition for forgiveness. See *Sin*.

ALILAT DAM see Blood Accusation.

ALIYAH

Hebrew term meaning "going up" and referring to the honor given a Jewish person to ascend the *Bimah* (reading desk platform) in the synagogue to recite the blessings over the Torah. It is also used as a term meaning "Immigration" into the Land of Israel. Some migrations to Israel are known by their numbers, thus the First Aliyah (immigrants of 1880–1905); the Second Aliyah (immigrants of 1905–14); the Third Aliyah (1919–24); the Fourth Aliyah (1924–29); and the Fifth Aliyah (1933–39).

ALLIANCE ISRAÉLITE UNIVERSELLE

World Jewish organization founded in

Immigrants of the Second Aliyah work the land in Palestine, and in this fashion was the Psalmist's words, "They that sow in tears, shall reap in joy," fulfilled by the establishment of the State of Israel.

Paris in 1860 by a group of influential Jewish citizens of France owing to anti-Semitic outbreaks and persecutions of Jews in several Jewish communities the world over. The purposes of this central international Jewish organization were to defend the good name of the Jews; to protect their civil and religious liberties; to offer financial help to distressed Jewish communities and to furnish educational facilities to backward Jewish groups. The Alliance founded the first agricultural school at Mikveh Israel in the Jewish homeland. It was particularly active in protecting and aiding the Jews of Morocco, Algeria, and Persia, and it also intervened in the blood accusation trials against Jews in several countries. The Alliance is operated by an executive committee, half of whose members reside in France and the other half in various other countries.

ALMEMAR see Bimah.

ALPHABET, HEBREW

Consists of twenty-two letters, all of them consonants. Five letters have an additional form used at the end of a word, and five variants created by placing a dot inside or above the letter. There are several separate vowel signs made up of lines and dots placed below, in the center or above the letters. The Hebrew square-character alphabet is a development of the ancient Hebrew alphabet, probably closely related to the Canaanitish. Each Hebrew letter has a corresponding numerical value, as follows: Aleph-1; Bet-2; Gimmel-3; Dalet-4; Hé-5; Vav-6; Zayin-7; Het-8; Tet-9; Yod-10; Kaf-20; Lamed-30; Mem-40; Nun-50; Samekh-60; Ayin-70; Pé-80; Tzade (Tzaddik)-90; Kof-100; Resh-200; Shin-300; Tav-400. Combinations of the above are used in the Hebrew numbering system,

9

especially in the Jewish Calendar. (See articles on each individual letter.)

ALROY, DAVID

False messiah of the 12th century, and hero of Benjamin Disraeli's famous novel by that name. He was born in Kurdistan, Persia, and was reared in Bagdad. His fantastic plans for the restoration of the Jewish kingdom in Jerusalem are related in the memoirs of Benjamin of Tudela, his contemporary and famous world traveler. David Alroy declared himself messiah to the Jews of Babylonia, and called upon the Jews of his native city to revolt against the Persian ruler. The rebels were defeated, and according to Benjamin of Tudela, Alroy escaped, but was later assassinated by his father-in-law. His life and activities have been the theme of numerous tales.

ALTAR

A term known in Hebrew as *Mizbe-ah*, which in early Biblical times referred to a stone, or a pile of stones, used as the place for the offering of sacrifices. In the regulations laid down for the Holy Sanctuary in the *Book of Exodus*, there are two altars, one of brass for burnt-offerings, and one of gold for the burning of incense. During the days of the Temple the altar symbolized the sanctity and the unity of the Jewish people.

PRINTED FORM	SCRIPT FORM	ENGLISH TRANSLITERATION	PRINTED FORM	SCRIPT FORM	ENGLISH TRANSLITERATION
א	lc	Aleph	ל	ℓ	Lamed
ב,ב	ג,ב	Bet, Vet	ם,מ	ᴅ,ᴎ	Mem, Final Mem
ג	c	Gimmel	ן,נ	l,J	Nun, Final Nun
ד	ꝰ	Dalet	ס	o	Samekh
ה	ꜛ	Hé	ע	ɤ	Ayin
ו	I	Vav	ף,פ,פ	ƒ,ꝰꝰ	Pé, Fé, Final Fé
ז	ꜜ	Zayin	ץ,צ	ᵹ,ᴣ	Tzade (Tzaddik), Final Tzade
ח	ɳ	Het	ק	ꝓ	Kof
ט	ʊ	Tet	ר	ꝛ	Resh
י	′	Yod	ש,שׂ	ꝍ,ꝍ	Shin, Sin
ך,כ,כ	ꝭ,ꝭ,ꝭ	Kaf, Khaf, Final Khaf	ת	ꝰ	Tav

Chart showing the twenty-two letters of the Hebrew alphabet in print and in script with their modern Israeli transliterations. This alphabet is also used in such languages as Yiddish, Ladino and Aramaic.

AMALEK

A people dwelling in Biblical times in the south of Palestine and the first to wage war with the Israelites in the wilderness. Thus the name Amalek became synonymous with "enemy" of the Jewish people. The wicked Haman of the story of Purim is said by tradition to have been a descendant of Amalek.

AMALGAMATED CLOTHING WORKERS OF AMERICA

A workers' organization in the men's clothing industry, founded at Nashville, Tenn. in 1914. It has a membership of over 250,000 workers of many nationalities, including a large number of Jewish members.

Stone altar from Megiddo used for burning incense, ca. 1000 b.c.e. Horns of the four corners were grasped by those who sought sanctuary.

The New York Joint Board of the Amalgamated Clothing Workers of America parade in support of President Harry Truman's veto of the Taft-Hartley labor bill which Congress, in 1947, enacted into law.

In the course of time this organization has been successful in reducing long weekly working hours and eliminating sweatshop conditions as well as child labor from the clothing industry. It advocated the principle of collective bargaining in relations between employers and workers, and sought to provide unemployment insurance in the major centers of the clothing industry. In addition to its sponsorship of cooperative housing projects which provide low cost rental for its members, the Amalgamated established workers' banks in New York and Chicago. It has also contributed large amounts of money for various causes, including many of Jewish character. The Amalgamated operates a Department of Cultural Activities offering a variety of correspondence courses dealing with workers' problems. See *Hillman, Sidney; International Ladies' Garment Workers' Union.*

AMARNA LETTERS see Archeology.

AMEN

Hebrew term meaning "so be it" or "truly," used by Jews and Christians as a word of affirmation of and response to a prayer or benediction.

AMERICAN ASSOCIATION FOR JEWISH EDUCATION

A coordinating agency for Jewish education in the U.S., founded in 1939, with headquarters in New York. It seeks to help Jewish schools, bureaus, and boards of Jewish education throughout the country to raise the standards of Jewish education. It encourages the establishment of communally supported local central agencies for Jewish education, and it helps them to develop educational facilities for all Jewish ideological groups in the community. It has several major departments, each designed to serve all types of Jewish educational institutions.

Masthead and front page of the first edition of "The Israelite," America's oldest Jewish weekly.

AMERICAN COUNCIL FOR JUDAISM

A body of extremist reform rabbis and laymen, organized in 1942, which took up the fight against Jewish nationalism in general, and Zionism in particular. Although it has a small membership, its leadership consists of wealthy and influential Jews.

AMERICAN HEBREW, THE

A weekly journal of Jewish interest, founded in 1879 in New York City. It represented the then reform anti-nationalist viewpoint, giving as its purposes the spread of knowledge of Judaic principles; the defense of the rights of Jews wherever threatened; and the interpretation of Judaism to non-Jews. True to its purposes, it was deeply concerned with Jewish persecutions in Tsarist Russia (1881) and assisted in the formation of the Hebrew Immigrant Aid Society (HIAS). Its distinguished contributors endeavored to lay the ground for better understanding between Jews and Christians, and were par-

American Jewish Committee delegation in Washington, D.C., December 1911, requesting termination of the Russo-American commercial treaty of 1832 for discriminating against American Jewish citizens.

ticularly articulate in attempting to rouse public opinion against Nazi propaganda and atrocities. In 1956 it combined with the Jewish Examiner to become the American Examiner.

AMERICAN ISRAELITE, THE

The oldest Jewish weekly in America, founded in Cincinnati, Ohio, in 1854 by Rabbi Isaac M. Wise for the purpose of spreading the principles and teachings of reform Judaism. Its files form an invaluable record of Jewish history in the United States, especially with reference to Jewish immigration from Germany, and the development of reform Judaism.

AMERICAN JEWISH COMMITTEE

A national body formed in 1906 for the purpose of: a) protecting the civil and religious liberties of Jews in all parts of the world; b) hindering the occurrence of discrimination; c) securing for Jews equality in economic, social and educational op-

portunities; and d) helping to alleviate the consequences of persecution.

It was originally organized chiefly in reaction to the anti-Semitic outbreaks and pogroms in Russia, and continued to intervene to protect the rights of Jews abroad. In the United States its activities are directed against the spread of anti-Semitic literature, and against all forms of discrimination and prejudice, through a program of education and civic action. It prepares the "American Jewish Yearbook" and publishes the monthly magazine "Commentary" on culture and politics.

AMERICAN JEWISH CONGRESS

Formed in 1917, and subsequently reorganized in 1922. Its major objective is to protect the rights of Jews the world over and to combat prejudicial discrimination wherever it may appear. It also furthers the development of the democratic organization of Jewish communities in the United States, and seeks to strengthen Jewish

13

historic identity, religion and culture. It is an affiliate of the World Jewish Congress. The American Jewish Congress includes various national Jewish organizations which are represented through their delegates at its annual sessions.

AMERICAN JEWISH HISTORICAL SOCIETY

Organized in 1892 by a group of Jewish scholars for the purpose of collecting and publishing materials bearing upon the history of Jews in America and Jewish history in general. It operates and maintains an extensive library and museum located at The Jewish Theological Seminary of America. Among its first presidents were Oscar S. Straus and Dr. Cyrus Adler.

AMERICAN JEWISH JOINT DISTRIBUTION COMMITTEE see Joint Distribution Committee, American Jewish.

AMERICAN ZIONIST COUNCIL

Founded in 1939 to serve as public relations arm of all the American Zionist organizations, and as their spokesman in all representations before the American government with regard to Zionist interests.

AM HA-ARETZ

Hebrew term meaning literally "people of the land," generally understood to designate "an ignorant Jewish person" or one who is uneducated in Jewish matters. The phrase recalls the English "country yokel," one not as knowledgeable as his city brother.

AMIDAH

The meaning of the Hebrew word *Amidah* is "Standing." This term is applied to the prayer which is recited at every service, while the worshipper stands. The structure of this prayer is threefold: three opening benedictions (Adoration), three closing benedictions (Thanksgiving), and intermediate benedictions. On weekdays there are thirteen intermediate benedic-

tions, and on Sabbath and festivals there is one. The intermediate benedictions on weekdays are in the nature of "Petitions," while the one intermediate benediction on Sabbath and festivals is known as the "Sanctification of the Day."

On Sabbath, festivals and Rosh Ḥodesh an additional Amidah, called *Musaf*, is recited after the conclusion of the morning service. The Musaf consists of seven benedictions, with the exception of the Rosh Hashanah Musaf which has nine. Following the afternoon service on Yom Kippur, the *Neilah* (Service of Conclusion) is recited, and its Amidah also consists of seven benedictions. See *Shemoneh Esreh*.

AMNON OF MAYENCE see U-Netanneh Tokef.

AMORA (AMORAIM)

A Talmudic term meaning "interpreter" or "speaker," applied to scholars in the Academies of Palestine and Babylonia who interpreted the Mishnah, from the beginning of the third century c.e., until the completion of the Talmud (500 c.e.). The *Amoraim* followed the group of great scholars called *Tannaim*. An ordained *Amora* was called "Rabbi" in Palestine, and "Rav" or "Mar" in Babylonia.

AMOS

The first of the *literary* prophets; that is, one whose compositions were preserved in written form. He was active about the middle of the 8th century b.c.e. Living a quiet life as a shepherd and a tender of sycamore trees in Judea, he became outraged by the immorality and corruption of the people and its rulers in the prosperous kingdom of Israel. He went to Beth-el in the north to plead for justice, to cry out against oppression of the poor, and to foretell the ruin of Israel. His prophecies are in the *Book of Amos*, one of "The Twelve" books which form the last unit of the second part of the Hebrew Bible.

AMPAL

Abbreviated name of the "American Palestine Trading Corporation," founded in 1942. It seeks to develop trade relations between the U.S. and Israel and assists in the development of economic and agricultural resources of Israel.

AMSTERDAM

Largest city in Holland, historically important Jewish center, having a Jewish population of about 70,000 before the Second World War. The first Jews to settle in Amsterdam were Marrano refugees from Spain and Portugal. The first synagogue in Amsterdam was erected in 1598. In the 17th century Amsterdam became an important Jewish community in Europe with a number of famous rabbis and Jewish leaders of whom Menasseh ben Israel is best known. Two Jewish personalities, Uriel Acosta and Baruch Spinoza, lived in Amsterdam during that period. Amsterdam became known as the center of Jewish printing shops where many volumes of Jewish sacred literature were published. The first community of Ashkenazi Jews was founded about the middle of the 17th century, and later augmented with large numbers of persecuted Jews from eastern Europe, especially from Poland.

AMULET see Kamea.

ANAN BEN DAVID

Founder of the Jewish sect of *Karaites*, first known as *Ananites*. He lived during

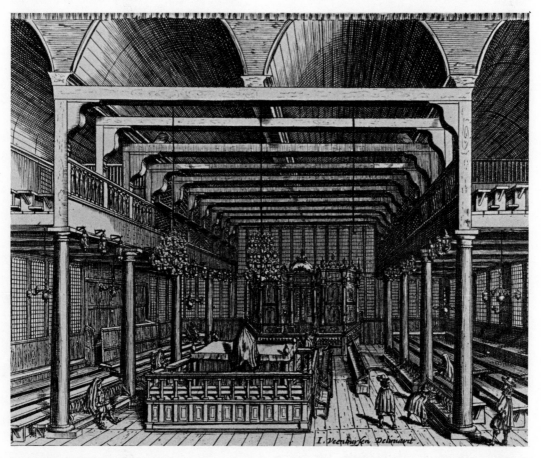

Amsterdam's old Spanish and Portuguese Synagogue. Here, in 1640, Uriel Acosta publicly recanted his heretical opinions, and here, too, in 1656, Baruch Spinoza's excommunication took place.

ANATHEMA

the latter part of the 8th century. Because
of a dispute with the *Geonim* (Rabbis),
he founded his own school in Jerusalem,
and started a bitter attack against the
Talmudists and the Talmud. He soon had
many followers who maintained that the
commandments of the Torah are the sole
true faith of the Jews, and that the Talmudic interpretations had distorted the
real meaning of the Laws of Moses. Despite the fact that Anan and his followers
claimed that no interpretations or adaptations may be made of the Laws of the
Torah, nevertheless they themselves wrote
a great number of books of commentary
and interpretation.

ANATHEMA see Herem.

ANGEL OF DEATH

The Hebrew name for God's messenger
whose function it is to destroy life and
take it away is *Malakh ha-Mavet*. The concept of "Angel of Death" is found chiefly
in rabbinical literature; in Jewish folklore
there are numerous legends on this subject.

ANIELEWICZ, MORDECAI (1919–1943)

Heroic leader and commander of the
armed Jewish revolt against the Nazis in
the Warsaw Ghetto. Born in Warsaw, Poland, he was raised in the midst of extreme
poverty. Showing exceptional abilities of
learning and leadership, he attended a Hebrew gymnasium (high school), and
became a trusted and able leader of "Hashomer Hatzair," a Zionist youth organization. In 1942, when the Nazis began
their mass deportations of Jews from the
Warsaw Ghetto, carrying them off to extermination centers, Anielewicz organized
the Jewish youth for armed resistance. In
January 1943, he led the first armed attack
on the Germans and was the only one of
the group who escaped death. Two weeks
before his heroic death in the last battle
against the Germans, he wrote to one of

his friends: "My life dream is fulfilled.
The Jewish self-defense in the Ghetto is
a fact. The Jewish armed resistance has
been established. I bear witness of the
glorious heroic battles of the Jewish
rebels." The memory and name of Mordecai Anielewicz have been honored in
Israel through the establishment of the
Kibbutz (workers' settlement) "Yad
Mordecai."

AN-SKI, S. (1863–1920)

Pen name of Solomon Seinwil Rapoport,
Russian Yiddish writer, especially known
as a folklorist and dramatist. His play
"The Dibbuk," published in 1916 and
based on a mystical legend of Hasidic
lore, has enjoyed great popularity and
success on both the Yiddish and the non-
Jewish stage. As a result of his revolu-

S. An-Ski (left), writer, whose play "Dibbuk"
is a Yiddish classic, is seen here with S. Niger.

16

tionary activities An-Ski had to flee Russia. In contact with Jewish political refugees in Paris and Switzerland, he wrote his popular Yiddish revolutionary hymn, the "Shevueh" (Oath), which many regard as the Jewish "Marseillaise."

ANTI-DEFAMATION LEAGUE see B'nai B'rith.

ANTIOCHUS EPIPHANES

Syrian king from 175 to 164 b.c.e., who because of his tyranny was nicknamed by the Jews "Epimanes" (madman). He sought to unify his kingdom through a common religion and the Hellenistic culture, and consequently tried to suppress the Jewish religion and mode of life. Because of his military defeats in Egypt, he turned his anger against the Jews of Judea by forbidding them to observe their laws and customs, by plundering the Holy Temple,

and by ordering them to worship Zeus. This led to the Judean revolt against Syrian rule, under the leadership of the Hasmoneans, particularly Mattathias and his sons. See *Hanukkah; Maccabees.*

ANTI-SEMITISM

A term generally applied to the hostile attitude of non-Jews toward individual Jews and the Jewish people. Numerous reasons are given for the milder as well as the more cruel forms of anti-Jewish discrimination. Hostility toward the Jew because of his religion is as old as, and older than, the Christian era. In recent times, anti-Semitism became less the product of opposition to the Jewish faith and more of social, economic, political and racial reasons: 1) The Jew, being in one way or another different from his surroundings, is looked

Nazi soldiers round up Jewish men, women and children from the Warsaw Ghetto for deportation to the death camps. Nazi anti-Semitism, and racial theories resulted in history's most ruthless genocide.

upon as a stranger toward whom there exists among people an instinctive hatred; 2) As a result of the rise of nationalism there came about a feeling of intolerance and often overt hatred toward members of minority groups; 3) The Jew as a city dweller, engaging in certain areas of the land's economy, often arouses the envy and animosity of groups in other fields of work or business; 4) The prominence of some Jews in the financial world created the myth of the "Jewish millionaire," and the naive belief that the Jew in general controls national and world economy; 5) The Jew is often the scapegoat for many evils befalling a country, such as economic distress and defeat in wars; 6) Participation of Jewish individuals in liberal movements arouses the anger of reactionaries and causes persecution of the entire Jewish group; 7) During the Nazi regime, the discredited racial theory claiming the existence of superior and inferior races was revived, and brought untold suffering to "non-Aryans," causing the annihilation of six million European Jews.

The consequences of anti-Semitism range from restrictive laws against Jews, denial of civil liberties, social and physical isolation of Jewish groups, to pogroms and the vicious physical destruction of entire Jewish communities.

ANTOKOLSKY, MARK (1843–1902)

Russian sculptor. As a young boy, while attending "Ḥeder" (Hebrew school), he displayed his talent as a woodcarver. His woodcarving of a later period, "The Jewish Tailor," gave him international recognition. His best known sculptures are: "Moses," "Spinoza," "The Jews Surprised by the Inquisition," "Ivan the Terrible," and "Peter the Great."

ANUSIM see Marranos.

APIKOROS see Epicurus.

APOCRYPHA

A Greek term applied to a group of 14 Jewish writings excluded from the Hebrew version of the Bible. They were written during the last two centuries b.c.e. and the first two centuries c.e., and were preserved by the Christian Church. Of special historic interest to the Jews are the apocryphal writings, *Ben-Sira* and the books of the *Maccabees*. The Apocrypha includes historical writings, prophecies, religious poems, proverbs, etc. The Protestant churches also exclude the Apocrypha from the canon.

APOSTATE see Meshummad.

AQABA (Akabah) see Eilat.

ARAB LEAGUE

Federation of the various Arab States organized in 1944. It was set up with the help and encouragement of the British government in order to strengthen its own international position, and to fight Jewish aspirations in Palestine. The governments of the Arab League, although split among themselves on many issues, united in 1948 to make war on the State of Israel. Following the crushing defeat of their invading armies by the Israelis, the Arab nations united through the Arab League, refused to make peace with the State of Israel, and have constantly threatened its peaceful development.

ARABS

A Semitic people, who according to Jewish and Mohammedan tradition, are the descendants of Ishmael, the son of Abraham the Patriarch and Hagar, Sarah's handmaid. Historically they are the Arabic speaking people, mostly Moslems (Mohammedans), and the inhabitants of Syria, Iraq, Israel, Transjordan, the Arabian peninsula, Egypt, Tripoli, Tunisia, Algeria and Morocco. The Arab population consists of bedouins (nomadic tribes), fellaheen (peasants), city-dwellers, and effendis (rich land-owners). Each Arab tribal group or village is headed by a sheikh, the elder and leader of the community.

The language and culture of the Arabs has had great influence on the culture of the Jewish people. Many literary and scientific works were written in Arabic during the period between the 8th and the 12th centuries, when the Arabic language and religion reached Babylonia, Syria, Palestine, North Africa and Spain. To that period belong the great works written in Arabic by Saadiah Gaon, Judah Ha-Levi, Moses ibn Ezra, Maimonides and many others. Arabic is spoken today by Jews living among the Arabic speaking people.

Before the establishment of the State of Israel, there lived in what was then Palestine over half a million Arabs, including about 70,000 of the Christian faith. The steady Jewish immigration into Palestine following the Balfour Declaration (1917) was not welcomed either by the Palestinian Arabs or those of the neighboring countries. The Palestinian Arab leaders had constantly incited the Arab peasants to riots and even bloody pogroms against the growing Jewish settlements in order to deter them from building the Jewish National Home as promised to the Jewish people by Britain and confirmed by the League of Nations after World War I. The partition of Palestine between Jews and Arabs decided upon by the United Nations, and the declaration of the estab-

Arab bedouins taking their siesta in the market place of Beer-sheba. Though many of the local Arabs left Israel after the 1948 War of Liberation, almost a quarter of a million, mostly in Galilee, remained.

lishment of the State of Israel in 1948, aroused the Arab nations in the Middle East, and they launched an unsuccessful war against the defenders of the Jewish homeland. During the War of Liberation, most of the Palestinian Arabs fled the country, and only about 160,000 remained to become lawful citizens of the State of Israel. The bitterly defeated Arab nations, although forced to sign an armistice, still refused to sign a peace-treaty with the government of the State of Israel.

ARAMAIC

A Semitic language, somewhat similar to Hebrew. It was first adopted as a common Jewish tongue by the Jews in Babylonia, (probably about 525 b.c.e.), then by the Jews in Egypt, and later by the Jews in Palestine (about 325 b.c.e.). It flourished as the Jewish tongue until the seventh century c.e., when Arabic became the language of the East. During much of this period, Aramaic was the language spoken by many non-Jews as well. Major Jewish literary works were either translated into Aramaic, such as the *Targum* (translation of the Hebrew Bible), or created in that language, such as parts of the Biblical books of *Daniel* and *Ezra*, as well as portions of the two Talmuds and much of the Midrashic literature. The Aramaic of the Bible and the Palestinian and Babylonian Talmuds are each in different dialects. In addition there are many legal Jewish documents and important Jewish prayers which were written in Aramaic. In the present day, e.g., the *Ketubah* (Jewish marriage contract), the *Get* (Jewish writ of divorce), and the *Kaddish* (mourner's prayer) are in Aramaic. When Aramaic ceased to be the common Jewish vernacular, it became, like Hebrew, a sacred language of the Jews. Much of the mystical literature (Kabbalah), written in Aramaic, remains important.

Foundation stone of a proposed Jewish colony at Grand Island, New York, laid in September 1825, which was to have been called "Ararat."

ARARAT

The mountain mentioned in the Bible as the place where Noah's Ark rested after the Flood. It is also the name of the projected Jewish settlement on Grand Island, Niagara, proclaimed by Mordecai Manuel Noah in 1825. His plan never materialized, but the foundation stone is kept at the Buffalo Historical Society. See *Noah, Mordecai Manuel.*

ARBA KANFOT (Kanfos)

Hebrew term meaning "four corners" applied to the four-cornered "small shawl" (Tallit Katan) traditionally worn during the day by orthodox Jewish men under the upper garments, as distinguished from the larger Prayer Shawl (Tallit), usually worn by worshippers for the morning service. The *Arba Kanfot* has "Tzitzit" (fringes) on each of its four corners and a central opening for passing it over the head. It is believed that the practice of wearing the Arba Kanfot originated during the time of religious persecutions when it was not safe for a Jew to be seen wearing the Tallit. See *Tallit.*

ARBA KOSOT

Hebrew term for the four cups of wine used at the Passover Seder. They are a reminder of the liberation from Egyptian bondage, which is described in the Bible by the use of four verbs: "bring out," "deliver," "redeem," and "take." See *Seder.*

ARBA KUSHYOT see Four Questions; Seder.

ARBEITER RING see Workmen's Circle.

ARBOR DAY, JEWISH see Tu Bi-Shevat.

ARCH OF TITUS see Titus, Arch of.

ARCHEOLOGY

The branch of science dealing with the investigation of ancient Jewish culture. It is especially concerned with the study of Jewish history and culture beginning with the Biblical period and ending with the Talmudic period.

Jewish archeological studies make use of both written and non-written materials. The written materials include the texts of the Bible, the literature of the period of the Second Temple, the Talmudic and Midrashic texts, as well as the literature of early Christianity; the non-written materials consist of archeological discoveries through excavations and other means in terms of architecture, monuments, inscriptions, utensils, coins, art, and many other artifacts bearing on customs, religion, and social and economic life.

Jewish archeological excavations in Palestine began during the second half of the 19th century, first by French, and then by English, German and American archeologists. Under the British Mandate over Palestine the activities of archeological research in Palestine was intensified, and the first Jewish society for archeological research in Palestine was founded in 1919. In 1926 the Hebrew University in Jerusalem established an archeological department. Following the birth of the State of Israel in 1948, the Israel Government Department of Antiquities took over the supervision of archeological research, and the Israel Exploration Society embarked on an intensive and systematic program of research in Jewish antiquities.

Jewish archeology, especially the study of the Biblical period, concerns itself with the excavations made in Palestine as well as with those made in the neighboring countries. Following is a description of the more important archeological excavations and discoveries, listed in alphabetical order:

Amarna Letters: Discovered in 1887 in Egypt, on the site of an ancient capital, now known in Arabic as Tel El Amarna. Some of the letters were written by vassal kings in Canaan to the Pharaohs (1413–1377, and 1377–1361 b.c.e.) complaining about the disorder caused by the invasion of the Habiru (probably Hebrews), requesting the assistance of the Pharaohs because of the frequent wars among the vassal kings. See *Catacombs, Jewish.*

Bet-Alpha: On the site where there is now a cooperative settlement in Israel (Valley of Jezreel), a synagogue of the 6th century c.e. was excavated. Its mosaic floor depicts ritual symbols, the sacrifice of Isaac, and contains inscriptions in Hebrew, Greek and Aramaic.

Bet-Shean: Excavations north of the present town of the same name have uncovered the remains of this ancient and important Palestinian city which is mentioned in Egyptian inscriptions of the 2nd millennium b.c.e.

Bet-Shearim: Excavations since 1936 unearthed a synagogue and numerous tombs of the second to the fourth centuries, with inscriptions in Hebrew, Greek, Aramaic and other dialects. Bet-Shearim was an important center of learning, and the seat of the Sanhedrin during the days of Judah Ha-Nasi.

Bet-Shemesh: Excavations have revealed the remains of this ancient walled city with its underground water tanks.

Bet-Yerah: Excavations since 1936 have revealed a 5th century synagogue, as well as traces of civilization dating as far back as 5000 b.c.e.

Caesarea: Excavations have revealed relics of Roman and Byzantine origin, as well as the remains of a synagogue.

(Top left) The containers in which the Dead Sea Scrolls were discovered. (Top right) The actual seventh Dead Sea Scroll before being unrolled. (Bottom right) Professor James Biberkraut unrolls the last of the seven Dead Sea Scrolls now in Israel's possession. At first thought to be the Book of Lemech, before it was deciphered by Hebrew University archeologists, it is now known to be a commentary on the Book of Genesis, and part of it is devoted to a description of the beauty of Sarah, wife of the Patriarch Abraham. (Bottom left) Cast of the Hammurabi Stelle dated ca. 1780 b.c.e. The original is now in the Louvre Museum in Paris.

Caesarea, capital of the Procurators of Judea 19 centuries ago under Roman occupation, still has a Roman amphitheater and hippodrome, and Roman and Crusader city walls to testify to its greatness.

Relics of the temple at Hazor are on display at the Haifa Museum. Hazor was one of the Canaanite fortified towns which, in the Biblical account, Joshua destroyed probably during the 13th century b.c.e.

23

(Top left) 2nd century c.e. tomb of the "Sanhedrin" in Bet-Shearim near Haifa. (Top right) Ancient fortress of Masada in the Negev was built by the Hasmoneans and fortified by King Herod the Great. (Below) Reconstruction of Capernaum's synagogue.

Capernaum: The remains of a synagogue of the 2nd to the 4th centuries are well preserved.

Dead Sea Scrolls: Ancient manuscripts, the first few of which were discovered in 1947 at Khirbet Qumran, a few miles from Jericho. These scrolls contain several books and portions of books of the Hebrew Bible, Biblical commentaries, fragments of Apocrypha and Pseudepigrapha, as well as completely unknown books, some of which describe in detail the local way of life, teachings of a Jewish sect (akin to the Essenes) which flourished during the pre-Christian era, whose members wrote and preserved the scrolls. These scrolls influenced subsequent study of the Bible and religion.

Ezion-Geber: Nelson Glueck excavated the remains of the ancient port at the Gulf of Aqaba, and found "Solomon's mines."

Gezer Calendar: A Hebrew inscription of the 10th century b.c.e., listing agricultural seasons and details of various tasks connected with them.

Hammurabi Code: Discovered at the beginning of the 20th century, represents the legislation of a Babylonian king (1728–1686 b.c.e.). This code resembles in some details the legislation in the Pentateuch.

Hazor: Ancient city in Galilee, mentioned in Egyptian inscriptions from the 19th century b.c.e., where excavations began in 1928, and where Yigael Yadin began in 1955 to do extremely important archeological research.

Jericho: Excavations which began in 1906 yielded evidence of the existence of walled villages in Palestine as early as 5000 b.c.e.

Lachish Letters: Excavated in 1935 on the site of Lachish. These are Hebrew letters from military personnel inscribed on 21 potsherds, probably in 589 b.c.e., when Lachish was threatened by the Babylonian empire.

Mamre: A site near Hebron, mentioned in the narrative about Abraham, where excavations have uncovered a wall erected by Herod.

Mari Texts: Discovered in 1933–38 at Mari, Mesopotamia, as part of a library of an excavated palace of the 18th century b.c.e. These texts throw much light on the narrative of the Patriarchs contained in Genesis.

Masada: Famous fortress west of the Dead Sea, where the remains of Herod's palace, as well as those of another palace of Hasmonean origin were excavated in 1955–56.

Megiddo: Ancient town in the Valley of Jezreel, where excavations made between 1909 and 1939 uncovered many strata of settlement, in one of which the stables of Solomon's horses were found.

Moabite Stone: Found in 1868 at the Moabite capital Dibon. It was inscribed by Mesha, king of Moab, on the occasion of his successful uprising against Joram of the northern Kingdom of Israel. This stone, now in the Louvre, is written in Moabitic, a language similar to Hebrew.

Nirim: A settlement in the Negev, in the vicinity of which the remains of a mosaic floor of an ancient synagogue were discovered.

Samaria: Capital of the northern Kingdom of Israel, was excavated in 1908–10 and in 1931–35 by Jewish, but mostly by non-Jewish archeologists.

Shaar Ha-Golan: A settlement in the Central Jordan Valley where excavations have uncovered a pre-historic settlement (c. 10,000 b.c.e.).

Shechem: Ancient Canaanite town, excavated by German archeologists in 1913–34.

Sinai Inscriptions: Discovered in 1906 in the southern part of the Sinai peninsula. Originated in the 15th century b.c.e., these inscriptions illuminate the development of the ancient Hebrew alphabet.

ARK OF NOAH

Ugarit Documents: Discovered in the ancient Canaanite city now known as Ras Shamra. Written in cuneiform in Ugaritic, a language akin to Hebrew, these documents illuminate Canaanite religion and culture with striking similarities to parts of the early Biblical narrative.

Ur: Excavations in the ruins of this Babylonian city, home of Abraham, show traces of a high civilization in Abraham's time, as well as evidence of a great flood in the early history of mankind.

ARK OF NOAH see Noah.

ARK OF THE COVENANT

This term, known in Hebrew as *Aron ha-Berit*, refers to the Ark made by the Biblical artisan Bezalel by divine inspiration

One of the many reconstructions of the Ark of the Covenant showing Egyptian influences.

at the direction of Moses. It was placed in the Tabernacle and was carried by the Levites during the wandering of the Israelites in the wilderness. After the conquest of Canaan, the Ark of the Covenant was moved to the sanctuary at Shiloh. It was later brought to Jerusalem by David, and following the erection of the Holy Temple it was placed there by King Solomon.

ARON HA-KODESH

Hebrew term for the "Holy Ark," referring to the artistically wrought cabinet situated in the center of the east wall of the synagogue, in which the Scrolls of the Torah are kept. It is covered with a beautifully embroidered curtain called "Paro-

khet," and above the doors in front hangs the *Ner Tamid* (Eternal Light). Also above the door of the *Aron ha-Kodesh* there is usually an inscription of a sacred message, or the text of the Ten Commandments. The Aron ha-Kodesh is the holiest part of the house of worship, because of the sacred Scrolls within it as well as serving as a reminder of the "Holy of Holies" in the ancient Temple at Jerusalem.

ARYANISM

The term, originally used to designate the group of "Indo-European" and "Indo-Germanic" languages, was subsequently applied to the discredited racial theory. According to this theory, the Aryan-speaking people are descendants of the original Aryan race, which exclusively possesses the highest human capacities for the best cultural attainments in the fields of literature, art, science and statesmanship. This theory, although rejected by all scientists, became popular in Germany, and with the rise of the Nazi regime the theory of the existence of "superior" and "inferior" races was used to launch a campaign of hatred and annihilation of those people, especially the Jews, whose supposedly "inferior blood" and culture were likely to contaminate the pure-blooded "Nordics" and especially the German "Master Race."

ASARAH BE-TEVET see Fast Days.

ASCH, SHOLEM (1880–1957)

Yiddish novelist and dramatist, born in Poland. His first great work, placing him among the foremost Yiddish writers, was "Dos Shtetl," an idyllic novel about Jewish life in Poland. This was followed by a drama, "The God of Vengeance," successfully produced on the Yiddish and non-Jewish stage. After his visits to Palestine and the United States, he wrote other important novels, such as "Uncle Moses,"

Ceremonial Torah Ark which was a gift to the synagogue of Urbino, in Italy, in the year 1451. The Ark's three upper partitions symbolize the three parts of the Bible: Pentateuch, Prophets, and Writings.

"Kiddush Ha-Shem," and "Motkeh the Thief." After World War I he published "Three Cities," a novel dealing with the current period of Jewish life in Russia. He later published "Salvation," a famous novel about Ḥasidic life in Poland. In later years he published, while living in the United States, the controversial historical novels "The Nazarene," "The Apostle," and "Mary." These three novels, like many of his other works, were translated into English, and caused the author to become unpopular in Jewish circles because of his apparent acquiescence in certain Christian traditions, even where critical scholarship rejected them. His last book of this series, "The Prophet," did not do much to enhance his reputation. In 1955 he settled in

Sholem Asch, Yiddish writer, whose powerful evocations of the "Shtetl" and ancient Palestine have aroused both acclaim and controversy.

27

Israel. After his death there appeared a willingness in Jewish circles to overlook the evil that he may have wrought in later years, and to reinstate him in the galaxy of Jewish talents, keeping in mind the important work he had done in his earlier days.

ASHAMNU

Hebrew word meaning "we have trespassed"; the opening word of a confession of sins arranged in alphabetical order, and recited during the Yom Kippur services. To show real repentance, the person reciting the confession beats his breast as he utters each transgression.

ASHI (352–427)

One of the last and foremost Babylonian *Amoraim*, (interpreters of the Mishnah). As the head of the Academy of Sura and Mata Meḥasya for 52 years, his major work was the compilation and editing of much of the Babylonian Talmud. Because of his influence as a teacher and his social prestige, the Talmud remarks that from Rabbi Judah the Prince to Rabbi Ashi "learning and dignity have never thus been united in one person."

ASHKENAZIM

The Hebrew term "Ashkenaz" has, since the 10th century, been applied to Germany, and "Ashkenazim" was applied to those Jews living in Germany and northern France, in contradistinction to the Jews living in the Spanish and Mediterranean countries, called "Sephardim." Later the Jews of Poland, Russia, and the Scandinavian countries were also called Ashkenazim. The Ashkenazim differ from the Sephardim in culture, ritual and social customs. The Sephardi Jews adopted the Spanish language to form their own dialect called *Ladino*, whereas Ashkenazi Jews spoke the German language and formed their own language, which developed and survived as the *Yiddish* language. The Hebrew pronunciation of the Ashkenazim differs from that of the Sephardim. The Sephardi pronunciation of Hebrew (with some modification) was adopted in modern Israel and subsequently gained in popularity and currency wherever modern Hebrew was spoken.

ASIDEANS see Hasideans.

ASSYRIA

One of the important empires in western Asia at the time of its greatest strength. It played a significant role in the history of Israel and Judah between 900 and 600 b.c.e., i.e. during the period of the two kingdoms. The security of the Jewish states as well as that of their neighbors frequently depended on the vicissitudes in the royalty and in the military power of Assyria. It was in 721 that Sargon destroyed the Northern Kingdom, deporting many Israelites to Assyria and, in turn, bringing many pagans from Assyria to Israel. In 700, King Sennacherib besieged Jerusalem, but due to a plague breaking out in his camp, was forced to retreat. In the latter part of the century, Assyria was succeeded by Babylonia in importance as a power.

The Assyrians were notorious for their cruelty, especially the harsh manner in which they conducted war and treated prisoners, a phenomenon alluded to in many places in the Bible. It is written that the prophet Jonah was commanded by God to preach to the inhabitants of Nineveh, capital of Assyria, to exhort them to change their evil ways. Jonah is reported to have been chagrined that they repented and that, therefore, his prophecy of their destruction was not fulfilled.

ASYLUM, RIGHT OF see Cities of Refuge.

ATONEMENT, DAY OF see Yom Kippur.

Alabaster relief of Assurbanipal (Asenappar in Hebrew), last of the great Assyrian emperors, who lived about 669–633 b.c.e. Conqueror of Egypt and Chaldea, he is shown here as a cavalry archer.

AUSTRALIA

Continent and British Dominion where 60,000 Jews lived in 1960. Jewish immigration to Australia began in 1817, and consisted mainly of British Jews, to which east European Jewish immigrants were added in later periods. The largest Jewish communities are found in Sydney, Melbourne and Perth. From the beginning the Jews of Australia enjoyed religious and political freedom and contributed greatly to the economic and industrial life of the island. Politically the Jews of Australia occupied prominent positions. Sir Isaac Isaacs was Governor General, the highest governmental function. There have been Jewish prime ministers and members of parliament, and many cities have had Jewish mayors and judges. The Jewish community takes an active interest in local and world Jewish affairs. It has its own Jewish religious and cultural organizations.

AUSTRIA

Jewish history in Austria can be traced to the 4th century. In spite of persecutions and expulsions between the 15th and the 18th centuries, the Jewish community in Austria continued to exist, and especially flourished in the 19th century when Jews were accorded equal rights and religious freedom. Both in the Middle Ages and in modern times the Jews in Austria have occupied important positions in the economic and political life of the country and have made great contributions to Jewish culture and Jewish national movements. Many important rabbis and scholars, Jewish financiers, journalists and political leaders were active in Austria and influenced Jewish life elsewhere. In 1938 there were about 200,000 Jews in Austria, with the largest Jewish community in Vienna. The decline of Austrian Jewry began with the Nazi occupation, and fol-

29

A Spanish painting, vintage ca. 1500, in the National Gallery in Madrid, showing the judges and victims of the Inquisition's Auto-Da-Fe.

lowing the Second World War it almost completely disappeared. In 1960, there were about 12,000 Jews in Austria, the remnants of what was once a flourishing Jewish community.

AUTO-DA-FE

A Portuguese term for "The Act of Faith" applied to the judgment rendered by the Court of the Inquisition and the place of execution (mostly death-sentence by burning) of those accused of being unfaithful and disloyal Christians. Although established as punishment against heretics and infidels in general, the Jews of the Spanish countries, especially those converted by intimidation to Christianity, bore the brunt of these ghastly public executions.

There is a record of at least 2,000 Autos-Da-Fe, most of which took place in Portugal and Spain, involving some 400,000 martyrs tried for their loyalty to Judaism. Beginning at the end of the 13th century, the Autos-Da-Fe continued until the early part of the 19th century. There were also Autos-Da-Fe held in the Spanish and Portuguese colonies on the American continent. See *Marranos*.

AUTO-EMANCIPATION see Pinsker, Leo.

AV

The 11th Hebrew month, corresponding to July-August, and consisting of 30 days. In the history of the Jewish people a number of tragic events occurred during the month of Av, and its first nine days are traditionally considered days of sorrow. See *Tishah Be-Av*.

AV, NINTH DAY OF see Tishah Be-Av.

AVINU MALKENU

Two Hebrew words meaning "Our Father, Our King," beginning a well known litany recited during the Penitential Days, from the New Year to the Day of Atonement, as well as on the other fast days. God is seen here in the twofold aspect of divine mercy (Father) and divine justice (King).

AVOT

A popular tractate of the *Mishnah*, also known as *Pirke Avot* or "Ethics of the Fathers." It comprises the selected wisdom, sayings, ethical and religious principles and rules of conduct as expressed by the teachers of the Mishnah. It contains six chapters, which are read sequentially every Sabbath between Pesaḥ and Rosh Hashanah. *Avot* teaches good human relationships, the value of studying the Law, how to serve God, love of peace, and the importance to all mankind of charity, modesty and humility.

AYIN (ע)

The sixteenth letter of the Hebrew alphabet. It is a consonant, but like the Aleph it has no sound. In Yiddish, Ayin is a vowel representing the sound equivalent to the English letter *e* in the word *let*. The numerical value of Ayin is seventy.

AYIN HA-RA

Hebrew term, also pronounced "Ayin Horre," meaning "evil eye" or, more literally, the eye of the evil one, i.e., the devil. It refers to a superstition that certain individuals possess the evil power to injure others by looking at them. It is also believed that even seeing a person enjoying good health or being successful, can have a damaging effect. From antiquity to our own day, all over the world, people believed that the glance of the eye can cause material harm even when operating at a distance. It is therefore customary with Yiddish-speaking people to say "Kein Ayin Horre" (no evil eye) when referring to someone's good health, prosperity or success. People affected by such superstitions have resorted to a variety of remedies for those stricken with the "evil eye," such as reading the Bible, wearing a talisman, and using certain incantations. Although still popular with some Jewish groups, this superstition has largely disappeared in the more modern Jewish communities. Our English word "fascinate" derives from the Latin phrase relating to the "evil eye"; the widespread nature of such belief may further be noted from the fact that in Italian the expression "evil eye" is contracted into a single word "malocchio."

B

BENEDICTIONS

Soon may there be heard in the cities of Judah, and in the streets of Jerusalem, the voice of joy and gladness, the voice of the bridegroom and the voice of the bride, the jubilant voice of bridegrooms from their canopies, and of youths from their feasts of song. Blessed art Thou, O Lord, who makes the bridegroom to rejoice with the bride.

TALMUD

BAAL

BAAL

A term meaning "master," "husband," "possessor." In Biblical times it was used to designate local gods of the West Semitic peoples. The Baalim (plural of Baal) were gods possessing the power to control nature, such as fertility and harvest. After the conquest of Canaan many Israelites worshipped the Baal. The Hebrew prophets strongly opposed idol worship, and the prophet Elijah was especially active in fighting Baal worship in the Kingdom of Israel, spread by the Phoenician-born queen of Israel, the infamous Jezebel, the wife of King Ahab.

BAAL HA-BAYIT

Hebrew term meaning "the master of the house." In Yiddish it is pronounced "Balebos," and commonly applies to a well-to-do person enjoying a privileged stature in the community.

BAAL KORE

Hebrew term meaning "master reader," applied to the official reader of the designated portion of the Torah read during Sabbath and festival services in the synagogue before the congregation.

BAAL NES

Hebrew term meaning "a performer of miracles." Jewish tradition refers to the *Tanna*, R. Meir, as "Rabbi Meir Baal Nes," and special charity boxes were commonly placed in Jewish homes in his name.

BAAL SHEM

Hebrew term meaning "Master of the Name," traditionally applied to a person who, by divine inspiration and by the use of God's name, possesses the power to perform miracles. Such persons were known for their acts of piety and for their expert knowledge of Jewish mysticism called Kabbalah. The "Baal Shem" par

An idol of Baal Hammon, one of the many primitive nature deities worshipped in various animal and human forms in the ancient Near East.

excellence always refers to the *Baal Shem Tov*, leader of the Ḥasidim.

BAAL SHEM TOV (1700–1760)

Father of the Ḥasidic movement whose given name was Israel ben Eliezer, also known as the "Besht," abbreviated form of "Baal Shem Tov." He was orphaned as a young child, and during his early years was reared by the Jewish community of Okup, province of Podolia. He was a dreamy boy who preferred roaming in the fields and forests to studying in the *ḥeder* (Hebrew school). As he grew older he became an assistant to a teacher, then a *shoḥet*, a clay-digger, and finally he opened his own school for beginners. He married the sister of a scholar who did not think much of the untutored brother-in-law. Israel and his wife moved to an isolated place in the Carpathian mountains. In the quiet of the mountains and forests, Israel communed with God and learned much about the healing power of various kinds of herbs. When he later moved to a larger town, he became known as a healer of people, and many gave him the name of "Baal Shem," (Master of the Name). When people were troubled they came to him for good advice, for benedictions, and for cheerful promises of better times. It soon became known in many Jewish communities that the *Master of the Good Name* (Baal Shem Tov) had found a new way of teaching Judaism. He preached to hundreds of people who flocked around him that the first duty of a Jew is to seek God, and that God is in all places and in all things of the universe. He further explained that in order to reach God one does not need much technical learning, but rather simplicity and sincerity. A simple but heartfelt and sincere prayer is all one needs for communion with God. He also said that the way to commune with God was through joy rather than through sadness.

The *Baal Shem Tov* gave new hope to thousands of simple people who felt that not only the learned, but they too, could now reach God and serve Him in their own way. Later, when many rabbis opposed the teachings of the *Baal Shem Tov*, his followers formed the Ḥasidic sect which became a great and influential movement in Jewish life for many generations to come. See *Ḥasidism.*

BAAL TEFILLAH see Ḥazzan.

BAAL TEKIAH see Baal Tokea.

BAAL TESHUVAH

Hebrew term applied to a person who sincerely repents of sins he has committed. Jewish tradition has high regard for the *Baal Teshuvah*, whose sins are believed forgiven even if repentance comes late.

BAAL TOKEA

Hebrew term applied to the person who sounds the *Shofar* during services on the High Holy Days.

A young Ḥasidic boy wearing the ritual earlocks and skullcap carries on the traditions of the Baal Shem Tov, the saintly father of Ḥasidism.

BABEL, TOWER OF

According to the Bible, the people of the early history of mankind spoke one language, and they decided to build in the land of Shinar (Babylonia) a tower "whose top may reach into heaven." This attempt was frustrated by God when He confused their language so that they did not understand one another; the people thereafter scattered upon the face of the earth. The name "Babel" is said to mean "confusion," and the word with a small "b" has this meaning in modern English.

BABYLONIA

An ancient Asian empire on the shores of the Euphrates, known second only to Palestine as the greatest and most important center of Jewish life and culture for a period of about 1500 years. Abraham emigrated from Babylonia (Ur of the Chaldees) about 2000 b.c.e., and Jewish history had continual contact with what was one of the earliest centers of civilization since then. In the 6th century b.c.e., Babylonia,

35

Reconstruction of ancient Babylon with a temple (or ziggurat) dedicated to Marduk, believed to be the chief god of Babylonia. In the foreground are the Euphrates River, and the walls of Babylon.

under its king Nebuchadnezzar, conquered Judea and carried off into exile large numbers of the Judean captives. The Jews in Babylonia enjoyed religious freedom and economic prosperity, and were able to establish houses of study and worship. Even after the conquest of Babylonia by the Persian king Cyrus who permitted the Jews to return to Judea, many Jews continued to live in their adopted country. During the period of the Second Temple in Jerusalem, the Jews in Babylonia developed their community and there was continued contact between them and the Palestinian Jews.

Following the Bar Kokhba revolt against Rome in 135 c.e., new waves of Jewish immigrants came to Babylonia, and the period of the great Jewish academies began, where the Babylonian Talmud was gradually created and developed by hundreds of *Amoraim* (interpreters of

Ishtar's Gate, built in 6th century b.c.e. by Nebuchadnezzar II, was dedicated to the fertility goddess. Note the "Hanging Gardens of Babylon" (upper right), one of the "seven wonders" of the ancient world.

the Mishnah). After the completion of the Talmud, the academies existed under the leadership of the *Saboraim* and later the *Geonim*, who continued the tradition of Jewish learning, and made Babylonia the center of Jewish legal authority for all Jewish communities. During that period Aramaic was the language of the Jewish people, and continued to be so until the period of Islam, when the Arabic language was gradually taken over by the Jews of Babylonia. In this language too, the Jews of Babylonia created many important philosophical and scientific works, as exemplified by the works of Saadiah Gaon. During the 12th century, however, the Jewish community in Babylonia began its downward period, until it practically disappeared, and Jewish communities began to develop and flourish in Spain, Italy and Germany. Babylonia is now known as Iraq. See *Academies, Babylonian*.

37

BABYLONIAN EXILE

The period of seventy years, between 586 b.c.e. when the First Temple was destroyed and 516 when the Second Temple was built. When Judea was conquered by the Babylonians in 586 b.c.e., many captives were carried off to Babylonia. They lived there in prosperity and enjoyed religious freedom. However, they did not forget their desolated homeland and longed for their return to it. Babylonia was conquered by Cyrus, king of Persia, in 539 b.c.e., who issued a proclamation allowing the Judeans to return to their homeland. As a result many returned, though others remained behind and continued to live in Babylonia, which later developed into an important Jewish cultural center.

BADGE, JEWISH

During the Middle Ages and until the 18th century there were many countries where Jews were ordered to wear a special mark (badge) on their clothes, or a special garment to distinguish them from the non-Jewish population. The badge of discrimination was first imposed in Moslem countries in the 9th century on both Jews and Christians, and at the beginning of the 13th century it was imposed on the Jews by the Christian Church. England and continental European countries imposed the Jew-badge during the next several centuries.

The Jew-badge was of different sizes, shapes, and colors, depending on the whims of the Jew-haters; quite frequently it was a yellow badge bearing other distinguishing designs. During the Nazi period, beginning in 1933, the use of the yellow badge was revived in Germany and later also in the Nazi-occupied countries. First it was introduced in the form of a yellow identification card for Jewish students in Germany, and later in the form of a yellow piece of cloth bearing the sign of the *Magen David* (Jewish Star).

The Yellow Badge the Nazis required Jews to wear in Germany and Nazi-occupied countries.

BAECK, LEO (1874–1956)

Reform rabbi and theologian. Born in Germany, he became a rabbi in 1897. From 1912 he ministered in Berlin, where he also lectured on Midrashic literature. Rabbi Baeck soon became the spiritual leader of Liberal Judaism in Germany, and was head of the *Rabbinerverband* (Union of Rabbis). During the Nazi regime he became the chief representative of German Jewry, and served in that capacity until 1943 when he was sent to a concentration camp. He survived, and in 1946 settled in London, where he subsequently organized the World Union of Progressive Judaism, of which he was the first president. He frequently traveled to the United States to serve as visiting professor at the Hebrew Union College, Cincinnati, Ohio. A school bearing his name was established in Israel.

BAHUR, ELIJAH see Levita, Elijah.

BAHYA B. JOSEPH IBN PAKUDA

Religious philosopher living in Spain during the 11th century, and author of a widely read book on moral conduct entitled "Hovot Ha-Levavot" (Duties of the Heart). Originally written in Arabic, this book was translated into Hebrew about a century later by Judah ibn Tibbon. For many generations its influence in the Jewish world was very great. In the ten chapters of the book, Ibn Pakuda writes on the unity of God; the duty of man to search for and to recognize God's ways; the best ways of serving God; the duty of having faith; the duty of cultivating good habits and manners, modesty and love.

BAIS see Bet.

BALFOUR DECLARATION

An important document in the form of a letter issued by the British Government on November 2, 1917, and signed by the Foreign Secretary Lord Arthur James Balfour. The letter, addressed to Lord Roth-schild, reads in part: "His Majesty's Government view with favour the establishment in Palestine of a national home for the Jewish people, and will use their best endeavors to facilitate the achievement of this object . . ." The Declaration was then approved by France, Italy, Japan and the United States.

This recognition of the claim of the Jewish people to their historical homeland gave new hope to the Zionist movement and started a period of mass immigration and the establishment of Jewish settlements in Palestine, which in the course of thirty years paved the way for the establishment of the State of Israel.

BAMIDBOR see Numbers.

BAR-ILAN UNIVERSITY

An institution of higher learning in Israel, founded in 1955 and located at Ramat Gan, near Tel Aviv. The University is sponsored by the Mizrachi Organization of America, and was named after the late

Leo Baeck, rabbi and Reform leader, was a Jewish theologian of merit and great influence.

Lord Arthur James Balfour, British statesman and author of the famous Balfour Declaration.

BAR KOKHBA

The large auditorium of Bar-Ilan University in Ramat Gan, near Tel Aviv. Founded in 1955 under American Mizrachi auspices, the University aims at synthesizing secular and religious Jewish culture.

Rabbi Meir Bar-Ilan (Berlin), prominent leader of the World Mizrachi Organization, the Zionist religious group.

The University was created to fill the need for an institution of higher learning conducted in the spirit of orthodox Judaism, and to provide for the practical educational needs of the country, such as the training of personnel for various governmental agencies and institutions. Its program of studies is based on a synthesis between traditional Jewish culture and general secular culture and science.

The University opened with a body of 100 students, a large number of whom came from the United States; others were from Europe, South America, Morocco, Egypt and Iraq. In 1956 the University doubled its enrollment and offered 42 different courses in mathematics, physics, chemistry, biology, languages and literature, history, psychology, economics, Bible and Talmud.

BAR KOKHBA

Great hero and leader of the Jewish revolt against the Roman oppressors (131–135 c.e.). His given name was Simeon, and he was considered by many as the *Messiah;* he also won the support of the leading

scholar of that period, R. Akiva. He came from the town of Koziba, and was therefore known as the "Man of Koziba" (Bar Koziba); this name was changed to the optimistic Bar Kokhba—the "Son of the Star." Bar Kokhba's call to arms was answered by most Jews, even by many living in communities outside of Judea. With great skill and heroism he succeeded in a short time in defeating the Roman armies and capturing Jerusalem, in honor of which event he struck coins bearing the inscription "Le-Herut Yerushalayim" (to Jerusalem's liberation). After repeated defeats of his armies, the Roman emperor Hadrian sent his foremost general Julius Severus with a fresh army which succeeded, after a long struggle, in defeating the Jewish rebels. The last battle took place at the remaining fortress Bettar which fell in 135 c.e., where Bar Kokhba perished together with his heroic men. The failure of the Bar Kokhba revolt brought a new wave of Roman terror and caused great suffering and martyrdom to the defeated and helpless Jewish people.

1800-year-old papyri from the Bar Kokhba era recently discovered by a Hebrew University team of archeologists. The inscribed fragments were military orders from Bar Kokhba to a deputy.

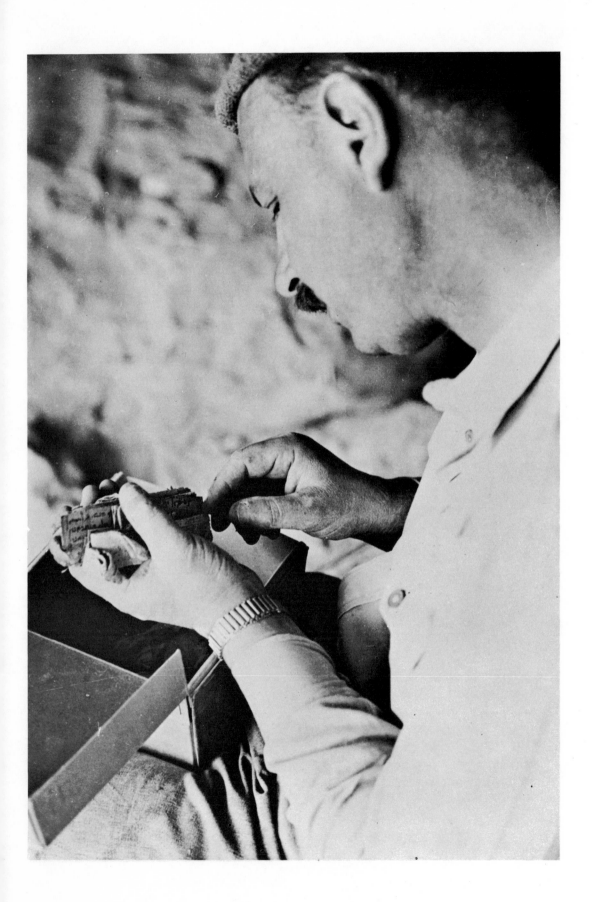

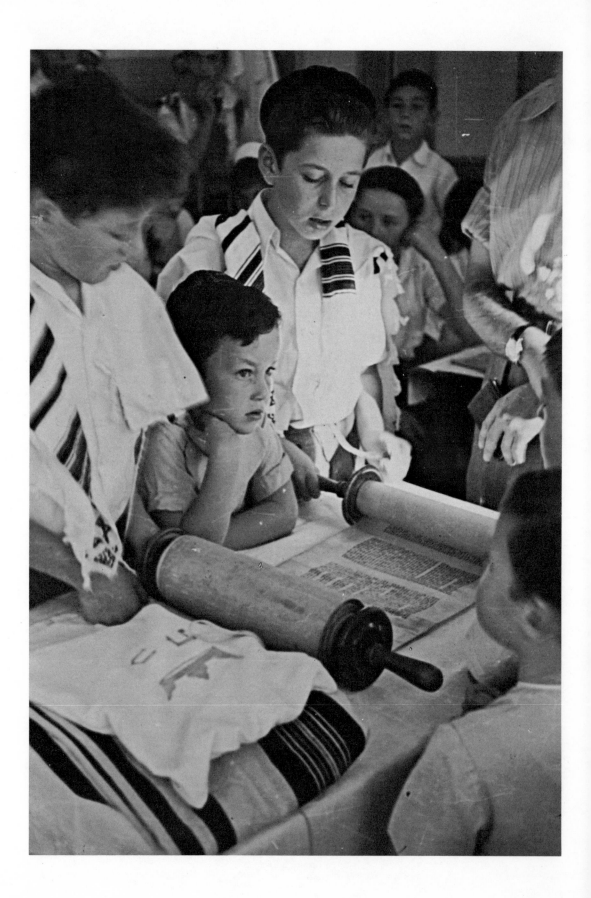

BAR MITZVAH

Hebrew term meaning "Son of the Commandment," or more accurately, a person who is duty bound to observe the commandments of Judaism, applied to a Jewish boy reaching his thirteenth birthday. From then on it is his duty to assume the religious responsibilities of an adult Jew; it is his duty to wear phylacteries ("Tefillin") during the morning weekday prayers; and he is included in the *Minyan*, ten male adults, the quorum required for public prayer. The Bar Mitzvah celebration is a festive occasion, usually taking place on the Sabbath following the boy's 13th birthday. At the synagogue the boy is honored with an *Aliyah* and usually reads the *Haftarah*, after which he may deliver a *Derashah* (discourse), which may be of hortatory or scholarly nature.

Bar Mitzvah is one of the most universally celebrated events in Jewish life. Every branch of American Judaism celebrates it, as do many secular Jews. In earlier days of *Reform*, there was some sentiment for eliminating Bar Mitzvah in favor of *Confirmation*, one ground being that the confirmant is more mature and more able to understand the significance of the occasion, and his new responsibilities. Today, many reform and conservative congregations encourage the Bar Mitzvah as well as subsequent confirmation. All branches of Judaism oppose the cessation of Jewish education after Bar Mitzvah is reached. Some congregations have instituted a corresponding ceremony for girls called Bat (Bas) Mitzvah.

BARSIMSON, JACOB

Known as the first Jew to settle in New Amsterdam (now New York), in 1654. He was a poor, but a proud and righteous

Young Israeli boys after their Bar Mitzvah are permitted to conduct regular synagogue services for themselves and for their younger friends.

man. Together with Asser Levy, he fought for equal rights for the Jews of the Dutch colony. After a prolonged fight they compelled Governor Stuyvesant to yield to their request that Jews in the colony be given the right to perform guard-duty instead of paying a substitutionary tax.

BASLE PROGRAM

The manifesto stating that the aim of Zionism is to establish for the Jewish people a publicly recognized, legally secured homeland in Palestine. This declaration was adopted at the first Zionist Congress held in Basle, Switzerland, in 1897, convened by Dr. Theodor Herzl. The Basle Program also included a number of recommendations for specific activities to be undertaken by Zionists the world over.

BATH-SHEBA

King David's wife and mother of King Solomon. The Bible relates that in order to marry the beautiful Bath-sheba, David intentionally gave her husband Uriah a dangerous military assignment, as a result of which he was killed. Outraged by this act, the prophet Nathan admonished David and foretold the misfortunes and consequences that he would suffer during his lifetime.

BATLAN

A Hebrew-Yiddish term commonly applied to an impractical man having little knowledge of worldly affairs. It also designates an idler, having no definite occupation of his own. Traditionally *Batlan* referred to a person who spent most of his time attending to the affairs of the community, such as making sure that there was a *Minyan* (quorum) for divine prayer services.

BBYO see B'nai B'rith.

BEACONSFIELD, EARL OF see Disraeli, Benjamin.

43

Beer-sheba and its mosque. Mentioned in the Bible in connection with all three Patriarchs, the city became a part of Israel in 1948, and is both the gateway to and the chief Jewish town of the Negev.

Mendel Beilis, innocent victim of Tsarist anti-Semitism in a 1913 "ritual murder" trial in Kiev.

BEDIKAT ḤAMETZ

Hebrew term applied to the old Jewish tradition of searching on the evening before the first Passover night for crumbs of bread or remains of leaven to be burned before the Passover festival during which *Ḥametz* (leavened food) is forbidden. The burning of the Hametz is called "Biur Ḥametz." Before collecting and burning the Ḥametz, the head of the family recites an appropriate blessing.

BEER-SHEBA

A predominantly Jewish city of the northern part of the Negev in the State of Israel. It is called the gateway to the Negev. Beer-sheba is as old as Jewish history itself; it is mentioned in the Bible as the place where Abraham worshipped and where Isaac and Jacob built altars. Through the period of King Saul's rule,

44

Samuel Belkin, scholar, educator and noted authority on Hellenistic literature and Judaism.

Beer-sheba was at the southern boundary of the Jewish kingdom, whereas the city of Dan was at the northern boundary, hence the commonly used phrase "from Dan to Beer-sheba."

BEILIS AFFAIR

World-famous blood-libel trial of a Russian Jew, Mendel Beilis, accused of having murdered a twelve year old Christian boy, whose blood was to be used for ritual purposes during the Passover festival. The trial taking place at Kiev in 1913 was used by the Russian government, and by anti-Semitic clergymen and press to stir up anti-Jewish riots in the country. The Beilis case attracted world-wide attention, and thanks to the skillful defense and to the expert medical evidence produced at the 34-day trial, as well as to pressures from the civilized nations of the world, the innocent victim was cleared by the court and acquitted. A broken man, Mendel Beilis went to Tel Aviv, Israel, and in 1924 settled in the United States, where he died ten years later. See *Blood Accusation*.

BEKHOR

Hebrew term applied to a first-born male child. See *Pidyon ha-Ben*.

BELGIUM

Country on the North Sea, where 75,000 Jews lived before the Second World War. Jews came to Belgium as early as the second century, during the Roman rule in Palestine. The Jewish community developed under favorable conditions, but following the persecutions during the black death period in the middle of the 14th century, there were practically no Jews left in Belgium. After the expulsion from Spain Jews returned to Belgium, and at the end of the 18th century the Jewish community was accorded equal civil rights. The largest Jewish communities developed in Antwerp and Brussels, where Jews distinguished themselves as diamond-cutters, goldsmiths and merchants. As a result of the Second World War and Nazi persecutions, the Jewish population was reduced to about 35,000.

BELKIN, SAMUEL

President of Yeshiva University. Born in Poland in 1911, he was ordained rabbi at Radin when he was 17, and settled in the United States shortly thereafter. He received his doctorate at Brown University and taught Greek at Yeshiva College. He rose quickly on the faculty, becoming in turn professor and dean (1940), and finally president (1943). Under his leadership the institution developed into Yeshiva University (1945), which at present is comprised of 17 schools and divisions. In addition to his profound scholarship in

rabbinics, he is expert in Hellenistic Jewish literature, and has written on Philo and other religious and philosophic subjects. His latest work, "In His Image," develops a contemporary philosophic presentation of orthodox Judaism.

BEMIDBAR see Numbers.

BENDERLY, SAMSON (1876–1944)

Educator and founder of the first Bureau of Jewish Education in New York. Born in Palestine, he studied at the American University at Beirut, Lebanon. In 1898 he settled in the United States and began his work in Jewish education, as well as his studies for a medical career. In 1910 he became the director of the Bureau of Jewish Education in New York, and for over 30 years devoted himself to the task of Hebrew education in the United States. He advocated the teaching of Hebrew as a living language, and sought to modernize the methods of Hebrew instruction. He had great influence on other Jewish educators, who later became important leaders in the field of Jewish education.

BENEDICTIONS

Referred to in Hebrew as "Berakhot" meaning blessings, giving of thanks, praise; and connected with the word for kneeling. It is an old Jewish tradition, dating at least from the days of Ezra, to offer blessings and thanks to God on frequent occasions. A Jew recites benedictions as part of the daily ritual; when he partakes of food; when performing certain commandments (*Mitzvot*); and when witnessing certain natural phenomena, such as thunder. Each benediction begins with the words "Barukh Attah Adonai" (Blessed art Thou, O Lord).

David Ben-Gurion, pioneer Labor Zionist, scholar and statesman, was one of the moving spirits and chief founders of the State of Israel, its first Prime Minister and Minister of Defense.

BEN-GURION, DAVID

One of the most influential Zionist political leaders and first Prime Minister and Minister of Defense of the State of Israel, which was created in no small measure through his determination. Born in 1886 in Poland, he went to Israel at the age of twenty, where he worked as a laborer in the orange groves. He became active in political affairs, and in later life rose to the highest position of leadership in the Labor Zionist Movement, both in Israel and abroad. Because of his political activities he was expelled by the Turkish Government from Palestine and went to the United States, where he helped organize the Jewish Legion, in which he served during World War I until the occupation of Palestine by the British. After the war he worked in London for the *Poale Zion* (Labor Zionist) movement, and in 1933 he became a member of the executive committee of the World Zionist Organization and chairman of the Executive of the Jewish Agency for Palestine. Following the decision of the United Nations in 1947 to partition Palestine between the Arabs and the Jews, Ben-Gurion and his associates drafted the Declaration of Independence of the Jewish State, and during the invasion of the Arab countries he led the War of Liberation both as Prime Minister and Minister of Defense of the Provisional Government of Israel. For a short time he gave up governmental functions and settled in one of the settlements of the Negev (southern desert area), thus serving as an inspiration and example for younger people to settle on and cultivate the desert land of the Jewish State. In 1955 he was again called to head the Government of Israel. In 1959 his party (Mapai) won the fourth parliamentary election held in the history of the State, and he organized a new coalition government. See *Knesset*.

BENJAMIN

In addition to his political activities Ben-Gurion was continuously active as a journalist. He won his extensive general education not so much through formal schooling as through self-discipline and his great thirst for knowledge. He is considered one of the most scholarly heads of state in human history.

BENJAMIN

Jacob's youngest son, and whole brother of Joseph. His mother Rachel died at the time he was born. One of the twelve Jewish tribes named after him settled west of the Jordan, an area which included the city of Jerusalem. King Saul was of the tribe of Benjamin which later joined the tribe of Judah to form the Kingdom of Judah, as a result of the division of the United Kingdom after the death of King Solomon.

BENJAMIN, JUDAH PHILIP (1811–1884)

Prominent statesman of both the United States and the Confederate States, orator and successful British lawyer. Born in the West Indies, he was reared in the United States, where he became a prominent lawyer, and was offered a seat in the U.S. Supreme Court, which he declined in favor of his law practice and political career. Twice he was elected by the State of Louisiana to the U.S. Senate, where he distinguished himself as a great orator. When his state seceded from the Union, Benjamin became Attorney General and then Secretary of War of the Confederate States. Unjustifiably blamed for the loss of a battle, he was promptly rewarded by being promoted to Secretary of State. He became known as "the brains of the Confederacy." When the war ended in the defeat of the Confederacy, Benjamin went to England where in a short time he became an honored member of the English bar. Benjamin took little interest in the Jewish community. He was, however,

Judah Philip Benjamin, after serving the Union as a U.S. Senator, had a very brilliant career as a lawyer and statesman of the Confederacy.

Eliezer Ben-Yehudah, editor of the prominent Hebrew dictionary, was one of the very first to champion use of Hebrew as a living language.

48

proud of his ancestry, and often defended the name of his people against unjust attacks and prejudices.

BENJAMIN OF TUDELA (SPAIN)

Renowned Jewish traveler of the 12th century. He traveled in connection with his business in Europe, Asia and North Africa, and kept a detailed record of the Jewish communities which he visited. His diary, written in Hebrew, was edited after his death, and published in the 16th century under the title *Massaot shel Rabbi Binyamin* (The Travels of Rabbi Benjamin). The book contains descriptions of the Jewish communities, their religious, political and social status. This remarkable diary has been translated into many languages, and has become a source for Jewish historical research.

BEN-SIRA, JOSHUA

The author of an ancient book entitled "The Wisdom of Jesus the Son of Sirach." In Hebrew the book is commonly referred to as "Ben-Sira." Its Latin title is "Ecclesiasticus." This is probably the oldest book of the Apocrypha (ancient books not included in the Bible). The author probably lived about the third century b.c.e., since he mentions the high priest Simon ben Onias who died in 199 b.c.e. Despite the fact that the book was not included among the canonized books of the Bible, it was very popular with the Jews. "Ben-Sira" was originally written in Hebrew, but only its Greek translation was subsequently known. In 1896 a fragment of the original Hebrew text of "Ben-Sira" was found by Dr. Solomon Schechter in the Cairo Genizah (archives). Later other manuscripts were recovered, which together make up about two-thirds of the lost Hebrew text, and recently published in Israel.

The content of "Ben-Sira" is similar to the *Book of Proverbs* in the Bible. It gives a valuable account of Jewish social life of that period, dealing with moral conduct and daily life experiences. The book praises the treasures of wisdom, and the invaluable service of physicians, artisans and scholars. He teaches that the highest virtues of man are modesty, goodness, forgiveness, mercy, and love of peace. Probably because of its known late authorship, it was rejected by many Jewish authorities and not included in the Canon. Translated into many languages, it has become the object of scholarly research.

BEN-YEHUDAH, ELIEZER (1858–1922)

Pioneer of the revival of the Hebrew language in Israel. Born in Lithuania, he settled in Jerusalem in 1881 where he began his fanatic fight to introduce Hebrew as the language of instruction in the schools. He was a journalist and editor of several Hebrew journals. In his writings he demanded that Hebrew be used as the spoken language by young and old. In this he never compromised, and in his private life he would refuse to speak any other language to members of his family or to his friends. He organized and built the *Vaad Ha-Lashon* (Council for the Development of Hebrew), and devoted himself stubbornly and heroically to his life-work, the *Dictionary of the Hebrew Language*. This outstanding dictionary is to this day an invaluable source for the study of the Hebrew language. In recognition of his pioneering work, two main streets, one in Jerusalem and one in Tel Aviv, have been named after him.

BEN-ZVI, ITZHAK

Second President of the State of Israel, leader of the Zionist Labor Movement and scholar. Born in 1884, Ben-Zvi was one of the founders of the *Poale Zion* (Labor Zionists) in Russia (1905), and other European countries. He settled in Jerusalem in 1908 where he was one of the founders and teachers of the Hebrew gymnasium (high school), and became one of the leaders of the Poale Zion World Federation. During World War I he went to the United States and returned to Palestine in 1918 as a member of the Jewish Legion, which he helped organize. He represented the workers' organization in many important capacities, and in 1931 became president of the *Vaad Leumi* (National Council of Palestine). After the death of Chaim Weizmann in 1952, he was elected President of the State of Israel.

In addition to his political career, Ben-Zvi gained the reputation as a contributor to Russian, Yiddish and Hebrew journals, writing especially on subjects concerning the history of eastern Jews and Arabs. He is the author of "The Exiled and the Redeemed," a Bialik Prize-winner.

BERESHIT see Genesis.

BERIT (Beris) MILAH see Circumcision.

BERURIAH

Scholarly wife of Rabbi Meir, who lived in the second century in Tiberias, Palestine. She was the daughter of Rabbi Hananiah ben Teradyon, one of the martyrs of the Roman persecution. The Talmud mentions Beruriah in a number of passages, and refers to her wisdom and learning. Her life was used as a theme by modern writers.

BES see Bet.

BESAMIM see Havdalah.

BESHT see Baal Shem Tov.

BESSARABIA

Formerly a Rumanian province, and at present divided between the Moldavian SSR and the Ukraine. German and Polish Jews began to settle in Bessarabia in the 16th century. From about 5,000 Jews in 1812, the Jewish community reached a

quarter of a million in 1919, when Bessarabia was annexed to Rumania. Bessarabia had a large number of Jewish agricultural settlements. There, as in the cities, Jews engaged in commerce and industry. The Bessarabian Jews showed great interest in Jewish cultural activities; they had a Yiddish press, and a number of elementary and high schools with Hebrew as the language of instruction, and which were under the supervision of the Rumanian government.

Bessarabian Jews were known for their Zionist activities, and many young Jews emigrated to Palestine as part of the Pioneer Movement (Halutzim). Most of the Jewish population in Bessarabia perished in concentration camps set up by the Nazis in Transnistria, and the Jewish communities were completely wiped out. The few that escaped the Nazi ordeal settled in Czernowitz, Bukovina, after the war.

BET (VET) (ב ,בּ)

The second letter of the Hebrew alphabet. Its meaning is "house," and its numerical value is two; when followed by an apostrophe its value is two thousand. In Ashkenazic it is called *Bes* or *Bais* (*Vais*). With a *dagesh* (dot in letter) it is sounded B, and without the dagesh its sound is V. In an unvoweled text there is no visible distinction between *Bet* and *Vet*. In this volume the Hebrew letter *Tav* has been transliterated with the letter T as in the Sefardic pronunciation. Therefore phrases such as *Bes Din* or *Bes ha-Mikdash* appear as Bet Din, or Bet ha-Mikdash. See *Aleph* for its use in the word alphabet.

BET-ALPHA see Archeology.

BET DIN

Hebrew term applied to a Jewish religious or civil court of law. The *Bet Din* originated early in Jewish history, and during the period of the Second Temple

A typical Bet Ha-Midrash scene with the Hebrew books lining the walls, and men and boys gathered. The men's dress, "Tallit" and "Shtreimel" (Ḥasidic fur hat), suggest the east European "Shtetl."

it was known as the *Sanhedrin*. A Bet Din in our day in the United States, is a voluntary arbitration court in the Jewish community for settling disputes.

BET HA-MIDRASH

Hebrew term meaning "house of study," applied to a place where Jews congregate for prayer and study. It is sometimes distinguished from the *Bet ha-Keneset*, which is designated for prayer only The term is also applied to a rabbinical school for higher studies.

BET HA-MIKDASH

Hebrew term meaning "sanctuary," applied to the Holy Temple in Jerusalem which was the spiritual and religious cen-

ter of Jewish life in ancient times. There were two Temples in the course of over one thousand years of Jewish history. The First Temple, built by King Solomon, stood over 400 years and was destroyed by the Babylonians in 586 b.c.e. The Second Temple, built about 70 years later by the returned Jewish deportees from Babylonia, was destroyed by the Roman general Titus about 70 c.e. The Temple, a masterful structure, built out of freestone, was situated on the site of the sacred Mount Moriah, opposite the Mount of Olives. It had two major divisions, the outer sanctuary or the Holy Place, and the inner sanctuary or the Holy of Holies. The Holy Place, to which only the priests were admitted, contained the altar of incense, the table of the shewbread (*Leḥem ha-Panim*), and the *Menorah* (candelabrum). The Holy of Holies, which only the High Priest was permitted to enter, and then only on Yom Kippur, housed the Ark of the Covenant in the First Temple. In the Second, because the Ark had been lost, its place was taken by what is known in tradition as the *Even Shetiyah* or Foundation Stone. The Temple was surrounded by a large court where the sacrificial altar and other utensils were located, and which was divided into three major sections as assembly places for men, women, and priests, separately. The Temple, administered by the High Priest, his assistant and other functionaries, was supported through popular taxation and through special gifts. It was both the duty and the privilege of every Jew in the land to visit

Beth-lehem, storied Biblical country town in the hills south of Jerusalem, is the legendary birthplace of King David. Though mostly peopled by Arabs today, it remains a shrine to Jew and Christian alike.

the Temple and take part in the public services three times a year, on Shavuot, Sukkot, and especially on Passover, when men, women and children from all parts of the land made their holy pilgrimage to the city of Jerusalem to participate in the general festivities, and to bring their sacrifices, both animal and vegetation, to the Temple where special rituals were conducted by the Kohanim (priests) and the Levites.

The Second Temple was remodeled about 20 c.e. There the *Sanhedrin* (Jewish High Court) was housed as well as a number of houses of study. After the destruction of the Temple by the Romans, its remains gradually disappeared, except for one wall, believed to be the western wall of the Temple, now known as the *Wailing Wall*, a traditional place of prayer for Jewish pilgrims. The Mosque of Omar, erected in the seventh century, now stands on the site of the Temple. See *Wailing Wall*.

BETH-LEHEM

Ancient city in the Land of Israel, sacred to both Jews and Christians. The Bible mentions it for the first time when Jacob the Patriarch buried his beloved wife Rachel near Beth-lehem. Rachel died after giving birth to Benjamin. The famed shrine of "Rachel's Tomb" still stands about 9 kilometers from Jerusalem. Bethlehem is also remembered as the place where King David was born. The locale of much of the story of Ruth (the great grandmother of David) is Beth-lehem. According to Christian tradition, Beth-lehem was the birthplace of Jesus. Beth-lehem is inhabited largely by Arabs of the Christian faith, and its many churches and sacred shrines emphasize it as a place of special interest to Christians the world over. In 1949, after the War of Liberation, Bethlehem came under Jordanian rule.

BET-SHEAN see Archeology.

BET-SHEARIM see Archeology.

BET-SHEMESH see Archeology.

BET-YERAH see Archeology.

BEZALEL SCHOOL

Famed school of arts and crafts in Jerusalem. Founded in 1906 by Boris Schatz, and named after the skillful artisan Bezalel, mentioned in the Bible as the one whom Moses put in charge of building the Tabernacle. Beginning with classes in drawing, painting, carpet-weaving, it later added other classes in wood-work, metal-work and ceramics. After World War I the Bezalel School was reorganized and it now houses a museum of art as well as a library of its own.

BIALIK, ḤAYYIM NAHMAN (1873–1934)

Foremost national Hebrew poet. Born in Russia, he mastered both Jewish and secular knowledge. Living for a number of years in Odessa, then an important Jewish cultural center, he published (under the sponsorship of Aḥad Ha-Am), his first Hebrew poem expressing longing for Zion, which attracted wide attention. His poetical works published afterwards gained him the reputation of the most outstanding and brilliant Hebrew poet. The major

Jerusalem's Bezalel Museum is famed for its art library and exhibitions of Jewish ritual art.

Hayyim Nahman Bialik, poet of "wrath and sorrow," is the father of modern Hebrew poetry.

theme of his widely read poetry concerned itself with the cultural and political existence and problems of the people. In contrast to the other writers of the *Haskalah* (enlightenment) period, he considered the traditional Jewish institutions of learning (the Heder and the Yeshivah) as the fountain of life for the Jewish people, and as a major source of cultural inspiration and vitality for the succeeding generations amidst the precarious Jewish existence. His poetry reflects great admiration for the lonely Talmudical student, and great concern for the neglect and eventual disappearance of traditional Jewish learning. As a result of pogroms and inhuman persecution of Jews in Russia and elsewhere, Bialik wrote his vigorous and stirring poems of "wrath and sorrow," protesting not so much against the cruel enemy, but more against the humiliating passivity of the Jewish masses confronting the inhuman oppressors. His heartfelt call for active resistance and for

retaliation inspired Jewish able-bodied men and women to organize Jewish self-defense groups to protect the lives and property of the constantly menaced Jewish communities in eastern Europe. As a natural consequence of Bialik's poetic and often prophetic writings, he became one of the spiritual leaders of the Zionist movement, calling for the restoration of the historic Jewish homeland.

In addition to his original poetic creations in Hebrew, such as "In the City of Slaughter," "The Dead of the Wilderness," and the "Scroll of Fire," Bialik has also written some fine stories (such as "Aftergrowth") and together with Ravnitzki rendered into modern Hebrew much of the folklore of Talmud and Midrash in their "Sefer Ha-Aggadah" (Book of the Aggadah). With other collaborators he published an anthology of medieval Hebrew poetry ("Shirat Yisrael") and critical editions of medieval Hebrew poets, as well as a commentary on the first section of the Mishnah, and school texts of the Bible. He recognized the importance of translating the world's classics into Hebrew, and stimulated others to do so with his own translation of "Don Quixote" and "Wilhelm Tell." His writings in Yiddish are also well known.

After settling in Tel Aviv in 1924, he took an active part in the life of Palestinian Jewry. He initiated and took part in many cultural and literary projects. The "Bet-Bialik" (Bialik Center) on Bialik Street in Tel Aviv became a popular meeting place for Jewish writers and important cultural events. The city of Tel Aviv established the "Bialik Prize" as an annual award for the best writings in Hebrew. His house has been made a national museum by the State of Israel.

BIBLE

The basic and most sacred collection of

books of the Jewish people, also referred to as the *Holy Scriptures*, the *Hebrew Canon*, and the *Hebrew Bible;* Christians call it the Old Testament, to distinguish it from the New Testament. The common name for the Bible, TaNaKh, is made up of three initials indicating its major sections, namely *Torah* (Pentateuch), *Neviim* (Prophets), and *Ketuvim* (Writings).

The Torah consists of the Five Books of Moses: *Genesis, Exodus, Leviticus, Numbers,* and *Deuteronomy,* which give an account of the creation of the universe; the lives of the Patriarchs, Abraham, Isaac and Jacob; the story of the Israelites in Egypt, and the Exodus led by Moses; the wanderings in the wilderness; the giving of the Torah on Mount Sinai; and also the vast body of social and religious law, known as the Law of Moses (Torat Mosheh). The Torah concludes with the death of Moses.

The second section of the Bible, called *Neviim,* includes in its first part the historical books, *Joshua, Judges, Samuel* and *Kings,* and in its second part the books *Isaiah, Jeremiah, Ezekiel,* and *The Twelve* (sometimes called the *Minor Prophets*). The historical works tell the story of the Jewish people from their entrance into Canaan until the destruction of the First Commonwealth by the Babylonians in 586 b.c.e. The second part of this section of the Bible contains the prophetic utterances of the Hebrew prophets.

The third section of the Bible, *Ketuvim,* contains the following books: *Psalms, Proverbs, Job,* the Five Scrolls (*Song of Songs, Ruth, Lamentations, Ecclesiastes* and *Esther*), *Daniel, Ezra, Nehemiah,* and *Chronicles.* In these books are found some of the world's greatest religious and nature poetry, prayers, wisdom literature and historical narrative.

The Bible is written in Hebrew, with a very few passages in Aramaic, and is there-fore referred to as the Hebrew Bible. As the fundamental record of Jewish religion, ethics, law, history, prophetic ideals, prayers and wisdom, it is also known as the "Book of Books." Much of the sacred post-Biblical literature such as the *Mishnah* and *Gemara,* and the writings of later periods, are based on the Bible, and at least in form, as well as largely in content, are an elaboration and interpretation of the basic content of the Bible. The Bible is also the sacred book of the Christians, for whom the word Bible includes the Hebrew Bible (which they call the Old Testament) as well as the New Testament. The Mohammedan Koran includes some Biblical and Rabbinic material. The Bible has been translated into almost every language and dialect of the world, including such important translations as the *Septuagint* in Greek and the *Targumim* in Aramaic. Exposition of and commentaries on the Biblical text, structure and meaning were composed by an untold number of scholars throughout the ages, and the Bible is still the object of scientific research, with new translations constantly in the making, and continues to be a chief source of inspiration and enlightenment for all varieties of artistic and intellectual expression.

BIKKUR HOLIM

Hebrew term meaning "visiting the sick" applied to the traditional obligation of a Jewish person to visit the sick and comfort them during their illness. Jewish thinkers consider this practice one of the higher virtues. Many Jewish congregations and fraternal organizations appoint special committees whose duty it is to visit sick members and their families.

BIKKURIM see First-Fruits.

BILU

Initials of the Hebrew words "Bet Ya-akov Lekhu Venelekhah" ("O House of

Jacob, Come Ye, Let Us Walk"), name assumed by groups of Jewish students in Russia in 1882, who, after the outbreak of pogroms, decided to emigrate and to establish agricultural settlements in Palestine. They were the first pioneers who began to rebuild the land of their forefathers. They built the early Jewish colony, *Rishon Le-Zion*.

BIMAH (Almemar)

The elevated platform on which is placed the reading desk in the synagogue from which the Torah is read during public services. Traditionally, it was situated in the center of the synagogue, but in modern conservative synagogues it is placed in front of the Ark on a dais; in reform synagogues the same desk is generally used for reading the prayer book and the Scrolls of the Torah.

BIRKAT HA-MAZON see Grace after Meals.

BIRKAT KOHANIM see Blessing, Priestly.

BIRO-BIDJAN

A region in the Far East belonging to the Union of the Soviet Republics, which in 1928 was declared by the Soviet Government a territory for the colonization of Russian Jews, eventually to become a Jewish Republic of the Soviet Union, with Yiddish as the national language. In 1939, there were in Biro-Bidjan about 45,000 Jews who established a number of towns and agricultural settlements. By 1960 the Jewish population had not increased at all.

BIUR ḤAMETZ see Bedikat Ḥametz

BLACK DEATH

About the middle of the 14th century a deadly epidemic (the bubonic plague)

A mid-19th-century engraving of the interior of the oldest synagogue in Prague, the famed Altneuschul. Note curious arrangement of the pews and the very interesting design of the Bimah.

raged throughout Europe and killed about one-third of its population. This plague was called the "black death" and as a result of prejudice, superstition and ignorance, a rumor spread among the people that it was caused by the Jews, who were said to have conspired against the Christians by poisoning the wells. The fact that the Jews, too, perished from the plague, did not stop the people from believing this myth. Perhaps fewer Jews in proportion contracted the plague because of their observance of the dietary laws. Jewish communities in Europe, especially in Germany, were subjected to massacres and frequently complete annihilation by the savage mobs. Even the intervention of Pope Clement VI, who denounced this rumor, did not bring relief to the Jewish martyrs. In Germany alone 300 Jewish communities were wiped out during that dreadful period.

BLESSING, PRIESTLY

The special benediction chanted in the synagogue, as part of the Festival and Holy Day services, by the *Kohanim*, (descendants of the priestly family). In the Sephardic congregations this benediction is also recited on the Sabbath. The Kohanim recite the blessing with raised arms, standing near the Ark and facing the congregation, while the worshippers cover their heads with their prayer-shawls. This tradition dates back to the time of the Holy Temple in Jerusalem when the Kohanim (priests) blessed the people from the steps of the fore-hall, the *dukhan*. This latter term, or its variant "dukhanen," is now commonly applied to this priestly blessing, which is also referred to in Hebrew as the *Birkat Kohanim* (Priestly Blessing). In many congregations in Israel, the "Dukhan Service" takes place every day. In the reform as well as in many conservative congregations in the United States, the

A Nuremberg woodcut dating from 1493 shows the burning of Jews as punishment for the usual and spurious charges of ritual blood guilt.

priestly blessing is occasionally recited by the rabbi.

BLOCH, ERNEST (1880–1959)

Well-known composer of Jewish themes. Born in Geneva, Switzerland, he began his musical career at an early age, both as a lecturer and composer. Starting with general musical themes, he later found his best and deepest musical expression in Hebraic motifs. He expressed his enthusiasm for Jewish content in the following words: "It is the Jewish soul that interests me, the complex, glowing, agitated soul that I feel vibrating in the Bible . . . the freshness and naiveté of the Patriarchs; the violence of the prophetic books; the Jewish savage love of justice; the despair of Ecclesiastes; the sorrow and immensity of the Book of Job; the sensuality of the Song of Songs. . . ."

His Hebraic compositions are: "Two Psalms," "Trois Poèmes Juifs," "Jezebel," "Pictures of Ḥasidic Life," "Baal-Shem Suite," "Shelomo," and "Israel Symphony." In 1916 he settled in the United States, and three years later he received the Coolidge Prize for his Symphony "America." Following a period of lecturing and writing, he was appointed director of the San Francisco Conservatory of Music. Later he traveled in Europe and returned to the United States in 1934 where he continued to create his important compositions, and to influence young American composers.

BLOOD ACCUSATION

Commonly referred to in Hebrew as "Alilat Dam," the wicked and false accusation, dating back to the 12th century, that Jews use Christian blood for the Passover ritual, that is, for the preparation of *Matzot*. Despite the fact that not one bit of evidence was ever produced by the accusers, these accusations persisted for centuries, causing violent attacks against the Jews. Blood-thirsty individuals, quite often leaders of the clergy and functionaries of the government, found an accomplice who would murder an innocent Christian child whose mutilated body would secretly be placed at the residence of some respectable Jewish family, or even secreted in the synagogue. Such cruel acts were most often perpetrated before the Passover festival, thus turning the holiday occasion into a horrible ordeal. Beginning in 1171 in England, these accusations were repeated in almost every country, including the United States. The last world-famous blood accusation trial, of Mendel Beilis, took place in Russia in 1913. Other cases attracting world attention were the Damascus affair (1840), the Tisza-Eszlar case (1882), and the Polna case (1889).

The Jewish religion not only prohibits the use of human blood (which would be cannibalism), but even objects to the use of animal blood, and enjoins the eating of meat unless much of the blood is previously drawn and washed away under detailed ritualistic regulations.

BLUM, LÉON (1872–1950)

Statesman, writer and first Jewish Prime Minister of France. Early in life he gained recognition as a literary and dramatic critic

Léon Blum, socialist lawyer and writer, was the first Jewish Prime Minister of France in the Popular Front governments of the 1930s. After France fell, he was tried and imprisoned by the Nazis.

and published a number of important books. A lawyer by profession, he entered political life, and in 1899 joined the Socialist movement. During the First World War he became executive secretary of the Ministry of Public Works. As the

respected leader of the French Socialist Party, he was elected several times to the Chamber of Deputies. In 1936 he became Prime Minister of France, supported by a strong coalition of leftist parties, the so-called "Popular Front." As head of the government he initiated a number of reforms for the benefit of the working class. In 1938 he was appointed Prime Minister for the second time, remaining in that office for a short period. When France capitulated to Nazi Germany in 1940, he was imprisoned and later put on trial; the world admired his heroic self-defense, but he was deported by the Germans to the concentration camp in Buchenwald in 1943, from which he was freed two years later by the U. S. Army. During the critical postwar years he headed the government for a third time in 1946. Blum took great interest in Jewish affairs, and warmly supported many Zionist projects. In recognition of his leadership in behalf of the working class and his interest in the Jewish homeland, "Kfar Blum," a workers' settlement in Israel, was named after him.

B'NAI B'RITH

Hebrew name, meaning "Sons of the Covenant." The oldest and largest Jewish fraternal and service organization. It was founded in 1843 by a group of German Jews in New York, and since developed and grew to an international membership of over 400,000 and a national membership of 325,000. Throughout the years, its manifold activities spread out to reach all significant Jewish communities in the United States and abroad. It started as a purely fraternal organization seeking to provide health insurance and sick benefits for its members. These were given up in time, and the main purpose of B'nai B'rith became the helping of others. In many Jewish communities it established orphan homes, old age homes and hospitals, many of which are still in existence. The work of B'nai B'rith grew to include civic work, such as the organization of Americanization classes for Jewish immigrants, and the establishment of the important *Anti-Defamation League* whose chief purpose is to

fight anti-Semitism and to promote better relations between Jews and non-Jews. B'nai B'rith eventually extended its welfare work to Jewish communities overseas. It spent large amounts of money to fight anti-Jewish discrimination in European countries, and to give relief to needy Jewish communities, especially during great emergencies. B'nai B'rith was especially interested in the upbuilding of the Jewish homeland and, with the cooperation of other Jewish organizations, it undertook and carried out many important Zionist projects.

In addition to its philanthropic work, B'nai B'rith maintains a rich Jewish cultural and educational program. In 1924 it established the *Hillel Foundation*, which conducts cultural, religious and social programs for Jewish college students at major universities. It also operates the *BBYO* (B'nai B'rith Youth Organization), offering a varied program of religious, cultural and social activities and sports. B'nai B'rith sponsors a number of publications, especially the *National Jewish Monthly*, having the largest circulation among the Anglo-Jewish journals. In 1959 it held its convention in the State of Israel. See *Aleph Zadik Aleph*.

BOARD OF DEPUTIES OF BRITISH JEWS

Representative body of the Jewish communities in England, founded in 1760 for the purpose of protecting the civil and political rights of the Jews. When Moses Montefiore became its president in 1835, the Board of Deputies became a protective agency for Jews of other countries as well. In 1840 the Board of Deputies intervened in connection with the Damascus and Rhodes ritual murder accusations. It has since become the recognized body of British Jewry, and a most influential political and relief agency in international Jewish affairs.

BONDS FOR ISRAEL

Securities issued by the Government of Israel and sold in the United States by an underwriting agreement with the Development Corporation for Israel, in New York. These Bonds offer the purchaser specified dividends, depending on the denomination and maturity date. The funds raised from the sale of Bonds are used by the Government of Israel to increase the cultivated and the irrigated areas of farmland; to establish industrial plants and develop the natural resources of the country; and to extend its transportation and communication systems. Sales of Israel Independence Issue Bonds, issued after the establishment of the State of Israel, totalled $145,542,900 at the end of the period of flotation, May 1, 1954. In 1958 Bonds for Israel were sold in the amount of $45,000,-000 in the United States alone.

Independence Bond Issue signed by Premier Ben-Gurion and the Finance Minister Kaplan.

BOROCHOV, BER (1881–1917)

Leader and theoretician of the *Poale Zion* movement, and Yiddish philologist. Born in the Ukraine (Russia), he was a student of exceptional ability. He first joined the Russian socialist party and later the *Poale Zion* movement. His major accomplishment was the formulation of his theory of blending Marxism with Zionism. Holding to the ideals of socialism, he disagreed with those who believed that a socialistic order would solve the Jewish problem. He argued that even socialists are not free from anti-Semitism, and that Jewish socialists living among non-Jews would eventually assimilate and lose their Jewish identity. He therefore urged Jewish workers to settle in Palestine, their historic homeland, where they would endeavor to build a Jewish civilization based on the principles and ideals of socialism. Borochov went to the United States in 1914, where he became active in the Poale Zion movement. He edited the Labor Zionist Weekly, the *Yiddisher Kempfer,* and contributed to many other publications. He made significant contributions as a student of the Yiddish language, literature and philology.

BRANDEIS, LOUIS DEMBITZ (1856–1941)

Justice of the United States Supreme Court, and Zionist leader. Born in Louisville, Kentucky, he became one of the outstanding lawyers of the United States. He gave up many opportunities for making "big money" and devoted himself to causes affecting the welfare of the underprivileged. He acted successfully as counsel in a number of cases involving workers' minimum wage and hour laws, and as a result he became known as "the people's lawyer." His popularity and exceptional legal work led President Wilson to appoint him in 1916 a member of the Supreme Court of the United States. In 1910

Louis Dembitz Brandeis, U.S. Associate Supreme Court Justice. A brilliant legal theorist, he was also known as "the people's lawyer," and as a symbol of blending the Jewish and American spirits.

he became interested in Zionism, and he rendered great service to the Zionist organization, especially when American Jewry was called upon to continue the work in the Jewish homeland which had been interrupted during the World War. From 1918 to 1921 he was honorary president of the Zionist Organization of America. His memory has come to symbolize the true spirit of the blending of Americanism and Judaism. The Brandeis University at Waltham, Mass. bears his name.

BRANDEIS UNIVERSITY

Inaugurated in 1948 and located at Waltham, Mass. It is the first Jewish sponsored non-sectarian university in the Western Hemisphere. It is open to all students who meet academic standards without reference to race, color or religious affiliation. Courses of instruction under the Faculty of Arts and Sciences are offered by four schools, Creative Arts, Science, Social Science, and Humanities. It offers Bachelor of Arts and Bachelor of Science degrees. In its graduate school it offers masters' degrees in Arts and Fine Arts as well as the Doctor of Philosophy in many more fields. It was named after Justice Louis D. Brandeis, eminent for his contributions to jurisprudence and education and to the welfare of his country and his people.

The Student Center, one of the buildings on Brandeis University's campus. Named after the late Justice Brandeis it is the first Jewish sponsored non-sectarian University in the Western hemisphere.

BRAZIL

There are in Brazil about 125,000 Jews (1959 statistics), a great number of whom live in Rio de Janeiro. Jews first settled in Brazil when the Portuguese conquered it in 1531. Many of the first Jewish settlers were Marranos who hoped to escape the Inquisition in Portugal and be able to return to the Jewish faith on the new continent. However, the Inquisition kept a watchful eye on the Jews of Brazil and many suspected Marranos were either sent back to Portugal or dealt with harshly by the Inquisition established in Brazil. When the Dutch fought the Portuguese, the Marranos helped the former, and when

they conquered Brazil, they extended full religious liberty to the Jews. Many Jews settled in Recife, which became a prosperous Jewish community. The Jews developed the sugar industry which they originally brought from the island of Madeira. The peaceful period under Dutch rule was short-lived since the Portuguese recaptured Brazil in 1654. The Inquisition was reintroduced and most Jews had to flee to Holland, to the West Indian Islands and elsewhere. It was at that time that 23 Jews migrated to North America from Brazil and landed in New Amsterdam (now New York). Not until 1823, when Brazil freed itself from Portuguese rule, did the Jews

63

regain their religious liberty and the Jewish community began to develop as a result of a new Jewish immigration, mostly Sephardic. Immigration of Ashkenazic Jews began in the 20th century, when the ICA (Jewish Colonization Association) established a number of agricultural settlements. The Jewish community in Brazil is well organized and maintains educational, Zionist, religious and other vital Jewish institutions.

BREAD OF AFFLICTION

Refers to the first words ("Ha Laḥma Anya") of the declaration read in the *Haggadah* at the beginning of the Passover Seder. Written in Aramaic, it states that the *Matzah* is "the bread of affliction" that our forefathers ate when they left Egypt. It also contains an invitation to the poor to come and partake of the Seder meal. It finally expresses the hope of the redemption of the Jewish people and their return to their homeland as free men. In Jewish life, the invitation to the poor to partake of the Seder is brought to reality by the practice of "Maot Ḥittim," providing for the poor person's Passover needs prior to the festival.

BRIGADE, JEWISH see Jewish Brigade.

BRITH ABRAHAM see Indepedent Order of Brith Abraham.

BRITH (BERIT) MILAH see Circumcision.

BUBER, MARTIN

Scholar, religious philosopher and interpreter of Ḥasidism. Born in Vienna in 1878, he studied in a number of German universities and became a Zionist writer and editor of important German-Jewish periodicals. He advocated spiritual Zionism and encouraged the pioneer colonization movement in the Jewish homeland. His major work was devoted to the study of Jewish mysticism and Ḥasidism. He is the author of many stories based on the Ḥasid-

Martin Buber, philosopher of Jewish mysticism and Ḥasidism, is also an eminent Jewish leader.

ic tradition and of books on the meaning and influence of Ḥasidism. In 1933 he fled Germany as a result of Nazi persecution, and in 1938 he became professor of philosophy at the Hebrew University in Jerusalem. His philosophy of religion has had a profound impact on religious thought, both Jewish and Christian.

BUKOVINA

As a result of World War I, Bukovina was transferred from Austria to Rumania. Its Jewish population was then about 190,-000. The Jews of Bukovina had well organized Jewish communities, the largest of which was in Czernowitz. It was a center of the Jewish enlightenment movement (Haskalah), and of Zionist activities. At an international conference of Yiddishists held in Czernowitz in 1908, the Yiddish language was proclaimed the national language of the Jewish people. The first modern Yiddish schools were established there. In 1940, northern Bukovina became a part of Soviet Russia. Many war refugees settled in Czernowitz. There are no available figures regarding the present size and status of the once flourishing Jewish community in Bukovina.

BULAN see Khazars.

BULGARIA

The history of the Jews in this Balkan

64

country began in the second century. The Jewish community in Bulgaria flourished in the 8th and 9th centuries, when it is believed that under its influence the Khazars embraced Judaism. The Jews prospered particularly during the reign of John Alexander, who married a Jewess. During that period (the 14th century) and later, Jews from other countries found refuge in Bulgaria. The majority of Bulgarian Jews are of Sephardic origin. In 1941 there were in Bulgaria about 60,000 Jews, which number was reduced after World War II to about 6,000 (1960).

BUND

Common Yiddish name of the Jewish social democratic workers' organization in Russia, Poland and Lithuania, founded in 1897. The *Bund* fought vigorously against the Tsarist regime in Russia, and in Jewish life it claimed the right of the Jewish people to national cultural autonomy wherever they lived. The Bund opposed Zionism, and proclaimed Yiddish the national language of the Jewish people. It demanded that the government support Yiddish schools, and established numerous Yiddish cultural institutions and clubs for the education of the Jewish masses. Following the Bolshevist revolution, most of the Bundists became staunch opponents of communism. With the annihilation of the Jewish communities in eastern Europe by the Nazis, the organization and the activities of the Bund were disrupted. Some of its leaders found refuge in the United States aided by the Jewish Labor Committee.

BUREAU OF JEWISH EDUCATION

Common name of the central agency in the United States for Jewish education in Jewish communities operating a number of Jewish schools. In some cities this agency is variously known as the Board of Jewish Education, Associated Talmud Torahs, or Jewish Education Committee. The Bureau of Jewish Education is to the Jewish schools what the Board of Education is to the Public Schools. The first Bureau of Jewish Education was founded in 1910 in New York, and others have since been established in all major Jewish communities in the United States. Bureaus of Jewish Education receive their funds from the local Jewish welfare fund or from Jewish federations.

The more important functions of a Bureau of Jewish Education are: a) to help increase enrollment in all types of Jewish schools; b) to give grants or subsidies to needy schools; c) to offer supervision and educational guidance; d) to help train Jewish teachers; e) to prepare courses of study, teachers' manuals, and other instructional materials; f) to arrange for inter-school activities; g) to encourage the establishment of Jewish parent-teachers associations; and h) to encourage the establishment of new Jewish schools.

BUSTANAI (c. 618–670)

The first Exilarch of the Jews in Babylonia under Arab rule. A legend tells that by order of the king of Persia his father and all other descendants of the House of David were killed, and only he was miraculously saved. Bustanai married a Persian princess, and after his death the two sons of his Jewish wife refused to recognize the rights of the other sons born to the non-Jewish wife. This family quarrel became an important issue for the entire Jewish community in Babylonia, and the matter was finally settled in favor of the sons of the princess.

C

CENTER, THE JEWISH

He that planted the ear, shall He not hear?

He that formed the eye, shall He not see?

He that instructeth the nations, shall not He correct,

Even He that teacheth man knowledge?

PSALMS

CABALAH see Kabbalah.

CAESAREA

A seaport on the Mediterranean coast of Israel south of Haifa, built by King Herod in honor of the emperor, Augustus Caesar. It was the seat of the Roman procurator in Judea, in the latter period of the Second Commonwealth. The Jewish revolt against the Romans started in Caesarea, and following Bar Kokhba's defeat, Rabbi Akiva was put to death there. During the 3rd and the 4th centuries Caesarea had a flourishing Jewish community and a center of Jewish learning led by *Amoraim* (interpreters of the Mishnah). Only the ruins of Caesarea and its port still exist, and because of its significant archeological excavations it is a center of

attraction for tourists. The archeological excavations have revealed relics of Roman and Byzantine origin, as well as the remains of a synagogue.

CAHAN, ABRAHAM (1860–1951)

Socialist labor leader, journalist, writer and editor. Born in Lithuania, he joined the socialist movement in Russia, which country he had to leave because of his revolutionary activities. He migrated to the United States, where he organized the first socialist group among the Jewish workers. To reach the Jewish masses, he preferred the use of Yiddish as an education medium. Except for 1898-1902, he was chief editor of the Yiddish daily, the "Forward," for some fifty years, from 1897. The Forward became one of the

The Mediterranean seashore at Caesarea, so named after the Roman emperor, Augustus Caesar. Its importance in Jewish and Roman history, and its excavations have made it a great tourist attraction.

most widely read foreign language newspapers in the country. In 1925 and in 1930 he visited Palestine, and became a supporter of the Zionist movement. Because of his activities both as a socialist leader and as an educator of the Jewish masses, he gained an international reputation among the working people. He was an able journalist and writer both in Yiddish and in English. He wrote a "History of the United States" in Yiddish, and a popular novel "The Rise of David Levinsky" in English, as well as five volumes of memoirs and other writings. He was a strong opponent of communism.

CAIN AND ABEL

Two sons of Adam and Eve. Cain was, according to the Bible, a farmer, and Abel

Abraham Cahan, editor of the Yiddish newspaper "Forward," was a novelist and educator.

a shepherd. When God accepted Abel's burnt-offering and refused that of Cain, the latter killed his brother in a fit of jealousy. God condemned Cain to become a "fugitive and a vagabond," whose only protection would be a mark on his forehead (the Sign of Cain). Tradition holds Cain to be the symbol of greed and sin. Some scholars interpret the strife between Cain and Abel as symbolic of the animosity that existed between the wandering shepherds and the settled agricultural tribes in the early history of mankind. The tale of Cain and Abel has been used by artists as a theme for artistic and literary works.

CALENDAR, JEWISH

The rules for setting up the Jewish calendar (called in Hebrew and Yiddish "Luaḥ") were definitely fixed and published about the middle of the 4th century c.e. by the Patriarch Hillel II. Before that time the formula used for the arrangement of the calendar was known only to Jewish authorities, who publicized information at fixed and appropriate times to advise the people about the dates of Jewish holidays and other seasonal events.

The Jewish calendar system starts with the year in which the "Creation of the Universe" presumably took place, though it is important to point out that the acceptance of this as the date of that event is not a dogmatic requirement in Judaism. The Jewish year is lunar (since each new month begins with the appearance of the new moon), and is adjusted to the solar year by adding an extra month on each leap year. The ordinary Jewish year has 12 months composed of 30 or 29 days each, totaling approximately 354 days a year. In order to adjust the Jewish lunar year to the solar year composed of approximately 365 days, Jewish leap years occur in the 3rd, 6th, 8th, 11th, 14th, 17th, and 19th year of each cycle of 19 years.

These and other minor adjustments were made in order to make sure that festivals occur in their proper season. Thus Passover must be celebrated in the month of Nisan, called in the Bible the month of Abib (Spring), and never before the vernal equinox. This explains why the extra intercalated month is always inserted right before the Passover holiday. Shavuot is a barley harvest festival, and Sukkot a general harvest season. It was also necessary to make sure that certain Jewish observances do not occur on prohibited days, such as the Day of Atonement (Yom Kippur), which can never occur on Sunday, or Friday.

It appears that, in the classical period of Jewish history, at least two calendars were used. One considered the spring month (*Abib*, our *Nisan*) to be the first of the months. Throughout the Torah and some prophetic books too, the months are thus designated "the first month," "the second month," etc. However, it is also recorded that the New Year was celebrated in the fall, so that it was feasible to arrange the calendar with Tishre as the first month.

The Bible records only four original

THE JEWISH CALENDAR

TISHRE, 30 days, coincides with September-October
  ROSH HASHANAH (New Year), 1st & 2nd day
  TZOM GEDALYAH (Fast of Gedaliah), 3rd day
  YOM KIPPUR (Day of Atonement), 10th day
  SUKKOT (Tabernacles), 15th through 21st day
  SHEMINI ATZERET, 22nd day
  SIMHAT TORAH, 23rd day

HESHVAN (Marheshvan), 29 or 30 days, coincides with October-November

KISLEV, 30 or 29 days, coincides with November-December
  HANUKKAH (8 days), 25th is 1st day [1]

TEVET, 29 days, coincides with December-January
  ASARAH BE-TEVET (Fast of 10th of Tevet), 10th day

SHEVAT, 30 days, coincides with January-February
  TU BI-SHEVAT or HAMISHAH ASAR BI-SHEVAT (New Year of the Trees), 15th day

ADAR [2], 29 days, coincides with February-March
  TAANIT ESTER (Fast of Esther), 13th day
  PURIM, 14th day

NISAN, 30 days, coincides with March-April
  PESAH (Passover), 15th through 22nd day

IYAR, 29 days, coincides with April-May
  YOM HA-ATZMAUT (Israel Independence Day), 5th day
  LAG BA-OMER, 18th day

SIVAN, 30 days, coincides with May-June
  SHAVUOT (Pentecost), 6th & 7th day

TAMMUZ, 29 days, coincides with June-July
  SHIVAH ASAR BE-TAMMUZ (Fast of 17th of Tammuz), 17th day

AV, 30 days, coincides with July-August
  TISHAH BE-AV (Fast of 9th of Av), 9th day

ELUL, 29 days, coincides with August-September

NOTE A. The days between Tishre 1 and 10 are called *Aseret Yeme Teshuvah* (the Ten Days of Penitence); those between Passover and Shavuot are known as *Sefirah* (Counting of the Omer); and those between Tammuz 17 and Av 9 are called "The Three Weeks" (of mourning for the destruction of both Temples).

NOTE B. In Israel all Jews, and in the diaspora reform Jews, observe Simhat Torah together with Shemini Atzeret on Tishre 22; Passover for only 7 days, Nisan 15-21; and Shavuot one day, Sivan 6. Reform Jews observe Rosh Hashanah one day, Tishre 1.

NOTE C. It is ordinarily forbidden to observe a general fast on the Sabbath, the one exception being Yom Kippur, because it, like the Sabbath, is ordained in the Torah. When any of the other fasts fall on Saturday, their observance is postponed to the next day. In the case of *Taanit Ester* the fast cannot take place on Sunday because of Purim and it therefore is observed on the preceding Thursday.

[1] Because Kislev may have either 30 or 29 days, Hanukkah may end either on Tevet 2 or 3.

[2] In an intercalative (leap) year, an additional month is inserted after Adar, and is called *Ve-Adar* or *Adar Sheni*. In this situation, the first Adar will have 30 days and the added month 29 days. The Fast of Esther and Purim are observed in the added month.

A rabbinical calendar dated 1276 was found inserted in a 13th-century Bible manuscript. On its outer rim is inscribed the 28-year great, or sun cycle; on the inner, the 19-year small, or moon cycle.

Hebrew names of the months. However, the Hebrew names were subsequently replaced by names of Babylonian origin, which have been used ever since. Some of them appear in the later books of the Bible. See *Chronology, Jewish*.

CANAAN

Land of the Canaanites, the descendants of Canaan, the grandson of Noah. The Canaanites lived in the Promised Land (Palestine) before it was conquered by Joshua. Although the Canaanites were descendants of the son of Ham, according to tradition, their language was Semitic, and very similar to Hebrew. See *Palestine*.

CANADA

Jewish history in Canada began about the middle of the 18th century. After the first 150 years of Jewish immigration, there were less than 20,000 Jews in Canada. However, in the following 50 years the Jewish community in Canada grew in numbers, reaching about 246,000 Jews in 1960, of which the city of Montreal had the largest number, followed by Toronto and Winnipeg.

71

The first Jewish settlers in Montreal were of Spanish-Portuguese origin, and founded the synagogue "Shearith Israel" in 1768. Eastern European Jews began to emigrate in larger numbers about the end of the 19th century because of persecutions in Russia and other east European countries. The largest numbers arrived after the First World War, and smaller groups of immigrants were added since 1933 during the Nazi regime in Europe and the period following the Second World War.

The Jews in Canada are represented in all trades, professions and industries. Some live in agricultural settlements established by the ICA (Jewish Colonization Association). The Jewish communities in Canada have a highly developed cultural, social and institutional life. There are a large number of flourishing Hebrew and Yiddish schools, some of which are all-day schools. There is an important Zionist movement in Canada which has carried out significant projects in Israel. The Jewish Congress is the representative body of Canadian Jewry. There are, in addition, federations of Polish, Rumanian, Lithuanian and Ukrainian Jews. Religious life is organized through congregations in which orthodox Jewry plays the leading role.

CANDLES, LIGHTING OF

Jewish religion attaches much significance to the lighting of candles or lamps. In the Bible the priests are told to keep a lamp continually burning in the Tabernacle. The lighting of lamps or candles in the synagogue during the service is an old custom. The lighting of candles in the Jewish home as a ceremonial for ushering in the Sabbath and all major Jewish holidays is ordained in the *Mishnah* and has become one of the most solemn duties and privileges of the Jewish woman. According to tradition, light symbolizes the Torah and

man's soul. Events of joy or sorrow are customarily commemorated by candle-lighting, such as lighting candles during the marriage service, yortzeit candles and the placing of lit candles beside the dead. See also *Hanukkah*.

CANON

A term used to designate all the books included in the Bible, and generally referred to as the Holy Canon. See *Bible*.

CANTONISTS

Name applied to Jewish boys in Tsarist Russia who were drafted for military service at the age of 12 or younger. This was one of the schemes of Tsar Nicholas I to involve the Jews of Russia in the process of enforced Russification. Russian soldiers were at that time conscripted at the age of 18, for a period of 25 years of military service. In 1827, Nicholas I ordered that Jews be drafted at the age of 12 instead of 18. The Jewish boys were placed in special camps or "cantons," and were trained by proverbially cruel sergeants. Few of the children could survive the conditions of those inhuman training camps. Every Jewish community was ordered to produce a certain quota of young draftees, and because Jewish parents made every effort to keep their children from being drafted, Jewish community officials resorted to actual kidnapping of Jewish children, thus spreading terror among the Jews. This conscription practice continued until 1857, when it was abolished by Alexander II. Some of the Cantonists were baptized under duress, though many proved loyal to Judaism despite their hard life and the enticements held out to them.

CANTOR see Hazzan.

CAPERNAUM

An ancient town, called in Hebrew "Kfar Nahum," which lies on the western shore

The ruins of a two-story synagogue originally built at Capernaum on Lake Tiberias during the Roman era, about 3rd century c.e. Note the Ark of the Covenant carved on the fallen pillar (bottom right).

of Lake Tiberias (Sea of Galilee or Kinneret), in Israel, north of the city of Tiberias. It is sacred to Christians because Jesus made his temporary home there. The remains of a synagogue, the excavation of which began in 1905 by the Franciscans, indicates that an important Jewish community existed in Capernaum in the second century, as well as in later periods. Part of the ancient synagogue has been reconstructed, and the interesting relics are cared for by the Franciscan Fathers, whose church is established there.

CAPTIVES, RANSOM OF see Pidyon Shevuyim.

CARDOZO, BENJAMIN NATHAN (1870–1938)
Great liberal jurist and Associate Justice of the Supreme Court of the United States.

Benjamin N. Cardozo, Associate Supreme Court Justice and a leading American liberal jurist.

73

Haifa and its magnificent bay as seen from the heights of Mt. Carmel. Famous as the spot where Elijah defeated the prophets of Baal, Carmel is today the site of numerous Jewish settlements.

Born in New York, he was the descendant of a famous Sephardic family. He never attended a law school, but graduated from Columbia University at the age of nineteen. His brilliant legal work made it possible for him to become justice of the New York Supreme Court in 1913, and in 1926 he became Chief Judge of the Court of Appeals. His appointment by President Hoover in 1932 to the Supreme Court of the United States was warmly acclaimed by the entire nation. During his long legal career he was known for his liberal interpretation of the Constitution, and was the author of many incisive opinions on New Deal laws during the Roosevelt Administration. Cardozo took a vital interest in Jewish affairs, and was a life-long member of the Spanish and Portuguese Synagogue of New York. He was also a member of the American Jewish Committee.

CARMEL

Name of a famous twelve-and-a-half mile

Interior of the Bet-Shearim catacombs shows a large seven-branched candelabrum sculptured in stone. Menorahs were often used to ornament Jewish burial grounds and catacombs.

mountain-ridge on the sea coast of Israel, beginning at Haifa and extending toward the southeast. Mount Carmel is mentioned frequently in the Bible, and is known as the place where the prophet Elijah contested the activities of the prophets of Baal. Carmel is famous for its beauty and healthful climate, and is the site of numerous Jewish settlements in modern Israel. Especially known is the beautiful quarter of Haifa known as the "Hadar Ha-Karmel," where several monasteries and the important Israeli vocational and engineering school, the Technion College, are located.

CARO, JOSEPH see Karo, Joseph.

CATACOMBS, JEWISH

Underground natural or artificial galleries or caves designed as graves for the burial of the dead. This system of burial, already mentioned in the Bible, such as the purchase of *Machpelah* by Abraham as a family burial-place, came to be used extensively during the early centuries of the Christian era. Many Jewish catacombs have been discovered in Italy, North Africa and other places where important

75

Jewish communities had flourished. Of special significance are the catacombs discovered in recent years in Bet-Shearim, Israel, which was the seat of the *Sanhedrin* during the period of the great *Tannaim* (scholars mentioned in the Mishnah). One of the discovered catacombs in Bet-Shearim is believed to be the burial place of the great Rabbi Judah Ha-Nasi (the Prince), the editor of the *Mishnah*. The design of the catacombs follows a certain pattern, that is, they usually contain benches hewn out of rock, hollowed graves in the floor or in niches cut into the walls, and a variety of inscriptions and designs. The inscriptions are in Greek, Latin or Aramaic, depending on the time and place of the catacombs. The ornamentations in the Jewish catacombs are usually in the form of a seven-branched candelabrum, a *Lulav*, a *Shofar*, an Ark with scrolls of the Torah, etc. It seems that the catacombs were often robbed or desecrated, as evidenced from an Aramaic inscription in one of the catacombs in Bet-Shearim, which contains a curse and a warning to such intruders.

CENSUS see Population, Jewish.

CENTER, THE JEWISH

Jewish Community Center is the name of the organization created by more than 200 local Jewish communities in the United States and Canada to provide for their leisure-time recreational, informal educational and cultural needs as a Jewish group. In 1960 there were 334 such centers which in some communities were known as YM-YWHAs.

Their combined membership totalled 621,000 people ranging in age from 3 to 83. Annual attendance at all Center activities and programs reached 23,000,000. Building facilities designed for Center purposes were valued at nearly $90,-000,000. Centers conducted 209 day and 71 country camps and sponsored 115 nursery schools and 125 programs of recreation for older adults. Centers employed 1600 professionally trained social group workers.

At the beginning of 1960 these Centers and Ys were spending approximately $23,000,000 annually.

The Jewish Community Center and YMHA movement had its beginnings in the Jewish literary societies organized by Jewish youth in the United States during the 1840s. These Young Men's Hebrew Literary Associations were the forerunners of the YMHAs, the first of which was founded in Baltimore in 1854.

By 1900 there were 100 YMHAs, all contributing enormously to the adjustment of the masses of Jewish immigrants. In 1913 the first permanent national body of YMHAs was organized as the National Council of Young Men's Hebrew and Kindred Associations. In 1921 this Council merged with the National Jewish Welfare Board, generally known as JWB.

After World War I the YMHAs expanded rapidly in facilities, staff and program. Emphasis shifted from primary concern with serving youth to growing inclusion of all elements in the Jewish community. The change in name to Jewish Community Center followed.

In the 1920's and 1930's, there was a powerful movement, particularly within conservative Judaism, for the establishment of synagogue centers, whereby all the facilities of a Y would be available in the synagogue's building and under its auspices. A number of institutions incorporating this concept were thus established and are still in existence. See *National Jewish Welfare Board*.

CENTRAL AMERICA

The region comprising the republics of Guatemala, Honduras, El Salvador, Nicaragua, Costa Rica and Panama. It was conquered by the Spanish in the early part of the 16th century, and its first Jewish settlers were Spanish Marranos. Because of the Inquisition, Jewish immigration was negligible until the middle of the 19th century. As the Central American states became independent in the 1870's, Sephardic Jews from Syria, Turkey and Egypt settled in Costa Rica and Panama. Immigration of German Jews as well as Polish and Russian Jews began later, especially after the First World War. Nazi persecutions in the 1930's brought large numbers of German Jews to Panama and other states. In 1957 the estimated Jewish population in the Central American states was about 5,500, mostly concentrated in Panama, Costa Rica and Guatemala.

CENTRAL CONFERENCE OF AMERICAN RABBIS

Association of reform rabbis in America, founded in 1889 by Rabbi Isaac M. Wise, is the oldest rabbinical organization in America. According to its constitution, the purpose of this association was fourfold: a) to advance the teachings of Judaism; b) to create uniformity in observance and worship in religious instruction and in the functions of the rabbis; c) to create a united effort for the lawful development of Judaism; and d) to prevent discord in Judaism, and see to it that major issues pertaining to Judaism should be decided upon by men of learning and authority.

The Conference started with a membership of 32 rabbis, including the first graduates of the Hebrew Union College. In 1960 it had a membership of 767, serving congregations in the United States, Canada, and other countries. In 72 years of activity, the Conference succeeded in raising the standing and prestige of reform rabbis, and to create uniformity of observances practiced in the congregations. The Conference published the Union Prayer Book in two volumes, which became the standard prayer book in almost all reform congregations. The Conference also published the *Union Haggadah* for Passover, the *Union Hymnal*, a handbook for rabbis, and annual Yearbooks containing the proceedings of its conventions. The first president of the Conference was Isaac Mayer Wise, and its president in 1960 was Bernard J. Bamberger.

CENTRAL YIDDISH CULTURE ORGANIZATION
see CYCO.

CEREMONIAL OBJECTS, JEWISH

Judaism has always maintained the importance of ceremonial observance as a fulfillment of God's will and as a channel of communication with Him. The basic such observance is prayer. While much of prayer may be uttered without further aids, Jewish law prescribes specific means and objects to be used in many prayers. Some prayers cannot be recited without the ceremonial object ordained. A great deal of artistic imaginativeness has been expended in the creation of such objects. Some of the ceremonial objects are described in detail in their alphabetical order in this work. Below many are listed under certain classifications.

CEREMONIAL OBJECTS USED IN PRAYER:

1. *Kittel*, (from the German for smock). A loose white garment worn during services on Yom Kippur and by the head of the household at the *Seder*. Religious functionaries, such as the *Hazzan* and the *Baal Tokea*, also wear it during the services on Rosh Hashanah and Hoshana Rabbah. Pious Jews are buried in their *Kittel*.

2. *Tallit*, (also pronounced *Tallis*). Prayer shawl. Worn by men during the morning service every day of the year. (On Tishah Be-Av it is worn only for the afternoon service, and on Yom Kippur for every service.)

3. *Tefillin*. Phylacteries. Worn by men

(males who have reached their thirteenth birthday) during the morning service on weekdays. (On Tishah Be-Av they are worn in the afternoon service.)

CEREMONIAL OBJECTS IN THE HOME:

1. *Candlesticks.* A minimum of two candles are kindled by the housewife before sundown on Sabbaths and holy days.

2. *Dietary Utensils.* In traditional homes certain utensils are needed in preparing meats before cooking. In addition, dishes used for meat are not used for dairy foods, and dishes used the year round are not used for Passover.

3. *Havdalah Objects.* On Saturday nights and on the nights after the expiration of a holy day, the head of the household recites the *Havdalah* over a cup filled with some beverage other than water. On Saturday night, as well as on the night after the observance of Yom Kippur, a blessing is recited thanking God for having created light. For this blessing a double light is needed (the wording of the blessing speaks of "lights," in the plural, therefore a minimum of two). A braided candle is generally used for this purpose. Also on Saturday nights, a blessing over spices is recited. For this a box specially designed for spices (*Besamim*) is used.

4. *Kiddush Cup.* The head of the household pronounces the *Kiddush* over a cup filled with wine on Friday nights and on the eves of the holy days. The *Kiddush* may also be recited over the *Lehem Mishneh* (two loaves of bread).

5. *Megillah.* Scroll (of Esther), handwritten on parchment. This is the one book of Holy Scripture which is read at home as well as in the synagogue, since Purim commemorates the deeds of a woman, and the Scroll should be read at home for the women who cannot attend synagogue themselves. Many Jewish homes have a *Megillah*.

6. *Menorah.* Special candelabrum used for the Hanukkah lights, making provision for nine lights (eight plus *Shammash*). Either candles or oil and wicks are used. In Israel this candlestick is known as *Hanukkiah*.

7. *Mezuzah*, attached to the doorpost and containing the first two paragraphs of the *Shema*.

8. *Seder Objects.* Some Jewish homes have a special plate for the *Seder* known as the Seder plate, placed at the head of the table and containing the several objects required. Some also have a special container for the three *Matzot*. Some also have a special "Elijah Cup," a special pitcher and container for washing the hands at the table, and a special cup for wine for every member of the family for the "four cups."

9. *Sukkot Objects.* Every traditional Jew will make every effort to provide himself with a *Sukkah* (booth). In addition, he will obtain for himself and his family an *Etrog* (citron) and *Lulav* (palm branch). Attached to the base of the Lulav will be two *Aravot* (willow branches) and three *Hadassim* (myrtle branches).

10. *Tallit Katan.* Small *Tallit* known as *Tzitzit* or *Arba Kanfot*. Every pious male wears this during waking hours.

CEREMONIAL OBJECTS IN THE SYNAGOGUE:

1. *Ammud.* Reader's desk. Placed in the front of and below the Ark. The leader of the services faces the Ark.

2. *Aron Ha-Kodesh.* The Holy Ark where the Scrolls of the Torah are kept. The Ark has a long covering in the front, called the *Parokhet*, and a narrower valance above (*Kapporet*). Reform temples, as a rule, do not have the Parokhet or Kapporet. Above the Holy Ark there usually is placed a double tablet inscribed with the opening words of each of the Ten Commandments.

3. *Bet Ha-Midrash.* Historically the synagogue has been not only a House of

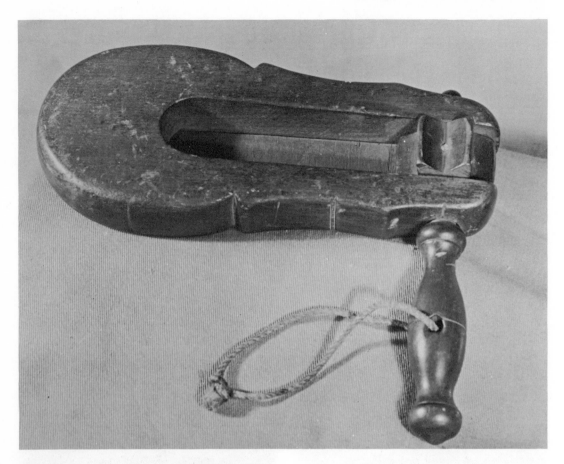

(Top) Early 19th-century Russian "grager." (Bottom left) 17th-century silver Sabbath lamp from Frankfort-am-Main, Germany. (Bottom right) 19th-century embroidered skullcap, Russian or Polish.

(Left) A graceful silver holder for the "Havdalah" candles from Frankfort-am-Main, Germany, ca. 1750. Note the man in the top hat holding a pitcher and cup, and supporting a drawer for fragrant spices above as well as the candelabrum. Pitcher, cup and spices are used here as symbols of the Havdalah ceremony which ends the Sabbath. (Right) 18th-century German Torah mantle, and east European silver Torah crown with an 18th-century Galician breastplate and pointer.

(Right) Late 17th-century silver and gilt "Etrog" box from Augsburg, Germany. (Below) Faience "Seder" plate from Pesaro, Italy, dated 1614, is now in New York's Jewish Museum. On the rim are two scenes from the Bible: Joseph revealing himself to his brothers, and Jews hastily baking "Matzot" in Egypt. On four separate cartouches are Moses, Aaron, David and Solomon. Text on the plate is the "Kiddush" and the order of the Seder.

18th century Polish circumcision plate shows the sacrifice of Isaac. Note all the signs of the Zodiac.

15th-century Passover Haggadah from Spain, and 19th-century Polish Elijah's cup and Seder plate.

A 19th-century European Torah Scroll, probably Polish, is opened to the Biblical Book of Genesis.

Silver Torah breastplate from Nuremberg, Germany, 1752. Note the horned unicorns and the lions.

Early 20th-century bronze version of a Hanukkah "dreidl" at Israel's Bezalel Museum in Jerusalem.

19th-century engraved silver "Tefillin" cases from Warsaw for both the hand and head phylacteries.

Prayer, but also a House of Study. Therefore, synagogues maintain a library, providing the worshipper not only with prayer books and copies of the Bible, but also other works for study, such as Talmud, Responsa, Codes, books on ethics, mysticism, etc.

4. *Bimah* or *Almemar*. The desk placed in the center of the synagogue for the reading of the Torah. One of the innovations of reform (joined later by conservative) Jews was to move the *Bimah* near the Ark and to use it for the leader of the services as well, who now faced the congregation. Even where a lectern (Ammud) was retained, it too was on the same level with the Ark and flanked alongside the Bimah with the *Hazzan* facing the congregation.

5. *Mehitzah*. Partition. In Jewish law, there must be a partition of minimum height between men and women worshippers. Sometimes the women worship in a balcony especially prepared for them. An innovation introduced by conservative and reform Jews was the family pew, where the whole family, men and women, sat together, doing away with the *Mehitzah*.

6. *Ner Tamid*. Eternal light. Hangs high and in front of the Ark, as a remembrance of the light which burnt continuously in the ancient Temple. It also alerts people to the fact that there are holy Scrolls of the Torah within the Ark, and that they should therefore act in a respectful manner.

7. *Sefer Torah*. Scroll of the Torah. Every synagogue must have at least one Scroll, and most have several. See *Sefer Torah* under alphabetical listing.

8. Every traditional synagogue has a *Mezuzah* on the doorpost, a cup and wine for *Kiddush* and *Havdalah*, a braided candle and spicebox for the Havdalah, a *Megillah*, a *Hanukkah Menorah*, and generally also skullcaps and prayer shawls for those who do not bring their own. Some traditional synagogues also have the prophetic books in scroll form.

MISCELLANEOUS CEREMONIAL OBJECTS:

1. *Burial*. Traditionally, Jews must be buried in a plain box, unornamented, and having no metal. He is clothed in simple garments, made of white cloth (Takhrikhin) and also in his *Tallit* and *Kittel*. A stone marker (Matzevah) is placed over the grave in the course of the year of mourning.

2. *Circumcision Knife* or *Izmel*, used by the *Mohel*. Other objects used in the circumcision ritual are the "Chair of Elijah" and the cup for drawing the blood (Metzitzah).

3. *Hallaf* or knife for slaughtering the fowl or animal in *Shehitah*, used by the *Shohet*. Ritual slaughter must be as rapid and painless as possible.

4. *Head Covering*. Traditional Jews will not ordinarily have their head uncovered. They will wear a hat or cap, or frequently the skullcap, known as *Kappel* (from German *Kappe*), or *Yarmulke* (etymology unknown), or in Hebrew, *Kippah*. To cover one's head is imperative for reciting prayers or for reading of religious books. Pious married women never show their hair in public, and have it covered frequently by a wig, known in Yiddish as *Shaitel* (from German *Scheitel*) or Peruk (French *Perruque*, German *Perruecke*).

5. *Huppah*. Canopy under which the groom and bride stand during the marriage ceremony. It is generally made of some textile, such as velvet; but sometimes a bower of flowers is used. The *Huppah* is symbolical of the new home the pair are building for their personal lives. Also essential to the marriage ceremony are the marriage band (ring), wine, and *Ketubah*, which is the marriage agreement.

6. *Mikveh* or the pool used for ritual purification.

CEREMONIAL FOODS:

1. *Ḥallah*. The piece of dough which is thrown into fire in lieu of the original gift to the *Kohanim* in Temple times. The word *Ḥallah* also denotes the special white bread eaten on the Sabbath and festivals.

2. *Hard boiled egg* taken as the last meal before Tishah Be-Av and the first meal by the mourner on returning from the funeral.

3. *Leḥem Mishneh*. Two loaves of bread to commemorate the double portion of manna on Friday. These loaves are used at the meals of the Sabbath and festivals, and the Kiddush may be recited over them if wine is not available.

4. *Matzah*. Unleavened bread for Passover use.

5. *Seder Foods*. Jewish law prescribes *Matzah*, wine, special vegetables (*Karpas* and *Maror*) and *Ḥaroset* to be taken at the *Seder*. Other symbols are the shank bone, the roasted egg and salt water.

6. It is customary to partake of honey on Rosh Hashanah, as a symbol for a sweet new year. Usually a piece of *Ḥallah* and an apple is dipped into the honey. On the second night of Rosh Hashanah it is customary to partake of a fruit not yet eaten that season, so as to be able to recite the benediction "*Sheheḥeyanu*."

7. Certain foods have become identified with several of the holidays, such as pancakes on Hanukkah, *hamantashen* and chick peas and broad beans on Purim, *knoedel* (matzah balls) on Passover, carob (bukser) or other Israeli fruit on Tu Bi-Shevat, dairy products on the second day of Shavuot, and *cholent* on the Sabbath.

CHAF see Kaf.

CHAGALL, MARC

Prominent painter of the surrealist school. Born in Russia in 1887, he studied at St. Petersburg (Leningrad) and went to Paris in 1910. In many of his paintings he gave

Marc Chagall, Russian painter, whose canvases depict the humble life of the European ghetto.

expression to the humble environment of his native village, and drew many of his themes from life in the Jewish ghetto. In 1914 Chagall returned to Russia where, under the Soviet regime, he became commissar of arts in Vitebsk. In 1923 he returned to France. He achieved great fame, and his works are found in the art galleries of many countries, including the United States. His popular paintings on Jewish themes are: "Rabbi," "Over the Town," "The Green Jew," and etchings for the *Book of Genesis*.

CHARITY

The essence of Jewish charity is expressed through two Hebrew terms, *Tzedakah* (righteousness), and *Gemilut Ḥasadim* (bestowing kindness). The giving of charity is one of the oldest and most sacred Jewish traditions, since the Bible not only commanded it, but described in full detail the manner in which the poor, orphans and widows should be provided for. The Bible even indicated

The alms box above is typical of those which were used for charity in a place of mourning.

what one is required to give for charitable purposes in the following words: "Every man shall give as he is able, according to the blessing of the Lord thy God which He hath given thee." Because agriculture was the basic industry in those days, the Bible prescribes for the farmer and tells him how he should provide for the needy from his produce, *Leket*, *Shikhah*, and *Peah*. Several volumes of the Mishnah are devoted to these and other types of charity. The Jewish concept of "charity" has, both in the Bible and later, been refined to mean more than the mere giving of alms; it has been considered as "Tzedakah," an act of justice and righteousness. Being poor should not be considered degrading for the individual; furthermore, the individual has the right to share the blessings of others which were accorded to them by the Almighty. The concept of Jewish charity was further developed and refined to mean "Gemilut Ḥasadim" (bestowing of kindness), that is, the giving of charity should be performed with grace, kindness

and humility. The Rambam (Maimonides) listed eight categories of donors, one of the higher of which is the one who not only gives charity in a secret manner in order not to humiliate the recipient, but does not even know who the recipient of his charity is. However, the highest category is one in which the needy individual is not only offered alms or gifts for temporary relief, but where an attempt is made to rehabilitate him, that is, "to help him to help himself," and to put him on his own two feet.

Throughout Jewish history the giving of charity was not only the concern of the individual Jew, but became the responsibility of the entire community. Also Jewish communities have always answered the call of distress of other Jewish communities during persecutions and in other unfortunate circumstances. As in the past, there is not now any Jewish community that does not have charitable societies.

CHARITY BOX

Called in the Yiddish language "Pushke," referring to a box or receptacle where charitable contributions are placed. Traditionally, every Jewish home had a charity box in which to deposit money for some charitable purpose. Charity boxes are also found in synagogues, cemeteries and other public places. Customarily, housewives put money into the Pushke, before lighting the Sabbath candles.

CHAUTAUQUA SOCIETY, JEWISH see
Jewish Chautauqua Society.

CHAZARS see Khazars.

CHILDREN OF ISRAEL

A translation of the Hebrew "Bene Yisrael," a name for the Israelite nation. Since the Patriarch Jacob was given the name "Israel," this implied a common ancestry from Jacob for all the Jewish people. The Bible uses this term both in the

CHILE

Torah and subsequent books. The Jewish tribes conquering the land of Canaan, and later living separately during the period of the Judges, are referred to in the Bible as "Bene Yisrael." The term also applies to people of the Jewish faith in general, including proselytes.

CHILE

The Jewish population of this South American republic was over 30,000 in 1960. The first Jews to settle in Chile were Marranos (secret Jews), who were exposed to the dangers of the Inquisition established there in the 16th century. The Chilean population persisted for centuries in its opposition to the settlement of Jews in Chile. The largest Jewish immigration to Chile was that of the 19th and 20th centuries. In 1910 Chile became an independent republic and Jews were accorded religious liberty. During the period of persecution of Jews in Germany in the 1930's, many German Jews settled in Chile. The Jewish communities are organized and Zionist and cultural activities are well-developed and long-established.

CHINA

The first reports received by the western world about the existence of Jews in China came in the 17th century, when a community of Mongolized Jews was discovered in the city of Kai-Fung-Foo. Exactly when the first Jews settled in China is not certain. Some believe that the prophet Isaiah referred to Jews in China when mentioning the land of the "Sinim." It is, however, certain that in the 7th century Persian Jews came to China through India. There are about 4,000 Jews in China who still observe certain Jewish customs but are otherwise not to be distinguished in appearance from the Chinese. The first influx of European Jews to China began in 1918. Since 1933 the Chinese

Jewish population increased substantially through immigration of German-Jewish refugees. The largest Jewish settlements were formed in Shanghai, Harbin and Tientsin, with a combined population of about 36,000 in 1940. These new immigrants resettled elsewhere after the Second World War, and there were only about 1,000 Jews in China in 1960.

CHOSEN PEOPLE

A term used to identify the Jewish people. According to the Bible, God chose the people of Israel to be the "holy people unto the Lord." The concept of the "Chosen People" for Jews was the prophetic idea that the God of the entire universe chose the Jewish nation, not for special favors, but as the people with a special mission to spread His teachings and to serve as an example to other nations. When the Nazis spoke of the Germans as the master race, they included the demand that the rest of the world must become their slaves. The Jewish concept of "Chosen People," on the other hand, involves the Jews as teachers of God's will to the world, and therefore as serving both God and man in the process. Anti-Semites have found the phrase a useful stick with which to beat the Jews, despite what is the term's clear meaning in Jewish life and thought.

CHRIST see Jesus of Nazareth.

CHRISTIANITY

The religion built around the figure of Jesus of Nazareth, regarded by Christians as the "Messiah" or "Son of God."

Traditional Christianity is based on the doctrine of the Trinity, that is, a God in three Persons: "God the Father," "God

T'ang Dynasty (618-906 c.e.) glazed terra cotta figure of Chinese trader with Semitic features. Travelling from Persia via India, Jews traded with the Chinese as early as the 7th century.

the Son," and "God the Holy Ghost." Differing branches of reform Christianity, which attempt to restore the Christian teaching of earlier times, vary greatly in their acceptance or interpretation of the doctrine of the Trinity, the most liberal, Unitarianism, rejects it entirely.

In historical Christianity, Jesus, called Christ, is revered as the incarnate second person of the Trinity. The teaching that God could possibly be incarnate constitutes Christianity's essential break with the teachings of Jewish monotheism.

The most significant difference between Christianity and Judaism is Christianity's acceptance of the doctrine of the Trinity as opposed to the absolute monotheism of the Jews. Closely related to this difference is the Christians' view of Jesus as their Savior. Christians unite in regarding Jesus as the Messiah, with different interpretations as to what that term may mean. And they look forward to a "Second Coming" in which Jesus Christ—or his teachings— shall reign supreme on earth. The Jews, on the other hand, regard the Messianic prophecies of the Bible as having reference to some undetermined time in the future, perhaps at the "End of Days."

Another basic doctrine of Christian dogma is that of original sin: the belief that, after the expulsion from Eden, all men were born into evil—an evil from which Christians believe that Jesus, as their personal Savior, offers the only hope of deliverance. Judaism rejects not only the concept of Jesus' Messiahship but the entire doctrine of original sin.

The virtue of "Christian love" is an essential feature of Christian teaching. Ideally, this love parallels the love that Jesus showed for the poor and needy and for all mankind, a love which—turned the other cheek to the aggressor and willingly suffered many indignities. Judaism teaches the goodness of love as set forth in the

Book of Leviticus 19:18, "thou shalt love thy neighbor as thyself," and in the Talmud, where the sage Hillel says, "Whatever is hateful unto thee, do it not to thy fellow." Indeed, Jesus drew much of his teaching on love from Hebrew Scripture and tradition, but Judaism balances love and mercy by an equal emphasis on the necessity for law and justice. See *Jesus of Nazareth.*

CHRONICLES

The name of the last book of the Bible, called in Hebrew "Divre Ha-Yamim" (Annals). The book consists of two parts, and gives a short history of the Jews from creation to the destruction of the First Temple by the Babylonians. It summarizes briefly the important genealogy from Adam to King Saul, and in more detail the content of the books of Joshua, Judges, Samuel, and Kings, concentrating mainly on the history of the Kingdom of Judah. There is no conclusive evidence as to time and authorship, but the Talmud attributes the book to Ezra and Nehemiah.

CHRONOLOGY, JEWISH

The Jewish people have used a number of methods of counting time. The method used currently is Biblical chronology, according to which time is measured from the creation of the world. However, the above method has not always been employed by the Jewish people. The Bible tells us that the Israelites counted time from the Exodus from Egypt, as for instance, the building of the First Temple was recorded as having taken place in the year 480 after the Exodus. During the time of the Jewish kingdoms, time was figured from the year that the king in question had ascended the throne. After destruction of the First Temple, years were counted from that date. After Greek ruler Alexander died, accession of the

Embroidery of a circumcision bench cushion (Germany, 1749) depicting the ceremony, inscribed, "And Abraham circumcised his son Isaac when he was eight days old, as God had commanded him."

Seleucidan kings in 312 b.c.e. marked the beginning of a new Jewish chronology.

It is not definitely known when the counting of time from Creation began. Some believe that it started in the second century c.e. The accepted differential between Jewish and general chronology is 3,760 years. By adding this figure to the current secular year one arrives at the year in the Jewish calendar. Thus the year 1960 c.e. is equivalent to the Jewish year 5720. In Jewish chronology it is customary to mark the years before One as "b.c.e." (before common era), and the years after the year One, as "c.e." (common era). See *Calendar, Jewish.*

CIRCUMCISION

A religious rite called in Hebrew "Berit Milah." Although it dates back to primitive times, and is practiced to this day by Moslems and other peoples, the rite is one of the basic commands of Judaism. In Judaism it represents the covenant between God and Israel. The first Hebrew to perform circumcision was Abraham, obeying God's command that "every male child among you shall be circumcised." This rite is therefore also referred to as the "Covenant of Abraham," and its influence on Jewish life at all times has been so remarkable that it is practiced to this day by all Jews, even by those who may discard other Jewish ceremonial institutions. Jews perform circumcision on the eighth day after birth of the male child, and the operation is delayed only on the doctor's advice. Circumcision consists of cutting off the foreskin of the male organ, and is performed by a *Mohel* (circumcisor), in the presence of the father of the child, the *Sandek* (godfather), and a religious quorum (Minyan). The child is usually named during the blessings recited at the completion of the operation. The ceremony is sometimes referred to as the Initiatory Rite.

CITIES OF REFUGE

Those cities which were, according to the Bible, designated as a place of asylum for unintentional murderers. There were six such cities in the Land of Israel, three west and three east of the Jordan. To be protected from the authorities or blood avengers, the unintentional murderer had to be confined to a "City of Refuge," and could only leave it on the death of the High Priest. In later periods additional places of asylum were designated, such as the Levitical cities or the court of the Holy Temple.

CITY OF DAVID see Jerusalem.

CODES

Every advanced society has found it necessary at one time to arrange in systematic fashion the laws and customs which grad-

ually evolve out of years of community life. Thus the Jews too, have codified their laws many times in the course of the millenia. The basic Jewish code is the written Torah (Pentateuch, also called Five Books of Moses). Some scholars find several codes within the Torah which are listed as follows: "Code of the Covenant" in Exodus, the "Code of Holiness" in Leviticus, the "Code of Deuteronomy," and the "Priestly Code" (Torat Kohanim) derived from the entire Pentateuch.

The next great code of Judaism is known as the *Mishnah*, redacted by R. Judah Ha-Nasi in the third century c.e. Subsequent centuries witnessed the development and completion of the *Gemaras* in the academies in Palestine which produced the Jerusalem Talmud (fourth century) and those in Babylonia which produced the Babylonian Talmud (fifth to sixth centuries). The accumulation of decisions in the Talmud and later teachers (Geonim) made further codifications necessary. Throughout the Middle Ages, and even to this day, individuals and communities turn to recognize Rabbinical authorities with problems in religious law. These questions and answers are known in Hebrew as *Sheelot U-Teshuvot* and in English we use the term Responsa. Numerous decisions thus recorded became incorporated in the several Codes in the course of scholarly revision.

Listed below are some of the later codes from the medieval and modern periods which have gained wide acceptance.

The "Code of Maimonides," known in Hebrew as *Mishneh Torah* or *Yad Ha-Ḥazakah*, in fourteen sections, deals with Jewish law in its entirety, including those laws which are no longer practiced because there is no Temple or sacrifice.

Arbaah Turim, by Jacob ben Asher, in four sections, omitting those laws no longer applicable.

Shulḥan Arukh, by R. Joseph Karo of Safed, in four sections, following the pattern of Arbaah Turim. Because Karo was a Sephardi he did not record the usage of east European Jews. R. Moses Isserles of Cracow therefore made additional notes. The basic text plus the notes have become the authoritative code for orthodox Jewry to this day. A late condensation, known as *Kitzur Shulḥan Arukh* is generally used by laymen.

Ḥaye Adam (Life of Man) and *Hokhmat Adam* (Wisdom of Man), by R. Abraham Danzig, in the 18-19 centuries, combines in simple form the first two sections of the Shulḥan Arukh, also used mainly by laymen rather than by scholars.

Writers whose decisions have been accepted as authoritative are known as *Posekim* (Deciders). Those who flourished until the sixteenth century are called *Rishonim* (Early Authorities); subsequent personalities are called *Aḥaronim* (Latterday Authorities). See *Halakhah*.

COHANIM see Kohen.

COHEN

Very common and oldest Jewish family name, and a term applied to Jewish males of priestly descent, even to those whose surname is not "Cohen." There are a number of different spellings of the name "Cohen," and a variety of other names derive from it. See *Kohen*.

COHEN GADOL see Kohen Gadol.

COLLEGE OF JEWISH STUDIES

A school of higher Jewish learning in Chicago, organized by the local board of Jewish education in 1924. The College trains teachers and youth leaders for all types of Jewish schools, and offers an adult education program. Its major courses are in Jewish history, Hebrew language, literature, religion, philosophy, sociology and education.

Christopher Columbus, discoverer of the New World. The portrait above is believed to be the only such based on a contemporary painting.

COLOMBIA

A South American republic where Jews numbered about 9,000 in 1960. Jewish immigration began in the 16th century, but because of religious persecution the Jewish community did not develop substantially. The early settlers were of Spanish origin, but the modern Jewish community in Colombia consists chiefly of east European and German Jews, the latter arriving during the Nazi regime in Europe. The Jewish Federation of Colombia represents all Jews in the different communities, the largest of which is in Bogota, the country's capital, and those in Cali, Baranquilla, and Medellin.

COLUMBUS, CHRISTOPHER (1451–1505)

Discoverer of the New World. Columbus' origin was for a long time a topic of speculation. Investigations cast doubt as to his presumed Italian birth, and much evidence was forwarded to strengthen the belief that his parents were Marranos (se-

93

cret Jews) who fled from Spain to Italy. It is known that his expedition was helped by Jewish scientists, financiers and statesmen. Some historians believe that Queen Isabella did not actually pawn her jewels to finance the expedition, and that most of the funds came from the confiscated wealth of Spanish Jews, especially that of the Marrano Luis de Santangel. A professing Jew, Abraham Zacuto, provided Columbus with scientific maps for the expedition, and a number of Marranos were members of his crew. It is recorded that the *secret Jew*, Luis de Torres, Columbus' interpreter, was the first white man who set foot on the soil of San Salvador, the first island of the New World to be discovered. Though Columbus did find the New World, it was named not for him, but for explorer, Amerigo Vespucci.

COMMANDMENTS, THE TEN see Ten Commandments.

COMMISSION ON JEWISH EDUCATION

An agency of the Union of American Hebrew Congregations and the Central Conference of American Rabbis, founded in 1923. It develops courses of study and prepares textbooks for Jewish education in reform religious schools throughout the United States. It publishes the "Jewish Teacher," a magazine for teachers of reform religious schools, curricula for the religious schools, and an annual catalogue of publications.

COMMUNITY CENTER see Center, the Jewish.

COMMUNITY COUNCILS

Many Jewish communities in the United States organized so-called "Community Councils" (also known as Jewish Federations or Welfare Funds), organizations through which representatives of the different Jewish groups could meet on a democratic basis for the purpose of dis-

Jews of the Warsaw Ghetto rounded up for transport to extermination camps. Six million Jews died in camps like Auschwitz, Dachau and Bergen-Belsen, names that symbolize Nazi German barbarism.

cussing problems facing the Jewish community and determining common action. The Community Councils, (numbering 231 in 1959), are in a sense a new form of the old European "Kehillah." The purpose of such Community Councils can be seen from the various activities in which they engage: raising funds for local, national and overseas needs; combatting anti-Semitism; conducting community surveys; sponsoring and stimulating Jewish educational and cultural activities; maintaining speakers' bureaus; supervising *Kashrut;* administering aid to refugees; coordinating the activities of community agencies; maintaining Jewish employment agencies.

CONCENTRATION CAMPS

The Hitler regime, which began in Germany in 1933, set out to free Europe from Jewish influence. In addition to depriving the Jews in Germany and in Nazi-occupied countries of their businesses, reducing their food rations, forcing them to wear the "Yellow Badge," and confining them into Ghetto walls, the government also resorted to mass deportation of Jews to concentration camps in Germany and in many occupied areas in eastern and even western Europe. There was no escape from these camps, which became virtual extermination places. The wholesale slaughter of Jews was speeded by the Germans through their use of gas chambers, where the victims were first poisoned and then disposed of in huge crematoria. About six million Jews were exterminated in the German concentration camps, a million and a half at Auschwitz alone. Some of the other extermination camps in Poland were located in Treblinka, Belsen, Chelmno, Sobibor and Maidanek. In Germany itself, the more notorious camps were Mauthausen, Buchenwald,

Jewish women and children packed into cattle cars for transport to the gas chambers. Nazi savagery and efficiency combined to wipe Europe "clean of the Jews" and so created a horrible genocide.

95

CONFESSION

Bergen-Belsen and Dachau. Other such camps were located in France, Holland, Italy, Estonia, and White Russia (Minsk). All the property of the victims was taken by the government, and their bodies were exploited for economic profit.

CONFESSION

As a Jewish ritual, confessions of sins are usually public confessions, that is, a part of public worship, such as the confession called *"Ashamnu"* recited on Yom Kippur. Confession, even in public, was solely between the penitent and his God. See *Sin; Viddui.*

CONFIRMATION

The custom observed in many synagogues whereby young people are formally confirmed as responsible members of the Jewish community. It is a development of the traditional Bar Mitzvah ceremony. The Confirmation ceremony generally takes place on the festival of Shavuot, which is the traditional season of the giving of the Torah and is thus an appropriate occasion for Jewish young people, usually fifteen or sixteen years old, to renew the pledge of their forefathers to observe the teachings of the Torah. In preparation for this event the confirmands spend a year or more studying the beliefs and practices of Judaism. Since Shavuot is also the festival of the First-Fruits, synagogues where confirmation takes place are decorated with flowers and greens, and during the confirmands' procession to the pulpit the girls usually carry flowers. The central point of the confirmation service is the reading of the Ten Commandments. The boys and girls participate in the services. Some recite prayers, some read selections from the Bible, and some speak briefly on the meaning of Judaism. The ceremony is concluded as the boys and girls face the Ark and are

blessed by the rabbi. Conservative congregations sometimes confine the confirmation ceremony to girls, and occasionally use the term "consecration" instead of the usual term "confirmation."

CONGRESS FOR JEWISH CULTURE

An organization established in 1948. It seeks to centralize and promote Yiddish culture and cultural activities throughout the world and to unify fund raising for these activities. It publishes a periodical "Bletter far Yiddisher Dertsiung" and "Kultur Naies." It is publishing two important works in Yiddish: "A Lexicon of Yiddish Literature" and "An Encyclopedia of Jewish Education."

CONSECRATION see Confirmation.

CONSERVATIVE JUDAISM

The movement of conservative Judaism in the United States began during the last decade of the 19th century, about 50 years after the first reform synagogue was established. The conservative movement came into being as a result of dissatisfaction with the orthodox synagogue service, and as an opposition to the extreme departures of reform religious services and practices. It may be said that the position of conservative Judaism is somewhere between reform and orthodox. Conservative leaders generally accept the doctrine of divine inspiration in some sense, but many hesitate affirming a literal revelation of the Torah by God at Sinai. The laws of the Torah and the Jewish customs transmitted from generation to generation are kept sacred by the conservative movement. They may not be discarded, but rather changed and adapted, if necessary, to modern conditions of Jewish life; but only by proper scholars and authoritative bodies. The Sabbath and *Kashrut* (dietary laws), for instance, are sacred traditions to be observed as fully as possible.

The conservative movement made a few changes in the traditional prayer book. They have tried, as their name implies, to "conserve" and to protect Jewish faith and culture, and maintain that Jews are not only a religious group, but a people with a distinct culture, a historic language, and a Holy Land. They advocate the duty of helping the development of the State of Israel, and in America the study of Hebrew and the creation of strong Jewish communities in order to preserve and strengthen the Jewish people, its religion and culture.

CONSTANTINOPLE see Istanbul.

CONVERSION TO JUDAISM see Ger.

COSSACK MASSACRES

During the years 1648 and 1649 savage outbreaks against Russian Jews took place as a result of the Cossack revolt against Polish noblemen. The leader of the Cossacks was the chieftain Bogdan Chmielnicki, who, with the help of Russian peasants, staged large scale massacres on Jews in the Ukraine, Volhynia and Podolia, because they were believed to be friends of the Poles. It is estimated that close to half a million Jews perished during that period. Unbelievable atrocities against the defenseless Jews were committed by the Chmielnicki hordes. There is a long record of Jewish martyrdom, of the destruction of entire Jewish communities, such as Tulchin, Nemirov, Homel and others. Thousands of men, women and children chose to die by the hands of the human beasts rather than to accept baptism. Over 700 Jewish communities were massacred. This disaster caused great changes in the structure and subsequent history of east European Jewry. Cossack anti-Semitism has persisted down to the present day.

COSTA, URIEL DA see Acosta, Uriel.

COUNCIL OF THE FOUR LANDS

For about two hundred years, from the 16th to the 18th century, the Jews of Poland were united under one governing body, called in Hebrew "Vaad Arba Aratzot" (Council of the Four Lands). The Council included representatives from four lands, namely, Great Poland, Little Poland, Ruthenia and Volhynia, and later also Lithuania. The Jews of each of these countries had their own autonomous organization, which was in turn affiliated with the great Council of the Four Lands. The Council was responsible to the Polish government; it coordinated the activities of the separate Jewish districts, and engaged in the following activities: a) collecting of taxes imposed upon the Jews by the respective governments; b) dealing with many of the economic problems of the Jewish communities; c) administering all matters pertaining to religion; d) providing education and social service; and e) arbitrating disputes between communities. The Council was headed by laymen, but religious matters were decided by rabbis. The Council's activities were recorded in a "Pinkas" (Record Book), transcriptions of which were preserved by a number of communities. The Council of the Four Lands was abolished by the government in 1764.

COUNCIL OF JEWISH FEDERATIONS AND WELFARE FUNDS

A national coordinating agency for local Jewish federations, welfare funds and community councils. It was founded in 1932, and in 1960 was servicing about 250 member organizations. The Council is subsidized through special foundations and subscriptions from member agencies. It operates a research department which helps in the budgeting, planning and interpreting necessary for the administration of the local and regional welfare and

A male child being brought in for the ritual Covenant of Circumcision (Berit Milah), from a 19th-century German painting by Moritz Oppenheim. Circumcision remains the Jew's mark of God's covenant.

health services. It holds annual conferences to discuss problems and policies of Jewish organizations, and it publishes and furnishes literature dealing with problems of Jewish community organizations. At its 1959 Convention it decided to embark on a cultural program as well. See *Federations*.

COVENANT (Berit)

Jewish tradition looks upon the relation of the Jewish people with God as covenantal. God has imposed certain obligations on and made certain promises to Israel. Israel, in turn, has accepted those obligations and

has been confident that He will fulfill those promises. In general, the purpose of this covenant was to spread among the peoples of the world knowledge of the true God, and to formalize the ritual and ethical requirements of the Law. The promise made by God was that the Jewish people were to be a blessing to all mankind, and a light to the nations.

This covenant was made and renewed with each of the Patriarchs, Abraham, Isaac and Jacob. The agreement between God and Abraham is explicitly described, both as regards the Jewish people as a whole (Genesis 15), and in relation to

A young boy's affirmation of Covenant takes place at Bar Mitzvah when he formally accepts all the obligations of an adult Jew. The French Bar Mitzvah scene above was painted ca. 1865 by E. Brandon.

each individual male Jew (Genesis 17). To this day the rite of initiation is called the "Covenant of Circumcision" (Berit Milah). The Sabbath is referred to in the Torah as "An eternal Covenant" between God and the Children of Israel; the Two Tablets on which were inscribed the Ten Commandments, as the "Two Tablets of the Covenant"; and the Holy Ark which housed them, as "Ark of the Covenant of the Lord." The prophet Ezekiel speaks of a "Covenant of Peace," "An everlasting Covenant" between God, and the Children of Israel, both descendants of the Household of Israel and the Household of Judah.

In recent years, some Jewish thinkers who reject the mystical implications of the covenantal relationship, reinterpreted it to mean not so much a promise between two parties (God and Israel) in the distant past as a formulation of what has actually taken place in human history. That the western world has accepted the Jewish Bible as a foundation for its thinking, and considered the cultural contributions of the Jews so great as to refer to our civilization as Judeo-Christian is considered to be evidence of the promise partially fulfilled that the Children of Israel were to become a blessing to all humanity. Orthodox and other branches of Judaism to a varying degree accept the doctrine of covenant as well as the "chosenness" of the Jewish people as an eternal fact, in the literal sense of an agreement between God and Israel. It may be noted here that historical Christianity considers itself the inheritor of this covenant doctrine.

In addition to the covenant between God and Israel, the Bible records another covenant made with Noah and binding on all mankind. The Rabbis list the following as the seven Noahidic prohibitions: idolatry, blasphemy, murder, incest, robbery, and eating the flesh of live animals. This covenant also imposed the obligation on man to establish law courts to maintain justice and order. After the deluge God promised Noah that never again would He destroy the world by flood, and He set the rainbow in the sky as an eternal sign of His promise.

CRÉMIEUX, ISAAC ADOLPHE (1796–1880)

French statesman, founder of the *Alliance Israélite Universelle*, and one of the most prominent Jews of the 19th century. An outstanding attorney and a brilliant orator, he settled in Paris, where he entered the field of politics, became a member of the Chamber of Deputies in 1842, and was appointed Minister of Justice in 1848. In 1873 he was appointed senator for life. As a political leader he succeeded in introducing important reforms, such as the abolition of slavery in the French colonies, abolition of capital punishment for political offenses, and the introduction of trial by jury.

He took a great interest in Jewish affairs and gained international recognition for his intervention during the Damascus blood accusation trial. He also used his political influence to help in the amelioration of the condition of the Rumanian and Balkan Jews. For the protection of Jewish

Isaac Adolphe Crémieux, an outstanding French Jew of the 19th century, was founder and first president of the "Alliance Israélite Universelle."

communities the world over from persecution, he called for the establishment of an international Jewish organization, and founded the "Alliance Israélite Universelle," becoming its first president. He was a wealthy man, and made large contributions to French patriotic causes and to Jewish institutions.

CRIMEA

Before the Second World War, there were about 50,000 Jews living in this peninsula (in south Russia on the Black Sea). Settlements of Jews in Crimea date back to the period of the destruction of the First Temple. Large Jewish settlements existed there in the seventh century, during the rule of the Khazars, whom it is believed they influenced to embrace Judaism. In addition to the Crimean Jews themselves (known as Krimchaks) there were also Jews from other Slavic countries, as well as Karaites. The Crimean Jews spoke the Tartar language, which they wrote in Hebrew characters, and observed many Jewish customs. When Crimea became a Soviet Republic, an attempt was made to create an autonomous Jewish community. A number of Jewish agricultural settlements were established, and a number of Yiddish schools were opened. As a result of the Second World War, these communities were almost completely wiped out by the Germans.

CROMWELL, OLIVER (1599–1658)

Lord Protector of England. Known in Jewish history for his religious tolerance and his friendship for the Jews. In 1655 he invited to London the famed Jewish scholar of Amsterdam, Menasseh ben Israel, known for his effort to secure readmission of the Jews to England. Although Council of the Government did not grant official permission for their return, the lawyers pointed out that no legal hindrance existed. In consequence Jews began to trickle in to England from then on. See *Menasseh ben Israel.*

CRUCIFIXION

The Greeks and the Romans used "crucifixion" as a form of capital punishment. This type of punishment was never used by Jews. The accusation made by some Christians that the crucifixion of Jesus was executed by Jews is not based on historical fact. For centuries the Jewish people have been exposed to untold suffering for this execution. The New Testament ascribes it to the Roman government, although it blames the Jews for instigating the trial. The usual representation in Christian art of the crucifixion of Jesus has him suspended on a cross of wood with arms outstretched and his hands and limbs nailed to the cross. A cross with the figure of Christ is called a crucifix.

CRUSADES

Holy wars waged by the Christian countries of Europe for the purpose of recapturing Palestine from the Mohammedans. These wars started at the end of the 11th century and continued to the beginning of the 13th century. The specific object of these religious wars was to free the sepulcher of Jesus, sacred to Christians, from the hands of the Moslem "unbelievers." There were four such major Crusades in the years 1096, 1146, 1187 and 1202. Based on the religious motif, the Crusades were actually waged for other reasons as well. Some of the Christian nobility taking part in the Crusades were fortune hunters looking for new lands to rule, and the thousands of peasants recruited for the holy wars looked for adventure and loot as an escape from their miserable existence. An important motivation for becoming a crusader was the cancellation of all debts on joining a Crusade.

The Crusades turned into a bitter and prolonged ordeal for the Jewish communities in Europe. The ignorant mobs were incited by the leaders of the Crusades to pillage and massacre whole Jewish communities. The cry was: "Before attempting to revenge ourselves upon the Moslem unbelievers, let us first revenge ourselves upon the 'killers of Christ' living in our midst!" Thousands of Jews perished, and entire Jewish communities were wiped out. To this day the Jewish liturgy contains prayers commemorating the martyrs of that dreadful period.

CRYPTO-JEWS see Marranos.

CUBA

The first white man to settle in Cuba was Luis de Torres, a Marrano (secret Jew) who was with Columbus when America was discovered. Other Marranos from Spain and Portugal settled there later, but because of the Inquisition immigration of

CULTURAL ZIONISTS

The last groups of the 11,000 Jewish refugees interned by the British as "illegal immigrants" in detention camps on Cyprus. After Israel's independence they were able to put the barbed wire behind them.

Jews was limited. Jews began to settle in larger numbers only after 1898 when Cuba was freed from Spanish rule. There were about 11,000 Jews in Cuba in 1960, the majority of whom came from eastern Europe during and after the Second World War. About two-thirds of the Cuban Jews live in Havana, where they developed several Jewish institutions, including a Hebrew school.

CULTURAL ZIONISTS

Toward the end of the 19th century, some persons felt that the political Zionism of Herzl gave a wrong emphasis to the age-old Jewish hope of returning to Zion. Such persons, among whom Aḥad Ha-Am was the chief theoretician, held to the belief that the main purpose of Zionism was to develop in the Jewish homeland a cultural center for Jews the world over. They maintained that so long as Jews are scattered all over the world, living among different nations and cultures, without any cultural center of their own, they

were exposed to the dangers of assimilation, and might eventually lose their national identity. Therefore, the only way to save Judaism was to rebuild the Jewish homeland where the Jewish settlers would develop a Hebraic culture, which would eventually serve as inspiration and unifying force for Jews all over the world. With the establishment of the State of Israel such differences among Zionists faded out in the reality of achieving both goals. See *Aḥad Ha-Am.*

CUP OF ELIJAH see Elijah's Cup.

CYCO

Abbreviated name of the "Central Yiddish Culture Organization," founded in 1938. It attempts to centralize, coordinate and develop Yiddish cultural activities in the United States. It publishes and distributes works of Yiddish authors; plans and organizes Yiddish cultural events with the cooperation of Yiddish speaking groups, fraternal orders and organizations; and sponsors the publication of an important

Jewish survivors of the Nazi holocaust form ranks in the streets of Bratislava, Czechoslovakia, to emigrate to Israel. Of the 450,000 Jews there in 1942, only 20,000 were left in the country by 1960.

Yiddish magazine, the "Zukunft," which had appeared under other sponsorship for many years.

CYPRUS

An island in the Mediterranean mentioned in the Talmud for its wine (Yen Kaphrisin) which was used as an ingredient in the incense prepared for the Temple. Jews are recorded as having lived there from time to time through the centuries. In contemporary history, it became notorious for its camp where the British interned 11,000 Jews deported from Palestine as "illegal" immigrants immediately after World War II (1945-49). In 1960 there were less than 200 Jews on Cyprus.

CYRUS THE GREAT

Founder of the Persian empire, over which he reigned from 558 to 529 b.c.e. He is remembered in Jewish history as a good king, who upon conquering Babylonia, issued a proclamation granting permission for the Jewish deportees to return to Judea and rebuild the Temple. This event is recorded in the Biblical books of *Ezra* and *Chronicles*.

CZECHOSLOVAKIA

In 1960 only about 20,000 Jews were left in the republic of Czechoslovakia. Close to 450,000 Jewish people had lived there in 1942. The Nazi victories in Europe and the Second World War which began in 1939 led to the almost complete annihilation of Czechoslovakian Jewry. The history of the Jews in Czechoslovakia can be traced to the Middle Ages. There were flourishing Jewish communities in Bohemia, Moravia, Silesia, Slovakia and Ruthenia (Carpatho-Russia), which areas in 1918 became provinces of the independent republic of Czechoslovakia. A truly democratic state, it granted equal political and religious rights to all citizens. In 1948, communists took control of the government by *coup d'état*, and Jews there have since suffered as they have in other communist countries.

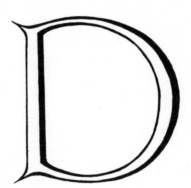

D

DAVNEN

Give ear to my words, O Lord,

Consider my meditation.

Hearken unto the voice of my cry,

    my King, and my God;

For unto Thee do I pray.

PSALMS

DALET (ד)

The fourth letter of the Hebrew alphabet. The word means "door" (delet), and its numerical value is 4; when followed by an apostrophe its value is four thousand. In Yiddish it is pronounced Daled. In the Greek the word becomes Delta. It is often used in place of the Lord's name, when it is also followed by an apostrophe.

DAMASCUS AFFAIR

An internationally known blood accusation trial staged against the Jews of Damascus, Syria, in 1840. Upon the disappearance of a Franciscan monk, Father Thomas, a rumor was circulated that he was killed by the Jews and his blood used for ritual purposes. The French consul started the inquiry and insisted that the governor Sherif Pasha prosecute the Jews. Following a forced confession extorted from a Jewish barber, a number of prominent Jews of Damascus were arrested and subjected to extreme tortures. One of the victims died in prison, another became a Mohammedan, and the others were forced to confess to the dreadful crime and condemned to die.

The news of this affair and of the anti-Jewish riots by the mobs of Damascus reached Europe. Two prominent Jews, Adolphe Crémieux of France, and Sir Moses Montefiore of England proceeded to Damascus to plead with the governor for the release of the surviving victims. They were eventually successful, and the blood accusation was publicly denounced as baseless.

DAN

One of Jacob's sons, and traditional ancestor of one of the twelve Israelite tribes of that name. After the conquest of Canaan, this tribe settled in the southern territory and occupied some of the northern territory as well, where the city of Dan was founded. This was the northernmost city of the land, just as Beer-sheba was southernmost city, hence the expression "from Dan to Beer-sheba," indicating the entire length of Israelite territory. Dan was a tribe of fearless warriors, and Samson is the most popular Biblical "hero of Dan."

DANIEL

A prophet whose book by the same name is included in the *Writings*, the third group of books of the Bible. Written partly in Hebrew and partly in Aramaic, the *Book of Daniel* deals with a number of topics: a) It tells of Daniel, who as a young boy of royal descent, was taken into Babylonian exile, and in spite of all perils remained true to the Jewish faith; b) It relates his prophetic visions and wisdom and his interpretation of the king's dreams, foretelling how the world will be ruled by different powers; c) It foretells the downfall of Babylonia as shown from Daniel's interpretation of the "writing on the wall" in the king's palace, which Daniel interpreted to mean: "Thou art weighed in the balance and found wanting"; and d) It contains a statement of life after death which says in part: "Many of them that sleep in the dust of the earth shall awake, some to everlasting life, and some to shame and everlasting contempt." Some scholars believe that the Book of Daniel, although telling of experiences in Babylonia, was written during the days of the Maccabees (about 165 b.c.e.) in order to encourage the Jews to resist the persecutions of the Syrian ruler Antiochus. The book has had great influence on the Christian Church because of its apocalyptic character.

Of great popular interest is the story of Daniel in the lions' den. Thrown into a pit filled with lions because of machination in the Persian court, he was found alive the next morning.

DANIEL DERONDA

A famous novel written in 1877 by the renowned and liberal English woman author, George Eliot. In this book, which has been translated into many languages, the author describes an assimilated Jew (Daniel Deronda) who not only returned to Judaism, but became an ardent advocate of the rebuilding of the Jewish homeland in Palestine. The book is important not only because of the author's sympathies toward the Jewish cause, but also for her knowledge of Jewish sources and her accurate descriptions of Jewish life, customs, and problems.

DAVID

Son of Jesse of Beth-lehem, second king of Israel, and most beloved and heroic figure in ancient Jewish history. He combined the talents of poet and warrior. As a young boy he was secretly anointed king by Samuel. He fought and killed the Philistine giant Goliath; he played the harp before the melancholic King Saul; he married the king's daughter Michal and won the friendship of the king's son, Jonathan. Because of Saul's jealousy David fled the country, became captain of outlaws, and found refuge among the Philistines. On the death of Saul and Jonathan, David lamented them in words which became famous in all literature: "How are the mighty fallen!" Thereafter David became king, first of Judah and then of all Israel. He fought the Philistines, conquered Jerusalem, and extended and fortified the now United Kingdom.

Remains of a private house at Megiddo, built during the reign of King David (11th to 10th century b.c.e.), were uncovered by archeological excavations, and indicate the crude architecture of the time.

The potash works on the Dead Sea. A small railway, built directly into the evaporation basin, is used to load and transport the crude mineral salts to the processing section where the chemicals are extracted.

View of the Dead Sea with the mountains of the Negev in the foreground. Deriving its waters mainly from the Jordan and Arnon Rivers, the Dead Sea is rich in minerals and an important Israeli natural resource.

The human shortcomings of David are overshadowed by his genius as warrior, ruler and poet. His abilities and accomplishments were extraordinary. According to tradition he organized the official religious service of priests and Levites, and wrote many of the Psalms. He was the founder of the Davidic dynasty (House of David) which provided kings for the Kingdom of Judah from about 1000 to 586 b.c.e., and later from 200 c.e. to 1000, Exilarchs in Babylonia. Tradition teaches that the Messiah will be a descendant of the House of David.

DAVNEN

Yiddish expression meaning "to pray." The origin of the word is not definitely established. Some say that it is connected with the Latin "divino." See *Liturgy*.

DAYAN

Hebrew term meaning "judge," applied to a functionary of a rabbinical court. A *Dayan* is usually an associate of the head of a Jewish religious court. In Sephardic communities a Dayan is an assistant to the chief rabbi.

DAYENU

The concluding word of each verse in a popular Passover song included in the Haggadah. The meaning of this one-word refrain is: "It would have been quite enough for us." Since the song lists all the favors that God bestowed upon the people of Israel, the refrain indicates that any one of the enumerated favors would have been sufficient and deserving of praise and thankfulness.

DAY OF ATONEMENT see Yom Kippur.

DAY OF JUDGMENT see Rosh Hashanah.

DAYS OF AWE see Penitential Days.

DEAD, PRAYER FOR THE see Kaddish.

DEAD SEA

A body of water, some thirty miles east of Jerusalem extending 47 miles southward. It has a surface of 360 square miles with no outlet, and is 1,300 feet below sea level. It was named the "Dead Sea" because of the fact that no living thing can exist there since the water is extremely salty and bitter and contains a very high percentage of minerals and other chemical elements. Its Hebrew name is "Yam ha-Melaḥ" (Salt Sea). The waters of the Jordan which run into it evaporate rapidly because the climate of that area is unusually dry. The Dead Sea contains a huge and unknown quantity of calcium, magnesium, potassium, sodium chlorides and bromides. One of the chief industries in Israel today is the extraction of minerals from the Dead Sea. The water is pumped from the Dead Sea, led into huge pans dug near the shore, where after evaporation, large quantities of minerals are left. There are a number of chemical companies in Israel which manufacture many useful products from the minerals thus extracted.

DEAD SEA SCROLLS see Archeology.

DEATH

In Judaism, death is looked upon from a twofold point of view. On the one hand, it recognizes the fact of a feeling of loss of a close relative and provides channels for expressing such natural grief through its laws of mourning. Judaism recognizes that mourning is made easier and more satisfactory from the psychological standpoint if the mourner knows what to do, what the society in which he lives expects him to do.

However, prolonged mourning is forbidden, because death is only a portal through which the deceased enters into the "world of truth," the next world. To mourn beyond the prescribed period may be interpreted as a denial of immortality. Judaism teaches that death is not the end, but does not undertake to give precise details as to what happens in the "world to come." Man can rely on the justice of God, and this is sufficient assurance for him.

Expressive of the Jewish conception of the ultimate bliss, is the picture we find in Jewish literature of the righteous sitted together with father Abraham, studying Torah. To the Jew, the most important activity of life is the study of God's will, and this is what he hopes for in the next world.

Most persons, with very few exceptions specified in the Talmud, whether Jews or non-Jews, will have a portion in the "world to come." No person is so wicked that his punishment will endure for more than twelve months after his death. At the end of time, with the coming of the Messiah, a general resurrection will take place, after which the righteous will enjoy the divine splendor for ever. Some hold that the ultimate punishment of the wholly wicked will be disintegration, so that they will not participate in such heavenly bliss. See *Hevra Kaddisha; Kaddish; Olam ha-Zeh; Resurrection; Shivah.*

DEBORAH

Prophetess and Judge of the Israelites. For her great accomplishments in behalf of her people she is known as "Mother in Israel." She inspired the armies of Israelite tribes under the leadership of Barak in their battle against the Canaanites. Her heroic song describing the battle and the decisive victory of the Israelites reflects the difficult times and the threats of the many enemies during the period of the Judges.

DECALOGUE see Ten Commandments.

DECIDERS see Codes.

DEDICATION, FEAST OF see Hanukkah.

DEGANIAH

The oldest cooperative workers' settlement (Kevutzah) in Israel, founded in 1909, on the shores of the Kinneret (Sea of Galilee), east of the Jordan river. Deganiah A and Deganiah B (founded in 1920), both on the land of the Jewish National Fund, served as models for numerous other such settlements in Israel. See *Kibbutz.*

DELILAH

The beautiful Philistine woman whom the Biblical hero, Samson, took as wife. She was responsible for the defeat of Samson, whom she betrayed to the Philistines. According to the Bible the secret of Samson's strength lay in his long hair. Under the pressure of her persistent demands and beguilements, Samson revealed the secret to her, and she in turn had his hair cut off while he was asleep and delivered him to the Philistines. This Biblical narrative inspired the French composer Camille Saint-Saens to write the well-known opera "Samson and Delilah."

DELUGE see Flood, the.

DENMARK

Sephardi Jews settled in Denmark on the invitation extended to them by King Christian IV in 1622. In 1960 there were about 6,500 Jews in Denmark, most of them concentrated in Copenhagen. In the modern period, the Jews of Denmark enjoyed civil, political and religious liberties. During the Nazi regime in Europe, the people of Denmark helped many Jews to escape the Nazi invaders and to find refuge in Sweden. King Gustav showed his sympathy toward the Nazi victims by wearing the "Yellow Badge," which Jews were compelled to wear in Nazi-occupied countries.

110

Deganiah, first communal settlement (Kevutzah) in Israel. Founded in 1909 and home of A. D. Gordon, leader of Palestinian workers, Deganiah served as a model for many subsequent Israeli settlements.

DERASHAH

A Hebrew term applied to a discourse on a Biblical or Rabbinic theme. Of the better known types are the sermon delivered by a rabbi, or the formal and public speech made by a Jewish boy as part of his Bar Mitzvah ceremony in the synagogue. The term also applies to the lectures of itinerant preachers. See *Maggid*.

DEREKH ERETZ

A Hebrew term, the literal meaning of which is "the way of the land." In common usage it applies to the good and respectful behavior of a person and his decorum in relation to other people. *Derekh Eretz* also implies a person's proper respect for himself. In traditional usage the term is also applied to a person's occupation and manner of earning a livelihood.

DERONDA, DANIEL see Daniel Deronda.

DEUTERO-ISAIAH see Isaiah.

DEUTERONOMY

Greek name of the fifth book of the Torah (Five Books of Moses), called in Hebrew *Devarim* (Words). The book relates some of the more important experiences of the Israelites while in the wilderness, and is in the form of discourses by Moses to the people when they were about to cross the Jordan for the conquest of Canaan. Moses reviews the highlights of the sojourn of the Israelites in the wilderness during the forty years of their wandering; he recites again the Ten Commandments with a few modifications; he urges the Israelites to keep the laws of the Torah, citing curses and punishments for the disobedient and blessings for the obedient. The famous *Shema* is found in this book. The book concludes with the Song of Moses, containing his blessings of the tribes, and the story of his death. The social and humane legislation of this book is noted for its high level of ethical concern with the individual's welfare. A noteworthy stylistic feature of the book is that it is mainly in the first person, with Moses as the speaker, whereas in the other books the narration is cast in the third person.

Some of the contents of Deuteronomy are a repetition of the laws found in the other books of the Torah. Some scholars maintain that this was the book found by the High Priest in the 7th century b.c.e., when the Temple was repaired, and which became the basis of the religious reformation under King Josiah.

DEVARIM see Deuteronomy.

DEW, PRAYER FOR see Tal.

DIALECTS, JEWISH see Languages, Jewish.

DIASPORA

A Greek term meaning "scattering," generally referring to the dispersion of the Jewish people outside of Israel. The Hebrew word "Galut" (Exile) is usually applied to the forced dispersion of Jews who historically had frequently been subjected to persecution either by the government under which they lived or by the people of the country.

Jews have lived outside of Palestine as far back as the period of the kings. After the downfall of the Kingdom of Israel destroyed by the Assyrians, and later the downfall of the Kingdom of Judah conquered by the Babylonians, Jewish settlements developed in Babylonia, Egypt and elsewhere. During the reign of Alexander the Great and subsequent Greek rule in the Middle East, new Jewish communities were established in Alexandria, Egypt, and Syria. Before and after the Roman con-

quest of Judea, Jewish settlements were formed in Europe, especially in Rome. From Rome Jews came to Spain, France, and later to England and Germany. Owing to religious, economic and political persecutions in Germany, Jews sought refuge in Poland and Russia. After the expulsion of Jews from Spain and Portugal at the end of the 15th century, new Jewish settlements were established in Holland, Turkey and North Africa, as well as on the American continent. Dispersion of Jews on a large scale also took place in 1881 as the result of persecutions in Russia and other European countries.

The First World War created great dislocation of Jews and the disruption of Jewish life in European communities, resulting in large scale emigrations. The period of the Second World War witnessed the annihilation of about six million Jews and the dispersion of the survivors to different countries, especially to the American continent and to Palestine.

The State of Israel, established in 1948, absorbed more than a million Jews from European and Arab countries. Most Jews of the world still live in the diaspora. Of about twelve million Jews in the world, only slightly over two million live in Israel. See *Exile*.

DIBBUK (DYBBUK)

A Hebrew term meaning "attachment," applied to the soul of a deceased sinful person, believed to have entered the body of a living person and thereafter refused to leave it until "driven out" by a religious rite. This belief in evil spirits and migrant souls was popular among many peoples throughout the world and found

An actor playing one of the roles in S. An-Ski's popular Yiddish play, "The Dibbuk," at the Habimah theater in Israel. "Dibbuks," or evil spirits which enter another individual's soul, are an age-old tradition in Yiddish folklore and writing.

112

expression in mystical literature. S. An-Ski in 1916 wrote a popular Yiddish play "The Dibbuk" dealing with this belief. In 1959, Paddy Chayefsky wrote "The Tenth Man," a play on this theme in relation to contemporary psychiatry.

DIETARY LAWS (KASHRUT)

The Jewish Dietary Laws are based on Biblical and Rabbinical ordinances. They distinguish between foods that are "kasher" (permissible) and "terefah" (forbidden). In popular Jewish speech, the terms for these are "kosher" and "traif." These laws, as old as the Jewish people themselves, have had great influence on Jewish life. Jewish history is replete with incidents where individual Jews or even entire communities courageously resisted religious persecution forbidding the observance of the Jewish Dietary Laws.

Some of the Dietary Laws provide: 1) Only the flesh of those animals which are cloven-footed and chew the cud (cattle, sheep, goats and deer) are permitted; 2) Animals living in the water that have both fins and scales are permitted; shellfish is forbidden; 3) Tradition specifies which types of fowl are permitted. In general, birds of prey are excluded; 4) Most locusts (with the exception of four types) and reptiles are prohibited; 5) It is forbidden to eat the blood of animals, and meat must be drained and "salted" before cooking; 6) Animals must be slaughtered according to ritual, and inspected as precaution against diseases; 7) It is prohibited to eat meat and milk at the same time or foods derived from them; that is, it is unlawful to mix "flaishig" (meat foods) with "milchig" (dairy). All other foods such as fruits, eggs, fish and vegetables are "pareve" (neutral). On Passover additional prohibitions obtain. See *Passover*.

Most dietary laws are still observed in varying degrees by Jews everywhere.

A 16th-century woodcut of a Jewish-Gentile debate. Such disputes were often deliberately imposed by hostile authorities and then used as a pretext for persecution and anti-Semitism.

DIN TORAH

A Hebrew term applied to a trial held according to the principles of Jewish law.

DISPUTATIONS

Public debates on religious matters held between Jews and non-Jews. Such debates date back to ancient times, when they were mostly of an intellectual nature. However, such disputations between Christians and Jews eventually became a means of forcing the Jews to accept Christianity, and often resulted in anti-Jewish outbreaks. The disputations stimulated public interest, and were often presided over by high officials or monarchs. Jewish and Christian theological experts were usually chosen as participants, and each of

Statesman, novelist and political essayist, Benjamin Disraeli was a distinguished British Prime Minister noted for his radical domestic reforms and for an aggressive foreign policy.

the opponents had to show thorough knowledge in defense of his point of view. Such disputations took place at different periods from the 13th through the 18th centuries in France, Spain, Italy and Poland. The most bitter and compulsory disputations took place in Spain during the period of the Inquisition, when they were used as a weapon against heretics or unbelievers. The disputations were mainly concerned with whether passages of the Talmud were offensive to Christianity. Since Jewish scholars were not permitted to question Christian dogma, the outcome was predetermined. See *Naḥmanides*.

DISRAELI, BENJAMIN (1804–1881)

Earl of Beaconsfield, prime minister of England during the reign of Queen Victoria, and novelist. He was born in London to Isaac D'Israeli, English author, and baptized at the age of 12. His conversion to Christianity enabled him to be admitted to the English Parliament. As a young man, he started his career as a novelist, which he continued through his life. His greatest fame was gained in the field of politics. In 1837 he became a member of the Parliament and soon became leader of the British Conservative Party. He was twice chancellor of the exchequer, and in 1866 he became prime minister, an office to which he returned in 1874. During his premiership, the British Empire extended its influence in the world, and Queen Victoria, referring to him as her "favorite prime minister," was made Empress of India. In recognition of his brilliant political career and his great service to England, he was elevated to the House of Lords as Earl of Beaconsfield. Although an aggressive imperialist in the foreign affairs of England, he nevertheless used his political influence and his talent as a writer to further the welfare of the working and underprivileged people.

Despite his conversion to the Christian faith he was proud of his Jewish descent, and used his influence to protect the Jewish name. He visited Palestine, and for his novels, such as "David Alroy" and "Tancred" he drew his themes from Jewish history. When frequently charged by his opponents in the Parliament that his Jewish emotions influenced his political policies, he encountered such accusations with courage, pride and wit. To this day he is remembered in England with great affection and admiration, and the anniversary of his death on April 19th is still commemorated by the observance of "Primrose Day."

DIVRE HA-YAMIM see Chronicles.

Meir Dizengoff, chief developer of Tel Aviv, was also founder of the city and its first mayor.

DIZENGOFF, MEIR (1861–1936)

Zionist leader, founder and mayor of Tel Aviv. Born in Bessarabia, he joined the "Hovevei Zion" (Lovers of Zion) movement, and later became one of the followers of Theodor Herzl, the founder of political Zionism. In 1905 he went to Palestine, and in 1909 broke the ground for the establishment of Tel Aviv, which became the largest modern city in Israel in less than fifty years. He was mayor of Tel Aviv from 1920 to 1925. The city of Tel Aviv honored his memory by naming one of its streets and a park after him.

DON JOSEPH see Nasi, Don Joseph.

DOWRY see Nedan.

DREIDEL see Hanukkah.

DREYFUS AFFAIR

World famous military trial and conviction for high treason of Alfred Dreyfus, captain of artillery attached to the general staff of the French army. Dreyfus was accused in 1894 of selling military secrets to Germany, the evidence based on forged

Alfred Dreyfus, hero of the Dreyfus Case, is here decorated with the Legion of Honor after he had been exonerated on charges of treason and reinstated as a Captain in the French Army.

documents. The case lined up the military, the Church and the royalist party against the republicans. Despite his complete innocence, supported by the liberals of France, Dreyfus was tried by a military court and sentenced to life imprisonment on Devil's Island, French Guiana.

This miscarriage of justice was contested by a minority group, consisting mainly of intellectuals, and called the Dreyfusards. It was Colonel Georges Picquart who discovered the fact that the trial documents were forgeries. He demanded a revision of the case by a civil tribunal. In this he was joined by the novelist Anatole France, the statesman Georges Clemenceau, the scholar Joseph Reinach, and the socialist Jean Jaurès. A significant role in the attempt to clear the victim was played by the prominent French novelist Émile Zola, who risked his life and reputation when he published an open letter to the President of the Republic which began with the words "J'Accuse" (I Accuse), in which he accused the general staff of the army of being in league with forgers and conspirators and he called the verdict of the court-martial "a crime of high treason against humanity." Aroused public opinion forced the military to reopen the case in which Dreyfus was again found guilty, but his sentence was reduced to ten years imprisonment. Émile Zola was imprisoned, but escaped to London. Dissatisfaction with the verdict persisted and continued efforts were made to vindicate Dreyfus, who was finally completely exonerated by the (civil) supreme court which had undertaken to revise the case in 1906. Dreyfus was reinstated in the army. Anti-Semitism played no little role in the entire affair.

This prolonged case, accompanied by anti-Semitic outbreaks in France and its colonies, awakened the nationalistic feelings of the Jews. Theodor Herzl, then a successful journalist in Vienna and foreign correspondent, was so shaken by its results that he vowed to devote the rest of his life to free the Jewish people from their precarious existence through the establishment of a Jewish national home in Palestine. He thereupon became the founder of political Zionism which opened a new era in Jewish history, and which finally culminated in the historic creation of the State of Israel.

DROPSIE COLLEGE FOR HEBREW AND COGNATE LEARNING

Established in Philadelphia, Pa. in 1907 as a post-graduate school, with funds bequeathed by Moses Aaron Dropsie. The college offers courses in Biblical and Rabbinical literature, in Jewish history and philosophy, in Jewish education, and in Semitic languages and Egyptology. It is non-sectarian, and confers the degree of doctor of philosophy; in its School of Education it grants the M. A. and Ed. D. degrees. Although its student body is limited, in the course of its existence many of its graduates have made valuable contributions in the field of Jewish learning, and have assumed positions of leadership in various Jewish communities in the United States. The college possesses an extensive library, which includes valuable collections, manuscripts and documents. Its staff consists of outstanding scholars in their respective fields. It publishes the *Jewish Quarterly Review* and other scientific publications.

DUBINSKY, DAVID

Prominent labor leader and president of the International Ladies' Garment Workers' Union. Born in Poland in 1892, he joined the Social Democratic Party, and because of his political activities in behalf of the working class was arrested many times and finally exiled to Siberia. Du-

Simon Dubnow, well-known historian, was an authority on Jewish diaspora nationalism.

binsky went to the United States in 1911, started as a garment worker in New York City, and soon rose to leadership, first as president of the Cutters' Union, and in 1932 as president of the International Ladies' Garment Workers' Union. As leader of the ILGWU he opposed communist tendencies, and advocated reasonable cooperation with employers. In 1935 he helped John L. Lewis in the creation of the Committee for Industrial Organization (C.I.O.). Under his leadership the ILGWU contributed hundreds of thousands of dollars for labor as well as Jewish and other causes. In 1936, he helped found the American Labor Party, but left it in 1944, because he felt it was too close to communism, and he helped to found the Liberal Party.

DUBNOW, SIMON (1860–1941)

Prominent Jewish historian and political writer. Born in Russia, he published his first valuable contributions on Jewish history and on *Hasidism* in Russian Jewish periodicals. His later work was devoted mainly to the history of the Jews of Poland and Russia, publishing the "History

Sketch of part of the city and city walls based on archeological excavations near where the Dura-Europos synagogue was found. The architecture unearthed indicates strong Hellenistic influences.

of the Jews in Russia and Poland," the "World History of the Jewish People," and school-texts on Jewish history. Some of his major works have been translated into many languages, including Hebrew and Yiddish.

His theory of diaspora nationalism has influenced Jewish thinking on matters concerning the meaning and function of Jewish nationalism and culture. Unlike Graetz, his predecessor in the field of Jewish history, Dubnow maintained that Jewish existence does not depend on culture and religion alone, but also on communal organization in the diaspora, whereby Jewish unity and Jewish spiritual values are kept alive. Although generally sympathetic to the Zionist movement and its aims, he did not think that Jewish unity necessarily depends upon a national territory or an independent state. He declared that Jewish minority groups, wherever found, should be considered as national groups entitled to cultural and communal autonomy. He was a staunch fighter for Jewish minority rights in the lands of their dispersion. Dubnow, the great advocate of national Jewish existence, shared the fate of millions of his brethren in Europe; he was killed by the Nazis in 1941.

DUKHAN, (DUKHANEN) see Blessing, Priestly.

DURA-EUROPOS

Archeological excavations, 1932–35, uncovered the ruins of a synagogue erected at Dura-Europos in the middle of the third century, c.e. A highly advanced and well-organized Jewish community on the Tigris River is evident. Scenes from the Bible and religious objects pictured on the walls point to a remarkable development of art among the Jews in those days.

DYBBUK see Dibbuk.

EDUCATION

Go up and down before their Houses of Study and

Houses of Worship. If you do not hear the voices of

their children chanting, you can overcome them. But if

you hear the chant of their children, you can never

subdue them.

MIDRASH

EBAN, ABBA

EBAN, ABBA

Minister of Education in Israel. Born in Capetown, South Africa, in 1915, he spent most of his early years in England. There he was graduated from Cambridge University, and subsequently taught at Pembroke College. From early youth he took a leading role in the Zionist movement. During the Second World War, he served as an officer in the British Army assigned to the Middle East, and afterwards settled in Jerusalem.

Soon he was made a member of the Jewish Agency delegation to the United Nations (1947), Israel's United Nations delegate (1948–1959), and Ambassador to the United States (1950–1959). In 1959 he was recalled to Israel and shortly thereafter appointed Minister of Education.

Eban's wide travels in the Near East, lecturing in Hebrew and Arabic, and his contributions to learned journals, added prominence as a scholar and speaker to an already fine reputation as a diplomat.

ECCLESIASTES

The Greek name of the book *Kohelet*, contained in the last section of the Hebrew Bible, called "Writings" (Ketuvim). According to the opening words in the book it was written by "Kohelet, the son of David," and tradition attributes it to King Solomon, the son of David. Some scholars believe that it was written during the period of the Second Temple. Some of the *Tannaim* did not think that the book should be included in the Canon.

In content, the book in many passages reflects a highly pessimistic outlook on life. It starts with the assertion "Vanity of vanities, all is vanity." The implication is that nothing in life is worthwhile; material and spiritual possessions, and all life experiences, pleasures, disappointments and wisdom have no real value, because "there is nothing new under the sun;" that "he

that increaseth knowledge increaseth sorrow;" that "a man hath no pre-eminence above a beast;" and that all men's effort is "only a striving after the wind." The philosophical conclusions of the book are, however, not irreligious. Kohelet advises that man should not grow impatient or become discouraged, because there are things beyond man's comprehension, and that in the end God will not fail him. It is, therefore, important to "fear God and keep His commandments, for this is the whole duty of man." The book is universally quoted because it contains numerous sayings of practical wisdom in reference to man's conduct, his relationship with other people and his manifold experiences in life.

ECCLESIASTICUS see Ben-Sira, Joshua.

EDEN, GARDEN OF see Gan Eden.

EDOM, EDOMITES

A Biblical people and country named after Esau who was called Edom after he sold his birthright to his twin-brother Jacob. The Edomites occupied the territory south of Canaan, between the Dead Sea and the Red Sea. Although Moses warned the Israelites, saying "thou shalt not hate an Edomite, for he is thy brother," there was constant warfare between the two nations, who traditionally had a close blood-relationship. The Edomites (now called Idumeans) were conquered by the Maccabees, and later by John Hyrcanus, who forced them to embrace Judaism. Herod, descendant of these converted Edomites, became king of Judea under Roman rule and is remembered chiefly for his cruelty to the Jews and his efforts to please the Romans. The Idumeans are also mentioned as the brave fighters who, together with the Zealots (Judean patriots), made the last stand in the revolt against Rome.

EDUCATION

Nothing was more important to the Jewish people throughout their history than the teaching of Torah to their children. The teaching of Jewish religious and ethical principles was based on the Biblical command "and thou shalt teach them diligently to thy children." In Biblical times children received their practical and religious education directly from their parents. During the Second Commonwealth, the synagogue became not only a house of prayer but also a house of study for adults, and perhaps also for younger people. The love of learning has long been a characteristic of the Jewish people, as has been respect for the man of learning.

Simeon ben Shetah is credited with the establishing of schools for young people during the first century b.c.e., and universal elementary Jewish education was introduced in 64 c.e. by the High Priest Joshua ben Gamala who compelled every community to conduct an elementary school of its own.

The role of schools for both children and adults increased in importance after the destruction of the Temple (70 c.e.) and the disruption of independent national life in Palestine. Education thus became the source of strength to the defeated nation and the primary means for spiritual salvation. In the course of time Jewish education became a well organized and regulated institution. The *Bet ha-Sefer* ("house of the book") was the common elementary school where children received instruction in the Bible, and the *Bet Talmud* or *Bet ha-Keneset*, and later the *Bet ha-Midrash* were the higher institutions of learning where Talmud was taught. Girls were generally excused from receiving a formal education, and their training for practical Jewish living was given to them

Young Hungarian boys after World War II follow in their fathers' footsteps. They are studying Jewish history and tradition, as well as the vocational subjects, in religious elementary-school classes.

in the home, though there were numerous women who had acquired a high level of Jewish knowledge.

These two institutions of learning, later better known as the *Ḥeder* (elementary religious school) and the *Yeshivah* (Talmudical Academy), have been maintained by Jews in all the lands of their dispersion. There were practically no Jewish children who did not receive at least an elementary Jewish education consisting of instruction in prayers and the Hebrew Bible.

The European type of Jewish school was taken over by the Jewish communities in the United States, where more than 490,000 children attended some sort of Jewish elementary school in 1960. The subject matter of these schools is religious and cultural in character, consisting mainly of prayers, Bible, Hebrew, Jewish history and current events. These schools are generally sponsored by orthodox, conservative and reform congregations, the latter emphasizing the one day a week religious school with a curriculum limited mainly to Jewish history and customs.

EGYPT

Jewish history in Egypt began with Abraham, the founder of the Jewish people. The Biblical record tells that Jacob's family of 70 settled in Goshen, Egypt, when Joseph was its popular viceroy. After several hundred years of sojourn in Egypt, during which period the Children of Israel multiplied and became slaves under the Pharaohs, they left as free men in the Exodus under the leadership of Moses.

Despite the Biblical restriction stating that "Ye shall return no more that way," the relationship of the Jewish people with Egypt continued to persist during the entire Biblical period. After the destruction of the First Temple, many Jews settled in Egypt, where the Jewish community grew steadily, and especially during the Greek

rule in the Middle East it developed into a most significant Jewish center. It is believed that close to a million Jews lived in Egypt, particularly in Alexandria, during the 4th century b.c.e. The decline of the Jewish community in Egypt began in the first century c.e., and it had almost completely disappeared in the sixth century. Jews, however, returned to Egypt later, so that in the Middle Ages the Jewish settlement grew in importance if not in size. Some of the most outstanding Jewish personalities, such as Rabbi Saadiah Gaon, and Moses Maimonides lived in Egypt during that period. Jews living in modern Egypt are mostly of Sephardic origin, and are found mainly in Alexandria and Cairo. With the establishment of the State of Israel in 1948, Egypt and the other Arab countries continued to consider themselves in a state of war with Israel, owing to their defeat by the Israeli army. As a result of the successful Sinai campaign carried out by the Israeli army in 1956 because of Egypt's constant provocations, thousands of Jews were forced to flee the country. In 1959 only 15,000 Jews remained in Egypt.

EHAD MI YODEA

The Hebrew name of a children's rhyme, meaning "One: Who knows?", which is a chant in the *Haggadah* and is sung with a special melody toward the end of the Passover Seder. The rhyme lists 13 questions starting with "One: Who knows?", then "Two: Who knows?", "Three: Who knows?", etc. The corresponding answers are: "One is God," "Two are the Tablets of the Covenant," "Three are the Patriarchs," etc. It probably originated in France and Germany in the 16th century, for the purpose of keeping the children awake to the end of the ritual.

EIBESCHÜTZ, JONATHAN (1690–1764)

Rabbi, Talmudist and Kabbalist. He was

the head of the Yeshivah (Talmudical Academy) of Prague which he founded, and later rabbi of Metz, Altona and Hamburg. He associated with the followers of Shabbetai Tzevi, the discredited "messiah," and because of this he came into an open and bitter quarrel with Rabbi Jacob Emden. The latter accused Eibeschütz of being a Sabbetaian himself, using as evidence the fact that the amulets which he issued to sick people and expectant mothers contained in a concealed form the name of Shabbetai Tzevi. This dispute caused great upheaval in the Jewish communities, and leading rabbis of Germany and Poland, as well as governmental authorities, took sides in this controversy between the two opposing parties. Although Eibeschütz was vindicated in the end, the bitter conflict between him and Rabbi Emden left a serious and unhappy atmosphere.

EIGHTEEN BENEDICTIONS see Shemoneh Esreh.

EILAT (Elath)

Hebrew name for the seaport of Aqaba (Akaba) on the Red Sea, and the southernmost point of the State of Israel. King Solomon used this seaport for his commercial expedition to Ophir. During the period of the Jewish kingdom, Eilat was under Jewish rule, and had Jewish inhabitants during the Arab period up to the end of the Middle Ages. When the partition of Palestine was ordered in 1947 by the United Nations, the seaport of Eilat was included as part of the Jewish territory. This promising seaport at the southern end of the Negev was placed under development by the State of Israel. Because of its strategic position and the hardships of living in a remote and somewhat primitive outpost, the government appealed to the patriotism of young immigrants to serve as *Ḥalutzim* (pioneers) and settle there. As a result of their efforts, in 1958 and 1959, its growth was spectacular.

EINHORN, DAVID (1809–1879)

Rabbi and leader of American reform Judaism. Born in Germany, he became active in the Jewish reform movement there, and met with opposition from both orthodox Jewry and the German government. He went to Budapest, where he met with the same difficulties, and therefore decided to go to the United States, where he was appointed rabbi in 1855 at Temple Har Sinai in Baltimore.

Einhorn was more radical than Isaac Mayer Wise in his interpretation of Judaism. He published a prayer book for use by reform Jews, omitting or modifying many of the traditional prayers. This prayer book was used as a basis for the *Union Prayer Book*, which was published some time later.

Before the Civil War Einhorn joined the anti-slavery movement, and because of his sermons denouncing the pro-slavery party, his life was actually threatened, and he moved to Philadelphia. In 1866 he was appointed rabbi of the Adath Jeshurun Congregation in New York, where he was active for the rest of his life. He wrote numerous articles and essays and also left to posterity a collection of sermons and important addresses.

EINSTEIN, ALBERT (1879–1955)

Most prominent physicist in modern times. Born in Germany, he published four important scientific papers in 1905, in some of which he formulated his world-renowned "Theory of Relativity." His work attracted the attention of the greatest physicists of the world, and he was invited to serve as professor of physics in the universities of Zurich, Prague, and Berlin. As his theories were authenticated by observation, his fame became universal, and he was accepted as a member of the world's outstanding academies of science. In 1922 he received the Nobel Prize for

physics. Because of the Nazi terror, he fled Germany in 1933 and went to the United States, where he was appointed to the Institute for Advanced Study at Princeton, N.J. It was Einstein's letter to President Franklin D. Roosevelt which alerted the American government to the manufacture of atom bombs.

Outside of his scientific work, which laid the ground for nuclear theory and the development of atomic energy, he showed great interest in humanitarian and liberal causes. He was particularly interested in Zionism and devoted much of his time in behalf of the Hebrew University in Jerusalem and other Zionist projects. His name enjoyed universal esteem; and as an expression of admiration by the Jewish people, it was suggested that he become president of Israel.

EISENDRATH, MAURICE

Born in Chicago in 1902, Eisendrath was educated at the University of Cincinnati and at the Hebrew Union College. He served as rabbi to congregations in Charleston, West Va., and in Toronto, Canada. In 1943, he was elected president of the Union of American Hebrew Congregations. In 1952, he was granted life tenure in this post. He is active in interfaith work and in Jewish community affairs.

EKHAH see Lamentations.

ELDAD HA-DANI

Name of an imaginative Jewish traveler of the 9th century. He said that he was a descendant of the tribe of Dan. According to his account of his travels in Egypt, Mesopotamia, Spain and North Africa, he discovered the Ten Lost Tribes of the Kingdom of Israel, which was conquered

One of the late photographs of Albert Einstein, Nobel Prize-winning physicist and father of the Theory of Relativity. A shy, retiring man, he was considered one of the age's great minds.

by the Assyrians. Three of the lost tribes lived in Ethiopia, and one tribe of the Sons of Moses (Bene Mosheh) lived nearby in a country encircled by the Sambatyon, a river renowned in legend. His stories, appearing in printed form in 1480, were widely read. The reliability of his accounts are questioned by historians. Some believe that he was one of the Falashas (Ethiopian Jews), others believe that he was a Karaite missionary and an impostor.

ELDERS OF ZION, PROTOCOLS OF THE

An anti-Semitic forgery, consisting of a document circulated also under the title "Protocols of the Learned Elders of Zion," and claiming to be the minutes of a secret international committee or congress of prominent Jewish leaders. According to this canard, these "Elders of Zion" devised a conspiracy whereby the Jewish people would dominate and control the world. After the First World War, this document, under different titles and in different languages, appeared in France, England, Germany, the United States, and other countries. The first document of this kind appeared in 1905 in Tsarist Russia. It was later discovered that the secret police of the Tsarist government used a brochure written by a Frenchman as an attack against Napoleon III, who it was alleged plotted to dominate Europe. This document was revised by the Russian secret police by substituting the Jews for Napoleon. Following the fall of the Tsarist regime, the forged document was reprinted and widely circulated to show that the Bolshevist revolution was plotted by the "Elders of Zion," whose scheme it was to "bore from within" and to place Jewish leaders in key positions of the governments of the world. Despite their obvious falsity, the "Protocols" were taken seriously by millions of people throughout the world, giving impetus to virulent anti-

Semitism. The most widespread dissemination of the Protocols in the United States took place between 1920 and 1927, when the "Dearborn Independent," which was controlled by Henry Ford, published excerpts periodically. Ford later publicly apologized, in order "to make amends for the wrong done to the Jews as fellow-men and brothers by asking their forgiveness." These blatant forgeries continue to be circulated by professional anti-Semites.

ELI

High Priest at the shrine of Shiloh and judge over the Israelites, near the end of the period of the Judges. His two sons Hophni and Phinehas caused him grief and shame through their misconduct as attendants at the shrine of Shiloh. Following the defeat of the Israelites by the Philistines, Eli fell from his seat and died when told that the enemy captured the Ark of the Covenant. The prophet Samuel was trained by Eli, whom he succeeded as judge over the tribes of Israel.

ELIJAH

Also known as *Eliyahu Ha-Navi* (Elijah the Prophet), and "Elijah the Tishbite." He was prophet in the 9th century b.c.e., during Ahab's reign in the Kingdom of Israel. In Jewish tradition Elijah is the most popular, most dramatic and most romantic among the Jewish prophets. He first appeared before King Ahab foretelling the coming of a drought, and then began his repeated attacks against Queen Jezebel, who introduced the worship of

The fresco on the south wall of the synagogue at Dura-Europos, built in the 3rd century, depicts the Biblical contest of sacrifices between the great prophet Elijah and the idolatrous priests of Baal.

the Phoenician Baal among the Israelites. In his fight against idol-worship Elijah had no fear. He attacked the priests of Baal with whom he waged a great contest on Mount Carmel. He performed many miracles, and when he went into hiding he was fed by ravens. He denounced Ahab for the legal murder of Naboth on trumped-up charges to make it possible for Ahab to take possession of his vineyard.

Jewish folklore has kept alive the name of the prophet who, according to the Bible, "went up by a whirlwind into heaven." Hundreds of tales have been preserved about Elijah as the protector of the poor, and as one who performed miracles in order to bring succor to the righteous in hours of danger and despair. He is thought of by tradition as the forerunner of the Messiah at the end of time. His cave on Mount Carmel has become a place of worship for Jews, Christians and Moslems.

ELIJAH'S CUP

A goblet of wine, bearing Elijah's name, placed on the table during the Passover *Seder*. Traditionally, Elijah is the prophet who will announce the advent of the Messiah, which is to take place on Passover eve. A glass of wine, which remains untouched, is therefore poured in his honor, and the door is opened at a certain point during the Seder to welcome his arrival. Some ancient authorities taught that at the Seder five cups rather than four should be taken; the fifth cup (not used) is called Elijah's because it is he who in the Messianic Era will resolve all doubtful matters in the law.

ELIJAH, GAON OF VILNA see Gaon of Vilna.

ELISHA

Prophet in the northern Kingdom of Israel, and successor to Elijah. Elisha is remembered for the many miracles he performed, and for the counsel and assistance he gave the royal family in times of peace and war. He denounced King Omri for spreading Baal worship, and anointed Jehu as king of Israel.

ELISHA BEN AVUYAH

A *Tanna* (Teacher of the Law) at the beginning of the second century c.e. He is known as the Tanna who became a heretic, abandoning Jewish laws and traditions. The cause of this is not definitely known, but it is believed that he was influenced by Greek philosophy, which

18th-century Russian version of Elijah's cup. Engraved on it is the Messiah on a donkey.

129

he studied. Because of his apostasy he is referred to in the Talmud as "Aḥer" (the other). Rabbi Meir, one of the great *Tannaim*, nevertheless, remained his faithful friend and disciple, accepting, as he said, the kernel of his teacher's learning and rejecting its husk.

ELLIS ISLAND

An island in upper New York Bay which served as a federal immigration station from 1890. During the ten-year period before the First World War, millions of immigrants came to the United States, among whom hundreds of thousands were Jews from eastern European countries. All immigrants were sent to Ellis Island for inspection and examination. Jewish immigrants named it the "Island of Tears" because of many unfortunate cases of individuals who were not allowed to enter the United States because of physical disabilities, and were consequently separated from their families and deported. In 1954, the government ceased using Ellis Island for purposes of processing immigrants, transferring all such immigration procedures to its Manhattan offices.

EL MALE RAHAMIM

The opening words (God who is full of compassion) of a prayer for the departed, recited by Ashkenazim at funerals, on the Sabbath of the week of *Yortzeit*, and during the *Yizkor* (memorial) service in the synagogue. It is believed that this prayer dates from the 17th century. Its popular Yiddish name is "Molay."

ELUL

The twelfth month of the Hebrew year, corresponding to August-September, and consisting of 29 days. Preceding the "Days of Awe" (Rosh Hashanah and Yom Kippur), Elul is traditionally the month of preparation for penitence. It is cus-

tomary to blow the *Shofar* (ram's horn) every weekday of the month, and to recite the *Seliḥot* (penitential prayers) during the last week of the month before daybreak. The *Sephardim* recite the Seliḥot during the entire month.

EMANCIPATION

The abolition of restrictions against Jews and the granting of equal religious, civil, and political rights to persons of Jewish descent, took place gradually in many countries through the 18th and the 19th centuries. During the period of the Roman Empire, Jews enjoyed citizenship rights with the exception of some minor limitations. These rights were lost to most of the Jewish communities in Europe during the Middle Ages when special restrictions were imposed upon them by the Christian church, accompanied by persecutions, attacks, and confinement in ghettos.

Political emancipation of the Jews was achieved in some colonies of North America in the 18th century and the Declaration of Independence of the United States formalized it, though without special thought of the Jews. In many states such equality for the Jews had to wait for the 19th century; in New Hampshire as late as 1876. The Jews of France were emancipated as a result of the French Declaration of the Rights of Man of 1789. Other countries followed suit, so that during the period following the First World War Jews were granted equal rights in most European countries. This emancipation was, in many instances only formal. Anti-Jewish legislation and many forms of restrictions were not uncommon. The Nazi regime, followed by the Second World War, brought Jewish emancipation to a tragic end. Since the war, efforts have been made in behalf of the remnants of the European Jewish communities to restore their once vigorous communal life.

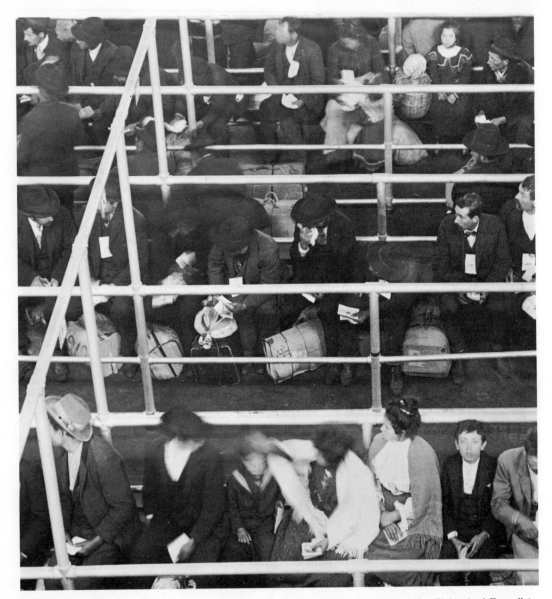

Immigrants to the U.S. in the early 1900s wait on Ellis Island, often called the "Island of Tears," to be "processed." Note the baggage tags pinned to their lapels or around their necks for identification.

EMDEN, JACOB ISRAEL (1697–1776)

Also known as Yaabetz (abbreviation of Yaakov ben Tzevi), Rabbi and Talmudist in Germany, and opponent of the followers of Shabbetai Tzevi, the discredited "messiah." He was the most controversial figure of his time, owing to his unrelenting fight against the adherents of the Sabbetaian sect, and especially against the famous Rabbi Eibeschütz of Hamburg.

Rabbi Emden gave up the rabbinate and established his own printing shop, where he published book after book denouncing the Sabbetaians. He was a brilliant writer on rabbinical subjects, and some of his manuscripts are in the possession of Columbia University. The modern family name Javits is probably derived from the old name Yaabetz, and has been used as an American surname in the revised form.

131

The Valley of Jezreel, popularly known as the "Emek," once a barren stretch of land dividing the mountains of Carmel and Samaria from those of Lower Galilee, is now a region of towns and farms.

EMEK JEZREEL (YIZREEL)

A stretch of land in Israel, popularly known as the *Emek* (the Valley par excellence), extending from Haifa and Acre, in a southeasterly direction to the valley of the Jordan. In this plain many *Kibbutzim* (cooperative agricultural settlements) are found. When the Jewish National Fund bought large tracts of this land in 1921–22, they were barren wastes infested with malaria. The Emek is now a flourishing area, telling the heroic story of pioneers who faced great hardships and dangers. In Biblical times this plain was the battleground of conquering armies. It is here that Barak, inspired by the prophetess Deborah, defeated the armies of Sisera, and Jael then killed the defeated Sisera.

EMUNOT VE-DEOT see Saadiah Gaon.

132

ENGLAND

In 1955 British Jewry celebrated the Tercentenary of Jewish resettlement in England. Jewish history in England began in the 11th century where for about two centuries Jews were persecuted, and finally expelled in 1290. For the next period of over three and one-half centuries, Jews who admitted to their faith could not live in England.

Menasseh ben Israel, an Amsterdam rabbi and scholar, won the friendship of Oliver Cromwell, Lord Protector and ruler of Britain, to whom he presented a petition in 1655 to allow Jews to settle in England with the liberty to practice their religion openly. This intervention was finally successful in an indirect manner, and Sephardic Jews began to settle in England. In the course of the next two centuries the Jewish community developed, and a number of synagogues were established. Toward the end of the 19th century, thousands of persecuted Russian Jews were admitted to England. These and many others from eastern Europe had an important effect on the previously established Anglo-Jewish community. They opened new synagogues, established a Yiddish press and theatre, and developed Jewish institutional life. There were close to half a million Jews in England in 1960, enjoying complete freedom; their official organization is the Board of Deputies of British Jews. The largest Jewish community is found in London, and other thriving Jewish communities exist in Manchester, Glasgow and Birmingham.

British Jews founded Jewish elementary schools and higher institutions of Jewish learning, and have played an important role in the general culture of the country. The *Jewish Chronicle*, founded in 1841, is the outstanding English language Jewish weekly publication in the world. The celebration of 300 years of the return of Jews to England marked the British Jewish community as the most important and the best organized in western Europe.

EN KELOHENU

The opening Hebrew words, meaning "There is none like our God," of a hymn included in the prayer book as the concluding part of the morning ritual. In the Ashkenazic ritual it is used only after the *Musaf* (additional) service on the Sabbath and the festivals. The Hebrew stanzas form an acrostic "Amen Barukh Attah."

ENLIGHTENMENT, PERIOD OF see Haskalah.

EN YAAKOV

Hebrew title, meaning "The Fountain of Jacob," of a popular compilation of Haggadic passages from the Talmud. The "En Yaakov" appeared in Salonica in 1515, and was compiled by R. Jacob ben Solomon ibn Haviv. In the usual editions are included many important commentaries, in addition to those supplied by the author himself. It appeared in numerous editions and for generations has been used as a text by study groups, especially among the less educated Jews.

EPHRAIM

Name of the younger son of Joseph, the brother of Manasseh, and founder of one of the important Jewish tribes which settled in Canaan. After the division of Solomon's kingdom, Ephraim became the most influential tribe in the northern Kingdom of Israel, which was often referred to as the "House of Ephraim."

EPICURUS

Name of a Greek philosopher of the 4th century b.c.e., and a term (also pronounced *Apikoros*) generally applied in Jewish literature to a person who is an "unbeliever" or lax in Jewish religious observance. This latter connotation of the term developed as a result of the interpretation of the teachings of Epicurus which circulated among the Jews during the period of the *Mishnah*. Epicurus denied that the gods had any effect on man's life and preached that man should live an unrestricted life of pleasure. Jewish teachers, therefore, regarded the Epicurean philosophy as contrary to the beliefs and teachings of Judaism. Jewish tradition teaches that an "Apikoros" will have no share in "the world to come," and that a Jewish person must understand the true principles of Judaism and be at all times ready to defend them against the contrary and misleading teachings of the Epicureans.

ERETZ ISRAEL (YISRAEL)

Hebrew term meaning "Land of Israel," applied to Palestine. The term is found in the Bible and Talmud and all the later literature. The Jewish State, proclaimed in 1948, calls itself Israel. See *Palestine*.

EREV

Hebrew term meaning "evening," generally understood to designate the day before the Sabbath or a holiday. Thus "Erev Shabbat," "Erev Yom Tov," "Erev Pesaḥ," "Erev Yom Kippur," refer to the day before the Sabbath (i.e., Friday), Pesaḥ, Yom Kippur, etc. The late afternoon hours preceding the Sabbath or festivals are traditionally the hours of preparation for the ushering in of the solemn events. Friday night is *Lel Shabbat;* when the sun sets on Erev Pesaḥ, *Lel Pesaḥ* begins.

ESAU

Twin brother of Jacob and older son of Isaac and Rebekah. The Bible tells that Esau sold his birthright to Jacob for "a mess of pottage," and thus relinquished his right to succeed Isaac as head or Patriarch of the Hebrew clan. Esau settled in Edom, and is considered the founder of the

Edomite nation. In Jewish tradition the word "Esau" became the symbol for an evil person.

ESROG see Etrog.

ESSENES

Name of a Jewish sect during the latter period of the Second Commonwealth. The mode of life of this sect is described by Philo and Josephus, with numerous inconsistencies. The Essenes were groups of pious people, living in communities of their own, close to the desert. They were vegetarians, doing manual labor, sharing their earnings, eating together and dressing very simply, usually in white. They washed and bathed frequently, and seemed to know something of the healing power of herbs, thus earning the reputation of healers of the sick. They were regarded as holy people because of their restricted and secret ways of life, and also because some of them would go out to preach among the people, urging them to mend their ways and to repent before it is too late, that is, before the coming of the Great Day of Judgment. Some scholars hold that some of the Dead Sea Scrolls are the product of Essene communities.

ESTHER

The heroine of the Biblical *Book of Esther*, relating the story of *Purim*. A beautiful orphaned maiden, she was raised by her cousin (or uncle) Mordecai. Her Hebrew name was Hadassah. King Ahasuerus chose her queen of Persia after he had removed the former Queen Vashti. Haman, the prime minister, became angry at Mordecai for not kneeling to him (as did the other

Reconstruction of the palace of Ahasuerus at Persepolis. Flanking the monumental entrance are a pair of stylized Assyrian winged bulls, intended to symbolize the great power that the Persian king sought to impress on his subjects. Note the frieze of lions across the propylaea.

Traditional Etrog, or pomegranate, and the Lulav, or palm-branch, used in the Sukkot festival. A fruit rare in east Europe, the Etrog became a symbol in many Yiddish tales.

courtiers), and succeeded in winning the king's consent to his plot to kill all the Jews of Persia on the 13th day of Adar. However, upon Mordecai's insistence, Esther intervened for her people, and Ahasuerus ordered that Haman be hanged on the gallows, and the Jews were granted the right to defend themselves. Thus the imminent disaster became an occasion for joy and festivities for the Jews of Persia and all the world, and is to this day commemorated by the celebration of Purim. The story of the Book of Esther has not been confirmed by archeological findings. Of interest is the fact that the Book of Esther does not mention the name of God. See *Ahasuerus; Purim*.

ESTHER, SCROLL OF

Another name for the *Book of Esther*, which is one of the five *Megillot* (Scrolls) in the third division of the Bible, the *Ketuvim* (Writings). It is popularly known as the *Megillah* (the Scroll, par excellence). See *Esther*.

ETERNAL LIGHT see Ner Tamid.

ETHICS OF THE FATHERS see Avot.

ETROG

A citrus fruit, pronounced "Esrog" in Ashkenazic and understood by tradition to be the Biblical "fruit of the goodly tree." The *Etrog* is used together with the *Lulav* in the service during the festival of *Sukkot* (Feast of Tabernacles). One of the many traditions as to which was the fruit whose eating was forbidden in the Garden of

Scene from Rekh-mi-Re's tomb at Thebes about 1450 b.c.e. showing Jewish slaves helping in Egyptian

Eden holds that it was the Etrog. The Etrog grows in Israel as well as in other Mediterranean countries. The law forbids the use of a defective Etrog for the Sukkot festival service.

EVE see Adam and Eve.

EVENING SERVICE see Maariv.

EVIL EYE see Ayin Ha-Ra.

EVIL INCLINATION see Yetzer Ha-Ra.

EXCOMMUNICATION see Herem.

EXILARCH

A title known in Aramaic as "Resh Galuta" (Leader of the Exile) carried by the head of Babylonian Jewry. This office was hereditary and was held by descendants of the House of David. Babylonian Jews were ruled by Exilarchs from the second through the eleventh century. The Exilarch was the all-powerful ruler of the Jewish community, and only responsible to the ruler of Persia. He collected taxes for the government, was the supreme judge of the Jewish people, had appointive power, was responsible for the public security, and controlled the trade and commerce of the Jewish community.

EXILE

The Hebrew term for "Exile" is *Galut* or *Golah*. Although Jews have suffered many exiles throughout their history, the term is specifically used in connection with the exile of the Jewish people from the Jewish homeland. Thus, the first was the Babylonian Exile, also known as the Babylonian Captivity. This Exile lasted from the destruction of the First Temple in Judea in 586 b.c.e. to 516 b.c.e., when the Second Temple was dedicated. The second exile began in 70 c.e., when the Romans conquered Judea. See *Diaspora*.

EXODUS

The story of the departure of the Israelites from Egypt, referred to in Hebrew as *Yetziat Mitzrayim*. The narrative is contained in the *Book of Exodus*. Some scholars think that the Exodus under Moses took place about the middle of the 13th century b.c.e., though tradition gives a date two centuries earlier. The Exodus, which marks the birth of the Hebrew nation, together with the prior enslavement in Egypt, is considered the greatest event in ancient Jewish history, to which constant reference is made in the Bible and in the Jewish liturgy. Passover, celebrating this event of "freedom from bondage," is one of the most beloved festivals of the Jewish people. See *Passover*.

EXODUS, BOOK OF

The second of the Five Books of Moses (Pentateuch), known in Hebrew under the title of *Shemot* (Names). The book is divided into 40 chapters which relate the following events: The slavery of the Israelites in Egypt, the birth of Moses and his activities as the leader of the Exodus; the crossing of the "Red Sea" (properly, Sea of Reeds) by the Israelites; the wanderings and the struggles in the wilderness;

construction work by carrying materials to the brickmakers and wall painters of Amenhotep II

the giving of the Ten Commandments at Mount Sinai; and the construction of the Tabernacle by Bezalel. Much important legislation is given in this book, including ethical and social regulations, as well as instructions for the building of the portable Tabernacle in the wilderness.

EXPULSION FROM SPAIN see Spain.

EZEKIEL

One of the major prophets and author of the *Book of Ezekiel*, contained in the second section of the Bible, called *Prophets*. As a young man of priestly descent he was exiled to Babylonia in 593 b.c.e., before the destruction of the First Temple. Living in the village Tel-Abib, near the city of Babylon, he became a spiritual leader of the Jewish community in Babylonia. Before the destruction of the Temple, Ezekiel, like Jeremiah, foretold the doom of Judea, and believed that God would use the king of Babylonia as his agent to punish the sinful Judeans and their unjust leaders. After the destruction of the Temple, Ezekiel sought to comfort the captives, and his prophecies were filled with visions of hope and promise of redemption. In his vision of "The Valley of the Dry Bones" he foretold the resurrection of the Jewish people, and their eventual return to their homeland. Contrary to the belief of the people, he assured them that God would not punish them for the sins of their fathers, and that reward and punishment is for the individual's own acts. This teaching of individual responsibility strengthened in the people the hope for redemption and their eventual liberation from captivity. In addition to his prophetic teachings, Ezekiel projects a detailed picture of the construction of the new Temple.

EZION-GEBER see Archeology.

EZRA

Scribe, traditionally the author of the *Book of Ezra*, and religious leader who, together with Nehemiah, helped many Jews to return from Babylonia to Judea. In the year 458 b.c.e., Ezra came from Babylonia to Palestine where he began his life work as the spiritual leader of his people. His first decree was directed against intermarriage, and advised the Judeans to divorce their non-Jewish wives in order to prevent the assimilation of Jews with the neighboring idol-worshipping nations. His major accomplishment, according to rabbinic tradition, was the restoration of the Torah after it had been forgotten. To facilitate the reading of the Torah, he introduced the use of "Assyrian" square characters, which constitute to this day the characters of the Hebrew alphabet. Ezra is said to have founded the Great Assembly, made up of the greatest legal and religious authorities, which undertook the compilation of the books of the Bible and their subsequent canonization. It was Ezra also, according to tradition, who introduced Torah readings on Monday and Thursday.

The *Book of Ezra*, contained in the *Writings* (Ketuvim), opens with the proclamation issued by King Cyrus, permitting the Babylonian Jews to return to their homeland, and continues with the events of the home-coming, the attempts to rebuild the Temple, and Ezra's decree regarding intermarriage. The book is written mainly in Hebrew with about a third written in Aramaic.

F

FESTIVALS

Blow the horn at the new moon,

At the full moon on our feast-day.

For it is a statute for Israel,

An ordinance of the God of Jacob.

PSALMS

FAITH, AFFIRMATION OF see Shema.

FAITH, THIRTEEN ARTICLES OF see Maimonides.

FALASHAS

Jews native in Abyssinia (Ethiopia). The existence of this community of black Jews was brought to the world's attention by a French Jewish scholar, Joseph Halévy, who in 1867 discovered about one hundred thousand such people who called themselves *House of Israel*. An investigation of the history of the Falashas was later made by Halévy's disciple, the explorer Jacques Faitlovitch, who spent much time with them over a period of many years. He found that the Abyssinians, although Christians or Mohammedans themselves, claimed to be descendants of their ancient ruler Menelik, the son of King Solomon and the Ethiopian Queen of Sheba, and that their kings use the title "Lion of Judah." The tradition of the Jews of Abyssinia tells that the priests and advisers whom Solomon sent to assist Me-

nelik spread the Jewish faith among the Abyssinians. Many scholars hold that the real ancestors of the dark-skinned Jews were those Jewish settlers who came to Abyssinia during the Second Jewish Commonwealth or later. The word "Falashas" probably means "exiles" or "strangers." Although a small minority, the Falashas remained faithful to Jewish traditions. They observe the Sabbath and some of the dietary laws; they perform circumcision and observe in some modified form the major Jewish festivals, though they do not observe Purim or Ḥanukkah. They do not know Hebrew, but they have their own prayer book and the Bible written in Geez, the old Ethiopic dialect. They live completely apart from the natives, and admission to their synagogues is forbidden to non-Jews. Their standards of living, such as sanitation and the status of women, is higher than that of their neighbors. The efforts of Dr. Faitlovitch succeeded in bringing the Ethiopian Jews closer to other

Falasha Jews in front of their place of worship at Woozaba, Ethiopia. The Falashas, or "Black Jews," number about a hundred thousand. Their prayer book and Bible are written in an Ethiopian dialect.

Jewish communities, and to the State of Israel.

FALSE MESSIAHS see Messiah.

FARBAND, LABOR ZIONIST ORDER

A fraternal benefit organization founded in 1912, known for over forty years as the "Jewish National Workers' Alliance of America" or "Farband." Initially established for the purpose of aiding the Jewish working masses, it provides its members with mutual aid, sick benefit, insurance, and assistance to families in times of distress and death. An essential part of its activities consists of a well-organized educational, cultural and social program reaching out to its entire membership in the major Jewish communities of the United States and Canada (36,000 members in over 400 branches as of 1960). The majority of its members are Yiddish-speaking and Zionist oriented. Although a non-political organization, the Farband is closely associated with the *Poale Zion* (Labor Zionists). Among its chief accomplishments are its endeavors and activities toward the rebuilding of the Jewish national homeland. In cooperation with the Labor Zionists, the Farband maintains in the United States and Canada a system of Jewish schools called *Folkshulen*, where Yiddish, Hebrew, Jewish history, literature, folklore, customs and ceremonies are taught. Its educational system consists of elementary and high schools, and of a Jewish Teacher's Seminary, offering adult education and a training program for teachers. In accordance with its Labor Zionist ideology, the Farband endeavors to improve Jewish communal life, based on democratic principles, and generally seeks the cultural advancement of the Jewish masses and the encouragement of a social order both in the diaspora and in Israel, based on economic and political democracy. See *Poale Zion.*

FAST DAYS

Fasting plays a relatively minor role in the Jewish religion. *Yom Kippur* (the Day of Atonement) is the only fast day prescribed in the Torah. Many other fast days came about in commemoration of great national calamities that befell the Jewish people in the course of their history. The destruction of the Temple, and the loss of independent Jewish life in Palestine, gave rise to four fast days commonly observed by orthodox Jews the world over. In calendar order they are: the Fast of Gedaliah (Tzom Gedalyah), commemorating the assassination of Gedaliah, the governor of Judah, appointed by the Babylonian king; the Fast of the Tenth of Tevet (Asarah Be-Tevet), commemorating the siege of Jerusalem by the Babylonians; the Fast of the Seventeenth of Tammuz (Shivah Asar Be-Tammuz), commemorating the first breach in the walls of the city; and the Fast of the Ninth of Av (Tishah Be-Av), commemorating the destruction of both Temples.

Another important fast is the Fast of Esther (Taanit Ester) on the thirteenth of Adar, the day before Purim, commemorating the fast of Esther before she petitioned the king of Persia. In addition to these fasts there are local or "private" fasts held by certain communities or individuals in commemoration of a particular communal or personal tragic event.

The fasting usually lasts from sunrise till sunset, with the exception of Yom Kippur and Tishah Be-Av, each of which lasts from sunset to sunset. In Judaism a fast day is observed by complete abstention from all food and drink.

FÉ

A letter of the Hebrew alphabet. See *Pé.*

FEAST OF BOOTHS see Sukkot.

FEAST OF CONCLUSION see Sukkot.

143

Hasidic Jews examine a bunch of thick-leaved myrtle branches. Together with the Etrog (citron), Lulav (palm) and willow, these branches are all used as the symbols of the ancient Sukkot harvest festival.

FEAST OF DEDICATION see Ḥanukkah.

FEAST OF GIVING OF THE TORAH see Shavuot.

FEAST OF LIGHTS see Ḥanukkah.

FEAST OF LOTS see Purim.

FEAST OF TABERNACLES see Sukkot.

FEAST OF WEEKS see Shavuot.

FEDERATIONS

Jewish communal agencies in the United States and Canada established for the purpose of raising funds for welfare institutions. The specific names of such agencies vary in different communities, and are known as Jewish Charities, Jewish Philanthropies, Jewish Federation, Federated Jewish Charities, Federation of Jewish Charities, etc. The first of such federations were established in Boston and in Cincinnati in the last decade of the 19th century,

and other communities followed at later dates. After World War I, these federations assumed other functions in addition to fund-raising, such as the general planning of Jewish social welfare and educational work of the Jewish communities.

In some communities the fund-raising activities of the federations were taken over by newly established Jewish welfare funds, Jewish community councils, and partly by local community chests. In the earlier period the leadership of federations was mainly in the hands of the wealthier Jews, but the trend has been to include a wider representation of organizations. See *Council of Jewish Federations and Welfare Funds*.

FESTIVALS

In the Jewish religious calendar there are three types of festival days: the High Holy

Bokharan Jews joyously celebrate the Simḥat Torah festival. Their Torah scrolls, encased in wood, Oriental style, are carried around the synagogue during the ancient and traditional Hakkafot service.

Days, the three pilgrimage festivals, and the so-called minor holidays. The High Holy Days (*Yamim Noraim*) are: *Rosh Hashanah* (the Jewish New Year), observed the first two days of the month of Tishre by Jews throughout the world (with the exception of some reform Jews who observe only one day), and *Yom Kippur* (Day of Atonement), observed by all Jews on the tenth day of Tishre. The first ten days of the Jewish year are days of solemnity and spiritual inventory, and are known as the Ten Days of Penitence (*Aseret Yeme Teshuvah*). The *Shofar* is sounded on Rosh Hashanah, and Yom Kippur is observed by all-day attendance in the synagogue and by fasting. These days are of a purely spiritual nature and not grounded in any event in Jewish history. They are devoted to praying for a good year and for forgiveness of sins.

The second category of festivals is *Shalosh Regalim*, the three pilgrimage festivals, so called because it was the duty of every Jew on those occasions to make a pilgrimage to Jerusalem and bring an offering to God. Each of these holidays has a threefold significance: agriculture, history and spirituality. Passover (*Pesaḥ*) is the early harvest festival, *Shavuot* is the festival of the first-fruits, and Tabernacles (*Sukkot*) is the general harvest festival. Historically, Pesaḥ is associated with the Exodus from Egypt, Shavuot with the Revelation at Mount Sinai, and Sukkot with the wandering of the Israelites for forty years in the wilderness during which time they dwelt in temporary booths or tabernacles.

All peoples, including pagans, have their nature and patriotic feast days. Judaism has given to these days certain spiritual

145

qualities which make them religiously significant, and it has interwoven the entire life of the individual Jew and the Jewish people with religious purpose. Thus Passover is *Hag ha-Matzot* (the Festival of the Unleavened Bread) as well as *Zeman Herutenu* (the Season of our Freedom). Shavuot (Festival of Weeks) is also known as *Hag ha-Bikkurim* (Festival of the First-Fruits) and *Zeman Mattan Toratenu* (Season of the Giving of our Torah). Sukkot (Festival of Booths) is called *Hag ha-Asif* (Festival of Ingathering) and *Zeman Simhatenu* (the Season of our Rejoicing), in thankfulness for all of God's blessings, both physical and spiritual.

Passover is observed for eight days (Nisan 15-22) by orthodox and conservative Jews in the diaspora, and for seven days (Nisan 15-21) by Israelis as well as by reform Jews. Shavuot is observed on the sixth and the seventh of Sivan, except that Israelis, as well as reform Jews, observe only the sixth. Sukkot is observed by the orthodox in the diaspora for nine days (Tishre 15-23) and by Israeli and reform Jews for eight days (Tishre 15-22). The three major festivals are known in Hebrew as *Haggim* or *Moadim*. The phrase *Yamim Tovim* (Good Days) is also applied to the High Holy Days. All the above days are prescribed in the Torah.

As just noted, the three pilgrimage festivals are observed for an additional day in the diaspora (Yom Tov Sheni shel Galuyot) by the orthodox and conservative groups. On Passover and Sukkot only the first and last days are full holidays. The intermediate days are half-holidays (Hol ha-Moed); thus in Israel Nisan 16-20 and Tishre 16–21 are Hol ha-Moed, whereas in the diaspora Hol ha-Moed days are respectively Nisan 17-20, and Tishre 17–21.

The lesser festivals are: *Purim* (Feast of Lots), observed on the 14th of Adar, in commemoration of deliverance from Haman's persecution. This is the only minor festival prescribed in the Bible (Book of Esther). *Hanukkah*, celebrating deliverance from the Syrian tyranny, is observed for eight days beginning on Kislev 25. The story is related in the two books of the Maccabees. *Lag Ba-Omer*, on the 18th of Iyar, celebrates deliverance from Hadrian's persecution. *Tu Bi-Shevat*, the 15th of Shevat, or Israel Arbor Day, is a festival celebrated both in Israel and in the diaspora. In tradition, *Tu Bi-Shevat* is also known as "Rosh Hashanah Leilanot" (New Year of the Trees). *Yom Ha-Atzmaut*, the 5th of Iyar, is Israel Independence Day.

Rosh Hodesh (the first day of each month) is observed as a half-holiday (with the exception of Rosh Hodesh Tishre which is also Rosh Hashanah). In Jewish tradition the most significant day in the week is the *Sabbath*.

FETTMILCH PURIM

The Thirty Years' War left many European cities devastated and thousands of people suffered from unemployment and general misery. This situation was used by demagogues seeking to obtain power to name the Jews as the source of all misfortunes, and to stage riots against them. The Jews of Frankfort were the victims of such a situation from 1612-1616. A baker, Vincent Fettmilch, aroused the populace to storm the ghetto and expel the Jews from Frankfort. Although the Jews defended themselves heroically, they were outnumbered by the savage mobs, and after having been pillaged and subjected to all kinds of atrocities, those who remained alive sought refuge in neighboring communities. As Frankfort was left without Jews, the city magistrates feared that the anger of the masses would turn against them. They therefore asked the

Pillaging of the Jewish quarter during the Fettmilch uprising in Frankfort in 1614 as shown in this contemporary copper engraving.

Louis Finkelstein, noted rabbi and leader of American conservative Judaism, is also a scholar and head of The Jewish Theological Seminary.

Emperor to intervene and send troops against the rioters. The Emperor ordered that the demagogue Fettmilch be arrested and punished. Fettmilch, who boasted of being "the Haman of the Jews," escaped arrest for a long time, but was finally captured and executed. The Jews were then invited to return to the ghetto, and by imperial command compensated for their loss of property. In commemoration of that event the Jews of Frankfort celebrated each year on the 20th of Adar the *Purim-Winz* (Vincent's Purim).

FIFTEENTH OF SHEVAT see Tu Bi-Shevat.

FINKELSTEIN, LOUIS

Rabbi, scholar, leader of conservative Judaism in America, and chancellor of The Jewish Theological Seminary of America. Born in 1895 in Cincinnati, Ohio, he was educated in New York and ordained rabbi by The Jewish Theological Seminary, with which he was associated from 1920. In 1931 he became professor of theology and in 1937 provost. In 1940, on the death of

Cyrus Adler, he became president of the Seminary, and in 1951 its chancellor.

He has written many important articles and books on Jewish history and literature, some of which are: *Jewish Self-Government in the Middle Ages* (1924), *The Pharisees, their Origin and their Philosophy* (1929), *Maimonides and the Tannaitic Midrashim* (1935), *Akiba—Scholar, Saint and Martyr* (1936), *The Pharisees* in 2 Volumes (1938), and in 1949 he edited *The Jews, Their History, Culture and Religion* in 4 volumes.

FINLAND

Immigration of Jews to Finland, which was under Russian rule until 1917, was limited. As Finland became an independent republic, larger numbers of Jews were permitted to settle, and in 1960 there were about 1,900, most of whom lived in Helsinki, the cosmopolitan capital of this Scandinavian country.

FIRST-BORN, REDEMPTION OF see Pidyon ha-Ben.

147

FIRST-FRUITS

According to the Biblical law of *Bikkurim* (First-Fruits), the Jewish farmers each year offered their first ripe fruits as a symbol of thankfulness for the blessings of God. These offerings usually began on Shavuot, hence its name of *Ḥag ha-Bikkurim* (the Festival of the First-Fruits). The law required that only the choicest produce be offered and brought as gifts to the Temple, where special services were held for the occasion. The farmers carried the first-fruits in a solemn procession to Jerusalem, where they were met by the Levites to the accompaniment of music and festivity. The traditional Bikkurim ceremony was revived in a modified form in modern Israel, where the week following the festival of Shavuot is designated for such celebration. Particularly centered in Haifa, school children of the agricultural settlements of the Emek bring offerings of the first-fruits as contributions to the *Keren Kayemet* (Jewish National Fund).

FIVE BOOKS OF MOSES see Torah.

FLAG, JEWISH

The Bible mentions special banners used by each of the twelve Israelite tribes. In post-Biblical times the literature makes reference to the "Lion of Judah" as a Jewish emblem, and to the banner adopted by Judah the Maccabee during his revolt against the Syrians in 168-165 b.c.e. The Maccabean banner is said to have borne the letters M K B I, which were presumably the initials of "Mi Khamokha Ba-elim Adonai" (Who is like unto Thee, O Lord, among the mighty). The modern Jewish flag of blue and white with the design of

Traditional Bikkurim (First-Fruits) festival as presently revived in Israel. Here, children present wheat (bread) and lamb to the "Keren Kayemet." Such festivities usually are celebrated during the week which follows the Shavuot festival.

The blue and white flag of the State of Israel with the Magen David was conceived by David Wolffsohn and adopted by the Zionists in 1898.

the *Magen David* (Shield of David) in the center was adopted by the Zionists in 1898 at the suggestion of David Wolffsohn, and is now the national flag of the State of Israel. It is reminiscent of the ritual prayer shawl, the *Tallit*.

FLAVIUS JOSEPHUS see Josephus, Flavius.

FLOOD, THE

The Biblical account of the deluge, referred to as the *Mabbul* (Flood), brought about by God to destroy most living creatures because the earth was "filled with violence." *Noah*, the only just man, was allowed to save himself and his family, together with a few beasts and birds— all lodged in Noah's ark. The flood lasted 150 days, and as the waters subsided the ark rested on Mount Ararat. Then God, in a covenant with Noah, promised that there shall not "any more be a flood to destroy the earth."

FOUR CUPS OF WINE see Arba Kosot.

149

Child chanting the "four questions" found in the traditional Haggadah and asked during the Passover Seder. Usually recited by the youngest of the house, the "questions" ask why Passover is "different."

FOUR LANDS, COUNCIL OF see Council of the Four Lands.

FOUR QUESTIONS

The text in the Passover *Haggadah* of the *Arba Kushyot*, in Yiddish "Fihr Kashes," (Four Questions), beginning with the words "Mah Nishtannah" (Why is this night different?). Literally this phrase means "How different this night is!". The questions are customarily asked by the youngest participant at the *Seder*, and their content is: a) why do we eat *Matzah* instead of bread? b) why do we eat bitter herbs? c) why do we dip herbs twice? and d) why do we sit in a reclining position during the reading of the Haggadah? The head of the family then gives the answer, which actually constitutes the rest of the Haggadah. The purpose of the questions is to motivate and stimulate the child's interest, thus fulfilling the prescription in the Torah to teach the child about the Exodus and God's providence and love for His people.

Briefly, the traditional answers can be summarized as follows: The Matzah represents the "Bread of Affliction" which the Israelites took with them when they left Egypt in such haste that the dough did not have time to rise. The bitter herbs represent the bitterness of the life led by our forefathers under Egyptian bondage. The dipping of the vegetable in salt water reminds us of the ancient practice of partaking of some vegetable preliminary to a big meal; and the dipping of the *Maror* in the sweet *Haroset* serves to alleviate its bitter taste. The Haroset itself symbolizes the mortar which the Israelites used during the Pharaonic oppression. Men of position, in ancient times, reclined while eating, so we recline at the Seder to show our non-servile state.

FRANCE

In 1960 there were about 350,000 Jews in France. It is believed that Jewish settlers came to France (Gaul) during the

The Grand Sanhedrin in session, composed of 46 rabbis and 25 laymen, was convoked by Napoleon to assure him of Jewish loyalties in France. Its opening session was held on February 9, 1807.

period of the Second Commonwealth. There was a considerable Jewish community in France during the 4th century c.e., with centers in Marseilles, Narbonne, Avignon and Bordeaux. Under the rule of King Charlemagne in the 8th century, Jewish immigration was encouraged, and France became a significant center of Jewish learning, particularly from the 10th through the 13th centuries. Among the great rabbis and spiritual leaders of that period were Rabbi Gershom, Rashi, and Rabbenu Tam. However, during that period the Jews of France were not free from persecution and anti-Jewish outbreaks. The *Talmud* was publicly burned in 1242, and in 1306 Jews were expelled from France. Although allowed to return, they were ultimately driven out of the country in 1334.

At the end of the 18th century, after the French Revolution, equal citizenship rights were granted to the Jews of France, and Jewish immigration increased, and in

Pierre Mendés-France, French socialist leader and post-Second World War Premier of France.

the 19th century there were many prominent Jews in the French government. The *Dreyfus Affair*, however, uncovered bitter anti-Semitism, arousing the entire world, and evoking the protests of French republicans, among whom were Émile Zola and Clemenceau.

Most of the Jews in France were Alsatian. Jewish immigration from Russia and Poland rose after World War I, and especially after Hitler's rise to power in Germany. When the Nazis occupied France, serious restrictions were placed against the Jews and nearly 100,000 were exterminated in concentration camps. After World War II, the Jews began to re-establish themselves, though many communities had been irreparably destroyed. Léon Blum and Pierre Mendès-France, outstanding socialist leaders, were both premiers of France.

Many important Jewish institutions were established by French Jewry, the most outstanding of which is the *Alliance Israélite Universelle*, an international organization for the protection of Jewish rights and the giving of relief to destitute Jewish communities the world over. The present Jewish community in France, absorbed large numbers of war refugees from other countries, is active and well organized, and in western Europe it is second only in number and importance to the Jewish community in England.

FRANK, ANNE (1929–1945)

Remembered for her remarkable "journal," now known as "The Diary of Anne Frank," which she wrote in her early teens while hiding with her family during the Nazi occupation of Holland. With unusual literary talent and psychological insight, Anne Frank depicts life under the Nazi terror. This diary was found after her death. It has been translated into many languages and successfully produced on the stage of many countries. In 1959 the Hollywood screen production of "The Diary of Anne Frank" was acclaimed by millions of viewers, and its showing in foreign countries has brought added plaudits.

FRANK, JACOB (1726–1791)

False messiah and founder of a sect called *Frankists*. Born in southern Poland, he traveled through southeastern Europe, stayed in Salonica where he came in contact with the secret followers of Shabbetai Tzevi, himself a messianic pretender. Frank declared himself the successor to Shabbetai Tzevi and proclaimed his new doctrine, which was in opposition to rabbinic Judaism and involved transgression of moral Jewish principles. Upon his return to southern Podolia he gained many followers from among the heretic Sabbetaians. The frequent and ever-growing gatherings of the so-called Frankists, accompanied by immoral orgies, aroused the indignation of the leading rabbis and the concern of the Jewish communities. In order to win the sympathy and support of the Catholic Church, the Frankists made violent attacks on the rabbis and the Talmud, and accused the Jews of using Christian blood for ritual purposes. The Frankists were frequently supported by the Catholic authorities against the Jews. The Church authorities ordered the Frankists and their opponents to appear at public disputations to defend their doctrines. Soon after, Frank himself and many of his followers embraced the Christian faith. However, because the separate activities of the Frankists continued, the Church doubted Frank's loyalty to the Christian faith. He was arrested, and after 13 years

Anne Frank, a young girl the Nazis murdered at Bergen-Belsen, wrote a "Diary" which was preserved. Its poignant description of Jewish life under Nazi terror gained it widespread acclaim, and later adaptations as a movie and drama.

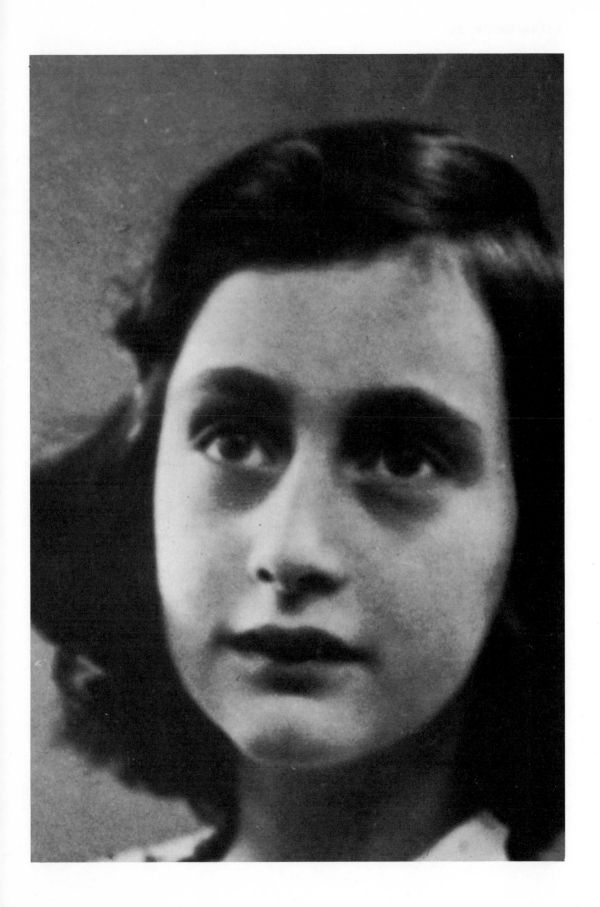

FRANKFURTER, FELIX

of imprisonment, when Poland was partitioned, he was released. He settled in a small German town, where he assumed the title of baron and lived in luxury, made possible through contributions of his secret followers. After Frank's death, his daughter Eve declared herself the head of the Frankists, but her followers gradually abandoned her and the sect eventually ceased to exist.

FRANKFURTER, FELIX

Associate Justice of the Supreme Court of the United States. Born in Vienna in 1882, he settled in the United States at the age of twelve. After graduating from Harvard Law School, he served as assistant United States Attorney in New York City, and later joined the staff of the Bureau of Insular Affairs, where he handled cases before the U. S. Supreme Court. In 1914 he became professor of law at the Harvard Law School. He advocated social reforms beneficial to the welfare of the masses. In 1927 he took a particular interest in the famous Sacco and Vanzetti case, two Italian workers who were tried and convicted of murder, and he wrote a vigorous defense of the two men maintaining that they were convicted because of their political views rather than on actual evidence of the facts.

In 1939, President Franklin D. Roosevelt appointed him associate justice of the Supreme Court of the United States, where he quickly joined the so-called liberals on the bench in rendering legal decisions. Many thought that he gradually became more conservative in his outlook over the years in the Supreme Court.

In spite of his busy schedule as a teacher and prolific writer, Frankfurter took an active interest in Jewish affairs. He was an active Zionist and in 1919 he presented the Zionist cause at the Versailles Peace Conference. He visited Palestine three

154

Felix Frankfurter, Associate Justice of the Supreme Court, is a teacher and writer of note.

times, assumed responsible leadership in political Zionism, and worked in behalf of the Hebrew University in Jerusalem. He gained national recognition for his outstanding contributions to Jewish life.

FRANKISTS see Frank, Jacob.

FREE WILL

Judaism teaches that God granted man freedom of will to determine his own conduct. Each individual is responsible for his own decisions and is rewarded or punished in accordance with his free choice between good and evil. The problem of Free Will is difficult, both in religion and science. Some religionists, in order to avoid limiting God's knowledge and power, teach that man has no free will. In Judaism we find the paradox stated quite

Sigmund Freud, father of psychoanalysis, was a great pioneer in the study of human psychology.

expressly by Rabbi Akiva: "Everything is foreseen by God, and yet free will is granted to man." Ethics (both in religion and philosophy) demands an acceptance of both concepts, although they seem to contradict one another, if man is to be held responsible for ethical behavior.

FREUD, SIGMUND (1856–1939)

A physician who became the world famous founder of psychoanalysis. Born in Germany, he studied in Vienna, where he spent most of his life, and became interested in hypnosis as a treatment for certain cases of hysteria. This was for Freud the beginning of his new theory of psychoanalysis based on "free association." His theory was designed to help understand the motives of people's actions, and as an aid in the treatment of the mentally ill. Because of his unorthodox and novel ideas, Freud met with great opposition on the part of the medical profession. In this opposition Freud recognized an expression of anti-Semitism. However, as a result of his success in the treatment of mental cases, he soon won many followers in the profession, and his theory, with some modifications, gradually became the basis for the modern science and practice of psychoanalysis. Finally Freud enjoyed world recognition. Because of the Nazi terror he fled to London, where many honors were bestowed upon him.

Freud did not take an active interest in Jewish affairs. However, on many occasions he demonstrated his concern with the Jewish people, and showed a special interest in the Hebrew University in Jerusalem. In his later years he wrote "Moses and Monotheism," in which the life of the Jewish lawgiver was described and analyzed, not in accordance with accepted tradition, and contrary to all historical and literary evidence.

FRINGES see Tallit.

FRISCHMAN, DAVID (1861–1922)

Prolific Hebrew and Yiddish writer, editor and translator. Born in a Germanized city in Poland, he combined Jewish traditional knowledge with western culture and languages, and became one of the architects of modern Hebrew literature and language and an influential literary critic. He edited several important Hebrew periodicals, and wrote fiction, poetry, essays, feuilletons, literary criticisms and translations. The painstaking care and artistic structure of his writings acted as a model, and served to raise the standards of Hebrew writing. His works were published in 17 volumes in Hebrew, and 7 volumes in Yiddish, of which several editions appeared.

155

GEMILUT ḤESED

He who sustains one life is regarded as if he had created

the world.

TALMUD

GABBAI

A Hebrew term meaning "collector," commonly applied to an official or honorary officer of a synagogue. The *Gabbai* is usually the treasurer and/or the vice-president of the congregation, and often the person in charge of the charity funds (*Gabbai Tzedakah*). This term was already in use during the period of the *Mishnah*, and applied to a tax-collector for the government.

GABIROL, SOLOMON IBN see Ibn Gabirol, Solomon.

GABRIEL

"Man of God," name of an archangel mentioned in the Bible. The only other angel mentioned by name in the Bible is *Michael*.

GAD

One of Jacob's sons, and founder of the Israelite tribe of that name. The tribes of Gad and Reuben, and half of the tribe of Manasseh, settled east of the Jordan.

GALICIA

After World War I, when the Austro-Hungarian Empire was broken up, Galicia became a province of Poland. Jews settled in Galicia as early as the 10th century, and at the outbreak of World War II the Jewish community numbered over half a million. The Jews of Galicia played an outstanding role in Jewish history, and many of its rabbis, teachers, scholars and communal leaders enjoyed a great reputation in the Jewish world, even if they were known as "Galicianer." See *Poland*.

GALILEE

The northern part of Palestine, called in Hebrew "Galil," traditionally divided into Upper and Lower Galilee. Its major cities and localities are: Haifa, Acre and Caesarea on the coast; Safed and Tiberias in the north; Capernaum and Nazareth in the east. Galilee played an important role in the history of Palestine. It was the major battlefield of the wars fought in the Holy Land, including the war waged by Bar

Galilee, the northern part of Palestine, has always played an important role in the country's history. Recently resettled with agricultural colonies, the once devastated area is now being rebuilt by Israel.

Kokhba against the Romans. Galilee later became an important center of learning, where both the *Mishnah* and the *Palestinian Talmud* were compiled. In the 16th century the city of Safed became the residence of the great teachers of *Kabbalah* (Jewish mysticism). For centuries the land of Galilee stood devastated. Its resettlement and cultivation began with the establishment of the first agricultural colonies by the Zionist pioneers of modern Palestine.

GALILEE, SEA OF see Kinneret.

GALLAH

Hebrew term meaning "shaved" and applied to a Catholic priest, presumably because of the way Catholic priests' hair is shaved or tonsured.

GALUT

Hebrew term (pronounced "Goless" in Yiddish) meaning "exile," generally referring to the lands of Jewish dispersion and particularly those lands where Jews were subject to persecution and treated as undesirable strangers. See *Diaspora*.

GAMALIEL (GAMLIEL)

Family name of a group of prominent *Tannaim* (teachers quoted in the Mishnah) and spiritual leaders of Palestinian Jewry between the first and the fourth centuries, c.e. The best known of these were: *Gamaliel I*, also known as Gamaliel Ha-Zaken (the Elder), who was the grandson of Hillel and the first to bear the title *Rabban* (master-teacher). He was held in high esteem and is mentioned with reverence in the New Testament. He was the author of many reforms "for the improvement of society," especially regulations designed to protect the rights of women. *Gamaliel II*, grandson of Gamaliel I, succeeded Rabbi Johanan ben Zakkai as *Nasi* (Patriarch) of the *Sanhedrin* (High Court

at Yavneh). He was the Jewish leader, recognized as such by the Romans, and used his authority against the views of other members of the Sanhedrin. He apparently contested the spread of Christianity, and some scholars say that it was he who added the additional prayer to the *Shemoneh Esreh* (Eighteen Benedictions) aimed against the *Minim* (heretics). *Gamaliel III* was the son of Judah the Prince (Ha-Nasi). In his time the compilation of the *Mishnah*, initiated by his father, was brought to completion.

GAN EDEN

The term *Gan Eden* (Garden of Eden) is used for "Paradise" or the abode of bliss reserved in heaven for the departed souls of the righteous. In the Bible the Garden of Eden is the garden that God planted "eastward of Eden" and where He placed Adam. Among the trees growing in the Garden of Eden were the "tree of life" and the "tree of knowledge." The fruit of the latter was forbidden to Adam and Eve. When they violated this prohibition, Adam and Eve were driven out of the Garden. Some ancient Jewish authorities maintained that this story had an allegorical meaning. However, many writers assume that the "Garden of Eden" was an "earthly paradise," a real geographical area located somewhere in the Euphrates valley.

GAON

A title meaning "Excellency," applied in common usage to a person of outstanding originality and Talmudic scholarship, such as the "Gaon of Vilna," the great 18th-century authority, Elijah of Vilna. As an official title it was held by heads of the Babylonian Academies of Sura and Pumbedita from the end of the 6th century to the 11th century, and to some extent even later. The *Geonim* (plural of

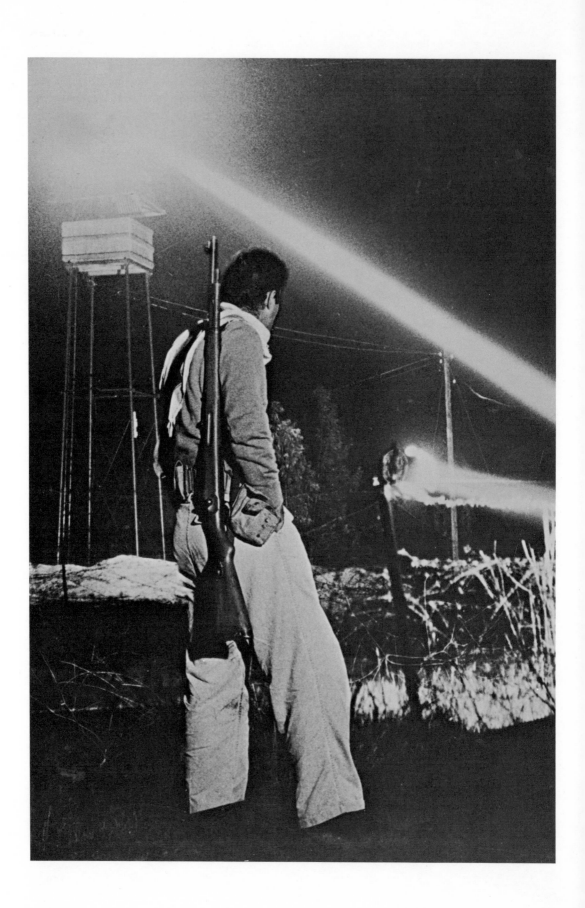

19th-century aquatint of the great Lithuanian Talmudic scholar, student of mathematics and resolute foe of Ḥasidism, the Gaon of Vilna.

"Gaon") were generally elected to the office of *Gaon* on the basis of high scholarship, and were paid from the income of the academies. The office of a Gaon served as a central and authoritative religious institution, and endeavored to spread knowledge of the Talmud and establish it as a guide in all matters of the life of the Jew as well as to encourage respect for learning in general. The Geonim exercised great authority, and were generally only nominally responsible to the *Exilarch*, the hereditary head of the Jewish community. Among the best known Geonim were *Saadiah*, *Sherira* and *Hai*.

GAON OF VILNA (1720–1797)

Title of honor by which the great Lithuanian Talmudist Elijah is called. At the

Israeli guards patrol the Gaza strip to prevent border infiltration by Arab terrorists, the Fedayeen groups organized by Egypt. One of the objectives of the 1956 Sinai campaign was to wipe out all of the Egyptian Fedayeen bases.

age of 20 he was already famed as a great Talmudic authority, whose counsel was sought by prominent rabbis of the time. In addition to his phenomenal knowledge of the entire range of rabbinic literature, he was a student of grammar, mathematics and other sciences. He is also remembered as the outspoken opponent of the *Ḥasidim* (followers of the Baal Shem Tov), whose leaders he excommunicated. He refused the official office of rabbi, and devoted his entire life to his studies, research, the writing of commentaries and other "notes" on many aspects of the legal literature. Numerous legends have been woven around his life indicative of the love and reverence in which he has been held by the people.

GARDEN OF EDEN see Gan Eden.

GAZA

The border "strip" between the State of Israel and Egypt. Following the war between Israel and the Arab nations in 1948, it became the scene of repeated attacks by Arabs on the neighboring Jewish settlements. Historically Gaza is the Greek transcription of the Biblical "Azzah," one of the chief cities of the Philistines. Jews lived in Gaza after the destruction of the Temple, perhaps throughout the entire medieval period. There were Jews there at the end of the 18th century when it was captured by Napoleon. Before the Gaza area was placed under Egyptian control, the administrative center of the Jewish settlements in that district was located in the city of Gaza.

GEDALIAH

The prince appointed by the king of Babylonia as governor of Judah after the destruction of the First Temple. He was assassinated by Jewish zealots, and thereupon many of the remaining Jews, who had escaped Babylonian captivity, settled

161

in Egypt. Tradition considered his assassination a national calamity, and this tragic event is still commemorated by orthodox Jews on the third day of Tishre, as *Tzom Gedalyah* (the Fast of Gedaliah). See *Fast Days*.

GEHINNOM (GEHENNA)

In common usage this term means hell or purgatory (the opposite of *Gan Eden* or Paradise), a place where souls receive punishment after death. The sinister connotation of this term probably derived from the Biblical phrase *Ge Hinnom* (or Ge ben Hinnom), the name of a valley south of Jerusalem, the location of a shrine where children, under ancient paganism, were sacrificed to Moloch.

GEIGER, ABRAHAM G. (1810–1874)

Scholar, rabbi and leader of reform Judaism in Germany. As a rabbi in Breslau and Berlin, and at several rabbinical conferences, he championed the cause of reform. He was not as radical as some others, but he aroused the opposition of the orthodox rabbis. He was one of the great Jewish scholars of his day; his studies opened new areas in the fields of Bible criticism, Jewish history, and the language and content of the *Mishnah*. He founded the scientific *Magazine for Jewish Theology*, in which he published numerous articles about the reform movement and other matters; he was also lecturer at the Institute of Jewish Science in Berlin.

GELILAH see Hagbahah and Gelilah.

GEMARA see Talmud.

GEMAR HATIMAH TOVAH see Ketivah va-Hatimah Tovah.

GEMILUT HESED (HASADIM)

A Hebrew term meaning "the bestowal of kindness," applied generally to the giving of charity or the granting of a loan to a needy person. Traditionally it was also applied to other acts of kindness such as visiting the sick, comforting those in mourning, etc. See *Charity*.

GENERAL ZIONISTS

The middle-of-the-road Zionist party. Many of the General Zionists believed that the main task of Zionism was to rebuild the Jewish homeland, and that questions regarding religion, capital and labor, and other issues should be decided by the Jews of Palestine themselves. Others held that the new state should establish free enterprise. Of the various Zionist groups, the General Zionists were for a long time the largest; however, in modern Israel they have been a minority in the general elections.

GENESIS

The first of the Five Books of Moses (the Torah), called in Hebrew *Bereshit* (In the beginning). The book begins with the story of Creation, and presents a detailed account of the lives of the Patriarchs Abraham, Isaac and Jacob, ending with the death of Joseph in Egypt. Some major points of the book are: God's selection of Abraham as the founder of the Jewish religion and nation, and God's selection of Canaan as the Promised Land of the Jewish people.

GENIZAH

Hebrew term meaning "hiding place" applied to a special storeroom for Hebrew books no longer physically fit for use but which could not be destroyed because they contained the name of "God." Such Hebrew materials were therefore commonly called "Shemot" (Names). The "Genizah" is usually found in the attic or the cellar of the synagogue. The best known Genizah was that of the old Ezra Synagogue in Cairo, Egypt, which held the largest and oldest collection of stored-

The famous Genizah of the old Ezra Synagogue in Cairo, Egypt, where many ancient, sacred manuscripts were stored. Above, Cambridge University Professor Solomon Schechter examines some of them.

away ancient Hebrew documents. Professor Solomon Schechter made the Cairo Genizah famous when he discovered those valuable documents there. It is, in addition, an old custom to bury Shemot with the remains of a pious Jew.

GENTILE

A term applied to a non-Jew. See *Goy*.

GEONIM see Gaon.

GER

Hebrew term for a convert to Judaism. The Bible uses this word for "stranger," or one who lived only temporarily in the land of Israel. Under Jewish law even though one did not embrace the Jewish faith, he was fully protected against discrimination and enjoyed many civil rights. The Talmud distinguishes between a *Ger Toshav* and a *Ger Tzedek*. The former is one who accepts monotheism (belief in one God) and the Noahidic laws, but not all the other *Mitzvot* (commandments of the Torah), such as dietary laws; the latter is one who accepts Judaism with all its religious obligations and requirements. The *Gere Tzedek* (genuine converts to Judaism), upon embracing the Jewish faith, are circumcised if they are male, and both male and female proselytes take the ritual bath (*Mikveh*). Men usually assume the name of the first Hebrew, Abraham, and women the name of Ruth,

163

View of the "Judengasse," or Jewish quarter, in Frankfort, Germany, vintage ca. 1870. The first Jewish settlement in this city can be traced as far back as the early part of the 13th century.

who became a Jewess in the Biblical story bearing her name. The *Ger Tzedek* is considered a full Jew in every respect.

GERIZIM, MOUNT

A mountain in Palestine, near the city of Shechem (modern Nablus), where, according to the Bible, blessings were pronounced on the Israelites. Mount Gerizim is especially sacred to the Samaritans who built their own temple there. To this day the high priest of the still existing, though small community of Samaritans, offers the Passover sacrifice on Mount Gerizim. See *Samaritans*.

GERMANY

The country where Jews over many centuries developed a high level of Jewish scholarship, and where they have been, at the same time, exposed to the most cruel types of anti-Semitism, culminating in the greatest disaster in Jewish history during the Hitlerian period.

There is evidence that Jewish settlers reached Germany during the early Roman period, and that later, in the 4th century, there existed a flourishing Jewish community in the city of Cologne. However, the larger concentration of Jewish settlements in Germany, which developed great and influential spiritual leadership in the Jewish world, began at the end of the 9th century. After many Jewish communities took firm roots on German soil, a long period of persecution and great suffering began, reaching disastrous proportions during the period of the Crusades, and resulting in the wiping out of entire Jewish communities. Despite the persecutions, the Jewish community in Germany of that period reached a high level of cultural development under the spiritual leadership of Rabbenu Gershom, Rabbi Judah Ḥasid, Rabbi Meir of Rothenburg and others. At that period also, the Jews in

A young girl lays a memorial wreath at a mass grave in the Bergen-Belsen cemetery. Belsen concentration camp, located near Celle, in North Germany, was one of the most infamous Nazi death camps.

the Rheinish provinces began to develop their own Judeo-German language, which in the course of later centuries became known as the Yiddish language, the spoken and written tongue of the east European Jewish masses.

The evil period of the Crusades was followed by other dark centuries of blood accusations, "black-death" massacres, and expulsions, during which time German Jews sought refuge in the Slavic countries, particularly Poland. In spite of their precarious existence and the numerous limitations to which they were exposed as a result of ghetto life, the Jewish communities in the German provinces continued to develop, and famous *Yeshivot*

(Talmud academies) became the centers of learning, spiritual leadership, and Jewish legal authority for Jewish communities elsewhere.

German Jewry is also credited with the opening of a new era in modern Jewish life through the *Haskalah* (Enlightenment) movement, which began during the second half of the 18th century under the leadership of Moses Mendelssohn. The gates of western culture and secular learning were opened to German Jews, and this learning later spread to eastern Europe. In this period the way was paved for the granting of civil rights to the Jews of Germany after the revolutions of 1848. Despite the persistence of anti-Semitism, the

165

Jews of Germany began to participate fully in the development of general German culture, science, music, finance and industry, and at the same time to further develop Jewish scholarship known as "Jewish Science." Following World War I, German Jewry reached the peak of development and influence, and when Hitler came to power in 1933, there were over 550,000 Jews in Germany. The Nazi regime and World War II resulted in the complete liquidation of the Jewish communities in Germany, as well as the annihilation of one-third of world Jewry. There were about 30,000 Jews in Germany in 1960, the remnants of a once flourishing Jewish cultural and economic center in western Europe.

GERSHOM BEN JUDAH (960–1040)

Known as "Rabbenu Gershom," surnamed "Light of the Exile," and considered the greatest Talmudic authority and spiritual leader of his time. He was the head of the *Yeshivah* (Talmudical academy) of Mayence, and founder of Talmudic schools in Germany and France. He enjoyed great esteem and popularity, and his rabbinical decisions found unquestioned acceptance in Jewish communities throughout Europe. With the aid of a rabbinical synod convened at Mayence, he established a number of legal provisions for the Jewish communities in western Europe. Among these were: a ban on polygamy; special changes in the divorce laws providing better security for women; provisions for the better treatment of those who sought to return to the Jewish faith after baptism under duress; and laws providing the right of privacy and forbidding the opening of correspondence except by the addressee. See *Takannah.*

GESHEM

The Hebrew title of the "Prayer for Rain," one of the oldest prayers, recited on *Shemini Atzeret* (eighth day of Sukkot). The recital of a prayer for rain, incorporated in the *Amidah*, is continued through the winter months until the first day of Passover; that is, for the duration of the rainy season in Israel. In the springtime, on the first day of Passover, a prayer for dew is recited. See *Tal.*

GET

Hebrew term for "Writ of Divorce." The "Get" is a document written in Aramaic and the text is strictly prescribed by law. According to Talmudic law it was possible for a man to divorce his wife against her will. At the beginning of the 10th century, Rabbenu Gershom of Mayence reformed the divorce laws, stipulating among other things that a wife cannot be divorced without her consent. Such a divorce is nevertheless valid. Where the rabbis had authority in the local community, they were also in a position to compel the man to give his wife a *Get* where such act was necessary and proper.

GEULLAH

Hebrew term meaning "redemption." One of the important Jewish religious concepts is that God is the redeemer of all mankind. The Jewish daily liturgy contains a prayer named "Geullah." In common usage this term has the opposite meaning of *Galut* (Exile), and is the symbol of the longing of the Jewish people to be freed from prejudice and persecution, and ultimately to return to the historic Jewish homeland.

GEZERAH

Hebrew term meaning "decree," which is used as a popular phrase applied to any anti-Jewish law or persecution conceived of as punishment from God and directed against a Jewish community.

GEZER CALENDAR see Archeology.

GHETTO

A term for the restricted quarters within a given city where Jews were required by the secular law to reside. The derivation of the term "ghetto" is not definitely established. Some authorities believe that *ghetto* is an Italian term for "foundry," and since the Jews of Venice, Italy, were confined in 1516 to a special quarter of the city where gun-foundries (ghettos) existed, the term was later applied to all such quarters reserved for Jews. Compulsory ghettos existed in Europe from the 16th to the 18th century, of which the best known were those in Rome, Venice, Frankfort-on-the-Main, Prague and Trieste. The enforced ghettos were intended as a means of persecution and as a measure for the prevention of contact between Jewish and the non-Jewish population. However, in the course of Jewish history there were also voluntary ghettos established by Jews themselves, in order to protect themselves behind walls when living in other areas of a city was dangerous, and often a tightly-knit self-government resulted.

The compulsory ghettos officially disappeared in the 19th century, although in a number of cities Jews continued to live in separate quarters for various reasons. Compulsory ghettos, under the most inhuman conditions, were re-established in Poland during the Nazi occupation after 1939. The ghettos, the largest of which was in Warsaw, became virtual annihilation centers. In April 1943 the Jews of the Warsaw Ghetto made an heroic armed revolt against the Germans in which the remnants of the Jewish population were martyred.

GIDEON

The fifth judge of Israel who lived dur-ing the 12th century b.c.e. According to the Bible he was a poor farmer who, by the command of God, fought against Baal worship, and led a successful and heroic war against the Midianites under the slogan "For the Lord and Gideon!" When asked to become king of the Jewish people he declined, saying that God is the only ruler of Israel. As a respected judge and chieftain, Gideon served his people for forty years.

GIMMEL (ג)

The third letter of the Hebrew alphabet. Its meaning is probably "camel," and its numerical value is three; when followed by an apostrophe its value is three thousand. In the Greek the word becomes Gamma.

GINZBERG, ASHER see Aḥad Ha-Am.

GLÜCKEL VON HAMELN (1646–1724)

Writer of invaluable memoirs in early Yiddish (*Ivre-Taitsh*), describing the conditions of Jewish life in the 17th century. A mother of twelve children who, when she became a widow, managed to keep her husband's business, provide her remaining unmarried eight children with a good education and substantial dowries, and write her excellent memoirs. Some of the memoirs, originally in seven volumes, were later copied by members of her family and translated into several languages. They are considered an excellent source for the study of Jewish cultural, social and economic life, and of great literary merit.

GLUECK, NELSON

Prominent archeologist and president of the Hebrew Union College–Jewish Institute of Religion. Born in Cincinnati, Ohio, in 1900, he was ordained rabbi in 1923, and studied in Europe where he received his doctorate. He served as professor of Bible and Biblical archeology at the Hebrew Union College, and was director of the American Schools of Oriental Research in Jerusalem. He gained prominence through his archeological research and excavations in and about the Jordan Valley, which yielded important knowledge about the history and culture of eastern Palestine. He also made the excavations of "Solomon's Mines" near Aqaba (Eilat) on the Red Sea. He published a number of studies dealing with scientific explorations.

Nelson Glueck, rabbi, college president and Biblical archeologist, is famous for his excavations in the Jordan Valley. He is shown here examining pottery remains which may date back as far as the time of the ancient Patriarchs.

GOD

Fundamental in Judaism is that God exists, that He is pure spirit, He is eternal, good, holy, true, faithful, just, loving and full of compassion. He is immanent in the world of nature and in human aspiration. He is the Author of the laws of nature as well as of ethics and morality. He is all-powerful, all-knowing, and both love and justice are of the essence of His Being. God's Providence is over all His creatures. He is a Person in the sense that He hears prayer and reveals His will to man. God is the only proper Object of worship. In order to stimulate men to live the good life He holds out the promise of reward and punishment, even though the ideal reason for doing God's will is out of love for Him, and not for the purpose of obtaining reward or avoiding punishment. God has implanted in man reason and a mind so that he may decide on his own to obey Him. One aspect of the dignity conferred on man is that he has been given the freedom of will to obey God.

During the early history of mankind, the Jewish people were the only community who worshipped the one God; all the rest were idolators, serving many gods. One of the Hebraic contributions to our civilization is that much of mankind now believes in the one true God.

The Hebrew prophets struggled against polytheism, atheism, and dualism. In the Middle Ages the philosophers sought to systematize proofs for His existence, and offered such arguments as the cosmological, teleological and ontological. Some hold that one cannot in logic prove His existence, but that our knowledge concerning Him derives from the empirical facts of human life.

Judaism recognized that the belief in one God who is just and mighty bears with it certain difficulties. On the ethical plane, one problem is that a good and powerful God permits evil in the world. Another problem which confronts the believer is that if God is omniscient and omnipotent, in what sense can it be said that man has the freedom of will to choose between good and evil, and if he does not have such freedom, where is the justice in divine retribution. On the plane of natural law, the problem is the relationship between an eternal God and matter, which according to science is indestructible and, by the same token, can not be created. In what sense, then, may God be called the Creator of the world? The philosophers have given varying answers to these problems, but most thinkers seem to agree that while belief in God may involve many difficulties, the negation of God creates a great many more. It appears that on balance philosophers are inclined to accept some sort of God idea. It is important to note that generally it is the pure Jewish God concept which the most profound philosophers accept.

Certain phrases in the Bible which speak of God in an anthropomorphic or anthropopathic vein (human form of thought) have given rise to some questioning. Apart from critical opinion, most religious men interpret such phrases in a metaphorical manner, as figures of speech. In order that men may get a better grasp of the great truths of religion, "the Torah speaks in the language of men." In Rabbinic literature, circumlocutions were used to avoid anthropomorphic implications. To avoid the appearance of anthropomorphism, the Aramaic *Targum* sometimes renders the Hebrew word "God" by the Aramaic phrase "Word of God." Other words and phrases used for God's activity in this world are: "the Holy Spirit" (*Ruah ha-Kodesh*); "the echo of the divine voice" (*Bat Kol*); the "Indwelling" (*Shekhinah* i.e. God's immanence); "The Holy One, Blessed be He" (*ha-Kadosh Barukh Hu*

or *Kudesha Berikh Hu*); "The Merciful One" (*ha-Rahaman* or *Rahamana*); etc.

Whatever difficulties may have arisen with regard to the belief in God and the vicissitudes which have befallen the Jewish people and all mankind, Judaism has throughout the ages proclaimed with clarity and depth God's unique Unity, the supremacy of His Being, and His just but merciful Providence of mankind. The affirmation of His Unity and Spirituality is the essence of all Jewish prayer, and Jewish martyrs throughout history have died with the words "the Lord our God is One" on their lips. See *Monotheism*.

GOLDEN CALF

The idol that the Israelites made and worshipped in the wilderness while Moses was on Mount Sinai receiving the Torah. When Moses descended from Mount Sinai and found the Israelites worshipping the Golden Calf, he broke the Tablets of the Law. Moses pleaded with God to forgive the people and after punishment was meted out to them, Moses made another set of Tablets.

GOLDFADEN, ABRAHAM (1840–1908)

Founder of the modern Yiddish theater, playwright, and poet. Born in Russia, he completed the rabbinic studies at Zhitomir, and became active as editor of several Yiddish journals. His theatrical career was started in Rumania where he organized the first modern Yiddish theater, wrote his own plays and made successful tours with his troupe of actors. He migrated to the United States in 1887, where he began the publication of an illustrated Yiddish periodical.

He started his literary career as a Hebrew and Yiddish poet, but his reputation as a Yiddish playwright and author of several operas surpassed that of all his other literary accomplishments. His most

Nahum Goldmann, famous as a Zionist leader, and president of the World Zionist Organization.

famous operas, based upon historical subjects, are *Shulamis* and *Bar Kokhba*. Undoubtedly, the best loved of his songs is *Rozhinkes mit Mandlen*.

GOLDMANN, NAHUM

Zionist leader. Born in Russia in 1894 and educated in Germany, he became interested in Jewish cultural and Zionist activities. He was one of the founders of Eshkol Publishing Company and helped in the publication of the *Encyclopedia Judaica*. He represented the Jewish Agency at the League of Nations (1935-39); was chairman of the executive and president of the World Jewish Congress. He was joint chairman of the Jewish Agency, and in 1955 he became president of the World Zionist Organization. Goldman was one of the chief negotiators with the government of West Germany concerning the payment of reparations to the Jewish victims who survived the Nazi regime. He resided in the United States from 1940.

GOLEM

A term used in Jewish folklore to describe a robot made out of clay or wood, given artificial life with the aid of magic or the use of the Divine name. As used in the Bible and the Talmud, the term had several connotations: "embryo," "formless substance," and "human body without a soul." The concept of the *Golem* as an artificially created human being by supernatural means was widely accepted during the Middle Ages. Tradition tells of automatons created by Solomon ibn Gabirol, Elijah of Chelm, and others. According to the legend, the most famous Golem was created in the 16th century by Judah Löw of Prague, one of the great rabbis. The express purpose of these living automatons was to protect the Jews from menacing dangers. The Golem created by the rabbi of Prague is said to have been made for the purpose of exposing a plot to involve the Jews in a blood accusation. The robots were usually under the spell and control of their creators, and could become destructive if not checked. Jewish folklore has numerous Golem stories, and several modern literary works have been written on that theme, such as the famous Yiddish play "Der Golem" by H. Leivick. In everyday usage, "Golem" describes a stupid person.

GOLIATH

Philistine giant who was killed by David. According to the Bible, David volunteered to fight Goliath, who had dared the Israelites to find one among them to encounter him in battle. Without armor, and using only a stone and a sling-shot, David downed the giant and cut off his head, after which event the Israelites routed the Philistines.

Samuel Gompers, influential founder and first president of the American Federation of Labor.

GOLUS see Galut; Diaspora.

GOMEL BENDCHEN

Yiddish phrase referring to a benediction that Jews customarily recite when delivered from peril or following a narrow escape from danger. Persons who recover from a serious illness, who return from a hazardous journey, or after similar occasions of relief from exposure to possible calamity, are honored with an Aliyah to the Torah in the synagogue, and they bless the Lord "Who bestoweth benefits upon the undeserving."

GOMORRAH see Sodom and Gomorrah.

GOMPERS, SAMUEL (1850–1924)

American labor leader and one of the founders of the American Federation of Labor. Born in London, he migrated to America at the age of 13, where he helped his father as a cigar maker. Gompers joined the cigar makers union, and soon became a militant labor leader, organizing a number of strikes and urging improvement in the conditions of employment. He organized the Cigar Makers International Union and in 1881 was a delegate to the first convention of the American Federation of Labor, whose president he became the following year. As president of the American Federation of Labor, an office which he held until his death, Gompers advocated a conservative, anti-socialist and non-political labor policy. During World War I, he led the workers of the nation in support of the Allies. The accomplishments of Gompers were well appreciated by the American people, and in 1933 a monument was erected in his honor in Washington, D.C., known as the Samuel Gompers Memorial. In 1941 a statue of Gompers was erected at Uniondale, Long Island.

GORDIN, JACOB (1853–1909)

Yiddish playwright. Born in Russia, he began his writing career as a journalist in Russian newspapers. In 1891 he settled in New York City, where he wrote a number of Yiddish plays. Encouraged by the success of his first play, he continued to write original plays as well as adaptations from outstanding European playwrights. Gordin's plays gave new life to the Yiddish stage, and his fame reached both Jewish and non-Jewish audiences. His more successful original plays were: "Gott, Mensh un Taivl," "Mirele Efros," "Elisha ben Avuyah," "Yiddisher Kenig Lear," "Kreutzer Sonata," and "Di Sheḥite." Two volumes of selected plays were published under the overall title "Yaakov Gordin's Dramen."

GORDON, AARON DAVID (1856–1922)

Leader and teacher of the Palestinian workers. Born in Russia, where he worked as a land official, he went to Palestine at the age of 48, where he became a manual laborer. A champion of the idea of the return of the Jewish people to the soil, he wrote his *Dat Ha-Avodah* (The Religion of Labor), which influenced the moral development of the Jewish pioneers in Palestine, and created the ideology of the *Hapoel Hatzair* movement. Believing that the Jewish people can be reborn through the re-education and moral conduct of the Jewish individual and through love of the soil, of work and fellow men, he himself served as a good example through his personal life and work. His writings, comprising many essays and "Letters from Eretz Yisrael," were published in 1935, and were translated into English and several other languages. *Bet-Gordon* (Gordon House) was dedicated in his memory at Deganiah, the oldest agricultural workers' settlement in Israel, and the Zionist youth organization "Gordonia," which is now part of *Habonim*, was named after him.

Aaron D. Gordon, champion of the Jewish return-to-the-soil movement, provided the Hapoel Hatzair movement with its fundamental ideology.

GORDON, JUDAH LOEB (1830–1892)

Foremost Hebrew poet of the Russian *Haskalah* (Enlightenment) period. Born in Vilna, he served for many years as a teacher in government sponsored Jewish schools, and was made secretary of the Society for the Promotion of Enlightenment among the Jewish masses in Russia. He contributed many of his poems to leading Hebrew periodicals, in most of which he criticized Jewish ghetto life. He advocated religious reforms, satirized bigotry and superstition in Jewish life, and attacked old-fashioned Jewish customs and practices as well as the tyranny and the restrictions imposed by the rabbis and leaders of the community. His writings and his activities for the promotion of the ideas of the enlightenment movement brought him in bitter conflict with orthodox Jewry. As a result of the pogroms in Russia in the 1880's he revised his views on the Haskalah as an answer to the Jewish problem. His poetic works were published on the occasion of his 25th anniversary as a Hebrew poet, and he received wide recognition as a militant and influential poet.

GOSHEN

The district in eastern Egypt where, according to the Bible, Jacob and his sons settled when Joseph was the ruler of the land. There the Israelites multiplied, and were enslaved by Pharaoh.

GOY

A Hebrew term applied commonly to a non-Jew. Literally the term *goy* does not have any derogatory meaning; it simply means "people." The Bible, for instance, refers to the people of Israel as *goy kadosh* (a holy people).

GRACE AFTER MEALS

The Bible says: "When thou hast eaten

and art full, then thou shalt bless the Lord for the good land which He hath given thee." Thus the practice of *Birkat ha-Mazon* (Grace after meals) is very old, although the formal texts of the grace or "bendchen" were composed at later periods. Grace is said after all meals at which bread has been eaten. The text of the grace is made up of four benedictions, including thanks to God, the creator and sustainer of all mankind; thanksgiving for the land of Israel; a prayer for God's mercy and sustenance; and a blessing of praise to God. The Grace after meals contains additional texts for Sabbath, the holidays, and other solemn occasions.

GRAETZ, HEINRICH (1817–1891)

Jewish historian. Born in Germany, he obtained his doctorate, taught at the Jewish theological seminary in Breslau, and at the university of Breslau. His greatest accomplishment was his eleven volume *Geschichte der Juden* (History of the Jews), which he published between 1853 and 1876. His history is considered the first standard work in the field. He wrote Jewish history with great knowledge, imagination and love of Judaism. He visited Palestine to study the historic scenes of the heroic events and people of ancient Israel. In many chapters of his great work he attacks the Christian world for its inhuman treatment of the Jews. He also published a shorter and more popular history of the Jews, as well as many other studies in the field of Jewish science. It must be noted that in his day there were few monographs of original research in the field, which meant that Graetz had to rely on primary source material, without the help of much secondary work. His own work has been one for historians to conjure with.

GRAND ISLAND, JEWISH COLONY OF see Noah, Mordecai Manuel.

GRATZ, REBECCA (1781–1869)

Pioneer in Jewish philanthropic work, and educator. Born in Philadelphia, Pa., of a famous American Jewish family, she became a popular figure both for her personal charm and her social activities. Sir Walter Scott, who knew her through Washington Irving, took her as the original for the character of Rebecca in his *Ivanhoe*. Rebecca Gratz became the secretary of the "Female Association for the Relief of Women and Children in Reduced Circumstances," and later founded the Philadelphia Orphan Asylum. She was interested in Jewish education, and in 1838 was one of the founders of the first Jewish Sunday School established in the United States.

GRATZ COLLEGE

The first college for the training of Jewish teachers in the United States, established in 1893 in Philadelphia.

It was named after Hyman Gratz, brother of Rebecca Gratz, who be-

Rebecca Gratz, founder of the American Jewish Sunday School movement, and the woman on whom Scott based Rebecca in his "Ivanhoe."

173

GREAT ASSEMBLY

queathed $150,000 for Jewish education. The college began its program on the premises of the Mikveh Israel Congregation, the religious school of which later became the "school of observation and practice" for student teachers. A total of over 500 teachers have been graduated from Gratz college, most of whom served in the congregational schools and Sunday schools of Philadelphia.

GREAT ASSEMBLY see Great Synagogue, Men of the.

GREAT BRITAIN see England.

GREAT SYNAGOGUE, MEN OF THE

The spiritual leaders of the Jewish people, known in Hebrew as the *Anshe Keneset ha-Gedolah*, members of the highest religious institution, *The Great Synagogue* or *The Great Assembly*, which according to tradition was established during the time of Ezra the Scribe (early period of the Second Temple), and continued for about two hundred years. Tradition maintains that the Men of the Great Synagogue formed a council of 120 members, and established numerous ordinances (*Takkanot*) with regard to prayer and other matters. They are credited with the arrangement of the *Shemoneh Esreh* (Eighteen Benedictions).

GREECE

Greece is mentioned in the Hebrew Bible (*Javan* i.e. Ionia) and there were Jews there as early as the second century b.c.e. It is also recorded that the Apostle Paul preached to the Jews of Salonica, Athens and Corinth. Little information is available about the Jewish communities in Greece during the Middle Ages, and only after 1890, when Greece won its independence, did the Jewish community there begin to play an important role. The Jewish population was greatly increased when Salonica came under Greek

Hayim Greenberg, leader of the American Labor Zionist movement, and noted writer and speaker.

rule in 1919, and in 1925 there were an estimated 125,000 Jews there. This figure was thereafter reduced, and the Jewish community was completely disrupted during the Nazi occupation and as a result of the Second World War. In 1960 there were only about 6,000 Jews in all of Greece.

GREENBERG, HAYIM (1889–1953)

Editor, essayist, lecturer, and leader of the Labor Zionist movement in the United States. Born in Bessarabia (Russia), he became one of the leaders of the *Tarbut* (Hebrew Culture) in Russia. Following the Bolshevik Revolution, he moved to Berlin where he edited *Ha-Olam*, a Hebrew periodical of the World Zionist organization. In 1924 he settled in the United States where he became editor of the *Yid-*

disher Kempfer and *The Jewish Frontier*, important publications of the Labor Zionist Organization. He won great recognition for his writings and lectures, and was the spiritual leader of the *Poale Zion*. In his last years he served as director of the department of education and culture of the Jewish Agency in America.

GUGGENHEIM FAMILY

An American family prominent in metal smelting and refining and in philanthropy. Meyer Guggenheim (1828–1905) was born in Switzerland, and came to the United States in 1847, where he eventually entered the embroidery importing business. In the late 1880's he bought a mine in Colorado, and then established smelters and refineries. His seven sons, Isaac, Daniel, Murry, Solomon, Simon, Benjamin, and William, all entered the business. Both Daniel (1856–1930) and Simon (1867–1941) established well-known philanthropic foundations. Solomon (1861–1949) endowed the Guggenheim Museum for modern art in New York City.

GUIDE FOR THE PERPLEXED see Maimonides, Moses.

H

HORAH

. . . with joy shall ye draw water

Out of the wells of salvation.

ISAIAH

HABAKKUK

HABAKKUK

One of the so-called Minor Prophets, thought to be a contemporary of Jeremiah, whose prophecy was probably uttered about 600 b.c.e. His book contains three chapters, in the first two of which he foretells the destruction of Judah by the Chaldeans. The prophet is disturbed by the possibility that the good will perish too, but he concludes that "the just will live by their faithfulness." The third chapter is a beautiful psalm in praise of God, and contains the often quoted words: "In wrath remember mercy."

HABDALAH see Havdalah.

HABIMAH

First and world renowned Hebrew theatre founded in Moscow in 1916. It was established by a great lover of Hebrew, Nahum Zemach, and a group of enthusiastic actors. Despite Bolshevik opposition to the Hebrew language and to Zionism, the Habimah acquired great friends among Russian writers and artists, and it flourished until 1926. In the following year the Habimah toured several European countries and the United States. There the company divided, and the larger group settled in Palestine, where the Habimah was reorganized and continued its great accomplishments as the foremost Hebrew theatre. Some of the better known performances of the Habimah are: An-Ski's *Dibbuk*, Pinski's *Wandering Jew*, Leivick's *Golem*, and Hofmann's *Jacob's Dream*. The above were translations, but the Habimah also successfully played a number of original Hebrew plays, and has remained a most influential cultural institution, reaching out to eager audiences in all major settlements in Israel.

HABONIM

Youth organization of the Labor Zionist Movement in the United States, England,

A scene from the original Hebrew play, "Most Cruel the King," staged at the Habimah theatre in Tel Aviv. The Habimah company's tours have met with widespread critical and popular acclaim.

South Africa, Canada, Holland and other countries. In the United States it was founded in 1935, and in 1960 it had a membership of 4,000. Habonim in America had its origin in the Young Poale Zion Alliance which was mainly a political organization. The basic program of Habonim is education toward Jewish values and Zionism, character building, and pioneer work in Israel. In the younger groups, devices such as scouting, handcraft and stories are the main tools for the attainment of the educational goals, while in the older groups greater emphasis is placed on discussions, seminars, participation in community affairs and fund raising. A successful educational feature of the Habonim movement is the summer *Camp Kvutzah*. In the twelve camps active in 1959 life was modeled after the Kibbutz (agricultural workers' settlement) in Israel. The Habonim Institute trains leaders for the movement. The Habonim organization has

become a training center for prospective *Halutzim* (Pioneers). A number of organized groups of Halutzim from the ranks of Habonim settled in Israel, and established their own *Kibbutzim*. In 1951, Habonim started the Youth Workshop in Israel. Under its auspices scores of Habonim members are given the opportunity of working and studying in Israel for a nine-month period. This program assures the continued well-being of the movement, spurs *Aliyah* (immigration) and preserves the essential character of American Habonim.

HADASSAH

Women's Zionist Organization of America founded in 1912 by Henrietta Szold. It is the largest Jewish women's organization in the world. It started with 12 women and in 1960 had reached a membership of 318,-000 in 1,320 chapters. Its initial objective was the improving of health conditions in

Children cared for by the Youth Aliyah ride a donkey at Kfar Szold, the Israeli village named in honor of Henrietta Szold, the founder of Hadassah, which is the Women's Zionist Organization of America.

ḤAD GADYA

Hadassah-Hebrew University Medical Center at Kiryat Hadassah is near the city of Jerusalem.

Palestine. During World War I, Hadassah sent an American Zionist medical unit to Palestine, which opened hospitals and dispensaries in the major centers to serve both Jewish and Arab patients. Following the war, Hadassah extended its activities by opening new hospitals, schools for nurses, various child care centers, playgrounds and school hygiene service.

One of the main activities of Hadassah was the organization of the Youth Aliyah (immigration) movement, under the auspices of the Jewish Agency for Israel.

Hadassah sponsors two Louis D. Brandeis Vocational Centers. Brandeis Center "A" in Jerusalem includes the Alice L. Seligsberg Vocational High School and the Vocational Guidance Bureau. Brandeis Center "B" in Romema includes The Fine Mechanics and Precision Instruments and The Printing Workshops.

Hadassah also helps support *Neurim*, a rural vocational center; raises money for the Jewish National Fund; and sponsors "Dollars for Supplies," a fund-raising project in America for purchase in Israel of hospital linens, garments, etc., all produced by Israel's industries.

In Israel Hadassah conducts a vast network of curative, diagnostic, and research activities. The Henrietta Szold School of Nursing, opened in 1918, had graduated over 800 nurses by 1960. The Hebrew University–Hadassah Medical School, the only medical school in Israel, which opened in 1949, had in 1960 a student

body of over 700. It provides post-graduate fellowships and facilities for research. The Hadassah–Hebrew University Medical Center was dedicated in August, 1960, and planned to begin functioning in 1961.

Hadassah conducts programs in the United States as well as in Israel. It is an N.G.O. (non-governmental organization) of the United Nations; it interprets Israel and its people to the American public; it promotes the education of the American Jew through study groups and special publications; and aids Zionist youth activities, as well as sponsoring Junior Hadassah. See *Youth Aliyah*.

ḤAD GADYA

Title and refrain of an Aramaic hymn "An Only Kid," found in the Passover Haggadah and chanted at the end of the *Seder*. Its content revolves around an only kid which father bought for two coins; it reaches a climax when God smites the Angel of Death who, in turn, then slew the butcher for killing the ox, who drank the water, which put out the fire, which burned the stick, which beat the dog, which bit the cat, which ate the kid that father bought. The "Ḥad Gadya" is an adaptation of similar old German and French doggerels and appeared for the first time in the Prague Haggadah in 1590. It has been interpreted allegorically as relating incidents in the history of the Jewish people. It may also be one of the techniques developed to maintain the children's interest till the end of the Seder.

HADOAR

The only Hebrew weekly paper published in the United States. It first appeared in 1921 as a daily Hebrew newspaper in New York City, but following its suspension it was taken over by the Histadrut Ivrit of America in 1923, and has since continued as a weekly. Until 1954 it was edited by

Menachem Ribalow, and after his death by M. Maisels. In 1959 Mosheh Yanon became editor. Hadoar also features a biweekly Hebrew supplement, *Hadoar Lanoar*, for the younger readers of the Hebrew language.

HAFTARAH

Hebrew term meaning "conclusion," applied to the selection from the Prophets read in the synagogue immediately after the reading of the Torah on Sabbaths and festivals. The reading of the Haftarah is preceded and followed by special benedictions. The child celebrating his Bar Mitzvah usually reads the Haftarah. The custom of reading a portion of the Prophets in addition to the reading of the Torah dates back to ancient times. The Haftarah generally is related in some way to the Torah portion or, if it is a special Sabbath, to the occasion.

HAGANAH

Hebrew term meaning "self-defense" applied to the "people's army" of the Jewish settlement in Palestine during the latter period of the British Mandate. The Haganah stemmed from *Hashomer* (The Guard), an organization established by the early Jewish pioneers in Palestine for the purpose of defending the Jewish colonies and workers' settlements from attacks by hostile Arabs. When the British government in Palestine opposed the armed units of Jewish self-defense, the Haganah went underground, and heroically defended the Jewish settlements from persistent Arab

Members of the Haganah, volunteer army of the Jewish settlers before the establishment of the State of Israel. Here, they are on patrol in the salt hills of Sodom near the southern end of the Dead Sea.

attacks. During World War II many of the Haganah members joined the British Army in Jewish units and fought along with the British against the German armies; undertaking daring military and humanitarian missions, they succeeded in rescuing many Jews from the Nazi forces.

The Haganah became especially active after World War II, when the British restricted Jewish immigration and brutally opposed the admission of thousands of "illegal immigrants" into Palestine. The underground units of the Haganah started a guerrilla warfare with the British military, though their main struggle was against Arab onslaughts. When the Jewish State was established in 1948, the Haganah reorganized and became part of the national Israeli army, which successfully fought the War of Liberation against the Arab invaders, and administered a swift and stunning defeat to the numerically superior Arab forces.

HAGAR

Sarah's Egyptian handmaid, who gave birth to Ishmael, the son of Abraham. After Sarah gave birth to Isaac, she insisted that Abraham expel Hagar and her son. According to tradition, the Arabic tribes are the descendants of Ishmael, the son of Abraham and Hagar.

HAGBAHAH AND GELILAH

Two Hebrew terms meaning "elevating" and "rolling-up" respectively. They refer to the practice of elevating and rolling-up the Scroll of the Torah after its reading in the synagogue. The raising and rolling-up of the Scroll of the Law are considered special honors. As the Torah is raised, the congregation rises and recites: "And this is the Law which Moses set before the Children of Israel." It is customary to finish the rolling of the Scroll before starting the reading of the Haftarah.

Elevating and rolling the Torah scrolls are a privilege for pre-Bar Mitzvah Jewish boys.

HAGGADAH (AGGADAH)

The subject matter contained in the Talmudic and Rabbinic literature is of two types: that which deals with the laws and ordinances governing religious or civil practice and life in the community is known as *Halakhah* (Law); all other matter which may be called lore, such as prayers, philosophy, theology, parable, wisdom, ethics, fable, saga, history, science, etc., is classified as *Haggadah* or *Aggadah* (narration).

The Halakhah, dealing with laws and legal discussions and interpretations, was the special province of the learned, whereas the Haggadah made its appeal also to the less educated masses. One of the *Amoraim* made this distinction: "One who teaches Halakhah is likened to one who sells precious stones which are needed and appreciated by the few; but one who teaches Aggadah is like one who sells simple but essential merchandise which is bought and needed by most people." In order to explain the meaning and implications of the Law, the Talmudists occasion-

A 15th-century Northern Italian parchment of the Passover Haggadah illuminated in colors.

ally used fables, stories and anecdotes as pertinent illustrations.

The Haggadic literature is very rich, making up one-third of the Babylonian Talmud and one-sixth of the Palestinian Talmud. It was developed during the days of the Second Commonwealth and in the course of the first six centuries c.e.; in the later period it was arranged in numerous collections. See *Midrash*.

HAGGADAH SHEL PESAḤ

The "Passover Haggadah" is the special book in Hebrew (with a few passages in Aramaic), which is used at the *Seder*. The Haggadah contains the story of the Exodus from Egypt, the explanations for the use of the symbolic objects of the Seder table, and certain prayers, psalms, hymns and songs. The contents of the Haggadah are an answer to the "Four Questions" asked at the beginning of the Seder. In effect it presents a religious philosophy of Jewish history. Much of the Haggadah text dates back to the period of the Temple in Jerusalem, with some additions from later

periods. The Haggadah has always been a popular book, and since the 13th century there have appeared hundreds of illustrated editions, some of which are extremely fine and of great artistic value.

HAGGAI

One of the so-called Minor Prophets, author of the book of the same name. Haggai prophesied during the period following the return of the Jews from Babylonia (520 b.c.e.). His book contains two chapters, in which Haggai urges the people and their leaders to rebuild the Holy Temple, and predicts the restoration of the House of David, and the coming glory of the Second Temple.

HAGIOGRAPHA

Greek term meaning "Holy Writings," applied to the books contained in the third division of the Bible. The Hebrew term for these books is *Ketuvim* (Writings). The Hagiographa contains the following books: *Psalms, Proverbs, Job*, the Five Scrolls (*Song of Songs, Ruth, Lamentations, Ecclesiastes, Esther*), *Daniel, Ezra, Nehemiah, Chronicles I* and *Chronicles II*. This division of the Bible was the last to be canonized.

HAIFA

Important and growing industrial and commercial city and seaport in Israel, at the foot of Mount Carmel. The name of Haifa is first mentioned in the Talmud; the early Jewish community there was wiped out by the Crusaders in 1100. The modern Jewish settlement in Haifa began in the 18th century, and developed especially after World War I. After the War of Liberation in 1948, most of the Arab population fled Haifa which subsequently had the third largest Jewish community in Israel. Haifa is known for its important harbor, oil refineries, mills and factories, its technical institute (Technion) and its workers' quarters and beautiful suburbs situated on the slopes of Mount Carmel (Hadar Ha-Karmel).

ḤAKHAM

Hebrew term meaning "wise man," "scholar"; also used as the title of rabbi among the Sephardi Jews.

HAKHNASAT KALLAH

A Hebrew term applied to the charitable act of providing poor girls with dowries and even trousseaus to aid their marriage. There were "Dowry Societies" in the Middle Ages.

HAKHSHARAH see Ḥalutzim.

HAKKAFOT see Simḥat Torah.

HALAKHAH

A term used to convey the sense of "legal decision," "rule of conduct," "guidance," "practice" or "law." The *Halakhah* is the foundation of Jewish religious life. The Talmud is commonly said to consist of *Aggadah*, which contains ethical teaching, theology, fable, history; and *Halakhah*, comprising the laws and ordinances of religious and civil practice in every phase of Jewish life and conduct. The Talmudists defined Halakhah as the final legal decision or concensus arrived at after thorough discussion by the teachers and the free expression of their opinions and interpretations.

Legal formulae called Halakhah were first drawn by the *Soferim* (Scribes) and later by the authorities of the Talmudic schools, such as those of Hillel and Shammai. The Halakhah was, to begin with, the *Oral Law*, those legal decisions which were handed down orally from generation to generation. With the accumulation of an extraordinary amount of legal traditions it became necessary to compile the material into some systematic classification. Thus Rabbi Akiva made a systematic collection

of *Halakhot;* Rabbi Meir based his on that of Rabbi Akiva and thereafter the final compilation of the Oral Law, called the *Mishnah*, was edited by Rabbi Judah Ha-Nasi. The next great compilation of Halakhot was made with the completion of the *Talmud*.

In the course of the ages, the Law or Halakhah became expanded as new situations developed in Jewish life, and the general principles were applied to newer cases by the rabbis, either sitting as courts of law, or expounders of the Law in the form of answers (Responsa) to those who submitted questions to them. This continuous process of legal development, which is carried on to this day, has from time to time led to further codifications for the purpose of facilitating study and decision. Some of the more famous codes were those by Maimonides (Mishneh Torah), by Joseph Karo (Shulḥan Arukh), and by Abraham Danzig (Ḥaye Adam and Ḥokhmat Adam).

The Conservative Rabbinate claims the right to interpret the Halakhah in such a way as to adapt it to modern conditions. The Reform Rabbinate, in general, disregards the Halakhah in practical life, though some of the leaders prefer to remain within the Halakhic frame of reference as much as possible. See *Codes*.

HA-LEVY, JUDAH see Judah Ha-Levi.

ḤALITZAH

The ceremony whereby a childless widow became free to be married to others than one of her deceased husband's brothers. The Jewish law, as prescribed in the Bible, enjoins such a woman from marrying anyone but her deceased husband's brother. If, however, the brother of the deceased refused to marry the widow, he might appear before the Jewish court and publicly declare his unwillingness to be united in marriage with the widow. The essence of the ceremony was the act of *Halitzah* (drawing off), that is, the widow drew off a (special) shoe from her brother-in-law, and declared: "So shall it be done unto the man that doth not build up his brother's house!" The act of Halitzah released the widow to enter a new marriage. Conveyance of real property was probably effected by the purchaser treading on the land. Hence, the removal of the shoe may symbolize the denial of taking possession. While the Bible provides two alternatives, the levirate marriage (i.e. to the brother-in-law) fell into disuse, and now only the Halitzah is practiced.

HALLAH

Hebrew name for the twisted loaf of bread eaten in Jewish homes on the Sabbath and festivals. This term was traditionally applied to the portion of the dough which was, in ancient times, separated by Jewish women and offered to the priest as a dedication to God. In later times when there was no priesthood, the separated portion of dough was instead thrown into the fire. See *Ceremonial Objects, Jewish* (Lehem Mishneh).

HALLEL

Word meaning "praise," used in the Talmud as a term for a group of Psalms (113–118 and 136) which constitute part of the ritual. Psalms 113–118 are called *Hallel ha-Mitzri* (the Egyptian Hallel), and Psalm 136 is called *Hallel ha-Gadol* (the Great Hallel). The Hallel ha-Gadol is recited during the morning service of Sabbaths and festivals, as well as at the Passover Seder. The Hallel ha-Mitzri is recited during the morning service of the festivals, on Rosh Hodesh (New Moon), on Hanukkah, and at the Passover Seder. However, on the last six days of Pesah (Passover) and on Rosh Hodesh only the so-called "half Hallel (in which the first 11 verses of

Psalms 115 and 116 are omitted) is said. The half Hallel is recited on Passover's last days, because with Egyptians dying in the Red Sea, the Talmud tells that God says, "How can you sing hymns while My creatures are drowning in the sea?"

HALLELUJAH

A refrain meaning "Praise ye the Lord," occurs at the opening or ending, or both of many Psalms. During the Second Commonwealth, the refrain was chanted during the *Hallel*. *Hallelujah* or *Alleluia* was later included in the Christian liturgy.

HALUKKAH

A Hebrew term meaning "distribution" applied to the collection of funds for the support of the pious poor Jews of Palestine. Such funds were collected in the diaspora (Jewish communities outside of Palestine), especially for the needy Jews of Jerusalem, Hebron, Safed and Tiberias, the "sacred cities." Such charity began in olden times and continued until replaced by modern fund-raising.

HALUTZIM

Hebrew term meaning "Pioneers," applied to groups of young Jews who emigrated to Palestine for the purpose of rebuilding the Jewish national homeland. The *he-Halutz* movement started in 1917, and its guiding spirit was Joseph Trumpeldor, a Russian Jew, who is also remembered as one of the chief organizers of the Jewish Legion during World War I. The main objective of the he-Halutz movement was to prepare young Jews, both physically and spiritually, for the task of settling in the Holy Land in cooperative communities—based on labor, equality and mutual ownership of economic goods. Before settling in Palestine, the he-Halutz groups underwent a training period in special *Hakhsharah* (training) farms. The

185

Hakhsharah program consisted of agricultural training, the study and use of the Hebrew language, and preparation for collective living.

The he-Halutz movement reached large numbers in Russia, Poland and Central Europe. It also developed on a smaller scale in the United States and Canada. In 1933 there were about 100,000 Halutzim throughout the world, but World War II destroyed most of the he-Halutz centers in Europe.

Most of the *Kibbutzim* (agricultural workers' settlements) in Israel were established by the Halutzim who, through labor, devotion, idealism and sacrifice, paved the way for the restoration of the Jewish homeland in Palestine.

HAMAN

Principal figure in the story of Purim who, as vizier of Persia, plotted to destroy all the Jews on the 13th day of Adar. The intervention of Mordecai and his cousin Queen Esther frustrated his plans. According to Jewish tradition, Haman was a descendant of the Amalekites, the most bitter ancient enemies of the Israelites. Haman thus became the typical Jewish enemy. As the villain in the story of Purim, he became the scorned figure in various Purim plays. During the reading of the *Megillah* (Scroll of Esther) in the synagogue, it is customary for children to stamp their feet and rattle gragers (noise-makers) at the mention of Haman's name. The special pastries eaten on Purim are called *hamantashen*. See *Purim*.

HAMELN, GLÜCKEL VON see Glückel Von Hameln.

HAMETZ

Hebrew term meaning "leavened," applied

Harvest time during the Second Aliyah shows the early Halutzim (Pioneers) in Palestine, and their primitive rakes and scythes, as they return home from the fields after the day's work.

to bread or any other baked product made of fermented dough. The Bible forbids the use of *Hametz* on Passover, and ordains the eating of *Matzah*, which is unleavened bread. The word Hametz is also applied to many other types of food and drink which tradition prohibits for use on the Passover, and also to the dishes with which Hametz has come in contact. See *Bedikat Hametz*.

HAMISHAH ASAR BI-SHEVAT see Tu Bi-Shevat.

HAMMURABI CODE see Archeology.

HANANIAH BEN TERADYON

Tanna (Talmud scholar) of the second century and one of the "Ten Martyrs" executed by the Romans during the Hadrianic persecutions. One of Hananiah's two daughters was Beruriah, mentioned in the Talmud for her piety, wisdom and scholarship. When Hadrian prohibited the teaching of the Torah under penalty of death, Hananiah disregarded the decree and was seized by the Romans, who sentenced him and his wife to death. He was wrapped in the scroll of the Torah and burned at the stake, while his daughter and disciples watched his agony. When asked "Master, what dost thou see?" he replied, "I see parchment burning, but the letters of the Torah soar upward." Thus he demonstrated the Jewish faith in the ultimate triumph of the spirit of Judaism. It is said that his executioner, overpowered by the suffering and courage of Hananiah, plunged into the flames.

HANINA BEN DOSA

Tanna (Talmud scholar) of the first century c.e., contemporary of R. Johanan ben Zakkai, and known as a miracle worker and healer of the sick. Despite his great piety, he lived in extreme poverty, and other Tannaim said of him that a voice from heaven was heard daily, declaring "The whole world is fed by reason of the

In the old Maccabean tradition, an Israeli soldier tells his young son the story of Ḥanukkah.

merit of My son Ḥanina, but Ḥanina himself is satisfied with a measure of carobs weekly." Some of Ḥanina's words of wisdom are: "He whose works exceed his wisdom shall have his wisdom endure"; and "He who pleases people, also pleases God."

HANNAH

Mother of the prophet Samuel. Childless, her silent prayer at the Shrine of Shiloh was answered by God. Hannah is also the traditional name of the heroic Jewish mother who chose to die with her seven sons rather than betray their faith, as enjoined by the tyrant Antiochus against whom the Maccabees were fighting.

ḤANUKKAH

Hebrew term meaning "dedication," and name of the post-Biblical holiday, the "Feast of Lights" or "Feast of Dedication." Ḥanukkah begins on the 25th day of the month of *Kislev* and lasts for eight days. It commemorates the Maccabean victory

over the Syrians in 165 b.c.e., and the re-dedication of the Temple which had been defiled by the tyrant Antiochus, king of Syria. Since the days of Judas Maccabeus, Ḥanukkah has been celebrated by lighting candles for eight days as a reminder of the miracle of the cruse of oil which burned for eight days instead of one. The lighting of the candles is accompanied by blessings and the chanting of the hymn *Maoz Tzur* (Rock of Ages). The festival of Ḥanukkah is popular with children, who enjoy lighting the candles, receiving traditional gifts of money (Ḥanukkah Gelt), and playing appropriate games, especially the "Dreidel," a top with four Hebrew letters: Nun, Gimmel, Hé, Shin, interpreted as the initials of the phrase *Nes Gadol Hayah Sham* ("A great miracle happened there"). Ḥanukkah in Jewish life represents the ever recurring attempts to destroy Judaism. It probably records the first struggle for religious freedom in human history. Purim speaks of physical anti-Semitism, where the enemy Haman urged the annihilation of the people; whereas Antiochus was concerned not with their physical destruction, but with the forsaking of their religion for paganism. Thus Purim and Ḥanukkah represent both sides of the coin of anti-Semitism, hatred of the Jew and hatred of the Jewish religion respectively.

ḤANUKKAT HA-BAYIT

Hebrew term meaning "inauguration or dedication of the house," referring to an ancient Jewish custom of celebrating the consecration of a new private dwelling or public building. The custom is still observed, and the completion of a home, a synagogue, or other community structure is usually celebrated with special rites.

HAPOEL HAMIZRACHI

Zionist labor organization of orthodox Jews established in 1921. Its main objective

Hapoel Hatzair dancers, imbued with the spirit of A. D. Gordon's "Religion of Labor," perform an Israeli folk dance. Hapoel Hatzair helped to establish the "Histadrut," and later became a part of the Mapai.

was the rebuilding of the Jewish homeland "according to the principles of the Torah." In Israel the Hapoel Hamizrachi is essentially a trade union movement, maintaining its own *Kibbutzim* (agricultural labor settlements). In 1957 it amalgamated with Mizrachi. See *Mizrachi.*

HAPOEL HATZAIR

Hebrew term meaning "The Young Worker," the first Jewish labor party in Palestine, founded in Petah Tikvah in 1906. From the outset, its primary objective was the rebuilding of the Jewish homeland through Jewish labor. Since private enterprise in Palestine often refused to hire Jewish workers, using instead cheaper Arab labor, the Hapoel Hatzair fought for *Kibbush Avodah* (conquest by labor). that is, the penetration of Jewish workers into all productive work enterprises of the land, especially agriculture. Side by side with its successful campaign to strengthen the position of Jewish labor

in Palestine, Hapoel Hatzair has also endeavored to raise the educational, social and cultural level of the Jewish worker, and was particularly successful in the revival of Hebrew as the spoken and literary language of modern Palestine. In 1907 it established its own weekly, *Hapoel Hatzair,* which is still a leading publication.

Hapoel Hatzair organized Deganiah, the first cooperative agricultural settlement in Palestine, which was later followed by other similar settlements. Among the leaders of Hapoel Hatzair were Aaron David Gordon, Joseph Sprinzak, Joseph Baratz and Ḥayim Arlosoroff. In 1920, Hapoel Hatzair helped to establish the *Histadrut,* and in 1930 merged with *Aḥdut Ha-Avodah* to form *Mapai.*

HARKAVY, ALEXANDER (1863–1939)

Prominent student of the Yiddish language, and journalist. Born in Russia, he was educated in Vilna and migrated to the United States in 1882. In addition to his

189

ḤAROSET

Alexander Harkavy, scholar and educator, was a prominent Yiddish philologist and linguist.

Yiddish journalistic work and his textbooks for the teaching of English to adults, his major accomplishment was the compilation of the "English-Yiddish Encyclopedic Dictionary" (1891), the "Dictionary of the Yiddish Language" (1898), and the two-volume "Hebrew-Yiddish-English Dictionary" (1926). Largely owing to his efforts, as well as to other circumstances, Yiddish became recognized as a modern language, and its literature and grammar became part of the curriculum of numerous academic institutions.

ḤAROSET

A mixture of apples, nuts, wine, and spices in which the *Maror* (bitter herbs) is dipped during the Passover *Seder* as a reminder of the clay used by the enslaved Israelites in Egypt to make bricks. It probably also serves as a condiment with which to flavor the Maror and make it more palatable. See *Seder*.

ḤASDAI IBN SHAPRUT (915-975)

Physician, diplomat and patron of Jewish learning in Spain, Ḥasdai served under two Cordova caliphs, and carried out important diplomatic missions.

A famous scholar, he surrounded himself with learned Jews of his day and sponsored important literary works. With him, it is said, was inaugurated the *Golden Era* of Jewish literature in Spain. As head of the Jewish community, he not only financially supported the Talmud academies in Babylonia, but also helped make Spain a new center of Talmudic studies. Ḥasdai's name is particularly remembered in connection with his correspondence with Joseph, king of the Khazars, who embraced Judaism.

HASHOMER HATZAIR

"The Young Guard," world socialist Zionist youth organization founded in Poland in 1914. It originally started as a Jewish national scout movement, but after World War I its program emphasized the training of pioneers (Ḥalutzim) for immigration and settlement in Palestine on collective farms (Kibbutzim). The movement spread from Poland to other European countries, the United States and Canada. Before World War II the total world organization of *Hashomer Hatzair* had a membership of about 60,000 with half that number in Poland. The first groups of the Hashomer Hatzair settled in Palestine in 1919. The Kibbutzim of Hashomer Hatzair are affiliated in the *Kibbutz Artzi*, a member organization of the *Histadrut* (General Federation of Jewish Workers in Israel). Hashomer Hatzair in Israel supported the *Mapam*, the left-wing workers' party in Israel.

Typical Ḥasidim from pre-World War II Poland wear the usual clothing, beards and earlocks.

HASIDEANS (ASIDEANS)

Greek form of Hebrew *Ḥasidim* (The Pious Ones), those Jews who readily martyred themselves in the strict observance of Judaism and vigorously opposed the infiltration of the Hellenistic way of life which began to spread among the Jews of Palestine in the third century b.c.e. The Hasideans were especially active during the period of the Maccabean revolt and many of them joined the army of Judas Maccabeus in the fight for religious freedom and for the restoration of Jewish worship in the Temple which had been defiled by the tyrant Antiochus. The Hasideans had no definite political program. Their only aim was to uphold the traditional Jewish way of life. The Hasideans gradually disappeared as a distinct group. It is thought that the Pharisees ab-

sorbed them, becoming ultimately the significant group in Jewish life in the last centuries before the destruction of the Temple in Jerusalem.

ḤASIDISM

A religious movement which originated among the Jews of Poland in the 18th century, and during the following two centuries affected almost half of world Jewry. Its adherents were then called and still are known as *Ḥasidim* (singular, *Ḥasid*—pious).

Ḥasidism came about as a result of a number of factors, some of which were: 1) The spiritual and economic depression resulting from the *Cossack Massacres* in the 17th century; 2) The frustration among the Jewish masses resulting from the collapse of the messianic movement initiated by Shabbetai Tzevi; 3) Talmudic scholarship and the intellectualism of the Talmudist was inaccessible, incomprehensible, and unsatisfying to the Jewish uninformed masses; 4) The Jewish masses were ready to accept mystic teachings that would assure them of new hope, promise of happiness and closeness to God.

The founder of Ḥasidism was Israel Baal Shem Tov or the *Besht* as he was popularly called. Starting as a *Kabbalist* and miracle worker, the Besht began to preach a living faith in which the ordinary individual found comfort and a way to approach God. He taught that sincere devotion, zeal and heartfelt prayers are more acceptable to God than great learning, and that He can best be served through deep-seated joy rather than solemnity and intellectualism.

The Ḥasidic movement spread rapidly, continuing to grow after the death of the Besht under new leaders. Under the guidance of Rabbi Baer of Meseritz, the Ḥasidim began to look upon the Ḥasidic "rebbe," called the *Tzaddik* (righteous man), as almost the intermediary between God and man. Dynasties of *Tzaddikim* were established, each Tzaddik having his own enthusiastic and devoted followers.

As the Ḥasidic movement grew, the Talmudists began to oppose and even persecute the Ḥasidim. They were called *Mitnagdim* (opponents) and in Lithuania the great Talmudist Elijah, known as the *Gaon of Vilna*, issued a ban against the Ḥasidim and synagogues established by them. It would seem that misguided enthusiasm led a number of the Ḥasidim to violate some basic religious precepts. The persecution of the Ḥasidim by the Mitnagdim led them to seek the intervention of the government. The Ḥasidic teacher, Rabbi Shneour Zalman, was imprisoned twice, but after investigations by government officials the Ḥasidic sect was given full freedom. However, the opposition continued and for many years there was no intermarriage between Mitnagdim and Ḥasidim. Later the rift diminished, and other issues became important in Jewish life, such as the *Haskalah* (enlightenment) movement of the 19th century which was felt as a threat to the teachings and beliefs of both the Mitnagdim and the Ḥasidim.

Ḥasidism, although still practiced, has lost its significance as a mass movement, even though its renewed vigor is expressed in the life of numerous smaller groups. The Ḥasidim modified the ritual by adopting some elements used by the Spanish Jews, and to this day Mitnagdim use the Ashkenazic (German) or Polish rite, while the Ḥasidim use a modified form of the Sephardic (Spanish) rite in their services. There are numerous variations within each rite. See *Baal Shem Tov.*

HASKALAH

A Hebrew term meaning "enlightenment" derived from the word "sekhel" (intelligence), and applied to a movement among Jews to bring "enlightenment" or to modernize Jews and Judaism. The movement of the *Haskalah* began in the middle of the 18th century in Germany, and spread to Austria, Poland and Russia.

The *Maskilim* (proponents of the *Haskalah*) believed that Jews were persecuted because they differed from the non-Jews in culture, language, education, dress and manners. Their contention was that as soon as Jews could modernize their schools, learn the spoken language of the land, increase their knowledge of modern science and art, and adapt their manners to those of their neighbors, they would be treated as equal citizens and become emancipated politically and socially.

The champion of the Haskalah movement in Germany was Moses Mendelssohn, who translated the Pentateuch (Five Books of Moses) into German with modern commentaries (Biur) written by himself and other Jewish scholars. The purpose of the translators was to teach German to the Jews. As a result of the efforts of the followers of Mendelssohn, modern Jewish schools were established in the major cities in Germany, and "Ha-Meassef," a Hebrew periodical, was started in order to "fight the battles of light against darkness" and to free the Jews from the shackles of ghetto life.

The Maskilim in Austria, Poland and Russia followed the pattern of the *Haskalah* movement in Germany, with the exception that in Poland and Russia Yiddish and Hebrew were used in addition to the Russian language as instruments for the modernization of contemporary Jewish life and culture.

As was to be expected, the work of the Maskilim was challenged and opposed by many leaders of orthodox Jewry. Many of the orthodox saw in Haskalah a great threat to Judaism and a source of assimilation. Indeed, many of the Maskilim did throw off the yoke of Jewish tradition, and in their effort to identify themselves with the culture of the land, became estranged from Judaism. In some instances they left the Jewish faith entirely. The Tsars favored the Haskalah and instituted "modern" schools in the Pale. The Jewish masses in Poland and Russia soon realized that the attempts of the government to encourage the Haskalah movement, by establishing such modern Jewish schools, were only a trap, a calculated means for the Russification of the Jewish people. The hopes of the Maskilim themselves were finally shattered because the modernization of Jewish life did not prevent the government from persecuting the Jews and provoking pogroms as well as decreeing anti-Jewish legislation. Consequently, many Jewish leaders came to believe that the only solution to the Jewish problem was the establishment of a Jewish national home. The movement of Haskalah became one of the potent factors in the initiation and propagation of the Zionist movement. See *Krochmal, N.; Levinsohn, I. B.; Lilienblum, M. L.; Mapu, A.; Smolenskin, P.; Wessely, N. H.*

HASMONEANS

Family name of the Maccabean dynasty that ruled in Judea from 141 to 37 b.c.e. The surname of *Ḥasmonai* is first associated with Simon, the father of Mattathias who, together with his five brave sons, rose up against Syrian rule. This revolt ended in the Maccabean victory celebrated on the feast of Ḥanukkah.

HATIKVAH

Hebrew term meaning "The Hope," name of the Jewish (and now Israel national) anthem. It was written by the poet Naphtali Herz Imber, and set to music by Samuel Cohen, one of the Palestinian colonists who presumably adapted a Sephardic

Copy of the Hatikvah, Jewish national anthem, published in 1886, and its author, N. H. Imber.

melody, or perhaps a tune from one of Smetana's works. It became the hymn of the Zionist movement in 1898, and the official national anthem of Israel on the establishment of the State, at which time the concluding words of the refrain were modified to suit the changed condition.

HAVDALAH

Hebrew term meaning "separation," applied to a special prayer and ceremony in the home and in the synagogue declaring the end of the Sabbath or a festival. Benedictions are recited over a cup of wine, (and on Saturday night, also over spices called *Besamim*, and a braided candle), and contain praise of the Lord "who maketh a separation between the sacred and the secular" (that is, between the holiness of the Sabbath or festival and the secular nature of the weekdays). If a festival is celebrated on Saturday night the words are "between

Havdalah, the ceremony in which leave is taken of the "Sabbath Queen," as shown in a Dutch woodcut of the Minhagim Book, 1662.

holy and holy" (that is, the greater holiness of the Sabbath and the lesser holiness of the festivals). In such case no spices are used, and instead of a braided candle, the candles which have been kindled in honor of the festival are used. The Havdalah ceremony, marking the conclusion of the day of rest, parallels the Kiddush which ushers in the sacred days.

HAZZAN

Hebrew name for "Cantor," the official in the synagogue who leads the worshippers in prayer. The term was originally used to designate "a servant of the synagogue," *Hazzan ha-Keneset*, who was sexton, beadle and superintendent. In recent centuries his function became limited to chanting the service. Larger congregations engage a *Hazzan* for the entire year, while in smaller congregations he is usually engaged only for the services on Rosh Hashanah and Yom Kippur.

In many congregations in the United States, the Hazzan also assumes the function of religious school director. Yeshiva University, The Jewish Theological Seminary of America, and Hebrew Union College sponsor special institutions for the training of Hazzanim.

194

HAZKARAT NESHAMOT see Yizkor.

HAZOR see Archeology.

HÉ (ה)

The fifth letter of the Hebrew alphabet. It is sounded like the English H. Final *Hé* is silent; when it has a *Mappik* (dot inside) it is aspirated. Its numerical value is 5. When followed by an apostrophe, it may have the value of 5000; or it may be a symbol for the Lord's name.

HEAVEN

The word "heaven" may either refer to the sky in the physical sense, or to the "spiritual heaven," the place where the righteous dead abide. In Hebrew it is called *Gan Eden*. See *Death; Gan Eden.*

HEBREW IMMIGRANT AID SOCIETY see HIAS.

HEBREW LANGUAGE

The language of the Jewish people since ancient times, in which Biblical and much post-Biblical literature is written. Hebrew belongs to the northwest Semitic family of languages. It is called *Leshon ha-Kodesh* ("the Holy Tongue," or perhaps "the language of the Sanctuary") because even when Aramaic displaced Hebrew as the daily language of the people during the Second Commonwealth, Hebrew remained the language used for holy purposes, such as the liturgy in the Temple and later in the synagogue, as well as much of the other literature, both legal and folkloristic.

The Jews throughout their history in the diaspora spoke the respective languages of the people among whom they lived. They would modify the languages in order to accommodate them to religious needs by introducing Hebrew ritualistic terms. Among such dialects are Judeo-Arabic, Judeo-Spanish (Ladino), and Judeo-German. The latter dialect developed into an independent language, Yiddish.

Despite the fact that Hebrew ceased to be the spoken language of the Jewish people some time during the period of the Second Commonwealth, it was kept alive in all periods of Jewish history. The knowledge of Hebrew has always been an essential requirement of Jewish education, consisting of the study of the Bible in the original, and a reading knowledge of the Hebrew prayers. Hebrew thus became one of the strongest links which held the Jew-

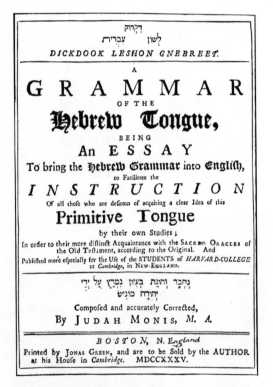

Title page of Judah Monis' "Grammar" published for Harvard College in the year 1735.

ish people together during the many centuries of Jewish existence in the diaspora.

The Hebrew language, the literature of which covers a period of over 3,000 years, has gone through many changes in grammatical form and vocabulary content. During the first thousand years of Jewish history, known as the Biblical period, Hebrew was a spoken language; during the following two thousand years Hebrew

was mainly used for literary purposes and as the language of worship; in modern times, especially through the *Haskalah* and Zionist movements, Hebrew once again became a living language with a rich and modern literature as exemplified in prose and poetry of Aḥad Ha-Am, Bialik and Tschernikhovski. Today it is the national language spoken in the State of Israel. See *Ben-Yehudah, Eliezer.*

HEBREW SHELTERING AND IMMIGRANT AID SOCIETY see HIAS.

HEBREW THEOLOGICAL COLLEGE

An orthodox rabbinical seminary, known in Hebrew as "Bet Ha-Midrash Le-Torah," organized in 1921 in Chicago, Illinois. Its purpose is to train orthodox rabbis and teachers, and to offer courses of higher Jewish learning for the general Jewish public. The seminary resembles, both in curriculum and method, the Yeshivot (Talmudical Academies) of most of eastern Europe.

HEBREW UNION COLLEGE—JEWISH INSTITUTE OF RELIGION

The oldest rabbinical seminary in the United States, founded by Rabbi Isaac Mayer Wise in 1875, in Cincinnati, Ohio, under the name of Hebrew Union College. It is the institution of reform Judaism for the training of American rabbis "who combine a modern American education with a knowledge of Jewish lore." The Board of Governors of the College is made up of 31 members, 19 of whom represent its original sponsoring body, the Union of American Hebrew Congregations, and the remaining members representing the Alumni Association and the Central Conference of American Rabbis.

In 1947 Hebrew Union College combined with the Jewish Institute of Religion, a graduate school, founded in New York City by Rabbi Stephen Samuel Wise in

1922, its purpose being to prepare students for the Jewish ministry, for research and for community service. Dr. Wise envisioned a non-denominational seminary. Thus its faculty included renowned scholars, orthodox as well as non-orthodox. The combined institution, known as Hebrew Union College–Jewish Institute of Religion, has since taken on a predominantly reform attitude.

In addition to training for the rabbinate, the College-Institute operates a school for cantors and educators; maintains one of the largest libraries of Hebraica and Judaica; and publishes scientific works through the Hebrew Union College Press. It has schools in New York and in Los Angeles, and in 1960 was in the process of building a post-graduate school in Jerusalem. Many outstanding scholars serve on the faculty of the College-Institute, headed by its president (1960), the distinguished archeologist, Dr. Nelson Glueck. Many of the rabbis ordained by the College-Institute have become leading figures in American Jewish life.

HEBREW UNIVERSITY OF JERUSALEM

At the first Zionist Congress in 1897, the plan of establishing a Hebrew University in Jerusalem was propounded, and 28 years later (1925) this plan was inaugurated on Mount Scopus. The University began as a research institution in the field of Jewish studies, but gradually added and developed other departments, such as Arabic and Oriental Studies, Palestine Natural History, Hygiene, Chemistry, Physics, Mathematics, Philosophy, History and Letters, Biology, Education, Medicine, Agriculture, Law, and Social Sciences. The University offers undergraduate and graduate courses leading to higher degrees in these various fields. The average number of students until 1933 was about 200. As of 1960 the student body numbered

Lord Arthur James Balfour addressing an audience at a dedication ceremony for Hebrew University on Mount Scopus in Jerusalem. Around him are Chaim Weizmann, Judah Magnes and Lord Herbert Samuel.

almost 7,500. During the Nazi rule many Jewish intellectuals of world reputation came to the University from Germany and other European countries to serve as professors and lecturers.

After the establishment of the State of Israel and the War of Liberation, the site of the University on Mount Scopus was isolated in Arab-held territory, and its various departments were as a result established in makeshift quarters in the Israeli sector of Jerusalem. By 1960 a great new central campus was being developed at Givat Ram and new schools of medicine and nursing were rising at Ein Karem.

The University is supported by endowments and through fund raising activities in the United States, especially by the organization known as American Friends of the Hebrew University.

HEBREWS

A term applied to persons of Jewish de-

scent. The Patriarch Abraham was the first to be known as a *Hebrew* (Ivri). Some authorities maintain that the word "Hebrew" is derived from *Eber* meaning "the other side," which refers to Abraham's crossing from the "other side of the river" (Euphrates or Jordan) upon entering the land of Canaan. In the course of its history the Jewish people were known under the names: Children of Israel, Israelites, Hebrews, Judeans and Jews. Some scholars believe that the term Hebrew is related to the "Habiru" mentioned in the Tel el Amarna tablets of the 15th century b.c.e. A citizen of modern Israel is known as an Israeli.

HEBRON (HEVRON)

Located about 200 miles south of Jerusalem. This is one of the four sacred cities of Palestine, the others being Jerusalem, Tiberias and Safed. It is mentioned in the Bible as the city near which the burial-

Some of the new buildings and part of the campus of Hebrew University of Jerusalem at its new location in Givat Ram. The original Mt. Scopus buildings were isolated in Arab-held territory in the 1948 war.

A typical old-fashioned Ḥeder scene giving the atmosphere and demonstrating the method of the schools in which generations of Jewish children were formally introduced to their fathers' tradition.

place of the Patriarchs (the Cave of Machpelah) is found, and as the capital of King David before the conquest of Jerusalem. Since the return from Babylonian captivity, Hebron has had a Jewish community, which at different periods has been exposed to persecution. Hebron is now located within the state of Jordan.

ḤEDER

Traditional Hebrew elementary school. It was an established institution in most Jewish communities and was attended by practically all boys, and occasionally by girls, where they received instruction in Hebrew reading, prayers, Hebrew Bible and Rashi's

Mosque above the Cave of Machpelah, the place where the Bible says the Patriarchs were buried. The land was originally bought by Abraham from the Hittites as a burial place for Sarah, and was used to bury his descendants.

commentary on the Torah, as well as Talmud. The child was started at a very early age, even as young as four years. Until modern times, the only education received by Jewish children was in the Ḥeder, since very few Jewish boys and girls attended secular government schools. The traditional Ḥeder was a one-room school, usually in the house of the "Rebbe" or "Melammed" (teacher of the very young), where boys attended most of the day, and in the case of more advanced pupils, in the evening as well. In the United States the term "Ḥeder" is occasionally applied to a Talmud Torah or a modern Hebrew school, open on weekdays during the afternoon hours, and on Sundays. See *Talmud Torah*.

HEFKER

A Hebrew term used in rabbinical literature to designate any unclaimed or ownerless property, both real and personal. "Hefker" is usually the property left by one who dies without heirs, property deliberately renounced by the owner, and property consisting of lost unclaimed objects. One who claims such property must assume the responsibilities of ownership.

HE-ḤALUTZ see Ḥalutzim.

HEIFETZ, JASCHA

Famous violinist. Born in Vilna in 1899, he became a sensation at the age of six when he made his debut playing Mendelssohn's Violin Concerto. At the age of eight he became a pupil at the St. Petersburg Conservatory, and soon started successful tours in the capital cities of Europe, where he was acclaimed as a great virtuoso. In 1917 he made his first appearance in the United States, and has since enjoyed world-wide reputation as one of the most accomplished violinists of his time.

HEINE, HEINRICH (1797–1856)

One of the most famous poets and essayists of the 19th century. Born in Germany, he gave up a business career and studied law at Bonn and other universities in preparation for public office. When he settled in Berlin, he published his first book of poetry which made him universally famous. He came under the influence of Moses Mendelssohn and Leopold Zunz and helped establish the "Society for the Culture and Science of Judaism." In 1825 he embraced Christianity to further his opportunities for receiving appointment to public office. Years later he openly expressed his regret for leaving the Jewish faith, and in many of his literary works such as "The Rabbi of Bacherach," "Hebrew Melodies" and others he showed great admiration for and interest in Judaism and its problems.

Because of his pro-French political attitude he chose to leave Germany and settle

Heinrich Heine, German poet and essayist, was known as an acute political critic and a significant influence on the Haskalah movement.

in Paris, where he continued his brilliant journalistic and poetic career. Despite his lack of popularity with the Jews because of his conversion, and with the Germans because of his criticism of Germany, he was admired for his great poetry. As a poet, Heine exercised great influence on the Jewish *Haskalah* (Enlightenment) movement, and on both Hebrew and Yiddish poetry.

HEKDESH

Hebrew term applied to an institution which used to serve as a poorhouse, an inn for strangers and as an infirmary for the sick and the aged. The *Hekdesh* developed in the Middle Ages, and continued to exist as a popular charitable institution in most European Jewish communities until recent times. The Hekdesh in its day was a useful institution, despite what in our day would be considered inadequate facilities. It was replaced by modern social service agencies and institutions.

HEKHSHER

Hebrew term applied to a permit issued by a religious authority such as a rabbi, attesting that the foods under question are ritually fit for use or "kosher" according to Jewish dietary laws. All meats throughout the year, as well as all foods for Passover, are under strict supervision of a Jewish religious authority (*Mashgiah*, supervisor), and when they meet with the requirements of the dietary laws, a *Hekhsher* for their use is issued in the form of a written declaration or special stamp or identifying mark. In the United States and Canada many foods bear the insignia of a U with a surrounding O. This "Ⓤ" testifies to the approval of the Union of Orthodox Jewish Congregations of America.

HELL

Judaism does not teach a specific concept of hell. It is assumed that evildoers will be punished, but the manner and place of chastisement are left to the justice of God. See *Death; Gehinnom.*

HELLENISM

A term applied to ancient Greek civilization in general, and in Jewish history to its influence on Jewish thinking and literature. The influence of *Hellenism* on the Jews began during the time of the conquest of Alexander the Great and lasted for about seven centuries. Judea was under the control of Hellenistic rulers for some two centuries, during which period Jews were brought into close contact with the modified Greek culture, language, art, literature and religion known as Hellenistic civilization. The attempt of the foreign rulers to impose Hellenistic culture and worship in Judea led to a bitter conflict resulting in the Maccabean revolt, and to Jewish independence from Hellenistic rule. However, in the diaspora (Jewish communities outside Judea), Greek cul-

ture continued to influence Jewish thought for several centuries. Under that influence the Bible was translated into Greek; Philo and Josephus wrote their works in Greek; and many Greek words are found in the Talmud. Jewish thinkers began to interpret the Jewish religion in the light of Greek philosophy, and some of the *Jewish Wisdom Literature* was influenced by Greek thought. Although Hellenism exercised its greatest influence on Judaism during the Greek and Roman periods, it was later revived after the Crusades and brought to the knowledge of Jews as well as Christians through translation into Arabic, Latin, etc. Attempts to harmonize Jewish and Greek ideas were made by Saadiah Gaon, Maimonides, Ibn Gabirol and others.

Matthew Arnold wrote a famous essay on "Hebraism and Hellenism." In summarizing the major difference between Hebraism and Hellenism it may be said that to the Jews virtue meant righteous life, and to the Hellenist, physical excellence; Jews sought the knowledge of God, and Hellenists sought the knowledge of nature. For Hebraism virtue is beauty; for Hellenism beauty is virtue. The Jew welcomed the ideals of the Greek but refused to be assimilated into the Greek ideal. Or, as the Talmud states it: "The beauty of Japheth (the Greeks) in the tents of Shem (the Jews)."

HEREM

Hebrew term meaning "excommunication" or "anathema." In ancient Jewish history the *Herem* was a prohibition placed upon the use of spoils taken during a war, which had to be destroyed. In later times the rabbis used the Herem as a punishment of individuals for certain offenses regarded as detrimental to the Jewish community. The milder type of Herem, called "Niddui," was a short-term ban by which the individual was cut off from social and business contacts. The more severe type of Herem, in the form of a complete boycott or excommunication for an indefinite period, was used as a punishment against heretics or followers of certain sects whose practices and ideas were regarded by the rabbis and Jewish communal leaders as detrimental to the welfare of the Jewish people and to the principles of Judaism. This type of Herem was proclaimed, for instance, against Uriel Acosta and Baruch Spinoza, and against the followers of the "false messiahs" Shabbetai Tzevi and Jacob Frank, as well as against some of the leaders of the Hasidic movement in its early beginnings.

The Herem was a powerful weapon against transgressors and wrongdoers. In modern times it has fallen into disuse.

HEROD

King of Judea from 40 to 4 b.c.e. and founder of the Herodian dynasty. Although surnamed "the Great," he is considered the most unpopular king in Jewish history because of his tyranny, extreme cruelty and slavish obedience to the Romans. He was the son of Antipater, a descendant of the Idumeans. As virtual ruler of Judea under the protection of the Romans, Antipater appointed Herod governor of Galilee. When he was proclaimed king of Judea after Antipater was poisoned, he perpetrated on the country an unparalleled reign of terror, including the wholesale murder of Jewish leaders as well as members of his own family. To counter the bad impression and to win the favor of the Jewish masses, he married Mariamne of the Hasmonean family, and remodeled the Temple which thus became known as the most beautiful structure of the time. However, there was nothing that Herod could do to befriend the people because of his total disregard for Jewish tradition and

national interests, and his mad thirst for power. In his constant fear of conspiracy against him, Herod put to death his wife Mariamne, her mother, his brother-in-law, his sons, and hundreds of Jewish scholars and other leaders. In order that his death should not become a cause of rejoicing in the country, it is said that he ordered the most prominent men to be killed on the day of his death.

HERUT

A political party in Israel known for its extreme militant and nationalistic stand on questions of foreign and domestic affairs of the country. Herut demands an aggressive policy against the Arab nations, and advocates the expansion of the territory of Israel. Many of the adherents of this party are former members of the *Irgun Tzevai Leumi*, an extremist military group during the British regime in Palestine under the Mandate. See *Revisionists*.

HERZL, THEODOR (1860–1904)

Founder of political Zionism, the World Zionist Organization, and the Zionist Congress. Born in Budapest, he studied for the bar in Vienna, but practised journalism as his career, and was successful both as journalist and as playwright. As correspondent and later literary editor of the "Neue Freie Presse" he became interested in various aspects of the Jewish problem.

The famous "Dreyfus Affair" in Paris, involving a Jewish captain in the French army who was falsely accused of selling military secrets to Germany, brought about a wave of anti-Semitism that hastened Herzl's decision to seek a solution to the plight of the Jewish people. In 1896 he wrote a brochure entitled "The Jewish State" in which he outlined a program of political Zionism, stating that the only solution to the Jewish problem was the establishment of a Jewish State, legally recog-

This unusual photograph of Theodor Herzl shows him with his family in the role of a father rather than as father of the Jewish state. The picture was taken in Austria about 1890 where Herzl then lived.

nized and sanctioned by most of the great world powers.

His ideas seemed fantastic and impractical, and aroused the opposition of assimilated Jews, many orthodox Jews and even some "Lovers of Zion," the leader of which group was the great Hebrew essayist *Aḥad Ha-Am*. Despite the opposition, Herzl almost single-handedly began his campaign to influence European statesmen in behalf of the Zionist cause. In 1897 he convened in Basle the first Zionist World Congress, out of which the World Zionist Organization was established. Herzl's major endeavor was to secure from the Sultan in Constantinople a charter legalizing free mass-immigration of Jews into Palestine to establish a Jewish autonomy.

To further this objective, he was received in audience by Wilhelm II, the German emperor, who seemed interested in the Zionist program. However, Herzl's

contacts with the major European statesmen, including the Sultan, did not bring any favorable results. In desperation Herzl was ready to accept a "Jewish Territory" elsewhere, such as Uganda in East Africa, proposed by the British colonial office as a temporary solution. However, Herzl's ardent followers in eastern Europe, representing the bulk of the Jewish masses, vigorously opposed any substitute for the Jewish historical homeland.

This defeat convinced Herzl and most of his followers that all the efforts of the Zionist organization must be directed to secure Palestine as the national home for the Jewish people. As a result of his visit to Palestine he wrote "Altneuland," a novel depicting a modern Jewish state in the ancient land of Israel, and ending in the words "If you will it, it is no legend," which became the slogan of Zionist hopes and activities for the years to come. Herzl's health was affected by his untiring activities and anxieties, and in 1904 he died of a heart attack.

He was mourned by the Jewish people, throughout the world, and his followers pledged themselves to continue his work and bring it to fulfillment. His dream came true in 1948, when the State of Israel was proclaimed. His remains were brought from Vienna to Jerusalem, where they rest on *Har Herzl* (Mount Herzl), as the symbol of a great leader who labored brilliantly and devotedly for the rebirth and salvation of his beloved people. Herzl is considered one of the greatest personalities of Jewish history. See *Zionism*.

ḤESHVAN

The second Hebrew month, also known as "Marḥeshvan," corresponding to October-November in the civil calendar, and having either 29 or 30 days.

HESPED

Hebrew term for a funeral oration, delivered in the home, the funeral parlor, the synagogue, or at the grave of the deceased. Such eulogies date back to Biblical times, and usually contain an account of the virtuous life, the good deeds and accomplishments of the departed one, as well as an admonition to the survivors to emulate the good life of the deceased.

HESS, MOSES (1812–1875)

Zionist philosopher and socialist. Born in Germany, he became an advocate of socialism and a champion of the cause of the proletariat. He was influenced by the philosophy of Spinoza and shared the socialist ideas of Marx and Engels. As a Jew he did not accept the idea that socialism, assimilation or religious reform would solve the Jewish problem. In his book *Rome and Jerusalem*, written in 1862, which has become a classic in Zionist liter-

Moses Hess, a forerunner of modern Zionism, influenced such men as Aḥad Ha-Am and Herzl.

ature, he calls for the return of the Jewish people to Palestine and the establishment of a Jewish commonwealth based on social justice. He also points to the peril of assimilation, and advocates Jewish independent existence and the revival and continuation of Jewish tradition, religion and Hebrew culture. His ideas had great influence on Theodor Herzl, founder of political Zionism, and on Aḥad Ha-Am, according to whom Palestine was to serve chiefly as a cultural and spiritual center for world Jewry.

ḤET see Sin.

ḤET (ח)

The eighth letter of the Hebrew alphabet, sounded like the *ch* in the Scottish word *loch*. In our day the *Ḥet* and the *Khaf* are pronounced alike; however, some Sephardi

A Ḥevra Kaddisha (burial society) glass painted in Bohemia in 1692 shows an old funeral.

Jews retain the difference which undoubtedly obtained in ancient times. Perhaps one is properly uvular and the other guttural. The numerical value of Ḥet is 8. See *Kaf*.

ḤEVRA KADDISHA

An Aramaic term meaning "holy society," denoting a Jewish burial society, which traditionally was a voluntary organization whose members attended the bedside of a dying person, washed and dressed the corpse, conducted the burial service and performed the burial itself. This type of society dates back to ancient times, and it existed until recently in every Jewish community in Europe and in some communities in the United States. As a rule, poor people were buried by the *Ḥevra Kaddisha* without charge, but others were required to pay for the burial plots. The

functions of the Ḥevra Kaddisha have been taken over by professional undertakers (morticians). The chief service of the Jewish burial societies existing today in the United States is that of paying the cost of burial for those families who are unable to assume such financial responsibility. In the Ladino spoken by Sephardim, the Ḥevra Kaddisha is called Lavadores.

HEVRON see Hebron.

HEZEKIAH

One of the prominent kings of Judah who ruled from about 720 to 692 b.c.e. Under the guidance of the prophet Isaiah, he destroyed the sanctuaries and shrines of the many gods, and enjoined the idolatrous practices introduced by his father Ahaz, restoring worship of the one God in the Temple of Jerusalem. He led a successful campaign against the Philistines, but was unable to stop the Assyrian armies from invading the country. A divine visitation (perhaps a plague) over the Assyrian camp, led to the raising of the siege and the city of Jerusalem was saved from the destruction which threatened.

HIAS

Initials of the "Hebrew Immigrant Aid Society," also known as "Hebrew Sheltering and Immigrant Aid Society," organized in 1884, its purpose being to: a) help Jews to migrate, generally from Europe for permanent settlement in North and South American countries or elsewhere; b) help them prepare for emigration; c) meet the immigrants upon their arrival and give them legal protection and temporary shelter; d) help immigrants in their economic and social adjustment. It is now called United Hias Service. See *United Hias Service*.

ḤIBBAT ZION

Hebrew name meaning "Love of Zion"

Meron is the place traditionally assigned to Hillel's tomb. Jews have a special affection for the gentle sage and scholar, Hillel, whose kindness, charity, patience and Golden Rule are truly without peer.

given to the movement for the settlement of Palestine during the latter part of the 19th century and before the creation of the World Zionist Organization by Theodor Herzl. This movement was extensive in eastern Europe. See *Hovevei Zion*.

HIGH HOLY DAYS see Festivals; Penitential Days; Rosh Hashanah; Yom Kippur.

HIGH PRIEST see Kohen Gadol.

HILLEL

One of the most revered spiritual leaders of the Jewish people who lived during the latter part of the first century b.c.e., and the beginning of the first century c.e. Born in Babylonia, he went to Palestine at the age of 40, where he became a distinguished student at the academy of Shemaiah and Avtalion, and because of his brilliant scholarship was later appointed president of the *Sanhedrin* (High Court). Together with his colleague Shammai he formed the last of the five pairs (Zuggot) mentioned in chapter one of *Pirke Avot*. Hillel established his own academy, the *Bet Hillel* (House of Hillel), which became known

for its liberal interpretation of the Laws of the Torah, as distinguished from *Bet Shammai* (House of Shammai), which advocated a strict adherence to the letter of the Law. Hillel introduced several legal reforms, chief of which was that of the *Pruzbol*. This reform kept private debts alive despite the Sabbatical year, which under Torah legislation voided them. The courts thereby required the individual to pay outstanding debts even after the seventh year. The poor were thus enabled to borrow money from the rich who were, according to the provisions of the Pruzbol, guaranteed full payment even after the Sabbatical year. The automatic cancellation of debts at the end of each six year period (*Shemitah*) was adopted in modified form by the English common law and most of the United States adopted a "Statute of Limitations."

Tradition credits Hillel with the formulation of the Golden Rule stating in its negative form "Do not unto thy fellow men what is hateful to thee; this is the whole Law; the rest is commentary." His

206

liberalism, mildness, love of peace, love of fellow men and of learning are set forth in numerous words of wisdom found in Pirke Avot, such as: "Be of the disciples of Aaron, loving peace and pursuing peace, loving thy fellow creatures, and drawing them near to the Torah"; "Do not separate thyself from the community"; "Judge not your neighbor until you have come into his place"; "Do not say: 'When I have leisure I shall study,' perhaps you will never have leisure."

HILLEL FOUNDATION see B'nai B'rith.

HILLMAN, SIDNEY (1887–1946)
Prominent labor leader. Born in Lithuania, he settled in the United States at the age of 20, and soon became active as a spokesman for the working people. In 1915 he became president of the Amalgamated Clothing Workers of America, and championed the principle of collective bargaining. In 1935 Hillman helped organize the C.I.O. (Committee for Industrial Organization). A supporter of the New Deal, he was appointed in 1933 by President Franklin D. Roosevelt as a member of the labor advisory board of the National Recovery Act. In 1940 Hillman became an important figure in the national defense program, being one of eight members of the National Defense Advisory Commission, and later associate director of the Office of Production Management.

Hillman also took an interest in Jewish affairs, being a member of the council of the Jewish Agency for Palestine and urging labor participation in many types of Jewish relief work.

HILLQUIT, MORRIS (1869–1933)
Socialist leader and publicist. Born in Latvia, he settled at a young age in the United States, studied law, and became active in the Socialist Labor Party. As a successful lawyer he championed the cause of labor,

appearing in behalf of the workers before the higher courts, promoting favorable labor legislation, and representing unions before arbitration boards. Hillquit represented labor at international gatherings and took an active part in American political life, polling record votes as candidate for congressional and municipal offices. Hillquit wrote: *History of Socialism in the United States* (1903), *Socialism in Theory and Practice* (1909), *From Marx to Lenin* (1921), and other important books, pamphlets and magazine articles.

HILLUL HA-SHEM
The profanation of God's name. Generally used of unethical conduct, which makes for a public scandal. See *Kiddush ha-Shem*.

HIRSCH, BARON MAURICE DE (1831–1896)
Philanthropist. Born in Germany, he inherited a fortune, and as a banker underwrote the financing of railroads in Turkey, Russia and Austria, increasing their progress. A member of a prominent family active in Jewish affairs, Hirsch first became interested in the *Alliance Israélite Universelle* and contributed large amounts of money for the maintenance of its schools in the Orient. Knowing of the plight of the Jews in Russia, he offered the Russian Government the sum of 50 million francs for the training of the Jewish masses for productive life in industry and agriculture. This offer having been refused, Hirsch directed his attention toward the resettlement of Jews elsewhere, especially in Argentine. To this end he established the Jewish Colonization Association (ICA) in 1894, which became and was for a long time the greatest Jewish philanthropic organization. The ICA bought large stretches of land in Argentine for the colonization of Russian Jews. In addition to this great undertaking, he founded the Hirsch School Fund in Ga-

Peretz Hirschbein, Hebrew and Yiddish playwright, was also a poet, novelist and traveller.

licia, which promoted Jewish trade schools for Galician and Bukovinian Jews. Hirsch also established the Baron Hirsch Fund in New York for the technical and agricultural training of Jewish immigrants from eastern Europe. When he died he left 500 million francs for charitable institutions. His charitable work benefited Jews and non-Jews alike.

HIRSCHBEIN, PERETZ (1880–1948)

Prominent Yiddish playwright, born in Russia. His first published play was *Miriam*, both in Hebrew and in Yiddish. In 1908 Hirschbein organized a Yiddish theatrical company which toured Russia and Poland, producing plays of Yiddish writers, including his own popular play *Di Neveyle* (The Carcass). In 1911 Hirschbein settled in the United States, where his plays *Di Puste Kretshme* (The Idle Inn), *Dem Shmids Tochter* (The Smith's Daughter), and *Di Griene Felder* (The Green Fields), were produced by the Vilna troupe under the direction of Maurice Schwartz. Hirschbein was also known as a poet, novelist and writer of impressions of his extensive travels. He has made an outstanding contribution to the modern Yiddish theater, especially with his idyllic

plays about simple Jewish people. His writings have been translated and produced in several languages.

HISTADRUT

The General Federation of Labor in Israel, comprising in 1960 over three quarters of its working people. Organized in 1920, the original basic principles of the *Histadrut* remain the same: non-exploitation, self-help and mutual aid. Membership in the Histadrut is open to all types of workers, both men and women, both of brawn and brain. The Histadrut engages in the following activities: a) Directs most of the trade unions; b) Sponsors the collective farms and labor settlements; c) Operates *Kuppat Ḥolim* (Workers' Sick Fund), the largest health organization in Israel; d) Provides unemployment, old-age, disability and other types of social security insurance; e) Operates an extensive educational program offering adult education, and maintains its own publishing house, choirs and orchestras, and numerous study groups; f) Operates cooperative projects such as housing, all types of consumers' and producers' societies, transportation, etc.; g) Operates a workers' bank; h) Owns many industrial plants, and *Solel*

Modern building in Tel Aviv which houses the offices of Histadrut, Israel's labor federation.

Boneh, the largest construction firm in the Middle East. As such it is the largest employer in Israel.

Since its establishment the Histadrut has played a vital role in the building of the Jewish homeland, and has exercised great political, economic and cultural influence in shaping the present and undoubtedly the future of the State of Israel.

HISTADRUT IVRIT

The Hebrew name for the Hebrew Culture Organization of America, founded in 1917 in New York. As a nation-wide organization for the promotion of the Hebrew language, education and culture, it has published, since 1923, *Hadoar*, a Hebrew weekly, and the children's and youth supplement, *Hadoar Lanoar;* it has also established its own publishing house *Ogen*, issuing several Hebrew volumes each year. It also sponsors *Hanoar Haivri*, the Hebrew Youth Organization. The local Hebrew Culture Organizations (branches of the central Histadrut Ivrit), existing in most major Jewish communities in America, conduct varied Hebrew programs consisting of lectures, concerts and forums, and engage in fund-raising activities for the support of Hebrew cultural institutions and Hebrew publications.

HITLER, ADOLPH (1889–1945)

Dictator of Germany, and Fuehrer (leader, actually dictator) and founder of the Nazi party; the worst anti-Semite of all time, who after coming to power in Germany (1933), destroyed the German Jewish community, and as a consequence of the Nazi occupation of Austria, Czechoslovakia, Poland, Lithuania, Belgium, France, Rumania, Hungary, and other European countries, six million Jews were annihilated under the most inhuman conditions.

In his book "Mein Kampf" he laid down his political philosophy, his plan for con-

Spanish and Portuguese Synagogue in The Hague, Dutch capital, as pictured in 1726.

quering the world, and his anti-Semitic policies, which served as a blueprint for his followers. Hitlerism brought about the greatest misery in the history of mankind, and a horrible catastrophe in the history of the Jewish people. It is estimated that his army horde destroyed over 25 million people in World War II, which he started. It is assumed that Hitler committed suicide when the Nazi hordes were finally crushed by the victorious armies of the United States and its allies in World War II. See *Anti-Semitism; Aryanism; Nazism.*

HOL HA-MOED see Festivals.

HOLIDAYS see Festivals.

HOLLAND

A kingdom in western Europe, also known as the Netherlands, where the Jewish community before World War II numbered about 120,000, half of whom lived in Amsterdam. The first Jewish mass immigration to Holland began in the 16th century, when Marranos from Portugal and Spain sought refuge from religious persecutions, and established there their Sephardic congregations. They were later followed by Jews from Germany and Poland, who established important *Ash-*

HOLY LAND

kenazic communities. The Jews of Holland have enjoyed religious freedom, and Amsterdam became a center of Jewish learning and the seat of important Jewish leaders and personalities, such as Menasseh ben Israel and Baruch Spinoza. In 1790 the Jews of Holland were given equal civil and political rights, and have since occupied positions of leadership in the affairs of the kingdom. As a result of the Nazi occupation in Holland, the Jewish community suffered greatly, and in 1960 the estimated Jewish population was about 26,000. Many Jews were saved by good Christian people of Holland during the Nazi occupation. Anne Frank, whose "Diary" written in her early teens and depicting life under the Nazis in Holland, was also hidden by Dutch people.

HOLY LAND see Palestine.

HOLY SCRIPTURES see Bible.

HOMILETICS

Jewish sermons are generally involved in the interpretation of Biblical or Rabbinic texts, known in Hebrew as *Derush* or *Derashah* (exposition, homily, sermon). The homily usually seeks to derive from the scriptural texts a lesson of practical application to life. Such Jewish sermons date back to the first century, and in the course of subsequent centuries became a part of the synagogue service on Sabbaths and holidays, and are customarily delivered by the rabbi in the language of the people. Numerous collections of such sermons have been made, the first of which was probably that of R. Tanḥuma in the fourth century. In modern times the religious sermon has become essential, and the effectiveness of the rabbi depends to a large extent on his skill in preaching.

During the Second Commonwealth, the interpreter (meturgeman) stood next to the Reader of the Torah (Baal Kore) and expounded the text, verse by verse. In the

Middle Ages the rabbi would generally preach twice a year, on the Sabbath before Passover (Shabbat ha-Gadol), reminding his people of the laws of the festival; and on the Sabbath before Yom Kippur (Shabbat Shuvah), rousing his flock to repentance. In the late Middle Ages, the institution of the *Maggid* developed. The Maggid was an itinerant preacher who traveled from town to town and offered his homily to the local people in their synagogue, generally addressing them on Sabbath afternoon.

HORAH

A popular folk dance in Israel, probably imported from Rumania, and introduced by the pioneer settlers (Ḥalutzim).

HOSEA

His book is the first in order of the *Twelve* (Tere Asar) *Minor Prophets*. He lived in the Northern Kingdom from about 784 to 725 b.c.e., and preached the coming of the doom of the Kingdom of Israel because of the widespread worship of idols and the corruption of the rulers. He likened the idolatry of the people to adultery. However, he believed that God was merciful, and that He loved His chosen people despite their many sins; that like a husband who stands ready to forgive his unfaithful wife because of his love for her, God also seeks to win back His people if only they would purify themselves and live according to the Laws of Moses. The last chapter of his book is the *Haftarah* of Shabbat Shuvah, the Sabbath between Rosh Hashanah and Yom Kippur, so called because the opening word of the Haftarah is "Shuvah" (Return), also known as *Shabbat Teshuvah* (Sabbath of Repentance).

HOSHANA (HOSHANOT)

The opening words of several prayers, meaning "Save, we beseech Thee." These

A group of young Israeli girls dancing the "Horah." Though probably Romanian in origin, the dance has come to be closely identified with the early Ḥalutzim and the pioneer spirit of the Zionist movement.

prayers are part of the Sukkot service and recited in the course of a procession around the *Bimah* while carrying the *Lulav* and *Etrog*. On the Sabbath of Sukkot, specially designated *Hoshanot* are recited and there is no procession.

HOSHANA RABBAH

The seventh day of Sukkot, and the twenty-first day of Tishre. It is so named because the liturgy contains repeated invocations by the worshippers during the processions held in the Temple of Jerusalem. Seven processions are made in the synagogue. The term "Hoshana" also applies to the willows used by each worshipper during the liturgy of Hoshana Rabbah. The beaten off leaves of the willows are said by some to symbolize the petitions to God to cast off the sins of the people. The services on Hoshana Rabbah are almost as solemn as those on Yom Kip-

pur, and by tradition Hoshana Rabbah is considered the day when man's blessings for the coming year are finally decreed in Heaven.

ḤOVEVEI ZION

Hebrew term meaning "Lovers of Zion," the name of the organization formed by east European Jewry during the 19th century to encourage the settlement of Jews in agricultural colonies in Palestine.

In the years following the anti-Jewish riots in Russia (1881), *Ḥovevei Zion* societies were formed in major Jewish communities in eastern Europe, and the first groups of pioneers set out for Palestine and founded *Rishon Le-Zion*, an early Jewish colony. Despite the opposition of the Russian government to the Ḥovevei Zion societies, the movement continued to develop, and other groups were organized in Germany, France, England and

211

An 18th-century French etching by Bernard Picart shows a Jewish wedding ceremony. The bride sits under the traditional wedding canopy (Ḥuppah) as the bridegroom symbolically smashes a glass.

the United States. When Theodor Herzl organized the World Zionist Organization in 1897, the Ḥovevei Zion societies joined the new Zionist movement.

HULEH

A lake in northeastern Israel, also called the "Waters of Merom." The lake covers an area of about 4,000 acres, and the marshes surrounding it extend over 5,000 acres. As a result of pioneer work in the Jewish resettlement of Palestine, the waters of the infested marshes were drained off, and flourishing settlements have been established on previously useless land.

HULLIN

A tractate in the Babylonian Talmud containing basic discussions relating to the Jewish dietary laws, such as the methods of *Sheḥitah* (slaughtering), the prohibition of diseased and unfit animals, the prohibition of eating the blood of slaugh-

tered animals, prohibitions against eating certain parts of an animal, prohibitions against cooking or eating milk with meat, and other dietary regulations.

HUMMASH

Hebrew term meaning "fifth," that is, one of the Five Books of Moses (Pentateuch). But the term is also applied to the entire Pentateuch. See *Bible*.

HUNGARY

Before World War II there were in Hungary about 650,000 Jews. It is assumed that the Jewish settlement in Hungary dates back to Roman times; it is established that in 960 c.e. Ḥasdai ibn Shaprut mentioned the Hungarian Jews in his letter to Joseph, king of the Khazars. Until the sixteenth century Jewish life in Hungary was comparatively normal, and many individual Jews occupied important governmental positions. There were, never-

212

Ḥuppah stone, the special stone on which the symbolic goblet-breaking of the wedding takes place, presumably memorializing the loss of the Temple. Ḥuppah stones were put in the north wall of synagogues. The one above is from the German synagogue at Altenkundstadt.

theless, periods of persecution, massacres, and even several expulsions, which ended in repeated readmittances to Hungary. During Turkish rule in divided Hungary in the 16th century, Jews enjoyed a more privileged position in comparison with those living under Christian rulers. In the 18th century, however, when Hungary was taken from the Turks, the Jewish communities were continuously exposed to persecutions and heavy taxation. Not until the middle of the 19th century were Hungarian Jews granted full citizenship. The Jewish community has since developed rapidly, and in the major Hungarian cities Jewish scholarship flourished. Jewish life was especially influenced by the bitter conflict between orthodox and reform Jews. Both camps have contributed to the advancement of Judaism and Jewish learning. In Pressburg and other cities there existed *Yeshivot* (Talmudical Academies) of world-wide fame, and in Budapest the reform rabbinical seminary earned high recognition. Following World War I, a wave of anti-Semitism swept Hungary, and World War II and the occupation of Hungary by the Nazis led to the almost complete destruction of the Jewish community. As of 1960 there were about 100,000 Jews in Hungary.

ḤUPPAH

Hebrew term for the canopy under which the bridal couple is married. The *Ḥuppah* consists of a silk or satin embroidered roof, supported by four poles fixed to the floor or held by relatives or friends of the bride and groom. The history of the Ḥuppah dates back to ancient times, when the term was applied to the bridal chamber. Traditionally marriages are solemnized under the open skies, and the Ḥuppah is thus the special enclosure for groom and bride. It is considered the symbol of the new home they are to build.

I

ISRAEL

I will bring back the exiles of my people Israel,

They shall build the waste cities and dwell in them,

They shall plant vineyards and drink their wine,

They shall make gardens and eat their fruit,

And I will plant them in their own land.

Never again shall they be uprooted

From the land which I have given them.

This is the promise of the Lord thy God.

AMOS

IBN DAUD, ABRAHAM HA-LEVI (1110-1180)

Philosopher, historian and astronomer, during the Golden Age of Jewish history in Spain. His main work in Jewish history, the *Sefer Ha-Kabbalah* (Book of Tradition) maintains the continuity of Jewish history and culture from Moses through the subsequent generations, as against the contention of the Karaites that the only authentic Jewish religious tradition is the *Written Law* handed down by Moses, and not the *Oral Law* developed by the Rabbis. His contribution to Jewish philosophy is in his especially important work, *Emunah Ramah*. Accepting Aristotle's philosophy, he sets out to reconcile it with the principles of Jewish religion. This pioneer attempt to prove that Jewish theology rests on sound philosophical foundations was later undertaken by others, especially by Maimonides, whose philosophical works overshadowed and fulfilled those of his predecessors.

IBN EZRA, ABRAHAM BEN MEIR (1092–1167)

Hebrew poet and scholar of the Golden Age of Jewish history in Spain. During the first half of his life Ibn Ezra lived in Toledo, Spain, where he enjoyed the reputation of scholar and poet. His major literary works were written during his many years of wandering in France, Italy, Egypt and Palestine. His poverty and his precarious existence as a vagabond are reflected in some of his elegant and witty poetical verses. His main contribution to Hebrew literature was in the fields of Hebrew philology and Biblical commentaries. His scholarly commentaries on the Bible have for centuries been an authoritative source for research by students of the Bible. His writings also include works in mathematics and astronomy.

IBN EZRA, MOSES BEN JACOB (1070–1138)

Religious and secular Hebrew poet of the Spanish period. He wrote a number of *Selihot* (penitential poems), which became part of the Jewish liturgy. He was therefore known under the name of *Ha-Salah* (writer of Selihot). His poetry is held by critics to be unsurpassed in perfection of form and style. He also wrote a philosophical work and a history of the Jews of Spain.

IBN GABIROL, SOLOMON (1021–1058)

Leading Hebrew poet and philosopher of the Spanish period. Beginning to write at an early age, he became known for his religious and secular poetry. Influenced by neo-Platonism, he wrote philosophical works, the greatest of which was *Mekor Hayim* (Fountain of Life), which in its Latin translation exercised considerable influence on Christian theology in the Middle Ages. Known as "Fons Vitae," it was thought to be the work of an Arab "Avicebron" until the 19th century, when Salomon Munk established Gabirol as its author. He is best known for his religious hymns, which have been incorporated in the Jewish liturgy. His greatest hymn is *Keter Malkhut* (Royal Crown), a poetical meditation on the greatness of God which evinced strong *Kabbalistic* influences.

IBN NAGDELA, SAMUEL HA-LEVI BEN JOSEPH
see Samuel Ha-Nagid.

IBN SHAPRUT, HASDAI see Hasdai ibn Shaprut.

IBN TIBBON

A famous family of translators into Hebrew of Arabic works by Jewish and Arabic scholars. The Ibn Tibbon family, originating in Spain, and active chiefly in southern France, flourished during the 12th and the 13th centuries. Listed in chronological order of their birth, the following members of this celebrated family are known for their valuable contributions: *Judah ben Saul ibn Tibbon* (1120-1190), physician and translator, who left

Spain and settled in Provence, France. He translated from Arabic into Hebrew the "Hovot Ha-Levavot" (Duties of the Heart) by Bahya ibn Pakuda; the "Kuzari" by Judah Ha-Levi; "Emunot Vedeot" (Doctrines and Views) by Saadiah Gaon, and others. *Samuel ben Judah ibn Tibbon* (1150-1230), son of Judah ben Saul, settled in France, and is best known for his translation of Maimonides' "Moreh Nevukhim" (Guide for the Perplexed), and parts of his other works. *Jacob ben Machir ibn Tibbon* (1230-1312), known for his translations into Hebrew of astronomical, mathematical and philosophical works written in Arabic, and for his original astronomical works, which were used by later astronomers as a basis of their scientific investigations. *Moses ibn Tibbon* (1240-1283) lived in France, and translated into Hebrew works in philosophy, astronomy and medicine, and the "Sefer Ha-Mitzvot" (Book of the 613 Commandments) by Maimonides. He also wrote a number of original works.

ICA see Jewish Colonization Association.

ICOR

Abbreviated name of an organization established in America in 1924 for the purpose of aiding the Jewish agricultural settlements in the Soviet Union. The organization was established by representatives of Jewish labor organizations and unions in the United States, and it concentrated on aid to the Jewish agricultural settlements in the Crimea, the Ukraine, and Biro-Bidjan. The organization was active until World War II.

IDOLATRY

The worship of idols or gods in the form of images. The Bible forbids idol worship in these words: "Thou shalt not make unto thee a graven image, even any manner of likeness, of any thing that is in heaven above, or that is in the earth beneath, or that is in the water under the earth. Thou shalt not bow unto them, nor serve them." After the conquest of Canaan, the Israelites lived among nations that worshipped idols, and for many centuries to come, from the period of the Judges through the period of the Kings, idol worship was frequently practiced by the people. The Hebrew prophets opposed idolatry, and constantly admonished the Israelites and their kings with regard to their idolatrous ways. It is not impossible that the people, in adopting Canaanitish practices, actually thought them to be the proper form in which to worship the true God. It was the people's experience in the Babylonian exile which led them to recognition of the truth of the prophets' teachings, and thereafter we do not find any more tendency to idolatry among the Jews. Even after all traces of idolatry were wiped out following the return from Babylonia, the injunction against idol worship was considered important by the leaders, the scribes, and later the rabbis who recognized the necessity of keeping aloof from paganism. The Jews were the only monotheistic people for thousands of years, and they lived among polytheists for the greater part of their history. One of the tractates of the Talmud is called *Avodah Zarah* (Idolatry). Maimonides looks upon Christianity and Islam as divinely sent to lead the masses of the people away from paganism, as a stepping stone to the right religion.

The Second Commandment prohibits the making of graven images for the purpose of worshipping them. In Jewish life, therefore, representations of animals and other forms, particularly in solid shape, have generally been frowned upon. However, we find the lion (the symbol of Judah), and the eagle (the symbol of Israel), used symbolically in synagogues.

Ancient Roman cult vessel. Note the image of the god Serapis at the handle base. It was probably defaced by Jewish users because of the strong prohibition against graven images.

Bronze statuette of a Canaanite god, presumably the god-king El, found at Megiddo, and dating from about the 13th century b.c.e.

Frescoes depicting Biblical scenes were found on the walls of the synagogue in Dura-Europos and mosaics representing astronomical bodies and Biblical characters in the Bet-Alpha Kibbutz in Israel. The human form, however, is never found, whether in three or two dimensions.

ILLUI
Hebrew word for an exceptionally gifted young person, particularly the traditional title given to a Talmudic student of unusual intellectual ability.

IMBER, NAPHTALI HERZ (1856–1909)
Hebrew poet and author of the Jewish and Israeli anthem, *Hatikvah*. Born in Galicia, he spent most of his early life wandering from country to country, including Palestine, where he lived among the Bedouin. His collection of poems, *Barkai*, included *Hatikvah* and *Mishmar Ha-Yarden*, a militant song which became popular among the pioneer settlers in Palestine. In 1888 he went to England where he met Israel Zangwill, who described him in a sketch of one of the characters of his novel "Children of the Ghetto." In 1892 Imber settled in the United States, where he spent the rest of his life, wandering from place to place while engaged in literary work. See *Hatikvah*.

IMMORTALITY see Resurrection.

INCUNABULA
A Latin term applied to all printed books published before 1500. There are about 200 known Hebrew books of this character printed in Italy, Spain, Portugal, and other places. The Hebrew incunabula cover a variety of subject matter, especially Biblical and Rabbinical literature. Two of such Hebrew books printed in 1475 are *Rashi's Commentary* on the Pentateuch (Five Books of Moses), and the *Turim* by Jacob ben Asher.

Naphtali Herz Imber, Hebrew poet and traveller, was the author of the Jewish national anthem.

INDEPENDENT ORDER OF BRITH ABRAHAM

A large Jewish fraternal insurance order, founded in New York in 1887. Its membership in 1960 was approximately 14,000. Outside of the insurance, medical, burial and other benefits which the Order provides for its members, it also takes a vital interest in Jewish affairs, and is especially interested in Zionist work.

INGATHERING, FEAST OF see Sukkot.

INDIA

It is believed that the Jews' association with India dates back to the days of Solomon. The *Book of Esther* mentions the name of *Hodu* (India). Other references to Jews in India are found in the Talmud, and in the written reports of Jewish travelers during the Middle Ages.

Indian Jewry may be divided into four groups. 1) *The Cochin Jews.* Their tradition claims settlement in India after the destruction of the Temple. The first written record, however, is a charter granted to a group of Yemenites who settled in Cranganore about 750 c.e. During the early part of the thirteenth century, the first community in Cochin was formed by Spanish, German, and Syrian refugees, as well as by converted slaves. There has been, in accordance with the Indian caste system, segregation of the so-called "White Jews" and "Black Jews" in this Jewish community in India. 2) *The Bene Israel.* Culturally similar to the native Indians, though they observe most traditional Jewish feast and fast days. This group of "Black Jews" dwells in the vicinity of Bombay. Their specific origins are unknown, but they are believed to have been living in India for centuries. 3) *Iraqi Jews.* This group from Baghdad, first settled in Bombay in 1680. Sizeable migration began in the 19th century, with most of the Jews returning to Baghdad, and many of them subsequently leaving India for Europe. The famous Sassoon family, most of whom later moved to England, played an important role in Indian finance and industry. 4) *European Jews.* Settled in India in small numbers during British rule, later joined by refugees from Germany. There were approximately 25,000 Jews in India in 1960, most of whom lived in Bombay and Calcutta.

INQUISITION

The tribunal of the Catholic Church set up in the 13th century in order to discover and punish heretics. Originally directed against Christian offenders of the Catholic Church, the Inquisition turned against the Jews who returned to Judaism after having previously embraced Christianity. In the 14th century, when mass forced conversions of Jews took place in Spain, many of these "New Christians" remained secretly loyal to the Jewish faith. The Inquisition set out to deal with the *Marranos* (secret Jews), and for over three centuries Jews of Spain and Portugal were exposed to the terrors of those reli-

219

gious tribunals. The most terrifying period of the Inquisition began when Thomas de Torquemada was appointed General Inquisitor of Spain in 1483. In Jewish history he is remembered as the most cruel and most fanatic inquisitor. He compiled a code of specific instructions for the trial of Marranos and the most ghastly methods of torture were devised. The Marranos were thrown into torture chambers, where they were forced to confess their allegiance to the Jewish faith and to disclose the names of others similarly suspected. Thousands of Jews were sentenced to die at the Auto-Da-Fe (literally, Act of Faith, used as a public place of execution) by burning at the stake. It is estimated that some 400,000 persons were tried by the Inquisition of Spain and Portugal, 8,000 of whom perished during the time of Thomas de Torquemada alone.

The Inquisition was also set up in the Spanish and Portuguese dominions in Mexico, Peru and Goa, and many Jews who fled its terrors in the *Old World* could not escape the Auto-Da-Fe, even in the *New World*. The Inquisition was also established in Europe against heretics. Its evil power persisted until the beginning of the 19th century.

INTERNATIONAL LADIES' GARMENT WORKERS' UNION

In the early part of the twentieth century the garment industry was comprised largely of immigrant Jewish workers, mostly centered in and around New York City. This group of workers were influential in organizing and building such labor unions as the Amalgamated Clothing Workers of America and the International Ladies' Garment Workers' Union.

Founded in 1900, the ILGWU grew from an original membership of 2,000 to a membership of 450,000 in 1960. Like other unions, the ILGWU was organized

David Dubinsky, ILGWU president, labor movement pioneer, and fighter against sweatshops.

in the United States during the period of intolerable sweatshop conditions, and its initial struggle was for a living wage, shorter working hours and better working conditions. In 1910 the ILGWU called a general strike of 60,000 cloakmakers, as a result of which an agreement was reached with the employers providing favorable terms for the employees. With the election of David Dubinsky as president in 1932, the ILGWU was reorganized, and much of the ground lost during unsuccessful and costly strikes in the years of the economic crisis after World War I, was gradually regained.

The ILGWU sponsors a program of cultural and educational activities for its membership, which is made up of different nationalities, including a large percentage of Jewish workers. It also maintains the Union Health Center, and a summer resort, Unity House. Outside of its purely trade union activities, the ILGWU has cooperated with other unions and organizations in giving substantial financial support to many national and international relief projects. In recent years, the proportion of Jews among the membership has been decreasing.

I.O.B.B. (Independent Order of B'nai B'rith) see B'nai B'rith.

IRAN see Persia.

IRAQ

The kingdom of Iraq occupies the territory of Mesopotamia or ancient Babylonia. Before World War II, there were in Iraq about 110,000 Jews, most of whom lived in the capital city, Baghdad, and in Mosul, famous for its oil fields. Despite the fact that some Iraqi Jews occupied positions of importance in the government of modern Iraq, the Jewish communities there were always exposed to limitations and even persecution. An Arabic country, Iraq sided with the Arabs in Palestine, and began a campaign of terror against its Jewish population in general and against Zionists in particular. Iraq is a member of the Arab League, and it was one of the seven Arab countries that started the war against Israel in 1948. The defeat of the Arab armies by the Israelis brought on a new wave of terror against the Jews of Iraq. Mass immigration of Iraqi Jews to Israel began, and by 1960 the once large Jewish community had dwindled to only 5,000. See *Babylonia*.

IRELAND

As of 1960 there were in the Republic of Eire about 5,400 Jews. According to a legend, the Irish are descendants of the Ten Lost Tribes, and it is believed that Jews came to Ireland in ancient times. However, the first reference to a Jewish settlement in Ireland is that of 1232. In 1745 the Jews of Ireland were accorded citizenship rights, and about a century later they were fully emancipated. Most of the Jews of Eire live in Dublin. Belfast in Northern Ireland (Ulster) also has a large Jewish population.

IRGUN TZEVAI LEUMI

The Hebrew name of the secret Jewish "National Military Organization" commonly known as the "Irgun," founded in 1936 in Palestine. Its major purpose was to take drastic military action against the Arab terrorists, and to fight for the establishment of an independent Jewish state in Palestine. The Irgun led a vigorous campaign against the British authorities for their anti-Jewish policy in Palestine. The extremist political aims of the Irgun are at present advocated by the *Herut* party in Israel.

ISAAC

Second of the Biblical Patriarchs, son of Abraham and Sarah. The Bible tells that God wanted to test Abraham's faith, and commanded him to offer his son Isaac as a sacrifice. At the last moment, however, as Abraham was ready to comply with God's command, an angel told him to spare Isaac and sacrifice a ram instead. Isaac married Rebekah, who gave birth to twins, Jacob and Esau. In his old age Isaac became blind and wanted to give his blessings to Esau, whom he favored. Rebekah, however, helped Jacob impersonate his brother, whereby he received Isaac's blessings. Isaac blessed Esau also. Isaac died when he was 180 years old, and was buried with his ancestors in the Cave of Machpelah.

ISAAC ELCHANAN THEOLOGICAL SEMINARY see Yeshiva University.

ISAIAH

One of the greatest of the Hebrew prophets. Scholars generally agree that the bulk of the first 39 chapters (of the *Book of Isaiah*) are the work of Isaiah, the son of Amoz, who prophesied between 740 and 701 b.c.e. His emphasis is on the holiness of God and the urgency of having faith in Him. He is known for his poetic imagery, for the nobility of his lines and for his wide interests, showing concern both for the international as well as the

local scene. Among the subjects he deals with are the social evils of his day, injustice to the poor, the inefficaciousness of sacrifices when offered with hands made unclean by unethical conduct, the doom of Israel because of unholy living, and the need for faith in God rather than reliance on alliances with foreign nations. Isaiah projects a vision into the future "at the end of days" when peace will be established on earth, the wolf shall dwell with the lamb, a scion of David will rule with wisdom and justice, and all the nations will stream toward Jerusalem, from which city will come forth the word of the Lord.

Some modern scholars, and even a few in the Middle Ages, hold that chapters 40 to 66 of the *Book of Isaiah* were composed no earlier than the middle of the sixth century b.c.e. Their basic theme is the restoration of the Jews to the Holy Land, and the concept of God as most exalted. The Persian Emperor Cyrus is mentioned by name, and a polemic against Zoroastrian dualism seems to appear quite clearly. The poetry and the beauty of phrase and conception are the work of a genius, but a genius unlike the Isaiah of history. We do not know the name of this prophet; he is sometimes called the Great Unknown Prophet of the Exile; he is frequently referred to as the Second Isaiah (Deutero-Isaiah) as a shorthand phrase. It is not even agreed among scholars whether he lived in Babylonia or Judah. His words of comfort to the people have rung through the ages, and the concept of the people as the suffering servant of God gave strength to them during the

Scroll fragments of a commentary on the Book of Isaiah. These were discovered by bedouins in the Fourth Cave at Qumran in 1952. The Qumran Caves have yielded some of the most important documents for study on the Jewish sects of the 1st century b.c.e. Fragments are studied at the Palestine Archeological Museum.

evils of persecution. The last seven Sabbaths of the year (prior to Rosh Hashanah) are known as the Seven Weeks of Comforting, and the *Haftarot* all come from this part of the Book of Isaiah.

ISHMAEL

Son of Abraham and Hagar, Sarah's Egyptian handmaid. The Bible tells that Sarah asked Abraham to expel Hagar and Ishmael. Ishmael lived in the desert as a hunter. He married an Egyptian woman, and is considered the ancestor of a number of Ishmaelite tribes. In the folklore of the Arabs, Ishmael is said to be one of their prophets, and the founder of the Arab people.

ISLAM

Also known as Mohammedanism, one of the three major monotheistic religions, founded by Mohammed in Arabia. Year one in the calendar of Islam commemorates the flight (Hegira) of Mohammed from Mecca to Medina and corresponds to the year 622 c.e. The holy book of the Moslems (followers of Islam) is the *Koran*. Islam worship prescribes: 1) a declaration that "there is no God but Allah, and Mohammed is his prophet"; 2) the observance of five daily prayers; 3) fasting from sunrise to sunset throughout the month of Ramadan; 4) giving of alms; 5) an obligatory pilgrimage, at least once in one's lifetime, to the holy shrine at Mecca.

Mohammed urged the spread of Islam by the sword, and the Jews of Arabia who failed to support the new faith were ruthlessly attacked and caused to suffer the results of oppressive legislation. However, at that time life for the Jews under Christian rule was even worse. Outside of Arabia, therefore, where Jews lived under Christian rulers, they often welcomed the conquering Moslems, and in Syria and Egypt the conditions of the Jews were improved under Islam. In North Africa, however, the so-called ordinances of Omar occasionally imposed forced mass-conversions of Jews, and during the Moorish rule in Spain in the 11th century, Jews were massacred and exiled. However, with the exception of some periods of persecutions, Jews had more freedom under the Ottoman rule in Turkey, and many of them rose to positions of considerable influence under the Sultans.

ISRAEL

According to the Bible, the Patriarch Jacob was named "Israel" by the angel of God with whom he wrestled. Thus the descendants of Israel were called *Bene Israel* (the Children of Israel), the name by which the Jewish people have since been identified. See *Hebrews*.

ISRAEL, KINGDOM OF

The name of the kingdom established by the ten Israelite tribes of northern Palestine as a result of their successful revolt against the "House of David" after the death of King Solomon. The Kingdom of Israel, established by Jeroboam, son of Nebat, lasted from 933-722 b.c.e. Its first capital was Shechem, until King Omri established the capital at Samaria. The kingdom, open to foreign invasions, suffered from frequent wars and from strife within the country resulting from warring and short-lived dynasties. Idol worship was widespread and frequently encouraged by the kings themselves. The prophet Elijah distinguished himself through his uncompromising fight against idolatry. Of the seven dynasties which ruled the Kingdom of Israel, the better known kings were: Omri (889-875), the founder of the capital Samaria; Ahab (875-853), successful military leader; Jehu (842-815), who fought idolatry; Jeroboam II (782-741),

whose long reign saw expansion and prosperity; and Hoshea (734-722), last king of Israel. The Kingdom of Israel was destroyed by the Assyrians in 722 b.c.e., and many of the people were led into captivity. Taking into exile a sizeable portion of a conquered people was standard practice in those days; but this exile was the source of many legends concerning the "Ten Lost Tribes." When 150 years later the population of the Southern Kingdom (Judah) also suffered exile, the new refugees were apparently met by the old refugees from the Kingdom of Israel, as attested by the prophet Ezekiel.

ISRAEL, PEOPLE OF

According to the Bible, the first Hebrews, a Semitic tribe of nomads, emigrated from Mesopotamia into Canaan about 2,000 b.c.e. Jacob and his family came to Egypt in search for food and settled in the area of Goshen, where they lived for several centuries, and their numbers increased greatly. Here the descendants of the Patriarchs, Abraham, Isaac and Jacob developed into twelve tribes, the "Children of Israel," or the *Israelites*. Enslaved by the Pharaohs, they were freed by Moses and finally returned to Canaan under the leadership of Joshua. At first disunited, and exposed to attacks by the neighboring nations, they were finally united under the rule of the first king, Saul, anointed by Samuel. David and Solomon, the succeeding kings, further cemented that unity and formed the united Kingdom of Israel. After Solomon's death, the country was divided into the Northern Kingdom (Israel) comprising ten tribes, and the Southern Kingdom (Judah). After less than 200 years of existence, the Northern Kingdom was destroyed by the Assyrians, and many of its people were carried off into exile. Judah thus became the sole organized survivor of the Hebrew nation. In 586 b.c.e., Judah was destroyed by the Babylonians and its people were exiled to Babylon. Fifty years later, when the Persians conquered Babylonia, the Judeans were permitted to return to their homeland. For several centuries the Judeans lived under Persian, Egyptian and Syrian rule. As a result of the Maccabean revolt of 168 b.c.e., Judea again became an independent kingdom until the year 63 b.c.e., when Roman rule began in Palestine. Judea lost its independence and was finally destroyed by the Romans in 70 c.e. The people of Israel had no national center until 1948. Their dispersion to many parts of the world in the diaspora had begun with the destruction of the Northern Kingdom in 722 b.c.e., and was increased in 586 b.c.e. and during the days of the Second Commonwealth, and was augmented in the year 70 c.e., when Titus destroyed the Second Temple. See *Jew*.

ISRAEL, STATE OF

The Jewish republic named *Israel* was established on May 14, 1948, as a result of the decision of the United Nations to partition Palestine into a Jewish and an Arab state. When Great Britain gave up its mandate over Palestine, Jewish authorities, headed by David Ben-Gurion, issued in solemn assembly the Proclamation of the State of Israel. The Arab nations, opposing the partition of Palestine and the establishment of the Jewish State, attacked Israel. As a result of the War of Liberation the Arabs were defeated, and an armistice between the Jewish State and the Arab nations was signed. The territory held by the Arabs became a part of the Kingdom of Transjordania, later known as *Jordan*. The section of Jerusalem held by the Jews, mostly the modern part of the city, became the capital of the newly created State of Israel.

The Tel Aviv assembly of founders in spring 1909. On the spot where the State of Israel was proclaimed there now stands the Tel Aviv Museum, and around it the city has grown to a great metropolis.

The Jewish population of Palestine was approximately 650,000 just before its independence. By 1960, 970,000 Jews had emigrated to Israel, bringing the Jewish population, with its natural increase, to almost 2 million. These included refugees from the European disaster, and from Arab countries, including all but a small fraction of the ancient communities of Iraq and Yemen. Many of these immigrants were in poor physical condition and in need of public assistance.

By 1960, Israel had made great progress in the economic field. One measure of her industrial expansion was the increase in electric power consumption from 1948, when it was 246 million kilowatt hours, to 1960, when it was 1,565 million. Among Israel's products are canned foods, chemicals, ceramics, cement, textiles and tires. Carefully planned efforts are being made to exploit her mineral resources, including oil and copper which, with the exception of the chemicals in the Dead Sea, are comparatively limited. Israel has a successful "productivity program," and is making special efforts to attract foreign investors.

Between statehood and 1960, agricultural production almost tripled, so that the country was self-sufficient in most foods. Over 60,000 acres were planted in afforestation projects, of which 50,000 were planted after independence.

Funds transmitted to Israel from abroad have been of great assistance in her unprecedented absorption of immigrants. These include monies collected by the UJA and similar organizations which between 1950 and 1959 amounted to over $530 million, over $324 million in loans and grants in aid from the United States, and over $750 million received from Germany as reparations and personal restitution payments.

The Declaration of Independence of the newly created State of Israel is read by David Ben-Gurion on May 14, 1948 at the Tel Aviv Museum under a portrait of Herzl, founder of the Zionist movement.

The end of the War of Liberation was marked by the signing of armistice agreements, but even by 1960 no Arab state had yet signed a peace treaty with Israel. Indeed, Iraq and Saudi Arabia had never even signed the armistice agreements. In 1960, despite many Security Council decisions and in direct contravention of international law, all cargoes to and from Israel were barred from the Suez Canal.

From the signing of the armistice, Israeli settlements were subject to almost nightly maraudings by Arabs from Jordan and the Gaza strip, a narrow finger pointing up the Mediterranean coast which was put under Egyptian control after the armistice. Around 1955, Egypt began to train and dispatch special terrorists called *Fedayeen*. These groups were to infiltrate Israel territory and destroy Jewish morale, in preparation for the final attack. In September, 1955, Soviet Russia agreed to supply Egypt with large amounts of armaments. In the fall of 1956, Jordan joined Syria and Saudi Arabia in placing her army under Egyptian control, for the expressed purpose of destroying Israel.

Faced with the avowed determination to destroy her, by enemies who were now well-armed and acquiring skill in the use of their weapons, Israel saw but one alternative: On October 29, 1956, she sent her armies deep into the Sinai peninsula, in what has come to be known as the Sinai campaign. In one week they defeated the Egyptian armies, destroyed the Fedayeen staging grounds, occupied the Gaza strip, and were, as a contemporary account noted, "Fourteen Hours to Suez."

Meanwhile, Britain and France announced that they were sending troops to capture Suez and protect the Canal. This provoked strong reactions in the United Nations, and in the week between the announcement and the actual attempt of occupation, the fighting ceased. The campaign ended with a United Nations emergency force occupying the Gaza strip.

The first president of Israel was Chaim Weizmann. After his death in 1952, Itzhak Ben-Zvi, who was re-elected in 1957, became President of the State. See *Haganah; Knesset; Palestine.*

ISRAEL, UNITED KINGDOM OF

According to the Bible, the United Kingdom of the Israelites was established in 1028 b.c.e. and existed for nearly 100 years under the rule of the first three Hebrew kings: Saul (1028–1006), David (1006-973), and Solomon (973-933). The United Kingdom marked a most significant advance in the history of the Jewish people, who previously had consisted of disunited tribes. The battles fought by Saul with the warring neighboring nations were continued with greater military ability and much greater success by the popular King David. David made extensive conquests, and made Jerusalem the capital of the united nation. King Solomon consolidated his father's territorial gains, and started a period of cultural and religious development and economic prosperity. His greatest accomplishment was the erection of the Holy Temple in Jerusalem, which for centuries continued to be the spiritual center of the nation. The period of the United Kingdom came to an end when, after Solomon's death, it was split into two separate kingdoms, namely the northern Kingdom of Israel, and the southern Kingdom of Judah.

ISRAEL INDEPENDENCE DAY

The fifth day of the Hebrew month of Iyar, when the State of Israel was proclaimed (May 14, 1948), became a national holiday, observed both in Israel and throughout the Jewish world. In Israel, the *Yom Ha-Atzmaut* (Israel Independence Day) is a legal holiday, celebrated through

227

Israeli Independence Day celebrations on the 10th anniversary of the founding of the State. The entire year was designated a Festival Year and here Israeli boys in Jerusalem parade with the national flag.

a special liturgy, public services in the synagogue, civilian and military parades and general mass festivities.

ISRAELITES

The phrase "Bene Israel" (Children of Israel) is generally translated into English by the word "Israelites." The Bible also refers to the Israelites as: *House of Israel*, and *House of Jacob*. The term *Israelites* appears in Jewish liturgy as well as in Jewish poetry of the pre-modern period. The term was frequently adopted as the name of Jewish organizations, societies and periodicals. The term "Israelite" is no longer popular as a modern term, and has generally been replaced by the term "Jew." Citizens of the State of Israel are known as *Israelis* (singular, Israeli).

ISRU HAG

Hebrew term applied to the day after each of the three pilgrim festivals.

ISSACHAR

One of Jacob's twelve sons, the fifth son by his wife Leah. The tribe of Issachar occupied sixteen towns in the Plain of Jezreel. Jewish folklore describes the descendants of Issachar as men of learning.

ISSERLES, MOSES (1520–1572)

Eminent Polish rabbi, Talmudist, and author. Isserles was the founder and head of the Yeshivah (Talmudical Academy) in Cracow. In addition to his many works, such as Biblical commentaries, responsa and philosophical writings, his chief work is held to be his notes (*Mappah*, "Table

228

Cloth"), to Joseph Karo's code, *Shulḥan Arukh* ("The Prepared Table"); and the two together, Karo's code and the notes of Isserles became the accepted general code of Jewish life in the Ashkenazic Jewish communities. Karo's basic text detailed the Sephardic practices. Isserles was a beloved teacher and revered for his saintliness and learning. The following words, inscribed on his tombstone in Cracow, "From Moses to Moses there was none like Moses," imply that from Maimonides to Isserles no others were equal in learning and character. See *Shulḥan Arukh*.

ISTANBUL

The old capital of Turkey, also known as Constantinople, attracted Jewish travelers since the 4th century c.e. Despite constant persecutions under the Byzantine emperors, there were, according to the famous traveler Benjamin of Tudela, over 2,000 Jews living in Constantinople in 1176, which was also the seat of great Jewish scholarship. In the middle of the 15th century, when Constantinople was conquered by the Turks, immigration began to increase rapidly. By the end of the 16th century the Jewish population had grown to about 50,000 and consisted of four types of communities: Greek Byzantine, Italian, Ashkenazic and Sephardic Jews. Each type of community had its own synagogues and ritual. The Jews of Constantinople occupied important economic positions, both as merchants and all types of workingmen. In the 17th century, however, a rapid decline of the Jewish community began. Only after World War I did a wave of Russian immigrants bring the Jewish population to 90,000. The modern Jewish community lost its cultural influence, and due to political limitations and unfavorable economic conditions, many Jews left the city, and as of 1960 its Jewish population shrank to 50,000.

ITALY

Jews came to Italy in the second century b.c.e. After the destruction of the Second Temple by the Romans (70 c.e.), many Jewish prisoners of war settled in Rome and other cities. During the Middle Ages, while the Jews in Europe suffered greatly, the Jews in Italy, especially those living in Rome, were protected against violence by the Pope, though they suffered many restrictive laws. From the 16th to the end of the 18th century, as a result of Catholic reaction, the position of the Jews in Italy was unfavorable. In 1555 they were forced to live in a ghetto under economic and other restrictions. In modern times, the Jews in Italy have not been exposed to severe forms of anti-Semitism, and have even enjoyed a fair position in the economic and political life of the country. In 1936 the Fascist government in Italy began an anti-Jewish campaign resulting in the emigration of many Jews. The Second World War and Nazi influence brought a further decline of the Jewish community, although Italian measures against Jews never matched Nazi barbarism. As of 1960 there were about 32,000 Jews in Italy.

Throughout the centuries of Jewish life in Italy, Jewish scholarship flourished, and a considerable number of great rabbis, poets and philosophers have acquired world-wide fame. The first Jewish printing press was introduced in Italy, and the first Hebrew book, Rashi's famous Commentary, was printed there in 1475.

IYAR

The eighth Hebrew month, corresponding to April-May. It consists of 29 days. Most of the *Sefirah* days occur during the month of Iyar. *Lag Ba-Omer* is observed on the eighteenth day of the month. Israel Independence Day is celebrated on the fifth of Iyar.

JEW

It hath been told thee, O man, what is good, and what

the Lord doth require of thee: only to do justly, and to

love mercy, and to walk humbly with thy God.

MICAH

JABNEH see Yavneh.

JABOTINSKY, VLADIMIR (1881–1940)

Zionist leader, writer, orator, and founder of the Revisionist-Zionist movement. Born in Odessa, Russia, he studied law in Italy and Austria, and was known as a brilliant journalist. As he became active in the Zionist movement, he saw the opportunity of freeing Palestine from Turkey as a by-product of World War I, and with the help of Joseph Trumpeldor he organized Jewish battalions which later became known as the Jewish Legion and which fought alongside the British armies in the conquest of Palestine.

Jabotinsky subsequently became a member of the Zionist Executive. He soon opposed the policies of Chaim Weizmann, president of the World Zionist Organization, and advocated the establishment of a Jewish state in Palestine, with a Jewish army and unrestricted Jewish immigration. In 1925 he organized the World Union of Zionist Revisionists. As its president he continued to press for a more militant Zionist policy. Jabotinsky and the Revisionists left the Zionist organization in 1935. As head of the new organization he continued his activities in London, and fought the plan of partitioning Palestine between Jews and Arabs. In 1940 he went to the United States, where he died unexpectedly while visiting a summer camp of the Revisionists.

In addition to his Zionist activities, Jabotinsky enjoyed the reputation of an outstanding writer in Hebrew, Yiddish and several European languages. His best known works are a Russian translation of Bialik's poems, "Short Stories," "Samson the Nazirite," "Judge and Fool," "The Jewish War Front," and a translation of Dante into Hebrew.

JACOB

The third of the Biblical Patriarchs, son of Isaac and Rebekah, and twin-brother of Esau. Given the name of *Israel*, after wrestling with an angel of God, he became, as the father of 12 sons and one daughter, the founder of the Israelite nation. Favored by his mother Rebekah, he impersonated his brother Esau and obtained the birthright and Isaac's blessings. Because of Esau's anger, he fled Canaan and went to Mesopotamia to live with his uncle Laban in Paddan-aram. Some 20 years later he returned to Canaan. His favorite son Joseph was sold into slavery, but subsequently Joseph became viceroy of Egypt. During the years of famine, Jacob and his sons settled in Egypt where they prospered and multiplied. After Jacob's death his body was carried into Canaan and buried in the Cave of Machpelah with his ancestors and his wife Leah.

Vladimir Jabotinsky, co-founder of the Jewish Legion and the founder of Revisionist Zionism.

Rachel, mother of Joseph and Benjamin, had died earlier.

JACOB, BLESSING OF

The Biblical text in Genesis chapter 49, consisting of the individual blessings given by Jacob to his twelve sons on his death-bed. The blessings include a characterization of each son, describing his positive and negative traits.

JACOB BEN ASHER (1269–1340)

Jewish codifier of the 14th century, also known as the "Baal Ha-Turim." Born in Germany, he declined the position of rabbi, and lived in Spain the greater part of his life. His fundamental work was the *Arbaah Turim* (Four Rows), a compilation of the essential Jewish laws intended as a practical guide for the average Jew. The book contained four parts: *Tur Orah Hayim* (Way of Life), containing the laws on prayer, the Sabbath and the Holy Days; *Tur Yoreh Deah* (Teacher of Knowledge), dealing with the dietary laws, cleanliness, circumcision, etc.; *Tur Even Ha-Ezer* (Stone of Help), laws on marriage and divorce; and *Tur Hoshen Ha-Mishpat* (Breastplate of Judgment) on Jewish civil and criminal law. The *Turim*, one of the first known printed Hebrew books, became the standard authoritative Jewish code, and the basis for the later popular code, the *Shulhan Arukh*, compiled by Joseph Karo.

JACOB BEN MEIR TAM (1100–1171)

Grandson of Rashi, leading Talmudic authority of France, popularly known as "Rabbenu Tam." He taught Talmud at Ramerupt, but after attack by the Crusaders, he settled in Troyes, where he headed several rabbinical conferences which issued a series of rabbinic ordinances known as the "Ordinances of Rabbenu Tam." Some of these ordinances dealt with improvements of women's rights. Rabbenu Tam was head of the French school of *Tosafists* (Talmudic commentators), having students from many lands. Jewish communities of western and central Europe sought his *Responsa* (answers) to questions on Jewish law. The *Tosafot* (notes) are published in many editions of the Talmud, and his book, *Sefer Ha-Yashar*, offers important explanations to thirty Talmudic tractates. Rabbenu Tam also wrote a number of liturgical poems (Piyyutim), some of which were incorporated in the prayer book.

Extremely pious Jews use "Rabbenu Tam's Tefillin" in addition to the *Tefillin* (Phylacteries) ordinarily used. The reason for this practice is that Rabbenu Tam held that the order of the Biblical texts inserted in the Tefillin be somewhat different than the order mentioned by Rashi, his illustrious grandfather.

JAFFA

The Joppa of the Bible. Ancient Mediterranean seaport in Palestine, mentioned in the Bible as the point of embarkation of the lumber brought from Lebanon for the building of the Temple in the days of Solomon, and as the port from which Jonah sailed, and was "swallowed by a big fish." The Maccabees, the Romans, as well as the Crusaders and Napoleon, conducted their military campaigns in Jaffa. At the beginning of the 20th century Jaffa became a center of Jewish colonization, and at the outbreak of World War I it had about 10,000 Jewish inhabitants and about 35,000 Arabs. Its Jewish population was steadily reduced as a result of Arab anti-Jewish riots; and Tel Aviv, first established as a suburb of Jaffa, became the largest all-Jewish city in Palestine. Following the establishment of the State of Israel and the War of Liberation, most of the Arabs fled from Jaffa, which is

The ocean front at Jaffa, Israel's ancient Mediterranean port and fishing village. Once primarily an Arab city, it is now peopled by Jewish immigrants, and part of the Tel Aviv municipal administration.

now predominantly populated by Jews. In 1949, Jaffa was incorporated into the municipality of Tel Aviv, which adopted the official name of Tel Aviv–Jaffa.

JAHRZEIT see Yortzeit.

JAHVEH see Tetragrammaton.

JAMNIA see Yavneh.

JAPAN

In 1960 about 1,000 Jews lived in Japan. Jews have begun to immigrate to Japan about a half a century ago, and most of them live in Tokyo, Yokohama and Kobe. Some writers have advanced a theory that the Japanese are descendants of the Ten Lost Tribes of the Kingdom of Israel. In the late 1950's a great deal of interest in

Judaism was aroused in intellectual circles, and there were a number of conversions to Judaism.

JAVNEH see Yavneh.

JEHOASH see Yehoash.

JEHOVAH

In Jewish tradition the name of God *Yod Hé Vav Hé* may not be sounded. It is customarily pronounced "Adonai," and when the ineffable name in Hebrew is vocalized it is given the vowels of that word (Sheva, Ḥolam, Kamatz). In Latin transliteration this became Jehova. It is clear that the word Jehova (Jehovah) is an artificial composite. Modern scholarship believes that the original pronunciation of the name was "Yahveh."

JEHU

King of Israel, anointed by the prophet Elisha. He ruled from 842 to 815 b.c.e., and founded a new dynasty of five kings, following the reign of Ahab. Although unsuccessful in his attempts to defend the kingdom from foreign invasions, Jehu did succeed, at least for a time, in rooting out Baal worship from Israel.

JEHUDAH see Judah.

JEPHTHAH

One of the Judges in Israel, remembered for his victory over the Ammonites who threatened to overrun Gilead east of the Jordan. At first Jephthah, who was of inferior birth, was exiled by his half-brothers and the elders of Gilead, but he was later recalled to lead the Israelites in the war against the Ammonites. The Bible tells that Jephthah made a vow that if he returned victorious from the battle against the Ammonites, he would sacrifice to God whatever came out of his house first. It turned out that his only daughter was the first to come out and greet him on the occasion of his victory. The Bible further tells of a civil war that started because the Ephraimites were angered by Jephthah's refusal to ask their help in his fight against the enemy. The Ephraimites were completely routed by Jephthah in their retreat to west of the Jordan. To detect the fleeing Ephraimites, Jephthah's men directed them to pronounce the word "shibbolet"; the Ephraimites could not pronounce the SH, and instead pronounced it "sibbolet." Based on this story the word "shibboleth" means criterion, test or watchword.

JEREMIAH

One of the major Hebrew prophets, whose book bears his name. Jeremiah prophesied from the 13th year of the reign of King Josiah in 626 b.c.e., until his death after 582 b.c.e. Jeremiah's prophecies reflect his great love for the people of Israel, and his great concern over the fate of the nation. He was most outspoken in his utterances against idolatry and social injustice. He taught that every individual was responsible for his conduct, and he emphasized personal religion. His famous "confessions" show his depth of feeling and his close sense of communion with God. In his anxiety to save the nation from destruction, Jeremiah advocated submission to the rule of Babylon, which he believed to be the instrument selected by God for the punishment of Judah. Because of his repeated predictions that the Temple would be destroyed, he aroused the anger of the king and the people, and his life was threatened. He was forced to live in hiding, where he dictated his prophecies, which were written down by his faithful disciple and secretary, Baruch ben Neriah. Jeremiah's warnings and good advice remained unheeded. He lived to see the fall of Jerusalem and the destruction of the Temple by the Babylonians, against whom King Zedekiah unsuccessfully rebelled. Jeremiah refused to join the captives, who were carried off to Babylon, and after the assassination of Gedaliah, the governor of Judah, he probably joined the remnants of the people who fled to Egypt. In a letter to the Jewish community in Babylon, Jeremiah advised the people to establish themselves in their land of exile, to build homes, marry off their children, and to pray for the welfare of the country in which they lived. This prophetic directive became the guiding principle of Jews throughout their subsequent history in the diaspora. According to tradition, Jeremiah also wrote the *Book of Lamentations*, describing the despair and the desolation of Jerusalem after the exile, the once glorious, prosperous and happy capital of Judah.

Overall view of Jerusalem, one of mankind's very oldest cities. In the foreground is the fine octagonal Mosque of Omar built on the probable site of King Solomon's Temple late in the 7th century.

JERICHO

An Arab village situated northeast of Jerusalem, near the site of the ancient city of the same name, mentioned frequently in the Bible. Jericho, the walls of which crumbled to the sound of the Shofar, was conquered by the Israelites, led by Joshua, when they entered the land of Canaan. Throughout the centuries Jericho was destroyed and rebuilt many times. Ancient Jericho was excavated by German archeologists in 1908 and 1910, and subsequently by English archeologists in 1930. See *Archeology*.

JEROBOAM I

Son of Nebat and first king of the northern Kingdom of Israel (c. 930–910 b.c.e.), which he founded after the death of Solo-

mon by separating it from the rest of the country. Jeroboam, elevated to a high position, rose against Solomon, and had to flee to Egypt. After Solomon's death he returned, and caused the division of the United Kingdom. As first ruler of the Northern Kingdom, in the capital of Shechem, he set up shrines for the worship of the sacred calf at Dan and Beth-el. Because he stimulated idol-worship, Jeroboam is regarded by Jewish tradition as a sinful king, who led others to sin.

JEROBOAM II

King of Israel (784–744 b.c.e.) who expanded the kingdom by annexing Aramean towns. The prophets Hosea and Amos denounced the corruption of his rule. There was great economic prosperity in his day.

JERUSALEM

One of the oldest cities, Jerusalem was in existence long before the Israelites conquered Canaan. David conquered it from the Jebusites and made it the capital of the United Kingdom of Israel. It attained its glory in the days of Solomon, when it became the spiritual center of the people after the erection of the Holy Temple. Jerusalem has since survived many wars and conquests by the empires of ancient, medieval and modern times. It has been estimated that during the days of the Second Commonwealth the Jewish population of Jerusalem probably reached a million. Jerusalem was successively conquered during the following major expeditions: The Babylonians in 587 b.c.e.; the Romans in 70 c.e.; the Moslems in 637; the Crusaders in 1099; the Moslems in 1187; and the British in 1918. There were Jews in Jerusalem throughout history with the exception of short periods. After the Moslem conquest, Jews were permitted to settle in Jerusalem, but the entire Jewish community was wiped out during the expeditions of the Crusaders. A more significant Jewish settlement in Jerusalem began in the 19th century, and grew in recent times to become the second largest Jewish community in the State of Israel. Jerusalem is divided into two major sections; the Old City, which after the War of Liberation in 1948 was placed under Arab rule; and the New City, which is predominantly Jewish, and the capital of the State of Israel.

Jerusalem is mentioned in the daily liturgy, and throughout the centuries of Jewish dispersion it was the symbol of the nation's glorious past as well as of hope for the ultimate restoration of the national Jewish homeland.

JESHURUN

Hebrew term meaning "righteous" or "valiant," used in the Bible as a poetic name for the people of Israel.

JESUS OF NAZARETH

Central figure of Christianity, and regarded by its adherents as the "Christ" (Greek for "Messiah"). Jesus (Hebrew: Yeshu) was born during the reign of the Emperor Augustus, Palestine then being a province of the Roman Empire. The day and month of Jesus' birth are not known, nor, with any certainty, is the year. The "Common Era" was thought to be reckoned from the time of Jesus' birth, but scholars believe that he was probably born four to eight years prior to the first year of the Christian calendar.

Gospel accounts of Jesus' boyhood, youth, and early manhood are meager. They state that he was circumcised, and that he early showed an active interest in Jewish teachings and religious questions.

At about the age of thirty, Jesus was publicly baptized by the famous preacher, John the Baptist, then after a brief period of withdrawal, began his career as preacher and teacher. Journeying throughout the country, he preached, especially in Galilee, to large crowds of fishermen, laborers, and other humble people. In sermons and parables he promised salvation in the "Kingdom of God."

When, in the third year of his ministry, Jesus set out for Jerusalem to keep the feast of the Passover, he apparently did so in anticipation of his death. Upon his entry into Jerusalem he was openly proclaimed by his followers as the Messiah. Of perhaps more concern to Jews who did not accept that claim was Jesus' statement that he was the "Son of God." Through succeeding centuries this statement of Jesus has been subject to differing manners and degrees of interpretation by various sections of the Christian faith.

In the eyes of Jewish authorities, Jesus'

claims to messiahship were particularly distressing because of their political implications, since Palestine had already suffered as the result of attempted insurrections against the Herodian rulers. As a probable rebel against Roman authority, Jesus was handed over to the Roman governor, Pontius Pilate, to be tried for treason. He was adjudged guilty, sentenced by Pilate to death by crucifixion, and the sentence carried out. Some of Jesus' disciples believed that he was resurrected on the third day after his death and burial. His teachings continued to be preached in and beyond Palestine, and a new faith, the Christian, began to take root and spread, developed by the Apostles, notably Paul.

Many of Jesus' teachings were similar to those of the Pharisees, yet the Gospels, set down some years after his death, indicate that a complete rift, even strong animosity, existed between Jesus and the Pharisees. This supposition can perhaps be explained by the fact that the Gospel accounts, in which the Pharisees are referred to as "hypocrites," reflect not a condition that existed in Jesus' lifetime, but rather hostility which sprang up after his death between Judaism and the new Christian church.

Of great concern to Jews is the lingering medieval accusation that the Jews as a people were responsible both for the fact of Jesus' execution and the manner of it. This old canard that the Jews were "Christ-killers" became in turn the excuse for much hatred and persecution of the Jews—the persecution reaching at times dimensions of mass brutality and hysteria.

There is no doubt among scholars that legal responsibility for the execution of Jesus rested squarely upon the Roman authorities, since they reserved to themselves the right to inflict the death penalty within the Empire. And the method of Jesus' execution was Roman, not Jewish.

Crucifixion was, in fact, the standard Roman punishment for treason or insurrection within the Empire, and other Jewish leaders before and after Jesus of Nazareth had suffered this death at the hands of the Romans.

The question of responsibility for turning Jesus over to the Romans for trial and judgment is also of great complexity, involving conflicting partisan currents among Jews and Romans and affected at all points by insufficient evidence. The Jewish population of Jesus' time is known to have presented not a monolithic front but clearly discernible tendencies to division, such as country Jew against city Jew, and to an extent, of poor against rich. Palestine, as a conquered province, even suffered the existence of a Herodian party in the Temple. Over all lay the shadow of the power of Rome. No act, and no decision taken under these circumstances, can be rightly construed as representing the corporate will of the "Jewish people."

The reason for Jesus' execution is left unclear in the Gospel story, appearing sometimes as a charge of heresy against Judaism and sometimes as a charge of treason against Rome. The Gospels appear to represent different layers of tradition on this matter. The earlier layers imply a threat of insurrection against Rome and Roman repression thereof. The later tend to clear the Roman authorities, particularly Pontius Pilate, of any responsibility in Jesus' death. It is perhaps significant that the later traditions grew up at a time when the early Christian church was becoming largely Gentile in composition and was dissociating itself from its Jewish origins. Both versions, mutually contradictory, appear together in the Gospel stories. See *Christianity*.

JETHRO

Father-in-law of Moses, a priest of the

Midianites; the English rendering of the Hebrew *Yitro*. When Moses fled Egypt after killing a cruel Egyptian slave driver, he came to Midian, married Zipporah, Jethro's daughter, and became a shepherd. When Moses returned to Egypt to deliver the Israelites, he left his wife and two sons with Jethro. Later, when Moses led the Israelites through the desert, Jethro came to greet him, and helped him set up a system of people's courts.

JEW

Designation of a member of the Jewish people, or an adherent of the Jewish faith. The term derives from its Hebrew equivalent *Yehudi* (Judean) which gradually became the generic term in the course of centuries, since the tribes other than Judah had mostly been assimilated into that tribe. See *Israel, People of.*

JEW BADGE see Badge, Jewish.

JEWISH AGENCY FOR ISRAEL

Article IV of the League of Nations mandate for Palestine, conferred on Great Britain in 1922, provided that a "Jewish Agency" as a representative body of the Jewish people be formed to assume the responsibility for Jewish immigration and settlement in Palestine, and to cooperate with the mandatory power in all matters concerning the development of the Jewish national home. The Jewish Agency was extended in 1929 by including 50 per cent of non-Zionist members, representing the Jewish communities of various countries. The president of the World Zionist Organization served as the president of the Jewish Agency. Despite the difficulties created by the mandatory power, the Jewish Agency exercised considerable influence in the development of the Jewish homeland in Palestine. The Jewish Agency took over from the Zionist Organization the Palestine Foundation Fund (Keren

Ha-Yesod), and through its fund-raising activities it provided for the training of immigrants, colonization, public health, housing, labor and public works. When the British government withdrew from its mandate for Palestine and the State of Israel was proclaimed in 1948, the Jewish Agency continued to function as the representative body of the Jewish people for the purpose of strengthening and developing the Jewish republic. The Jewish Agency is still active in cultural matters in the United States and throughout the rest of the world.

Aerial photograph of the Jewish Agency's headquarters buildings in the new city of Jerusalem.

JEWISH BRIGADE

A separate Jewish fighting force (in some respects similar to the Jewish Legion of World War I), formed in September 1944 as part of the British army. As the result of persistent urging of the Jewish Agency, under the leadership of Chaim Weizmann, the establishment of a Jewish Brigade, made up of Jewish military units in Palestine, was finally approved by the British government. First stationed in Egypt, and under the command of Brigadier A. P. Benjamin, the Brigade was subsequently moved to Italy. As part of the Eighth Army, it first went into action in north Italy in February 1945. The existence of the Jewish Brigade in a strategic area of World War II gave hope and encouragement to Jewish survivors of the concentration camps seeking to reach the shores of the Jewish homeland in Palestine. The Jewish Brigade accomplished a double task: it contributed to the final defeat of the Nazi army, and it also engaged in rescue work, aiding Jewish victims of Nazism. After serving for several months on the front line between Belgium and Holland, the Brigade returned to Palestine, and was disbanded in 1946.

JEWISH CENTER see Center, the Jewish.

JEWISH CHAUTAUQUA SOCIETY

An educational organization formed in Philadelphia in 1893 for the dissemination of Jewish religion and culture in America. The Society, founded by Rabbi Henry Berkowitz, conducted its educational work through study circles, a correspondence school, and assemblies and forums held during summer and winter vacation periods. In 1910 the Society started a program of summer school lectures at universities. These programs became very popular, and were attended by thousands of students in a large number of American universities. In 1939 the reform National Federation of Temple Brotherhoods took over the Society, and established its headquarters in Cincinnati, from which it later moved to New York. The Society is subsidized through membership fees, individual contributions and welfare fund grants.

JEWISH COLONIZATION ASSOCIATION

A philanthropic association commonly known as the ICA, founded by Baron Maurice de Hirsch of Paris in 1891 for the purpose of aiding east European Jews to settle in agricultural colonies. The major colonization project of the ICA started in Argentine, where thousands of Jews were settled on land purchased by Baron de Hirsch. Similar colonization activities were undertaken in Brazil, Canada, Palestine, Russia and Poland. The ICA also assisted the colonists through the establishment of schools, and cooperative loan and savings banks.

JEWISH EDUCATION COMMITTEE

An agency organized in 1939 in New York, with an endowment of $1,000,000 from the foundation established by Colonel Michael Friedsam. The J.E.C. seeks to meet the educational needs of the different groups in Greater New York through cooperation with the official educational agencies. The major functions of the J.E.C. are: 1) to provide educational consultants for the various types of Jewish schools; 2) to offer scholarship grants to the schools; 3) to conduct pupil enrollment campaigns; 4) to maintain a code of practice for schools and teachers; 5) to initiate experimental educational activities; 6) to maintain teachers' group insurance and a pension fund; 7) to help maintain the board of licenses for Hebrew teachers; 8) to maintain an in-service training program for teachers; 9) to maintain a pedagogic reference library; 10) to publish various teaching aids, manuals, textbooks, and the "World Over," a children's magazine; 11) to sponsor *Keren Ami*, a children's welfare fund project; 12) to maintain a department of youth education; 13) to operate a department of statistics and research; 14) to enlist community support for Jewish education, through a special Community Council.

JEWISH FOUNDATION FUND see Keren Ha-Yesod.

JEWISH HISTORICAL SOCIETY see American Jewish Historical Society.

JEWISH INSTITUTE OF RELIGION see Hebrew Union College-Jewish Institute of Religion.

JEWISH LABOR COMMITTEE

Founded in 1934, it is a representative body of organized labor in the United

Soldiers of the Jewish Legion pray near the Wailing Wall. Organized during World War I, and commanded by British General Allenby, the Legion fought on the Palestinian front and had a fine record.

States, including three international unions, trade unions, the Workmen's Circle, and other labor organizations. It was organized for the purpose of aiding Jewish and non-Jewish labor institutions overseas to help the victims of oppression and persecution, and to combat anti-Semitism and racial and religious prejudices in the United States and elsewhere. The Jewish Labor Committee was particularly active during and after World War II. It helped the Jewish population in Nazi-occupied countries, and rescued many Jewish and non-Jewish labor leaders from the Nazi terror. The Committee conducts a program of educational work consisting of lectures, meetings and publications. It is maintained through contributions from the labor organizations, and cooperates with the American Jewish Joint Distribution Committee, the ORT (Society for the Rehabilitation and Training) and the National Jewish Welfare Board.

JEWISH LEGION

Following the outbreak of World War I, Vladimir Jabotinsky and Captain Joseph Trumpeldor recruited over 600 Jews in Egypt who had been expelled by the Turks from Palestine, as fighting units in the British army. These units were, however, not used in the Palestine front for the liberation of Palestine from the Turks; they were, instead, sent to the Gallipoli front as the Zion Mule Corps. Owing to the efforts of Jabotinsky, and as a result of the Balfour Declaration in 1917, other Jewish fighting battalions were recruited from Palestine, the United States and elsewhere, for the Palestinian front exclusively. The total number of Jews in the Jewish battalions, known as the Jewish Legion, that fought under British command, was over 10,000.

In 1918, the victorious Jewish legionnaires entered Jerusalem, and Palestine was freed from Turkish rule. The Jewish Legion was highly praised by the British commander-in-chief, Marshal Edmund Allenby, for its heroic stand on the Palestinian front. Shortly thereafter, and over Jewish protests, the Legion was demobilized.

JEWISH NATIONAL FUND

World organization which is the instrument of world Jewry to acquire and develop land in Israel on behalf of the entire Jewish people. Its Hebrew name is *Keren Kayemet Le-Yisrael*. It was founded in 1901 at the fifth Zionist Congress on the proposal of Professor Hermann Zvi Schapira, famous mathematician and Zionist leader.

The Jewish National Fund acquires land in Israel as the eternal possession of the Jewish people; reclaims and improves the soil; plants trees and forests, and generally prepares the land for Jewish settlement.

The Fund organization, with its headquarters in Jerusalem, is administered by a twelve-man board of directors elected by the Zionist Congress. The Fund laid the foundations of the Jewish State through its land holdings on which there was a peasantry firmly rooted in the soil, and whose

The Golden Book, kept at Jewish National Fund headquarters in Jerusalem, records the names of many contributors to land purchase in Israel.

settlements served as a bastion of Jewish military defense.

With the establishment of the State of Israel, the scope of land activities was broadened. Out of 20,500,000 dunams within the boundaries of the state, only 5,000,000 dunams were under cultivation in 1960. The rest is desert, rock, swamp and sand dunes. It is the mission of the Fund to reclaim the land it has bought, and to turn the wilderness into arable soil. The government of Israel authorized the Fund to purchase abandoned Arab land in Israel.

The Jewish National Fund helps in the absorbing of new immigrants in three ways: a) it places land at the disposal of new villages and urban housing plans for new immigrants; b) it provides the newcomers with employment through reclamation works, afforestation, road building, etc.; c) through its land improvement program it helps the country feed its growing population.

The Fund raises funds all over the world through its traditional collection techniques, such as the Blue Box, inscriptions in the Golden Book, tree subscriptions, *Sefer Ha-Yeled* (Children's Book), *Sefer Bar Mitzvah* (Bar Mitzvah Register), and through various functions and provisions for bequests. The Fund in 1960 owned 3,343,000 dunams of land and raised, since its beginning, over two hundred million dollars, of which 72% were received from the United States.

JEWISH NATIONAL WORKERS' ALLIANCE see Farband, Labor Zionist Order.

JEWISH PUBLICATION SOCIETY OF AMERICA
Founded in Philadelphia in 1888 for the purpose of publishing and distributing books of Jewish interest in English. As a non-profit publishing house, it has published and distributed many of the foremost titles of Jewish literature.

JEWISH SCIENCE (Juedische Wissenschaft)

A school of scholarship established in Germany in the nineteenth century which influenced Jewish scholars throughout Europe. It was devoted to discovering and publishing factual material about Jewish history, literature, philosophy and religion. It utilized scientific research methods and is also commonly known as the "Science of Judaism."

JEWISH TELEGRAPHIC AGENCY

World-wide Jewish news service, established in 1917, with offices in London, New York, Berlin, Paris, Jerusalem, and special correspondents in major cities of Europe, Asia, South Africa, Australia and South America. The Agency services both the Jewish and the non-Jewish press.

JEWISH THEOLOGICAL SEMINARY OF AMERICA

Founded in 1886 in New York as the "Jewish Theological Seminary Association" for the training of rabbis and teachers, with Sabato Morais as its first president. Under the leadership of Solomon Schechter, its name was changed in 1902 to "The Jewish Theological Seminary of America," and it became the spiritual center of conservative Judaism. After the death of Solomon Schechter in 1915, Cyrus Adler succeeded as president. Louis Finkelstein, who followed him as president in 1940, later became its chancellor.

Strengthened by the United Synagogue of America, founded by Schechter in 1913, and the Rabbinical Assembly of America, the Seminary made rapid progress. It now maintains in addition to the rabbinical school, the Teachers' Institute, the Seminary Institute of Jewish Affairs, the Seminary School of Jewish Studies, the Leaders Training Fellowship, the Institute of Religious and Social Studies, and the Cantors' Institute. *Ramah* camps are under the educational supervision of the

New York City's Jewish Museum, maintained under Jewish Theological Seminary auspices.

Seminary. It also sponsors the Jewish Museum in New York City which was established in 1953, and the Seminary Israel Institute, established jointly with the Jewish Agency in 1952. The Seminary has one of the largest libraries of Judaica and Hebraica in the world. Together with its West Coast branch, *The University of Judaism* in Los Angeles, it had, as of 1960, an enrollment of over 2,500 students in all its schools and departments, and is staffed by recognized authorities in Jewish academic and professional learning. Its hundreds of graduates serve as rabbis, teachers, principals and educational directors in almost every important community throughout the United States and Canada.

JEWISH WAR VETERANS OF THE UNITED STATES

A nation-wide organization formed in 1923 from the previously existing organizations of Jewish war veterans. Eligible as members are Jewish men and women in the armed forces of the United States and who served in its wars. The aims of the Jewish War Veterans are: to maintain allegiance to the United States of America; to defend the good name of the Jew and his rights wherever attacked; to give assistance to veterans and their families whenever in need; to compile and keep records of patriotic services by Jewish men and women in the armed forces; and to honor the memory of Jewish war heroes. The organization, with its headquarters in New York City, had (in 1960) 110,000 members with about 790 posts located in every large city of the United States.

JEWISH WELFARE BOARD see National Jewish Welfare Board.

JEW OF MALTA, THE

A once popular play depicting a greedy blood-thirsty Jew, written by Marlowe in 1588. It is believed that this play was the basis for the characterization of "Shylock" in Shakespeare's "Merchant of Venice."

JEZEBEL

Wife of Ahab, king of Israel, and daughter of a Phoenician king. As the queen of Israel she introduced among the Israelites the customs of her people and the worship of the Phoenician Baal. She is regarded by tradition as a wicked and sinful woman. The prophet Elijah led a bitter fight against Jezebel and her idolatrous ways, and his curse that "the dogs shall eat Jezebel in the moat of Jezreel" finally came to pass during the uprising of Jehu against Ahab's dynasty.

JEZREEL, PLAIN OF see Emek Jezreel.

JOB

One of the greatest books of the Wisdom Literature, contained in the third section of the Bible, the *Ketuvim* (Writings). It deals with the problem of divine justice, seeking an answer to the question: "Why do the righteous suffer?"

The *Book of Job* contains 42 chapters and consists of a prologue (first 2 chapters), an epilogue (last chapter), and the bulk of the book in the form of a series of dialogues between Job and his friends. In the prologue Satan questions the sincerity of Job, known as a pious and virtuous man; he claims that Job is obedient to God only because of the favors He had bestowed upon him. To test Job's obedience, God permits Satan to bring upon Job all sorts of misfortunes: his wealth is taken away from him, then his beloved children die, and finally he is afflicted with a loathsome disease.

In the dramatic dialogue between Job and his three friends, the question of undeserved suffering is discussed. Job, shaken by many misfortunes and great suffering, pours out his soul in bitter protest against God's unjustifiable punishment as he proclaims his innocence. His friends, however, insist that Job confess his guilt, because God's punishment, though not understood by man, is nevertheless always deserved.

In the epilogue, describing God's appearance in a storm, out of which He spoke to Job, the latter is told to realize how insignificant man is in the face of God's omnipotence, and how futile is the attempt to understand God's actions.

JOCHEBED

Wife of Amram of the tribe of Levi, mother of Moses, Aaron and Miriam.

JOEL

One of the so-called Minor Prophets. His prophecies comprise the four chapters of the *Book of Joel*. Joel describes the doom of the land caused by a plague of locusts, and then repentance followed by alleviation of distress. He sees a vision of "The Day of the Lord," when the enemies of Judah will be judged and punished and the glory of Jerusalem will be restored.

Little is known about Joel's life. Some scholars maintain that he prophesied during the reign of King Joash (836–798 b.c.e.), while others believe that some of the prophecies contained in the *Book of Joel* belong to a much later period.

JOHANAN BEN ZAKKAI

Tanna, prominent disciple of Hillel and father of the academy at Yavneh (70 c.e.), of which he was president. According to tradition Johanan is believed to have lived 120 years, that is, from 40 b.c.e. to 80 c.e. Johanan foresaw the bitter end of the people's revolt against the Romans, and advised submission to the conquerors. When Jerusalem was besieged, he fled the city secretly and came before Vespasian to get permission to preserve the academy at Yavneh. With the fall of Jerusalem, Yavneh became the spiritual and intellectual center of the conquered nation. As head of the academy, Johanan became the most influential teacher of his time, and many of his pupils later became leaders of the people. Because of his wisdom, his piety, and his devotion to the study of the Law, Johanan is regarded as one of the beloved figures in Jewish history, and many of his sayings are quoted to this day. Johanan was among those teachers whose foresight and leadership helped adjust Jewish life to an existence no longer centered on the Temple.

JOHANAN (JOHN) OF GISCHALA (GISCALA)

Military leader and patriot during the Judean war with the Romans (66–70 c.e.). A native of the Galilean town Gush Ḥalav (Gischala), he attempted to rouse the Galilean population against the Jewish military leader Josephus, whom he suspected of treason. After the fall of Gischala, which was attacked by the Romans, Johanan fled with the remnants of his army to Jerusalem. There he contended against the other Jewish military leaders (such as Simon bar Giora) for control over the military operations of the city. However, during the Roman siege of Jerusalem the rival leaders united their efforts against the common foe. After the fall of Jerusalem, Johanan was carried off with other captives to Rome, where he died in prison.

JOHN THE BAPTIST

Considered by Christian tradition the forerunner of Jesus Christ, John (i.e. Johanan) the Baptist was a preacher in the first century c.e. He was probably a member of the Jewish sect of the Essenes, and as a wandering preacher through Galilee and Judea he called upon the people to repent in preparation for the approaching "Kingdom of Heaven" (Judgment Day). He had his many followers baptized in the waters of the Jordan as a symbol of purification of sin. The New Testament has John baptizing Jesus. Herod Antipas, then governor of Perea, feared that John might arouse his followers against him on account of his immoral marriage, and had him arrested and put to death.

JOINT DISTRIBUTION COMMITTEE, AMERICAN JEWISH

Chief agency of American Jewry for the relief of distressed Jews in foreign countries. It is commonly known as J.D.C. or "Joint." It was organized in 1914 through the efforts of outstanding American Jewish leaders, Felix Warburg, Julius Rosenwald and others, for the purpose of relieving the suffering of the Jewish victims of World War I, and has continued as the major agency for aid to Jews overseas. The activities of the J.D.C. have branched out into almost every country in eastern and central Europe, the Near East and Far East (including Israel), and North Africa. Outside of its emergency aid which

245

Some of the founders of the Joint Distribution Committee, November 27, 1914. It represents the relief organizations of all American Jewry. Felix M. Warburg (left, foreground) was the first Joint chairman.

reached millions of Jews the world over, the J.D.C. initiated programs of rehabilitation (such as child-care centers, trade schools, credit and loan societies, hospitals, summer colonies for tubercular and anemic children), and has aided and maintained various religious and cultural institutions. The work of the J.D.C. assumed great proportions during the rise of Nazism in Germany, the outbreak of World War II, and establishment of the State of Israel. Although the J.D.C. was started by well-to-do Jewish leaders of the American Jewish Committee, it has become representative of

Jewish girl from the ghetto in Teheran, Iran, clutches "loaves" of Persian bread. Living in dire poverty, as do various other Jews in Middle Eastern countries, such Jews were cared for by the Joint Distribution Committee's relief fund.

all Jewish groups in the United States, and its benefits have been and are extended to all Jews irrespective of their political or ideological differences.

JONAH

One of the so-called Minor Prophets, whose book by the same name contains a unique story. Jonah, the son of Amittai, a Hebrew prophet, was commanded by God to proceed to Nineveh, the capital of Assyria, and foretell the doom of the city because of its sins. Jonah disobeyed and embarked on a ship travelling from Joppa (Jaffa) to Tarshish. A storm broke out on the high seas and Jonah was thrown overboard by the sailors at his own request and insistence, after which he was swallowed by a big fish. In the belly of the

247

View of Palestine's historic river, the Jordan. A source of legend and folklore for Jews and Christians alike, the river is potentially very valuable as a present-day source of hydro-electric power for Israel.

fish Jonah prayed to God, and as a result he was cast up by the fish on dry land. Jonah then fulfilled his prophetic mission, going to Nineveh, where he prophesied its imminent doom. The people of Nineveh repented, and God saved the city from destruction. Jonah was angered because his prophecy remained unfulfilled. God then spoke to Jonah, teaching him that one must be merciful and forgiving to all people, even sinners, if they repent.

Although Jonah, the son of Amittai, is mentioned in the Bible as the contemporary of King Jeroboam II (782–741 b.c.e.), some students of the Bible believe the *Book of Jonah* to have been written at a much later period.

Because of its universalistic tone and its message of tolerance, mercy, repentance and forgiveness, the *Book of Jonah* is traditionally recited as the Haftarah for the afternoon service on Yom Kippur.

JONATHAN

Son of King Saul, mentioned in the Bible as a skillful warrior, and noted especially for his great friendship with David. Following Jonathan's death in a battle with the Philistines, David uttered a most touching eulogy, which is considered to be one of the finest examples of poetic expression.

JORDAN

Principal river of Palestine known in Hebrew as *Yarden*. Several springs at the foot of Mount Hermon are the source of the

Jordan, which runs southward through Lake Huleh, and the Kinneret (Sea of Galilee), and empties into the Dead Sea. It forms a natural dividing line between eastern and western Palestine, and because of its rapid flow and its narrowness in many parts, it is not navigable. The fall of the Jordan, especially between Lake Kinneret, which is 682 feet below sea-level, and the Dead Sea, which is 1292 feet below sea-level, is potentially usable as a source for the generation of hydro-electric power for the country. However, as a result of international tension, no progress has been made in the matter. Most of the smaller streams in the country flow into the Jordan, the most important of which are the Yarmuk and the Jabbok. The Jordan River has, through the centuries, been a source of Jewish folklore and a theme for both ancient and modern Hebrew poets. In Christian tradition too, the Jordan is considered a holy river.

JOSEPH

Beloved son of Jacob, Rachel's first-born, and father of Ephraim and Manasseh. The cycle of Joseph's stories as told in the *Book of Genesis* is considered among the most beautiful short stories in all literature. A dreamer of dreams and Jacob's favored son, Joseph aroused the envy and hatred of his brothers. He was sold as a slave and was brought to Egypt. With his personal charm, resourcefulness and intelligence, Joseph finally established himself as a gracious and reputable person. His wisdom included the ability to interpret dreams. When summoned to interpret Pharaoh's dreams he predicted the coming of seven years of plenty to be followed by seven years of famine. Pharaoh put Joseph in charge of the country's economy, and elevated him to the rank of viceroy. As famine spread to Canaan, Joseph's brothers came to Egypt to purchase grain. The

story of Joseph confronting his brethren has been dramatized frequently. In the end their wrongdoing was forgiven. Later Joseph's brothers and their families settled in Egypt together with Jacob, where they prospered under the protection of their illustrious brother and son. Joseph lived 110 years and his embalmed remains were ultimately brought to Canaan and buried near Shechem. The tribes of Israel bear the names of his two sons.

JOSEPHUS, FLAVIUS (c. 37–100)

Roman name of a Jewish historian and military leader. Known in Hebrew as *Yosef ben Mattityahu* (Mattathias), a descendant of a family of priests, he associated himself in his youth with the Essenes, and later became a Pharisee. At the age of twenty-six Josephus was sent to Rome to help free a number of priests arrested by the Romans. When he returned to Jerusalem, the Jewish revolt against Rome had begun. He was appointed military leader of the Galilee. Josephus apparently did not believe in the successful outcome of the revolt, and he was soon suspected by the Jewish patriots (especially Johanan of Gischala) of trying to suppress the rebellion. The attempts to recall Josephus as commander of the Galilean army failed, and the city of Jotapata, which he defended, was soon captured by the Romans. Fleeing Jotapata, he hid in a cave, but eventually surrendered to the Romans, praising the conqueror Vespasian, and predicting that he would soon become Emperor of Rome. Following the fall of Jerusalem, Josephus settled in Rome, where Vespasian and later Titus bestowed many favors upon him, and where he lived for the rest of his life.

Despite the fact that Josephus is traditionally considered a traitor and a Romanizer, he is superb as a Jewish historian. Apparently intending to please the Romans, he wrote his first historical work entitled

249

JOSHUA

The Jewish War, first in Aramaic and then in Greek. In this work he glorifies Rome, and attempts to put the blame for the Jewish revolt on the zealots (Jewish patriots). His second work, called *The Jewish Antiquities*, contains twenty books, designed as a complete history of the Jewish people from Creation to the time of the revolt against Rome. His other important works are *Autobiography* and *Against Apion*, a defense of the Jewish people against the anti-Jewish attacks by the Greek Apion of Alexandria. His historical works constitute the best available source for the study of Jewish life during the period of the Second Commonwealth.

JOSHUA

Son of Nun, successor of Moses and conqueror of Canaan. During the wanderings of the Israelites in the wilderness, Joshua, an Ephraimite, was the trusted and courageous lieutenant of Moses. After Moses died, Joshua led the Israelites into Canaan, and later divided the conquered land among the tribes. His life and activities are described in the Bible, largely in the *Book of Joshua*, though a number of incidents are also told in *Exodus*, *Numbers* and *Deuteronomy*. Tradition attributes the writing of the *Book of Joshua* to Joshua himself, but some modern critics believe that its final redaction took place at a much later date.

JUBILEE see Sabbatical Year.

JUDAH

Fourth son of Jacob and Leah, and founder of the tribe of Judah. The Bible tells that Judah intervened when his brothers wanted to kill Joseph, and persuaded them to sell him as a slave instead. The tribe of Judah was known for its warriors, and according to the *Book of Judges*, it was the first to enter Canaan and conquer the southern part of the land. The tribe of

Judah became influential after David was proclaimed king, first by the tribe of Judah and then by the other tribes. After the death of Solomon, the name of Judah was given to the separate kingdom of the southern tribes, established after the division of the country by Jeroboam. In the course of time the word Jew (contraction of Judean) became the generic term for the entire Jewish people, and Judaism the name of their religion.

JUDAH, KINGDOM OF

The Southern Kingdom established in 937 b.c.e. following the revolt of the northern tribes against the House of David. The capital of the Kingdom of Judah was always Jerusalem, and its kings were of the dynasty established by David. Judah was a small hilly state, the spiritual and intellectual center of the Jewish people for over a thousand years. To maintain its political independence Judah frequently had to rely on alliances with the rivaling world powers of Egypt on the southwest and Assyria on the northeast. With the rise of Babylonia, Judah was finally conquered in 586 b.c.e., when many of its inhabitants were carried off to Babylon. Fifty years later, after the conquest of Babylonia by Cyrus, king of Persia, the exiles of Judah were allowed to return to their homeland, which after a period of reconstruction, and the rebuilding of the Temple (in 516 b.c.e.), became once more an independent Jewish state known in history as Judea. See *Judea*.

JUDAH HA-LEVI (Yehudah Halevi) (1085–1140)

One of the greatest Hebrew poets of the Middle Ages. Born in Toledo, Spain, he lived in comfortable circumstances. He received a well-rounded Jewish and secular academic education, as well as training for the medical profession, which he successfully practiced first in Toledo and

One of the Bet-Shearim catacombs, burial place of Judah Ha-Nasi, compiler and codifier of the Mishnah. Note the Palmyrene inscription left of the archway, and the seven-branched Menorah carved on the wall.

then in Cordova. Judah began his writing career at an early age, and was soon recognized by his contemporaries as a gifted Hebrew poet. His early poems were written on secular themes such as love, friendship, the joy of life, dedications to great benefactors. His best known poetry consists of religious hymns and songs of Zion, which inspired the generations to come, and have been included in the liturgy of Jewish communities the world over.

In addition to his fame as the foremost Hebrew poet of the Spanish period of Jewish literature, Judah Ha-Levi is also considered an outstanding Jewish philosopher. His great philosophic work, the *Kuzari* (written in Arabic, and translated into Hebrew by Judah ibn Tibbon), was designed as the "Book of Argument and Demonstration in Aid of the Despised Faith." The *Kuzari*, written as a philosophic dialogue in defense of Judaism, is based on the story of the conversion to Judaism of the Khazars and their king Bulan in 740 c.e.

Both in his poetry and in the *Kuzari*, Judah Ha-Levi expressed his deep concern for the suffering of his people in the diaspora, and his longing for Zion, the land of his forefathers. In the latter part of his life he realized his dream of going to Palestine. Despite the hardships of the sea voyage he reached Egypt, where he was received with great acclaim by the Jewish community, and then proceeded to Jerusalem. A legend tells that while reciting his *Ode to Zion* in the streets of the Holy City, he was crushed to death by a galloping Arab horseman.

JUDAH HA-NASI (Judah the Prince) (c. 135–210)
One of the greatest personalities in Jewish history, redactor of the *Mishnah*. Commonly referred to in the Talmud as

Advanced students in a Talmud class. Study of the Talmud has been one of the links in the chain of the spiritual, religious and intellectual tradition which has bound Jews together over the generations.

"Rabbi" or "Rabbenu ha-Kadosh" (The Rabbi, par excellence, or our holy master), he was the son of the Patriarch Rabban Simeon ben Gamaliel II. He studied in Usha, and after the death of his father he succeeded him as the *Nasi* (Patriarch), and was the head of the famous academies in Tiberias, Bet-Shearim and Sepphoris. Judah Ha-Nasi was known for his wisdom, piety, as well as for his wealth, with which he used to support scholars, including his many famous pupils. Despite the fact that Aramaic was then the language of the Jewish people, he insisted on speaking only Hebrew with his family and friends. Because of his knowledge of Greek, and his position, he was influential with Roman government officials, as well as with Antoninus, the emperor of Rome.

His greatest accomplishment was the compilation and codification of the *Halakhah* into six orders known as the *Mishnah*. In the last years of his life Judah Ha-Nasi was bedridden; he was buried with great honor in Bet-Shearim with his ancestors before him.

JUDAH LÖW BEN BEZALEL (1520–1609)

Famous chief rabbi of Prague, popularly known as the *Maharal*, mystic, great Talmudic authority, writer, and student of astronomy, mathematics and geography. He also fathered important ordinances and legal reforms. He was held in great esteem not only by the Jewish community, but also in non-Jewish circles, and was received in audience by the emperor of Austria. In Jewish folklore he is said to have created by divine inspiration an automaton, the *Golem*, whose task it was to save the Jewish community from many dangers, notably ritual murder accusations. See *Golem*.

JUDAISM

A term used to describe the living faith

and the spiritual way of life of the Jewish people. The history of the Jewish religion begins in tradition with Abraham, the Father of the Jewish people, and has since passed many stages of development. The principles of Judaism are embodied in the sacred writings of the Jewish people, which include in addition to the Bible—the Talmud, the Commentaries on the Bible and Talmud, the Responsa and Decider literature, the liturgy, Kabbalistic and Ḥasidic literatures, and countless other religious writings of both past and contemporary Jewish religious thinkers and spiritual leaders.

Despite its contacts with other creeds and civilizations, Judaism has essentially retained its religious and cultural uniqueness, remaining true to the principles of ethical monotheism of the Prophets, and to the belief in godly living which is characterized by a devoted fulfillment of the *Mitzvot* as well as by righteousness and universal justice.

The inroads of modern life and science have failed to alter the essence of Judaism; they have, on the other hand, contributed to a fortification of the past and a clarification of its implementation for the future. See *Conservative Judaism; Mitzvah; Monotheism; Orthodox Judaism; Reconstructionism; Reform Judaism.*

JUDAIZERS

A term employed by the Christian church to designate either genuine Christians who observed some Jewish customs and ceremonies, or those Jews who, despite the fact that they had been forcibly converted to Christianity, secretly continued to practice Judaism. See *Marranos.*

JUDAS ISCARIOT

One of the twelve disciples of Jesus, who betrayed his master for thirty pieces of silver. According to the New Testament, Judas pointed out Jesus to the Roman soldiers by kissing him. Jesus was thereupon arrested and brought before Pilate, the Roman governor of Palestine, who ordered his crucifixion. The figure of Judas Iscariot and his role in the Jesus story have been subjected to much scrutiny by critical scholars. They question the need to identify Jesus only a few days after he had received a widespread public reception; also some claim the name Judas (Judah) points to anti-Semitic intent.

JUDAS MACCABEUS (Judah, the Maccabee)

Hero of the Maccabean wars against Antiochus, Hellenistic-Syrian king, who attempted by compulsion to impose paganism and deteriorated Hellenism on the Jews of Palestine. Judas was one of the five brave sons of Mattathias, a priest at Modin. Mattathias started a revolt against Syrian rule, and after his death his leadership was taken over by Judas. Judas started a guerrilla warfare with ill-equipped and untrained men against the powerful Syrian armies. He gradually mustered sufficient strength to overcome the enemy in the field of battle. With unparalleled bravery Judas' men won a number of decisive victories against the Syrian generals, and Jerusalem was finally freed and its defiled Temple cleansed and rededicated. However, the Syrians returned with a strong army, and in the ensuing battle in 161 b.c.e. Judas met his heroic death. The war was continued by Judas' successor, his brother Jonathan. An armistice was finally reached, and twenty years later, Simon the Hasmonean, became the High Priest and virtual ruler of Judea. See *Ḥanukkah.*

JUDEA

Ancient name of a province in Palestine, south of Samaria. The name of *Judea* appears for the first time in the books of *Ezra* and *Nehemiah;* the two men were leaders

The Judean hills of central Palestine, where David tended his flocks and the Maccabees fought against their oppressors. The 1948 Palestine partition left most of these hills in the hands of Jordanians.

of the Jewish returnees from the Babylonian captivity during the Persian rule. Judea gained its independence from subsequent Greco-Syrian rule on the successful Maccabean revolt which began in 167 b.c.e. Judea was overrun by the Romans in 63 b.c.e., and destroyed by them in 70 c.e. See *Judah, Kingdom of*.

JUDEO-GERMAN see Yiddish.

JUDEO-SPANISH see Ladino.

JUDGES

A term applied to the leaders of the Israelites for a period of 440 years, according to traditional chronology, from the death of Joshua to the anointing of Saul as king of Israel. The Israelite tribes, being ununited and unprotected, were harassed and often subjugated by the Canaanites from within and by the neighboring countries from without. Judges thus rose up among individual tribes to serve as military captains in times of trouble, and as leaders and teachers in peacetime. There were sixteen Judges in all, the best known of whom are Deborah, Gideon, Jephthah, and Samson. The Judges generally distinguished themselves as military leaders against the neighboring Moabites, Midianites, Ammonites, and Philistines. The Biblical record of the activities of the Judges is found in the *Book of Judges*.

JUDGES, BOOK OF

The second book of the second division of the Bible, called in Hebrew *Shofetim*.

It narrates the sagas of the tribes and heroes of the Israelites during the period from the death of Joshua to the ascension of King Saul. See *Judges*.

JUDGMENT, DAY OF

Known in Hebrew as *Yom ha-Din*, it refers to the Jewish New Year Day (Rosh Hashanah) as the day of universal judgment, when each person's fate for the coming year is decided by God. Traditionally the entire season of the High Holy Days is motivated by the idea of the Heavenly Judgment which is emphasized in the liturgy of the synagogue of those days. The phrase "Day of Judgment" is also used for the period of the end of time in the Messianic Era.

JUDITH

Heroine of a book by the same name included in the Apocrypha. The sixteen chapters of the book relate the story of Holofernes, one of Nebuchadnezzar's generals, and Judith, a loyal Jewess. Holofernes invaded Palestine, and when the fortress of Bethulia was about to be surrendered by its Jewish defenders, Judith, a beautiful and pious widow, appeared at the camp of the general. Attracted by her charm, Holofernes invited her to remain with him. One night, after Holofernes had been drinking and fallen asleep, Judith cut off his head with his own sword. Left without a leader, the army fled and the city and country were saved from imminent destruction.

Scholars generally maintain that the *Book of Judith* is a fictional story, written for the purpose of fortifying the Jewish people in their faith in God and in their religious observances. The courageous and self-sacrificing work of Judith has served also as a theme in art, music, and drama.

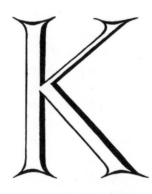

K

KIDDUSH

I will lift up the cup of salvation,

And call upon the name of the Lord . . .

PSALMS

KABBALAH

KABBALAH (CABALAH)

Hebrew term meaning "tradition" or "reception" (teachings received orally from generation to generation), applied to an important complex of Jewish and non-Jewish mystical philosophy and practice. The beginnings of Jewish mysticism are traced to ancient times in Palestine and Babylonia. Some Biblical passages may have mystical implications. Mysticism gradually appears more distinctly in the subsequent apocalyptic literature, the writings of the Essenes, and in the Talmud. It is in the Gaonic period (7th to 9th centuries) that such significant works as *Otiot de R. Akiva* and *Sefer Yetzirah* made their appearance. The following age (10th to 12th centuries) is one of eclecticism, with the appearance of *Sefer Raziel*, *Sefer Hasidim* and *Rokeah*. The crystallization of the Kabbalah took place in the 13th century when *Sefer Ha-Bahir* appeared and a number of Spanish personalities, philosophers and commentators lent their intellectual weight and fame to mysticism, men like Nahmanides (Moses ben Nahman, or Ramban), Abraham Abulafia, Joseph Gikatilla and Moses de Leon. The teachings of the *Kabbalah* spread to Germany where Rabbi Judah

Figurative presentation of the Ten Sefirot from a Kabbalistic treatise by Moses Cordovero.

258

Hasid was especially important, and reached their culmination during the 16th century in Palestine in the city of Safed, where Rabbi Isaac Luria created a new system of Jewish mysticism. The period of the 14th to 17th centuries may be looked upon as the aftermath of Kabbalistic creativeness; in addition to the personalities already mentioned, one must also name R. Isaiah Horwitz (Shelah Ha-Kadosh).

It should be noted that those Kabbalistic works which are anonymous are generally ascribed by tradition to very ancient authorship, such as of the *Tannaitic* period.

The basic work of the Kabbalah is the *Zohar* (Splendor) which appeared close to the end of the 13th century. The book is believed by some scholars to have been compiled by Moses de Leon of Spain, though mostly from earlier sources. Tradition ascribes it to the great *Tanna* R. Simeon ben Yohai, of the second century. The Zohar is in the form of a commentary on the Pentateuch and a few other Biblical passages.

The chief problems dealt with by the Kabbalah are the nature of God, the creation of the Universe, the destiny of man in the world, the nature of evil, and the ultimate meaning of the Written Law. The major teachings of the Kabbalah are:

1) God did not create the world directly, since He is above all existence; He is the Eternal, the *En Sof* (the "Endless"); the world and all higher and lower forms of life and conduct are emanations proceeding from God and then from one another, from the more spiritual to the less spiritual. The *Ten Spheres* (Sefirot) emanated in the following descending order, each succeeding one from the preceding one: Crown, Wisdom, Intelligence, Greatness, Strength, Beauty, Firmness, Splendor, Foundation, and Kingdom. The last Sphere, "Kingdom," created the physical world. Through these Spheres God rules

the world, and through them are explained all His activities.

2) Everything that exists is a part of Deity, and man can achieve union with God through his acts of piety and moral conduct. Through the observance of the commandments every Jew can influence the Spheres which, in turn, can influence God in behalf of mankind. The Jewish people were chosen to preserve the world by strict observance of the Law.

3) Man is judged by his soul, which is the most important part of his being. All souls were created at the same time during Creation, and the soul which remains pure after its contact with the body becomes after death a part of the world ruled by the Ten Spheres. The impure or contaminated souls must, after death, reinhabit another body, and continue to migrate from body to body, until they have been purified.

4) Evil does not exist in itself but is the negation of good, and can be overcome by prayer, repentance, self-affliction and strict observance of the Law.

5) The text of the Bible is filled with hidden meanings. Although written in the language of man, its words contain divine and mysterious concepts that man should strive to uncover. The Kabbalists, therefore, employed different techniques by which they tried to discover the hidden and divine meanings of Biblical terms.

Kabbalah had significant influence on many Jewish communities. It had prompted messianic movements, and influenced the rise of *Hasidism*. Christianity, too, was interested in Jewish mysticism and it used the teachings of Kabbalah for the interpretation of various Christian doctrines. See *Zohar*.

KABBALAT SHABBAT

Hebrew term meaning "the ushering in of the Sabbath," applied to the prayers with which the Sabbath services begin in the synagogue on Friday evening. The special prayers date back to the 16th century, when they were first introduced in Safed, Palestine, by the Kabbalists. They include such Psalms as "Lekhu Nerannenah" (O come, let us sing unto the Lord), and the hymn "Lekhah Dodi Likrat Kallah" (Come my friend, to meet the bride, i.e. the Sabbath) composed by R. Shelomoh Ha-Levi Alkabetz.

KADDISH

A word meaning "Sanctification," and the name of a prayer written in Aramaic. It was originally recited after study and at the end of important portions of the daily liturgy in the synagogue, but for many centuries has also been used as a mourner's prayer. In this latter function it is commonly recited by the mourner at the grave-side of parents or close relatives, and during the three daily prayers in the synagogue for the first eleven months following the death of a parent or relative. The Kaddish has no direct reference to the dead or to mourning. It is essentially a doxology, praising God, and praying for the speedy establishment of God's Kingdom on earth, and is to this day recited by the Reader several times during each public service. It is only the special burial Kaddish which incorporates a prayer for the resurrection of the dead. In the reform liturgy the Kaddish is recited only as a mourner's prayer and a paragraph concerning those who have died has been inserted. See *Death*.

KAF (KHAF) (כ , ך)

Eleventh letter of the Hebrew alphabet; its numerical value is 20. It is pronounced like the English K when it has a *daggesh* (dot in the letter), but like the Scotch CH when without it, and is then properly transliterated KH. The letter's form prob-

KAHAL

ably represents the palm of a hand, and derives its name therefrom. In an unvoweled text there is no visible distinction between *Kaf* and *Khaf*.

KAHAL (KEHILLAH)

Hebrew term meaning "community," applied to the administrative body of Jewish communities, which in recent history has been known as the *Kehillah*. Jewish communal representative organizations have been in existence since the time of the Jewish dispersion. During the Middle Ages and especially beginning with the 18th century, the *Kahal* became an important authoritative Jewish organization, officially recognized by the government. The Kahal played a significant role in eastern European countries, especially during the period of the existence of the Council of Four Lands. One of the chief functions of the Kahal during that period was the collection of taxes for the government from members of the Jewish community. Other important functions of the Kahal were: the organization and supervision of Jewish religious education; the administration of all types of charitable institutions; the supervision of *Kashrut* (Dietary Laws); the placement of community functionaries; the erection and maintenance of community buildings; the maintenance of Jewish law courts; and in general, supervision over the welfare, religious, educational, economic, and other social problems. Some of the functions of the Kahal have diminished in modern times, but most of the Jewish communities the world over still maintain some form of voluntary community organization.

KALIR, ELEAZAR

Prolific author of Hebrew liturgical hymns and poems. There is no biographical information about him, and it is assumed that he was active at some period between

the 7th and the 11th centuries. Some 200 of his religious hymns have been included in the *Mahzorim* (Holiday Prayer Books) of the Ashkenazic congregations all over the world.

KALISCHER, TZEVI HIRSCH (1795–1874)

Rabbi and promoter of Jewish colonization in Palestine. Born in Prussian Poland, he spent most of his life in Thorn, where he served without compensation as acting rabbi for a period of forty years. He was deeply interested in Jewish affairs, and became one of the earliest and chief advocates of the settlement of Jews in agricultural colonies in Palestine. In 1862 he published his book entitled *Derishat Zion* (Longing for Zion), in which he advanced the idea that the salvation of the Jewish people depends on self-help and on a program of colonization of Jews in agricultural settlements in Palestine. Kalischer conducted a propaganda campaign for this ideal, and secured the help of prominent Jews such as Moses Montefiore, Rothschild, Adolph Crémieux, and others. As the result of his efforts a number of societies for colonization in Palestine were established in Europe, and in 1866 eighty Jews bought land in Palestine and settled near Jaffa. He persuaded the Alliance Israélite Universelle to establish the first agricultural school in Mikveh Israel in 1870. Rabbi Kalischer is also known for his philosophic writings and commentaries. His best known work is the *Sefer Emunah Yesharah*, which is a study of Jewish doctrine and philosophy.

KALLAH MONTHS

Two months (Elul and Adar) of each year during which many laymen journeyed to the Babylonian academies of Sura and Pumbedita to study Jewish law and tradition. During the above months the farmers were usually free from much of their seasonal farm work, and thus enabled to devote their leisure time to studies. A different tractate of the Talmud was studied each month. This program of mass education flourished in Babylonia from 200 to 500 c.e.

The term *Kallah* has been used recently in the United States to refer to study groups, under the direction of the rabbi, which are held away from home.

KALONYMOS

A famous Jewish family which flourished during the Middle Ages, the members of which distinguished themselves as religious poets, rabbis, translators and philosophers. The more prominent members of this family, in alphabetical order, were: *Kalonymos ben Judah* (ca. 1160) lived in Speyer, and became known as a liturgical poet whose hymns, describing the sufferings of the Jews during the Crusades, are included in the *Maḥzor* (Holiday Prayer Book); *Kalonymos ben Kalonymos ben Meir* (1286–1328) lived in France and became known for his mission to Rome where he pleaded before the Pope in behalf of the Jews. He wrote some philosophic works in Hebrew, and translated works in astronomy, mathematics and medicine from Arabic into Hebrew; *Kalonymos, Meshullam ben Moses*, a liturgical poet who lived about the last quarter of the 11th century. During the First Crusade (1096) he took his own life rather than fall into the hands of the Crusaders; *Kalonymos ben Shabbetai*, liturgical poet and son of the president of the Jewish community in Rome. He served as rabbi in Worms, and was martyred during the First Crusade (1096).

KAMEA

Amulet used as a protection against evil spirits, sickness and other dangers. The *Kamea* is usually in the form of a piece of parchment or paper on which the name of

Kabbalistic text on parchment in a 17th-century Italian gold amulet. It is hung over a child's cradle as a protection against evil and danger.

God is inscribed, with other holy words, phrases, and prayer. This popular belief in the protective power of the Kamea is of ancient origin, and persists to this day. Many different peoples wear some type of protective charm.

KAPLAN, MORDECAI MENAHEM

Rabbi, educator, philosopher and founder of the Reconstructionist movement in the United States. Born in Lithuania in 1881, he came to the United States at the age of eight. He graduated from the College of the City of New York, received his M.A. degree at Columbia University, and was ordained rabbi at The Jewish Theological Seminary of America. He started his ca-

Mordecai M. Kaplan, rabbi and teacher, founded the Reconstructionist philosophy of Judaism.

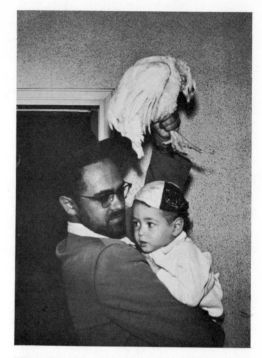

"Kapores shlogen" ceremony is observed with a rooster symbolically waved around the head.

reer in 1903 as rabbi at Kehilat Yeshurun Congregation in New York City, and later became principal and then dean of the Teachers' Institute of The Jewish Theological Seminary of America. In 1921 he organized the Society for the Advancement of Judaism, and subsequently formulated his philosophy of Judaism contained in such works as "A Program for the Reconstruction of Judaism" (1920), "A New Approach to the Problem of Judaism" (1924), "Judaism As a Civilization" (1934), "Judaism in Transition" (1936), and "The Meaning of God in Modern Jewish Religion" (1937). *The Reconstructionist*, a biweekly periodical, founded by Kaplan in 1934, has been devoted to the exposition and interpretation of the Reconstructionist philosophy of Judaism. This philosophy regards Judaism as a religious civilization, and advocates the reorganization of the Jewish community; the revitalization of the constructive and creative powers in Judaism; the rebuilding of

the Jewish homeland, and the creation of a Jewish way of life that will provide joyful experiences and opportunity for self-realization for the modern Jew.

KAPPARAH (KAPORES)

Hebrew word meaning "atonement." There is a custom among some Jews to designate, a day or two before Yom Kippur, a rooster (for men) and a hen (for women) to be slaughtered as a substitute and atonement for the sins committed during the past year. The rooster or the hen is waved three times around the head of the penitent following the recitation of certain verses from the Psalms. This ceremony, commonly known in Yiddish as "kapores shlogen," is observed to this day by orthodox Jews. The slaughtered fowl or its value is given to the poor. The custom is of ancient origin, and is believed to be a reminder of the use of the scapegoat in the times of the Holy Temple.

262

KARAITES, KARAISM

A Jewish sect founded in Babylon about 767 c.e. by Anan b. David. The Hebrew words for the members of this movement are *Karaim, Bene Mikra,* or *Baale Mikra* (the followers of the Scriptures). Karaism recognized only the Bible as the authoritative source of legal and practical faith, and opposed the "Oral Law," that is, the teachings and Scriptural interpretations of the Talmud and the other rabbinic literature. The defenders of the Talmud were known as the "Rabbinites," the followers of Rabbinical Judaism. In rejecting Rabbinic tradition, Karaism found itself compelled to impose highly restrictive regulations on its adherents. Thus Karaites are forbidden not only to make fire on the Sabbath, but even to enjoy its light and heat if kindled on Friday. The Karaite leaders very soon created interpretations and traditions of their own, realizing that Scriptural principles required further elaboration for practical application.

Their marriage laws were highly restrictive, creating many more cases of incest than in Rabbinic Judaism. It also prohibited intermarriage with the Rabbinites.

Despite the fact that Karaism caused a rift in some Jewish communities in the early days, it nevertheless had a certain positive influence upon Judaism at large. It encouraged the study of the Bible and Hebrew grammar, and by its criticism of Talmudic tradition it aroused its opponents, the "Rabbinites," to defend their teaching, resulting in the creation of important literary works. Chief among the opponents of Karaism was Saadiah Gaon (10th century), whose works did much to curb the spread of the influence of the new religious movement.

Karaism spread from Babylonia to Palestine, and from there to Egypt and Syria. Karaite communities were later formed in other countries, especially in Crimea (southern Russia), Constantinople, Lithuania, Poland and Turkey. Because some of the governments (especially in Russia) believed that the Karaites were descendants of the ten lost tribes of Israel, and were consequently not involved in Jesus' death, they were freed from the restrictions and persecutions to which non-Karaite Jewish communities were exposed. The number of Karaites has diminished in the course of the centuries. At present there still are several thousand Karaites in the world, most of whom live in Crimea, East Galicia, Istanbul, Cairo, and more recently there is a sizeable community in Israel.

KARO, JOSEPH (1488–1575)

Great Talmudic teacher and author of the "Shulḥan Arukh." Born in Spain, he was a child among the deportees during the expulsion of the Jews from Spain in 1492. He lived in Lisbon for five years, and then settled in Turkey where he became head of a Talmudical academy, and began his life-work as commentator on and codifier of Rabbinic Law. In 1536 he settled in Safed, Palestine, where he was ordained by the great Talmud authority, Rabbi Jacob Berab, and where he founded his own Talmudical academy (Yeshivah) and wrote most of his outstanding works. His most popular work, the *Shulḥan Arukh,* is a condensation and summary of his extensive work on Rabbinic Law, the *Bet Yosef,* which was originally planned as a commentary on Jacob ben Asher's code, the *Arbaah Turim.* Of all his many other important writings the *Shulḥan Arukh* has become the authoritative code of Jewish law. See *Shulḥan Arukh.*

KASHER see Dietary Laws.

KASHRUT

A Hebrew term meaning "fitness" or "legitimacy," as applied generally to foods, sacred objects and persons meeting the

263

19th-century European meat stamps used by the Mashgiah to indicate that the meat is Kosher.

religious requirements of traditional Jews. The basic laws of *Kashrut* are laid down in the Bible and were later expounded in the Talmud. The various codes of the Middle Ages all include them, and are observed by traditional Jews as they are set forth in the *Shulhan Arukh*. Most Jewish communities the world over set up Kashrut regulations and provide, through the appointment of special communal directors, for the supervision of the slaughtering and distribution of meat in accordance with Jewish dietary laws. See *Dietary Laws*.

KATZENELSON, BERL (1887–1944)

Writer and labor Zionist leader. Born in Russia, he became an active member of the *Poale Zion* (Labor Zionist) group in Russia. In 1909 he settled in Palestine as a laborer, and rose to leadership in the Labor Zionist movement, and was one of the founders of the *Histadrut* (General Labor Federation of Palestine). In addition to his political and organizational work, he distinguished himself as a journalist and writer, and in 1935 he became editor of the *Davar*, a workers' daily newspaper in Israel. In the mid 1940's *Mapai* founded in his memory the "Berl Katzenelson Institute" near Kfar Saba, Israel. This Institute, commonly known as "Bet Berl" (House of Berl), offers extensive courses in workers' education, and special leadership training courses for the Labor Zionist movement in Israel. "Ohalo," an institution

located on the outskirts of Tiberias, was founded in his memory by the Histadrut.

KEDUSHAH

Hebrew term meaning "sanctification," the name of the prayers inserted in the liturgy of the synagogue before the third benediction of the *Amidah* when it is repeated aloud by the Reader. The text of the *Kedushah* consists of verses from the Prophets *Isaiah* and *Ezekiel*, and from the *Psalms*, and is uttered as a proclamation of the majesty and holiness of God. The Kedushah of the *Musaf* also contains the *Shema* (Hear, O Israel, the Lord is Our God, the Lord is One).

KEHILLAH see Kahal.

KEREN AMI

Hebrew term meaning "the fund of my people" applied to the fund-raising projects of the pupils in Jewish schools throughout the United States. It is also referred to as the "Junior Welfare Fund Drive," through which the children in Jewish schools join the adult Jewish population in their efforts to raise funds for local, national and overseas Jewish charitable projects.

KEREN HA-YESOD

Hebrew term meaning "foundation fund" applied to the financial institution of the World Zionist Organization and of the Jewish Agency for Palestine, also known as "Palestine Foundation Fund" or "Jewish Foundation Fund." It was organized in 1920 for the purpose of assisting in the upbuilding of the Jewish national home. The *Keren Ha-Yesod* conducts annual fund-raising campaigns among Jews all over the world. Its funds are used for the development of agricultural settlements and urban colonization in Israel, for immigration, aid to immigrants established on land, for educational institutions, health services, industry, and for many other related projects. The headquarters of the Keren Ha-Yesod are in Jerusalem, and its funds are administered by a board of directors appointed by the World Zionist Congress.

KEREN KAYEMET see Jewish National Fund.

KERIAH

Hebrew term meaning "rending of garment." The custom of the mourner tearing his garment as a symbol of grief on the death of a near relative.

KERIAT HA-TORAH see Torah, Reading of.

KERIAT SHEMA see Shema.

KETIVAH VA-ḤATIMAH TOVAH

Hebrew phrase, also pronounced "Kesivoh va-Ḥasimoh Tovoh," the customary Jewish New Year greeting. Another form is "Le-Shanah Tovah Tikatevu ve-Teḥatemu" (Le-Shonoh Tovoh Tikosevu ve-Seḥosemu). According to Jewish tradition, the fate of the individual is inscribed in the heavenly records on Rosh Hashanah, and one therefore greets his fellow Jews with either of these phrases, wishing a good inscription and sealing in the book of life.

After Rosh Hashanah and until Hoshana Rabbah, the usual greeting is "Gemar Ḥatimah Tovah" (Gemar Ḥasimoh Tovoh) or "Gemar Tov," since one's fate for the year is sealed on Yom Kippur or finally on Hoshana Rabbah.

KETUBAH

Hebrew term for the marriage certificate. Since ancient times this document was used not so much as evidence of marriage, but chiefly as a protection of the woman's rights. The *Ketubah* contains the obligations of the husband to pay his wife a certain sum of money in the event of divorce, and specifications as to her property rights in the event of his death. The Ketubah is traditionally written in Aramaic, and is signed by witnesses.

Hand-illuminated Ketubah, or Jewish marriage contract, from Modena, Italy, dated 1757. Note the twelve signs of the Zodiac and the symbolic four seasons at each of the document's corners.

KETUVIM see Hagiographa.

KEVUTZAH see Kibbutz.

KHAF see Kaf.

KHAZARS

A Mongolian people who embraced Judaism and flourished from the 8th through the 10th centuries on the territory extending between the Don and the Volga rivers, and the shores of the Black, Caspian and Azov Seas. The story of the existence of such converts to Judaism reached the Jewish statesman Ḥasdai ibn Shaprut of Cordova in the 10th century. As a result, Shaprut wrote a letter which was ultimately received by Joseph, king of the Khazars, with the help of Jewish tradesmen from Germany and Hungary. In his reply King Joseph gave a detailed account of the history of the kingdom of the

A view of Kfar Orah, a Kibbutz village typical of those which have pioneered the remote areas of Israel. These settlements were also instrumental in training and providing bases for the Israeli armed forces.

Khazars and their conversion to Judaism. Bulan, the pagan ruler of the Khazars, in his desire to embrace the "true religion" had summoned representatives of the Christian, Moslem and Jewish faiths to expound their views on the superiority of their respective religions. Bulan thus became convinced of the truth of the Jewish faith, and he, as well as many of his noblemen, embraced Judaism, which later spread widely among the common people of the Khazar kingdom.

The Khazars were a warlike people, and succeeded in extending their rule and influence. They were subjected to occasional attacks by the Byzantines and later by the Russians. By the end of the 10th century they succumbed to the Russians, and after maintaining themselves for a short period in the Crimea, some gradually embraced the Christian or Moslem faith, ceasing to

exist as a separate people, though many joined with their Jewish brethren. The story of the mass conversion of the Khazars to Judaism was used by Judah Ha-Levi as background for his philosophic work the *Kuzari*, designed as a defense of the Jewish faith.

KIBBUTZ

Hebrew term for a collective agricultural settlement, now synonymous with *Kevutzah*. Historically there was a distinction between a *Kibbutz* and a *Kevutzah*. The Kevutzah was a completely integrated communal settlement where its members lived and worked together, usually in an agricultural community. The Kibbutz, however, was a communal settlement not necessarily integrated with its own farm, its members living communally, but possibly having jobs elsewhere, such as in industrial plants or in construction work. By the 1950's these differences were no longer significant, and the term Kibbutz included both Kibbutz and Kevutzah movements.

The first Kevutzah, Deganiah, was established in 1909 on land purchased by the Jewish National Fund. Nine members of *Hapoel Hatzair*, who were deeply imbued with A. D. Gordon's "Religion of Labor" were its founders. Many Kevutzot modeled after Deganiah were subsequently formed. It was about a decade later, during the Third Aliyah (1919–1924), that the Kibbutz type of settlement began.

Both the Kibbutz and Kevutzah are based on the socialistic idea of a community life, in which the members of such settlements have no private property and do not receive any wages. All income is the property of the settlement, which provides each member with all necessities in accordance with its ability to do so. Men and women are assigned to different tasks of work depending upon age and skills, and children are cared for in special nurseries and in communal schools. Members eat in a common dining room, but have private assigned living quarters so that they can lead their own lives. In 1960 there were over 200 collective settlements in Israel which have proven a successful experiment of communal living.

The importance of the Kibbutz in the forming of Israel cannot be overemphasized. In choosing their way of life, the *Halutzim* (Pioneers) dedicated themselves to a life of labor for the fulfillment of Zionism. Much of the area in which they settled was remote and disease-ridden. These settlements, because they were occupied territory, were later included within the boundaries of Israel. The *Palmach* and the *Haganah* were trained in these settlements, and the *Yishuv's* arms were secreted there. Many saw the Ḥalutz as the example of the Israeli Jew: a self-

This beautifully wrought silver Kiddush cup was fashioned by a contemporary Israeli craftsman.

respecting, self-reliant person who was not afraid to work with his hands at physical labor. See *Ḥalutzim*.

KIDDUSH

Hebrew term meaning "sanctification," the traditional benediction and prayer over a cup of wine or bread, ushering in the Sabbath or festivals. A *Kiddush* is also recited the following morning before partaking of the noonday meal. The Kiddush is generally recited by the head of the family. It is also recited during the

Friday and festival evening service in some synagogues, because wayfarers, especially in former times, would have no other opportunity to hear it uttered.

KIDDUSH HA-SHEM

Hebrew term meaning "Sanctification of God's Name," and signifying the highest standards of Jewish ethics. One hallows the name of God by exemplary and virtuous conduct, by readiness to defend the good name of the Jew in the face of danger, and by readiness for martyrdom for the sake of the truth, such as the Jewish faith. *Hillul ha-Shem* (Desecration of God's name), in contrast to *Kiddush ha-Shem*, is the lowest negative standard of Jewish morality, describing acts of disloyalty to ethical living and to the Jewish people and religion, and unworthy conduct which makes for a public scandal.

KIDDUSHIN

Hebrew term for marriage. It is also the name of a tractate in the Talmud dealing with the laws pertaining to marriage. See *Marriage Ceremony*.

KIMHI, DAVID (1160–1235)

Hebrew grammarian and Biblical commentator, also known under his abbreviated name *RADAK* (Rabbi David Kimhi). Born in Narbonne, France, the son of Joseph Kimhi, he wrote a number of important commentaries on the *Prophets*, *Psalms*, and *Chronicles*, as well as on the *Pentateuch*. His greatest contribution was in the field of Hebrew grammar. His major works are: the *Mikhlol* (Compendium), a systematic and scientific exposition of Hebrew grammar; and the *Sefer*

Awaiting his own execution, a Jew prays over the bodies of his brothers already murdered by Nazis watching in the background. Thus, on the brink of martyrdom do Jews proclaim "Kiddush Ha-Shem," or the Sanctification of the Name.

Ha-Shorashim (Book of Roots), a dictionary of the Bible, a highly original masterwork of Hebrew philology.

KINGS

The fourth book (in two parts), called in Hebrew *Melakhim*, found in the second division of the Bible called *Prophets*. In content the book is a continuation of the *Book of Samuel* and covers Jewish history from Solomon (970 b.c.e.) to the fall of Jerusalem (586 b.c.e.). In addition to chronicling the history of the kings of both the Kingdom of Israel and the Kingdom of Judah, the book gives an account of the activities of some of the prophets. It is written in a vivid narrative, and its authorship is attributed by tradition to the prophet Jeremiah.

KINNAH, KINNOT see Lamentations.

KINNERET

Also called *Yam Kinneret* because of its harp shape. Biblical name of a beautiful lake in the northern part of Israel on the western shore of which the city of Tiberias is located; it is therefore also known as *Lake Tiberias*, or *Sea of Galilee*. The Kinneret is 21 kilometers long, and from 8 to 12 kilometers wide. There are several Jewish settlements on the Kinneret, where a large fishing industry has developed.

KISLEV

The third month of the Jewish calendar, corresponding to November-December, and consisting of 30, and sometimes 29 days. The festival of *Hanukkah* begins on the 25th day of this month.

KITTEL

Used in Yiddish as the name of a special garment, a white robe worn by pious Jews, especially the rabbi, the cantor, and the *Baal Tokea* (one who blows the Shofar) during the services on Rosh Hashanah.

KLAUSNER, JOSEPH

Bialik Prize-winner Joseph Klausner was an authority on Hebrew literature and messianism.

On Yom Kippur many pious Jews wear it, as does the leader at Passover *Seder*. Pious Jews are also buried in a *Kittel*.

KLAUSNER, JOSEPH (1874–1959)

Veteran Hebrew writer and scholar. Born in Lithuania, he received his doctorate at the University of Heidelberg (1902), and upon his return to Russia he became interested in Hebrew literature, and was appointed editor of the Hebrew periodical "Ha-Shiloah." In addition to his numerous contributions in the field of literary criticism, he became known as a student of Jewish history. In 1919 he settled permanently in Palestine, where he later served as professor of modern Hebrew literature at the Hebrew University in Jerusalem. He wrote many volumes on Hebrew literature and philology, distinguished himself as historian of the period of the Second Commonwealth and is famous for the historical works *Yeshu Ha-Notzri* (Jesus of Nazareth) and *Ha-Bayit Ha-Sheni Bigedulato* (The Second Temple in its Greatness). His major work in the field of Hebrew literature is *A History of Modern Hebrew Literature*. In 1924 Klausner received the "Bialik Prize in Jewish

Learning" from the Tel Aviv municipality, and to his last day he continued his great career as an esteemed and prolific writer and scholar.

KNESSET

Hebrew name of the parliament in the State of Israel. Its members are chosen by all citizens over the age of 18, irrespective of sex, race or religion. The *Knesset*, created in 1949, consists of a single chamber (House) of 120 members representing the various political parties. Using the method of proportional representation, the Knesset assigns seats to each party in proportion to the number of votes gained in the country by the party's list of candidates. The Knesset has the sole power to make laws, and its approval is necessary before a government can take office. Elections for a new Knesset are held every four years or, if it so decides, at an earlier date. Candidates for election to the Knesset must be over the age of 25. The Knesset meets in its building in Jerusalem.

KODASHIM

The fifth of the six orders (Sedarim) of the *Mishnah*. It deals with the details of sacrifices, Temple regulations and services, and the duties and privileges of the priests. This division of the Mishnah is in turn subdivided into eleven tractates, one of which deals with the laws of *Kashrut*, including those of slaughtering.

KOF (ק)

Nineteenth letter of the Hebrew alphabet; its numerical value is 100. It is pronounced like the English K, but originally its sound was deeper in the throat, and is so pronounced by oriental Jews to this day. Some think that the meaning of the word is monkey. It is generally called *Koof*.

KOHELET see Ecclesiastes.

270

KOHEN (KOHANIM)

During the early period of Jewish history, until the fall of the Second Temple (70 c.e.), the priests or *Kohanim* (sing., *Kohen*) played a significant role in Jewish life. The Bible tells us that the priestly class derived from Aaron of the tribe of Levi. During the days of the First Commonwealth some laymen, such as judges and kings, occasionally functioned as priests. When Solomon built the Temple, Zadok became the founder of the Jerusalem priesthood. The principal duties of the priest were: to offer sacrifices at the altar or sanctuary of the Temple; to officiate at all sacred functions; and to serve as teacher. During the era of the Second Commonwealth, the authority to teach went into lay hands, the Pharisees, and on the destruction of the Temple, the priests lost practically all their prerogatives. With the decline of the authority of the priestly class, the rabbis took over the basic function of the priests, namely to teach and to decide the Law. In modern Judaism there are few symbolic re-

The Israeli parliament (Knesset) in session with Joseph Sprinzak presiding and Premier David Ben-Gurion on his right. Note the photo of Herzl overhead and the Menorah seal of state on the dais.

A reconstruction of the High Priest's vestments based on descriptions from the Book of Exodus.

Kaufmann Kohler, preacher and educator, was an ardent advocate of modernism in Judaism.

minders of priestly prerogatives. Among these are: the priestly benediction recited in the synagogue; the ceremony of the *Pidyon ha-Ben* (redemption of the first-born male), at which a Kohen must officiate; the restrictions of members of the priestly class to come in contact with a corpse; the first "Aliyah" in the reading of the Torah; and the prohibition of a Kohen marrying a divorcee.

KOHEN GADOL

Hebrew term meaning "High Priest." The

272

High Priest was the only one permitted to enter the "Holy of Holies" in the Temple once a year, on Yom Kippur. He exercised great authority and was at times the virtual ruler of the Jewish community in Judea during much of the period of the Second Commonwealth.

KOHLER, KAUFMANN (1843–1926)

Rabbi, scholar and foremost leader of reform Judaism. Born in Bavaria, Germany, he studied in German universities and at the same time pursued his Jewish studies. He was an orthodox Jew in his youth, but later changed his religious views and became an ardent advocate of modernism and religious freedom. In 1869 he settled in the United States, where he served as rabbi in Detroit, Chicago and New York. In 1903 he became president and head of the department of theology at the Hebrew Union College in Cincinnati. Kohler dis-

Alexander Kohut, rabbi and scholar, was a great exponent of conservative Judaism in America.

Rebekah Kohut, social worker, was active in many philanthropic causes in the United States.

tinguished himself as preacher, educator, scholar and prolific writer in almost all fields of Jewish learning. His major work is his *Jewish Theology*, a systematic and complete survey of the whole field of Jewish theology, in which he shows thorough mastery of Biblical, Rabbinic and philosophic sources. The major addresses delivered by Kohler, which reflect his great talent as a preacher and his interest in Jewish affairs, were published in a volume entitled *Hebrew Union College Addresses*. He also wrote *Heaven and Hell*, a study in comparative religion, and *The Origins of the Synagogue and the Church*, published after his death, in which he deals with the relationship between the Jewish sect of the Essenes and the early Christians, and the influence of Judaism on the origin of the Church. The "Jewish Encyclopedia" contains many articles by him. He is admired also for his piety to-

ward Jewish lore, his leadership, and his great influence on his disciples. Kohler contributed greatly to the advancement of Judaism and "Jewish Science."

KOHUT, ALEXANDER (1842–1894)

Rabbi and Talmudist. Born in Hungary, where he served as chief rabbi and as superintendent of the government school system, he settled in the United States in 1885, continued his career as rabbi, served as professor in Talmudic Methodology at The Jewish Theological Seminary, and became a great exponent of conservative Judaism. His chief contribution to Jewish scholarship was a monumental Hebrew work called *Arukh Ha-Shalem* (Aruch Completum), a dictionary of the Talmud. For this he earned wide acclaim.

KOHUT, REBEKAH (1864–1951)

Outstanding American Jewess, educator

273

Abraham Isaac Kook, scholar, Talmudist and Zionist leader, was a champion of orthodox Judaism in word and deed. Kook was chief rabbi and foremost leader of the Ashkenazic community in Palestine.

and communal worker. Born in Hungary, she came to the United States as a child, and received her education in California. She married Alexander Kohut, and embarked on her life-long career in educational and welfare work. In 1897 she was president of the New York Section, National Council of Jewish Women, and in 1914 she became the head of the Young Women's Hebrew Association Employment Bureau. With her expert knowledge of problems of unemployment, she headed important governmental commissions in the City and State of New York. In 1924 she was elected president of the World Congress of Jewish Women. She wrote several biographies and memoirs.

KOL NIDRE

The introductory words, meaning "All the Vows," of the opening prayer recited on the evening of the Day of Atonement (Yom Kippur). Written in Aramaic, the text of *Kol Nidre* contains a solemn declaration of the annulment of all personal vows made during the course of the year. This declaration does not, however, free the individual from obligation toward his fellow men. Preceding the Kol Nidre there is a declaration permitting transgressors to join the congregation in prayer, alluding perhaps to the Marranos, who were forcibly compelled to embrace Christianity but remained secretly loyal to Judaism. The solemn melody of Kol Nidre is a reminder of the sufferings of the forcibly converted Jews in Spain and Portugal, and of other Jews persecuted through the ages.

KOOF see Kof.

KOOK, ABRAHAM ISAAC (1864–1935)

Chief rabbi and head of the Ashkenazic community in Palestine, author and Zionist leader. Born in Latvia, he settled in Palestine in 1903, where he served as rabbi and founded a Yeshivah. After World War I, during which time he was stranded in Europe, he returned to Jerusalem and was appointed chief rabbi of Palestine. He was profoundly respected for his spiritual leadership, his scholarship and literary creativeness. In his memory the *Mizrachi* organization founded in Jerusalem the *Mosad Ha-Rav Kook* (Rabbi Kook Institute) for the purpose of publishing many of the unpublished works of Rabbi Kook, as well as the works of other scholars, and to promote the cultural and educational activities of the adherents of orthodox Jewry.

KOSHER

Hebrew term meaning "fit," "in proper condition," as a designation for ritually pure things, especially food permitted to be used in accordance with the dietary laws. See *Dietary Laws; Kashrut.*

KOSHER LE-PESAH

Hebrew phrase, meaning "fit for Passover use," designating food permitted to be used on Passover, in accordance with the dietary laws.

KOTEL MAARAVI see Wailing Wall.

KRISHMA

Popular term for "Keriat Shema" (the reading of the Shema). Pious Jews read the *Shema* every night before retiring. See *Shema.*

KROCHMAL, NACHMAN (1785–1840)

Historian, philosopher, and one of the founders of "Jewish Science." Born in Galicia, he became the spiritual leader and educator of Jewish Galician youth, and a pioneer in Jewish historical research. His writings were few, but he made a great contribution to the philosophy and history of Judaism through his important work entitled *Moreh Nevukhe Ha-Zeman* (Guide for the Perplexed of the Age), published after his death (1851) by Leopold Zunz which is still relevant to students of Jewish history and philosophy.

KU KLUX KLAN

A secret anti-Negro, anti-Catholic, and anti-Jewish organization, founded in Atlanta, Georgia in 1915, a revival of *Ku Klux Klan* organized in the south during the post-Civil War period. Klan members wore hooded gowns and carried fiery crosses, advocated "100 per cent Americanism," and resorted to attacks on Negroes, white foreign-born, and Catholics. The Klan had considerable success, and in 1922 reached a membership of four million. American common sense asserted itself and the influence of the Klan gradually diminished. By 1927 it had almost disappeared. It came to life again in 1939, and in cooperation with other fascist groups, especially the German Bund, it initiated a program of un-American and anti-Semitic activities. With the entry of the United States in World War II, the activities of the Klan were curbed.

KUPPAT HOLIM

Health organization of the *Histadrut* (General Labor Federation) in Israel. It provides medical care, health insurance, hospitalization and related services.

KUZARI see Judah Ha-Levi.

KVUTZAH see Kibbutz.

L

LAW

Hillel used to say: "Whatever is hateful unto thee, do it not unto thy fellow. This is the whole Law; the rest is but commentary."

TALMUD

LABAN

Brother of Rebekah and father of Leah and Rachel. The Bible tells that Jacob made his home with his uncle Laban in Paddan-aram (Mesopotamia), where he stayed for twenty years, married his two daughters, and became prosperous. Because of his attempts to exploit and cheat Jacob, Laban is considered in Jewish tradition the symbol of deceit.

LABOR ZIONIST ORGANIZATION see Poale Zion.

LACHISH

Important Biblical city situated sixteen miles east of Gaza and occupied by the tribe of Judah after the conquest of Canaan. Its name appears in the *Book of Joshua* as well as in ancient Egyptian documents. Lachish is mentioned as the fortified city which resisted the Babylonian invasion headed by Sennacherib. Archeological excavations made in 1935 at Tell ed-Duweir, the present site of ancient Lachish, disclosed eighteen inscribed potsherds (the so-called "Lachish Letters"). These documents parallel the Biblical account in the discourse of Jeremiah concerning the then imminent destruction of the First Temple. Following the establishment of the State of Israel, the Lachish area became the site of an important colonization project, "Operation Lachish," aiming at the expansion of Israel's agricultural production, the creation of a network of settlements for immigrants, and the establishment of a strategic military defense line.

LACHISH LETTERS see Archeology.

LADINO

Spanish Jewish dialect, also known as "Judeo-Spanish" or "Spaniolish," current among the *Sephardim* (Spanish Jews) living in the Balkan States, Morocco, Israel, Syria, and also to some extent among South and North American Spanish Jews. *Ladino* spread after the expulsion of the Jews from Spain in 1492. Ladino is basi-

Bas-relief showing Jews being exiled from the town of Lachish. The siege and surrender of the fortified town was the highwater mark of the Babylonian invasion of Judea commanded by King Sennacherib.

cally derived from the Castilian dialect, and contains numerous Hebrew elements, as well as Turkish, Arabic, Greek, Latin and some Slavic words. In many respects the relation of Ladino to Spanish is not dissimilar from that of Yiddish to German, and like Yiddish, it is written in Hebrew characters. There is a substantial literature written in Ladino, which began with translations from the Bible, religious poetry and folklore. The first printed book in Ladino appeared in Constantinople in 1510. There are numerous periodicals in Ladino published by the Sephardic communities throughout the world. Because of the widespread use of the native tongue in countries where Sephardic Jews live, Ladino as a spoken language has taken a serious decline and written Ladino is rarely used.

LAG BA-OMER

Hebrew term meaning "the thirty-third day of the Omer," a Jewish festival oc-

curring on the 18th day of Iyar, traditionally observed as a reminder of the cessation of a plague which threatened to destroy the students of Rabbi Akiva. It also recalls the Hadrianic persecution of the Jews which made it dangerous to study or teach Torah. *Lag Ba-Omer* is also observed as the anniversary of the death of Rabbi Simeon ben Yohai who, according to the tradition of the Kabbalists, was the author of the most sacred book of Jewish mysticism, the *Zohar*. Lag Ba-Omer is known as the Scholar's Holiday. In Israel pilgrimages are made on Lag Ba-Omer to the tomb of Rabbi Simeon ben Yohai at Meron in northern Galilee. Lag Ba-Omer is a favorite children's holiday, marked by excursions into the fields, the making of bonfires and illuminations, and playing with bows and arrows.

LAMED (ל)

The twelfth letter of the Hebrew alphabet, pronounced like the English L. Its

Lag Ba-Omer, the "scholar's holiday," is the customary time for orthodox three-year-olds to get their first haircuts. The boy cries as he gets his haircut near the tomb of Rabbi Simeon ben Yohai at Meron.

numerical value is 30. It means yoke (for oxen), and its meaning is clear when it is written horizontally.

LAMED-VAV TZADDIKIM

The secret "thirty-six righteous men" who, according to Jewish folklore, live in every generation, and by the merit of whose piety and saintliness the world is able to continue its existence. These men, popularly known as *Lamed-Vovniks*, lead a humble existence, and undetected among their neighbors they earn their living as ordinary persons, in unspectacular fashion. If by chance his identity is revealed, the *Lamed-Vovnik* loses his saintly usefulness. Hasidic folklore offers a great many stories about such *Lamed-Vav Tzaddikim*. The term "Lamed-Vav" is the alphabetical equivalent of 36.

LAMENTATIONS

The third of the "Five Scrolls" of the *Ketuvim* (Writings), the third section of the Bible. The book, composed of five chapters, contains elegies in poetical form on the fall of Jerusalem. Its authorship is attributed to the prophet Jeremiah, who was an eyewitness of the destruction of the First Temple in 586 b.c.e. In Hebrew the book is entitled *Ekhah* (the opening word of the book). The *Book of Lamentations* is recited in the synagogue on Tishah Be-Av (9th day of Av), in commemoration of the fall of Jerusalem and the destruction of the Temple. Many other lamentations (Kinnot) have also been composed for that day in the Middle Ages.

LANGUAGES, JEWISH

Jews have used, at different periods in their history, a number of languages other than Hebrew. The first major language was Aramaic, adopted by the Jews of Judea some time during the period of the Second Commonwealth. Aramaic was not only utilized as the common speech and in translating the Scriptures (Targum), but was later used for the *Gemara*, and a number of prayers and religious documents, as well as for the vast Midrashic and Rabbinic literature. During the Greek period in Jewish history, Greek became the common language of many Jews, and numerous Greek expressions were Hebraized. The vast Jewish literature originally written in the Greek tongue, includes some of the Apocrypha and Pseudepigrapha (non-canonical Jewish literature) as well as the works of Philo and Josephus. Much of this type of literature, even when originally written in Hebrew, was preserved only in some other tongue, such as Greek. Arabic was widespread among the Jewish people after the Islamic conquest, and they developed their own Judeo-Arabic dialect. Another important dialect was and still is *Ladino*, used by Spanish Jews, which consists of a mixture of Spanish, Hebrew, and Arabisms, and is written in Hebrew characters. The greatest and latest non-Hebrew language used by Jews is *Yiddish*, which branched off from the German language and in recent centuries became a literary as well as a spoken language used by millions of Jews of east European origin.

LATVIA

Formerly a part of the Russian Empire, Latvia became an independent Baltic republic in 1917, where close to 100,000 Jews lived before World War II. The major concentration of Jews was in three cities: Riga, Dvinsk and Libau. Jews had lived in Latvia since the 16th century and as in most European countries, they had for centuries been exposed to anti-Jewish discrimination. When Latvia gained its independence, Jews were granted minority rights and cultural autonomy. The government subsidized numerous schools

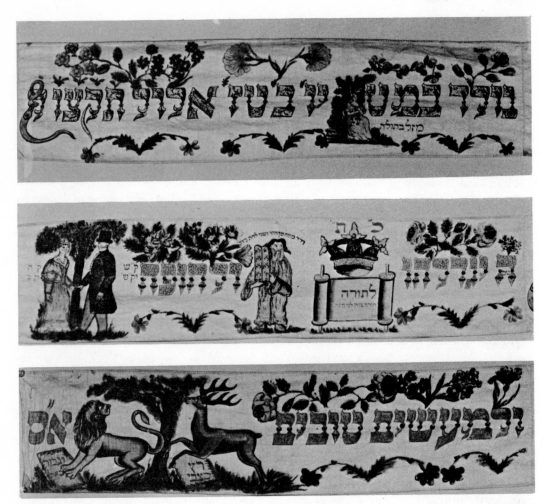

Parts of a painted linen Torah wrapper. Such covers are usually donated to a synagogue on a boy's first visit. His name and birthdate usually appear on the Torah wrapper with the Zodiac sign of the month.

maintained by the Jewish community, where the language of instruction was Yiddish, Hebrew, or both. Jewish life in Latvia was influenced by Jewish orthodoxy (Agudat Israel), as well as by Zionist and socialist factions. Many of the political and cultural freedoms of Latvian Jewry were curtailed in 1934 by a new authoritarian regime. In 1941 Latvia was occupied by the Nazis, and most of the Jewish population suffered the same fate as the Jews in other countries overrun by the Nazis.

LAW, THE JEWISH

The *Torah* (Pentateuch) forms the basis of Jewish law. Unlike other systems of law, Jewish law makes no clear distinction between the *human law* (relationship between a man and his fellow men), and the *divine law* (relationship between man and God). All types of secular, religious, material and spiritual relationships are considered an integral part of Torah, such as doctrine, aspiration, ethics, property, society, charity, domestic life, diet, ceremonial, the Sabbath and appointed times, marriage and divorce, relation of children to parents and parents to children, civil and criminal matters, Temple, priest, prayer, study, cleanliness, the personal, agriculture, etc.

281

Traditionally the Jewish law is divided into the *Written Law* (Torah Shebi-khetav) and the *Oral Law* (Torah Shebe-al Peh). The Written Law is that contained in the Five Books of Moses (Pentateuch), which according to tradition was written down by Moses through divine inspiration. The Oral Law, which according to ortho-dox belief was also revealed to Moses at Mount Sinai, consists of the vast body of explanations and interpretations of the Written Law. The Oral Law also includes all the ordinances and legal decisions and elaborations made by the rabbis of every generation, such as the *Soferim* (Scribes), the *Tannaim* (Interpreters of the Law of Moses), and the *Amoraim* (Interpreters of the *Mishnah*). The *Mishnah* and the *Gemara* (which in combination are known as the *Talmud*) are the basic Oral Law.

A number of codes have been made through the ages for the purpose of sim-plifying the study of the laws by arrang-ing them into logical classifications. One of the first and most important codifica-tions of the Oral Law was undertaken by Judah Ha-Nasi (135-210) who compiled the legal formulations and decisions and arranged them in six orders. This code is the Mishnah. In the Middle Ages Maimon-ides made another great codification and classification of the Jewish laws which he called *Mishneh Torah*. More generally it is known as *Yad Ha-Ḥazakah*. Observant Jews follow the *Shulḥan Arukh*, by Jo-seph Karo (1488-1575), which has become the authoritative code of Jewish religious practice. See *Codes*.

LAW, READING FROM THE see Torah, Reading of.

LAZARUS, EMMA (1849–1887)

American poetess of distinction. Born in New York to Sephardic parents, she re-vealed her poetic talent at an early age. In her younger days she showed little interest in Jewish affairs. In 1882 the per-secution of the Jews in Russia aroused Emma Lazarus to defend the cause of her people and to attempt to alleviate the mis-fortunes of her brethren. She began to study Hebrew, and her subsequent poetic work was inspired almost exclusively by Jewish themes. In addition to her poetic works, she published in *The American Hebrew* a series of articles entitled "An Epistle to the Hebrews," in which she advocated industrial training of Jewish im-migrants and the rebuilding of Palestine as a Jewish homeland. Some of her poems on Jewish themes are: "The Banner of the Jew," "The New Ezekiel," "In Exile," "By the Waters of Babylon," "Songs of a Semite," and "Translations from Hebrew Poets." In 1903 her great poem "The New Colossus" (i.e. the Statue of Liberty erected in the New York harbor), ex-pressing her love and aspiration for Amer-ica as a haven for the oppressed, was uni-versally acclaimed and it was inscribed on the base of the Statue.

LEAVEN, REMOVAL OF see Bedikat Ḥametz.

LEBANON

A mountain range in Syria at the north-ern boundary of Palestine. The moun-tain summits are always covered with snow, hence the name Lebanon, meaning "white." Lebanon is frequently mentioned in the Bible, and King Solomon used the beautiful cedars of Lebanon for the con-struction of the Temple. The poetry with which the Bible enshrined the "Cedars of Lebanon" has made it a phrase of frequent poetic usage through the ages.

Lebanon is also the name of an inde-pendent republic, formerly part of Syrian territory, having close to one million in-habitants, about half of whom are profes-sing Christians.

LEESER, ISAAC (1806–1868)

American rabbi, author and champion of

orthodox Judaism. Born and educated in Germany, he migrated to the United States at the age of 17, and in 1829 became "Ḥazzan" of Congregation Mikveh Israel in Philadelphia. Leeser devoted his entire life to the education of the American Jew and to the interpretation of Judaism. While maintaining liberal views and accepting certain reforms, he was a staunch defender of Jewish orthodox tradition. Leeser is credited with the following educational and cultural accomplishments: he published Jewish textbooks; established, together with Rebecca Gratz, the first Jewish Sunday School; organized the first Hebrew Education Society in 1849; founded the "Occident," the first important Jewish periodical in America; and in 1853 he published a translation of the Hebrew Bible into English, which for many years was the English version of the Bible generally used by Jews in the United States.

LEKHAH DODI

The opening Hebrew words (meaning "Come, my beloved") of one of the best known religious hymns sung on Friday in the *Kabbalat Shabbat* service. It was written about the middle of the sixteenth century by Shelomoh Ha-Levi Alkabetz. The initial letters of the first eight verses of the poem spell out the name of the author. Each verse of this hymn is followed by the refrain: "Come, my beloved, to meet the bride; let us welcome the presence of the Sabbath." See *Kabbalat Shabbat*.

LE-ḤAYIM

A popular Hebrew phrase meaning "for life," customarily used as a toast.

LEHMAN, HERBERT H.

Governor of New York State, United States Senator, and prominent Jewish

Herbert H. Lehman, politician and banker, was a U.S. Senator and Governor of New York State.

leader. Born in New York in 1878, he was active in finance, and became a partner in the Lehman Brothers banking firm. During World War I he served as an aide to Franklin Delano Roosevelt, then assistant Secretary of the Navy. For his outstanding services during World War I, he received the Distinguished Service Medal. He became active in the Democratic party, and in 1928 was elected lieutenant-governor of New York under Roosevelt as governor. In 1932 he became governor, an office which he held for 10 years, serving four terms. Following World War II, during which he served on important missions of the Federal Government, he was elected by the State of N. Y. to the U. S. Senate, an office which he held until 1956.

During his entire political career Leh-

LEIVICK, H.

H. Leivick, Yiddish writer, has devoted his work to the questions of freedom and social justice.

man showed an active interest in Jewish affairs and rendered outstanding service as a leader in the Jewish community. During World War I he served on the American Jewish Joint Distribution Committee, was vice-chairman of the Palestine Economic Corporation and a trustee of the Hebrew Sheltering Guardian Society. During and following World War II, he continued his valuable services in behalf of Jewish philanthropy. The State of Israel was a special concern of his. As a public servant, as a statesman and community leader, he is known for his liberal views and for his work in behalf of the common man.

LEIVICK, H.

Pen name of Levi Halpern, prominent Yiddish poet and playwright. Born in Russia in 1888, he was exiled to Siberia because of his revolutionary activities. With the help of his friends he escaped from Siberia and went to the United States in 1913. His literary career began in 1903, and he has published several volumes of poetry and some 20 plays. His major works are based on social motives, and reflect man's struggle for justice and freedom. His best known plays are: "Di Kaitn fun Moshiaḥ" (The Chains of the Messiah), "Der Golem," "Di Geula Komedie" (The Comedy of Redemption), "Shmates" (Rags), "Kaitn" (Chains), and "Hirsh Lekert." Some of his plays were produced on the Yiddish stage in New York as well as abroad with great success and also on the Hebrew stage in Israel.

LEON, MOSES DE see Zohar.

LESHANAH TOVAH TIKATEVU VE-TEḤATEMU see Ketivah va-Ḥatimah Tovah.

LESHON HA-KODESH

Hebrew term meaning "the Holy Tongue" which is applied to the Hebrew language and more specifically to the language of the Holy Scriptures and other sacred Hebrew texts such as the liturgy.

LEVI

Third son of Jacob, and father of the tribe of Levi. The *Levites* (members of the tribe of Levi) were the ministering persons of the Sanctuary, carrying the Tabernacle while Israel sojourned in the wilderness. Moses and Aaron were members of this tribe, and Aaron and his descendants became the priests. Following the conquest of Canaan, the Levites did not acquire a territory of their own, but were assigned a number of cities in the territories of the other tribes. In Temple times, especially in the period of the Second Commonwealth, the Levites were the singers, chanting the chorus during the services, while the priests (Kohanim) were in the process of offering the sacrifice and blessing the people.

284

LEVIATHAN

A legendary sea-monster mentioned in the Bible, and king of the creatures of the sea. According to Jewish folklore, all righteous people will partake of the flesh of the Leviathan in the Messianic era.

LEVI ISAAC OF BERDICHEV (1740–1809)

Prominent *Hasidic* rabbi (Tzaddik), and zealous defender of Hasidism. Born in Galicia, he became rabbi in his early youth. Because he openly professed Hasidism, he was persecuted by the *Mitnagdim* (anti-Hasidim) and was forced to wander from place to place, until he finally settled as rabbi in the city of Berdichev, where he spent the remainder of his life.

Because of his humble ways, his love of the common man and his great piety and saintliness, Levi Isaac became a legendary figure. His teachings, like those of the Baal Shem Tov, the father of Hasidism, were based on love of God and love of Israel. He believed that even the most humble and ignorant Jew is capable of reaching God. As a fervent preacher he dared to challenge God to stand by his people in spite of their occasional transgressions. His emotional prayers, which awed the worshippers, were often accompanied by melodies which thereafter became popular among the Hasidim.

LEVINSOHN, ISAAC BER (1788–1860)

Leader of the *Haskalah* movement in Russia, a man of great intellectual power and considerable Jewish and secular knowledge, and known as the "Russian Mendelssohn." Levinsohn's first major work in the Hebrew language was his *Teudah Be-Yisrael* (Testimony in Israel) in which he set forth a modern educational program for the Jews of Russia, advocating the study of foreign languages and science, and the rebuilding of Jewish economic and social life on the basis of agri-cultural and industrial occupations. In this effort he was aided by the Russian government, which embarked on a limited program of secular education and economic readjustment of the Russian Jews. His major literary work, published in 1829, was *Bet Yehudah* (House of Judah), designed as a modern interpretation of Judaism. Describing the major Jewish contributions to civilization, it advocated better relations between Jews and non-Jews. In order to encourage the study of modern Hebrew, Levinsohn published the first Hebrew grammar in the Russian language. As a defense of the Jew against the false blood accusations, he wrote his *Efes Damim* (No Blood), a book which was subsequently translated into English, and was used to good advantage by Sir Moses Montefiore in the *Damascus Affair*.

LEVITA, ELIJAH (1468–1549)

Also known as *Elijah Bahur*, Hebrew grammarian, student of the *Masorah* (a system of notes on the correct writing and reading of Scripture), Hebrew and Yiddish poet, and famous teacher of many prominent Christian Hebraists. Born in Germany, he lived an eventful life, rich in striking episodes and profitable contacts with outstanding non-Jewish scholars of his time.

Following the expulsion of the Jews from Nuremberg, his native city, he settled in Italy. His work as a teacher of Hebrew to Jews and non-Jews, and as a Hebrew grammarian, attracted the attention of Cardinal Viterbo, at whose request Levita wrote many of his books. His more important works are: *Sefer Ha-Bahur*, a Hebrew grammar; *Sefer Ha-Zikhronot*, a Biblical concordance; *Tishbi*, a dictionary of Talmud and Midrash; and the *Bovo Buch*, a Yiddish rendering of stories written in Italian, and based ultimately on a popular English character,

Portrait of Uriah Phillips Levy as a young U.S. Naval officer. A hero in the War of 1812, and an ardent Jeffersonian, Levy was responsible for the law abolishing corporal punishment in the American Navy.

Bevis of Hampton. The *Bovo Buch*, considered to be one of the oldest Yiddish writings, has been widely read for many generations, and is of special interest to students of Yiddish literature.

LEVITES see Levi.

LEVITICUS

The third of the Five Books of Moses (Pentateuch), called in Hebrew "Vayikra," the word with which the book begins. It was named *Leviticus* because it deals mainly with the functions of the priesthood, which was of the tribe of Levi. It is considered of great importance to Judaism since its 27 chapters are devoted to many vital laws of the Bible, such as the laws of sacrifice, the consecration of priests, the laws of purity, the ceremonial of the Day of Atonement (Yom Kippur), and the laws of holiness and sexual morality, as well as many dietary and festival regulations. Some scholars see a relationship between the Code of Holiness beginning with Chapter 19, and the legal system set up by Ezekiel in the latter part of his book.

LEVY, ASSER VAN SWELLEM

One of the first Jewish settlers in New Amsterdam (later New York), and champion of civil rights for his fellow Jews. There is no record of his birth date, but he was one of the first twenty-three Jews who sailed from Brazil and reached the Dutch settlement of New Amsterdam in 1654. Starting as a poor immigrant, he soon became a successful business man, being the first Jew to own property in New York and Albany. He is especially remembered for his legal contest with Governor Peter Stuyvesant over the civil rights of the Jews of New Amsterdam. Stuyvesant exempted the Jews from guard duty, in lieu of which he imposed upon them a special monthly tax. Levy refused to pay the tax, and demanded the right to do his civic duty instead. Despite Stuyvesant's persistent refusal, Levy finally won his case, as a result of which the Jews of New Amsterdam were finally granted full citizenship rights. Levy died in 1680.

LEVY, URIAH PHILLIPS (1792–1862)

Highest ranking officer in the United States Navy. Born in Philadelphia, Pa., he started his eventful career at the age of ten as a cabin boy. During the war of 1812 he volunteered his services, and was appointed sailing master on the *Argus*, which destroyed twenty-one British ships. However, in a subsequent attack upon a large British warship, Levy met with defeat, and for 16 months he was held prisoner in England. Levy's career in the U.S. Navy was not without disappointments. His troubles arose as a result of anti-Jewish prejudice, which caused him to fight a duel in which he killed his opponent; he was tried by court-martial several times, and lost his rank of captain to which he had previously been promoted. After ten years of retirement from service, he was vindicated, restored to captaincy, and subsequently attained the rank of Commodore of the American Navy, the highest rank held by a Jew up to that time.

Levy was an admirer of Thomas Jefferson and bought his estate at Monticello, which he turned over to the Government for the establishment of an agricultural school for orphaned children of naval officers. He himself wanted to be remembered as the father of the law which abolished corporal punishment of seamen in the U.S. Navy.

LIBYA

A territory in North Africa, between Egypt and Tunisia, an Italian colony from 1912. Jews were settled in its two provinces, Cyrenaica and Tripolitania, in pre-exilic times, and the Jewish communities developed, especially during the time of the persecution of the Jews in Judea by the Syrian ruler, Antiochus IV. In 1931 there were nearly 30,000 Jews in Libya. The position of the Jews deteriorated under Fascism. The Jewish communities also suffered greatly during World War II, when Libya became the battleground between the Fascists and the British military forces. In 1951, Libya became independent. As of 1960 the number of Libyan Jews was no more than about 3,750.

LILIENBLUM, MOSES LEIB

Moses L. Lilienblum was a writer, and a leader of Russia's Haskalah and Zionist movements.

LILIENBLUM, MOSES LEIB (1843–1910)

Hebrew writer and one of the pioneer Zionist leaders. Born in Lithuania, he first taught in a Yeshivah in Vilkomir, but soon began his career as a Hebrew writer. He joined the *Haskalah* (Enlightenment) movement, and wrote a series of articles, *Oreḥot Ha-Talmud* (Ways of the Talmud), a criticism of beliefs and practices which he thought outmoded, demanding important reforms in Judaism. Because of the opposition to Lilienblum by orthodox Jews, he moved to Odessa in 1869, where he wrote his *Ḥatat Neurim* (The Sin of Youth), a sharp criticism of the prevailing system of Jewish education.

Lilienblum's belief in the efficacy of the Haskalah weakened as a result of the pogroms of 1881. He came to the conclusion that a Jewish national home in Palestine was the only solution to the Jewish problem. As a result he joined the *Hibbat*

Zion (Love of Zion) movement, and in association with Leo Pinsker he organized a society for the colonization of Palestine, and became its secretary. To the end of his days Lilienblum was active in the Zionist movement, and devoted to the task of practical work for the establishment of agricultural colonies in the Holy Land.

Lilienblum wrote many other important works, both in Hebrew and in Yiddish, on questions of Judaism and on various literary topics.

LITHUANIA

One of the Baltic republics formed at the end of World War I, and occupied by Soviet Russia just before World War II. Jewish communities within the provinces of Lithuania have existed since the 14th century, and have experienced both periods of development and communal autonomy as well as periods of persecution and decline. There were once in Lithuania, with its capital at Kovno, close to 300,000 Jews, a number which as a result of emigration overseas and evacuations during World War I, was reduced to a little over 150,000 Jews. The Lithuanian Jewish community, with its remarkable cultural center at Vilna (the so-called "Jerusalem of Lithuania"), has made outstanding contributions to Jewish culture, both religious and secular. Lithuania became the cradle of Zionist and Jewish-socialist activities, as well as an important center of orthodox Judaism. Following World War I, the Jewish community in Lithuania was granted minority rights and an intensive Jewish educational system was developed, comprising about 300 Hebrew and Yiddish elementary schools, twenty high schools and a teachers' seminary. The Yiddish Scientific Institute (YIVO), now functioning in New York, originated in Vilna. Under the pressure of the Nazi occupation of Lithuania during World War II, the Jewish population was almost entirely annihilated.

LITURGY

Derived from the Greek, meaning "public worship," a term for the fixed order of divine services or prayers. Jewish liturgy dates back to the Holy Temple in ancient times when regular prayers, such as verses from the *Psalms*, were offered during the ritual of sacrifices. Jewish liturgy played a significant part in Jewish life during the Babylonian Exile, when the offering of sacrifices was replaced by special prayers recited in public assembly. Perhaps one of the earliest responses which the people made to the chanting of the Levites was *Ki Leolam Hasdo* (For His mercy endureth forever). In the course of time Jewish liturgy assumed the fixed pattern of three daily services known as *Shaharit* (morning prayer), *Minhah* (afternoon prayer), and *Maariv* (evening prayer). A fourth prayer known as *Musaf* (additional prayer) is recited on Sabbaths and festivals, and a special prayer called *Neilah* (closing prayer) concludes the Yom Kippur service. The basic prayers of the Jewish liturgy are the *Shema Yisrael* ("Hear, O Israel"), known briefly as the *Shema*, and the *Shemoneh Esreh* (also called "Amidah" or "Tefillah").

The prayers recited on weekdays and Sabbath are in the *Siddur* (Prayer Book), while those recited on festivals are found in the *Mahzor* (Holiday Prayer Book). There are two major versions of the Jewish liturgy; the so-called *Ashkenazic* ritual employed by east European Jews, and the *Sephardic* ritual followed by Jews of Spanish and Portuguese origin, and by several oriental Jewish communities. The Hasidic movement adopted much of the Sephardic ritual. The Jewish prayer service is built on the threefold structure of

adoration, thanksgiving and petition. The Jewish liturgy provides prayers and blessings for every occasion and for every important joyous or sad event in the life of the Jewish individual. Some prayers reflect events in Jewish history such as persecutions; others express the aspirations and longings of the Jewish people. In addition to blessing God before partaking of food, there is the *Birkat ha-Mazon*, the grace after meals. On retiring one recites the *Shema* and other prayers.

A significant feature of Jewish prayer is that man blesses God rather than the object over which he proclaims the blessing. At meals, for example, he blesses not the food he eats but God who provides it. Prayer is threefold in intent and action: praise, petition and thanksgiving. Few prayers in the Hebrew Prayer Book are of petition or supplication (tefillah), though some of those are particularly intense and moving.

LOD see Lydda.

LONDON, MEYER (1871-1926)

Labor leader and socialist member of the American Congress. Born in Russia, London settled in the United States in 1891, where he studied and engaged in the practice of law. His legal career was devoted to the cause of the working man and the trade union movement in America. London joined the Socialist party, and being particularly interested in the welfare of Jewish workers, he was a charter member and one of the prominent leaders of the Workmen's Circle (*Arbeiter Ring*). In 1914 he was elected to Congress, a public office to which he was twice reelected and which gave him the distinction of being the first socialist to become a member of the House of Representatives. As a Congressman he advocated unemployment insurance; fought anti-immigration laws; supported reduction in taxes,

LOPEZ, AARON

Meyer London, lawyer, labor leader and first Socialist member of the American Congress.

the anti-lynching bill, and legal measures designed to increase the welfare of the poor. Active in Jewish affairs, he fought anti-Jewish discrimination, and defended the economic, cultural and political interests of the Jewish masses. Despite his many opponents he became one of the most respected and beloved figures in American public life.

LOPEZ, AARON (1731–1782)

Leading American merchant before the Revolution. Born in Portugal, he went with his family to Newport, Rhode Island, in 1752. Together with Jacob Rodriguez Rivera, his father-in-law, he entered the whaling and sperm-oil industry, and became the owner of thirty ships which sailed to the West Indies, Africa and Europe. As a result of his efforts, Newport developed into an important commercial center, where a considerable

Jewish community had been formed. In 1763 Lopez laid the cornerstone of the Newport Synagogue, which is now a famous national shrine.

In the American Revolution and the subsequent occupation of Newport by the British, Lopez lost most of his wealth, and accompanied by other Jews he fled to Leicester, Mass. Upon his return to Newport at the end of the war, he died in an accident, and was mourned by Jews and non-Jews alike. The famous Christian scholar Ezra Stiles recorded in his diary that Lopez was "a merchant of the first eminence," and "without a single enemy and the most universally beloved by an extensive acquaintance of any man that I ever knew."

LOST TEN TRIBES see Tribes, Lost Ten.

LOT

Son of Haran and nephew of Abraham, whom he accompanied to the land of Canaan. According to the Bible, Lot subsequently settled in Sodom. When God destroyed Sodom and Gomorrah, Lot was forewarned by the angels to leave Sodom. Accompanied by his wife and two daughters, Lot fled the doomed city. His wife was turned into a pillar of salt when she disobeyed the warning not to look back on the flaming city. When Lot took refuge in a remote cave in the mountains, his two daughters made him drunk, and bore from him two sons, known as the ancestors of Moab and Ammon.

LÖW, JUDAH BEN BEZALEL see Judah Löw ben Bezalel.

Aaron Lopez, well-known merchant in Colonial America, contributed greatly to the early development of Newport, Rhode Island, where he was the leader of a flourishing Jewish community. He laid the cornerstone of the Newport Synagogue, now a National Historic Site, and when he died was mourned by the entire community.

LUAH

Hebrew word for "Calendar." See *Calendar, Jewish.*

LUBIN, DAVID (1849–1919)

American agrarian reformer and founder of the International Institute of Agriculture. Born in Russia, he went to the United States at the age of six. He began to work at the age of twelve, and in 1874 he went to California and opened a general store in Sacramento where he soon became known for his honesty and fair dealing. Upon his return from Palestine, which he visited in 1884, Lubin, now a successful business man, became interested in farming and in the problems of transportation, tariff, and reduced parcel-post rates for the benefit of both farmers and consumers. He then realized that farming problems can better be solved on an international basis, and that the welfare of the farmers in one country depends on the welfare of those in other countries. He advanced the idea of the establishment of an International Institute of Agriculture. This idea met with little support in the United States, England and France, but was accepted by King Victor Emanuel III of Italy, who called an international conference in 1905 at which forty-five nations joined in the establishment of the first permanent international agricultural corporation. David Lubin was then appointed representative of the United States to this Institute, which became a very successful organization benefiting both farmers and consumers the world over. He died in Rome, where his name is inscribed on a tablet in the Institute founded through his efforts and idealism.

Young boy at a Youth Aliyah settlement in Israel prepares to observe the Lulav and Etrog Mitzvah connected with the ancient harvest thanksgiving festival of Sukkot. The ritual is usually associated with reciting the Hallel.

LUHOT HA-BERIT, SHENE

Hebrew name for the tables (tablets) containing the Ten Commandments. See *Tables of the Law, Two.*

LUIS DE TORRES see Columbus, Christopher.

LULAV

Hebrew term for the palm-branch used together with the *Etrog* (citron) during the services on Sukkot (Feast of Tabernacles). A blessing is pronounced while holding the *Lulav* in the right hand and the *Etrog* in the left hand. The worshipper waves the Lulav in six directions (up, down, north, south, east and west), symbolizing God's Omnipresence. The ritual of waving the Lulav and Etrog is also associated with the recitation of the *Hallel.*

LURIA, ISAAC (1534–1572)

Kabbalist, founder of the so-called *Practical Kabbalah.* Born in Jerusalem to parents who had emigrated from Germany (hence his surname *Ashkenazi*), he was orphaned in early childhood and went to Egypt where he was raised and educated by his uncle. Luria mastered the Talmud at an early age, and began to study the *Zohar,* principal text of the Kabbalists. For thirteen years he lived as a hermit in Cairo, engrossed in the study of Zohar, and in 1569 he went to Palestine and settled in Safed, the center of the study of Kabbalah. His pupils and colleagues regarded him as the forerunner of the Messiah, as a performer of miracles, and named him the *Ari* (Lion) *Ha-Kadosh,* initials of three Hebrew words signifying the "Ashkenazi Rabbi Isaac" with the attribute "The Holy."

In the theoretical aspects of his system of Kabbalah, Luria explained the "Ten Spheres" through which God, the "Endless," rules the world. He also advanced the doctrine of transmigration of souls, suggesting that every soul, especially that of transgressors of religious duties, returns to this world, entering the body of another person in order to be purified. Luria's major contribution was his "Practical Kabbalah." In this system of mysticism, Luria suggested that *Kavvanah* (intense mental concentration) is capable of bringing man to a closer understanding of God and Creation. The attainment of a higher degree of mental concentration is made possible through repentance, self-affliction (such as persistent fasting), strict observance of the Law, and through mystical formulae, especially the use of the Hebrew alphabet both as letters and numbers in combination.

Except for a number of poems and religious hymns written in Aramaic and Hebrew, Luria left few writings. His ideas and teachings were written down and transmitted to posterity by his great disciple Ḥayim Vital.

LUZZATTO, MOSES ḤAYIM (1707–1746)

Kabbalist and Hebrew writer, known as the father of modern Hebrew literature. Born in Padua, Italy, he attained great Jewish and secular learning. Luzzatto's better known works in the field of Hebrew literature are: *Leshon Limmudim*, on rhetoric; *Migdal Oz* (Tower of Strength) and *La-Yesharim Tehillah* (Praise to the Upright), two allegorical dramas; *Mesillat Yesharim*, an ethical treatise which has become a classic of the *Musar* (moralist) literature; and 150 psalms and liturgical poems of which only a few have been preserved.

As a young man Luzzatto became interested in Kabbalah, and a devoted follower of the *Practical Kabbalah* of *Isaac Luria*. Because of his belief that he was destined to be the Messiah, he aroused the suspicion of the rabbis and was subsequently forced to leave Italy. He settled in Amsterdam, and then went to Palestine

Samuel David Luzzatto, scholar and commentator on Biblical and post-Biblical literature.

to continue his teachings of the Kabbalah. After a few years Luzzatto died in Acre (Acco) during an epidemic.

LUZZATTO, SAMUEL DAVID (1800–1865)

Father of modern Jewish scholarship. Born in Italy, and endowed with extraordinary abilities and talents, he began his literary career in his boyhood. Between his eleventh and fifteenth years he wrote a Hebrew grammar, and a commentary on the *Book of Job*, and studied the *Zohar*, coming to the conclusion that it was written at a later date than that accepted by tradition. In his early teens he published 37 poems and wrote a treatise dealing with the system of Hebrew vowels. At the age of twenty-nine he became a member of the faculty of the rabbinical college at Padua. His subsequent literary works, 37 volumes in Hebrew and 17 in Italian, were devoted to research work in many fields of Jewish knowledge and philosophy. Among other studies he analyzed the Samaritan writings, engaged in Biblical criticism, discussing the origin and authorship of several books of the Bible, and wrote critiques in the field of Hebrew poetry of the Spanish period. Luzzatto remained all his life a staunch defender of orthodox Judaism and believed in the rebirth of the Jewish people and culture in Palestine.

LYDDA

(Hebrew, Lod.) Ancient town in Palestine, southeast of Jaffa, the site of Israel's airport. According to the Bible it was founded by the tribe of Benjamin. After occupation by the Samaritans in the 4th century b.c.e., it was regained by Judea during the Roman rule. On the destruction of the Second Temple it became a haven for Jewish scholars, and Eliezer ben Hyrcanus founded an academy there. During the 4th century c.e., Lydda became a Christian center. It was destroyed during the Crusades, and in modern times it was re-established as the Arab city of Ludd. Since 1948, following the War of Liberation and establishment of Israel, Lydda became a Jewish city inhabited mostly by recent immigrants.

 **MEZUZAH**

For this commandment which I command you this day

Is not too hard for you, nor is it far off. . . .

But the word is very near to you;

It is in your mouth and in your heart,

So that you can do it.

DEUTERONOMY

MAARIV

Hebrew name for the evening service. It is one of the three obligatory services in the Jewish liturgy to be recited every day of one's life. The other two are the *Shaḥarit* (morning) and the *Minḥah* (afternoon) services. See *Liturgy*.

MAASER

Hebrew term meaning "one tenth," applied to the ancient Jewish religious duty of setting aside one tenth part of one's income for charity. The Bible enjoined the giving of Maaser (tithe) to the Levites and to the poor. There was also a Maaser

The Israeli Maccabi gymnastic group on Sport Day in Tel Aviv. Every three years a Jewish "Olympics," is held in Israel, sponsored by the Maccabi World Union and its more than 200,000 sportsmen.

which was to be brought to the Sanctuary. To this day many pious Jews contribute a tithe of their income to educational, religious and similar social service institutions.

MABBUL see Flood, The.

MACCABEES

The Hasmonean dynasty founded in Judea in the middle of the second century b.c.e. Mattathias, assisted by his five heroic sons, started a revolt against the despotic ruler of Judea, the Syrian king Antiochus. Following the death of Mattathias, Judas Maccabeus (Judah the Maccabee) led the war of independence which ended in a Maccabean victory and the rededication of the Holy Temple in 165 b.c.e. The Maccabean dynasty lasted for about 120 years, until Judea fell under Roman rule. The word Maccabee has come to mean patriotic hero. See *Hanukkah*.

MACCABI

An international association designed to promote athletics among Jewish youth, known as the Maccabi World Union. The first Maccabi athletic groups were organized in 1895 in Berlin. Prior to World War II, the Maccabi World Union consisted of thirty-eight organizations in different countries with a membership of about 200,000. The major project of the Maccabi is the organization of Maccabiads, or "Jewish Olympics," which have been staged in various countries, particularly in Tel Aviv, Israel.

MACHPELAH

The cave mentioned in the Bible as the burying place of the Patriarchs, Abraham, Isaac and Jacob, and the Matriarchs, Sarah Rebekah, and Leah. The *Cave of Machpelah*, in Hebron, was purchased by Abraham as a burying place for his wife Sarah. It has become a sacred shrine for

Jews, Christians and Moslems alike. Under Moslem ownership and supervision, it has for centuries been made inaccessible to members of other faiths.

MAFTIR

Hebrew term applied to the verses in the Pentateuch which conclude the *Reading of the Law* on Sabbaths and festivals. The person called to pronounce the benediction over the *Maftir* also reads the selection from the Prophets, the *Haftarah*. See *Haftarah; Torah, Reading of.*

MAGEN DAVID

Hebrew term meaning the "Shield of David" applied to the figure of the six-pointed star, or two interlaced equilateral triangles, which has come to be the accepted symbol of Judaism in general and

Terra cotta Magen David, believed to be from the Capernaum synagogue (ca. 3rd century c.e.).

Judah L. Magnes (center) appearing before the Anglo-American Commission on Palestine in Jerusalem (1946) to present the views of the "Iḥud" (Union of Palestine) group. (Martin Buber is at his right.)

of Zionism in particular. Though archeological discoveries have traced its use as far back as the 3rd century c.e. in the Capernaum Synagogue, it did not come into general use as a decoration for tombstones, synagogues, flags and other sacred objects until the 19th century.

The Magen David appears on the blue and white Israeli flag as a blue design on the white field. In Israel the *Red Magen David* (Magen David Adom) organization corresponds to that of the *Red Cross* in other countries.

MAGGID

Hebrew term for preacher. The *Maggid* (plural: *Maggidim*) was frequently an itinerant preacher who would go from town to town to give his homily, known as the *Derashah*. The Maggidim were usually gifted speakers, capable of stirring the listeners and moving them emotionally. Their sermons were of a religious, moral and instructional nature,

designed to comfort the listeners and give them hope for a better future for the people of Israel, or to admonish them for their human weaknesses or their indifference to the problems relating to the welfare of the Jewish community. The Maggidim were ordinarily well versed in *Midrashic* and *Haggadic* literature, and aptly used these sources for their public lectures. Some of the Maggidim acquired great fame in the Jewish communities of Poland and Russia. In recent times, however, this type of popular preaching has been on the decline.

MAGNES, JUDAH LEON (1877–1948)

Rabbi, Chancellor (1925), and President (1936), of the Hebrew University in Jerusalem. Born in San Francisco, he received his rabbinical ordination at the Hebrew Union College in Cincinnati, and studied in Europe, where he received the Ph.D. In 1905 he became active in the Zionist movement, and while serving as rabbi of Congregation Emanu-El in New York, he became known as a great community leader, organizing the short-lived *Kehillah* (Jewish Community) in New York, and laying the foundation of the Bureau of Jewish Education in New York, which existed until 1941. An active member and one of the founders of the American Jewish Joint Distribution Committee, Magnes went to Europe during World War I to help organize Jewish relief work.

Magnes is remembered for his activities in behalf of the Hebrew University in Jerusalem, for the organization of which he secured funds. In Palestine Magnes took an active part in the political life of the country, and advocated close cooperation between the Arabs and the Jews, even going to the extreme of suggesting the establishment of an Arab-Jewish State as part of an Arab Federation in the Near East. He was very well known as a pacifist and humanitarian.

MAHARAL see Judah Löw ben Bezalel.

MAH NISHTANNAH see Four Questions.

MAH TOVU

The opening two words of the prayer in the *Ashkenazic* prayer book recited on entering the synagogue. The text of the prayer is of Biblical origin, stating in part: "How goodly are thy tents, O Jacob, thy dwelling places, O Israel." According to the Talmud, the above quotation applies to the synagogue, hence the occasional custom of inscribing it over the entrance of houses of worship.

MAHZOR

Festival prayer book. Based on the *Siddur* (the weekday and Sabbath prayer book), the *Mahzor* contains additional prayers called *Piyyutim* (religious hymns) written by various poets, such as Kalir, Ibn Gabirol, Judah Ha-Levi, Moses ibn Ezra, and others. Jewish communities of east European origin use the *Ashkenazi Mahzor*, and those of Spanish origin use the *Sephardi Mahzor*. Many rites of the Sephardi Mahzor do not include most of the Piyyutim. Both the Ashkenazi and the Sephardi texts are based on the oldest and most comprehensive Mahzor, the *Mahzor Vitry*, compiled in the 11th century by a pupil of Rashi, R. Simhah ben Samuel of Vitry.

MAIMONIDES, MOSES (1135–1204)

Greatest Jewish philosopher and codifier of the Middle Ages, and distinguished physician, popularly known as the *RaMBaM*, from the initials of his Hebrew title and name, *Rabbi Mosheh Ben Maimon*. Born in Cordova, Spain, he received Talmudic and secular instruction from his learned father, Maimon ben Joseph. Because of religious persecution by fanatical Mohammedan sects, Moses fled Cordova at the age of 13, and together with his family wandered for 17 years from place to place in Spain, Morocco, and Palestine. During the years of wandering Moses studied Talmud, philosophy, mathematics, natural sciences and medicine, and began to write some of his famous works. In 1165 the Maimon family finally settled in Fostat near Cairo, Egypt. After the death of his father, Moses began to practice medicine, and enjoying an outstanding reputation in this profession, he became the personal physician of Saladin, the Sultan of Egypt. In the meantime Maimonides became known for his great scholarship and as the greatest Talmudic authority of his time. Taking an active part in the life of the Jewish community, he became the *Nagid* (Head) of the Jews in Egypt, and the recognized legal authority for Jewish communities elsewhere in the world.

Maimonides excelled in various fields of scholarship, such as Jewish law, phil-

The seven-branched candelabrum as illustrated in the first complete 13th-century manuscript of Maimonides' Mishneh Torah. Laws concerning candelabra made by Bezalel are in Exodus 37.

Italian portrait of Maimonides on a medallion, ca. 1700. Maimonides' major work was his philosophical book, "Guide for the Perplexed."

osophy, ethics, and medicine. His two greatest literary works, which left an indelible mark on Jewish life and scholarship, are the *Mishneh Torah* (Repetition of the Law) and the *Moreh Nevukhim* (Guide for the Perplexed). The Mishneh Torah, better known as the *Yad Ha-Hazakah* (The Strong Hand), is a gigantic religious code of fourteen books, written in Hebrew. This work, composed over a period of 10 years, appeared in 1180 and was designed as a systematic summary of the legal formulations of the Talmud and other rabbinic writings. In spite of the fact that the Mishneh Torah was attacked by those who feared that it might replace the study of the Talmud itself, it was quickly accepted as an authoritative code by most Jewish communities in Europe, Africa and the Near East, and was subsequently used by all codifiers and other scholars as the basis for their own works.

The Moreh Nevukhim (Guide for the Perplexed), Maimonides' greatest philosophical work, was written in Arabic, and completed in 1190. This work attempted to harmonize the teachings of Judaism with the philosophy of Aristotle, which was accepted by most thinkers at that time. In the words of Maimonides, the Moreh Nevukhim was written "to promote the true understanding of the real spirit of the Law, to guide those religious persons who, adhering to the Torah, have studied philosophy and are embarrassed by the contradictions between the teachings of philosophy and literal sense of the Torah." The book created a great furor among Jewish scholars and rabbis, many of whom attacked Maimonides bitterly, accusing him of embracing ideas which were contrary to the accepted Jewish tradition. The Moreh Nevukhim has, nevertheless, exercised great influence on both Jewish and Christian thinkers, and has been widely read and studied in the course of the succeeding generations. Among Jews the book has become popular through the excellent Hebrew translation of Samuel ibn Tibbon.

Other important works written by Maimonides are: A Commentary on the *Mishnah; Iggeret Ha-Shemad* (Letter on Apostasy) discussing the problem of those Jews who were forced to embrace another faith; *Iggeret Teman* (Letter to the Jews of Yemen), concerning the coming of the Messiah; *Responsa*, answers to questions on Jewish laws; and a number of medical works. The theology of Maimonides is summed up in the famous *Thirteen Articles of Creed* summarized by him, which have become a part of the daily ritual. These affirm the belief that: 1) God is the Creator and Guide of all things; 2) God is uniquely One; 3) God is incorporeal; 4) God is eternal; 5) God, and God alone, is the proper Object of worship; 6) God truly revealed His will through the prophets; 7) Moses was the greatest of all the prophets; 8) The Torah was revealed to Moses; 9) The Torah is eternal and unchangeable; 10) God is omniscient; 11) There is divine reward and punishment; 12) Messiah will surely come; and 13) The dead will be resurrected when God so wills.

Despite the opposition that arose against Maimonides in his own lifetime, and despite the burning of his books ordered by Christian authorities, he has remained one of the greatest and most revered personalities in Jewish history. As a tribute to his greatness it was said of him that "From Moses unto Moses there arose none like unto Moses."

MALACHI

The last of the *Twelve Minor Prophets*. Very little is known about the life of this prophet, and since "Malachi" is not otherwise used as a Hebrew proper name, and simply means "my messenger," the proph-

et's real name is probably unknown. From the content of his book, containing four chapters, it is assumed that he lived in Palestine during the period following the return of the Judeans from Babylonia, about the middle of the 5th century b.c.e. In his prophecies Malachi rebuked the people, both laymen and priests, for their unethical conduct, their worship of foreign cults, intermarriage and social injustices. He predicted the approach of the Day of Judgment, and pleaded eloquently: "Have we not all one Father? Hath not one God created us? Why do we deal treacherously every man against his brother, profaning the covenant of our fathers?" If the dating is correct, Malachi may have paved the way for the spiritual and social reforms of Ezra and Nehemiah.

MALAKH HA-MAVET see Angel of Death.

MAMRE see Archeology.

MAMZER

Jewish term for an illegitimate child, specifically the offspring of a forbidden marriage or of an adulterous woman. The Bible ruled that a "bastard shall not come into the congregation of the Lord," meaning that a *Mamzer* cannot marry a Jew.

MANASSEH

Eldest son of Joseph and traditionally father of the tribe that bears his name. According to the Bible, Jacob blessed Joseph's two sons and declared that Ephraim, although the younger, should take precedence over his older brother Manasseh.

MANDELKERN, SOLOMON (1846–1902)

Hebrew poet, scholar, and compiler of the Hebrew Concordance. Born in Russia, he turned from *Ḥasidism* to the *Haskalah* movement, studied in Russian and German universities, and in 1880 he settled in Leipzig. Mandelkern wrote in Hebrew, Russian and German, and distinguished him-

Young people celebrating Ḥanukkah are gathered around the holiday candles. After the candles are lit, the "Maoz Tzur," Mordecai's 13th-century hymn, known in English as "Rock of Ages," is usually chanted.

self as an original Hebrew poet and as translator of some of Byron's and Heine's poetry into Hebrew. His life work was the *Hekhal Ha-Kodesh*, a Hebrew-Latin concordance of the Hebrew and Chaldaic (Aramaic) words in the Bible, to which he devoted twenty years.

MANNA

Miraculous food or "food from heaven" which, according to the Bible, the Israelites ate for forty years during their wandering in the wilderness before reaching the Promised Land. The Bible describes *Manna* as "a fine, scale-like thing, fine as the hoar-frost on the ground," or as "white, coriander seed." The Manna fell during the night upon the dew, and the Israelites were instructed by Moses to gather each morning one "omer" (about four quarts), and a double portion on the sixth day of the week for the Sabbath, the day of

rest. The Manna was either baked or boiled, and tasted like wafers boiled in honey. An expedition of the Hebrew University discovered in 1927 that a certain secretion of some insect living on the leaves of the tamarisk is similar in taste to the description of that of the Manna in the Bible. The Bible derives the name from the question "man hu?" (what is it?) which the Israelites asked when they saw it for the first time.

MANTLE OF THE LAW see Parokhet.

MAOT ḤITTIM (Mo-os Ḥitim)

Hebrew term meaning "wheat money" applied to special funds traditionally raised before Passover by Jewish communities the world over, for the purpose of providing *Matzot* and other Passover needs for the poor. Thereby is fulfilled the invitation which the Jew utters at the Seder: "Let him who is hungry come and eat."

304

MAOZ TZUR

Opening words of the Hebrew hymn for Hanukkah, sung after the lighting of the Hanukkah candles. The hymn, known in English as "Rock of Ages," describes the Maccabean victory and compares it to the deliverance of Israel from Egypt, from Babylonia and from Haman. The hymn is believed to have been written in the 13th century by an unknown author called Mordecai, whose Hebrew name forms an acrostic of the initial letters of the five stanzas of the hymn.

MAPAI

Abbreviated name of *Mifleget Poalei Eretz Yisrael* (Workers' Party of the Land of Israel), the largest and most influential political party in the State of Israel. It was founded in 1930 through the merger of "Ahdut Ha-Avodah" and "Hapoel Hatzair." Since the establishment of the State of Israel *Mapai* has drawn the largest popular vote, is the leading party in the Knesset, and has successively been charged with the formation of the government. It has been the main party in the government coalition, though it has never attained an absolute majority in the Knesset.

MAPAM

Abbreviated name of *Mifleget Poalim Meuhadim* (Party of United Workers), a workers party in Israel, founded after the establishment of the State. It represents the leftist wing of the workers in Israel and has very few members in the Knesset.

MAPU, ABRAHAM (1808–1867)

One of the first modern Hebrew writers and author of the first Hebrew novel. Born in Russia, he was for many years a teacher of religion and German in a government school at Vilna. His first literary success was attained in the publication of the first Hebrew novel *Ahavat Zion* (Love of Zion) in 1853, which has since been translated into several languages. *Ahavat Zion* deals with the period of the prophet Isaiah, and was acclaimed in its day by the Hebrew reading public for its idyllic and romantic descriptions of the Land of Israel, and for its Biblical and somewhat florid language. Another Biblical novel *Ashmat Shomeron* (The Guilt of Samaria) published in 1863, dealing with the conflict between Jerusalem and Samaria, met with equal success. Mapu's other novel *Ayit Tzavua* (The Hypocrite), published in 1861, was a satire on aspects of contemporary Jewish life, describing certain religious fanatics and hypocrites.

Mapu's Biblical novels fortified in his readers their longing for Zion, and have indirectly served as a stimulus for the Zionist movement.

MARIAMNE

Hasmonean princess and wife of Herod the Great. Herod, the hated king of Judea, under the protection of Rome, married the beautiful princess of the Hasmonean dynasty in 37 b.c.e. Despite his love for Mariamne, the suspicious and cruel king killed the members of the Hasmonean family in order to wipe out any rival or pretender to the throne. Influenced by the intrigues of his sister Salome, who falsely accused Mariamne of infidelity and of conspiring to poison him, Herod had his wife executed on the scaffold when she was 28 years old.

MARI TEXTS see Archeology.

MAROR

Hebrew term applied to the bitter herbs eaten at the Passover *Seder* as a reminder of the experience of bitter slavery and the suffering of the Israelites in Egypt before they were led from Pharaoh's slavery to freedom by Moses. See *Seder*.

MARRANOS

Spanish word meaning "the damned," applied to those Jews who were forced to embrace Christianity and who, in many cases, remained secretly faithful to Judaism. The *Marranos* are called in Hebrew *Anusim* ("those compelled"), and are also known as *Crypto-Jews, Neo-Christians* or *Secret Jews*. The first forced conversion of Jews to Christianity began in Spain following the persecutions of 1381. As a result of those persistent persecutions, about 100,000 Jews adopted the Christian faith. The Church, however, continuously suspected the Jewish converts of unfaithfulness to the Christian faith, and in 1480 the *Spanish Inquisition* was established for the purpose of detecting and punishing the backsliders. In 1492, when all non-converted Jews were expelled from Spain, the *Marranos* were even more severely persecuted. The fate of the Jews in Portugal was even worse, because the entire Jewish population was compelled to embrace the Catholic faith. To escape the Inquisition, many Marranos of Spain and Portugal sought refuge in North Africa, Turkey and Italy, and later in southern France, Amsterdam and the Americas, and many eventually returned to Judaism. See *Portugal; Spain*.

MARRIAGE CEREMONY

Jewish tradition regards marriage a sacred undertaking; hence the Hebrew term for entering wedlock is *Kiddushin* (sanctification). Most Jewish marriage customs and ceremonies have an ancient origin, which have in the course of the ages acquired a fixed pattern followed in most Jewish communities the world over. Thus a traditional Jewish marriage begins with the *Tenaim*, a binding agreement between both parties, now commonly known as the "engagement." The marriage ceremony takes place under a *Huppah* (canopy) in the presence of two lawful witnesses as well as the families and friends of both the bride and the bridegroom, although for legal purposes only two valid witnesses are re-

Spanish Marrano family seated at the Passover Seder table are invaded by a gang of masked and armed Inquisitors. Though the consequences were torture and death, the old man continues the Haggadah.

A 17th-century woodcut from the Minhagim Book depicting a Jewish wedding of the time.

Louis Marshall, founder of the American Jewish Committee, vigorously defended minority rights.

quired. The person solemnizing the marriage (usually a rabbi) recites the betrothal blessing, whereupon groom and bride sip from a cup of wine. The bridegroom then places the wedding ring on the index finger of the right hand of the bride and utters the formula which makes them husband and wife: "Harey at mekuddeshet li betabaat zo kedat Mosheh ve-Yisrael" (Behold, thou art consecrated unto me by this ring according to the Law of Moses and Israel). Then the *Ketubah* is read by the officiant, who recites the "Sheva Berakhot" (the seven marriage benedictions), at the conclusion of which the groom and bride sip wine once again, though from another cup. The ceremony is concluded with the bridegroom breaking a glass by crushing it with his foot. This is symbolic of the sadness that always mingles with the happiness in human life, and reminds those present of the tragedies in Jewish history, especially the destruction of the Temple.

MARSHALL, LOUIS (1856–1929)

Outstanding Jewish leader. Born in Syracuse, N.Y., he became a successful constitutional lawyer who argued important cases before the highest courts. He became world famous for his great interest and leadership in Jewish affairs. He was founder and president of both the American Jewish Committee and the American Jewish Relief Committee; chairman of both The Jewish Theological Seminary of America and of Dropsie College; and founder of the Jewish Agency for Palestine. Among Marshall's many accomplishments, the following are of special note: he influenced the American Government to break diplomatic relations with Russia over the "passport issue" which involved the rights of American-Jewish citizens; and he was the leading spokesman of the Committee of Jewish Delegations which, after World War I, sought to secure at the Peace Conference "minority rights" for the defenseless Jews from Europe.

MARTYRS, THE TEN

The collapse of the Bar Kokhba Revolt against the Romans (132–135 c.e.) resulted in fierce religious persecutions and Jewish martyrdom. The *Asarah Haruge Malkhut* (the ten martyrs) were ten great Jewish teachers of the Torah who, when executed by the Romans, met their death

Cistern hewn out of rock at Masada, the 1st century b.c.e. stronghold of Herod the Great. Here, too, the Zealots, besieged for a whole year until starved into surrender, later made their last stand against Rome.

with exemplary courage out of their profound faith in God and His Torah. Among them were Rabbi Akiva, Rabbi Hananiah ben Teradion and Rabbi Judah ben Bava. Their martyrdom is described in a liturgical poem called "The Ten Martyrs" recited during the *Musaf* Service on Yom Kippur and also during the *Kinnot* on Tishah Be-Av.

MARX, KARL (1818–1883)

World famed theoretician and founder of modern "scientific socialism." Born in Germany, he was baptized at an early age when his father, a descendant of a rabbinic family, embraced Christianity. He entered the field of journalism and went to Paris where he began to advocate his philosophy of history and his theory of economics and socialism. Because of his radical ideas and his revolutionary activities, he was wel-

come neither in Germany nor in France, and he finally settled in London.

Marx was a prolific writer and the author of a number of important studies. His major works were: *The Communist Manifesto*, published in collaboration with Engels on the eve of the German Revolution of 1848, a militant proclamation ending with the call "Proletarians of all lands, unite!"; and *Das Kapital* (Capital), which came to be known as the Socialist bible. The first volume of Das Kapital was published by Marx himself in 1867, and the other two volumes were edited and published after his death by Engels. Das Kapital gives an economic interpretation of the functions of society, and deals with the price and profit system, with capital and labor and the functions of money.

Marx had no interest in Jewish affairs, and because he considered the Jews as representing the bourgeois class, his references to them are generally derogatory.

MASADA

Historically famous fortress on the west shore of the Dead Sea where the *Zealots* (Jewish patriots) made their last heroic stand in the Jewish war against Rome (66–72 c.e.). The name of this fortress became a symbol of Jewish heroism and fired the imagination of Zionist youth. Masada is also the name of a *Kevutzah* (cooperative agricultural settlement) established in 1937 in the Jordan Valley. See *Archeology*.

MASKIL (MASKILIM) see Haskalah.

MASOR (Moser)

Hebrew term for an informer (generally for money). The infamous and oppressive legislation of the secular government against the Jews compelled them to disregard much of it out of a sense of self-respect as well as loyalty to their faith. Out of greed or ill-will some Jews turned

Early 10th-century manuscript of the Masoretic text of the Bible with the various critical notes and commentary in the inner and outer margins.

informers. These informers (*Moserim*) have at different periods of Jewish history caused much suffering to Jewish communities. A *Masor* was obviously a much despised and hated individual and considered a traitor. Jewish communities took strict measures to protect themselves against Moserim.

MASORAH

Hebrew term meaning "tradition," applied to the work of Jewish scholars since ancient times to preserve the correct spelling and pronunciation of the Biblical text. They wrote critical notes, they counted the letters and the words of the text; they discussed grammatical rules, vowels, and accents. It is well-known that scribes have a tendency to make mistakes of omission or duplication. Also, Hebrew had ceased to be a spoken tongue, and in addition was written without vowel signs. The Masoretic scholars vigilantly guarded the text against all error.

The *Masoretes* were particularly active from the 6th to the 9th century. The *Masorah* encouraged the work of Hebrew grammarians and the minute study of every phrase, word and letter of the Bible. The introduction of a vowel system was helpful, as was the later invention of the printing press. However, even printed books have mistakes, and the labors of the Masoretes remain useful to this day. Tradition looks upon the entire apparatus of the Masorah as divinely revealed to Moses.

MATRIARCHS see Patriarchs.

MATTATHIAS

Judean priest of the Hasmonean family who started the revolt against the Syrians and Hellenists. After his death in 166 b.c.e., Judah the Maccabee, the most able of his five sons, waged a successful military campaign against the enemies of Judea. See *Hanukkah; Maccabees*.

19th-century Italian wedding band inscribed with "Mazzal Tov." Such rings were usually worn at the wedding and the week following by newly-wed women, but were generally owned by the synagogue.

MATZAH see Unleavened Bread.

MATZEVAH

Hebrew term used in the Bible as a designation of a sacred pillar of stone. Later it acquired the meaning of "tombstone."

MAZZAL TOV (Mazel Tov)

A customary Hebrew congratulatory expression or felicitation, meaning "good luck," and used on happy occasions or as a wish for success in an important enterprise. The term *Mazzal* was originally applied to a star, a constellation, a planet, and in particular to a sign of the Zodiac. The association of man's fate with the stars is ancient and universal, as witness the English word "disaster"—bad star. Judaism denies that human fate depends on the stars, and the original astrological significance is long forgotten; *Mazzal Tov* is now simply an expression of good will.

MEGIDDO see Archeology.

MEGILLAH see Esther, Scroll of.

MEHUTTEN

A Yiddish term derived from the Hebrew "Mehuttan" for a relation by marriage, such as the parents of the bridegroom and the bride in relation to one another.

MEIR, GOLDA

Minister for Foreign Affairs in Israel. Born Mabovitz in 1898 in Kiev, the Ukraine, she was brought to the United States at the age of 8. There in 1917 she married the late Meir Myerson whose first name she subsequently adopted as her surname. In 1921 she settled in Palestine. She became the first Ambassador of Israel to the Soviet Union (1948), Minister of Labor in Israel (1949–56), and Foreign Minister (1956). She has also held posts in Histadrut and the Jewish Agency.

MEIR BAAL HA-NES, RABBI

Tanna of the second century c.e., disciple of R. Akiva and son-in-law of R. Hananiah ben Teradion, both martyred during the Roman oppression. Meir's wife was the learned Beruriah who is mentioned in the Talmud numerous times.

His original name is believed to have been Measha, but he was called Meir (enlightener) because of his exceptional abilities as an expounder of the Torah. Rabbi Meir continued the work of Rabbi Akiva aimed at classifying Jewish law systematically, thus paving the way for the final classification and compilation of the *Mishnah* by R. Judah Ha-Nasi.

The head of the Academy of Usha in Galilee, R. Meir became one of the most frequently quoted authorities in the Talmud. He also had great talent as an Haggadic preacher, a teller of fables, and his sermons and lectures attracted large audiences. He had great respect for men of learning, and sought the friendship of both Jewish and non-Jewish scholars, one of whom was the heretic Elisha ben Avuyah, who because he renounced Jewish tradition was subsequently shunned by his other colleagues.

Jewish tradition refers to him as *Rabbi Meir Baal Ha-Nes* (Rabbi Meir, the Miracle Worker), whose tomb is said to be located in Tiberias. For centuries pious Jewish women kept charity-boxes, called *Meir Baal Ha-Nes Pushkes* in which collections of money were made for the purpose of helping the poor in the Holy Land.

MEIR OF ROTHENBURG, RABBI (1215–1293)

Prominent Talmudic scholar of the 13th century, sometimes called, because of his great authority, the "Light of the Exile." Born in Germany, he served as rabbi in a number of places, chiefly in Rothenburg. A recognized authority on Jewish law, Meir's chief work was the *Responsa* (answers to questions of law), of which many editions exist. He also wrote a commentary on the *Mishnah*, as well as liturgical hymns which are included in the services of Yom Kippur and Tishah Be-Av.

Because of persecutions of Jews in Germany, he decided to flee the country and settle in Palestine. He was, however, seized by the authorities and imprisoned for the rest of his life in the fortress of Ensisheim. Leaders of the Jewish community offered King Rudolph a large sum of money to free the scholar. Rabbi Meir, however, forbade them to pay any ransom in order not to create a precedent that would lead to the imprisonment of other prominent Jews for purposes of extortion. The saintly rabbi remained in prison, where he spent the last seven years of his life. His works are at present being published in Israel.

MELAKHIM see Kings.

MELAMMED

Hebrew term meaning "teacher," commonly applied to the traditional Hebrew religious teacher of small children. The term has acquired a somewhat derogatory meaning, and it is often used to describe any impractical or unsuccessful individual.

MELAVVEH MALKAH

A Hebrew term meaning "Escorting the Queen," applied to the meal and the special festivities which mark the termination of the Sabbath, which Jewish tradition compares to a "Queen." This post-Sabbath meal is of ancient origin and is still observed by orthodox Jews, especially Ḥasidim. In recent years a number of Jewish organizations have observed *Melavveh Malkah* in the changed form of special cultural events arranged for Saturday night.

MEM (מ)

Thirteenth letter of the Hebrew alphabet, pronounced like the English M. Its numerical value is 40. It means water (Hebrew, *Mayim*), and its script form N represents the water's waving. Both the Hebrew *Mem* and the Greek and Latin *M* come from a similar character in hieroglyphics.

MEMORIAL LIGHT see Yortzeit.

MEMORIAL SERVICE see Yizkor.

MENAHEM BEN SARUK

Tenth century Hebrew grammarian and compiler of the first complete Hebrew dictionary. Menahem was born in Spain and lived for many years in Cordova as the protégé and secretary of Ḥasdai ibn Shaprut, famous Jewish leader and statesman. It was Menahem who wrote Ḥasdai's letter to the king of the Khazars. His major literary work was the compilation of a Hebrew lexicon *Maḥberet*, in which he described the characteristic three-letter root of the Hebrew verb.

MENASSEH see Manasseh.

MENASSEH BEN ISRAEL (1604–1657)

Dutch rabbi, author, and negotiator for the readmission of Jews to England. His parents took him to Holland at an early age, and after receiving a rabbinical education, he served as rabbi in Amsterdam. Menasseh ben Israel was a prolific author whose works on the Bible, rabbinic literature, theology and history were widely read, and brought him in contact with the most prominent Jewish and non-Jewish scholars of his day.

Menasseh ben Israel is especially remembered for his untiring efforts to secure the readmission of Jews to England. He believed that before the coming of the Messiah, when all Jews would be restored to the Holy Land, they would first have to be dispersed all over the world, including England. This belief was held by Christians with regard to the second coming of Christ. Menasseh ben Israel was led to petition the Lord Protector, Oliver

Rembrandt etching of Menasseh ben Israel, the eminent rabbi of Amsterdam, in the year 1636.

Cromwell, the Puritan leader, to intervene in behalf of the Jews for their readmission to England, especially in view of the new spirit of religious freedom of the age. In 1655 Menasseh ben Israel was invited to England, where, supported by Cromwell, he presented his request to the Parliament. Unsuccessful at first, he finally won a partial victory, and Jews were thenceforth allowed, with some restrictions, to settle in England and were granted civil and religious freedom.

MENDELE MOCHER SEFORIM (1835–1917)

Pen name of Sholom Jacob Abramowitch, the so-called "grandfather" of Yiddish literature. Born in Russia, he spent a number of years wandering as a Yeshivah student from town to town gathering first-hand knowledge about Jewish life. He began his literary career as a Hebrew writer, and then turned to Yiddish, in which language he wrote several masterpieces, considered classics of modern Yiddish literature.

Mendele Mocher Seforim (Mendele the Bookseller) was a gifted writer and satirist whose works in Yiddish and in Hebrew are acknowledged classics. He is known as the "grandfather of Yiddish literature."

Mendele had great love for the Jewish masses and was mindful of their physical and spiritual well-being. He was known for his biting satire, and his works reflect his concern with the wretchedness of Jewish life in Russia and the need for economic and institutional reforms. His best known works are: *Di Kliatche* (The Nag), *Dos Vintchfingerl* (Wish Ring), *Fishke der Krumer* (Fishke the Lame), and *The Travels of Benjamin the Third*.

Mendele translated most of his Yiddish works into Hebrew, and is considered a master in both tongues.

MENDELSSOHN, MOSES (1729–1786)

One of the central figures in modern Jewish history; philosopher, critic, translator of the Bible, and father of the *Haskalah* (Enlightenment) movement. Born in Dessau, Germany, he received a traditional Jewish education from his learned father and especially from the local rabbi, David Hirschel Fränkel, whom he followed to

Berlin in 1743. There he studied European languages, literature and philosophy along with further studies of Jewish classical literature, especially the works of Maimonides. His close friendship with the German liberal writer Gotthold E. Lessing, and with other European intellectuals, paved the way for his subsequent literary career. Without Mendelssohn's knowledge, Lessing published his *Philosophische Gespräche* (Philosophical Chats) which attracted the attention of German literary circles. These were followed by other philosophical essays, and he was awarded the prize of the Academy of Sciences in Berlin. Mendelssohn's most popular work was *Phädon* wherein he argued for the belief in immortality of the soul. Challenged to explain how he could be at the same time a professing Jew and a philosopher, Mendelssohn wrote his *Jerusalem*, in which he asserted that there is no conflict in Judaism between belief and reason, outlined further the ideals of religious and

313

Portrait of Moses Mendelssohn, father of the Haskalah movement, is inscribed, "Humbly presented to King Frederick William the Second by the Berlin Jewish Freischule in 1787."

Medallion bearing portrait of Gracia Mendes, praised as "the heart of her people," and as savior of many Marranos escaping from Spain and Portugal, was engraved in Italy ca. 1555.

political toleration, and advocated equality for all citizens irrespective of creed.

Mendelssohn took an active part in Jewish affairs and used his influence to help Jewish communities in Germany and elsewhere. In Jewish history he is particularly known for his work to free the Jewish masses from ghetto existence, and for his endeavors to secure for them political and economic freedom, and the right to participate in European culture and education. He insisted, however, that the modernization of Jewish life ought not to be accomplished through relinquishing Jewish tradition and Jewish ceremonial laws. Consistent with his educational ideas, he compiled for the Prussian authorities the *Ritual Laws of the Jews*, and did a masterful German translation of the Pentateuch and the Psalms. These were followed by the *Biur*, a commentary to parts of the Five Books of Moses, later completed by his followers. His other literary contributions in the Jewish field comprise a commentary on *Kohelet*, a commentary on the *Millot Ha-Higgayon* by Maimonides, and the publication of a Hebrew periodical which was called *Kohelet Musar*.

Mendelssohn's work for Jewish cultural equality, progress and modernization were not without ill effects. His ideas were carried too far by some of his followers who, in their eagerness to avail themselves of the cultural and economic opportunities opened to them, became victims of assimilation, leading many of them to a complete break with Judaism, and some of his own children to embrace Christianity. Mendelssohn's own stature and his position in Jewish thought and history are fundamental in their permanent effect on Jewish life and thought.

MENDES (MENDESIA), GRACIA (ca. 1510–1569) Aunt of Joseph Nasi, the Duke of Naxos, protector of the *Marranos*, and Jewish

The upper part of the large eight-branched Hanukkah Menorah, cast in bronze about 1760, and originally from the Shnipishek synagogue in Poland, is on display in The Jewish Museum of New York.

philanthropist. Being a Marrano herself, under her Christian name of Beatrice de Luna, she left Portugal after becoming a widow, and lived in Antwerp and then in Venice. A woman of great wealth, she finally settled in Constantinople where she openly professed Judaism and became a Jewish leader famous for her philanthropic work designed to promote Jewish learning, and especially to help the Marranos who escaped from Portugal and Spain.

MENE, MENE, TEKEL UPHARSIN

The text of the famous Aramaic "Writing on the Wall" which appeared during a feast given by Belshazzar, king of Babylon. The incident is recorded in the *Book of Daniel*. The prophet Daniel was the only one of the king's wise men able to read the mysterious writing. Daniel's prophetic interpretation was the following: "God hath numbered thy kingdom and brought it to an end. Thou art weighed in the balances, and art found wanting. Thy kingdom is divided and given to the Medes and Persians." It is further recorded that Daniel's words came true as Belshazzar was slain the same night, and Babylon was captured by the Persians.

MENORAH

Hebrew name of the seven-branched candlestick originally made by the Biblical artisan *Bezalel* and placed in the sanctuary of the Tabernacle. In the First Temple, built by Solomon, there were ten golden Menorahs, and in the Second Temple there was one. The Menorah has since become

315

a universal symbol of Judaism. The Menorah now used in the synagogue has either more or less than seven branches so as to avoid the thought of any imitation of the ancient Temple. Reform temples permit the seven-branched Menorah. The *Ḥanukkah Menorah* has nine holders, one for each of the eight candles and one for the *Shammash*. The State of Israel made the Menorah its official symbol.

MERON

Ancient city in northern Galilee, now a small village not far from Safed, Israel. In the second century, Rabbi Simeon ben Yoḥai founded a rabbinic academy there. Because the tomb of Rabbi Simeon and that of his son Eliezer are said to be there, Meron has become the scene of annual pilgrimages and special festivities that take place on *Lag Ba-Omer*.

MESHUMMAD

A Jewish person who, of his own free will, forsook Judaism and embraced another faith; in short, an apostate.

MESSIAH

A modified form of the Hebrew word *Mashiaḥ* meaning "anointed," applied in the Bible to a person appointed for a special function, such as High Priest or King. Later the term *Messiah* came to express the belief that a *Redeemer*, that is a divinely appointed individual, will in the end bring salvation to the Jewish people and to the entire human race. During the Messianic era the scattered Jewish people will return to the Land of Israel, and all mankind will prosper through peace and justice. The prophets teach that in the *End*

With his young daughter wide-eyed in his arms, a Haganah soldier, modern-day descendant of the ancient warrior Maccabees, celebrates the "Feast of Dedication" in Palestine by lighting the Ḥanukkah Menorah's traditional eight candles.

of Days a just and wiser ruler, a descendant of David, will be king over Israel and the world, when peace will be established among the nations and the Law of the Lord will come from Jerusalem to all peoples.

The prophet Elijah will be the forerunner of the Messiah. There is also a tradition that *Messiah the son (i.e. descendant) of David*, will be preceded by *Messiah the son of Joseph*, who will pave the way for the real Messiah by waging war against the forces of evil (Gog and Magog), and will perish in the process.

The belief in the coming of the Messiah is one of the "Thirteen Articles of Creed" of Maimonides included in the daily Jewish ritual.

The mystical belief in the coming of a personal Messiah fortified the Jew during his precarious existence both in ancient Palestine and later in the lands of the dispersion. During periods of national disaster and persecutions, when hopes for immediate salvation were dim, the people's will to survive was given strong support by the ideal of ultimate justice and salvation that would come miraculously through divine help in the person of a redeemer or Messiah.

It is thus easy to understand why in the course of Jewish history there arose individuals who believed that it was within their power to bring salvation to their people. These individuals, whether inspired by a genuine love for their people and religion, or unscrupulous opportunists, succeeded during various periods of Jewish history in arousing the people and creating so-called messianic movements, which ended in great disappointment and despair, but which at the same time gave the people an inner sense of strength. Perhaps the most significant personality in Jewish history, who was looked upon as Messiah, was Simeon Bar Kokhba, who lead the unsuccessful revolt against Rome in the 2nd century with the support of Rabbi Akiva.

Most leaders of messianic movements are known as *false messiahs*. The most important of these were *David Alroy* in the 12th century; *David Reubeni* in the 16th century; *Shabbetai Tzevi* in the 17th century; and *Jacob Frank* in the 18th century. It is important to note that some of the so-called *false messiahs* had the support of the great intellects and spirits of their day. Shabbetai Tzevi was accepted enthusiastically by scholars, rich men and poor men alike. The word "false" does not really evaluate either their purpose or their character.

In our day many Jews still await the coming of the true Messiah "in the End of Days." In the 19th century Jewish nationalists and socialists sought to replace the belief in a personal messiah with the belief that through political action, economic reforms, and cultural revival the Jewish people would be able to restore their national homeland and also continue to survive in the diaspora in a universal social order based on peace and justice for all. Reform leaders in the 19th century substituted the concept of a messianic era for a personal messiah. Since the establishment of the State of Israel, the official rabbinate of Israel looks upon the State as *Athalta di-Geullah*—the Beginning of Ultimate and Universal Redemption.

METHUSELAH

The proverbial old man of the Bible, according to which he lived 969 years. He was one of the ten antediluvians in the Biblical list from Adam to Noah.

MEXICO

Republic in the southern part of North America, where Jews first settled in the early part of the 16th century. Its first Jewish immigrants came from Spain and

Late 18th-century silver Mezuzah case contains a Pentateuch text on a parchment scroll.

Portugal, seeking vainly to escape the Inquisition. Because of the religious persecutions to which Jewish immigrants were constantly exposed, there were in Mexico only about 10,000 Jews by 1910. Larger numbers of east European Jews began to settle in Mexico, especially in Mexico City, after World War I. In 1959 there were over 25,000 Jews living in Mexico, where Jewish life is fairly well organized. The Jewish schools in Mexico City, especially those of the Yiddish speaking group, have become well known.

MEZUMMAN

Hebrew term applied to a minimum of three adult Jewish males required in order to recite in unison the traditional blessings after the completion of a meal. If there are less than three, then each one recites the grace privately. The term basically means invited, prepared, ready, and has therefore been used in recent times to designate "ready cash," though when used in English slang it is almost always mispronounced "mezumah."

MEZUZAH

A small metal or wooden case with a strip of parchment placed in it on which are inscribed the first two sections of the liturgical *Shema* (i.e., *Shema* and *Vehayah Im Shamoa*, Deuteronomy 6:4-9 and 11:13-21) each of which prescribes this commandment. The Scriptural verses in the *Mezuzah* speak of the Jew's obligation to love God and obey His commandments. The reverse side of this parchment bears the name "Shaddai" (Almighty) which word is visible when the parchment is folded and placed in the case. This case is attached to the right (as one enters) doorpost of the house and of each room used for living purposes. The word Mezuzah literally means doorpost.

MICAH

Name of one of the Twelve so-called Minor Prophets, and of his book of prophecies contained in the Bible. Micah was a contemporary of the prophet Isaiah and preached about 735-705 b.c.e. His book of seven chapters, written in beautiful Hebrew, contains a vigorous protest against the idolatry and injustice that had swept the country. Predicting the doom of Samaria and Jerusalem, he also foretells the coming of the Messianic era, when justice and peace will be established. One of the most significant quotations from the *Book of Micah* is: "It hath been told thee, O man, what is good, and what the Lord doth require of thee; only to do justly, and to love mercy, and to walk humbly with thy God."

MICHAEL

One of the most important angels, called in the *Book of Daniel* a prince of the angels. Michael and Gabriel are the only angels mentioned in the Bible.

MICHELSON, ALBERT ABRAHAM (1852–1931)

Physicist and Nobel Prize-winner. Born in Germany, he arrived in the United States at the age of three and lived in San Francisco. He studied in the United States and Europe, and became professor of physics, first at Clark University and later at the University of Chicago. He is best known for his experiments and writings connected with research on the velocity of light, for which he won international fame. In 1907 he was awarded the Nobel Prize, and in 1923 he was elected president of the National Academy of Science.

MIDIAN, MIDIANITES

Country and people mentioned frequently in the Bible. The Midianites lived in northwestern Arabia, and were merchants, warriors, and shepherds. Jethro, Moses' father-in-law, was a priest of Midian. The Midianites had frequent wars with the Israelites and were defeated by Gideon.

MIDRASH

Hebrew term meaning "investigation" or "study," applied to a special type of broad interpretation of the Biblical text. There were two areas of such interpretations: the *Midrash Halakhah*, aiming to define the full meaning of Biblical laws; and the *Midrash Aggadah*, the purpose of which was to derive from the Biblical text a moral principle or lesson.

The Midrash Halakhah applied the legal principles of the Biblical legislation to specific cases and new life situations as they arose. There are three collections of Midrash Halakhah: *Mekhilta* on Exodus (beginning with chapter 12) relating to Passover; *Sifra* on Leviticus; and *Sifre* on Numbers and Deuteronomy. There is no Midrash Halakhah on Genesis because there is no Halakhah in Genesis (with the exception of three *Mitzvot*).

The Midrash Aggadah, generally referred to as Midrash, comprises many volumes. These *Midrashim* constitute a rich source of Biblical folklore, which began to develop in the early history of the people, and continued into the Middle Ages. Modern scholarship has tried to determine the relative age in which a specific Midrash may have been made. It must be noted here that each volume of the Midrash may contain both early and later Midrashim. Some center on major Biblical events, such as the Creation and the Exodus.

Among the better known Midrash collections may be listed: 1) *Midrash Rabbah*. Elaborate Midrashic collections on each of the Five Books of Moses, as well as on the Five Scrolls (Megillot). 2) *Tanhuma*. In several versions, some known as *Midrash Yelamdenu*. A homiletic work. 3) *Shoher Tov*. A series of homilies on the Book of Psalms. 4) *Pesikta de-Rav Kahana*. Homilies on calendar occasions. 5) *Pirke de-Rabbi Eliezer*. Elaborations of the narratives in Genesis and part of Exodus. 6) *Yalkut Shimoni* (13th century). Arranged according to Bible verses, containing much earlier material.

The Midrash to this day serves as a source for preacher, *Maggid*, and homilist.

MIGRATIONS OF THE JEWS

No other people in the world have been exposed to as many migrations as the Jewish people, hence the legend of the "Wandering Jew." In the course of their long history, Jews have wandered from place to place because of deportations, expulsions, religious persecutions, economic and political limitation, and because of the never forgotten vow to return to Zion. Too numerous to mention, only the major Jewish migrations are listed here: 1) During the 7th and the 6th centuries b.c.e., Jews were deported, first from Israel to Assyria and then from Judah to Babylonia, after the destruction of the kingdoms of Israel and Judah respectively; 2) In 538 b.c.e., the Judean refugees began to return to Judea by the permissive decree of the benevolent King Cyrus of Persia, who had conquered Babylonia; 3) In the 3rd century b.c.e., Jews migrated voluntarily from Palestine to Egypt during the reign of the liberal Ptolemies; 4) During the period of the Roman persecutions in Palestine in the 1st and 2nd centuries c.e., Jews again migrated to Babylonia; 5) In the 7th and 8th centuries c.e., during the conquests of the Moslems, Jews migrated from Babylonia to Egypt, North Africa and Spain; 6) In the 14th century c.e., a Jewish migration, because of German anti-Semitism and Polish friendliness, proceeded to Poland from previously established Jewish settlements in Germany; 7) In the 15th century many Jews migrated from Spain to the Turkish Empire; 8) In the 16th century Jews migrated from Spain to Holland; 9) As a result of the Russian pogroms in 1881, thousands of Jews migrated to England and hundreds of thousands to the United States; 10) After the first and second World Wars Jews migrated to the Americas and especially to the State of Israel, established in 1948. Israel has also become the haven for thousands of uprooted and persecuted Jews of the Arab countries; 11) Under the Nazi regime, as many Jews as could save themselves did so.

Survivors of the Nazi holocaust aboard the "Exodus." The British Navy intercepted the ship as it attempted to land the immigrants "illegally" in Palestine and deported them all to Hamburg, Germany.

MIKVEH

Hebrew term meaning "gathering of water," applied to the public ritual bath that has for centuries been maintained by every Jewish community. The use of a *Mikveh* is a requirement of traditional law for the purpose of purification and clean-liness of the body. The Mikveh, about two cubic yards in size, had to be filled with no other than running water. Pious Jewish men immerse their bodies in the Mikveh every Friday and on the day preceding each festival as physical and spiritual purification in preparation for the

321

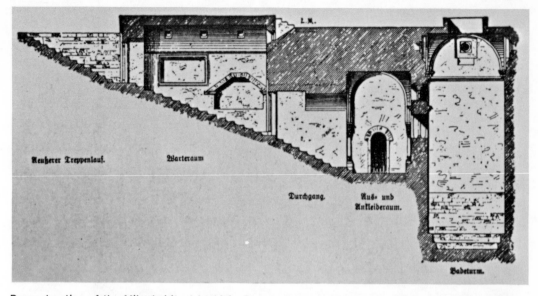

Reconstruction of the Mikveh (ritual bath) in Speyer, Germany. The bathing area is on the right hand, then dressing room, passageway, waiting room, and outer stairway. The bath was heated with hot stones.

Sabbath or the festival. Especially important, according to tradition, is the Mikveh for Jewish women, required by Jewish law after each menstrual period. On the modern scene, as with the men, it is observed only by the more pious women. This ritual obligation is one example of the practices of bodily cleanliness which, in former times, distinguished the Jews from other groups in matters of personal hygiene.

MIKVEH ISRAEL

A Jewish colony in Israel near Jaffa where the *Alliance Israélite* established the first agricultural school in 1870. One of the founders of this pioneer institution was Charles Netter, who is buried there.

MILAH see Circumcision.

MINHAG

Hebrew term applied to any well-established Jewish custom, either local or universal. Despite the fact that the Talmudic Law (Halakhah) is fundamental in Jewish life, certain persistent customs practiced in various Jewish communities have been accepted by the rabbis as part of the Jewish unwritten laws, some of which were incorporated in the *Shulhan Arukh*. The *Ashkenazi* and the *Sephardi* Jewish communities frequently have different customs (Minhagim).

MINHAH

Hebrew term for the Jewish daily afternoon service. In Biblical times the term *Minhah* was applied to the "meal-offering," but it acquired its present meaning in the days of the *Mishnah*. The *Minhah* prayer is recited before sunset.

MINORITY RIGHTS

Before the end of the 18th century, during the period of absolute monarchy, Jews living in a given country were subjects of the king and dependent on the will of the monarch. However, during the period following the American Revolution (1776) and the French Revolution (1789), which ushered in the era of nationalism and democracy, minority groups began to think of freedom and equality. These expectations were in great measure fulfilled when, during the 19th century, many minority groups gained their political autonomy and some new independent states were established. During this period the idea of political Zionism was born, and some leaders of the Jewish people in Europe, headed by Theodor Herzl, sought to secure from the powers a legally guaranteed national home in Palestine. The objectives of the Zionists, and other similar territorial plans for the Jewish masses of Europe, seemed far-fetched or impractical to other Jewish leaders. They saw the need for an immediate working solution to the problem of the Jewish minority groups in Europe. Thus the idea of a "Jewish Autonomy" was born. The historian Simon Dubnow, and later the socialist and revolutionary Chaim Zhitlowsky and others formulated the principle of Jewish autonomous rights to be demanded for the Jewish minority groups in those countries where they were denied civil and political equality. Under this program, Jewish minorities were to be granted by the different European governments the right to control their own educational system and their own philanthropic and communal organization, as well as the right to proportionate representation in the parliaments.

Following World War I, Jewish organizations in European countries and in the United States jointly submitted to the Versailles Peace Conference (1919) demands in behalf of Jewish minority groups, according to which they were to be guaranteed civil and political rights as well as religious and linguistic autonomy under the protection of the League of Nations. They were successful, at least in theory, and for most countries where Jews had previously been denied civil and political rights, provision was made in their peace treaties for such minority rights.

These guarantees regarding minority rights were short-lived. They failed because the League of Nations was too weak to enforce them. The rise of Nazism in 1933, and World War II "solved" the Jewish problem in the most tragic manner, the almost complete annihilation and disruption of the Jewish communities in eastern Europe. So drastically was the Jewish population of the area reduced that much of the problem of Jewish minority rights disappeared with it.

MINOR PROPHETS

The twelve small books of prophecies contained in the Bible, which are also known as *Tere Asar* (the Twelve). The books are: *Hosea, Joel, Amos, Obadiah, Jonah, Micah, Nahum, Habakkuk, Zephaniah, Haggai, Zechariah* and *Malachi*. These are called "Minor Prophets" not because they are less important, but because they are smaller in size by comparison with the larger prophetic books.

MINYAN

Hebrew term meaning "number" applied to the minimum number of ten Jewish males above the age of 13 required for public services. According to Jewish law a *Minyan* is required for community prayer, for the recital of the *Kaddish* (mourner's prayer), and for reading the Torah.

MIRIAM

Sister of Moses and Aaron. The Bible recounts how she watched over the infant Moses when he was left in a basket on the Nile river, and was found and adopted by the daughter of Pharaoh. Miriam, regarded by tradition as a prophetess, led the women in song when the Israelites crossed the Red Sea. Miriam protested Moses' marriage to a Cushite woman and to his sole leadership of Israel, and as a result was stricken with leprosy. But Moses prayed to God for her and she was able to recover.

MI SHEBERAKH

The two opening words of the Hebrew prayer offered in behalf of the person who is "called" up during the reading of the Torah in the synagogue. The prayer asks of God, who bestowed His blessings upon Abraham, Isaac, and Jacob, also to bless the given individual for the reason that he had performed a *Mitzvah*, such as coming up to the Torah or contributing an amount of money for a charitable cause.

MISHKAN see Tabernacle.

MISHLE see Proverbs.

MISHLOAH MANOT see Purim.

MISHNAH

Hebrew term meaning "learning" or "repetition," applied to the oldest post-Biblical collection of Jewish laws redacted by Judah Ha-Nasi. The *Mishnah* includes the vast mass of oral interpretations and applications of the Biblical law and the decisions based thereon, which had accumulated from the days of Ezra (about 450 b.c.e.) until the time of their final compilation, about 200 c.e. The Mishnah is not the produce of one author, but rather the work of many teachers. The compilation of the Mishnah had become necessary because of the great number of laws which it would be difficult to remember unless they were organized into some logical classification. But for a long time the Mishnah was kept literally as the Oral Law, and was not written down.

The Mishnah is both code and reporter, laying down decisions and also giving contrary legal opinions of other teachers. Written in the rich idiom of later Hebrew (which is now called Mishnaic Hebrew), it deals with many matters, including much that was not mentioned in Biblical law. It is organized into six main sections called *Sedarim* (Orders): 1) *Zeraim* (Seeds), dealing with the laws pertaining to agriculture, taxation, and charity; 2) *Moed* (Festivals), dealing with the laws of the Sabbath and the holidays; 3) *Nashim* (Women), laws pertaining to marriage, divorce and problems of family life; 4) *Nezikin* (Damages), dealing with civil and criminal law, and court procedure; 5) *Kodashim* (Holy Matters), dealing with laws concerning sacrifices and the services at the Temple; 6) *Tohorot* (Purities), containing laws of purity and impurity.

The structure of the Mishnah is highly systematic. The basic unit is the *Masekhta* (or *Masekhet*, tractate, tome, volume) which deals in the main with one subject of the law; e.g., *Masekhet Shabbat* presents the laws of the Sabbath. Each Masekhta has several chapters (*Perakim*; sing. *Perek*), and each chapter is divided into paragraphs (Mishnayot; sing. *Mishnah*). The word Mishnah is thus used in two senses, both for the smallest unit—the paragraph—and for the entire Code. The *Masekhtot* dealing in the main with one large area of the law are grouped together as one *Seder* (Order; plur. *Sedarim*). There are in the whole Code of the Mishnah, as has already been said, six Orders or Sedarim. It should be noted that the first Masekhta of the Mishnah deals with the laws of prayer and the liturgy. The last tractate of the fourth Seder is *Avot* (Ethics of the Fathers, or ethical sayings of the fathers or teachers of the Mishnah. This book is also called *Pirke Avot*, Chapters of the Fathers). The fifth Seder, though it deals with sacrifices, includes a volume on the dietary laws to be observed by laymen as well. The last, or sixth, Seder includes a Masekhta on the laws dealing with the purity of family life.

Once the Mishnah was published, it in turn became the basis for further study and discussion in the academies. After many centuries such discussions were compiled, to form the *Gemara*. The Mishnah and the Gemara together are called the *Talmud*. The Talmud is frequently called

Rabbi Meir Bar-Ilan (formerly Berlin) was the leader of Mizrachi, the Zionist religious group.

"Shas," an abbreviation of the two words *Shishah Sedarim* (The Six Orders). The teachers quoted in the Mishnah are called *Tannaim* (sing. *Tanna*), and those quoted in the Gemara are called *Amoraim* (sing. *Amora*). The title of a Tanna as well as a Palestinian Amora is Rabbi; e.g., Rabbi Judah, Rabbi Johanan. The title of a Babylonian Amora is Rav; e.g., Rav Ashi, Rav Ḥisda.

MISHNEH TORAH see Maimonides, Moses.

MITNAGDIM see Ḥasidism.

MITZVAH (MITZVOT)

Hebrew term for a religious and moral obligation. In tradition all commandments, statutes, ordinances, observances, teachings and testimonies are considered *Mitzvot*. The Talmud speaks of 613 (Taryag) Mitzvot of the Torah, 248 positive commands and 365 negative.

MIZRACHI

A Zionist organization of religious Jews which has as its objective the building and the development of the Jewish homeland on the basis of traditional Judaism. Its motto is: "The Land of Israel for the People of Israel, in accordance with the Torah of Israel." The Mizrachi organization was founded in 1902, five years after the first Zionist Congress. As a section of the World Zionist Organization, the Mizrachi takes part in all Zionist political, economic, and colonization activities, and has been especially active in promoting traditional Judaism and religious-educational activities in Palestine, now Israel. Foremost among the leaders of the Mizrachi movement were the late Rabbi Meir Berlin (Bar-Ilan) and Rabbi J. L. Fishman (Rabbi Maimon).

The Mizrachi Organization of America, established in 1911, has become the backbone of the World Mizrachi Organization with its headquarters in Jerusalem. In 1957 it merged with *Hapoel Hamizrachi*, the orthodox labor pioneer movement, to form "Religious Zionists of America, Mizrachi–Hapoel Hamizrachi." The organization sponsors two youth movements, called *Bnei Akiva* and *Mizrachi Hatzair*. Also affiliated are the *Mizrachi Women's Organization of America*, and the *Women's Organization of Hapoel Hamizrachi*.

MOAB

An ancient country located south of what is now Jordan. According to the Bible the *Moabites* were the descendants of Lot, a nephew of Abraham. They had many wars with their neighbors, but disappeared as a nation after the rise of the Babylonian empire. The Biblical injunction against intermarriage between Israelites and Moabites was modified by the rabbis on the theory that the nations were all intermingled by the Assyrians when they built their empire and conquered Israel, and that there were no longer any pure races. This kind of universalistic note is frequently found in the rabbinic literature.

To explain how Ruth the Moabitess (who in the Biblical account lived long before the said event of the intermingling of peoples) was permitted to be married to the Jew Boaz and become the great grandmother of King David, the rabbis maintained that the Biblical injunction applied only to the Moabitish man but not the Moabitish woman ("Moabite" says Scripture, but not "Moabitess").

MOABITE STONE see Archeology.

MOETZET HA-POALOT

Hebrew name for the *Working Women's Council* of the General Federation of Labor in Israel (*Histadrut*). The council protects the interests of women in the political, economic and social life of Israel. It maintains an extensive program of practical social welfare work aimed at improving conditions of women and children. It takes care of over 20,000 children in nursery schools, institutions and camps. It also maintains agricultural schools for boys and girls. The Pioneer Women's Organization of America conducts fundraising campaigns for the *Moetzet Ha-Poalot* in Israel.

MOHAMMEDANISM see Islam.

MOHEL see Circumcision.

MOHILEVER, SAMUEL (1824-1898)

Leading rabbi and founder of the *Hovevei Zion* (Lovers of Zion) movement in Russia. As rabbi in Bialystok, he became known for his Zionist activities and as a staunch advocate of Jewish colonization in Palestine. He urged Jewish emigrants, who fled Russia during the pogroms in 1881, to settle in Palestine. He founded the *Hovevei Zion* organization in 1882, and persuaded Baron Edmond de Rothschild of Paris to start a colonization project in Palestine. The first Jewish colonies in Palestine were thereupon established. Despite opposition from many or-

thodox rabbis, Mohilever worked without let-up for the Zionist cause, and later became one of the most devoted supporters of Theodor Herzl.

MOLKO (MOLCHO), SOLOMON (1500-1532)

Marrano, messianic visionary. Born in Portugal to Marrano parents, his Christian name was Diego Pires, and he held the position of royal secretary. Influenced by David Reubeni, who appeared in Portugal on a "messianic" mission to drive the Turks out of Palestine with the help of Christian powers in Europe, Molko was circumcized and became a professing Jew. He fled Portugal, became a student of Kabbalah, and joined the famous group of Kabbalists at Safed, Palestine. In 1529 he returned to Europe where he predicted the coming of the Messiah in 1540. In Italy he joined Reubeni and continued to preach openly the imminent arrival of the Messiah. Denounced as heretic to the tribunal of the Inquisition, he was sentenced to die at the stake. Molko and Reubeni fled to Germany, where they sought an audience with Emperor Charles V, whom they intended to win for their messianic mission of conquering Palestine. The Emperor, however, turned them over to the Inquisition in Italy, where Molko was made a martyr and died.

MONOTHEISM

The belief in one God, and basic characteristic of the Jewish religion. Abraham was, according to Jewish tradition, the father of Jewish monotheism. The belief in the existence of one God, in the course of early Jewish history, underwent a process of gradual development. Many of the early Hebrews, although perhaps accepting monotheism in principle, did not deny the existence of other gods. According to the Talmud, the First Temple was destroyed because of the practice of idol-

Portrait of Sir Moses Montefiore at the age of 100, painted by Madure Peixotto. Philanthropist, financier and civic leader, Montefiore's major contribution was in improving Jewish political and economic rights.

atry. It was not before their experience in the Babylonian exile that the masses of the people came to realize the truth of the continued prophetic teaching and warning to give up the worship of false gods as well as the wrong methods of worshipping the true God. The phrase "ethical monotheism" connotes several formulations: it is a belief of one God as against more than one God; it also affirms that the worship of God, without leading the ethical life, is false worship. God Himself is the highest ethical personality, and demands of man to imitate Him in this regard as much as finite man can. The doctrine of *ethical monotheism* describes God as uniquely One, as Creator, Holy, both transcendent and immanent, ever-living, omnipresent, omniscient and omnipotent. In His relation to man He is responsive to prayer; He is righteous and just, truthful and merciful. He is King of the universe and Redeemer of mankind; He is both Father and Friend of man who, as the child of the living God, contains within himself a spark of the Divine Creator, and is the bearer of moral and spiritual aspirations and purposes. See *God*.

MONTEFIORE, MOSES (1784–1885)

British communal leader and philanthropist. Born in Italy, he was brought as an

A pewter Purim plate to be used for "Shalah Mones," the holiday exchange of gifts, shows Haman hanging and Mordecai on horseback in triumph. The plate comes from Germany and is dated from 1768.

infant to England, where he lived the rest of his life, and became a famous financier. Out of his interest in civic affairs and his popularity, Montefiore was elected sheriff of London, was knighted by Queen Victoria, and received other civic honors.

Montefiore is best known for his lifelong outstanding Jewish leadership and philanthropic work. By virtue of his position and the esteem in which he was held, he succeeded in bettering the political and economic status of the oppressed Jewish masses abroad. He personally intervened in the famous *Damascus Affair* (1840), securing the release of Jews falsely accused of having committed ritual murder. He visited Russia, Rumania, and Morocco, obtaining assurances from the respective governments that anti-Jewish discrimination and practices would be terminated. Montefiore was especially interested in the welfare of the Jewish community in Palestine, and encouraged its colonization projects. He visited Palestine seven times, where he founded and helped maintain a number of educational and welfare institutions. To this day there are in Jerusalem a number of institutions bearing his name, and one of the older quarters of Tel Aviv is named after him.

328

Montefiore was a strictly orthodox Jew, and although of Sephardic descent himself, he sought to break down the traditional barriers between the Sephardi and the Ashkenazi Jewish communities. He was a most esteemed and popular Jewish personality of his age, and the portrait of "Sir Moses Montefiore" adorned many Jewish homes.

MORDECAI

One of the principal heroes of the *Book of Esther*. A cousin of Esther, the Jewish queen of Persia, Mordecai became prominent in the court of King Ahasuerus whose life he had saved by discovering a plot against the throne. Haman, the prime minister, became Mordecai's bitter enemy, and conceived of a plan to kill the Jews of Persia. Upon Mordecai's urgent demands, Esther intervened, and Ahasuerus permitted the Jews to defend themselves. See *Esther; Purim*.

MOREH NEVUKHIM see Maimonides, Moses.

MORGENTHAU, HENRY, JR.

Gentleman farmer, financier, and Secretary of the Treasury of the United States. Born in New York in 1891, he studied farming conditions in the United States, and became a successful farmer. His agricultural knowledge and his interest in social welfare brought him to the fore of public life. He served in a variety of important capacities in the government of the United States, reaching the high office of Secretary of the Treasury under the Roosevelt Administration. Because of his financial expertness, administrative ability, and interest in social and cultural affairs, his name became connected with scores of institutions, organizations, and agencies. He maintained a keen interest in Jewish affairs, and served in behalf of a great many Jewish philanthropic and Zionist campaigns.

MORIAH

Biblical name of the mountain on which the Holy Temple was built. It was also the scene of the binding of Isaac (Akedat Yitzḥak) by Abraham.

MORNING SERVICE see Shaḥarit.

MOROCCO

In 1960 there were about 200,000 Jews living in the French and Spanish protectorates of Morocco, including those living in the international zone of Tangiers. The Jewish community in Morocco dates back to the beginning of the first century c.e. During the first period of the Moslem conquest of Morocco which began in the 8th century, Jewish communities enjoyed a measure of freedom, but a period of persecution, expulsion and forced conversions to Islam began following the conquest by the Almohades in 1146. Jewish settlements in Morocco increased in number after the expulsion of Jews from

Henry Morgenthau, Jr., U.S. Secretary of Treasury, and also a financier and philanthropist.

Spain in 1492. Because of continuous suffering, the Jews of Morocco nursed lively messianic hopes, and during the days of Shabbetai Tzevi, they became among his most ardent followers. The ghetto-like conditions of the orientalized Jews of Morocco improved somewhat during the 18th and the 19th centuries when the Alliance Israélite Universelle and other Jewish organizations brought them economic aid and political protection.

With the granting of independence to French Morocco in 1956, the future of these ancient Jewish communities was called into serious question.

MOSER see Masor.

MOSES

Greatest Biblical figure and, according to many, the greatest historical figure of all time, commonly known as *Mosheh Rabbenu* (Moses our Teacher), Servant of God, Lawgiver, Liberator, and molder of the people of Israel. He was born to Amram and Jochebed, Levites, during the period when, according to Pharaoh's edict, all newly born Hebrew male children had to be slain. Left adrift on the waters of the Nile, he soon was found by Pharaoh's daughter, and was henceforth reared and educated in the king's court. As a grown man he defended the Hebrew slaves. He once killed an Egyptian task-master for striking a Hebrew slave, an act which forced him to flee to Midian. There he lived as a shepherd, and married Zipporah, the daughter of the Midianite priest Jethro.

The Bible tells us that while Moses was tending his flock in the desert, God spoke to him from a "burning bush," commis-

An elderly Jewish man in Casablanca, capital of French Morocco, works as a scribe, writing the letters of those who cannot write. Poorly paid, his work brings him only enough money for a subsistence level Moroccan standard of living.

sioning him to free the Hebrews from the bondage of Egypt. Joined by his elder brother Aaron, Moses appeared before Pharaoh demanding the release of his people. According to the Bible, Pharaoh broke his repeated promises to free the Israelites, and God thereupon sent "ten plagues" on Egypt. The people were finally freed and Moses took them out of Egypt, miraculously crossing the Red Sea. At Mount Sinai, God revealed Himself to Moses and the people, and amidst thunder and lightning, the Israelites received the Ten Commandments.

Moses spent forty days and nights on Mount Sinai receiving the Torah. Toward the end of that time the Israelites persuaded Aaron to make a golden calf, which they worshipped. Descending Mount Sinai, Moses found the Israelites dancing around the golden calf. In disappointment he broke the Tablets. The Lord wanted to destroy the people, but on the plea of Moses in their behalf, God forgave them. Moses once more spent forty days on Mount Sinai to prepare new Tablets of the Law.

The biography of Moses is inextricably bound up with the early history of the Israelites, and is found in the last four books of the Pentateuch (Torah). Before his death on Mount Nebo, overlooking the Promised Land, he charged his assistant Joshua with the task of leading the people across the river Jordan. Probably to avoid his deification, the Torah tells us his burial place was unknown.

Midrashic and Haggadic sources abound in stories related to the historical figure of Moses, revered as the profound believer, the faithful leader, the great lawgiver; founder of the Tabernacle and its divine service, and of the Levitic priesthood, as the greatest of the prophets, laying down the principles of love and justice as the proper basis of human society.

331

A ballet performance in the open air theater of Hebrew University on Mount Scopus before the establishment of the State of Israel in 1948. The area was then cut off by Arabs and made inaccessible.

In the history of the Jewish people the figure of Moses looms large for his divine inspiration, high ethics and deep concern for his fellow men. Though the Torah emphasizes that Moses was a man like other men, and by no means perfect, it also stresses that he was nevertheless greater than all other men. He laid the foundation for a community which he conceived as a "holy nation" based on monotheistic religion and principles of justice. His legislation, called *Torat Mosheh* (the Law of Moses), became the basis of Jewish religious life and all subsequent legislation; the Oral Law is known as *Halakhah le-Mosheh mi-Sinai* (Law given to Moses at Sinai). The influence of his work has spread to all humanity.

The essential human characteristics of Moses are devotion to and love of his people, extreme patience and forgiveness, and above all humility. In the words of the Bible (Numbers 12:3) "The man Moses was very meek, above all the men that were upon the face of the earth."

MOSES BEN MAIMON see Maimonides, Moses.

MOSES BEN NAḤMAN see Naḥmanides.

MOSES DE LEON see Zohar.

MOSES IBN EZRA see Ibn Ezra, Moses ben Jacob.

MOSHAVAH (MOSHAV)

The first farmers' villages in modern Palestine, which allowed the use of hired labor. Many of these villages, such as Rishon Le-Zion and Petah Tikvah, have expanded into large towns.

MOSHAV OVEDIM

An Israeli "smallholders' settlement" on Jewish National Fund land. While each farmer cultivates his own fields, the use of equipment as well as the marketing of his product is on a cooperative basis. As in

MUSAR MOVEMENT

other settlements affiliated with the *Histadrut*, exploitation of labor is forbidden. There is much emphasis on mutual aid. The first major *Moshav Ovedim* was Nahalal, established in 1921. After Israel became an independent state, the Moshav Ovedim proved to be an attractive type of settlement for many immigrants. There were in 1960 over 300 Moshavim, with a total population of over 100,000.

MOSHAV SHITTUFI

This settlement form combines the collective enterprise of the *Kibbutz* with the individual family life of the *Moshav*. Children are raised by their own parents and enjoy most of the privileges of normal home living.

MOSHAV ZEKENIM

Hebrew term for an old-age home.

MOSHEH RABBENU

Moses our Master or Teacher. See *Moses*.

MOUNT GERIZIM see Gerizim, Mount.

MOUNT SCOPUS

Mountain overlooking Jerusalem, upon which the Hebrew University was erected in 1925. The Hadassah Hospital is also there. A part of the Old City of Jerusalem, it is under the rule of Jordan. A new university campus has been erected in the New City.

MOURNER'S PRAYER see Kaddish.

MOURNING see Death.

MUSAF

Hebrew term for the additional service recited after *Shaharit* (morning prayer) on Sabbaths, festivals, and Rosh Hodesh (New Moon).

MUSAR MOVEMENT

The Moralist Movement in Judaism especially developed in the 19th century. The adherents of this movement, known as *Musarnikes*, emphasized the doctrine of ethical study and conduct. They were interested in the analysis of human conduct and in the presentation of moral principles governing the relation of man to man. The literature of the *Musar Movement* is written mainly for the masses, and deals with such subjects as family-life, education, relations between Jews and non-Jews, the care and treatment of animals and questions of hygiene.

N

NER TAMID

Let us now praise famous men,

Our fathers in their generations. . . .

But these were men of mercy,

Whose righteous deeds have not been forgotten. . . .

Their seed shall remain for ever,

And their glory shall not be blotted out. . . .

Peoples will declare their wisdom,

And the congregation telleth out their praise.

ECCLESIASTICUS

NABLUS

City in Palestine, situated between Mounts Ebal and Gerizim, near the site of the Biblical city of Shechem. Nablus was erected by the Roman emperor Vespasian in 72 c.e., and he called it Flavia Neapolis, the Flavian New City, Flavian being one of his names. The name Neapolis became Nablus. The population is predominantly Arab. There still exists in Nablus a small community of Samaritans, for whom Mount Gerizim has sacred memories of the time when they erected their holy temple there. See *Gerizim, Mount.*

NADAN see Nedan.

NAGDELA (or NAGRELA), SAMUEL HA-LEVI IBN see Samuel Ha-Nagid.

NAHMANIDES (1195–1270)

Also known as *RaMBaN*, initials of Rabbi Moses ben Naḥman, Talmudic authority, commentator on the Bible and mystic philosopher. Born in Gerona, Spain (hence his surname Girondi) he practiced medicine, and became the authoritative Talmudist of his time. He is best remembered for his famous dispute in defense of the Jewish religion. In 1263 he was compelled by King James I of Aragon to take part in a public religious disputation with Pablo Christiani, a renegade Jew. Naḥmanides defended Judaism and refuted the messianic ideas of Christianity so brilliantly that he was rewarded by the king. The Dominicans, however, would not concede defeat, and accused Naḥmanides of

Samaritans pitch their tents on Mt. Gerizim, near Nablus, to celebrate Passover. This spot is sacred to the Samaritans who consider it the Mt. Moriah where the sacrifice of Isaac was to have taken place.

blasphemy; he was thereupon banished from Spain. Naḥmanides set out for Palestine in 1267, where he wrote his commentaries on the Bible, and helped revive the Jewish community in Jerusalem.

NAḤMAN OF BRATZLAV (1771–1811)

Ḥasidic rabbi and founder of a Ḥasidic sect. A great grandson of the *Baal Shem Tov*, father of the Ḥasidic movement, he was born in the Ukraine, and was especially active in Bratzlav; hence his popular name "the Bratzlaver." Rabbi Naḥman did not found a dynasty, but remained, even after his death, the "Rebbe" and teacher of his many followers. His teachings, based on the general principles of Ḥasidism laid down by the Baal Shem Tov, especially emphasize the importance of joyful, heartfelt prayer; the belief in the authority of the true *Tzaddik* (the "righteous one"—leader of the Ḥasidim); that one may pray to God in any language at any time and place; and that friendship, brotherly love and moral conduct are basic to good living. Rabbi Naḥman visited the Holy Land (Palestine), which became to him and to his followers a vivid source of inspiration and living. He is remembered as a gifted story teller and as a master of the parable and the allegorical tale. His tales, created in the Yiddish language, became very popular, and are considered classics of Yiddish literature.

NAHUM

One of the *Twelve Minor Prophets*, whose place and time of birth are unknown. In his prophecies, contained in three chapters, he foretells the destruction of Nineveh and the downfall of the Assyrian empire.

NAOMI

Important character in the *Book of Ruth*. According to the Biblical story, Naomi returned from Moab to her native Bethlehem after the death of her husband and two sons. Her devoted daughter-in-law, Ruth the Moabitess, followed her into the land of Israel, and accepted the Jewish faith. Naomi advised Ruth to marry Boaz, and King David was one of their illustrious descendants. The meaning of the name Naomi is "sweetness."

NAPHTALI

One of Jacob's twelve sons, and father of the Israelite tribe of that name. The tribe of Naphtali occupied a strip of land in the northern part of Palestine, and its men were known as courageous warriors. They were cited for bravery in the vigorous chant of the *Song of Deborah*.

NASI, DON JOSEPH (1510–1579)

Prominent Jewish statesman of the 16th century, known also as the *Duke of Naxos*. Like other Marranos, he fled his native Portugal together with his aunt, the famous Gracia Mendes. Staying shortly in Antwerp and Venice, he settled in Constantinople, where he lived openly as a Jew. Because of his exceptional abilities, he was a favorite of Sultan Selim, became a most influential statesman, and was made Duke of Naxos. In recognition of his accomplishments, the Sultan gave Joseph a stretch of land near Tiberias, Palestine, and helped him in his attempt to establish settlements there for persecuted European Jews. After the death of Selim, Joseph Nasi's influence underwent decline. Joseph Nasi and Gracia Mendes used their influence and their wealth to help the refugee Marranos of Italy and Turkey.

NATHAN

Prophet and influential personality in the courts of King David and King Solomon. According to the Biblical account, Nathan objected to David's plan of building

337

the Holy Temple, advising him that this should be the work of his successor. He harshly reproved David for marrying Bath-sheba, but he subsequently supported her son, Solomon, in his claim to become heir to the throne.

NATIONAL CONFERENCE OF CHRISTIANS AND JEWS

Organization of Protestants, Catholics and Jews, founded in 1928 for the purpose of promoting interfaith understanding and cooperation and to combat prejudice, misinformation and hatred arising among religious groups in the United States. The educational program of the Conference consists of: 1) "Round-table" discussions by representatives of the three major faiths which bring the message of interfaith understanding and cooperation to schools, churches, clubs, labor unions and business and youth groups; 2) A human relations institute or seminar held periodically by religious and lay leaders for an interchange of knowledge of, and judgments on problems related to work of the National Conference; 3) The observance of Brotherhood Week, held each year during the week of Washington's Birthday; 4) The operation of a religious news service serving secular newspapers, religious journals of the three major faiths and radio and television stations throughout the country; 5) The publication of books, pamphlets and other literature which are distributed to study groups and individuals; 6) The issuance of special pronouncements signed by leaders of the three major faiths.

NATIONAL COUNCIL FOR JEWISH EDUCATION

An association of superintendents, executive directors, supervisors and principals of Jewish schools, as well as other professional leaders in the field of Jewish education. The Council was founded in 1926 for the purpose of serving as "a meet-

ing ground for the exchange of experiences and for establishing a basis for cooperation among Jewish educators in America, and to stimulate the study of Jewish education and the development of professional standards in the field of Jewish education." The Council holds annual national conferences and sponsors regional conferences of Jewish educators. It founded the national organization called *American Association for Jewish Education*, and it publishes *Jewish Education*, a magazine issued three times a year, and *Sheviley Hahinuch* (The Paths of Education), a Hebrew language quarterly.

NATIONAL COUNCIL OF JEWISH WOMEN

Founded in 1893 by Hannah G. Solomon of Chicago, in 1960 had 240 Sections with a total membership of 110,000. The Council carries out community service programs to meet welfare and educational needs; public affairs programs to stimulate informed, active citizenship; and provides services to Jewish communities abroad. The Council has an official observer at the United Nations and a Washington representative. To assist in the upbuilding of Jewish communities abroad, the Council provides scholarships for graduate study in the United States for educational and welfare specialists who return to strengthen these fields in their own countries. It also conducts a volunteer fellowship program. The Council helps support the Hebrew University's John Dewey School of Education in Jerusalem and is now building a new campus for the Hebrew University High School. In the Ship-A-Box program, local Sections send work and play materials to Jewish children's institutions abroad, mainly in Israel.

NATIONAL FEDERATION OF TEMPLE BROTHERHOODS

Affiliate of the Union of American He-

338

brew Congregations; founded in 1923. The Federation had in 1960 a membership of 60,000, affiliated with 400 brotherhoods. The purpose of the Federation is to stimulate religious and educational activities of reform congregations by helping them sponsor forums, round-tables, lecture courses, study groups, musical programs, and similar activities dealing primarily with problems pertaining to Judaism and Jewish culture. The Federation sponsors the Jewish Chautauqua Society, dedicated to the spreading of Jewish education and knowledge in America, especially on college campuses.

NATIONAL FEDERATION OF TEMPLE SISTERHOODS

Affiliate of the Union of American Hebrew Congregations, founded in 1913. It had in 1960 a membership of 106,000 with 563 units throughout the United States. The Federation aims to establish closer cooperation between the sisterhoods of reform temples and to stimulate religious and educational activities. Some of the Federation's important projects are: The Hebrew Union College scholarship and religious education fund; the annual Jewish art calendar; and a Jewish Braille library for the blind.

NATIONAL JEWISH WELFARE BOARD

Often called the JWB. It was founded in April 1917 at the request of Newton D. Baker and Josephus Daniels, the then Secretaries of War and Navy, respectively, to meet the religious and welfare needs of Jews in the American armed forces. In 1921 JWB also became the national association of Jewish community centers and YM-YWHAs when it merged with the National Council of Young Men's Hebrew and Kindred Associations. This Council had been created in 1913 as the first permanent organization of centers

Jacob Frankel, first U.S. Army Jewish chaplain, was appointed by President Abraham Lincoln. His commission, issued in March 1864, appears below. The National Jewish Welfare Board now ministers to Jewish men in the armed forces.

and Ys. The JWB makes available to centers in all parts of the United States and Canada year-round field service, technical help and skilled guidance. As part of its cultural program, it sponsors the Jew-

339

ish Book Council and the Jewish Music Council as well.

At the beginning of 1960 there were 150,000 Jews and their dependents in the U. S. Armed Forces and in Veterans Administration hospitals. Through the Commission on Jewish Chaplaincy, representing the orthodox, conservative and reform rabbinates, JWB recruits, ecclesiastically endorses and serves all Jewish military chaplains. At the beginning of 1960 there were 336 full and part-time Jewish chaplains serving 987 overseas areas.

The Armed Services Division as of 1960 was divided into 271 local committees, having a professional staff of 26 and a total membership of about 10,000 volunteers. This division directs religious, cultural, and recreational programs for the Jewish chaplains and soldiers as well as supplying them with religious equipment, literature, and *Kosher* food. More than 1,000,000 gifts were distributed in 1959.

As the Jewish agency in the USO, JWB is responsible for 25 clubs and operations at home and abroad. It also conducts servicemen's programs in Japan, England, France, Alaska, Panama Canal Zone and France. See *Center, the Jewish.*

NATIONAL REFUGEE SERVICE

An organization founded in 1939 for the purpose of aiding Jewish refugees arriving in the United States. From 1933, when the Nazi regime began in Germany, until 1942, over 200,000 Jewish refugees entered the United States. The program of the Refugee Service included the following: aid on arrival of refugees, financial assistance, employment service, retraining for employment, capital loan service, professional assistance, resettlement, migration service, and Americanization assistance. The National Refugee Service maintained throughout the United States local refugee service committees which generally

were beneficiaries of the local welfare fund drives. In 1946, the National Refugee Service combined with the United Service for New Americans, which later (1954) merged with HIAS and became United Hias Service. See *United Hias Service.*

NAZARETH

A picturesque city in lower Galilee, Israel, believed to have been the place where Jesus spent his youth. The city is not mentioned in the Bible or the Talmud. Until the 7th century it was a Jewish town, but currently is inhabited chiefly by Christian Arabs, enjoying civil and religious freedom as citizens of the State of Israel.

NAZIR see Nazirite.

NAZIRITE

The English form of the Hebrew Biblical term *Nazir*, applied to a person who consecrated himself by means of a special vow not to drink wine or liquor, not to cut his hair, and not to touch a dead body. This vow was a form of self-dedication to lead a sacred and priestly life. Samson is described in the *Book of Judges* as a *Nazir* (Nazirite) from birth, by angelic direction. Judaism does not favor asceticism as a universal practice.

NAZISM

Adolph Hitler's political and sociological system as adopted by the National Socialist German Workers Party. This system is based on the theory of the supremacy of the "Aryan" race, the so-called "Herrenvolk" (master race) whose function in life was to rule the so-called "inferior races." With Hitler's rise to power in Germany (1933) the Nazi Party initiated a program of violent anti-Semitism, which finally led to the annihilation of about six million Jews in Nazi-occupied Europe.

The violent expansion of German military power into eastern Europe in 1939

The Nazis:

    truck Jews to death camps

    degrade the religious

    murder in the woods

The Warsaw Ghetto—The Nazis crush the rising.

The Warsaw Ghetto—The survivors are marched off.

342

The Warsaw Ghetto—The dead and wounded lie broken.

The Warsaw Ghetto—The Ghetto is burned to the ground.

Legendary dragon with a serpent's head, lion's body, and eagle's hind legs, in glazed brick, is set into the Ishtar Gate in Babylon, and is dated from the reign of King Nebuchadnezzar II, 6th century b.c.e.

not only opened World War II, but brought Nazi "schrecklichkeit" to some of the oldest and most fruitful Jewish communities in all of Europe.

NEBUCHADNEZZAR (NEBUCHADREZZAR)

King of the Babylonians (604 to 562 b.c.e.), mentioned in Jewish history as the ruler whose armies conquered Jerusalem, destroyed the Temple and carried the Judeans into the historic Babylonian captivity (586 b.c.e.).

NEDAN

Popular term, also pronounced *Nadan*, applied to the dowry offered by the parents of the bride to her prospective husband. In earlier times, the *Nedan* (Biblical *Mohar*) was the gift presented by the bridegroom to the father of the bride.

NEDER see Vows.

NEGEV

A stretch of arid and mostly uncultivated land in the southern part of Israel, extending to the Gulf of Aqaba. The *Negev*, which was in Biblical times an inhabited and even productive area, but which had been barren for centuries, is now a vital part of the territory of the State of Israel, where important colonization projects have been initiated. To aid its development, a pipeline, fed by underground springs and waters from the Yarkon river, runs through a large part of the Negev, where many new settlements are flourishing. The development of the port of Eilat at the Gulf of Aqaba has both military and economic importance for the communications of the Jewish State.

NEHEMIAH

Governor of Judea and rebuilder of the walls of Jerusalem and of the Jewish com-

344

munity during the period following the return of the Judeans from Babylonian captivity. The cupbearer to the Persian king, Artaxerxes I, he was given permission to go to Judea to help the returned exiles and rebuild the walls of Jerusalem. Despite the difficulties created by the foreign inhabitants, Nehemiah succeeded in fortifying the city, and in re-establishing its Jewish community. Aided by the spiritual leader Ezra, he fought against mixed marriages, introduced a taxation system, and stimulated the observance of the Jewish festivals and the reading of the Torah. The *Book of Nehemiah*, following the *Book of Ezra* in the Biblical canon, gives an account of Nehemiah's appointment as governor of Judea, of his activities as the rebuilder of Jerusalem, and of his and Ezra's religious and civil reforms in the reconstituted community in Palestine.

NEILAH

Hebrew term meaning "conclusion" applied to the closing service on the Day of Atonement (Yom Kippur). In the days of the Holy Temple in Jerusalem, the *Neilah* was a daily prayer recited during the closing of the Temple gates. Regarded as the most solemn service in the synagogue, the Yom Kippur Neilah symbolizes the closing of the gates of heaven on the Day of Atonement, when the fate of man is "sealed." The Neilah service is concluded by the blowing of the *Shofar*, which marks the end of the fast.

Negev bedouins astride their camels, with their new modern farm machinery behind them. Until the early 20th century, the Negev was a desert until irrigated and cultivated by Zionist pioneer groups.

345

Late 18th-century silver Ner Tamid (eternal light) originally found in a Moscow synagogue.

Ner Tamid, designed by a contemporary craftsman hangs in The Jewish Museum in New York.

NER TAMID

Hebrew term meaning "eternal light," referring to the lamp of silver or bronze which hangs in every Jewish house of worship in the front of the *Aron ha-Kodesh* (Holy Ark), within which is an ever-burning light. The tradition of the *Ner Tamid* dates back to the days of the Temple, where the *Menorah* was never permitted to go out. The Ner Tamid symbolizes the immanence of God, and reverence for the Torah.

NETHERLANDS see Holland.

NETTER, CHARLES (1826–1882)

Founder of the first Jewish agricultural school in Palestine. Born in France, he took an active interest in Jewish life and

A 1726 etching depicts the blessing of the New Moon in the courtyard of a Fürth synagogue in Germany. Many Jews the world over still observe this ancient custom of blessing the New Moon in the open air.

was one of the organizers of the *Alliance Israélite Universelle*. He fought for the recognition of political rights of Jews in the Balkan countries, and for the protection of the Jews in Morocco, and he organized relief work for Jewish refugees from Russia. He is best remembered for his endeavors to improve the living conditions of the Jewish settlers in Palestine by means of agricultural projects. To this end he founded the agricultural school at Mikveh Israel (near Jaffa) in 1870, which has become a model of successful Jewish colonization projects. Netter died in Mikveh Israel and was buried on the school grounds. See *Mikveh Israel*.

NEW MOON see Rosh Ḥodesh.

NEW MOON, BLESSING OF

The practice of reciting special prayers at night (particularly on a Saturday night), in the first half of the lunar month while the moon is waxing. The blessing of the new moon, recited in the open air, offers praise of God, the Master of the universe, and makes reference to the kingdom of David, which will be restored by the grace of God, just as the full brightness of the moon is restored after a period of eclipse and waning. In early days, the appearance of the new moon was the occasion of the official proclamation of the new month by the *Sanhedrin*.

NEWPORT

A seaport in Rhode Island, famous for its

347

Exterior view of Newport's Touro Synagogue. Built in American mid 18th-century Colonial style, it was carefully restored to keep its original spirit intact, and declared a National Historic Site in 1946.

Jewish historical background. Jews came to Newport in 1658, and formed the second important Jewish settlement in what is now the United States. The development of Newport as an important commercial center was largely accomplished through its early Jewish merchants, especially Jacob Rodriguez Rivera and Aaron Lopez. Newport has two famous Jewish landmarks, namely, one of the oldest Jewish cemeteries in the United States, founded in 1677, and the little synagogue, founded in 1763, and later endowed by the great Jewish philanthropist Judah Touro. The "Touro Synagogue" is maintained as a national shrine by the Government of the United States.

The cemetery at Newport has been enshrined in famous poems by Emma Lazarus and Henry Wadsworth Longfellow.

Longfellow's tribute to the Jews still remains fresh and poignant today:

Pride and humiliation hand in hand
Walked with them through the world
where'er they went;
Trampled and beaten were they as
the sand
And yet unshaken as the continent.

Jewish prosperity in Newport was in great measure the result of Rhode Island's tradition of religious dissent. Founded by Roger Williams, himself a religious dissenter, the state provided a haven for Jews, so that they could build their large and thriving community in Newport.

On the facing page is the Holy Ark section of the famous Touro Synagogue. On the following pages President George Washington's August 21, 1790 letter to the Newport Jewish Congregation. It is an affirmation of religious freedom.

348

To the Hebrew Congregation in Newport
Rhode Island.

Gentlemen.

While I receive, with much satisfaction,
your Address replete with expressions of affection
and esteem; I rejoice in the opportunity of assuring
you, that I shall always retain a grateful remem
brance of the cordial welcome I experienced in
my visit to Newport, from all classes of citizens.

The reflection on the days of difficulty and
danger which are past is rendered the more sweet,
from a consciousness that they are succeeded by days
of uncommon prosperity and security. If we have
wisdom to make the best use of the advantages with
which we are now favored, we cannot fail, under the
just administration of a good Government, to become
a great and a happy people.

The Citizens of the United States of America
have a right to applaud themselves for having given
to mankind examples of an enlarged and liberal
policy: a policy worthy of imitation. All possess
alike liberty of conscience and immunities of
citizenship. It is now no more that toleration is
spoken of, as if it was by the indulgence of one
class of people, that another enjoyed the exercise
of their inherent natural rights. For happily
the

the Government of the United States, which gives to bigotry no sanction, to persecution no assistance, requires only that they who live under its protection, should demean themselves as good citizens, in giving it on all occasions their effectual support.

It would be inconsistent with the frankness of my character not to avow that I am pleased with your favorable opinion of my Administration, and fervent wishes for my felicity. May the children of the Stock of Abraham, who dwell in this land, continue to merit and enjoy the good will of the other Inhabitants; while every one shall sit in safety under his own vine and figtree, and there shall be none to make him afraid. May the father of all mercies scatter light and not darkness in our paths, and make us all in our several vocations useful here, and in his own due time and way everlastingly happy.

G. Washington

1790. August
Reply of Genl Washington
to Address of the Hebrews
of Newport Rhode Island
with Autograph Signature
of G. Washington
Original & Valuable

New York City's Lower East Side in the early 1900s, then the Jewish section. Note the pushcarts selling various commodities, and the store signs painted for the benefit of those who could read only Yiddish.

NEW TESTAMENT

The Gospels, Epistles, Acts of the Apostles, and the Apocalypse, dealing with the life of Jesus, the history of the early church, Christian theology and ethics. The *New Testament* is the second part of the Christian Bible, the first being the *Old Testament*, that is, the Hebrew Bible.

NEW YEAR see Rosh Hashanah.

NEW YEAR OF THE TREES see Tu Bi-Shevat.

NEW YORK CITY

The largest city in the United States, with a total population of about eight million, including over two million Jews, forming the largest Jewish community in the world. The first group of Jewish settlers arrived in New York (then New Amsterdam) in 1654, and the first Jewish cemetery was founded in 1656. The Sephardi congregation "Shearith Israel," estab-

lished in 1693, and its later offshoot, the Ashkenazi congregation "B'nai Jeshurun," established in 1826, were the beginnings of Jewish communal life in New York. These were followed by numerous other congregations, philanthropic and educational institutions. In 1847 there were in New York about 15,000 Jews, predominantly of Sephardi and German origin. This number increased rapidly after 1881, when a large wave of Jewish refugees from Russia and Poland reached the shores of New York City. By 1912 the Jewish population grew to 1,200,000 and was further increased after World War I with new immigrants.

Jewish immigrants contributed greatly to the cultural, commercial and industrial development of New York City, particularly in the garment industry and in the trade-union movement. New York City has become the largest center of Jewish

352

New York City's oldest Jewish cemetery, 1656, is located in busy downtown at Chatham Square. Owned by Cong. Shearith Israel, it numbers among its graves those of Jewish fighters in the American Revolution.

philanthropy, culture and education. The Jewish community maintains numerous welfare institutions, societies, fraternal and cultural organizations; it operates teachers' and rabbinic seminaries serving the needs of the various religious and cultural groups; it maintains a system of Jewish education consisting of Sunday schools, elementary and secondary Hebrew and Yiddish schools, as well as higher institutions of learning, including a medical school; it publishes Jewish dailies, weeklies and periodical literature in English, Hebrew and Yiddish, and it maintains Yiddish theaters. In New York City are the national headquarters of the major Jewish organizations, institutions and agencies. New York Jews have also helped maintain the universities and libraries of the city, both financially and intellectually, and have been important in social service

(e.g., hospitals) and in the political life of the city, state and country.

NEW ZEALAND

A British dominion southeast of Australia, in which there were 4,500 Jews in a total population of about two million in 1960. A few Jews first settled in New Zealand in 1840, larger numbers arrived after the discovery of gold in 1861, and some after the rise of the Nazi regime in Germany in 1933. Despite their small number, the Jews of New Zealand have taken an active and important part in the country's political and cultural life, and a number of them have held high governmental positions.

NIGER, SAMUEL (1883–1955)

Pen name of Samuel Charney, "dean of Yiddish literary critics," literary historian, and journalist. Born in Russia, he began

353

his literary career in connection with early political activities in the Zionist and socialist movements. He became a Yiddish writer in 1902 and subsequently edited political and literary magazines in Vilna. Even before his arrival in the United States (1919), he was recognized as a leader of the *Yiddishists*, publishing important works of literary criticism. His literary work flourished especially in the United States, where he made special studies of great figures in Yiddish literature, such as Mendele Mocher Seforim, Sholem Aleichem and H. Leivick, in addition to his many works of literary criticism and history dealing with almost every Yiddish writer, and with a broad spectrum of the problems of Yiddish literature.

Niger also excelled as a journalist, contributing innumerable articles to Yiddish dailies and periodicals. He was in the forefront of many cultural projects and institutions, such as the Jewish Teachers' Seminary, the Yiddish Scientific Institute, and the Sholem Aleichem Folk Institute.

NINEVEH

Ancient capital city of Assyria mentioned frequently in the Bible, especially in connection with the prophecy of Jonah. Excavations of that city on the left bank of the Tigris have yielded valuable information bearing on the ancient civilization. Nineveh was destroyed in 606 b.c.e.

NINTH OF AV see Tishah Be-Av.

NIRIM see Archeology.

NISAN

The seventh Hebrew month corresponding to March-April, and consisting of 30 days. It is the month during which the Exodus took place, and the festival of Passover begins on its 15th day. In the Torah, this month is called "Abib," and is designated as the first of the months. See *Calendar, Jewish*.

At left is an Akkadian lamassu, which has the head of a man on a bull's body. It and others like it flanked the Assyrian King Sargon II's (721-705 b.c.e.) throne room in Nineveh to protect it from evil spirits and destructive demons.

NOAH

Biblical figure of the tenth generation from Adam, and father of Shem, Ham and Japheth. The only righteous man of his generation, Noah was commanded by God to build an ark in which to save himself and his family during the flood brought upon the world because of its moral corruption. Noah took into the ark his family and several of each kind of animal. The ark floated for 150 days, and finally rested on Mount Ararat. Noah thus was the savior of mankind, and the second father of the peoples of the world.

NOAH, MORDECAI MANUEL (1785–1851)

American journalist, playwright, diplomat and Jewish leader. Born in Philadelphia, he studied law, but became a successful

Mordecai Manuel Noah once advocated a Jewish colony at Grand Island near Buffalo, New York.

Max Nordau, Herzl's collaborator in "political Zionism," was a physician by profession who then became a journalist and author. A brilliant orator, he was an active leader at the first nine Zionist congresses.

journalist and playwright. He became interested in the conditions of world Jewry as a result of his travels and his diplomatic post in Tunis, North Africa, where he served as American consul (1813-1816). Upon his return to the United States he became an advocate of Zionism, but realizing that the creation of a Jewish state in Palestine was then impracticable, he conceived the idea of establishing a Jewish settlement at Grand Island, New York,

near Buffalo. He named the proposed Jewish colony "Ararat," proclaimed himself its governor, and issued a solemn appeal to Jews the world over to join him in this venture. On September 15, 1825, the foundation stone for the "City of Refuge for the Jews" was laid. However, his scheme was deemed fantastic and his appeal remained unanswered. The only remaining trace of this project is the foundation stone, which is kept at the Buffalo

Historical Society. For the rest of his life Noah remained an ardent Jew, and continued his efforts to find a solution for Jewish difficulties.

NORDAU, MAX (1849–1923)

Zionist leader and author. Born and educated in Budapest, he settled in Paris as a practicing physician, but soon embarked upon a successful journalistic career. He gained international reputation for his literary works, especially the "Conventional Lies of Our Civilization," "Paradoxes," "The Maladies of the Century," and "Degeneration," all cultural criticism.

Equipped with a good Jewish background, he was very active in Jewish affairs, and was one of the staunchest advocates of political Zionism and a close collaborator of Theodor Herzl, father of political Zionism. He was a brilliant orator, and participated actively in the first nine Zionist congresses.

NORWAY

Scandinavian kingdom where only about 1,000 Jews lived in 1960. Although some Jewish settlers came to Norway at the end of the 17th century, Jewish immigration was not encouraged by the government until 1851, and the first Jewish community was not established until 1892. Most Jews live in Oslo. Norway is remembered as the protector of many Jews during the Nazi regime.

NUMBERS

The fourth of the *Five Books of Moses* (Pentateuch), known in Hebrew as *Bemidbar* (In the Wilderness), so named after the first significant word in the text. It is called "Numbers" because it opens with a census of the people after they came into the wilderness, and later the book records a second census before entering the Promised Land.

The Hebrew title Bemidbar is a better description of the contents of the book, which deals with many experiences of the Israelites in the desert, such as the Sinai legislation, the role of the Levites, and the major episodes of the wanderings from Sinai to the land of Moab, such as the sending of spies to the land of Canaan, the rebellion of Korah, the wars in the desert, the story of Balak, and the conquest of East Jordan. In common speech, this book is frequently called "Bamidbor."

NUMERUS CLAUSUS

A Latin term meaning "closed number" applied to the limitations imposed upon Jews desiring to enter universities, vocational schools and other institutions of higher learning. Only a limited number or a certain percentage of Jews in many European countries were allowed to pursue a higher academic or professional education. Such anti-Semitic legislation dates back to the 16th century, but was especially practiced during and after the 19th century in Russia, Poland, Rumania, Hungary and Germany.

NUN (נ)

The fourteenth letter of the Hebrew alphabet, pronounced like the English N. Its numerical value is 50, and its probable meaning is fish.

NUREMBERG LAWS

Special anti-Jewish legislation during the Nazi regime in Germany, put into effect on September 15, 1935. On the basis of these laws, issued as a protection of "German blood and honor," Jews were deprived of German citizenship, forbidden either marriage with or courtship of Germans. Jews were excluded from any significant economic and cultural jobs though many Jews had previously held positions of some importance.

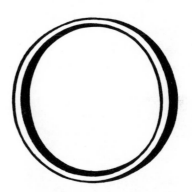

OMER

Seven weeks shalt thou number unto thee; from the time the sickle is first put to the standing corn shalt thou begin to number seven weeks. And thou shalt keep the feast of weeks unto the Lord thy God after the measure of the freewill-offering of thy hand, which thou shalt give, according as the Lord thy God blesseth thee.

DEUTERONOMY

OBADIAH

One of the *Twelve Minor Prophets* whose book of prophecies consists of one short chapter of twenty-one verses. It is believed that Obadiah lived after the destruction of the First Temple (586 b.c.e.), since in his prophecy he castigates Edom for not standing by the people of Judah during the attack of the Babylonians. Obadiah forecasts vengeance on the enemies and the return of the Judeans from the Babylonian captivity.

OCHS, ADOLPH SIMON (1858–1935)

Publisher of "The New York Times" and philanthropist. Born in Cincinnati, Ohio, he started his career in journalism in 1873 as a "printer's devil" on the Knoxville "Daily Chronicle," and later worked on the "Louisville Courier" and the Knoxville "Daily Tribune." In 1878 he became the owner of the Chattanooga "Daily Times"; he was one of the founders of the Southern Associated Press, and soon became an important official of the Associated Press, which he helped organize. After his arrival in New York in 1896, he took charge of "The New York Times" which he reorganized and subsequently developed into one of the leading dailies in the world, offering "all the news that's fit to print." Outside of his newspaper work, he was interested in a number of other important projects, and financed the publication of the *Dictionary of American Biography*, and also of the *American Year Book*.

Ochs was the son-in-law of Rabbi Isaac M. Wise, and contributed $500,000 to the endowment fund of the Hebrew Union College. He was a member of Congregation Emanu-El in New York, and attributed much of his success to his Jewish upbringing and the spiritual strength he gained from the Jewish religion. Ochs received honorary degrees from a number of leading universities, and "The New York Times" was awarded many distinctions for meritorious public service.

OHEL MOED see Tabernacle.

OLAM HA-BA see Olam ha-Zeh.

OLAM HA-ZEH; OLAM HA-BA

Hebrew terms meaning "this world" (man's present life on earth) and "the world that is to come" (life in the hereafter) respectively. The term *Olam ha-Ba* (world to come) refers, according to Jewish tradition, to both the life of the soul after death and to the Messianic Age of bliss (the Millenium). These two concepts originated in the teachings of the Prophets, and were further developed in classical Jewish literature. *Olam ha-Zeh* is only a preparation for *Olam ha-Ba*, and the sufferings of the individual in "this world" will be amply compensated for "in the world to come." Because of the wickedness and cruelty of the present world, Olam ha-Zeh is often referred to as the *Olam ha-Sheker* (the world of falsehood),

Adolph S. Ochs, the publisher of The New York Times and organizer of the Associated Press.

19th-century Omer calendar, by Maurice Mayer, goldsmith to Napoleon III, with date in center.

while on the other hand Olam ha-Ba is called *Olam ha-Emet* (world of truth). See *Death; Messiah; Resurrection.*

OMER

Biblical term having two connotations. Its first meaning applies to "a dry measure of grain" (a tenth of an "ephah"). The second meaning of *Omer* is "sheaf" applied to the sheaf of the First-Fruits which the Israelites were commanded to offer in the sanctuary on the second day of Passover. The counting of the days of the Omer between Passover and Shavuot (*Sefirah*) is to this day part of Jewish ritual. See *Lag Ba-Omer; Sefirat ha-Omer.*

ONEG SHABBAT

A Hebrew term meaning "joy of the Sabbath" applied to a special Sabbath celebration, which may be held on Friday night or Saturday afternoon. The *Oneg Shabbat* celebration, introduced by the

Hebrew poet Ḥayyim Naḥman Bialik in Tel Aviv, Israel, has been adopted by many Jewish institutions, organizations and synagogues in the United States. The program of the Oneg Shabbat celebration usually consists of musical selections, a lecture or dramatic presentation, and the serving of refreshments.

ONKELOS

Reputed author of the Aramaic translation of the *Pentateuch* (Five Books of Moses), called *Targum Onkelos.* Onkelos was a teacher of the second century. According to the Babylonian Talmud, he was a proselyte and of the Roman imperial family. Some authorities believe that Onkelos was mistakenly taken to be the author of the *Targum,* being confused with Aquila, who also lived in the second century and was the translator of the Bible into Greek. Aquila also is believed to have been a Jewish proselyte.

OPATOSHU, JOSEPH (1887–1955)

Yiddish writer. Born in Poland, he settled in the United States in 1907 where he pursued an uninterrupted career of Yiddish literary activity. Opatoshu's greatest novel, published in 1915, is *In Polishe Velder* (In Polish Woods), the first part of a trilogy which has since been translated into Hebrew and several European languages. In addition to hundreds of masterfully written short stories, his other larger works include: *A Tog in Regensburg* (1932), and *Rabbi Akiva* (1940).

ORAL LAW

The body of Jewish laws and traditions not contained in the "Written Law" (the Torah). The "Oral Law," (*Torah Shebe-al Peh*), believed to be divinely inspired, was transmitted from generation to generation without being written down. At the time of persecution and unstable conditions of

A machine shop in Givatayim, Israel, one of the many ORT Vocational Centers the world over. These not only help to train and rehabilitate young people, but provide a source of skilled labor for the new state.

Jewish cultural life, it became necessary to commit to writing the vast body of accumulated oral laws and traditions. The *Mishnah* and later the *Gemara*, are known as the "Oral Law" despite the fact that they were written down by the Mishnaic and Talmudic teachers.

The Oral Law was sustained by the Pharisees, and has been kept sacred throughout history. The Sadducees, and later the Karaites, as well as some early reform Jews maintained that the Oral Law was not divinely inspired, and was therefore not binding. However, at present, most Jews, though they may deviate from certain of its practices, believe the Oral Law to be divinely inspired and therefore eternally pertinent and valid.

ORDER BRITH ABRAHAM see Independent Order of Brith Abraham.

ORDINATION see Semikhah.

ORT

Abbreviation of three Russian words meaning "Society for Rehabilitation and Training," name of an international Jewish organization for the promotion of skilled trades and agriculture among Jews, founded in Russia in 1880. The ORT, originally designed to help Russian Jews, widened its scope during World War I, when it became a world organization with branches in France, Germany, England, America, and elsewhere, in addition to those in former Russian territories like Poland, Lithuania and Bessarabia.

Aiming to provide "help through work," the ORT operates employment bureaus; organizes trade schools; provides tools, machinery and materials; sets up special courses for apprentices; and maintains farm schools as well as cooperative agricultural colonies and workshops.

The ORT has been especially active from 1933 helping to rehabilitate thousands of Jews who became either destitute or displaced as a result of the Nazi regime in Germany. The ORT is subsidized from funds collected in South America, Australia, South Africa, and especially in the United States, where an American ORT Federation was founded in 1925, and where in 1942 the first vocational school for Jewish refugees was opened in New York City.

ORTHODOX JUDAISM

Jews were referred to for the first time as "orthodox" by Furtado during the time when Napoleon convened the Sanhedrin of Paris. In its broader sense the term "orthodox Judaism" applies to the historic religion of the Jewish people; but in modern times, especially since the birth of reform Judaism, it has been applied to the adherents of strict traditional Judaism. The foundation of orthodox Judaism rests on the teachings of the *Torah*, consisting of the *Written Law* as contained in the *Pentateuch* (Five Books of Moses), and the *Oral Law* as represented by the *Mishnah, Gemara, Responsa*, and the Codes of the *Posekim*. Orthodox Jews believe in the literal doctrine of revelation, that the Torah (both written and oral) was given to Moses by God on Mount Sinai and is,

therefore, the everlasting and only true guide of Jewish life and conduct. The Torah is considered by orthodox Jews as a way of life, expressed by practices, ceremonies and in conformity with the *Mitzvot* (commandments of the Law, good deeds). Orthodox Jews advocate unswerving loyalty to Jewish traditions, chief among which are: devoted study of the Torah, daily prayer, and strict observance of the Sabbath, the holidays, dietary laws (Kashrut), and laws of family purity. In accordance with the ethical principles of the Jewish law, orthodox Judaism requires every Jew to lead a pious, righteous and charitable life. A large number of American orthodox synagogues have banded together in an organization known as the Union of Orthodox Jewish Congregations of America.

OSE (OZE)

Abbreviation of three Russian words meaning "Jewish Health Society," international organization for the protection of the health of Jews, organized in Russia in 1912. Beginning its work in Russia, OSE extended its activities to most east European Jewish communities. During World War I it helped thousands of Jewish war victims, extending relief and medical aid, and assisting in the resettlement of refugees. At the start of World War II in 1939, OSE established dispensaries, hospitals, school hygiene, milk stations, and summer camps in Poland, Lithuania, Latvia and Bessarabia. A substantial part of the budget for the activities of the OSE came from the American Jewish Joint Distribution Committee.

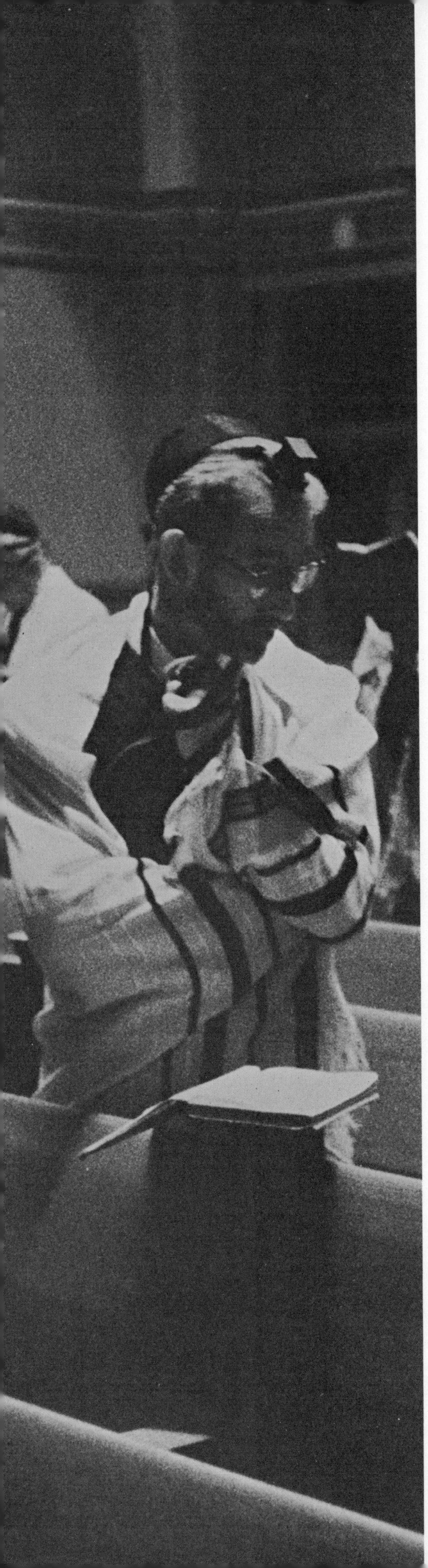

P

PHYLACTERIES

And these words which I command thee this day, shall

be upon thine heart. . . . And thou shalt bind them for

a sign upon thine hand, and they shall be for frontlets

between thine eyes.

DEUTERONOMY

PAGANISM

A term applied to the worship of idols or national gods, as contrasted with *Monotheism*, the worship of the one true God. Although Judaism has advocated tolerance to individuals of pagan peoples, it did not compromise with paganism as a religion. Biblical and post-Biblical literature abounds in injunctions against idol worship, and heathen customs and practices. Jewish tradition taught the Jew to prefer death rather than to engage in pagan practices, which were frequently of an immoral nature.

Palestinian idol of the goddess Astarte (in Hebrew, Ashtoreth), pagan goddess of fertility and love, probably used as a household god ca. 900 b.c.e. Such idols, common in ancient Israel, aroused the wrath of the Prophets at that time.

PALE OF SETTLEMENT

The provinces and districts in Tsarist Russia in which Jews were permitted to reside. Established in 1791 in the territory of the old Polish state, the Pale included areas in western and southern Russia. Jews were restricted to the Pale in order to minimize their "evil" influence on the Russian masses. Under the laws of 1882 they were forbidden, even within the confines of the Pale, to live in rural areas, and were compelled to reside in the crowded cities with limited economic opportunities. Some categories of Jews, however, such as students and merchants, were occasionally permitted temporary residence in cities outside the Pale. Over 90 per cent of the Jews in Russia lived in the Pale of Settlement, which extended over only 4 per cent of imperial Russia. Following the Kerensky Revolution in 1917, the Pale was finally abolished.

Life in the Pale of Settlement was cruel and oppressive. The six Tsars who ruled Russia from 1772 to 1917 not only used the Pale to isolate Jews from such opportunities in Russian life, commerce, culture and education as existed, but also tried to suppress Jewish communities under their sway.

But the Pale and its miseries, combined with Russian pogroms, boycotts, excessive taxation and other anti-Semitic depredations to produce the reverse of their intentions. They forged and hardened the national will and determination of the Jewish community. The *Haskalah* movement flourished, the Zionist movement developed, and Jewish Socialist activities involved a large part of the Jewish working

A typical old-style house and courtyard in the Polish town of Cracow. These houses are part of the Pale of Settlement, the ghetto area to which Jewish rights of residence were limited under the Tsars. Such large interconnected houses had many stores, workshops and homes.

Two photographs showing other aspects of the Pale. Above, the truckman or taxi-driver of the ghetto, called the "Baalagole" (literally, the master of the wagon). Below is a view of the Pale's market place. It was here, because of the commercial restrictions imposed on them, that Jews conducted most of their business. Note the primitive pump on the left which was the sole source of all the ghetto's drinking water.

people. A vigorous and varied Hebrew and Yiddish literature emerged, and Jewish religious life, culture and institutions gained a new depth and significance, even in the face of iron-fisted oppression.

PALESTINE

Called in the Bible *Canaan*, and including also part of the land of the Philistines when occupied by them. It was subdivided after Solomon's death into the northern Kingdom of Israel, and the southern Kingdom of Judah. Following the return from the Babylonian exile, the land came to be known as *Judah* or *Judea*. The Greeks and the Romans were the first to refer to the country west of the Jordan as *Palestine*, while the Jews referred to it as *Eretz Yisrael* (Land of Israel), the *Holy Land*, the *Promised Land*, the *Land of the Bible*, or the *Land of the Fathers*. Since 1948, following the establishment of the Jewish State, the land is known as *Israel*.

Palestine is situated in the southwestern corner of Asia on the eastern coast of the Mediterranean Sea, and borders on Africa. It is divided into eastern and western parts by the Jordan river. The whole territory of Palestine covers 66,000 square kilometers, of which 26,330 are in western Palestine. Palestine contains four zones: the coastal plane with a sub-tropical, moderate climate; the mountainous area with a colder climate; the Jordan valley with a tropical climate; and the plateau east of the Jordan with a varied climate. The hill country between the Negev and the Syrian boundary is divided into three main regions: *Judea* in the south, *Samaria* in the center, and *Galilee* in the north. The territory east of the Jordan river, which was known as Transjordania, is now the kingdom of Jordan.

Jewish history in Palestine began about 2,000 b.c.e., when Abraham left the city of Ur, traveled along the edge of the fertile crescent with his kinsmen, and settled in the land of Canaan. About two hundred years later, the Hebrews, driven by famine, migrated to Egypt where they lived for several centuries. After being enslaved by the Pharaonic regime of the 18th century b.c.e., the Hebrew tribes left Egypt under the leadership of Moses, who laid the foundation of the Israelite nation and its religion. Under the leadership of Joshua, Canaan was reconquered by the Israelites, and following hostile pressure from the neighboring peoples, especially the Philistines, the first monarchy was established under King Saul. The United Kingdom was extended over the whole of Palestine by King David and his son Solomon, who erected the First Temple in Jerusalem. After the death of Solomon, the United Kingdom split into the northern Kingdom of Israel and southern Kingdom of Judah. In 586 b.c.e., the First Temple was destroyed, and the people were taken into Babylonian captivity. Fifty years later, when Persia conquered Babylonia, the captives returned to Judea and later rebuilt the Temple, reconstructing their national life and making the Torah the foundation of Jewish life and thought. About 330 b.c.e., Alexander the Great conquered the Persian Empire, and after his death his own empire was divided among his generals. The Syrian and Egyptian dynasties battled over Palestine over a period of several centuries.

About 170 b.c.e., Palestine was conquered by the Syrians, and the spread of Hellenistic culture and persecution of the Jewish faith led to the Maccabean revolt and then to national independence under the Hasmonean dynasty. In 63 b.c.e., Palestine became a Roman province, and because of oppression by Roman rulers, the country was under constant strife and frequent rebellion, which was crushed by the conquerors who destroyed Jerusalem and the

Temple in 70 c.e. The Jewish dispersion, which had started several centuries earlier, finally became permanent, and only a remnant stayed in Palestine.

For over five hundred years Palestine remained under Roman and Byzantine rule, until the Arabs swept the Middle East. Jerusalem was then rebuilt and one of the early caliphs built the Mosque of Omar (in the 7th century) on the site of the destroyed Holy Temple. Following a period of about four hundred years of Arab rule, invasions began from Christian Europe in 1096 c.e. These invasions are known as the Crusades. By the end of the 12th century Palestine again fell under Moslem rule. In 1517 it was conquered by the Turks in whose hands the country remained until the British conquered Palestine in 1917-18. The British issued the "Balfour Declaration" in 1917, which promised the establishment of a Jewish national home in Palestine. Despite the opposition of the Arabs, who did little to recultivate the devastated land, thousands of Jewish pioneers from eastern Europe flocked to their historic homeland, beginning a new period of resettlement and colonization. Great Britain, the mandate power in Palestine, frequently interfered with Zionist aspirations, curtailing Jewish immigration. However, events following the Nazi regime, under which six million European Jews were annihilated, led to the establishment of the Jewish State in 1948, in part of western Palestine, known as the State of Israel. See *Israel, State of.*

PALESTINE FOUNDATION FUND see
Keren Ha-Yesod.

PALESTINIAN TALMUD see Talmud.

PARADISE see Gan Eden.

PARAGUAY

An inland South American country where, as of 1960, the Jewish population was about 2,500 out of a total population of about 1,500,000. Jews began to settle in Paraguay in 1900. As a result of persecutions in Germany during the Hitler regime, several hundred Jews were permitted to enter this country. Most Jews live in Asuncion, the capital city.

PARASHAH

Hebrew term applied to the portion of the Torah read at public services in the synagogue. In common usage, the word "Parashah" also refers to the entire *Sidrah* (or Sedrah), or to any of the various sections or paragraphs in the scroll of the Torah. The Torah is subdivided into *Sidrot* (sections), the reading of which is completed in a one year cycle; and each Sidrah is further subdivided into Parashiyot (sing. Parashah).

PARNOSEH

Popular Jewish phrase derived from the Hebrew word "Parnasah," which means a man's "livelihood."

PAROKHET (Porohes)

Hebrew term for the curtain which in most synagogues hangs in front of the Ark of the Law. It is made of satin or silk and is richly embroidered with various Jewish symbols, such as the Lion of Judah, the Crown of the Law, the Magen David and Temple vessels. It usually bears significant Hebrew inscriptions.

PASSOVER

The Jewish festival called in Hebrew *Pesah.* The first day of the festival falls on the 15th of Nisan (March-April) and lasts for eight days. It commemorates the deliverance of the Israelites from Egypt, and

Torah Ark curtain, or Parokhet, of embroidered velvet, comes from Germany, 1772. The main motifs are the seven-branched Menorah, the two sacred Solomonic columns, and the Crown of the Torah (top) held by two rampant griffins.

Stylized print, showing the Passover Seder at home, dates from the turn of the century. The print was an advertisement for selling tea; hence the woman of the house is seen (left) brewing the advertised brand.

is celebrated as "the Season of our Freedom" (*Zeman Ḥerutenu*). Only the first two and the last two days of Passover are observed as full holidays, and the four middle days are known as *Ḥol ha-Moed* (secular days of the holiday), and are observed as half-holidays. On the first two nights a special home ceremony or Passover ritual known as the *Seder* (Order) is observed. At the Seder ceremony the youngest participant asks the "Four Questions," and the head of the household, accompanied by the other participants, responds to the questions by reading the Passover story from the *Haggadah*. Reform Jews as well as Jews living in Israel celebrate only one Seder and observe the festival for seven days.

The festival of Pesaḥ is also called *Ḥag ha-Matzot* (the Festival of the Unleavened Bread), since only *Matzah* (unleavened bread) and other unleavened food are tra-

ditionally permitted to be eaten during the eight days of the holiday. This is done in commemoration of the Matzah that the Israelites baked in haste following their deliverance from Egyptian bondage by Moses. See *Seder*.

PATRIARCHS

A term applied to the founders of the Hebrew people, Abraham, Isaac and Jacob. Tradition also reveres the memory and merits of the four "Matriarchs," Sarah, Rebekah, Rachel and Leah. According to the Rabbis, the lives of the Patriarchs are a guide and example for all Jews. Their names are mentioned in the liturgy, especially in the first paragraph of the *Amidah*, called *Avot* (Patriarchs).

When Jewish tradition speaks of the Patriarchs or of any of the personalities mentioned in the Bible, it is not only the actual Biblical events that are referred to, but the entire complex which the *Aggadah* wove about them. Thus the Abraham story calls to mind the famous *Midrash* about the young lad contemplating the beauties of the sun and moon; about the sturdy faith of the young man who chose death rather than adopt the harsh and ugly paganism of King Nimrod. It is only through the rabbinic elaboration of the Biblical tales that one may achieve a deeper understanding of these great spiritual heroes.

PÉ (FÉ) (פ ,ף)

The seventeenth letter of the Hebrew alphabet. It is pronounced like the English P when it has a *Dagesh* (a dot inside), and like the English F without the Dagesh. It is then called *Fé*, and is sometimes trans-literated Ph, as in Joseph, because of classical influences. Its numerical value is 80, and its meaning is "mouth." In an unvoweled text there is no visible distinction between Pé and Fé.

PENITENTIAL DAYS

The "Ten Days of Repentance" known in Hebrew as *Aseret Yeme Teshuvah*, which begin on Rosh Hashanah (New Year) and end on Yom Kippur (Day of Atonement). These days are marked as days of solemnity. Special penitential prayers, known as *Seliḥot*, are said before morning devotions on these days. See *Festivals*.

PENTATEUCH

A Greek term for the *Five Books of*

Page from the Book of Deuteronomy of the first Hebrew edition of the Pentateuch, printed in Italy in 1482. The printed text includes the Biblical cantillation (Trope) used when the Torah is publicly read.

The huge relief of Darius I, king of ancient Persia, at Persepolis, Iran. It shows him receiving a foreign dignitary, with his son Prince Xerxes (the Biblical Ahasuerus), successor to the crown, behind him.

Moses, the translation of the Hebrew term *Ḥumash*. These books are Genesis, Exodus, Leviticus, Numbers and Deuteronomy. Since ancient times the Pentateuch has been the basis of Jewish religion and education. Every synagogue has at least one Scroll, which contains the handwritten text of the Pentateuch, and which is generally known as *Sefer Torah* (Scroll of the Torah).

PENTECOST see Shavuot.

PERETZ, ISAAC LEIB (1851–1915)

"Father" of Yiddish literature. Born in Poland, Peretz began his literary career as a Hebrew writer, but in order to reach the Yiddish speaking masses, he turned to Yiddish. He soon became the standard-bearer and the center of the Yiddish literary movement. He was the moving force at the Yiddishist conference held at Czer-

nowitz, Bukovina, in 1908, where Yiddish was proclaimed the Jewish national language. Peretz was a master of the dynamic Yiddish short story in which he described both the misery and the virtues of Polish Jewry. He embraced socialist ideas, and in much of his writing he decried social injustices and advocated the improvement of the status of the poor. Peretz was most successful in his romantic and symbolic stories known as "Hasidic Tales" and "Folk Tales" based on Jewish legend and mysticism. He also wrote two mystic dramas, "Di Goldene Kait" (The Golden Chain), and "Beinacht Oifn Alten Mark" (Night in the Old Market), and was editor of the literary compilations "Di Yiddishe Bibliotek" and the "Yom-tov Bletter." Peretz exercised great influence on younger writers, and was highly esteemed by his contemporaries. When he died in Warsaw more than 100,000 Jewish men and women came to his funeral. Jewish schools in many lands have been named after him, and the Yiddish Pen Club in the United States as well as a street in New York bear his name.

PERSIA

One of the larger states in central Asia, now known as Iran, whose capital city is Teheran. In 1960 there were about 80,000 Jews in Persia with a general population of less than twenty million. Persia has played an important part in the history of the Jewish people. In the sixth century b.c.e., Persia conquered Babylonia, and King Cyrus issued a proclamation which granted the right of return of Jewish captives to Judea and permitted them to rebuild the Holy Temple in Jerusalem. This event is recorded in the books of *Ezra* and *Nehemiah*. The story of Purim, as told in the *Book of Esther*, is also part of the history of the Jews of Persia. Although Persian rule in Palestine terminated in the 4th century b.c.e. with the conquest of Alexander the Great, Persia continued for many more centuries to play an important role in Jewish history. In Persia as well as in Babylonia there existed many flourishing Jewish communities with outstanding academies. The decline of the Jewish communities in Persia began in the 13th century following the invasion of the Mongols, and subsequent persecutions and massacres. A limited number of Jews lived in Persia during the following centuries. In the middle of the 19th century, the *Alliance Israélite Universelle* undertook relief work in behalf of the persecuted and impoverished Jewish community in Persia by extending economic help, improving their political status, and initiating a program of Jewish education. Jews of Persia now reside in Teheran, Hamadan, Ispahan, Seneh, Shiraz and Kermanshah.

PERU

South American country with 3,000 Jews out of a total population of close to nine million in 1960. The first Jews who settled in Peru were Marranos, and at the beginning of the 16th century these settlers occupied a dominant position in the life of the country. The Inquisition was introduced in Peru in 1569, and as a result most Jews lost their religious identity and became absorbed in the general population. The first Jewish settlers from eastern Europe came to Peru during World War I, and during World War II German refugees found new homes there. Most Jews live in Lima, the country's capital.

PERUSHIM see Pharisees.

PESAH see Passover.

PETAH TIKVAH

One of the oldest and largest Jewish colonies in Israel, near Tel Aviv. Founded as an agricultural settlement in 1878, its pioneers were later assisted by Baron Edmond de Rothschild. Petah Tikvah is known as the "mother" of Jewish colonies in Israel. Wine and oranges are its main products.

PETHAHIAH BEN JACOB OF REGENSBURG

Twelfth century traveler. Born in Prague, he traveled through Russia, Poland, Crimea, Armenia, Persia, Babylonia, Palestine and Greece. His records contain valuable geographical information and an account of life in the Jewish communities with which he came in contact. The notes of his journeys were collected by Judah He-Hasid and published under the title of *Sibbuv*. The book was subsequently translated into several languages.

PHARAOH

A title used in the Bible for the rulers of Egypt. It is derived from the Egyptian term *pero* meaning "the great house," referring to the royal court.

375

PHARISEES; SADDUCEES

Two major parties or sects among Palestinian Jews during the period of the Second Commonwealth, the third smaller sect being the *Essenes*. The *Pharisees* are known in Hebrew as *Perushim*, a word probably derived from *Parosh* which may mean "to separate" or "to expound." Such connotations explain two major characteristics of the *Pharisees* as compared with the *Sadducees*.

The Pharisees were "separatists" in that they emphasized observance of such practices as ritual purity and tithing, which kept them apart from the less observant Jews. They were "expounders," encouraging a liberal interpretation of the Scriptures and the adaptation of its laws to the changing conditions of life. This contrasts with the Sadducees who adhered strictly to the letter of the Law. When it became necessary to make new legislation, the Sadducean priests issued decrees without looking for support in the Torah, whereas the Pharisees were proponents of Scriptural interpretation which was known as the *Oral Law*.

Some relate the name Sadducees to *Zadok*, High Priest during King Solomon's reign. The Sadduceeans and their affiliates were mainly priests, as well as rich people, aristocrats and military leaders. The fellowship of the Pharisees consisted of lay leaders, teachers and scholars. The Sadducees were politically more influential, and apparently advocated greater assimilation of Hellenistic attitudes. The Pharisees, on the contrary, advocated a spiritually strong nation, were proponents of peace, and aimed for the spreading of Judaism by persuasion. The Pharisees, being more democratic and progressive, won the sympathy and fellowship of the Jewish masses. They introduced popular Jewish education; developed the liturgy of the synagogue; popularized the doctrines of immortality and resurrection; and instituted many reforms which benefited the Jewish masses. The Pharisees are therefore regarded as those authorities who helped develop and preserve traditional Judaism as it is known today.

Statements about the Pharisees found in the New Testament, where they are referred to as "hypocrites," are not to be taken as factual or true characterizations. The writings in the New Testament were set down after the rift between Judaism and the newly born Christian Church had taken place. Thus partisanship and rivalry had much more to do with the portrayal of the Pharisees in the New Testament than historical reality. The Talmud speaks of several classes of Pharisees, some of whom were not acceptable religiously; but by and large the Pharisees were worthy and great men.

PHILISTINES

An ancient people who settled in the Land of Canaan at about the same time as the Israelites. They probably had come from Crete, and occupied the southwest coastal plain known as *Philistia*, where they built the cities of Gaza, Ashkelon, Ashdod, Ekron and Gath. From "Philistia" was later derived the name of *Palestine*, given to the entire land of Canaan.

The Philistines were a sea-going people, famous as traders, and because of their superior weapons they became a serious menace to the Israelites. During the period of the Judges they overran a good part of the Land of Canaan until they were temporarily stopped by Saul, the first king of the Israelites. David, who as a youth fought the Philistine giant Goliath, later completely subdued the Philistines. Subsequently Jewish kings waged wars against them, until they were finally conquered by the Assyrians, after which they disappeared as a separate people.

PHILO

Jewish philosopher of the first century c.e. He lived in Alexandria, Egypt, and enjoyed a great reputation as a Biblical interpreter and philosopher of Hellenistic Judaism. Of a distinguished Jewish family, he took an active part in the life of the Alexandrian Jewish community. He headed a Jewish delegation to the half-mad Emperor Caius Caligula in Rome, to petition the revocation of a humiliating decree against the Jews of Alexandria. He described this successful mission in his book, *Embassy to Caius*. He is also known to have made a pilgrimage to Jerusalem to worship at the Temple on Passover.

His writings, all in the Greek language, include an allegorical commentary on *Genesis;* a systematic compilation of the teachings of the Torah; books on the Creation, the Patriarchs and Moses; as well as a number of philosophical treatises in which he attempted to reconcile Greek philosophy with the contents of the Bible. In this endeavor to harmonize religious thought with the prevailing philosophy, he was followed by all subsequent Jewish and Christian philosophers and theologians. Philo had little or no influence on Jewish thought, but the impression he made on Christianity seems very deep. His doctrine of the Logos (Word) is apparently reinterpreted by the author of the fourth gospel and made by him the basis of what later came to be a keystone in Christian theology. The Christian Fathers refer to him as *Philo Judaeus*.

PHOENICIANS

An ancient people on the northern coastal strip of Palestine, and southern Syria, identified in the Bible as the Tyrians. Phoenicia was a rich forest land, and the Bible tells of Hiram, king of Tyre, who provided Solomon with timber for the construction of the Holy Temple. The Phoe-

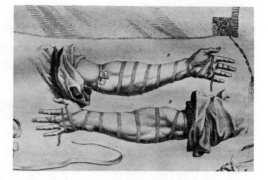

18th-century etching of Tefillin (phylacteries) shows the leather straps tied on a man's arm.

nicians were successful traders both on sea and land, and are known to have developed a high civilization. Of Semitic origin, their language was a Hebrew dialect, and the Hebrew-Phoenician alphabet was adopted by Greek and other Western languages.

PHYLACTERIES

Greek word for "Tefillin," applied to the two black leather cubes provided with long leather straps which are worn during the daily morning prayer (except on Sabbaths and holidays) by the Jewish male over the age of thirteen. The cases contain prescribed passages from the Torah written on strips of parchment, which relate to the injunctions concerning *Tefillin*. One Tefillin cube, called *Shel Yad*, is placed on the left arm facing the heart, and the other cube, called *Shel Rosh*, is placed on the center of the forehead. The long leather thong of the Shel Yad is wound seven times around the left arm, and the strap of the Shel Rosh is looped to permit the adjustment of the cube to the skull. The wearing of Tefillin is in conformity with a Biblical commandment and a reminder that the Torah must be studied and obeyed every day. There are detailed regulations relating to the arrangement of their texts, the manner in which they are to be worn and the time. There is a difference of opinion between Rashi and Rabbenu Tam as to the

18th-century east European brass plate used in the Pidyon ha-Ben ceremony for first-born sons.

order of the texts contained in the Tefillin, hence the use of two kinds of Tefillin by some pious persons.

PIDYON HA-BEN

Hebrew term meaning "redemption of the son," applied to the ceremony of redeeming the first-born male child 30 days after his birth, which is a Biblical requirement. The father offers five *Shekels* (or half-dollars) to a Kohen (member of the priestly family) in redemption of the child. At the *Pidyon ha-Ben* ceremony the father redeems the child and recites appropriate blessings. A first-born male is one who is the mother's first-born child. If either parent is a Kohen or a Levite (a descendant of the tribe of Levi), no Pidyon ha-Ben ceremony is required.

PIDYON SHEVUYIM

Hebrew term meaning "redemption of captives," applied to the honorable Jewish practice of ransoming those Jews who had fallen into captivity, or who had been ar-

rested by the authorities on false pretenses. This practice is of ancient origin, and Jewish legal codes offer detailed specifications and provisions for the ransoming of captives. Jewish history is replete with cases of Jewish individuals or groups who were redeemed by Jewish communities. The readiness of the Jewish communities to free their brethren has in many instances encouraged the captors to demand exorbitant ransom. To discourage such extortions, provisions had to be made, even as early as Talmudic times, that no individual or community undertake to pay unreasonable amounts of ransom. In some cases, such as that of the famous Rabbi Meir of Rothenburg, captives refused to be redeemed to discourage extortion.

PILGRIMAGE FESTIVALS

According to a Biblical ordinance, every male Israelite was required *to go up* to Jerusalem three times each year, namely on *Passover, Shavuot,* and *Sukkot,* in order to offer sacrifices at the Holy Temple and to bring gifts from the produce of the fields. These pilgrimages, which became very popular during the Second Commonwealth, even among Jews living outside of Palestine, became occasions for important religious experiences in Jerusalem, both joyful and solemn. The Hebrew term for these three pilgrimage festivals is *Shalosh Regalim,* and for such a pilgrim *Ole Regel.*

PINKAS

A term applied to a register of the Jewish community, or a minute-book in which important events, decrees, names of taxpayers, etc., were recorded. Such records, containing valuable historical information, have been kept by Jewish communities since the Middle Ages, and those that are preserved serve as a valuable source for current knowledge of the life of the people during those times.

A present-day pilgrimage to Mount Zion by a host of Oriental Jews during Passover. They are greeted by the Shofar as they ascend the mountain. Such pilgrimages were an ancient commonplace.

PINSKER, LEO (1821–1891)

Forerunner of political Zionism. Born in Poland, he was a physician by profession, and was acclaimed by the Russian government for his distinguished work during a cholera epidemic. At first he embraced assimilationist ideas, and advocated the improvement of Jewish conditions through the acquisition of civil rights. However, as the result of anti-Jewish riots in 1881, his ideas on Jewish survival underwent a radical change. In 1882 he published his famous *Auto-Emancipation*, in which he argued that the salvation of the Jews lies in self-emancipation in their historic homeland. This pamphlet received much attention in east European Jewish communities, and Pinsker joined the Ḥo-vevei Zion (Lovers of Zion) movement, which paved the way for subsequent Jewish colonization in Palestine.

PINSKI, DAVID (1872–1959)

Yiddish playwright and novelist. Born in Russia, he became interested in the Yiddish literary movement and in the enlightenment and progress of the Jewish working class. He settled in the United States in 1899 where he became a favorite writer for the Yiddish stage. His early plays depict Jewish suffering in Russia, whereas those of the later period are both poetic and symbolic presentations of Jewish historic themes. Some of his more successful plays are: *Der Oitzer* (The Treasure), *The Eternal Jew*, and *Shabbetai Tzevi*. He

379

also wrote a number of novels and short stories. Pinski showed an active interest in Jewish affairs, and identified himself with the Labor Zionist movement, serving from 1933 as president of the Jewish National Workers' Alliance. He died in Haifa, Israel, where he had resided in the last years of his life.

PIONEER WOMEN'S ORGANIZATION

The Women's Labor Zionist Organization of America, founded in 1925. It had in 1960 a membership of 50,000, organized in more than 500 clubs and groups in most of the states and in Canada. It is dedicated to the support of the *Moetzet Ha-Poalot* (Working Women's Council) in Israel. Together they are engaged in training and educating immigrants of the orient and Europe for life in Israel. The Pioneer Women help maintain and build farm schools, vocational training schools and courses, kindergartens, nurseries, hostels and youth centers. In addition to its fundraising activities for the Moetzet Ha-Poalot, the Histadrut, and the Jewish National Fund, the Pioneer Women's Organization promotes a cultural and educational program for its members, calling for a positive approach to Jewish life in America.

PIRKE AVOT see Avot.

PIYYUT

Hebrew compositions in poetical form which are included in the prayer book as additions to the established liturgy. The *Piyyutim* (plural of *Piyyut*) date back to Talmudic times and were especially cultivated during the Middle Ages. In content, the Piyyutim reflect the conditions of Jewish life in given periods of time, and have frequently originated in periods of religious persecution. The better known of the earlier masters of the Piyyut were *Kalir* and some of the famous Hebrew poets in Spain, namely *Ibn Gabirol, Moses*

ibn Ezra, and *Judah Ha-Levi*. The *Selihah* (Penitential Prayer) is the commonest form of Piyyut; most Piyyutim serve as interpolations in the services on holidays and special Sabbaths, such as *Shabbat Shekalim* and *Shabbat Zakhor*.

PLAGUES, THE TEN

The punishments and afflictions which, according to the Bible, God visited upon Egypt when Pharaoh refused to free the Israelites. The last plague, the slaying of the first-born, compelled Pharaoh to yield. The Ten Plagues are enumerated in the *Haggadah*, which is read each Passover at the *Seder* as a reminder of the Exodus from Egypt. Following are the names of the plagues: *Dam* (Blood), *Tzefardea* (Frogs), *Kinnim* (Lice), *Arov* (Swarms of beasts), *Dever* (Murrain), *Shehin* (Boils), *Barad* (Hail), *Arbeh* (Locusts), *Hoshekh* (Darkness), and *Makkat Bekhorot* (Death of the first-born). As the word for each plague is pronounced at the Seder, the reader pours off a drop of wine from his cup symbolizing the concept that even though the Egyptians deserved punishment, they were nevertheless creatures of God whose suffering causes us to lose a drop of joy from the cup of life.

POALE ZION

Hebrew name meaning "Workers of Zion" under which the world Labor Zionist Party is known. The first *Poale Zion* groups were formed in Russia and other east European countries soon after the first Zionist Congress in 1897. The political aspirations of the Labor Zionist Party are based on the ideals of both *Zionism* and *socialism*. Although the primary objective of the Poale Zion was the establishment of a Jewish national commonwealth in Palestine, it nevertheless emphasized that such commonwealth be based on socialistic principles. The Poale Zion party advocated the establishment in Palestine of cooperative agricultural workers' settlements, and hoped to create in the Jewish homeland a society where capitalist exploitation would be reduced to a bare minimum.

Outside of efforts to send pioneers to Palestine, the major activities of the Poale Zion prior to World War I were mainly educational. The party engaged in Zionist propaganda among anti-Zionist Jewish workers; it sought to win support for the Zionist cause among non-Jewish socialists; and it initiated a program of Jewish secular education based on the principles of Zionism and socialism.

In the years following World War I the center of the Poale Zion movement shifted to Palestine, where it gradually became the most influential of the political Zionist parties.

The American Poale Zion movement began in 1903. Its main endeavor was to win sympathy among Jewish and non-Jewish workers, and the establishment of Yiddish folk schools, a secular Jewish educational system. During World War I, the Poale Zion of America took the initiative in organizing the Jewish Legion, in which many of its members enlisted. The Poale Zion also organized the Jewish National Workers' Alliance (now called Farband Labor Zionist Order), the Pioneer Women's Organization, the Labor Zionist Youth Organization known as *Habonim*, and a number of summer camps and institutes offering labor Zionist educational programs for both children and adults. The Poale Zion and its affiliated groups organized the National Labor Committee for Palestine which gives substantial annual support to the *Histadrut*, the General Federation of Labor in Israel. The Poale Zion party of America publishes a Yiddish language weekly, the *Yiddisher Kemfer*, and an English language monthly, the

Jewish Frontier. In 1946, Poale Zion in the United States and Canada adopted the name, Labor Zionist Organization of America–Poale Zion.

POGROM

A Russian word meaning "riot" or "devastation" applied since 1881 to all violent anti-Jewish attacks. Hundreds of such large-scale massacres and anti-Jewish riots took place under the Tsarist regime in Russia and Poland. During "pogroms" thousands of Jews were killed and many Jewish communities suffered destruction and ruin. Despite protests of the civilized world, pogroms recurred periodically in Russia. The Russian authorities did little to defend the Jewish population against these outbreaks which, in many instances, were instigated by the government itself.

The most severe pogroms took place in 1881, in 1903 (the "Kishinev Pogrom") and in 1918-1921 after the fall of the Tsarist regime (the "Petlura" and "Denikin" pogroms). Under the subsequent Soviet regime, anti-Jewish outbreaks came to an end, although anti-Semitism under the Communist regime has developed vicious covert and overt anti-Jewish and anti-Israel attitudes and practices.

POLAND

Republic in east central Europe which, before the outbreak of World War II, had three and one-half million Jews in a total population of about 33 million. According to recent studies, Jewish history in Poland dates back to the 9th century, and the first Jews there are assumed to have been descendants of the Khazars, a people who had embraced the Jewish faith. During that early period Jews seem to have enjoyed a privileged status, evidenced from current tales about a Jewish king of Poland, and from the fact that some Polish coins had Hebrew inscriptions.

381

Two generations of typical east European Jews from Warsaw, in Poland. For four centuries Jewish communities in Poland flourished and were protected, so that Jewish culture was steadily developed.

The great influx of Jews to Poland took place in the 11th and 12th centuries when German Jews sought new homes because of the persecutions of the Crusaders. From the middle of the 13th century to the middle of the 17th century, Jewish communities in Poland steadily developed and flourished. Jewish contributions to the economic development of the country were invaluable, as a result of which Jews were granted special legal protection and security, especially under the rule of Casimir the Great (1333-1370) who, accord-

Young Jewish girl watches the market place in a Polish town. Here the peasants brought the produce of their farms to sell to the townspeople, and with the money they earned were then able to buy their manufactured goods.

ing to tradition, married a Jewess named Esterke (Esther).

The Jewish community in Poland flourished particularly in the 16th century, when it became the largest Jewish cultural center in the world, with a high degree of autonomy, under the authority of the famous *Council of the Four Lands*.

Years of suffering, persecution and devastation of the Jewish communities began with the uprising of the Cossacks against Poland in 1648, and subsequent wars waged against Poland by Russia and Sweden. In these catastrophes hundreds of thousands of Polish Jews perished, and hundreds of Jewish communities were wiped out. The remnants of the impoverished Jewish communities in Poland were then exposed

383

Pogrom and persecution later impoverished Polish Jews. Their synagogues were then modelled on fortresses for communal protection. Above is a rare, beautiful wooden synagogue built at Wolpa.

to untold persecutions by the Catholic Church and its people. Because of the miserable conditions, Polish Jews welcomed any hope of relief and redemption. They were given to mysticism and to the influence of *Kabbalah*, and zealously supported the false messiah *Shabbetai Tzevi*. About the middle of the 18th century the Ḥasidic movement arose among Polish Jews and gave new hope and comfort to the oppressed masses.

When Poland lost its independence in 1795, and its territory was divided among Austria, Prussia and Russia, the fate of the Jews depended on specific conditions in the countries to which they belonged. Austrian Poland was known as Galicia. When the Poles rebelled against Russia, first in 1830 and then in 1863, many Jew-

An elderly Polish Jew imitates a Gentile beggar who sings folk songs. Note the peasant boots.

The interior of a wooden synagogue at Parzeczew, in Poland, probably built some time around the end of the 18th century. Though there was a marked lack of ornament in the interior, the Holy Ark and Ammud were richly decorated.

ish leaders, including famous rabbis, sided with the Poles. The Jewish community in Poland subsequently enjoyed some measure of freedom and independent cultural development. The Ḥasidic movement gained in strength; and afterwards there arose the movement of Jewish nationalism linked with Zionism.

Following World War I, Poland regained its independence, and the Jewish minority in Poland, the largest and most vital Jewish community in Europe, was accorded minority rights. However, modern anti-Semitism, in the form of economic boycott and other limitations, was on the increase. Despite continuous persecution, Polish Jewry continued as the most significant Jewish cultural center, where outstanding rabbis, Hebrew and Yiddish writers, and leaders in both the socialist and the Zionist movements, made their lasting contribution to Jewish life and survival.

The greatest catastrophe of Polish Jewry followed the conquest of Poland by Nazi Germany in 1939. The Nazi hordes virtually annihilated the Jewish population and destroyed Jewish communal life. The Jews of the Warsaw ghetto made their last heroic stand against the Nazis in 1943, and afterwards Jewish life in Poland practically ceased to exist. In 1960 there were 41,000 Jews in Poland, not possessing sufficient strength or opportunity to develop an effective Jewish communal life.

POLL TAX

The Bible makes reference to a system of taxation in the form of a poll tax or a per capita tax of a "half-shekel," for the purpose of supporting the Sanctuary. The tax used during the Second Commonwealth for the upkeep of the Temple was later diverted by the Romans for the temple of Jupiter in Rome. During the Middle Ages, and into the 19th century, Jews in most European countries had to pay a special poll tax, either for the right of residence or for the right to engage in business.

POPULATION, JEWISH

Jewish tradition speaks of six hundred thousand males twenty years and over during the wanderings in the Sinai wilderness. The Bible records several other censuses also. In general there are very few verifiable data not only of Jewish population but of the general population, until relatively recent times. It is estimated by some scholars that during the second and first centuries b.c.e. there were probably a million Jews in Jerusalem and another million in Alexandria, with perhaps a total of three and one-half million throughout the world.

In the eleventh century the largest Jewish communities in central Europe were Mayence and Worms, each of which had about one thousand Jews. In the 18th century, Prague, the largest Ashkenazi center, had 10,000 Jews. In the middle of the 17th century the total Jewish world population was less than two million divided almost equally between Sephardim and Ashkenazim. Immediately prior to World War II there were 17 million Jews in the world, less than two million of whom were Sephardim. At the end of World War II there were 11 million. By 1961 the figure had risen to 12 million.

Europe was, of course, the largest Jewish center in the world until recently. As a consequence of heavy anti-Semitic outbreaks in Russia, Rumania and other areas in eastern Europe in the latter part of the 19th century, some three to four million Jews migrated to the west, including the U.S. In 1910 there were left in Europe about 10 million Jews. In the next quarter of a century, over 3 million left the continent for the U.S., Latin America and the British Commonwealth. In 1933 there were

6,382,000 Jews in Europe; in 1961, reflecting the Nazi holocaust, the population was reduced to 746,500. In Poland, the Jewish population dropped from 3,300,000 in 1933 to 30,000 in 1961; in Germany, from 550,-000 to 30,000; in Austria, from 190,000 to 10,000; in Hungary from 400,000 to 80,000; in Czechoslovakia, from 315,000 to 18,000; in Rumania, from 850,000 to 180,000; in the Netherlands, from 150,000 to 23,000; in Yugoslavia, from 75,000 to 6,500; and in Greece, from 75,000 to 6,000. It must be noted that the number of Jews in 1961 already includes a certain increase in Jewish population since 1945.

In 1961 there were about two million Jews in Israel, five million in the United States, three million in the Soviet Union, 700,000 in Latin America, and over half a million in Africa. The remaining Jewish population was distributed throughout the world in about 90 countries, many of them Jewish communities of considerable size and importance.

PORTUGAL

Republic in southwestern Europe with a Jewish population of 750 out of a total population of under nine million (1960). Jews settled in Portugal in the 10th century, and later occupied an important position in the life of the country. Following the expulsion from Spain in 1492, many Spanish Jews found refuge in Portugal. A few years later Portuguese Jews were subjected to mass conversions to the Catholic faith. Portugal hence became the land of the *Marranos,* large numbers of whom secretly observed their Jewish practices and ritual. The Marranos were, as a result, constantly under suspicion, and were frequently tortured by the Inquisition. Later many of the Marranos escaped to Holland where they returned to the Jewish fold.

POSEKIM see Codes.

POTOCKI, COUNT VALENTINE (c. 1700–1749)

A Polish nobleman, famous "Ger Tzedek" (proselyte) of Poland, and martyr. According to a tradition, Potocki, while living in Paris, became interested in Judaism and subsequently went to Amsterdam where he embraced the Jewish faith. He then settled in Vilna under the name of Abraham ben Abraham. Detected by the authorities, he was brought to trial and, despite inhuman tortures, remained true to Judaism. As a result he was burned at the stake. His ashes were buried in Vilna, and there is a story that an immense tree grew upon his grave, which was for many years a shrine for pious Jews.

PRAGUE

Capital of Czechoslovakia, famous metropolis of European Jewry. Jews lived in Prague from the 10th century, and from the beginning of the 13th century to the 18th century they lived in its ghetto, a quarter of the city which became known as the "Judenstadt" (city of the Jews). The Jewish community of Prague became famous for its great rabbis and *Yeshivot* (Talmudical Academies). One of its leading rabbis was Judah Löw ben Bezalel, the putative creator of the *Golem.* Under the

View of the outside of the famous Altneuschul in Prague. The Jewish City Hall is at the right.

Jews at morning prayer in Israel. The Hasidic boy in ritual hat and earlocks, and the boy in shorts and sandals are present-day contrasts in the Holy Land. The Tallit and Tefillin suggest a weekday morning.

Nazi occupation in 1939 thousands of Jews were massacred or deported, and the Jewish population of Prague was reduced from 65,000 to about 15,000 (1942); by the end of World War II, the Jewish community was disseminated.

PRAYER

The act of praying, collectively or individually, is mentioned frequently in the

Interior of the Altneuschul, which was the symbol and center of the Prague, Czechoslovakia, Judenstadt (Jews' town). Its vaulting Gothic architecture is very ancient, and in all probability dates from as early as the 12th century.

Bible. Sacrifices were offered on high places, as well as in the Tabernacle at Shiloh, and ultimately in the Temples, both first and second. Prayers accompanied the sacrifices, though we find prayers without sacrifice, such as Isaac praying in behalf of his wife, Moses praying for his sister, and Hannah praying for a child.

Sacrifice was accompanied by prayer. The Levites formed the chorus, chanting prayers while the priests offered the sacrifice. The Synagogue developed apparently during the Babylonian exile; on their return, the Jews continued to pray in their local synagogues, parallel with the services in the Temple. On the destruction of the Temple, the Sages instituted the prayer system in lieu of sacrifice.

Some important traditions regarding prayer are: 1) Praying in the synagogue and with the congregation is preferred to private prayer in one's own home; 2) Prayers should be in Hebrew, but may be offered in the vernacular if necessary; 3) Prayers should be offered regularly; that is, three times daily, morning, afternoon and evening; 4) During the recitation of the *Amidah*, the worshippers stand with legs together and head bowed; 5) Prayer requires the fullest concentration, without interruption, or distraction; 6) While praying it is customary to face eastward, or in the direction of Jerusalem; 7) Prayer must not be offered for an ulterior motive or for the impossible. In Jewish tradition there are three kinds of prayers: *Adoration, Thanksgiving,* and *Petition*. The Psalms are used as a sourcebook of prayer.

PRAYER BOOK

In ancient times Jews recited their prayers by heart, and the compilation of prayer books was traditionally forbidden. The first book by Gaon Amram, containing the order of prayers and benedictions for the entire year, appeared in the middle of the 9th century under the title "Seder Rav Amram." By 928 Saadiah Gaon had compiled his "Collection of Prayers and Songs of Prayer." The most popular and most comprehensive book of prayers for every purpose was the *Maḥzor Vitry*, which appeared in 1208. Subsequently two kinds of prayer books came into use, the *Siddur* and the *Maḥzor*. The latter contained, in addition to the basic prayers, collections of *Piyyutim* (religious hymns) written by various liturgical poets. It was primarily used during the holiday services and on special Sabbaths. In the course of time many important Jewish communities de-

veloped their own *Minhag* (version) of prayer books. Thus the Ashkenazi and the Sephardi Jewish communities used different *Minhagim* (versions of prayer books) and within each Minhag there were numerous variations. To fulfill the needs of some Jewish communities in Europe, there appeared translations of the Siddur and the Maḥzor in several European languages, such as Italian, French, German and English. With the rise of the Jewish reform movement in Germany, England and America, new versions of prayer books appeared in order to serve the needs of reform Judaism. A reform prayer book, called *Minhag America*, by Rabbi Isaac Mayer Wise, appeared in 1857. In 1895 the reform rabbis published the *Union Prayer Book* for Jewish worship. This remains the standard prayer book used in reform congregations in the United States, although it has been revised several times. The Conservative and Reconstructionist groups have also published their versions of the prayer book. See *Maḥzor; Siddur*.

PRAYER FOR THE DEAD see Kaddish.

PRAYER SHAWL see Tallit.

PRIESTLY BLESSING see Blessing, Priestly.

PRIESTS see Kohen.

PROPHETS, READING OF see Haftarah.

PROPHETS, THE TWELVE see Minor Prophets.

PROPHETS AND PHOPHECY

From the earliest times, and especially from the time of Moses until the early days of the Second Temple, the people of Israel had prophets (and prophetesses) in almost every generation. The Bible considers Moses not only the greatest of all prophets, but also the greatest human being. The activities of the Prophets are recorded in the main in the books contained in the second division of the Bible, and is called *Neviim* (Prophets).

The Hebrew word for prophet, *Navi*,

meaning "utterer," applies to a person who brings the word of God to man. A prophet was often called a "seer," a divinely inspired person who was able to predict future events. Some of the early prophets (such as Elijah and Elisha) were endowed with supernatural powers as performers of miracles.

The Prophets are chiefly remembered for their role as divinely inspired thinkers and teachers in the religious and political life of the Hebrew people. They were fearless fighters against idolatry and preachers of the belief in one God, Creator of the universe and Father of all mankind. They taught that all men were brothers, and the duty to love God and man. They cried out against injustice and immorality; they advocated humility and obedience to God; they were forceful national leaders and political agitators in times of great emergency; and they emphasized the sanctity of Jerusalem and the importance of the "House of David."

The Prophets are generally grouped as "Oral Prophets" and "Writing Prophets." The former are the earlier prophets, whose prophecies and messages were not committed to writing. The latter were called the literary prophets. Their orations and important national incidents occurring during their lifetime were written down in beautiful literary form. The works of the earlier prophets are described in the narratives contained in the books of *Judges*, *Samuel* and *Kings*, and the literary works and prophecies of the later prophets are contained in separate books such as *Isaiah*, *Jeremiah* and *Ezekiel*, as well as in the books of the *Twelve Minor Prophets* (Hebrew, *Tere Asar*). Numerous other personalities are held by tradition to have been prophets, e.g., the Patriarchs, Miriam and certain other persons mentioned elsewhere. The *Book of Daniel* is found in *Ketuvim*, the third division of the Bible. (Note: All the literary prophets are dealt with under their respective names.)

PROSBUL see Hillel.

PROSELYTE

A person of non-Jewish birth who adopts the Jewish faith. See *Ger*.

PROTOCOLS OF THE ELDERS OF ZION see Elders of Zion, Protocols of the.

PROVERBS

The second book of *Ketuvim* (Writings), the third section of the Bible. It contains 31 chapters, some of which bear the superscription "Proverbs of Solomon." Tradition attributes the authorship of much of it to King Solomon. However, some scholars hold that parts of the book consist of several collections of a later time.

The book consists of aphorisms and sayings about proper conduct, the importance of wisdom, relations between teacher and pupil, fear of God, admonitions against adultery, advice for public officials, the folly of intemperance and envy. It concludes with the famous eulogy on women (Eshet Ḥayil) which, in Jewish tradition, the husband recites prior to the Friday night meal.

PRUZBOL see Hillel.

PSALMS

First and most popular book of *Ketuvim* (Writings), the third section of the Bible. Tradition attributes the authorship of the *Psalms* to King David, the "sweet singer of Israel." Numerous Psalms are ascribed to David, Solomon, and the descendants of Korah. One is ascribed to Moses. The *Book of Psalms* is called in Hebrew *Tehillim* (Songs of Praise), and its religious poems are of different types and content, such as hymns of praise, trust in God, thanksgiving, penitence, and supplication.

Second only to the Five Books of Moses, the Book of Psalms is the most sacred to

Joseph Pulitzer, publisher of the St. Louis Post-Dispatch and New York World, and founder of the Pulitzer Prizes and Columbia University's journalism school, was a major figure in American journalism.

Jews. Many of the Psalms have become an integral part of the Jewish liturgy, and many of its hymns are customarily recited or chanted on various occasions of joy or sorrow. Traditionally there existed in Jewish communities "Tehillim Societies" for community recitation of the Psalms. The Book of Psalms is extensively used in the Christian liturgy, of both Catholic and Protestant churches.

PSEUDO MESSIAHS

False messiahs. See *Messiah*.

PULITZER, JOSEPH (1847–1911)

Newspaper publisher, philanthropist and founder of the "Pulitzer Prizes." Born in Hungary, he settled in the United States in 1864. Although he studied law, he carved a brilliant career in the field of American journalism. In 1883, following prior connections with the *St. Louis Post-Dispatch*, he bought the *New York World*, which became one of the leading newspapers in the country. Pulitzer was also active in politics and in philanthropic work. He gave two and one-half million dollars toward the establishment of the School of Journalism at Columbia University and left money in his will for various scholarships, and for the "Pulitzer Prizes," the highest award given in the United States for various types of literary works, including plays, novels and biographies as well as prizes for the best American journalism each year.

18th-century French puppets in a Purim scene with Queen Esther kneeling before King Ahasuerus, while in the background the hated Haman is hanged on the gallows he planned for the Jews.

PUNCTUATION see Vowels, Hebrew.

PURIM

Jewish festival observed annually on the 14th day of the Hebrew month of Adar (February-March). It commemorates the miracle of survival from Haman's plot to kill all the Jews of Persia. Purim is also called *Feast of Lots*, because of the lots which Haman cast to determine the proper day for the destruction of the Jews. The story of the Purim event is told in the *Book of Esther*, where Esther, Mordecai and Ahasuerus are well-delineated.

The *Fast of Esther* is observed on the day before Purim, and after sundown the *Megillah* (Scroll of Esther) is read with a special melody. The following morning the Megillah is read again and in the late afternoon of that day the *Seudah*, or traditional Purim meal, is begun and generally lasts for several hours.

Purim is also observed by merry-making and Purim plays (Purim Shpieln), with local talent called "Purim Shpielers." The Purim plays are generally a parody of the Purim story. On the day of Purim it is established practice to send Purim gifts, *Mishloaḥ Manot* (in common speech *Shalaḥ Mones*), to relatives, friends, and to the poor.

Purim is a most popular festival in Israel, especially in Tel Aviv, where the festivities take the form of a three-day colorful carnival, called *Adloyada*. See *Adloyada; Esther; Shushan Purim.*

RABBI

It is not incumbent upon thee to complete the work;

but neither art thou free to desist from it.

ETHICS OF THE FATHERS

RABBAN

Honorary title meaning "teacher" given in the Mishnah to presidents of the *Sanhedrin* (High Court), such as Rabban Gamaliel, Rabban Johanan ben Zakkai, and many others.

RABBENU GERSHOM see Gershom ben Judah.

RABBENU TAM see Jacob ben Meir Tam.

RABBI

Originally an honorary title meaning "my master," given in the Talmud to all *Tannaim* and Palestinian *Amoraim* as distinguished from the title "Rav" used in Babylonia. In the Middle Ages the office of the rabbinate was created, with the rabbi as the recognized leader of the community and the official Jewish legal authority. This title is now held by men officially ordained as competent to decide questions of Jewish law; this ordination may be done either by rabbinical academies or by individual rabbis.

RABBI ISAAC ELCHANAN THEOLOGICAL SEMINARY see Yeshiva University.

RABBINICAL ASSEMBLY OF AMERICA

The organization of conservative rabbis in the United States and Canada. Organized in 1901, its membership is primarily made up of graduates of The Jewish Theological Seminary of America. The Rabbinical Assembly aims "to conserve and promote traditional Judaism; to cooperate with The Jewish Theological Seminary of America and with the United Synagogue of America; to advance the cause of Jewish learning; to promote the welfare of its members; and to foster the spirit of fellowship and cooperation among rabbis and other Jewish scholars in America."

Some of the major activities of the Rabbinical Assembly are carried out by standing committees, such as the committee on Jewish law, concerned with the promotion of traditional Judaism in America, and the committee on social justice concerned with the interpretation of traditional Judaism in terms of present-day social and economic problems in the United States. The Rabbinical Assembly operates a placement bureau which recommends rabbis to conservative synagogues and centers; and it publishes annual reports of the proceedings of its conventions, as well as the *Rabbinical Assembly Bulletin*. Another publication is *Conservative Judaism*, a quarterly periodical. It also published a "Sabbath and Festival Prayer Book" in 1946 and a "Weekday Prayer Book" in 1961.

RABBINICAL COUNCIL OF AMERICA

Organized in 1924 as The Rabbinical Council of the Union of Orthodox Jewish Congregations, it merged in 1930 with the Rabbinical Association of the Rabbi Isaac Elchanan Theological Seminary under the new name of *Rabbinical Council of America*, which was incorporated as such in 1936. In 1943, the Alumni Association of the Hebrew Theological College of Chicago joined its ranks. The membership of the Rabbinical Council in 1960 numbered approximately 800 rabbis.

Some of its purposes as set forth in its constitution are: to advocate, teach and promote the practice and study of orthodox Judaism; to champion the right and the dignity of the Jewish people everywhere; to help build and strengthen the religious and general welfare of the State of Israel; to serve as a unifying force among orthodox rabbis in order that there be an authoritative voice expressing Torah views on all questions of proper interest to the American Jew.

The Rabbinical Council publishes bi-

One of the great Rembrandt van Rijn paintings of Jews, dated 1635. Like many of his other portraits of Jews, Rembrandt titled this one "Rabbi" too, though it was probably a Jewish merchant from Morocco then in Amsterdam.

Photograph of what is very likely the medieval tomb of some Islamic dignitary, but which is the place venerated as the "Tomb of Rachel" by Jews and Moslems alike. Rachel died en route to Beth-lehem.

monthly the *Rabbinical Council Record;* the semi-annual *Hadorom* in Hebrew; and the semi-annual *Tradition* in English. In 1960 there was published under the auspices of the Rabbinical Council "The Traditional Prayer Book, for Sabbath and Festivals."

RABBINITES see Karaites.

RACHEL

Younger daughter of Laban and favorite wife of Jacob. The Bible recounts that Jacob served Laban seven years in order to marry Rachel, but instead her elder sister Leah was substituted by ruse. Jacob was then compelled to work another seven years for the woman he loved. Childless for many years, Rachel later gave birth to Joseph. When Jacob left Laban and returned to Canaan, Rachel died on the way to Beth-lehem as she gave birth to

Benjamin. She was buried there, and her tomb still is a shrine on the road from Jerusalem to Hebron. Rachel is a favorite Biblical figure and the subject of many works of art as well as belles-lettres. The prophetic imagery of Rachel weeping for her exiled children is incorporated in the liturgy for the High Holy Days.

RADAK see Kimḥi, David.

RAIN see Geshem.

RAMBAM see Maimonides, Moses.

RAMBAN see Naḥmanides.

RANSOM OF CAPTIVES see Pidyon Shevuyim.

RAPHAEL

One of the seven angels who are mentioned frequently in Jewish and Christian folklore. Tradition has it that Raphael was one of the three angels who appeared to

This commentary on the Later Prophets by Rashi was written in France about 1250. Scarcity of vellum then forced the scribe to write around the holes and in the margins. The writing is in Rashi script.

Abraham. He is said to be endowed with the power of healing.

RAPOPORT, SOLOMON JUDAH LÖB (1790–1867)
Rabbi, leader of the *Haskalah* (Enlightenment) movement and historical researcher. He served as rabbi of Tarnopol and Prague, and was one of the founders of modern "Jewish Science." In addition to his several historiographical works, he completed the first volume of an encyclopedia of Judaism called *Erekh Millin*.

RASHBAM (ca. 1089–1174)
Abbreviated name of R. Samuel ben Meir, one of the great Bible commentators of northern France. He was a grandson of Rashi. As an author of commentaries, he completed some of Rashi's commentaries on the Bible and the Talmud, and wrote notes on several books of the Bible. He

is known for his use of the "Peshat," that is, the natural and simple meaning of the Biblical text, and for his clear and precise style. He was the brother of the well-known commentator Rabbenu Tam.

RASHI (1040–1105)
Abbreviated name of Rabbi Solomon Yitzḥaki or ben Isaac, author of the most popular commentary on the Bible and the Talmud. At the age of 25 he became rabbi at Troyes, France, where he spent most of his life. He founded a Talmudical academy which attracted students from many Jewish communities outside of France. His greatest and unsurpassed lifework were his written commentaries on almost the entire Talmud and on most of the books of the Bible. These commentaries soon became an indispensable aid in the study of both the Talmud and the Bible. Their

popularity grew during succeeding centuries, and even today they are the delight of young and adult students. Because of the extreme popularity of Rashi's work, his commentary on the Pentateuch had the unique distinction of being the first Hebrew book to be printed (1475). The texts of Rashi's commentaries are usually printed on the same page with those of the Bible and Talmud.

The distinguishing features of Rashi's commentaries are their simple, compact and precise Hebrew style. Whereas in his commentary on the Talmud Rashi attempted to convey the simple, natural and literal meaning of the text, his commentary on the Torah is often based upon *Midrashim* (Rabbinic folklore), the lessons of which he adapted as illustrations and elaborations of the literal meaning of the text. This combination of the literal with the folkloristic made the study of the Torah tremendously popular through the ages.

Because of his unequalled and gigantic work, Rashi became one of the most revered personalities in Jewish history. His work made the study of the Bible and Talmud accessible to the average student, and contributed to the widespread study of the Torah. It is therefore not surprising that the life of this great teacher is veiled with beautiful legends.

RASHI SCRIPT

While in the first place Rashi's commentaries were published as independent works, the custom of publishing them as part of the text to which they were written as commentary has spread. Text and commentary appeared on the same page. In order not to confuse the reader, printers ingeniously developed a special lettering for the commentary of Rashi. Thus this type of lettering came to be known as *Rashi Script*, and has since been used for other commentaries as well.

RATHENAU, WALTER (1867–1922)

German statesman, industrialist and philosopher. Born in Berlin, he became a successful engineer and subsequently wealthy industrialist. He became interested in politics, and during World War I helped the German government in the organization of its industry. In the post-war period he worked for the rehabilitation of Germany.

Rathenau was repeatedly exposed to anti-Semitic attacks by his political opponents, and in 1922, while in office as Foreign Minister, he was assassinated by a group of nationalist terrorists.

Although an assimilated Jew, Rathenau opposed conversion for personal advantage, and believed in Israel's mission among the nations. Influenced by Martin Buber's writings, he showed a keen interest in Biblical literature. In his own writings he expressed liberal economic and social views, and while upholding the capitalist system, he advocated humane and just treatment of the working class.

READING, MARQUESS OF, RUFUS DANIEL ISAACS (1860–1935)

First British Jew to be Lord Chief Justice, ambassador to the United States, and Viceroy of India. A member of a prominent Jewish family in Britain, Reading became a lawyer of note, rising to the office of Lord Chief Justice in 1913. During World War I he became one of the chief financial advisers of the British Government, going on important missions to the United States, where he served as ambassador in 1918. In 1921 he was appointed Viceroy of India where, despite the mistrust of the British, he succeeded in introducing important social reforms. For his invaluable services to Britain, many honors were conferred upon him, including the rank of Marquess, which is the highest of the four orders of knighthood.

Following the issuance of the Balfour

The Marquess of Reading, a leading Zionist and one of the British Empire's outstanding Jews.

Declaration, Reading, who always took pride in his Jewish ancestry, became interested in Zionism. He collaborated with Justice Louis D. Brandeis on Zionist economic projects, and in 1926 became president of the Palestine Electric Corporation. He visited Palestine in 1932 and became active in the political struggle of the Zionist movement.

REBBE

Common title (in contrast to that of "Rabbi") given to a Hasidic leader, that is, a *Tzaddik* or "Guter Yid." The term was also traditionally applied to a teacher in a Hebrew school.

REBEKAH

Wife of Isaac and mother of Esau and Jacob. The Bible recounts that she was chosen to be the wife of Isaac by Eliezer, Abraham's servant. Of her twin sons she preferred Jacob, whom she helped obtain his father's blessings.

RECIFE (PERNAMBUCO)

Seaport in Brazil where the earliest Jewish community in America was established. Recife became a Dutch colony in 1631, and because of its proclamation of religious freedom, the Marranos returned to their Jewish faith. In 1654 Recife was conquered by the Portuguese, and the Jewish community there came to an end. Twenty-three of those Jews who fled Recife set out to New Amsterdam (New York), and became known as the first Jewish settlers in North America. The modern small Jewish community of Recife dates back to 1900.

RECONSTRUCTIONISM

A modern religious movement in America, the principles and theory of which were formulated by Rabbi Mordecai M. Kaplan of New York. Followers of this movement, called "Reconstructionists," are rabbis and laymen who conceive of Judaism as being a "religious civilization," and not a religion exclusively. Judaism is a way of life based on religion, language, literature, customs and folkways, music and art, and a definite pattern of Jewish communal organization. To be a positive Jew one must identify himself with all aspects of Jewish life and be an active participant in the work for the survival of the Jewish community.

Emphasizing the need for a maximum Jewish life based on Jewish tradition, the Reconstructionists also maintain that Judaism must undergo constant change and development in accordance with the needs of modern conditions. Jewish life in America must thus be "reconstructed" to enable the modern Jew to derive full satisfaction from his association with the Jewish people.

The program of reconstructionist Judaism calls for: the need of having strong Jewish communities based on democratic

401

The Red Sea at sunset with coastal hills in the background. In the Biblical account of the Jews' departure from Egypt, Moses led them across the "Sea of Reeds," which later readers took to be the Red Sea.

organization; the importance of the State of Israel as a Jewish homeland and especially as a strong and influential cultural center for Jews throughout the world; the need of an intensive and effective Jewish educational system; and the need for a cooperative society based upon justice, freedom and peace as a condition for continued Jewish existence. The Reconstructionist Press publishes prayer books, a journal, and numerous pamphlets.

REDEMPTION OF THE FIRST-BORN see Pidyon ha-Ben.

RED MAGEN DAVID

Known by its Hebrew name *Magen David Adom*. The purpose and functions of this Jewish organization are similar to those of the Red Cross. It was first organized in 1918 in order to provide medical aid to the Jewish Legion in Palestine. The American Red Magen David was organ-

ized and supported by contributions from the Order of Sons of Zion.

RED SEA

The body of water referred to in the Bible as *Yam Suf* (Sea of Reeds), crossed miraculously by the Israelites after they were led out of Egypt by Moses. The Red Sea lies southeast of the Sinai Peninsula and is divided at its northern tip into the Gulf of Suez and the Gulf of Aqaba. The port of Eilat near the Gulf of Aqaba is the southernmost point of the State of Israel.

REFORM JUDAISM

A religious movement among Jews which began early in the 19th century in Germany and later developed in other European countries. Its main development was in the United States and it has become a most influential religious movement in American Jewry.

402

Reform Judaism came about as an opposition to some of the basic doctrines and practices of Judaism. The religious philosophy and practices of reform Jews relate themselves to the following: 1) That the belief in revelation should be rejected by modern Jews. It is inconceivable that God spoke directly to people, or that the Torah is God-given in the strictest sense of the word. The Torah is rather a creation of the Jewish people, who were inspired by God to make laws of righteousness. The story of Creation is simply an account of how the Israelites imagined the creation of the world; 2) That the Torah was conceived by divinely inspired men and not God-given, and therefore every generation has the right to accept only those laws of the Torah and those practices which are essential, and to reject those which are no longer necessary or practicable; 3) That since the Torah represents the highest conception of the God-idea as taught in the Holy Scriptures, the Jewish people were destined to fulfill a great mission among the nations of the earth—the teaching of the belief in God and the ethical ideals of brotherhood, justice and peace.

In accordance with the above principles, reform Judaism emphasizes the ethical teachings of the Torah, the Talmud and the other sacred writings, and the ritual is given secondary importance. Reform Jews do not adhere to the tradition of daily public prayer, and services are held on Sabbaths and holidays only. In the reform synagogue or temple, as it is generally called, men are usually not required to cover their heads, or to wear a *Tallit* (prayer shawl), men and women sit together during the services, and the organ is played even on the Sabbath and the sacred days.

Reform Judaism does not obligate its adherents to refrain from work on the Sabbath and the holidays. To assure greater participation of the worshippers, the prayer book used in the reform congregations includes more English than Hebrew prayers, and many traditional prayers have been omitted. Reform Jews further believe that the traditional laws of *Kashrut* (Dietary Laws) as well as many of the practices and ceremonies in the home and the synagogue, have outgrown their purposes, and are no longer considered essential.

The growth of reform Judaism in the United States was in no small measure due to the quality and zeal of its leadership. Among the early leaders of reform Judaism in America were Rabbi Isaac M. Wise and Rabbi David Einhorn who were active in the latter part of the 19th century. To unite the efforts of reform congregations, Rabbi Isaac M. Wise formed the Union of American Hebrew Congregations in 1873 and established the Hebrew Union College in Cincinnati in 1875, and the Central Conference of American Rabbis in 1889.

REHOVOT

One of the largest and most flourishing of the older agricultural colonies in Israel. Situated a few miles southeast of Tel Aviv and Jaffa, it was founded in 1890 by Russian Jews. It became a center for the cultivation of citrus fruits and has become the Agricultural Experimental Station established by the government. Rehovot is also famous for its important Weizmann Research Institute, named after Dr. Chaim Weizmann, renowned as a scientist and first President of the State of Israel.

REISEN, ABRAHAM (1876–1953)

Yiddish poet and short story writer. Born in Russia, he settled in the United States in 1914, when he already had an international reputation as a Yiddish writer. In his many volumes of poetry and short stories, he deals chiefly with problems of the simple and poor people, their daily life struggles, ambitions and disappointments. Many of his poems possess the quality of genuine folk songs, and have been set to music. Much of his literary work reflected socialistic sympathies and gave expression to his yearning for a new social order free of prejudice and exploitation. Reisen was one of the most favored and widely read poets among the Yiddish masses.

REJOICING OF THE TORAH see Simhat Torah.

REPENTANCE

The Hebrew term for "repentance" is *Teshuvah* (return), meaning that an individual will have his sins forgiven by "turning back to God," that is, by turning from the ways of wrongdoing to the ways of righteousness. Repentance as a condition for the salvation of Israel or the individual, Jew or non-Jew, is stressed both in the Bible and in rabbinic literature. Thus it is said that "the gates of prayer (*Tefillah*) may be shut, but the gates of repentance (*Teshuvah*) are ever open." Jewish law distinguishes between sins committed against God and those committed against man. Offenses against God may be forgiven if the sinner will confess and promise not to repeat the sin; but offenses against man will not be forgiven by God unless the sinner first makes amends to the person wronged. Jewish tradition regards repentance so important that one who truly repents is considered superior to the sinless. See *Sin*.

RESH (ר)

The twentieth letter of the Hebrew alphabet. It is pronounced like the uvular R of Parisian French. Its numerical value is 200. Its probable meaning is "head."

RESH GALUTA see Exilarch.

RESPONSA see Sheelot U-Teshuvot.

RESURRECTION

The earliest definite references to the belief in the resurrection of the body are found in the books of *Isaiah*, *Ezekiel*, and *Daniel*, although verses in the Torah and other Biblical books have been interpreted by the Rabbis as referring to this doctrine. During the period of the Second Temple the Pharisees emphasized the importance of this belief, and the Sadducees denied it. In the course of time the doctrine of Resurrection was discussed by many thinkers. Some Jewish teachers believed that only the righteous would be resurrected, and others maintained that both the just and the wicked would be resurrected, but the former will be rewarded, while the latter will be punished. Orthodox Jews believe in *Tehiyat ha-Metim* (Resurrection), and reform Jews generally reject this idea. There are discussions in rabbinic literature and in medieval philosophic and mystical literature to the effect that resurrection will take place in relation to "the End of Days," the coming of the Messiah. Resurrection is a fundamental belief in Jewish tradition, as it is in Christianity. Many reform Jews, while rejecting the doctrine of the resurrection of the body, accept the doctrine of immortality of the soul. Conservative Jews have no uniform doctrine in the matter. Reconstructionism denies resurrection, and accepts a modified idea of immortality. See *Death*.

REUBEN

Eldest son of Jacob and ancestor of the tribe of the same name. His mother was Leah, Jacob's first wife. The Bible recounts that Reuben pleaded with his brothers not to kill Joseph but to cast him into a pit instead. The tribe of Reuben was permitted by Moses to settle east of the Jordan on condition that it would later join the other Israelite tribes in the conquest of Canaan.

REUBENI, DAVID (c. 1491–c. 1535)

Messianic pretender. Born in Khaibar, Arabia, he appeared in 1522 in Egypt and Italy claiming to be the brother of the king of Khaibar, presumed ruler of a Jewish state. As the apparent emissary of the Ten Lost Tribes, his mission was to obtain military assistance from the Christian rulers of Europe to fight the Turks. He was received by Pope Clement VII, and later by the king of Portugal, who promised him a military alliance. However, Reubeni's prestige at court caused a great sensation among the persecuted secret Jews, the Marranos, who now saw a possibility of returning to Judaism. One of them, a young government official, became Reubeni's devoted follower, returned to Judaism, and under the name of Solomon Molko went to Turkey and then to Italy, where he was hailed as messiah. The agitation caused by Reubeni among the Marranos forced him to leave Portugal. He joined Molko in Italy, and both aroused messianic hopes among the Jewish masses. Meanwhile they lost the favor of the pope, and as they went to Ratisbon in order to interest Emperor Charles V in the crusade against the Turks, they were both arrested. Molko was burned at the stake, but Reubeni was brought back to Spain where he died as a prisoner of the Inquisition.

REUTER, BARON PAUL JULIUS VON (1816–1899)

Founder of Reuter's News Service and Agency. Born in Germany as Israel Josephthal, he settled in France where he founded a pigeon post service. He went to London (1851) where he established the Reuter Telegraph Agency. In 1865 he laid the first cable between America and France, and thus developed the largest telegraph agency in the world.

REVEL, BERNARD (1885–1940)

Founder and president of Yeshiva College and leader of orthodox Jewry in America. Born in Lithuania, he settled in the United States in 1906, where he continued his advanced studies combining great Jewish and secular learning. Despite a successful business career, he agreed in 1915 to head the Rabbi Isaac Elchanan Theological Seminary which became the Yeshiva College in 1928. This was the first college of liberal arts and sciences under Jewish sponsorship in the diaspora. In 1937 Revel founded a graduate school for Jewish studies, later named the Bernard Revel Graduate School. Revel became a recognized leader of orthodox Jewry, and his influence was felt in various orthodox Jewish organizations in America. He was a devoted supporter of Zionism, and in recognition of his Zionist activities a forest bearing his name was planted on the land of the Jewish National Fund in Israel. See *Yeshiva University*.

REVELATION

One of the fundamental beliefs of orthodox Judaism is that God makes known His will through revelation of Himself or His teachings to a single man or a group of men. From Adam till the latest Prophets, God revealed Himself to men. The greatest of all was God's revelation at Sinai, where the Israelites received the Law. Since the Torah was given by God directly, according to the orthodox view, its teachings are therefore unalterable and fundamental for all time and all generations.

REVISIONISTS

A Zionist party, particularly active before the establishment of the State of Israel. Founded in 1925 by Vladimir Jabotinsky, the Revisionists became an extremist Zionist group. Dissatisfied with moderate Zionist political aspirations and with the slow pace set by the other Zionist groups for the attainment of the Zionist political and economic program in Palestine, the Revisionists, as their name implies, demanded drastic and even militant revisions of the Zionist program.

The political objectives of the Revisionist party were: the establishment of a Jewish commonwealth in the historic land of Israel on both sides of the Jordan; the establishment of a Jewish majority through mass immigration controlled by Jews; and the organization of a Jewish army that would protect the colonization efforts from Arab interference. The Revisionist economic program called for large private capital investments and for unlimited capitalist enterprises. They were strongly opposed to the program of the labor party and *Histadrut*.

In 1935 the Revisionists withdrew from the World Zionist Organization and established the New Zionist Organization with its own strong youth organization *Brit Trumpeldor* (Betar).

The Revisionists had followers both in Palestine and the diaspora. Out of its ranks emerged the *Irgun*, an illegal military organization during the time of the British mandate in Palestine. The program of *Herut*, an Israeli political party, is largely dedicated to the principles and aspirations of the former Revisionist party.

RIBALOW, MENAHEM (1899–1953)

Important figure in American Hebrew literature. Born in Russia, he settled in the United States in 1921 and became associated with the *Histadrut Ivrit* (Hebrew Organization) of America, and served for over 30 years as editor of the Hebrew weekly *Hadoar*. He wrote several volumes of essays on ancient and modern Hebrew literature; compiled an anthology of Hebrew poetry in America; edited six volumes of the American Hebrew Year Book, and contributed to various periodicals in Hebrew, Yiddish and English. Ribalow's

literary and cultural activities had a considerable influence on the revival of the Hebrew movement in the United States.

RIESSER, GABRIEL (1806–1863)

Champion of Jewish emancipation in Germany. Born in Hamburg, Germany, he studied law, but being a Jew was denied admission to the bar. He thus began an unrelenting fight for the emancipation of Jews in Germany, denouncing the assimilationists and demanding political and civil liberties for the Jewish masses. Despite classical German anti-Semitism, his efforts were crowned with success after the Revolution of 1848. Riesser himself was elected to the parliament and in 1860 was appointed member of the high court in Hamburg, thus being the first Jewish judge in Germany. Riesser was considered by German Jewry as one of its most esteemed spokesman.

RISHONIM see Codes.

RISHON LE-ZION

An early agricultural colony in modern Israel. Situated a few miles southeast of Jaffa, it was founded in 1882 by the *Biluim*, the early pioneers among Russian Jews. It first became known for its wine cellars, built by Baron Edmond de Rothschild, but later developed as an important center of orange cultivation.

RITUAL BATH see Mikveh.

RITUAL MURDER see Blood Accusation.

ROCK OF AGES see Maoz Tzur.

ROME

The Jewish community in Rome is one of the oldest in Europe. Jews settled there during the Hasmonean period (2nd century b.c.e.) and their number increased considerably during the Roman wars in Palestine. The early settlers enjoyed almost equal rights, exercised great influence on the public and economic life of the city, and established academies, synagogues, and a Jewish communal organization. Both under pagan and Christian rule, the Jewish community of Rome continued its uninterrupted existence from ancient times to the present day. The flourishing Roman Jewish community began to decline after 1555, when the Jewish ghetto was established. For over two centuries the miserable conditions of ghetto life persisted with its poverty, pestilence, heavy taxation and forced baptism of Jewish children. The ghetto system was abolished after the French Revolution in 1798, but was restored after the fall of Napoleon in 1814. Conditions improved during the time of Pope Pius IX (1846-1878), but the ghetto system continued until 1870 when Rome became part of the kingdom of Italy. Since then, and until Mussolini's Fascist government joined hands with the Nazi regime in Germany, the Jews enjoyed complete equality, and contributed greatly to the economic, commercial and cultural life of that ancient and great city.

ROSENBLATT, YOSSELE (1880–1933)

World-famous cantor. Born in Russia, he began his public appearances at the age of nine, and ultimately became one of the greatest cantors of his time. At seventeen he studied music at Vienna, later served as cantor at Munkacs, Hungary, then at Hamburg, Germany, where he published original compositions titled *Zemirot Yosef*. Rosenblatt's first position in the United States was with the Hungarian Congregation Oheb Zedek of New York. During World War I, he made many appearances for Liberty Bonds and other public purposes. His popularity became worldwide through his numerous recordings of liturgical music and his appearances in the United States and Europe. Being an orthodox cantor, he declined an offer of 2,000

Yossele Rosenblatt, brilliant 20th-century cantor known for his lyrical voice and cantillations.

dollars per appearance made by the Chicago Opera Company. Among his better known publications are *Psalm 113* (1921), *Psalm 114* (1922), and *Tefillot Yosef* (1927). When engaged to sing in a Jewish film, *The Dream of My People*, he went to Palestine in 1933, where he died of a heart attack.

ROSENFELD, MORRIS (1862–1923)

One of the most significant Yiddish poets. Born in Russia, he began writing at the age of fifteen. As a Russian emigrant, he worked in Amsterdam, Holland as a diamond-cutter, and then in London as a tailor. In 1886 he went to the United States, where he worked in the sweatshops which he immortalized in his dynamic poetry. In his first book of poetry, *Di Gloke* (The Bell, 1889), he described the plight of workers. He later published his second book of verse *Di Blumen-Kaite* (The

ROSENWALD, JULIUS

Morris Rosenfeld, Yiddish poet, wrote many revolutionary lyrics about America's sweatshops.

Flower Wreath), and at the same time contributed to several Yiddish publications. His revolutionary songs were widely sung and recited at workers' meetings and concerts. Rosenfeld himself made numerous appearances both in the United States and Europe, where he recited and sang his popular poems. Professor Leo Wiener of Harvard University became attracted to Rosenfeld's third book of verse *Dos Liederbuch* (The Book of Songs, 1897), and later published a complete English translation of his poetry entitled *Songs of the Ghetto*. Despite his popularity, Rosenfeld died a poor man.

ROSENWALD, JULIUS (1862–1932)

One of the greatest American Jewish philanthropists. Son of Samuel and Augusta Rosenwald, both immigrants from Germany, he started in the clothing business,

and in 1893 joined Sears, Roebuck and Company, which, under his direction, became the greatest mail-order business in the world. As the head of the firm he became a multi-millionaire, and spent a large share of his wealth on humanitarian causes.

Rosenwald is especially remembered as the benefactor of the Negro people in the United States. With the help of his generous contributions, Y.M.C.A. buildings for Negroes were erected in twenty-five cities. He further subsidized, in the amount of some 28 million dollars, various educational facilities for the Negro population, and provided for the building of elementary schools for Negroes in the South. He also established the Julius Rosenwald Fund (1917) with a capital of thirty million dollars for the administration of his charitable work for Negro and other humanitarian causes.

Rosenwald's major contributions to Jewish causes include the following: The Associated Jewish Charities of Chicago; Jewish relief during World War I, Jewish colonization projects in Russia, and to a smaller extent, in Palestine; and substantial gifts to the Hebrew Union College in Cincinnati, and The Jewish Theological Seminary in New York. He contributed additionally and substantially to the University of Chicago, as well as to the International Ladies' Garment Workers' Union for the purpose of combatting sweatshop conditions.

ROSH HASHANAH

Hebrew term meaning "the head of the year" applied to the Jewish New Year observance. Rosh Hashanah is celebrated on the first and second days of the month of *Tishre* (September-October), and marks the beginning of the *Ten Days of Penitence*. Rosh Hashanah, traditionally regarded as the first day of Creation, is also called *Yom ha-Zikaron* (The Day of Re-

Here shown in an old print is "Tashlikh," one of the Rosh Hashanah ceremonies in which Jews at a river bank cast their sins symbolically "into the depths of the sea" while reciting the related prayers.

membrance), and *Yom ha-Din* (Day of Judgment), in which God remembers all His creatures and passes judgment on all human beings, thus determining their lot for the year to come. Rosh Hashanah is also named *Yom Teruah* (The Day of the Blowing of the Ram's Horn) as a symbol of God's summons to the people for self-judgment, self-improvement and atonement. During the entire month of *Elul* it is customary to sound the *Shofar* in the synagogue as a solemn announcement of the approach of Rosh Hashanah. Before dawn during the week prior to Rosh Hashanah, penitential prayers (*Seliḥot*) are recited as part of a special service.

The days of Rosh Hashanah are devoted to prayer, solemn festivities and rest from work. At mealtime it is customary to eat sweets, such as apples and honey, as a symbol of the hope for a sweet and good year to come. A special ceremony of Rosh Hashanah is *Tashlikh*, the "casting out of sins." It takes place on the afternoon of the first day of Rosh Hashanah (or the second day if the first is on a Sabbath), when Jews go to the banks of a river, and recite prayers relating to the forgiveness of sins. Reform Jews observe only the first day of Rosh Hashanah.

ROSH ḤODESH

Hebrew term meaning the "beginning of a month" applied to the religious half-holiday observed in connection with the appearance of the New Moon; that is, the beginning of each new month of the Hebrew calendar. In ancient times the celebration of *Rosh Ḥodesh* was more important than it is today. In the Jewish year, based on the lunar system, the arrival of the New Moon was used by the *San-*

409

Baron Edmond de Rothschild, philanthropist and banker, pioneered Zionist colonization.

hedrin (Jewish High Court) as a means of fixing the calendar, and was therefore heralded with great solemnity. After the destruction of the Temple and the weakening of the Jewish community in Palestine, the times for the observance of Rosh Ḥodesh and the holidays were established from a universally known calendar formula. On the Sabbath preceding the New Moon, a special prayer is offered for a good month.

ROTHSCHILD, BARON EDMOND DE (1845–1934)

Famous philanthropist and father of Jewish colonization projects in Palestine. As the head of the Rothschild bank in Paris, he was known in Hebrew as *ha-Nadiv ha-Yadua* (the well-known Benefactor) because at first he declined to reveal his identity as the benefactor of the Jewish community in Palestine. As a result of the anti-Jewish riots in Russia in 1881, he be-

came interested in philanthropic work in behalf of the persecuted Jews of east Europe. Influenced by the famous "lover of Zion," Rabbi Samuel Mohilever, Rothschild undertook to finance a number of colonies established by the early Jewish pioneers in Palestine. He subsequently built the famous wine cellars in Rishon Le-Zion and Zikhron Yaakov, and invested over 50 million dollars in various colonization projects under the management of the PICA (Palestine Jewish Colonization Association). The gratitude of the Jewish community in Palestine for his selfless humanitarian work and for his unequalled contributions to the rebuilding of the Jewish homeland was universal, and during his several visits to Palestine he was given most enthusiastic receptions. *Binyaminah*, one of the colonies in Israel, as well as one of the famous boulevards in Tel Aviv, bears his name.

ROTHSCHILD, HOUSE OF

Internationally known family of financiers and philanthropists. Originating in Frankfort, Germany in the 16th century, the Rothschild family lived in a house in the Judengasse (Jew Street) identified by a red shield, hence the name of Rothschild. The founder of the first Rothschild bank in Frankfort was Amschel Moses Rothschild. His five sons subsequently headed the five major branches of the Rothschild banking enterprises in Germany, Austria, France, Italy and England. Until the first quarter of the 20th century, the Rothschild House occupied a most important place in international finance and banking enterprises. The Rothschilds had undertaken important international financial transactions and projects; organized loans to governments; financed the building of railroads; and in general did much to aid progress in the modern world.

The Rothschilds also became famous

for their interest in Jewish affairs and for their Jewish philanthropic work. Best known for his humanitarian work is Baron Edmond de Rothschild, who financed Jewish colonization projects in Palestine. The Rothschilds protected Jewish communities against political and religious discrimination, and frequently refused loans to governments which mistreated the Jewish population.

The prominence and wealth of the Rothschilds declined considerably during the second quarter of the twentieth century, as did their influence.

RUMANIA

South European country which until the Second World War had about a million Jews out of a total population of 19 million. Some authorities believe that Jews settled in the territory of Rumania, the ancient Roman colony Dacia, in the first century c.e. During the 8th century, when the Khazars ruled in that territory, there were a number of Jewish communities there. Following the expulsion from Spain (1492), several Sephardi Jewish communities were established in the Rumanian provinces, and between the 16th and the 18th centuries Jewish immigrants from Poland and the Ukraine increased the Jewish population.

Persecutions of Jews in Rumania were almost constant and the Jewish communities were subjected to blood accusations, expulsions, and medieval discriminatory laws. Rumania failed to live up to the provisions of the Berlin Congress of 1878, in which the Jews were promised equal political and civil rights. As a result of the annexation of Bessarabia, Bukovina and Transylvania after World War I, the Jewish population of Rumania almost trebled. Despite the official recognition of Jewish minority rights, the underprivileged status of the Jews continued to exist during the

post-war period. Because of persistent anti-Semitism, Rumanian Jews emigrated in large numbers to the United States, Palestine and South American countries.

The annexation of Bessarabia and Bukovina by the Soviet Union in 1940, and the Nazi atrocities, caused the Jewish population in Rumania to dwindle to less than a quarter of a million.

The Jewish community in Rumania produced a number of distinguished rabbis, scholars and Jewish leaders, such as Rabbi Nathan N. Hanover, Rabbi Moses Gaster and Rabbi Solomon Schechter. Rumania is also known as the cradle of the modern Yiddish theatre, founded by the playwright Abraham Goldfaden.

RUSSIA

One of the largest countries in the world, extending over east and north Europe and north and mid-Asia. Until 1917 Russia was ruled by Tsars, and following the Bolshevist revolution it became known as the Union of Soviet Socialist Republics. Jews came to Russia as early as the 9th century from the Kingdom of the Khazars, and later from Crimea, Ukraine, Lithuania, Poland, Galicia, and Bessarabia, which had at different periods been under Russian rule. During the 11th and the 12th centuries, and still later during the 15th century, large numbers of Russians embraced the Jewish faith, and the early Jewish settlers, mainly merchants and physicians, were under suspicion of conversionist activity and therefore subject to the anger of the Russian clergy and to persecution by Ivan the Terrible. Most of the Tsars were known as outspoken foes of the Jews, and after the annexation of Poland and the Ukraine, anti-Jewish decrees multiplied. In 1804 the *Pale of Settlement* was established, in which the residence of Jews was restricted to certain districts of the Russian empire.

411

Large synagogue in Leningrad, Russia, completed in 1893. Note the Russian-style architecture. The cultural and political capital of Russia, Leningrad was also the center of Jewish press and publishing.

For a short period during the reign of Alexander I (1801–1825), the condition of the Jews improved somewhat, but under the rule of Nicholas I (1825–1855), the anti-Jewish policy was renewed. Nicholas I initiated a policy of forced conversion of Jews to Christianity by means of recruiting Jewish boys for a twenty-five year period of military service. Since each community had to meet a certain quota of such recruits, known as *Cantonists*, the recruitment was carried out against bitter protests of the parents and by the use of official kidnappers. The government also attempted to Russify the Jews by providing Russian schools for Jewish children, the real purpose of which was to wean the younger Jews from Jewish traditions and lead them to eventual baptism. During the more liberal reign of Tsar Alexander II, the recruitment of the Cantonists was abolished, but Alexander III adopted the restrictive "May Laws" and encouraged widespread terror against the Jewish population, and frequent pogroms. The anti-Jewish riots of 1881 resulted in mass emigration of Russian Jews to America, England and Palestine. It was during that period that the *Ḥovevei Zion* (Lovers of Zion) movement, as well as the Jewish socialist movement ("Bund") were created. Conditions became even worse during the reign of Nicholas II (1894–1917) who, despite the fact that he was forced to liberalize the government and to institute parliamentary rule, nevertheless used the Jews as scapegoats for the miserable conditions of the Russian peasants, and accused them of being the instigators of the revolutionary activities of the Russian socialists. The Tsar provoked repeated pogroms, as well as the infamous Beilis trial of 1913.

The Kerensky revolution of 1917 brought an end to the Tsarist regime as well as to anti-Jewish limitations. Under the subsequent Soviet regime Jews were theoretically granted complete political and civil equality. The Soviet government, although presumably encouraging Jewish cultural autonomy, and the establishment of Yiddish schools, strongly opposed all Zionist and Hebrew cultural activities. The Soviet regime attempted to establish a Jewish autonomous state in Biro-Bidjan, but the project attracted only a few Jewish farmers. After World War II the Stalin regime in Soviet Russia became anti-Semitic, gradually much of the cultural autonomy of Soviet Jews was liquidated, and most of the Yiddish writers were accused of counter-revolutionary activities and consequently imprisoned or annihilated. Behind the so-called "Iron Curtain" of the Soviet regime in 1960, the fate of the three million Russian Jews was uncertain. While the Soviet Union joined the other great powers in favoring the establishment of the State of Israel in 1947, it subsequently adopted a violent anti-Israel and pro-Arab policy.

RUTENBERG. PINHAS (1879–1942)

Engineering industrialist and developer of hydro-electric power in Palestine. Born in Russia, he became active in the social revolutionary movement there. He studied engineering in Italy, became interested in Zionism, and during his subsequent stay in the United States supported the formation of the Jewish Legion in Palestine during World War I. After visiting Palestine under the British mandate, he studied the water resources of the country and devised his plan of using the falls of the Jordan River for hydro-electric power. With the consent of the British he formed the Palestine Electric Corporation in 1923. This project contributed greatly to the development of modern Palestine, and Rutenberg attained an international reputation. He served for a short time as a member of the *Vaad Leumi* (the Jewish National Council of Palestine). When he died he was mourned by millions throughout the Jewish world, and was buried on the Mount of Olives.

RUTH

One of the books contained in the *Ketuvim* (Writings), the third section of the Bible, and the second of the Five Scrolls, read in the synagogue on the festival of Shavuot. The book tells the charming story of a Moabite woman who embraced Judaism. After the death of her Judean husband, Ruth left her native Moab and went, together with her mother-in-law, Naomi, to Beth-lehem, in Judea. Here she married Boaz, a wealthy farmer, and King David was one of their descendants.

S SYNAGOGUE

Build Thy Temple as of yore,

Establish Thy sanctuary on its site.

PRAYER BOOK

SAADIAH GAON

SAADIAH GAON (882—942)

Title of R. Saadiah ben Joseph, leading philosopher, Talmudist, Bible translator and Hebrew philologist. Born in Egypt, he became the greatest Jewish legal authority of his time, and was among the early Jewish scholars who concerned themselves with Arabic philosophy. Saadiah Gaon played a decisive role in two major controversies in Jewish life, which had nearly caused a complete rift and disunity among the Jewish communities the world over. Thanks to his great scholarship, reputation and leadership he successfully fought the disrupting influence of the Karaite sect which rejected the authority of the Talmud. He also prevented the acceptance of certain revisions of the traditional Jewish calendar advocated by Ben Meir, the head of an academy in Palestine. For these and other accomplishments his fame reached every major Jewish community; he was appointed head of the Academy of Sura by the Exilarch of Babylonia, and he brought to it additional distinction and authority. A man of great integrity, he soon aroused the anger of the Exilarch for his refusal to give approval to an unjust legal decision. Saadiah Gaon was forced to flee to Baghdad where he lived for seven years before he was reinstated to his position as the Gaon of the Academy of Sura.

Saadiah Gaon made important contributions to Jewish learning and philosophy. At the age of twenty-one he compiled a Hebrew dictionary, *Agron*, and years later he wrote an Arabic translation of and commentaries to the Bible. His greatest philosophic work, written in Arabic, was his *Book of Beliefs and Opinions*, later translated into Hebrew under the name of *Sefer Ha-Emunot Veha-Deot*. This book, in which he attempted to reconcile Greek philosophy with the teachings of the Bible, had great influence on Jewish and Chris-

tian thought and became one of the basic works of medieval religious philosophy. As a defender of traditional Judaism he produced some great polemic writings against the heresies of his time.

SABBATH

Weekly day of rest observed in Judaism on the seventh day of the week in accordance with Biblical injunction, and called *Shabbat* in Hebrew. The observance of the Sabbath is one of the chief foundations of Judaism. It is frequently mentioned in the Bible, and specifically ordained in the Ten Commandments: "Remember the Sabbath day, to keep it holy. Six days shalt thou labor and do all thy work, but the seventh day is the Sabbath of the Lord thy God." In the Friday night *Kiddush*, the traditional benediction (over wine or bread) for ushering in the Sabbath, the observance of the Sabbath is symbolically associated with both the creation of the world and the exodus from Egypt.

The Talmud contains a special tractate called "Shabbat" which deals with the regulations and laws governing the observance of the Sabbath. Such regulations were necessary in order to implement the spirit of the Sabbath under the changing conditions of life. Historical records of the Maccabean wars show that because of the holiness of the Sabbath, Jews had refused to defend themselves on that day even in the face of attack by the enemy, and did so only by special permission of Jewish legal authorities.

Despite numerous restrictions connected with its observance, the Sabbath is traditionally regarded not as a burden, but rather as a day of physical and spiritual joy. The traditional observance of the Sabbath calls for solemnity, the eating of special foods, the wearing of one's best garments, participation in public services in the synagogue, the chanting of *Zemirot*

This 19th-century painting by Viennese artist Isidor Kaufmann shows a Jewish woman ushering in the Sabbath with the ritual lighting and blessing of the Sabbath candles just before the onset of evening.

(Sabbath songs), physical rest, and periods of study and reading from the Scriptures and other holy books. The following practices are noted: 1) The blessing over the candles prior to sunset on Friday generally by the housewife; 2) Attendance at public services in the synagogue; 3) Upon returning from the synagogue, evening and morning, the *Kiddush* is recited; 4) Partaking of *Shalosh Seudot* (three Sabbath meals), one on Friday evening, one at noon on the Sabbath day, and the last in the late afternoon, frequently in the synagogue. The third meal is technically called *Seudah Shelishit*, but popularly known as "Shalesh Sudes"; 5) The singing of *Zemirot* during meals; 6) Study, and in particular the reading of the week's Torah section, with *Targum* (translation)

or commentary; and 7) The *Havdalah* ceremony on Sabbath night, marking the conclusion of the Sabbath.

In our days many synagogues and other institutions have adopted the *Oneg Shabbat* (Joy of the Sabbath) celebration, which they hold on Friday night or Saturday afternoon, and which generally includes musical selections, a lecture or dramatic presentation, and the serving of various refreshments.

SABBATH, SPIRIT OF THE

The idea that man is entitled to a day of rest each week is so widely accepted today that it is hard to realize that, when established in the Bible as an obligation of man, it was a revolutionary contribution to civilization. Tradition considers the Sabbath

417

a foretaste of the *Olam ha-Ba* (world to come). Not only was man and his household commanded to rest, but even his animals. The Sabbath is to be also a day of joy.

The stories of writers like I. L. Peretz convey some idea of what the Sabbath meant in the life of east European Jews. Even the humblest man became a king, and his wife a queen on the Sabbath. The best meals of the week were eaten then, and it was a particular *Mitzvah* to have a guest, preferably poor, for the Sabbath. It was customary to sing at the table, and to use one's finest linens, dishes, and silverware. No work was to be done, and the day was devoted to study and resting.

The Sabbath was likened to a "Queen," and to a beautiful bride. Thus the traditional celebration on Saturday night is called *Melavveh Malkah*—the leavetaking of the Queen. The historical significance of the Sabbath in Jewish life is epitomized in Aḥad Ha-Am's profound statement: It is not the Jew who has preserved the Sabbath, it is the Sabbath which has preserved the Jew."

SABBATHS, SPECIAL

Those Sabbaths which are connected with special occasions such as holidays, half-holidays, and fast days. Such Sabbaths are generally marked by an additional Torah reading making reference to the specific occasion, or a special *Haftarah*, or both. On many of these special Sabbaths, added prayers (Piyyutim) are also recited. During the month before the Passover (i.e., the month of Adar), several Sabbaths have interesting historical connotations. The Sabbath before Adar begins (or Rosh Ḥodesh Adar when it falls on a Sabbath) is called *Shabbat Shekalim*, a reminder that the universal poll tax of a half-shekel for the support of the sacrifices in Jerusalem was collected in Adar. The Sabbath before

Purim is *Shabbat Zakhor*, a reminder of the eternal enemies of Israel. *Shabbat Parah* deals with the laws of purification (necessary prior to partaking of the paschal lamb). *Shabbat ha-Ḥodesh* (Sabbath of the Month) is observed on the Sabbath preceding the month of Nisan (or on Rosh Ḥodesh Nisan if it falls on the Sabbath), because the Bible designates the month of Nisan (or Abib) as the first of the months. The Sabbath before Passover is *Shabbat ha-Gadol* (the Great Sabbath).

Among the other special Sabbaths may be mentioned: *Shabbat Ḥazon*, the Sabbath before Tishah Be-Av; *Shabbat Naḥamu*, the Sabbath after Tishah Be-Av (the first of the seven "comforting" Sabbaths preceding Rosh Hashanah); *Shabbat Shuvah* or *Teshuvah* (the Penitential Sabbath), the Sabbath between Rosh Hashanah and Yom Kippur; *Shabbat Bereshit* (Genesis), the first Sabbath after Simḥat Torah (when the annual cycle of reading the Torah is begun); and *Shabbat Hanukkah*. On the last Sabbath of each month (except Elul), a prayer is recited asking that the month to come be a good one, both spiritually and materially. Such a Sabbath is called *Shabbat Mevarekhim* (the Sabbath on which one prays for a good month). If the beginning of the month (Rosh Ḥodesh) falls on a Sabbath, an additional Torah portion and a special Haftarah are read; if Rosh Ḥodesh comes on the next day (that is, on Sunday), then a special Haftarah is recited, but there is no special Torah reading.

SABBATICAL YEAR

Every seventh year, called in Hebrew *Shemitah*, in which, according to the

The Hebrew year 5719 (1958-59) was a "Shemitah," or Sabbatical year. Right, its official ending is marked on Mt. Zion by rabbinical proclamation on the second day of Sukkot, thereby permitting the land to be worked again.

Young Sabras (native-born Israelis) at a kindergarten on a Kibbutz settlement. On most Kibbutzim, children are raised communally by people chosen by Kibbutz members rather than in individual homes.

Bible, the land had to lie fallow and both the soil and the farmer have complete rest in the land of Israel. Also during that year all outstanding debts were cancelled. This last provision was subsequently modified by Hillel through the institution of the *Pruzbol*. The sabbatical principle is followed in the statute of limitations of the modern western world, as well as in the periodic sabbatical leave in academic circles. In modern Israel, certain religious and juridical accommodations are permitted by the rabbinate.

SABBETAIANS see Shabbetai Tzevi.

SABORAIM

Aramaic term meaning "reasoners" applied to a group of Babylonian teachers (the followers of the *Amoraim*), who completed the Babylonian Talmud. Their activity was confined to several decades in the sixth century. See *Gaon*.

420

Large altar for burnt-offerings was discovered at Megiddo. This primitive method of idolatry frequently involved human sacrifice and other bestial practices, and was prohibited by the Bible and the Prophets.

SABRA

Hebrew term applied to the native-born of Israel. It is in fact the proper name of a prickly cactus plant of Israel, which is sturdy, enduring, and able to withstand hardship, and yet good-tasting. It has thus become descriptive of Israeli-born youth, and by extension refers to all native Israelis.

SACRIFICE

From the earliest times, people felt the need to offer something precious to their God or gods, either as an expression of gratitude for the blessings bestowed on them, or perhaps as a way of saying to the mysterious gods who were as frequently maleficent as beneficent: here, take this and please do not destroy the rest. Primitive people frequently offered their first-born children, animals and earth products as sacrifices.

The Bible prohibits human sacrifice and

421

View of Safed, one of Palestine's four "holy cities." Called the "mystic" town because it was the home of the "Kabbalah" movement, it overlooks the Mediterranean and Sea of Galilee from the hills.

regulates other types of sacrifice, taking into consideration the practices of other peoples, as a means of weaning the Israelites away from pagan cultic practices. It is difficult for modern man to understand completely the frame of mind of the ancients who looked upon animal sacrifice as a proper way of worshipping. Even Greek philosophers such as Socrates, and Jewish philosophers such as Philo accepted these sacrifices as proper and normal. The Hebrew prophets attacked the practice of their day. Some scholars hold that they rejected animal sacrifice outright, and others that the prophetic objection was to sacrifice as a substitute for ethics. The Rabbis of the Talmud and the later centuries, men of intellect and refinement, took animal sacrifice for granted.

Verbal prayer became a more and more important practice in the days of the Second Temple, both as an accompaniment to the sacrifice and as a substitute for it for those who dwelt too far for regular attendance at the Temple. By the time the Temple was destroyed and all animal sacrifice thereby abolished, verbal prayer was well established among the Jewish people, and was considered an adequate substitute for animal sacrifice.

This is the view taken in the rabbinic literature, which was written down after the destruction of the Temple, and which goes into great detail concerning the sacrifices which had been offered generations and centuries before. At the same time it prescribes with care the content and mode of verbal prayer which, in theory at least, remained the substitute for animal sacrifice. In the Middle Ages, the earlier codifiers retained the old sacrificial laws; but later codifications, including the *Shulḥan Arukh*, deleted them because they were no longer applicable.

SADDUCEES see Pharisees.

SAFED

A picturesque city in the Upper Galilee, Israel, known in Hebrew as *Tzefat*. (In Bible translations the name is rendered Zephath.) Although Safed is known from ancient times, it became famous during the 16th century as a center of Jewish learning. As one of the four "Holy Cities" of Palestine, (the others being Jerusalem, Hebron and Tiberias,) it became the seat of the *Kabbalists*, under the leadership of R. Isaac Luria and R. Ḥayim Vital. It was in Safed that Joseph Karo wrote the *Shulḥan Arukh*, the accepted legal code of modern Jewish life. In recent times Safed was inhabited mainly by Arabs, but following the Arab-Israel war in 1948 the population of the city became almost entirely Jewish. Because of its healthful climate and the natural beauty of its location, Safed became an attractive vacation resort and a haven for artists. It is near the village of Meron, famous for the tombs of R. Simeon ben Yoḥai and other rabbis.

SALK, JONAS EDWARD

Medical researcher, educator, and discoverer of the polio vaccine. Born in 1914 in New York City, he embarked upon a distinguished career as medical researcher, and in 1947 was made consultant in epidemic diseases to the U. S. Secretary of the Army. From 1949 he was director of the virus research laboratory, and professor of bacteriology at the University of Pittsburgh. From 1954 he was head of its Department of Preventive Medicine. He was made fellow of the American Public Health Association, and member of the American Association for the Advancement of Science. In 1951-53 he became internationally famous as the discoverer of the polio vaccine, which mitigated greatly the incidence of poliomyelitis.

Jonas E. Salk, discoverer of the polio vaccine and prominent medical research bacteriologist.

SALOMON, HAYM (1740–1785)

American patriot and financier of the American Revolution. Because of anti-Jewish persecution, he left his native Poland, and at the age of 32 settled in New York. His experience in matters of finance, brokerage and exchange, and his knowledge of languages helped him start a successful career as a broker. He soon became interested in the patriotic activities against the British, and joined the "Sons of Liberty." Because of his anti-British activities he was twice imprisoned, but managed to escape. Leaving his wife and infant, he went to Philadelphia, where he re-established his fortune and wealth as well as his patriotic activities.

In the meantime the Revolutionary army fighting the British was on the verge of collapse and mutiny. General Washington pleaded for money for his army. Robert Morris, the Superintendent of Finance for the Continental Government, used the services of Haym Salomon, as "broker of United States Government." Salomon not only helped keep the nation financially stable through the sale of subsidies to France and Holland, but also turned over to the government all the commissions he had earned. He gave his entire fortune for the cause of the Revolution and made personal loans to a considerable number of men in public office. Government records show that Haym Salomon wanted no interest on the financial transactions in behalf of the government. Neither he nor his heirs were ever repaid what was due him by the government.

Haym Salomon was also active in Jewish religious and philanthropic affairs. His stature as true patriot of his adopted country remains unsurpassed. A Congressional committee reported the following in 1850: "The Committee, from the evidence before them, are induced to consider Haym Salomon as one of the truest and most efficient friends of the country at a very critical period of its history."

SALONICA

Seaport in Greece and the seat of one of the oldest Jewish communities in Europe. When the apostle Paul came to Salonica in 53 c.e., he found a Jewish community there. Jewish emigrants from France, Poland, Italy and Germany settled there in the 13th and 14th centuries. After 1492 Sephardi Jews from Spain and Portugal became the largest segment of the flourishing Jewish community. During the Turkish rule, which began in 1430, Salonica became famous for its synagogues, *Yeshivot* (academies), and a Hebrew printing press (1515). Especially active in Salonica were the *Kabbalists,* as well as the followers of Shabbetai Tzevi, the false messiah. Among the notable individuals of this community were Joseph Karo and Judah Benveniste.

Jews formed a majority of the city's population, and distinguished themselves in trading and handicrafts.

In 1913 Salonica came under Greek rule, and Jews continued to occupy a prominent place in the public and political life of the city. During World War II and the subsequent occupation of Salonica by the Nazis (1941), the Jewish community was almost completely destroyed as a result of mass-deportations and famine; in 1960 there were only 1800 Jews remaining there.

SALVADOR, FRANCIS (1747–1776)

American patriot. Born in London, the son of Jacob Salvador, a member of a distinguished family of Portuguese Jews whose original family name was Rodriguez. Salvador inherited a large fortune, which was swept away by an earthquake. He went to America in 1773, where he became the successful owner of a large plantation. A passionate patriot, he joined the rebels of the South, and was elected a member of the first and second Provincial Congress of South Carolina (1775). At the outbreak of the Revolutionary War, the British incited a band of Indians to overrun the frontiers. Salvador led the colonists' counter-attack, and in one of the skirmishes he was shot by the Indians and scalped.

SAMARIA

Ancient city in Palestine built by King Omri, which became the capital of the northern Kingdom of Israel. Samaria was destroyed many times and rebuilt, through foreign military conquests. Excavations of recent years revealed interesting remains of the once famous city, including palaces, fortifications and Hebrew inscriptions. Samaria is also the historic name of a fertile district of Palestine. Extending north and west of Jerusalem, it comprises

The High Priest, head of the Samaritan community, and his family prepare to celebrate Passover on Mt. Gerizim. Samaritans claim direct descent from the earliest Israelite settlers in the Holy Land.

most of the Plain of Sharon, the coast to Haifa, as well as the city of Nablus (Shechem). The entire district made up the so-called Kingdom of Israel, as distinguished from the Kingdom of Judah to the south. See *Archeology*.

SAMARITANS

A Jewish sect which originated in Samaria after Assyria conquered the Kingdom of Israel in 722 b.c.e. The conquerors populated Samaria with people from other lands with whom the remaining Israelites intermingled. This mixed population in part gradually adopted heathen religious practices, but kept some essentials of the Jewish faith, such as the belief in one God and the adherence to the Laws of Moses

as prescribed in the *Pentateuch* (Five Books of Moses).

Many years later when the Judeans began to rebuild the Temple in Jerusalem, the Samaritans offered their help, but were regarded as a heathen-group and their offer was rejected. The Samaritans consequently built their own temple on Mount Gerizim. They continue to exist to this day, but their population has been in steady decline. The present Samaritan community in Jordan numbers about 200 people, with a high priest as their religious leader. On Passover eve they congregate on Mount Gerizim, where their temple once stood, and celebrate the Passover by slaughtering the paschal lamb in accordance with ancient tradition.

SAMBATYON

A legendary river, the turbulent waters of which are active on six days of the week and rest on the Sabbath. Apparently deriving its name from the word Sabbath, the river was mentioned by Josephus, Pliny and R. Akiva. In the course of time tales were circulated that the Ten Lost Tribes lived near the Sambatyon. The traveler Eldad Ha-Dani (9th century) claimed to have found the lost tribes on "the other side" of the Sambatyon, and even the famous scholar Menasseh ben Israel (17th century) took these tales seriously. Many attempts were actually made, even in modern times, to locate the Ten Lost Tribes at the Sambatyon as well as in other places, such as Mesopotamia, India, East Africa, China, Japan, Caucasia and Spain. There is also a story that the descendants of Moses (Bene Mosheh) lived on the other side of the Sambatyon.

Samaritan priests prostrate themselves on rugs, Oriental style, while saying their prayers on their major holiday festival: the Passover. The Samaritans live only according to the laws of the ancient and traditional Five Books of Moses.

SAMEKH (ס)

The fifteenth letter of the Hebrew alphabet. It is pronounced like the English S. Its numerical value is 60. See *Shin*.

SAMSON

Known in Hebrew as "Shimshon Ha-Gibbor" (Samson the Hero), one of the most popular heroes of the Bible, listed as the last of the Judges in Israel. A descendant of the tribe of Dan, he was reared as a Nazirite, forbidden to shear his hair or drink alcoholic beverages. As he grew up he possessed preternatural strength which he used in fighting the Philistines, though mostly to avenge personal insults rather than as the protector of his people. He fell in love with Delilah, a Philistine woman, who in the end led to his downfall. Revealing that his strength lay in his hair, she betrayed him to the enemy. Once his hair was shorn, Samson lost his strength and was captured and blinded by the Philistines. When called upon by the Philistines to make sport before the people gathered at a festival, Samson leaned with all his strength against the front two pillars of the temple and brought down the roof of the building, dying together with thousands of his Philistine enemies.

SAMUEL

Priest, prophet, and one of the great leaders in Israel following the period of the Judges (11th century b.c.e.). Of the tribe of Ephraim, he was consecrated by his mother Hannah to God and His service at the sanctuary of Shiloh, as assistant to Eli the priest. There he heard the voice of God, and the message about the imminent fall of the sanctuary at Shiloh. This happened when the Israelites were defeated by the Philistines and the Ark of the Covenant was captured. The House of Eli came to an end, and Samuel went to

SAMUEL, HERBERT LOUIS

Ramah, where he became known as a seer and judge of the people.

After more than twenty years of leadership, Samuel led the people to victory in a battle with the Philistines who renewed their attacks. As Samuel grew old, the people demanded of him that he choose for them a king who would protect them in times of danger. In a famous passage on the disadvantages of monarchy, Samuel warned the people about the possible dangers of selfish kings, but yielded to the popular demand, and finally chose Saul as the first king of Israel. Samuel was soon displeased with Saul's conduct, and proceeded secretly to anoint David as the successor to the throne.

The life of Samuel is recorded in the first of the two *Books of Samuel* contained in the Bible. These books relate the history of the Israelites from the birth of Samuel to the end of David's rule. Tradition attributes the authorship of *I Samuel* to Samuel himself, and *II Samuel* to the prophets Gad and Nathan. Some Bible scholars believe that the books were compiled from different sources during the period of the First Temple.

SAMUEL, HERBERT LOUIS

British statesman, philosopher, and first High Commissioner of Palestine under the British mandate. Born in Liverpool, England in 1870, he started his political career early in life, and entered parliament in 1902. He held many important government offices, and between 1931 and 1935 he was leader of the Liberal Party in the House of Commons. He was president of the British Institute of Philosophy and wrote several important philosophical works for publication.

Always active in Jewish affairs, he helped in the deliberations which preceded the issuance of the Balfour Declaration of 1917, which guaranteed the

Viscount Herbert L. Samuel, first Palestine High Commissioner under the British Mandate.

establishment of a Jewish national home in Palestine. The appointment of Sir Herbert Samuel as the first High Commissioner for Palestine in 1920 was applauded by world Jewry. But despite his attempt to serve Jewish and Arab interests objectively, his administration was often criticized by both Jews and Arabs. Upon leaving Palestine in 1925, he continued his services to the British government, and his activity in the interests of the Jewish community. In 1937 he was made viscount by King George VI.

SAMUEL BEN MEIR see Rashbam.

SAMUEL HA-NAGID (993–1055)

Popular name of Samuel ben Joseph ibn Nagdela (or Nagrela), Spanish statesman, Hebrew poet and Talmudic scholar. Born in Cordova, Spain, he acquired several languages, and excelled in the art of calligraphy. Through his work as a copyist he attracted the attention of the vizier of Malaga, who employed him as his secretary. Samuel was later appointed vizier by King Habus, and retained this position under his son Badis, who entrusted him with the foreign affairs of Granada.

For his learning and his support of Jewish scholars, he became the *Nagid* (spiritual leader) of the Jewish community in Granada. Samuel's own literary activity extended to various fields. He wrote the *Mevo Ha-Talmud* (Introduction to the Talmud), in which he set down the rules of the Talmudic form of discussion, as well as a commentary on the entire Talmud, and also works on Hebrew grammar. He is best known as the first of the important group of Spanish Hebrew poets of the Middle Ages. Although not considered as great a poet as his friend Solomon ibn Gabirol, his religious poetry as well as his other poetic works on various themes are marked by their force and elevation despite their frequent lack of clarity of expression.

SANCTIFICATION OF THE NAME see Kiddush ha-Shem.

SANDEK see Circumcision.

SANHEDRIN

The Hebrew form of the Greek word "Synedrion" (assembly), applied to the highest Jewish court and legislature which functioned during the latter period of the Second Commonwealth and was the supreme legal institution of the state, perhaps successor to the "Great Assembly" (Keneset ha-Gedolah) apparently established during the days of Ezra and Nehemiah (5th century b.c.e.). The Talmud refers to two kinds of Sanhedrin, the Great Sanhedrin of 71 members which met in the Temple at Jerusalem in the "Chamber of the Hewn Stones," and the smaller Sanhedrin of 23 members which met both in Jerusalem and in other major districts of Palestine. Generally speaking the Great Sanhedrin probably served as high court as well as legislature, while the

lesser Sanhedrin was only authorized to handle specific litigation including the most serious, such as cases involving capital punishment. At the head of the Great Sanhedrin stood two chief functionaries, the *Nasi* (prince, chief patriarch) and the *Av Bet Din* (elder of the court). The members were chosen on the basis of their character and authoritative knowledge of Jewish law. Under Roman rule in Palestine, the civil and political jurisdiction of the Sanhedrin was limited, and as early as four decades before the destruction of the Temple, it could no longer pass death sentences. Following the destruction of the Temple, the seat of the Sanhedrin was moved to Yavneh, near Jerusalem, and later to Usha, Bet-Shearim, Sepphoris and subsequently Tiberias.

In the Talmud there is a tractate entitled "Sanhedrin" which deals with the composition and jurisdiction of the various courts, judicial procedure and other aspects of criminal law.

SANTANGEL, LUIS DE

Chancellor of the royal house of Aragon, and financier of the expedition of Columbus for the discovery of America. A member of a prominent Marrano family, he succeeded his father in 1476 as farmer of the royal taxes. A favorite of King Ferdinand and Queen Isabella, he rose to financial and political power. Because of his financial support, Columbus was enabled to undertake his expedition for the discovery of the New World. For his services to the crown, and the role he played in the discovery of America, the Inquisition was forbidden by royal decree to investigate the religious faith and practices of Luis Santangel and his heirs. An esteemed statesman, Santangel died in 1505.

SARAH

Wife of Abraham and mother of Isaac,

who was born in her advanced age. The Bible recounts that Sarah induced Abraham to drive out his Egyptian handmaid Hagar and her son Ishmael whom she bore to him. Sarah was the first of the four Matriarchs of the Jewish people, the others being Rebekah, Rachel and Leah. She died at the age of 127, and was buried in the Cave of Machpelah, purchased by Abraham for this purpose. Sarah's original name was Sarai.

SATAN

In Jewish tradition Satan is the name of the archangel whose functions are to tempt man to sin, test his loyalty, and inflict punishment upon the sinner. He does not possess independent power, but appears only as the servant of God, whose permission he must seek for his schemes of evil-doing. Satan is mentioned only a few times in the Bible, particularly in the *Book of Zechariah* and in the *Book of Job*. In later Jewish folklore Satan is identified with *Sammael*, the angel of death, or the overseer of *Gehinnom* (Hell). In the Christian tradition Satan is represented as the chief of the Fallen Angels.

SAUL

The first king of Israel (1028-1013 b.c.e). A son of Kish of the tribe of Benjamin, he was anointed king by the prophet Samuel, and crowned after his successful war against the Ammonites. The real threat to the country was the Philistine horde whom Saul frequently fought without decisive victory. He was more successful in routing the Moabites, the Arameans, and the hated Amalekites.

Despite his courage on the battlefield, he failed to win freedom and independence for the Israelites. He was moody, melancholic and suspicious. He lost the friendship and support of Samuel, and out of jealousy turned against his son-in-law, Da-

vid, the popular young hero who was his personal attendant and armor bearer. Warned by his best friend Jonathan, Saul's son, David saved himself by going into hiding and seeking refuge with the Philistines. In the meantime the Philistines took advantage of the instability of Saul's kingdom by invading the country. In the battle at Mount Gilboa, the Israelites were completely routed and Saul took his own life to avoid falling into the hands of the enemy. David's beautiful lament over the death of Saul and Jonathan has become a classic eulogy.

SAYINGS OF THE FATHERS see Avot.

SCHAPIRA, HERMANN (1840–1898)

Zionist leader and founder of *Keren Kayemet Le-Yisrael* (Jewish National Fund). He served as professor of mathematics at Heidelberg, Germany and, intensely interested in Jewish affairs, he became an active Zionist and a follower of Theodor Herzl. He attended the first Zionist Congress at Basle (1897) at which time he proposed the creation of the Jewish people's fund, which became known as the *Jewish National Fund*, for the redemption of the land in *Eretz Israel* (Land of Israel). A Hebraist and advocate of Hebrew cultural revival, he originated the plan for the establishment of a Hebrew University in Jerusalem, which was realized in 1925.

SCHATZ, BORIS (1866–1932)

Sculptor, painter, founder and director of the Bezalel School of Arts and Crafts in Jerusalem. Born in Lithuania he studied art in Warsaw and in Paris, and soon was recognized for his original work as a sculptor. In 1896 he settled in Sofia, Bulgaria as the court sculptor of Prince Ferdinand, and became one of the founders of the Bulgarian Academy of Fine Arts. An active Zionist and a follower of Theodor Herzl,

Self-portrait of Boris Schatz, founder of the Bezalel School of Arts and Crafts in Jerusalem. Painter and sculptor, Schatz's influence on the exhibition and collection of Jewish art in Israel has been profound.

he went to Palestine in 1906 where he established the now famous Bezalel School of Arts and Crafts in Jerusalem. The purpose of the school was not only to teach arts and crafts, but to create and to collect Jewish art. The school soon became a great success and despite periods of decline, it was reorganized by the efforts of Boris Schatz, who traveled to the United States where he exhibited Bezalel art objects, as well as his own works of art, and raised funds for the Bezalel School. He died at Denver, Colorado on his second visit to the United States, but in accordance with his will he was then taken to Palestine for burial.

SCHECHTER, SOLOMON (1847–1915)

Rabbi, scholar, and president of The Jewish Theological Seminary of America. Born in Rumania, he received his rabbinical education from his father, and continued both his Jewish and secular studies in Vienna, Berlin, and London, and became Reader in Rabbinics at Cambridge University, and Professor of Hebrew at the University College, London. His first essay "The Study of the Talmud," as well as a series of other essays published in the *Jewish Quarterly Review*, later appeared in three volumes entitled *Studies in Judaism*.

Schechter's reputation became universal when he discovered a great many documents in a synagogue Genizah in Cairo and brought them to England, presenting them to the Library of the University of Cambridge. Scholars are still poring over the ancient fragments. Many important learned articles and books based on them have already been published. Schechter identified several leaves as part of the lost Hebrew original of the *Book of Ecclesiasticus* (Ben-Sira) which had been known only in translation.

In 1902 Schechter was appointed president and professor at The Jewish Theological Seminary of America, where he served with great distinction until his death. In the United States, Schechter became a leading figure in Jewish scholarship, the spokesman of conservative Judaism, and one of the founders of the United Synagogue of America (1913). He was co-editor of the *Jewish Publication Society*, the *Jewish Quarterly Review* and the *Jewish Encyclopedia*. His principal writings include: *The Wisdom of Ben-Sira, Documents of Jewish Sectaries, Some Aspects of Rabbinic Theology, Studies in Judaism*, and *Avot of Rabbi Nathan*.

SCHIFF, JACOB HENRY (1847–1920)

Financier, philanthropist and Jewish leader.

Born in Germany to a distinguished family in Frankfort. At the age of 18 he went to the United States, and ten years later he became a partner and later head of the private banking firm, Kuhn, Loeb and Co. Through this firm Schiff financed the building of railroads and other business enterprises and transactions, both in America and abroad.

A pious Jew and a lover of Jewish learning, he gave generously for the support of Jewish charitable and cultural causes. Some of his major contributions and accomplishments were: he erected buildings for the Young Men's Hebrew Association, and The Jewish Theological Seminary in New York; supported the Hebrew Union College in Cincinnati; helped erect the building for the Semitic Museum at Harvard University; established Jewish departments in the New York Public Library and the Library of Congress; provided funds for the translation of the Bible by the Jewish Publication Society; and subsidized the Montefiore Hospital and the Henry Street Settlement in New York City. He also gave financial assistance to many non-Jewish institutions and offered special gifts to Barnard College, Columbia University, and Cornell University at Ithaca, New York.

By virtue of his generosity and active interest in Jewish affairs he became one of the recognized leaders of American Jewry. His Jewish sympathies influenced his business relationships, so that he refused, for instance, to deal with Tsarist Russia because of her unjust treatment of the Russian Jews. For the protection of Jewish rights the world over, he joined in founding the American Jewish Committee. Al-

Solomon Schechter, father of conservative Judaism in America, was one of the founders of the United Synagogue of America, president of The Jewish Theological Seminary, and a leading figure in Biblical scholarship and writing.

Rudolph Schildkraut, famous character actor, in a montage of the many roles he played on the stage. He was famous for bringing the best of the European drama to the Yiddish-speaking public of America.

though not a Zionist, he donated generously for the founding of the Haifa Technion; purchased stock in the Jewish Colonial Trust, and financed loans for the wine-growers in Palestine. His name is permanently memorialized in Israel, as well as in New York City.

SCHILDKRAUT, RUDOLPH (1862–1930)

Famous Yiddish actor. Born in Constantinople, he became known as a character actor on the Austrian and German stage. On his first visit to the United States (1910) he became interested in the Yiddish theatre, and in 1920 he joined the Yiddish Art Theatre. Schildkraut is well remembered for his portrayal of Jewish characters and for presenting to the Yiddish speaking public the masterpieces of the European theatre. His son Joseph Schildkraut became a celebrated film star in Hollywood.

own dramatic company in New York, which became known as the Yiddish Art Theatre. During his career as a director and producer, he brought to the Yiddish stage over 150 plays, including some of the great plays of the European theatre. Schwartz is best remembered for his outstanding character portrayals and production of original Yiddish plays or dramatizations of the works of the following Yiddish authors: Peretz Hirschbein, Sholem Aleichem, S. An-Ski, Sholem Asch, Ossip Dymov, H. Leivick, and I. J. Singer. He toured internationally with his company of outstanding Yiddish actors.

SCIENCE OF JUDAISM see Jewish Science.

SCRIBES see Soferim.

SCRIPTURES see Bible.

SCROLL OF THE LAW see Sefer Torah.

S'DOM see Sodom and Gomorrah.

SEA OF GALILEE see Kinneret.

SEDER

Hebrew term meaning "order," applied to the ceremony held in Jewish homes on the first two nights (first night only in Israel and among reform Jews) of Passover. The *Seder* is a reminder of the Passover meal and the offering of the paschal lamb during the days of the Temple. As the occasion which commemorates Israel's miraculous deliverance from Egypt, the Seder has become a very colorful and solemn religious ritual, symbolizing as well the hope for the ultimate redemption of the people of Israel.

The essential features of the Seder are as follows: 1) recitation of the *Kiddush;* 2) reading of the *Haggadah* (narrative of the Exodus) which begins with the "Four Questions" asked by the youngest participant; 3) partaking of the unleavened bread (Matzah), and the bitter herbs (Maror); 4) the festival meal, followed by grace; 5) drinking of the *Arba Kosot* (four cups

Maurice Schwartz, actor, director and producer, was founder of the famous Yiddish Art Theatre.

SCHOLARS' HOLIDAY see Lag Ba-Omer.

SCHWARTZ, MAURICE (1887–1960)

Yiddish actor, director and producer. Born in Sudilkov, the Ukraine, he came to the United States in 1902. At the age of seventeen he joined a dramatic club of amateur Yiddish players. He soon joined the professional Yiddish theatre in Brooklyn, New York, under the directorship of David Kessler. In 1918 Schwartz organized his

A Passover Seder commemorating the Jewish flight from Egypt is celebrated in an old-age home in Israel. Ceremonies are conducted by the oldest member of the home who wears an all-white "Kittel."

of wine) at stated intervals; 6) recitation of *Hallel* (Psalms of Praise) and the singing of songs. Among the most interesting aspects of the Seder is the emphasis on children's participation.

It is often customary for several families to participate together in the Seder, and in recent years some Jewish organizations have arranged a public celebration during the Passover week known as the "Third Seder," which is, however, not traditional in either content or form.

SEDOM see Sodom and Gomorrah.

SEDRAH see Parashah.

SEFER TORAH

Hebrew term meaning "Book of the Torah" applied to the Scroll of the Torah, that is,

the roll of parchment upon which the Five Books of Moses are written, and from which the designated portion of the Torah is read in the synagogue. The Scroll of the Torah is made up of separate rolls or leaves of parchment sewn together, and the texts are written by a special copyist known in Hebrew as a *Sofer* (Scribe), who must be a pious and learned man.

The Scroll is rolled on two wooden poles, called in Hebrew *Etz Ḥayim*, each having an ornamental headpiece or crown. The rolls are tied together by a sash, and covered with an embroidered mantle (Meil). Other decorations are the breastplate (Ḥoshen Mishpat) and pointer (Yad) used in the reading of the Torah. The Scrolls of the Torah are kept in the *Aron*

436

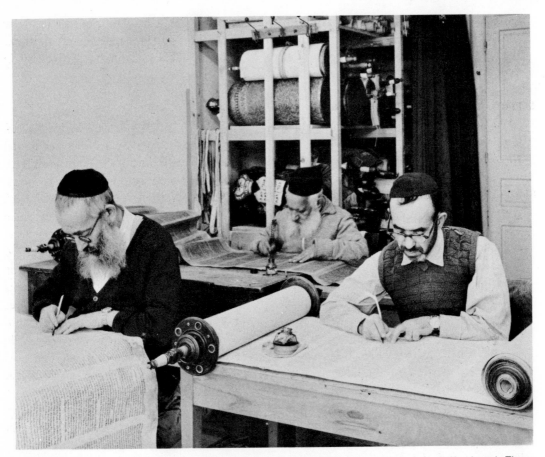

Old Torah scrolls found unfit for ritual use are here corrected in a workshop in Jaffa, Israel. These scribes are skilled in all of the complex and painstaking task of correcting a "Sefer Torah" properly.

ha-Kodesh (Holy Ark) in the synagogue, when not in use.

It is desirable to have more than one *Sefer* should the synagogue's only Scroll be found "pasul" (ritually unfit for use until corrected). It is also convenient to have several *Sefarim* so that, on the festivals, each can be ready in advance for the Scriptural reading taken from two (or three) different parts of the Torah. On Simhat Torah all the Scrolls are taken from the Ark to be carried around the synagogue in festive processions called *Hakkafot.*

The Sefer Torah is a most sacred object, and it is considered a great honor for one to be called upon to write in one of the letters of a newly dedicated Scroll, or in

any other way to be associated with its handling or reading.

SEFIRAT HA-OMER

Hebrew phrase meaning "the counting of the *Omer*," referring to the Jewish tradition of counting seven weeks from the second day of Passover (when the Omer was offered) to Shavuot. These 49 days are known as the *Sefirah days,* or *Sefirah.* This is traditionally a period of mourning on account of the persecutions suffered by the Jews during the Roman rule in Palestine as well as the death of many scholars. Many Jews refrain from various types of rejoicing, such as solemnizing of marriages, the exception being Rosh Hodesh and Lag Ba-Omer, when rejoicing is per-

437

mitted. As of 1959, the Israeli rabbinate allowed a similar relaxation on the 5th of Iyar, Israel Independence Day. See *Lag Ba-Omer; Omer.*

SEFIROT, THE TEN

"Ten Spheres" or powers through which God manifests Himself in the world. See *Kabbalah.*

SEIXAS, GERSHOM MENDEZ (1745–1816)

American rabbi and patriot. Born in New York, he served as minister of the Spanish and Portuguese Congregation *Shearith Israel* of New York City, and at the outbreak of the Revolutionary War he sided with the American patriots. Rather than perform his duties under the British, he closed his synagogue and eventually moved to Philadelphia where, with the help of other Jewish patriots, he founded the *Mikveh Israel* congregation. After the Revolutionary War he returned to his congregation in New York. At the inauguration of George Washington as first President, he was one of the clergymen attending the ceremony. From 1787 to 1815 he served as a trustee of Columbia College.

Seixas was active in Jewish philanthropic work. He was buried in the old

Medallion portrait of Gershom Mendez Seixas, Minister of New York's Spanish and Portuguese Synagogue and a trustee of Columbia College.

cemetery at Chatham Square in New York. His portrait appears on a bronze medal struck by Columbia University in his memory.

SELIHOT

Plural form of the Hebrew word *Selihah* (forgiveness), applied to the penitential prayers recited during the High Holy Day period, as well as on Jewish fast days. Some compositions of *Selihot* date back to the first century, but most of them were written by the great Hebrew poets of Spain and by the *Payyetanim* (liturgical poets) of the 12th and 13th centuries, the period of severe persecutions and great suffering of Jewish communities in Europe. There are over 2,000 Selihot written by more than 250 authors at different periods in Jewish history. The content of the Selihot varies with the occasion on which they are recited. Many of them deal with Jewish martyrdom during the Middle Ages in particular, and with Jewish suffering in general. Some commemorate the destruction of the Temple in Jerusalem, expressing the hope of ultimate salvation for the Jewish people, and others deal with the subject of human weakness, confessions and God's forgiveness and mercy.

SEMIKHAH

Hebrew term meaning "laying on of hands" referring to the act of transmitting authority. Moses placed his hands on the head of Joshua, giving him authority to become the leader of Israel. In the days of the Second Commonwealth, and later during the Talmudic period, one generation of teachers would grant *Semikhah* to future teachers, who were thus ordained to exercise religious and legal authority. Technically, Semikhah ceased some two thousand years ago, and was not established anew until the 14th or 15th century.

In modern times rabbinical students are granted Semikhah, that is, they receive a rabbinical diploma and become ordained as rabbis upon graduation from a rabbinical school or *Yeshivah*. Private ordinations are also still practiced.

SEMITES

A term derived from *Shem*, the son of Noah. Since the middle of the 18th century this term has been used as a designation for those people who speak the "Semitic languages." Scientifically the word *Semite* is strictly a technical term for the Semitic family of languages and has no racial implication. The term "anti-Semitism" implies opposition to all Semitic races, but in its popular usage it signifies only hatred of the Jewish people, and was created in the 19th century as a term for this phenomenon when it no longer was motivated by religion alone, and it was considered more polite because on the surface it did not pinpoint hatred of the Jew alone.

SEPHARDIM

Hebrew term applied to Jews of Spanish and Portuguese origin. The expulsions from Spain and Portugal at the end of the 15th century forced the Sephardi Jews to disperse in the lands of the Turkish Empire, such as Turkey, Syria, Palestine, North Africa, also in Greece, Bulgaria, Italy, Holland, Germany, England, and still later in North and South America. The Sephardi Jewish communities preserved their own ritual, traditions and customs, as well as their own dialect called *Ladino*, a form of Castilian with an admixture of Hebrew elements. They use the Sephardi pronunciation of Hebrew, which is basically that which is used in Israel as well as among many persons in the diaspora. The Sephardi Jews made great contributions to Jewish learning; they developed their own institutions and congregations, and had great rabbis and famous Jewish personalities. In language, form of ritual, traditions and customs, the Sephardim differ markedly from the east and west European Jews, the Ashkenazim.

SEPTUAGINT

A Latin word meaning "seventy" used as the name of the early Greek translation of the Hebrew Bible. The translation was apparently made in Alexandria, Egypt, and much of it during the reign of Ptolemy Philadelphus (284-247 b.c.e.). Tradition tells us that the king invited 70 (or 72) scholars (hence the name "Septuagint") from Jerusalem to make the translation. The scholars were put in different cells (or islands), each working on the translation independently, and in the end every one was found to have produced an identical translation.

Research leads modern scholars to hold that only the *Pentateuch* (Five Books of Moses) was translated first, and that the other books of the Bible were translated at later periods. The Septuagint was a significant cultural accomplishment since it helped make the contents of the Bible accessible to both Jews and non-Jews at a period in world history when Greek was

Page of a 9th-century c.e. manuscript of the Septuagint, the Greek translation of the Bible. The Septuagint itself is from the 2nd century.

SEX, JEWISH ATTITUDE TOWARD

the language of educated persons. To this
day it is invaluable for Biblical research.

SEX, JEWISH ATTITUDE TOWARD

In contemporary phraseology, the Jewish
attitude toward sex might be characterized
as "healthy." Judaism avoids the extremes
of asceticism and indulgence and teaches
affirmations and obligations of its own.
The attitude of Judaism toward sex is far
from "puritanical." Sex is not only not
sinful, but a normal and necessary function
of the human being. The basic principle
in Judaism with regard to sex is "Tzeniut,"
modesty. The high ideals prevailing in
Judaism have made the Jewish family a
sacred and abiding institution.

Judaism teaches the duty to marry and
have children. The first *Mitzvah* (Commandment) in the Bible is "Be fruitful and
multiply." In Jewish tradition this is interpreted as an obligation on every family
to have a minimum of two children. In
general to abstain from God's blessings is
sinful; what is required is a proper use of
them, neither abuse nor abstention is right.

SHAAR HA-GOLAN see Archeology.

SHABBAT see Sabbath.

SHABBETAI TZEVI (1626–1676)

Most popular of the messianic pretenders,
creator of a stormy messianic movement
among Jews, with telling effects for many
years after his death. Born in Smyrna,
Turkey, he was a gifted Talmudist and at
an early age became interested in Jewish
mysticism and an ardent student of *Kabbalah*. Endowed with a hypnotic personality and a rich imagination, he was encouraged by the prophecy of the *Zohar*
that 1648 was the year when Messiah
would appear, and he announced himself
to his friends as the "Elect," destined to
put an end to universal suffering and return the persecuted Jewish people to the
land of their forefathers. Because of his

extravagant claims and his sacrilegious act
of pronouncing the ineffable name of God,
which was permitted only to the High
Priest in the Holy of Holies on Yom
Kippur, he shocked the community and
was forced to leave Smyrna. He began years
of wandering from country to country,
including Palestine. In the meantime his
fame had reached Jewish communities the
world over, and many rabbis and other
leading Jews became his faithful supporters. Upon his return to Smyrna he was
given a royal reception, and was hailed by
his many followers as the true messiah.

Jewish mystics believed that the Messiah
would actually appear in 1666, and would
then open the Messianic Era. In that year,
therefore, Shabbetai was challenged to
dethrone the mighty Sultan, proclaim the
establishment of his universal kingdom,
and lead his people to the land of Israel.
Shabbetai set out on this fantastic mission, but upon arrival in Constantinople
he and his followers were imprisoned in
the fort of Abydos. Shabbetai was allowed
many liberties and comforts and was even
permitted to hold court and receive delegations of Jews from communities the
world over. The Sultan eventually was led
to believe that Shabbetai's activities were a
threat to his throne, and the would-be
messiah was given the choice of either
becoming a Moslem or being executed.
Standing before the Sultan, Shabbetai lost
his courage and put on the fez as a sign of
his conversion. Pleased with his compli-
ance, the Sultan gave Shabbetai the title
"Effendi" and made him a royal official.

Shabbetai's conversion caused great dis-
illusion among his thousands of followers,
but many of them believed his conversion
to be a necessary tribulation of the messiah
and followed his example. These converts
formed a Jewish-Islamic sect of *Donmeh*
(Turkish for "apostates"). For many years
the legend of Shabbetai Tzevi persisted.

440

Jewish mystics continued to believe in his divine mission, and some of them later proclaimed themselves as successors of Shabbetai Tzevi by initiating new and equally unsuccessful messianic movements. To this day there are several groups of Donmeh in Turkey. The followers of Shabbetai Tzevi are known as Sabbetaians.

SHABUOT see Shavuot.

SHADKHAN

Jewish term for marriage broker. The profession of matchmaking among Jews was already well established in the Middle Ages, when some rabbis and laymen made it a legitimate source of income and considered it a pious act. Very popular in east Europe, the profession of the *Shadkhan* flourishes in modern Jewish communities, including some in the United States, and his services are considered quite valuable.

SHAHARIT

Hebrew name for the daily morning service. The *Shaharit* service includes very old prayers, such as *Shema* and *Amidah*, as well as other prayers. The word "Shaharit" means morning.

SHALAḤ MONES see Purim.

SHALESUDES see Shalosh Seudot.

SHALOM

The Hebrew word *Shalom* means peace. It is also used as a greeting on meeting or departing. The ideal of peace was considered so important in Jewish tradition, that the ancient books took the word Shalom to be one of the names of the Lord.

SHALOM ALEKHEM

Literally "peace upon you," a Hebrew religious hymn sung on Friday evenings by the master of the house upon returning from the services at the synagogue. It is a song of welcome and greeting to the "Angels of Peace" who, according to tradition, visit every Jewish home when the holy Sabbath is being ushered in. The phrase is also used as a general greeting such as the English "Hello."

The pen name which the famous Yiddish writer Solomon Rabinowitz used, and by which he is best known was Shalom Alekhem, but was spelled when written in Latin characters Sholem Aleichem. See *Sholem Aleichem*.

SHALOSH SEUDOT

Hebrew term meaning "three meals" and popularly pronounced "Shalesudes," applied to the traditional meal eaten at home or in the synagogue on Saturday after the *Minhah* service. According to the Talmud every Jew should honor the day of the Sabbath with *Shalosh Seudot*, three festive meals, one on Friday evening and two the following day. However, eventually, the term came to be used as a particular designation for the third meal, literally called "Seudah Shelishit."

SHAMMAI

Tanna of the first century b.c.e. He was the colleague of Hillel, and together they formed the last of the illustrious *Zugot* (Pairs). See *Hillel*.

SHAMMASH (Shammesh)

The beadle or sexton of a synagogue. His duties often combine those of a custodian, a collector of dues, a secretary, an assistant to the *Hazzan*, and other functions connected with the synagogue and public service. The office of the *Shammash* is still maintained in most orthodox and conservative congregations.

The additional light in the Ḥanukkah ritual, which is used to kindle the other lights, is also called *Shammash*.

SHAPRUT, ḤASDAI IBN see Ḥasdai ibn Shaprut.

SHAS

Initial letters of *Shishah Sedarim*, the "Six Orders" of the Mishnah: *Zeraim, Moed, Nezikin, Nashim, Kodashim* and *Tohorot*. The term is usually applied to the entire Talmud. The term *Ḥevrah Shas* refers to a group or organization of men devoted to the study of the Talmud. See *Mishnah*.

SHAVUOT

Hebrew name of the Feast of Weeks, one of the three pilgrimage festivals (Shalosh Regalim). *Shavuot* is observed on the 6th and 7th days of *Sivan* (May-June) by orthodox and conservative Jews in the diaspora; Israelis as well as reform Jews observe the 6th day only.

It is also known as *Pentecost*, since it begins on the 50th day after the completion of seven weeks of the counting of the *Omer*. On the second day of Passover a sheaf (Omer) of the new barley was offered as a sacrifice, and the fifty days were counted from then. Wheat is harvested after barley, so that on the fiftieth day, or Shavuot, two "wave-loaves" of bread made from wheat were offered, or the first-fruits of the harvest. The holiday is therefore also called *Ḥag ha-Bikkurim* (Festival of the First-Fruits).

In Jewish tradition a further meaning is attached to Shavuot, the time when God gave the Ten Commandments on Mount Sinai, and hence its additional name of *Zeman Mattan Toratenu* (the Season of the Giving of our Torah). Because of its agricultural significance, it is customary to decorate Jewish homes and synagogues with plants and flowers. The synagogue liturgy of Shavuot includes the chanting of *Akdamut*, a medieval hymn (in Aramaic), extolling the glory of God and His revelation, and of the *Book of Ruth* reminiscent of Jewish agricultural life, and of Ruth's acceptance of the Jewish faith. Shavuot is also the date of the birth and death of King David, the descendant of Ruth. Since the early 1800's Shavuot has been generally the time when annual confirmation exercises are held in reform synagogues. Confirmation has spread of late to conservative groups, which frequently call it Consecration.

SHECHEM see Archeology; Nablus.

SHEELOT U-TESHUVOT

Hebrew term meaning "questions and answers," commonly referred to as *Responsa*, a branch of rabbinic literature comprised of opinions and rulings on matters of Jewish law in response to queries. Extending from the 7th century to the present, this type of literature began in Babylonia during the *Gaonic* period. The *Geonim*, whose authority was universally accepted by Jews the world over, issued written decisions on legal questions addressed to them by Jewish communities and individuals. With the end of the Gaonic period, Jewish communities in Europe turned to their own rabbis with questions on Jewish law, and the Responsa frequently assumed a more local character, and reflected local conditions of Jewish life. Covering the development of Jewish law for a period of about 1200 years, the Responsa provide us with valuable information about the religious, social, economic, moral and political life of Jewish communities at different periods of Jewish history.

SHEHEHEYANU

Hebrew word meaning "who has kept us in life" contained in the benediction of that name pronounced by Jews on many important occasions: on tasting fruit for the first time in the season; on putting on new clothes; on the first nights of Jewish festivals; before sounding the *Shofar*; before lighting the candle on the first night of Ḥanukkah; before reading the *Megillah*.

The week after the Shavuot festival is the time for the "Bikkurim" ceremonies in Israel. Here, Israeli children bring their offerings of First-Fruits as contributions to Jerusalem's Jewish National Fund.

SHEHITAH

A Hebrew term meaning "slaughtering" applied to the Jewish laws and regulations which must be observed by the *Shohet* (slaughterer) in performing the act of slaughtering animals for food. In addition to his knowledge of the *Shehitah* laws, the Shohet must be a pious man and in good health, and must take minute care that the animal which is to be slaughtered is caused as little pain as is humanly possible. Any imperfection found in the slaughtered animal renders it *Terefah*, that is, forbidden to be used as food by Jews. Because of the tremendous cranial hemorrhage which follows instantly on the act of slaughtering, the animal loses consciousness immediately, making it a humane method of slaughtering.

SHEITEL

Yiddish term for a wig of artificial or real hair worn, according to an old Jewish practice, by pious Jewish married women, as a sign of modesty. Rabbinic literature teaches that it is sinful for a Jewish woman

443

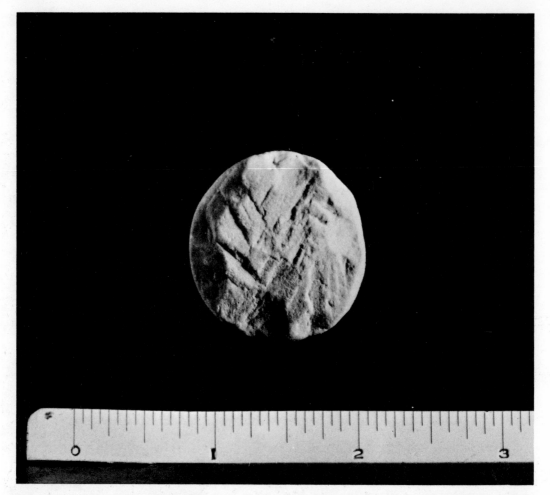

Unique seal-weight found at Nebi Rubin is of dome-shaped limestone. Unit sign, looking like a two-pronged paper clip with ends crossed to form a "v," indicates the equivalent of a "Shekel" in weight.

to be seen by any man other than her husband or to listen to the recital of prayers with her hair uncovered. Some very pious Jewish women used to cut their hair off on their wedding day and keep their head covered with a kerchief. This custom is still observed in some Jewish communities, but has been largely discarded in many parts of the world.

SHEKEL

An ancient Hebrew unit of weight, later used as the name of Hebrew coins from 66 c.e. on. Today, the *Shekel* is used to symbolize an individual's affiliation with a Zionist organization.

SHELIAH TZIBBUR

Hebrew term meaning "messenger of the congregation" originally applied to the High Priest in Jerusalem who served as the advocate of the people before God. In our day the *Hazzan* or any other person who leads the congregation in prayer is called *Sheliah Tzibbur*. In Jewish worship any male person who has passed his thirteenth birthday may lead the congregation in prayer.

SHELOSHIM

Hebrew term meaning "thirty," applied to the first thirty days of mourning after the burial of a deceased relative.

SHEM see Semites.

SHEMA

One of the oldest and most important Hebrew prayers. Deriving its name from its first word, the *Shema* is held to be in a sense Israel's affirmation of faith: "Hear, O Israel, the Lord our God, the Lord is One." When the Shema is recited in the morning and evening services, it is accompanied by the reading of three other selections from the Pentateuch. Before retiring, only the first paragraph (Veahavta) is read. The reform practice is to read only the one paragraph even at services.

SHEMINI ATZERET see Sukkot.

SHEMITAH see Sabbatical Year.

SHEMONEH ESREH

Principal prayer in Judaism, constituting the main section of each of the three daily prayers. It is a collection of blessings, called *Amidah* (standing) by the Sephardim because they are recited by the worshippers in a standing position; they were also called "Tefillah," or the prayer par excellence. It is customary for the worshippers to recite these benedictions in a low voice, facing east, and then for the *Ḥazzan* to repeat them aloud during the morning and afternoon services. The *Eighteen Benedictions* date back to the period of the Second Commonwealth; the prayer probably consisted originally of 17 blessings, to which one more was added later, and another still later. Despite the fact that there are actually 19 blessings, the name "Shemoneh Esreh" (eighteen) has continued to be used.

From a structural point of view, the *Shemoneh Esreh* has three principal divisions. The opening three benedictions are *Adoration* (*Avot, Gevurot, Kedushat ha-Shem*), the thirteen intermediate ones are *Petitions* (personal as well as communal prayers), and the concluding three are in the nature of *Thanksgiving* (*Avodah, Hodaah, Shalom*, or the "Priestly Benediction"). On Sabbath and festivals there is only one intermediate prayer, the "Sanctification of the Day"; thus on those days the Amidah consists of but seven blessings. See *Amidah*.

SHEMOT see Exodus, Book of.

SHEVAT

The fifth month of the Jewish calendar, consisting of 30 days, and corresponding to January-February. The 15th day of this month is celebrated as the New Year of the Trees and is known as *Tu Bi-Shevat* or *Ḥamishah Asar Bi-Shevat* (the 15th of Shevat).

SHIELD OF DAVID see Magen David.

SHIN (שׁ, שׂ)

The twenty-first letter of the Hebrew alphabet. It is pronounced like the English SH if it is dotted above its right leg; and like the English S if the dot is over its left leg, and it is then called *SIN*. *Sin* and *Samekh* are pronounced alike in contemporary Hebrew, though probably a distinction was made in ancient times. In an unvoweled text no visible difference between *Shin* and *Sin* appears. The value of the letter is 300; its shape suggests a tooth (Hebrew *Shen*). For pronunciation of *Sav, Suv*, see *Tav*.

SHIR HA-SHIRIM see Song of Songs.

SHIVAH

Hebrew term meaning "seven," referring to the first seven days of mourning after burial by the close relatives of the deceased. It is customary to "sit Shivah," that is, the mourners stay at home and, as a mark of bereavement, do not sit on chairs but on the floor or on a low stool. The *Shivah* is not observed on the Sabbath; also the major festivals cancel out whatever may remain of the Shivah days. For the purpose of Shivah (and *Sheloshim*), the following seven are considered closed relatives: spouse, father, mother, son, daughter, brother and sister. See *Death*.

SHIVAH ASAR BE-TAMMUZ see Fast Days.

SHLEMIEL

A common Yiddish expression applied to an individual who gets into many awkward situations and has innumerable mishaps, perhaps largely through his own ineptness. The term is occasionally used in American literature, and particularly in Hollywood motion picture dialogue. In modern psychological terminology, the *shlemiel* would be called accident-prone.

SHLIMMAZEL

A Yiddish phrase describing bad luck. The term is a combination of the German word "schlimm" (bad) and the Hebrew word "mazzal" (luck), and is used for the occurrence of the bad luck itself as well as the person to whom it happened.

SHNEOUR ZALMAN BEN BARUCH OF LIADI (1747–1812)

Hasidic rabbi and founder of the *Habad* movement. Born in Russia, he became a follower of the Hasidim, and after he settled in Mohilev he founded a sect of Hasidim known as "Habad," a name consisting of the initial letters of three Hebrew words: "Hokhmah" (wisdom), "Binah" (understanding), and "Daat" (knowledge). He differed from other leaders of the Hasidic movement in laying greater stress on the importance of study and learning. Shneour Zalman had many thousands of followers, but was unsuccessful in his attempt to overcome the opposition of the great Talmudist, R. Elijah of Vilna to the Hasidic movement. Denounced to the Russian government as a heretic in 1799, he was arrested and imprisoned, but was freed a year later. He then settled in Liadi.

Shneour Zalman wrote several works, the best known of which is *Tanya*, in which he laid down the principles of the Habad movement in Hasidism.

SHNORRER

A term commonly used as a designation for beggars among Jews, but more accurately applied to a certain type of beggar which originated during the Middle Ages. Because of economic plight and severe persecutions, hundreds of uprooted Jews began wandering from one Jewish community to another, and in time became entirely dependent on individual and communal charity. The typical *shnorrer*, begging from door to door, considered the receiving of alms as his vested right, and the giving of charity to him as the traditional moral duty of the better-to-do Jews. These men were often somewhat impudent, relying on their wit as well as their learning to convince the rich that they can not do without the poor if they want to share in the bliss of "the world to come."

Jewish folklore abounds in humorous stories about "shnorrers." Israel Zangwill immortalized this typical Jewish beggar in his masterpiece *King of the Schnorrers*. Organized Jewish charity in modern times led to the gradual disappearance of this unique type of beggar.

SHOFAR

Hebrew term applied to the horn of a ram which is sounded in the synagogue during the month of Elul, and particularly during the services of Rosh Hashanah and once at the closing service of Yom Kippur. In Biblical times the *Shofar* was blown in

Oriental Jew (right) blows the "Shofar," maintaining the Biblical custom of blowing the ram's horn on every festival. Note the long, curved horn used as distinguished from the shorter, more regular one used by Westernized Jews.

connection with many important occasions: for signals of alarm in time of war; for the purpose of proclaiming important national events; and for announcing and ushering in the Sabbath and festivals. The blowing of the Shofar is called *Tekiah* (blowing), and the person blowing it is called the *Baal Tokea*. In modern Israel, the Shofar is sounded every Friday afternoon as the Sabbath approaches.

SHOFETIM see Judges, Book of.

SHOHET see Sheḥitah.

SHOLEM ALEICHEM (1859–1916)

Pen name of Solomon Rabinowitz, greatest Yiddish humorist, "the Jewish Mark Twain." Born in Russia, he began writing in Hebrew and Russian at an early age, but earned his greatest literary success as a Yiddish writer, becoming one of the "fathers" of modern Yiddish literature. Sholem Aleichem contributed forty volumes of short stories, novels and plays to Yiddish literature. His writings offer a comprehensive picture of Jewish life in Russia in his lucid portrayals of hundreds of individuals in every walk of life, their social relationships, their ways of expression, their struggles and ambitions, as well as their mannerisms and physical appearance. Through his realistic depiction of literary characters and his profound and sparkling humor, he became one of the most widely read and best beloved literary figure in Yiddish literature. Among his admirers the world over were and still are thousands of Jewish children, for whom he wrote scores of stories with genuine understanding, humor and sympathy. He is best known today for: *Menahem Mendel*, the typical Jewish "Luftmensch,"

Sholem Aleichem, Yiddish humorist and satirist, is sometimes known as "the Jewish Mark Twain," and as "the father of Yiddish literature." A prolific writer in three languages, Aleichem's work achieved lasting fame chiefly in Yiddish.

the ne'er-do-well, a *shlemiel* failing in all sorts of fantastic business ventures; *Tevye der Milchiger* (Tevye the Dairyman), the simple and kindly small-town Jew, professing an endless faith in God and in the ultimate salvation of His chosen people despite all mishap; *Funem Yarid*, his autobiography; and *Shver Tzu Zain a Yid* (It's Hard to be a Jew), a comedy. Sholem Aleichem died in New York, where he had lived from 1914. Jewish libraries, schools, and institutes the world over have been named after him.

SHOLEM ALEICHEM FOLK INSTITUTE

A Yiddish cultural organization founded in 1918 for the purpose of establishing and maintaining Yiddish secular schools, and to promote Yiddish culture and literature. It administers and maintains the Sholem Aleichem Folkshul, where Yiddish language and literature, Hebrew and Bible, Jewish history, Jewish life in America and Israel are taught. It publishes the *Kinder-Journal*, a Yiddish magazine for children, and maintains the *Farlag Matones*, a publishing house for modern Yiddish literature and textbooks.

SHTADLAN

Hebrew term meaning "advocate," applied to a representative of the Jewish community chosen to plead the cause of the Jews before kings, princes, and governments. This title was first known in Germany (in the Middle Ages), and later in Poland and other countries. The *Shtadlan* was appointed by virtue of his wealth, his business connections, his eloquence and his relations with high dignitaries of the government. The Shtadlan was often successful in alleviating discriminatory measures against Jewish communities.

SHULḤAN ARUKH

Hebrew title of the Code of Jewish Law,

composed by Joseph Karo, and published in 1555. It is composed of four parts, dealing with all phases of life, both religious and civil. The first part is called *Orah Hayim*, and deals with prayer, Sabbath and the holidays. The second part, *Yoreh Deah*, deals with a miscellany of subjects, such as the dietary regulations, proselytism, etc. The third division, *Even Ha-Ezer*, covers the laws of domestic relations, and the fourth division, *Hoshen Mishpat*, deals with other civil laws. Unlike earlier codes, it omits the laws of animal sacrifices and the ancient Temple, since it was meant as a practical guide for Jews living in the modern world where such regulations do not obtain.

This Code received acceptance on the part of Jewish community the world over immediately upon its publication. Because it was written by a Sefardi Jew, the east European Jewish community found many of its statements at variance with its own practices. Rabbi Moses Isserles of Cracow therefore added notes to the text of the *Shulhan Arukh*, giving the manner of observance of the Ashkenazi Jew. To this day in all printed editions of the Shulhan Arukh, the basic text of Karo appears in square Hebrew letters, and the notes of Isserles appear in *Rashi Script*. Since the basic text is called "Prepared Table" (Shulhan Arukh), the notes of Isserles are called "Tablecloth" (Mappah). In common usage, the *Mappah* is called RAMA, a word made of the initial letters of the Hebrew name of Rabbi Moses Isserles.

While later codes written by great authorities made their appearance in recent centuries, the Shulhan Arukh has remained to this day the authoritative code for observant Jews. See *Codes; Isserles, Moses; Karo, Joseph*.

SHUSHAN PURIM

The day after Purim (15th of Adar). It is related in the *Scroll of Esther* that the Jews of the capital city, Shushan (Susa), observed Purim for two days. According to tradition, *Shushan Purim* was observed in those cities which had walls built around them in the days of Joshua. See *Purim*.

SIDDUR

Hebrew term meaning "order" applied to the Jewish daily prayer book, as distinguished from the *Mahzor*, the festival prayer book. Editions of the *Siddur* generally use the same order of services, including first the three daily services, *Shaharit* (morning service), *Minhah* afternoon service), and *Maariv* (evening service), followed by the *Sabbath* service. Different editions of the Siddur vary as far as inclusion of other liturgical materials is concerned. Besides the regular prayers, the Siddur often includes blessings for various occasions, *Psalms*, the *Passover Haggadah*, the *Song of Songs*, *Zemirot* (chants), and other liturgical matter. Modern editions of the Siddur are generally based on the oldest prayer book, compiled in the 9th century by R. Amram Gaon. The oldest prayers included in the Siddur are the *Shema*, which was recited daily in the Second Temple, and the *Amidah* or *Shemoneh Esreh*. In the course of the centuries, many other prayers composed by famous men were gradually added to the daily liturgy. In accordance with the customs of different Jewish communities, varying versions of the Siddur are used, such as the *Nusah Sephardi* (the Sephardi version), *Nusah Ashkenazi* (Ashkenazi version), and others. The basic prayers of the liturgy are recorded in the *Mishnah* and *Gemara*. See *Prayer Book*.

SIDRAH see Parashah.

SILOAM INSCRIPTION

One of the oldest known Hebrew inscriptions, found on the side wall of a tunnel cut through the rocks in the days of King Hezekiah. This tunnel was one of the two conduits which brought the waters of the Gihon river to the water reservoir in Jerusalem, called Siloam (Shiloaḥ). The inscription giving the details of the digging and completion of the tunnel was discovered by a group of children in 1880.

SIMEON

Second son of Jacob and ancestor of the tribe of the same name. The Bible recounts that Simeon together with Levi massacred the people of Shechem in revenge for the violation of their sister Dinah. Simeon was kept as hostage by Joseph when the brothers first came to Egypt to buy food supplies. After the conquest of Canaan, the tribe of Simeon settled in the extreme southern part of the land.

SIMEON BEN SHETAH (SHATAH)

One of the great Pharisaic teachers of the first century b.c.e., and president of the *Sanhedrin*. He is especially remembered for introducing compulsory elementary education in Palestine.

SIMEON BEN YOHAI

One of the most prominent *Tannaim* of the second century c.e., to whom tradition attributes the authorship of the *Zohar*. He was a pupil of Rabbi Akiva, and himself the head of an academy at Meron, near Safed. Because he agitated openly against the oppression of the Romans during the period following Bar Kokhba's unsuccessful revolt, he had to flee for his life, and for 13 years he and his son hid in a cave, living on carobs and water. Despite his difficulties with the Romans, he was a member of a Jewish delegation which went to Rome for the purpose of requesting the repeal of anti-Jewish decrees. In addition to his high

A devout Jew kisses the tombstone of Rabbi Simeon ben Yoḥai at Meron during his Lag Ba-Omer pilgrimage, while his family waits its turn.

scholarship, he was known for his saintliness, and to this day pious Jews in Israel make a pilgrimage to his tomb at Meron on the Lag Ba-Omer festival to pay homage to him and his accomplishments.

SIMHAH BEN SAMUEL VITRY

Compiled *Maḥzor Vitry*. See *Maḥzor*.

SIMHAT TORAH

Hebrew term meaning "Rejoicing of the Torah," the ninth and final day of the festival of Sukkot, devoted traditionally to rejoicing over the Torah. The characteristic feature of the services in the synagogue on *Simḥat Torah* is the series of processions (Hakkafot) with the Scrolls of the Torah which take place during the evening and morning services. Simḥat Torah marks the completion of the annual cycle of the reading of the Torah, and the beginning of a new cycle. Special honors are accorded to the person called up for the reading of the last lines of the

Painting of a Simḥat Torah celebration inside the synagogue at Leghorn, Italy, by Solomon A. Hart, London, 1841. The ceremonial procession with the Torah scrolls, called "Hakkafot," is a part of the festival.

Pentateuch who is called *Ḥatan Torah* (Bridegroom of the Torah), as well as to the person called up for the reading of the beginning portion of *Bereshit* (first book of the Torah), who is called *Ḥatan Bereshit* (Bridegroom of *Bereshit*). The holiday is a joyous occasion for children, who not only join in the procession of the *Hakkafot* carrying special Simḥat Torah flags sometimes topped by lit candles, but they are also given the exceptional privilege of being called up for the reading of the Torah (Kol ha-Nearim). Pious Jews celebrate Simḥat Torah by dancing, drinking of wine, and visiting friends, as an expression of rejoicing with the words of the Torah. In Israel and in reform congregations throughout the world, the festivi-

452

ties of Simḥat Torah take place on the preceding day, which is generally known as Shemini Atzeret. See *Festivals*.

SIN

A letter of the alphabet. See *Shin*.

SIN

In Judaism a sin is a violation of the will of God and thus an offense against Him. A sin is committed wilfully if the person committing the sin is: a) aware of what he is doing, and b) at the same time knows that the act is wrong. If either or both of these two elements are missing then the sinner is held to have acted inadvertently (Beshogeg).

Another classification of sins is that

"Ben Adam la-Makom" (a sin committed against God alone and not involving another human being) and "Ben Adam la-Havero" (an offense against a fellow man). Offenses against God alone may be atoned for by repentance, prayer, the giving of charity, and the proper observance of Yom Kippur. However, in cases of offense against other people, all these in themselves are inadequate; they must be accompanied by the forgiveness granted by the victim. The victim need not forgive unless every effort has been made by the aggressor to rehabilitate him as much as the circumstances allow.

True repentance involves sincere regret for the past act and the undertaking not to repeat it in the future. If a person sins with the intention of repenting afterwards, such a sin is never forgiven.

In general, sin is one of the areas in human life where Judaism and Christianity diverge. These differences are manifested in the Christian concept of original sin, which Judaism does not accept, and also the rejection by Judaism of the Roman Catholic practice of confession to another human being. In Judaism confession is to God alone, without any human intermediaries or intercessions.

The formula for the public confession of sin in Judaism is always couched in the plural number, "*We* have transgressed"; "For the sin which *we* have sinned" (Al het shehatanu), and never *I* have sinned. The confession of sins is uttered during every service on Yom Kippur except Neilah. The confession is also recited in the afternoon service on the day prior to Yom Kippur. Many Jews recite a private confession (Viddui) silently immediately before *Kol Nidre*. Very pious persons will confess their sins before God every month on the day prior to Rosh Hodesh, which is thus called the small day of atonement (Yom Kippur Katan).

Some persons confess their sins every night before going to bed. The devout Jew will also recite the confession (Viddui) on his deathbed.

SINAI

The Biblical name of the sacred mountain where, according to Jewish tradition, God gave the Israelites the Ten Commandments. Mount Sinai is also referred to in the Bible as Mount Horeb. The mountain is located somewhere in the Sinai peninsula between Israel and Egypt. However, the exact location of the sacred mountain is unknown. It is questionable whether the mountain now known as Sinai is the original Mount Sinai. Some authorities maintain that Mount Sinai is what is now known as Jebel Musa (the mountain of Moses), where a Christian church is located, housing a large and old library.

SINAI INSCRIPTIONS see Archeology.

SIRACH see Ben-Sira, Joshua.

SIVAN

Ninth month in the Hebrew calendar, corresponding to May-June, and consisting of 30 days. The Ten Commandments were given to the Israelites during this month, and the festival of Shavuot is celebrated on its 6th and 7th days. See *Festivals; Shavuot*.

SIYYUM

A Hebrew term meaning "end" or "completion," applied to a number of festive occasions in Jewish religious or scholastic life, such as *Siyyum Sefer Torah*, the ceremony of completing the writing of a Scroll of the Torah; *Siyyum ha-Sefer*, the conclusion of the reading of one of the tomes of the Talmud; *Siyyum ha-Torah*, the completion of the reading of the Five Books of Moses on Simhat Torah, the 23rd day of Tishre; and *Siyyum ha-Zeman*, a more recent term signifying the completion of a school term and taking the form of a graduation ceremony.

SKULLCAP see Ceremonial Objects, Jewish.

SLAUGHTERING, RITUAL see Sheḥitah.

SLOUSCHZ, NAHUM

Philologist, archeologist, Hebrew writer and Zionist leader. Born in Odessa, Russia in 1872, he spent about twenty years traveling in North Africa, including Algeria, Tunisia and Tripoli, where he studied the history of the Jews in those regions. He also studied the antiquities of the Phoenician civilization, headed scientific expeditions sponsored by French institutes, and made important archeological excavations in Tiberias and Jerusalem. An ardent Zionist and Hebraist, he published books on the renaissance of Hebrew, including a history of *Modern Hebrew Literature* and several other important studies. Many of his writings were published in French and in English, as well as in Hebrew. After World War I he settled in Palestine.

SMOLENSKIN, PERETZ (1842–1885)

Hebrew novelist, journalist and Jewish nationalist. Born in Russia, he was a Yeshivah student and spent his youth in hardship and wandering. In 1862 he arrived in Odessa where he became interested in the *Haskalah* movement, and began his literary career as contributor to the Hebrew publication *Ha-Melitz.* In 1888 he went to Vienna, where he founded the Hebrew periodical *Ha-Shaḥar,* becoming its editor and chief contributor. Smolenskin became a widely read Hebrew writer, and he used Ha-Shaḥar as a platform for propagating his idea of Jewish nationalism. In one of his best known theoretical articles, entitled *Am Olam* (Eternal People), he called for Jewish national revival through political and spiritual independence. Gaining firsthand information about conditions of the Jews in Rumania, which he investi-

gated in behalf of the *Alliance Israélite,* and knowing of the deplorable conditions of Jewish life in the diaspora, Smolenskin became an advocate of Zionist settlements in Palestine. He wrote a number of Hebrew novels, the best known being *Ha-Toeh Bedarke Ha-Hayim,* based on his own life, and depicting east European Jewish life in the 19th century.

SOCIETY FOR THE ADVANCEMENT OF JUDAISM

A congregation founded in 1922 by Rabbi Mordecai M. Kaplan. Functioning in New York City, the Society was designed to become a laboratory for the implementation of the ideas and objectives of the *Reconstructionist* movement. It thus aimed to offer Jews the opportunity to experiment with modern forms of Jewish living in terms of worship, education, and other cultural and group activities. See *Kaplan, Mordecai M.; Reconstructionism.*

SODOM AND GOMORRAH

Two cities which, according to the Bible, were situated in the "plain of the Jordan," the people of which were notoriously wicked as well as inhospitable. God decided to destroy them by a rain of brimstone and fire. Lot, Abraham's nephew, who lived in Sodom, was warned in time to escape; but his wife, who disobediently looked back on the flaming city, turned into a pillar of salt.

SOFER

Hebrew term meaning "scribe" commonly applied to a professional copyist of the Scrolls of the Torah and other sacred texts written on parchment in a characteristic form of lettering. The term is also

In Israel an Oriental scribe (Sofer in Hebrew) patiently and in exacting detail inscribes the Pentateuch on parchment to fashion a new Sefer Torah. Oriental scribes usually use a reed to write, Western scribes generally use a quill.

Tables and benches reconstructed from the long room at Qumran, which probably served as a writing room for the scribes of the Essene community. Ink wells were also discovered in the remains.

applied to one of the groups of teachers and interpreters of the Scriptures who lived and worked in the early period of the Second Commonwealth.

SOFERIM

Hebrew term meaning "scribes" or "bookmen" applied to professional copyists of the Bible as well as a group of religious leaders and interpreters of Jewish laws who were active in the period of the Second Commonwealth. Though the word "Sofer," probably meaning secretary, was used as early as the First Temple, the first known Sofer is Ezra (5th century b.c.e.).

Until the time of the Hasmonean dynasty's reign, the *Soferim* were the recognized authorities on the texts of the Bible. The Talmud records that the Soferim preserved the tradition of the correct text though they made a number of changes in the lettering to avoid misinterpretation. These glosses are referred to in the Talmud as *Divre Soferim* ("the words of the Scribes"), and used to clarify the text.

SOKOLOW, NAHUM (1860–1936)

Father of modern Hebrew journalism and prominent Zionist leader. Born in Poland, he earned early recognition as scholar and

456

Nahum Sokolow (left), prominent Zionist leader, follower of Herzl, and journalist, is shown with Menahem Mendel Ussishkin (right) in the Herzl Room of the Jewish National Fund's headquarters in Jerusalem.

linguist. In 1887 he became editor of the Hebrew periodical *Ha-Tzefirah*, and was soon acclaimed as a foremost Hebrew journalist and promoter of Hebrew culture. He later became editor of *Ha-Olam*, official organ of the World Zionist Organization, in which he played an active role. As member of the Zionist Executive Committee he toured many countries, including the United States, in the interests of Zionism. For his ability as a political leader, his erudition and wide range of experience as well as for his refined manners, dignity and dress, he received popular acclaim. Between 1931 and 1935 he served as president of the World Zionist Organization. He died in London in 1936, and in 1955 his remains were taken to Israel and buried next to the tomb of Theodor Herzl, the father of political Zionism, of whom he was a distinguished follower.

SOLOMON

The third king of Israel, son of David and Bath-sheba, who ruled from 973–933 b.c.e. Solomon consolidated the kingdom created by his illustrious father, and kept the country at peace by making friendly alliances with the neighboring countries. He devoted himself to the administration of the

457

country; he developed commerce with other nations, sending his fleet to Ophir to bring back gold, silver and other precious products, and established smelting works at Ezion-geber.

Solomon's greatest accomplishment was the erection of the Holy Temple in Jerusalem which became the religious and cultural center of the country. He is regarded by tradition as a man of great wisdom, and Jewish folklore is replete with tales of his remarkable powers of judgment. Tradition ascribes to him the authorship of the Biblical books of *Proverbs, Song of Songs* and *Ecclesiastes*.

Because of his extensive building program in Jerusalem and elsewhere, and his extravagant expenditures in the maintenance of his luxurious court, he resorted to forced labor and heavy taxation. Bitter opposition to his rule thus engendered the division of the United Kingdom which occurred after his death.

SOLOMON IBN GABIROL see Ibn Gabirol, Solomon.

SOLOMON MOLKO see Molko, Solomon.

SONG OF SONGS

First of the Five Scrolls (*Megillot*), called in Hebrew *Shir Ha-Shirim*, contained in the third division of the Hebrew Bible. The theme of the *Song of Songs* is the reciprocal love between man and woman. This collection of beautiful love lyrics has been canonized in the Bible despite its secular content and the absence of any reference to God. Tradition has, nevertheless, justified its inclusion in the Bible by interpreting the love between the maiden and her admirer as the love between God (the (Bridegroom) and Israel (the bride). The authorship of the book is traditionally at-

Remains of a wall around a large building, probably the governor's house, near the stables of Solomon at the southern edge of the Megiddo mount. During his reign (10th century b.c.e.), Solomon built a trade route between Egypt and Phoenicia where Megiddo was a way-station for horses and chariots.

tributed to King Solomon, but judging it from the standpoint of language and style some scholars consider it the literary product of later times.

SOUTH AFRICA

The Jewish community in South Africa began in the middle of the 17th century, its first settlers being immigrants from Holland, Germany and England. In 1891 its Jewish population numbered about 3,000, but with the influx of Jewish immigrants from eastern Europe, the Jewish community grew steadily, and in 1960 numbered about 110,000, a large percentage of whom were concentrated in the cities of Johannesburg and Capetown.

Jews have played an important role in the industrial, commercial, political and cultural life of South Africa, and prominent Jewish names appear among the leading personalities of the country. The Jewish community has developed several important institutions and agencies, the most vital and most influential being the Zionist Federation, which contributed about one-fourth of the budget of the World Zionist Organization. With the establishment of the State of Israel, South African Jews distinguished themselves by undertaking and developing important colonization projects there.

SOVIET RUSSIA see Russia.

SPAIN

Jews settled in Spain as early as the first century, and discrimination against them was ordered by the Council of Elvira in 303 c.e. Jews were treated well during the early reign of the Visigoths, but upon the conversion of the Visigoths to Catholicism, Jews were given the alternative of either

Reconstruction of a palace, probably the provincial governor's residence, in Megiddo during the Solomonic era. Megiddo was used both as a fortress to command and protect the caravan routes, and also as a great storehouse for the variety of goods Solomon traded with the Egyptians and Phoenicians.

embracing the Catholic faith or leaving the country. The Jews who remained, therefore welcomed the Arab invasion of Spain in 711. Under subsequent Arab rule, the Jewish community began to flourish, and inspired by the relative religious freedom accorded to them, they contributed significantly to the economic and cultural development of Spain. Jews became prominent figures in Arab culture, philosophy and science, and they made great strides in the development of Jewish culture. The establishment of Talmudical academies headed by famous rabbis led Spain to become the most significant center of Jewish learning in the Middle Ages. During this "Golden Period" of the Jewish community in Spain, Jews played a prominent role in the political life of the country, and great Hebrew scholars and poets made a lasting contribution in the fields of Jewish philosophy, and Hebrew poetry and philology. Prominent in this period were such names as Ḥasdai ibn Shaprut, Samuel Ha-Nagid, Baḥya ibn Pakuda, Solomon ibn Gabirol, Moses ibn Ezra, Judah Ha-Levi, Abraham ibn Ezra, and many others.

After the decline of Arab rule which began in 1212 and the subsequent domination of Spain by Christian rulers, Jewish existence became increasingly threatened. The year 1391 marked a turning point in the history of the Jewish community in Spain. On Ash Wednesday of that year, under the pressure of religious passions, the Jews of Seville were attacked and thereafter most Jewish communities in Spain were subjected to massacre resulting in tens of thousands of deaths, and in forced baptism. Both faithful Jews and Marranos continued to live in Spain under constant terror, which culminated in the establishment of the Inquisition, and the final banishment of all Jews from Spain in 1492 under the reign of King Ferdinand and Queen Isabella. According to the testimony of Don Isaac Abravanel, the great Jewish statesman of Spain who unsuccessfully intervened against the expulsion, some 300,000 Jews fled Spain and found refuge in Portugal, Italy, Morocco, Turkey, and elsewhere. Thus ended the history of the Jewish community in Spain. For centuries Jews refused to return to Spain. During the 19th century, small numbers of Jews settled in Spain. After the seizure of power by the Franco government, restrictions were placed on the public worship of all non-Roman Catholic groups. In 1960 the Jewish community there numbered about 3,000.

SPANIOLISH see Ladino.

SPINOZA, BARUCH (1632–1677)

One of the greatest philosophers of modern times. Born in Amsterdam, Holland, he came from a family of Spanish Marranos who had returned to Judaism. Spinoza studied Talmud, Jewish medieval philosophy, Kabbalah, classical languages, natural sciences, general philosophy and especially the works of the French philosopher Descartes. His unorthodox ideas brought him into sharp conflict with the traditional Jewish outlook on theological questions. Refusing to renounce his views, he was excommunicated by the rabbis. He left Amsterdam and wandered from town to town until he settled at The Hague, where he earned a modest living as a grinder of optical lenses and where he wrote his most important works. He died there of tuberculosis at the age of 45.

Spinoza's first important work, entitled *Theological-Political Treatise* (1670), aroused bitter opposition from both Jewish and Christian religious leaders. It developed the thesis that the state must encourage free thought. Advocating the principles of freedom of thought and religious tolerance, Spinoza initiated modern

Bible criticism, attempting to refute the idea of revelation. In his greatest work, the *Ethics*, published after his death (1677), Spinoza developed his philosophic system based on the doctrine of *pantheism:* God and Nature are identical, and all natural phenomena are manifestations of a single independent being or substance, called God or Nature. In the *Ethics* Spinoza further states that everything is predetermined and that man has no free will to choose between good and evil, and that neither prayer nor reward and punishment can change the fate of men. Man's true happiness lies in knowledge, his ability to control his emotions through his intellect, and the highest knowledge leads to the understanding and love of God.

Spinoza had a lasting influence on modern philosophy; and despite earlier indifference or opposition, modern Jewish and Christian philosophers and religious thinkers have shown interest in his works, and a reappraisal of his philosophical ideas has gradually taken place.

STAR OF DAVID see Magen David.

STATISTICS see Population, Jewish.

STRAUS

A prominent family which came to the United States from Germany, and whose members have become known in business, politics, public affairs and philanthropy. The chief members of the family were: 1) *Isidor Straus* (1845–1912), successful merchant and one of the founders of the Educational Alliance in New York City, generous contributor to welfare and cultural agencies. He and his wife met a tragic death on the steamship *Titanic* which sank after striking an iceberg in 1912; 2) *Nathan Straus* (1848–1931), most generous philanthropist (particulars are given below under separate heading); 3) *Oscar Solomon Straus* (1850–1926), U.S. Ambassador to Turkey, Secretary of Com-

merce and Labor, member of the Permanent Court of Arbitration at The Hague, leader of American Jewish Committee, and of the American Jewish Joint Distribution Committee.

STRAUS, NATHAN (1848–1931)

Prominent American philanthropist. Early in life he became a business associate in his father's firm, and later joined the R. H. Macy Co. in New York which became a successful business enterprise. In 1898 he was president of the Board of Health of New York City.

Nathan Straus is remembered for his unselfish philanthropic work for the poor masses of the American people in times of depression, and for his health projects in Palestine. In 1890 he established laboratories for the pasteurization of milk for the poor children of New York and elsewhere. He also organized the distribution of food and coal to the suffering poor during the crisis of 1893–94, and in 1909 founded a Tuberculosis Preventorium for children. During World War I he spent millions for the relief of war victims everywhere. He made several visits to Palestine, where he established the Nathan Straus Hadassah's Child Welfare Stations and later the Nathan and Lina Straus Health Centers in Jerusalem and Tel Aviv. His wife, Lina, also showed her social and Jewish concerns by giving all her jewels to Hadassah. When Straus died in 1931 thousands of humble people paid their last respects to their great benefactor. The town of Netanyah in Israel bears his name.

STYBEL, JOSEPH

Famous publisher of Hebrew books. In 1918 he founded his publishing company in Moscow; in 1926 he transferred it to Berlin; and in 1930 to Tel Aviv. He extended himself to help unknown Hebrew writers as well as established ones.

461

Jewish festival painting by Martin Engelbrecht, 18th-century Augsburg artist, shows five booths (called Sukkahs in Yiddish) in which part of the Sukkot holiday is celebrated. Inscriptions beneath the different booths are Biblical and post-Biblical quotations on how to use the Sukkah in observance.

SUKKAH see Sukkot.

SUKKOT

Hebrew name of the Feast of Tabernacles, the fall festival which begins on the 15th day of *Tishre*. The Bible prescribes that the eighth day shall be observed as a *Feast of Conclusion* (Shemini Atzeret). This is looked upon as a separate festival. In the diaspora, the day following Shemini Atzeret is known as *Simḥat Torah*. In Israel (as well as in reform congregations throughout the world) both days are celebrated on Shemini Atzeret.

Thus in the diaspora, the first and the last two days of Sukkot are full holidays, and the five middle days are half-holidays, called *Ḥol ha-Moed*. The seventh day of the festival bears the special name of *Hoshana Rabbah*.

Sukkot is first a harvest thanksgiving

festival, the *Ḥag ha-Asif* (Festival of Ingathering), and one of the *Shalosh Regalim* (three pilgrimage festivals), when it was the duty of every Israelite to go up to Jerusalem to attend services and the celebration in the Temple.

Sukkot is also celebrated in commemoration of the period when the Israelites wandered in the wilderness and dwelt in booths (sukkot). Because of the joyous nature of the festival, Sukkot is also called *Zeman Simḥatenu* (Season of our Rejoicing). The essential practices of this festival are living in a *Sukkah* (booth), and waving the *Lulav* and *Etrog*, thereby symbolizing the agricultural nature of the holiday.

Young Ḥasidic boy in the "Meah Shearim" quarters in Jerusalem helps to decorate the traditional Sukkah. The Sukkah is intended to commemorate the time when the Israelites in the wilderness lived in booths (Sukkahs).

SURINAM

The American Thanksgiving Day, derives from the festival of Sukkot. The pilgrims after a winter of hunger celebrated their first successful harvest in America by creating this holiday, modeled after this Biblical harvest festival.

SURINAM

Known as Dutch Guiana, historically important for its oldest Jewish permanent settlement in the Western Hemisphere. Jews settled in Surinam as early as 1639 as emigrants from Holland and Italy, and later from England and other European countries. The Jewish community there prospered under Dutch rule, but in later years it has been on the decline and now numbers only several hundred Jews.

SUV

A letter of the alphabet. See *Tav*.

SWASTIKA

Sanskrit name of a hooked cross used by ancient civilizations as a symbol of fertility. In India, in China, and in Japan it is still used as a symbol or decoration. It also appears as a decoration of ancient Jewish synagogues in Palestine, such as those found in the excavated synagogue of Capernaum of the 2nd century c.e. In modern times it was adopted by anti-Semites as their symbol, and in Nazi Germany it was especially popularized as a symbol of German or "Aryan" supremacy.

SWEDEN

There was no Jewish settlement in Sweden before the last quarter of the 18th century. Until the middle of the 19th century Jews lived under discriminatory laws. But thereafter the Jewish community grew under a regime of civic and religious freedom. Both the Swedish government and church demonstrated their sympathy for the Jews during the Nazi persecutions, and many Jewish refugees from Norway and elsewhere found asylum in Sweden. During the post-war period the Jewish population steadily increased, and grew to about 13,000 in 1960.

SWITZERLAND

Jewish settlements in this central European republic existed in the Middle Ages. Until the period following the French Revolution the fate of the Jews there was not brighter than in most European countries. In modern times Jews have equal citizenship rights. *Sheḥitah*, however, was forbidden in 1893 on "humanitarian" grounds. During the period of World War I many young Russian Jews went to Switzerland to enroll in its universities. Jews live mostly in Zurich, Berne and Basle. The latter was the city where the first Zionist Congress was convened by Theodor Herzl. In 1960 the Jewish population of Switzerland was about 19,000.

SYNAGOGUE

The most important religious institution in Jewish life, serving three functions, as a place of public worship, assembly, and study. It is also called *Temple* by reform and some conservative Jews, and *Shul* by Yiddish speaking orthodox Jews. The origin of the Synagogue is traced back to the period of the Babylonian exile when Jews assembled in private homes for services and religious instruction. During the period of the Second Commonwealth the synagogue existed as a gathering place for religious services and study, in addition to the Temple in Jerusalem. After the destruction of the Temple, the synagogue became the exclusive place for public services and instruction, and every Jewish community, both in Palestine and in the diaspora, had its synagogues.

The synagogue served as a place of worship, a communal center, as well as a

(Top) Ruins of the ancient synagogue at Capernaum, in Israel, on the Sea of Galilee. (Above, left) 18th-century engraving of a Frankfort, Germany, synagogue. (Right) Rodeph Shalom Synagogue on New York City's Clinton Street, 1853, built in the old Romanesque style. Note the two doors at street level leading to the first-floor galleries for women.

(Left) The "Scuola Spagnola," or Sephardic Synagogue, in Venice, Italy. Built in 1584 and later more lavishly ornamented in 1635, its elaborate Torah shrine, its lovely and ornate chandeliers, and its richly decorated ceiling, combine to give it a special Mediterranean flavor. Above the Ark is seen the balustraded balcony which is the women's gallery. (Top right) Architect's drawing of New York City's Temple Emanu-El at Fifth Avenue and 65th Street, which can seat more than 2,000 people. Its very early Romanesque architecture is an adaptation of the style used in Syria, the Middle East and also in parts of Sicily. (Bottom) Frank Lloyd Wright's celebrated modern synagogue at Elkins Park, Pennsylvania. Sometimes called a "mountain sheathed in glass," Beth Shalom has a unique cantilevered triangular marquee, a glass tower and an ingenious system of ramps which Wright designed to eliminate all of the staircases.

Interior of New York City's Spanish and Portuguese Synagogue is based on the traditional Sephardic plan. Framed by paired Corinthian columns, the Ark is crowned by the Decalogue on volutes and a pediment.

place of assembly and of study, as evidenced from the various Hebrew terms by which it was known, such as *Bet ha-Tefillah* (House of Prayer), *Bet ha-Keneset* (House of Assembly), *Bet ha-Midrash* (House of Study), and perhaps also *Bet Am* (House of the People).

Earlier functionaries of the synagogue were the *Parnas* (head of the synagogue), an honorary official, and the *Hazzan*, an official whose duties included the reading of the service, the upkeep of the building, and often that of religious instructor for the young. The *Shammash* became another official when the duties of the Hazzan were limited only to the reading of the service. The office of the Rabbi as the official head of the synagogue was introduced at a much later period.

Synagogues generally are so planned that during the services the worshippers are able to face toward Jerusalem. Traditionally each synagogue provided for a special women's section, which in recent years was eliminated in reform and conservative congregations in which men and women sit together during the services.

SYNAGOGUE, MEN OF THE GREAT see Great Synagogue, Men of the.

SYNAGOGUE COUNCIL OF AMERICA
Organized in 1926 to represent the majority of congregationally affiliated Jews of America through its constituent organizations, listed as follows: The Rabbinical Council of America and the Union of Orthodox Jewish Congregations of America (orthodox); the Rabbinical Assembly of America and the United Synagogue of America (conservative); the Central Conference of American Rabbis and the Union of American Hebrew Congregations (reform).

Through the Council these national bodies cooperate with one another. One of its major activities is the dissemination of good will and understanding between Christians and Jews in cooperation with the National Council of the Churches of Christ in America and other groups.

SYRIA
Ancient country, north of Palestine, known in the Bible as *Aram*. Formerly a province of Turkey, it became a mandate territory of France after World War I, and thereafter became an independent republic. In ancient times the territory of Syria extended over parts of Palestine, and under Roman rule important Jewish communities existed in Syria, especially in Antioch. Its most ancient city is Damascus, where most of its 5,500 Jews were living in 1960. Syria was one of the Arab states which attacked the newly proclaimed State of Israel in 1948, and continued to be one of the hostile neighbors of the Jewish republic. Syria and Egypt combined to form the United Arab Republic in 1958, which Syria broke from in 1961.

SYRKIN, NAHMAN (1867–1924)
Leader of the *Poale Zion* (Labor Zionist) movement, and writer. Born in Russia, he became interested in both Zionism and socialism, and formulated a program of Zionist socialism which advocated the establishment in Palestine of a Jewish socialist state as the ultimate solution of the Jewish problem. Unlike some other Jewish socialists, he opposed assimilation and called for the revival of the Hebrew language and culture. An accomplished publicist, he settled in the United States in 1907, where he became an active leader of the Poale Zion party.

SZOLD, HENRIETTA (1860–1945)
American social worker, leading Zionist and founder of *Hadassah*. Born in Baltimore, Maryland, she started her career as a teacher, and distinguished herself in con-

ducting Americanization classes. In 1893 she became editor in the Jewish Publication Society, was its secretary, and did translation and editorial work including collaboration as editor of the *American Jewish Year Book*.

Henrietta Szold is best remembered for her long career in Zionist work and leadership. In 1916 she was given the task of organizing the project known as American Zionist Medical Unit for Palestine. In connection with this project, she left for Palestine in 1920 where she subsequently became director of the School of Nursing in Jerusalem, which now bears her name. She also helped in the establishment of the Hadassah University Hospital and the Alice Seligsberg Trade School for Girls.

In 1927 she was chosen to be a member of the Zionist Executive, and in 1930 she was elected a member of *Vaad Leumi* (National Council for Palestine), in charge of social service activities. When the Nazis came to power in Germany (1933), she became director of *Youth Aliyah*, the immigration and rehabilitation of boys and girls from Germany.

For her leadership, devotion and untiring work in the field of social welfare in Palestine, she was the most respected woman among Zionist leaders, and the recipient of honorary degrees and other distinctions. *Kfar Szold*, a settlement of young German graduates of Youth Aliyah, was established in her honor. See *Hadassah; Youth Aliyah*.

Henrietta Szold, leading woman Zionist and the founder of the Hadassah, the Women's Zionist Organization of America. She was the active leader of the Youth Aliyah which saved thousands of Jewish youth from Nazi extermination.

T

TALLIT

Speak unto the children of Israel, and bid them that they make them throughout their generations fringes in the corners of their garments, and that they put with the fringe of each corner a thread of blue. And it shall be unto you for a fringe, that ye may look upon it, and remember all the commandments of the Lord, and do them. . . .

NUMBERS

TAANIT ESTER see Fast Days.

TABERNACLE

Translation of the Hebrew term *Mishkan*, or *Ohel Moed*, applied to the portable sanctuary of the Israelites in the wilderness, and constructed by Bezalel, as directed by Moses. It was a tent-like structure, having of an outer court where the priests burned offerings on the altar, and an inner "dwelling" leading to the *Holy of Holies*—the Ark of the Covenant—accessible only to the High Priest on Yom Kippur. The Tabernacle moved with the Israelites during their wanderings in the wilderness, and after the conquest of Canaan it is mentioned for the last time as being situated at Shiloh during the time of Eli the Priest.

TABERNACLES, FEAST OF see Sukkot.

TABLES OF THE LAW, TWO

Also known as "Tablets of the Law," translation of the Hebrew *Shene Luhot ha-Berit*, applied to the two stone tablets of the covenant or testimony on which Moses inscribed the Ten Commandments given to the Israelites at Mount Sinai. To this day the *Tables of the Law* are a distinctive symbol of the Torah and are seen in every synagogue at the upper part of the *Aron ha-Kodesh* (Holy Ark). The Ten Commandments are customarily represented by the first two Hebrew words of each Commandment which are inscribed on the Tables of the Law.

TAHANUN

Hebrew name of a prayer of supplication and penitence recited daily, excepting Sabbaths and festivals, as part of the morning and afternoon services after the *Shemoneh Esreh*.

TAKKANAH

Hebrew term meaning "improvement" or "establishment," applied to an ordinance or statute issued by a recognized Jewish authority to meet the needs of the time in relation to religious, social and moral problems of the Jewish community. Such *Takkanot* (Ordinances) were not necessarily based on Biblical or Talmudic legislation, but on current needs resulting from changes in social and economic conditions. The Takkanot, considered by Jewish communities to be as binding as the Written Law, date back to ancient times and have increased in number during the course of Jewish history. Examples of Takkanot enacted in ancient times are: the institution of the daily prayer; the reading of the *Megillah* on *Purim;* the use of the *Ketubah* (marriage contract); the *Pruzbol*, enacted by Hillel (the suspension of the Biblical law relieving debtors on Sabbatical years). In later periods numerous other Takkanot were enacted, such as the ordinance permitting a Jewish wife to sue her husband for a divorce; the prohibition of polygamy and forcible divorce of a wife, enacted by Rabbenu Gershom (10th century).

TAL

The Hebrew word for dew. In a country with a geographic and topographic climate such as Israel's, dew is as important as rain for the farmer. On the first day of Passover at the *Musaf Service* a prayer for dew (*Tefillat Tal*) is recited. In the Sephardi ritual, dew is mentioned (*Morid ha-Tal*) in the second benediction of the *Tefillah*, between Passover and Sukkot. In the weekday Tefillah during the winter months (December 4 or 5 to Passover) a prayer for "dew and rain" (*Tal u-Matar*) is inserted in the benediction asking for a fertile year. See *Geshem*.

TALLIT (TALLIS)

A Hebrew word for the prayer shawl in which male worshippers wrap themselves during the morning services throughout the year. The Tallit is rectangular in shape, made of silk or wool, with black or blue stripes, and with *Tzitzit* (fringes) at each of its four corners. The Tzitzit is the important part of the Tallit; the Bible commanded its use in order "that ye may look upon it and remember all the commandments of the Lord, and do them." The Tallit often has an embroidered band which serves as a collar upon which is inscribed the text of the blessing recited when it is put on. It is customary to bury a pious man wrapped in his Tallit, with one of the four fringes removed.

The leader of the service (Ḥazzan) wears the Tallit also during the afternoon service (Minḥah). On Yom Kippur the Tallit is worn by all male worshippers for every service; on Tishah Be-Av it is not worn in the morning, but during the afternoon service.

TALMID ḤAKHAM

Originally this Hebrew term referred to a disciple of a learned man (that is, a teacher of the Oral Law), as its literal meaning implies. Later it applied to any Talmudic scholar of high reputation, and in its present usage it applies to any individual of high Jewish scholarship.

TALMUD

A term meaning "study" applied to the second greatest literary achievement of the Jewish people, which after the Bible is the most authoritative source of Judaism. The Talmud consists of the *Mishnah*, the first Jewish code of laws after the Bible, and the *Gemara*, an elaboration of the Mishnah. The Gemara is actually more than a commentary on the laws of Mishnah, for it deals with almost everything concerning Jewish life, including a great variety of subjects such as historical events and personalities, religious and ethical material,

folklore, science, prayers. The teachers whose discussions are recorded in the Gemara are known as *Amoraim*, to be distinguished from the *Tannaim*, the teachers mentioned in the Mishnah.

The terms *Talmud* and *Gemara* are often used interchangeably. There are two separate compilations of the Gemara or the Talmud: the Babylonian and the Palestinian. The Babylonian Talmud or *Talmud Bavli* was developed by the Amoraim of Babylon, and the Palestinian Talmud, known as *Talmud Yerushalmi*, originated in Palestine.

The scholars who began the discussions which culminated in the Babylonian Talmud were Rav and Samuel, but its com-

19th-century Russian Tallit, or prayer shawl, with embroidered Hebrew initials on the front. Note, too, the embroidered neckband at the top.

A group of Yemenite Jews studying the Talmud in Jerusalem. Because books were then scarce, several people shared one book, and many learned to read upside down so they could take part in discussions.

pilation is ascribed to Rav Ashi. The year 500 c.e. is the approximate date of the final editing of the Babylonian Talmud. The initial compilation of the Palestinian Talmud is ascribed to Rabbi Johanan ben Nappaḥa (third century), and the date usually accepted for its completion is about 425 c.e.

Both the Babylonian Talmud and the Palestinian Talmud are written mainly in Aramaic, although in different dialects of the language, with an admixture of Hebrew. The quoted texts of the Mishnah are entirely in Hebrew. The Babylonian Talmud is about three times as large as the Palestinian Talmud, and is more comprehensive; it is the authoritative Talmud and is most influential in Jewish life.

The contents of the Talmud may be divided into *Halakhah* (the law) and *Aggadah* which includes everything that is not of a legal nature, and deals with the religious and ethical aspects of life. Thus while the Halakhah deals with legal discussions and decisions, the Aggadah contains historical material, ethical teachings, and folkloristic interpretations. While the texts of the Halakhah are technical and difficult, the texts of the Aggadah are more popular and appeal to the general imagination.

For centuries the Talmud served as the recognized source of Jewish knowledge and influenced every aspect of Jewish internal life. Its study spread to all important Jewish communities the world over; it stimulated further study and interpretation of Jewish law and survived the impact of other cultures as well as the

Young Ḥasidic children enrolled at an early age at the Etz Ḥayim Yeshivah in Jerusalem. At a somewhat later age, they will be studying Talmud, and will remain in religious school until young manhood.

attacks made upon it during periods of persecution in Christian countries. To this day the Talmud is the great library of Jewish life.

TALMUD BAVLI see Talmud.

TALMUD TORAH

The literal meaning of this Hebrew term is "the study of the Torah" or the "teaching of the Torah," but it is commonly used as a designation for an elementary Hebrew school. Whereas the traditional *Ḥeder* was a private religious school, the *Talmud Torah* was a public institution maintained and administered by the community in order to provide education for orphans or children of parents who could not afford private teaching. In America, Talmud Torah generally refers to a school which meets in the afternoon after the secular school session is over. Its curriculum includes the study of Bible, Hebrew, Jewish history, customs and ceremonies, and other phases of elementary Jewish knowledge.

TALMUD YERUSHALMI see Talmud.

TAM, RABBENU see Jacob ben Meir Tam.

TAMMUZ

The tenth month in the Jewish calendar, corresponding to June-July, and consisting of 29 days. The *Fast of the 17th of Tammuz* commemorates the breach in the walls of Jerusalem made when the city was besieged, and marks the first day of the traditional three weeks of mourning ending with the *Fast of Tishah Be-Av* (Ninth of Av). See *Bet Ha-Mikdash*.

477

TANAKH

TANAKH see Bible.

TANNAIM

A group of about 225 Jewish scholars active in Palestine for two and one half centuries after the death of Hillel. They are considered to be the recognized authorities on the Oral Law, their opinions being recorded in the *Mishnah* which was finally edited in 220 c.e. Some of the well-known *Tannaim* (meaning "teachers") include such figures as Rabbi Akiva, Rabbi Meir, and Rabbi Judah Ha-Nasi.

TARGUM

The literal meaning of this term is "translation," and may therefore mean translation from any language. The term is, however, applied specifically to the Aramaic translation of the various books of the Bible. The best known is the *Targum Onkelos*, the Aramaic translation of the Five Books of Moses by *Onkelos*. This and the other existing *Targumim* (translations) had become necessary when Aramaic replaced Hebrew as the spoken language of the Jewish people. In recent centuries the Targum Onkelos has been printed side by side with the Hebrew text of the *Pentateuch*. See *Onkelos*.

TARYAG MITZVOT

Hebrew term meaning "613 Commandments." The word "TaRYaG" is the numerical equivalent of "613." According to an ancient Jewish tradition God revealed 613 commandments to Moses. Of these, 365 are prohibitions, and 248 positive commands. The *Rambam* (Maimonides), among others, compiled a list of the *Taryag Mitzvot*, grouping them into different categories, and giving the Biblical source of each commandment.

TASHLIKH see Rosh Hashanah.

TAV (ת ,תּ)

The last (twenty-fourth) letter of the Hebrew alphabet. In the Ashkenazi pronunci-

Tel Aviv's Mograbi Square, now one of the city's busiest commercial centers, as it looked in 1921, a dozen years after the town was founded. Jaffa, in the background, was merged with Tel Aviv in 1949.

ation a distinction is made, depending on whether or not the letter has a *Dagesh* (dot inside the letter). In this case it is sounded like the English T and is named *Tuv*. If it is written without a Dagesh, it is sounded like the English S and called *Suv*. In the Sephardi pronunciation it is always sounded T. It is likely that in early days the *undageshed* letter was sounded TH, as in the English THin. It seems probable that *Samekh*, *Sin* and *Suv* had their own distinctive pronunciations at one time, and similarly so the *Tet* and the *Tav*. The numerical value of Tav is 400, and its meaning is "mark."

TEFILLAH

Hebrew term dating to Biblical times and still used as a designation for any prayer. The Yiddish term "tefille tun" means "to say a prayer." Technically, the word "Tefillah" is applied to the prayer known as *Shemoneh Esreh* or *Amidah*. See *Shemoneh Esreh*.

TEFILLIN see Phylacteries.

TEHILLIM see Psalms.

TEHINNAH

Hebrew term applied to a book of private prayer written in Yiddish and intended primarily for women. The *Tehinnot*, which first appeared in the 16th century, reflect the life of the Jews in that period, since many of the prayers make reference to oppressive times and ask for deliverance from false accusations and persecutions by the enemies. The word may be used for any individual supplicative prayer.

TEL AVIV

The largest and most modern city in Israel, with an all Jewish population. It was founded in 1909 on the sand dunes near Jaffa. Despite its slow development in the beginning, it showed a remarkable growth after World War I, and in 1960 it had a population of about 400,000. Cosmopolitan in nature, it has become the nerve center

Aerial photo of Tel Aviv, Israeli industrial and commercial center, shows the famous Dizengoff Square. Now the largest city in Israel, Tel Aviv contains about a fifth of the total population of the country.

479

of industrial, commercial and cultural life in the State of Israel. The name Tel Aviv was taken from the name of the Babylonian city Tel-abib. In 1949, the joining city of Jaffa was incorporated, and the official name changed to Tel Aviv–Jaffa.

TEMPLE see Bet ha-Mikdash.

TENAIM see Marriage Ceremony.

TENAKH see Bible.

TEN COMMANDMENTS (DECALOGUE)

The fundamental law of the Jewish people, known in Hebrew as *Aseret ha-Dibrot*, which according to the Bible were revealed to Moses and the people at Mount Sinai. An abbreviated form of the *Decalogue* follows: 1) I am the Lord thy God, who brought thee out of the land of Egypt, out of the house of bondage; 2) Thou shalt have no other gods before Me; 3) Thou shalt not take the name of the Lord thy God in vain; 4) Remember the Sabbath day to keep it holy; 5) Honor thy father and thy mother; 6) Thou shalt not murder; 7) Thou shalt not commit adultery; 8) Thou shalt not steal; 9) Thou shalt not bear false witness against thy neighbor; 10) Thou shalt not covet anything that belongs to thy neighbor.

The Ten Commandments are basic to civilized society and are regarded by all peoples, Jews and non-Jews alike, as the foundation of ethics and religion. They are commonly represented symbolically in the form of two tablets, called *Tables of the Law*, used as a sacred design in the synagogue, and as an ornament on different articles and objects. The Protestant numbering of the Commandments differs from the Jewish, and the Catholic differs from both.

TEN DAYS OF PENITENCE see Penitential Days.

TEN PLAGUES see Plagues, the Ten.

TEN TRIBES see Tribes, Lost Ten.

TERE ASAR see Minor Prophets.

TEREFAH see Dietary Laws.

TESHUVAH see Repentance.

TET (ט)

The ninth letter of the Hebrew alphabet, pronounced like the English T. In Ashkenazi its name is TES, but the sound of the letter is the same. Its numerical value is nine. See *Tav*.

TETRAGRAMMATON

The four-lettered word (Hebrew: Yod, Hé, Vav, Hé) which is the name of God. This name, whose real pronunciation is uncertain, is forbidden to be pronounced except by the High Priest in the Holy of Holies on Yom Kippur. Whenever this term appears in the Bible or elsewhere, it is pronounced *Adonai*, and is reverently referred to in Hebrew as the *Shem ha-Meforash* (Ineffable Name). Jewish mystics were thought to have known how to pronounce the *Tetragrammaton* and how to make mysterious use of it. Christians erroneously pronounce the word "Jehovah," and modern scholarship suggests that its original pronunciation was "Yahveh."

TEVET (TEVES)

The fourth month of the Jewish calendar, corresponding to December-January, consisting of 29 days. The last two or three days of *Hanukkah* and the fast of *Asarah Be-Tevet* (the tenth day of Tevet), which commemorates the beginning of the siege of Jerusalem by the Babylonians, fall in this month.

THIRTEEN ARTICLES OF FAITH see Maimonides, Moses.

THIRTY-SIX TZADDIKIM see Lamed-Vav Tzaddikim.

THOMASHEVSKY, BORIS (1866–1939)

Actor, playwright, producer, and one of the founders of the Yiddish theatre in America. Born in the Ukraine, he started

Israel's ancient town of Tiberias is situated on the shores of the Sea of Galilee and its hot springs have made it popular as a winter resort. In the foreground is the ancient tomb of Rabbi Meir Baal Nes.

to sing professionally at an early age, and after arriving in the United States in 1881, he organized the first Yiddish theatre group in New York City. He began writing his own plays, produced and directed many others, and became the idol of Yiddish theatre audiences. He brought new talents to the Yiddish stage, who later became famous as outstanding actors.

TIBERIAS

Ancient city in Israel on the western shore of the Sea of Galilee (Lake or *Yam Kinneret*) founded by Herod Antipas in the year 26 c.e. in honor of the Roman Emperor Tiberius. It became known as one of the four holy cities in Palestine, the others being Jerusalem, Safed and Hebron.

During the days of the *Tannaim*, as well as in later periods, Tiberias was an important center of Jewish learning. During the Middle Ages, the Jewish community in Tiberias declined, but in the 16th century the city was rebuilt by Joseph Nasi, the Duke of Naxos, to whom it was presented by Sultan Suleiman. As early as Talmudic times, Tiberias was famous for its hot mineral water springs, which have been modernized in recent years making the city an attractive winter spa. According to Jewish tradition, the graves of Maimonides and Rabbi Meir Baal Nes are located in Tiberias. Following the War of Liberation in 1948, the Arabs fled the city, and its present population is predominantly Jewish.

481

18th-century bronze, cast from the relief on the Roman Arch of Triumph erected to Titus for his conquest of Jerusalem in 70 c.e. Note the trumpets, Menorah and other Roman loot from the Temple.

TIBERIAS, LAKE OF see Kinneret.

TISHAH BE-AV

Hebrew term for "The Ninth Day of the Month of Av," observed by Jews as a day of fasting and mourning in commemoration of the destruction of the First and Second Temples. Later other disasters, such as the expulsion from Spain, were also remembered on that day. Part of the ritual of the day is the reading of the *Book of Lamentations* and the *Kinnot* (elegies). During the services the worshippers sit on the floor of the synagogue or on low stools as an expression of sorrow.

TISHRE (TISHRI)

The first month of the Jewish calendar, corresponding to September-October, consisting of 30 days. Several Jewish holidays occur during this month: *Rosh Hashanah* (the Jewish New Year), on the first and second days of *Tishre; Yom Kippur* (Day of Atonement) on the 10th day; and *Sukkot* (Feast of Tabernacles) on the 15th.

TITHE see Maaser.

TITUS, ARCH OF

A triumphal arch erected in Rome in honor of the victory of General Titus over Judea, conquering Jerusalem and destroying the Temple in 70 c.e. The Arch depicts the victorious general, the captive Jews, and the furnishings of the Temple and its sacred objects. Jews living in the Ghetto of Rome customarily avoided passing under the Arch. The Arch of Titus is still standing.

TOMBS see Catacombs, Jewish.

TORAH

In a limited sense this term refers to the *Five Books of Moses* (Pentateuch), known as *Torat Mosheh* (The Torah of Moses) as revealed to him by God at Mount Sinai. However, in its broader sense the term *Torah* generally applies to all the teachings of Judaism, its laws, doctrines, ethics, philosophy, and customs and ceremonies. The Torah is technically divided into the *Writ-*

A Torah Scroll is held open by three Yemenite Jews. The Talmud says that Jews are forbidden to sell Torah scrolls except to get money to learn Torah, to redeem captives, and to make a marriage.

ten Law or Mosaic Code as embodied in the Bible; and the *Oral Law*, consisting of the Talmudic teachings (*Halakhah* and *Aggadah*) and subsequent rabbinic teachings and literature.

TORAH, READING OF

In Jewish life study is an integral part of prayer. Public services therefore include reading from Scripture. It is an ancient Jewish practice to read portions of the *Pentateuch* (Five Books of Moses) as part of the Sabbath and festival services in the synagogue. The whole *Torah*, divided into portions, is read in annual cycles; the first portion is read on the first Sabbath after Sukkot (Shabbat Bereshit), and the last on Simḥat Torah (the last day of Sukkot). The public recitation of the Pentateuch is usually followed by the reading of a supplementary portion from the Prophets, called *Haftarah*. The Haftarah generally has a thematic connection with the Torah reading.

The weekly Torah portion is called *Sidrah;* the word *Parashah* may also be applied, though this generally denotes the subdivisions within the portion. For the Sabbaths the number of such subdivisions is seven, and seven different persons are invited to pronounce the benedictions prior to and following the reading of each Parashah. The last few verses are repeated for an eighth person, the *Maftir*, and it is he also who is called on to recite the prophetic selection (Haftarah).

In view of the great reverence in which Jews hold Torah and study, the invitation to pronounce the benedictions associated with reading the Torah is held a high honor, and the person so invited or "called" is said to have an "Aliyah," an ascension. The number of "Aliyot" for the festivals including Rosh Hashanah is five plus the Maftir; and for Yom Kippur it is six. The Maftir to be read on the festivals deals with the respective days. During the Sabbath afternoon (Minḥah) service, the first Parashah of the following week's Sidrah is read and is subdivided into three Aliyot. There is no Haftarah. On the festivals, the Torah is not read in the afternoon service, except if the festival falls on the Sabbath. In the Minhah service of Yom Kippur, there are three Aliyot (the third Aliyah being the Maftir), and the Haftarah which is read is the *Book of Jonah*.

According to tradition, one of Ezra's "Takkanot" (ordinances) was the institution of reading the Torah on Mondays and Thursdays, which were market days, so as to make it possible for the farmers to hear the Torah read. This procedure was continued and is still practiced. The reading is similar to that of the previous Saturday afternoon. The Torah is also read in the public services on Rosh Hodesh, the middle days of the festivals (Hol ha-Moed), Hanukkah, Purim, and the fast days. On such days, as on the festival days themselves, the Scriptural reading relates to and explores the theme of the day. See *Sabbaths, Special*.

TORAH SHEBE-AL PEH
Hebrew term for Oral Law. See *Oral Law*.

TORAH SHEBI-KHETAV
Hebrew term for Written Law. See *Written Law*.

TORQUEMADA, THOMAS DE see Inquisition.

TOSAFOT
Hebrew term meaning "additions" applied to the explanatory and critical notes to the Talmud written by a number of teachers from the 12th century on. These teachers are known as *Tosafists*, and were active in Germany and Italy, and especially in France. The most famous of them was Rabbenu Tam, illustrious grandson of Rashi. The *Tosafot* did not comment on the entire text of the Talmud, but only on especially difficult passages. Only advanced Talmudists are able to understand the highly subtle and complicated Tosafot, which are usually printed side by side with the texts of the Talmud and *Rashi*.

TOSEFTA
Literally the meaning of the term is "addition" or "supplement" applied to a collection of teachings of the *Tannaim*, which serves as a supplement or an addition to the text of the *Mishnah*. Very often the text of the *Tosefta* is a variant of the teaching of the Mishnah.

TOTZERET HA-ARETZ
Hebrew term meaning "produce of the land" applied to products of the home-industry and agriculture of Israel. In order to encourage Israel's industrial and agricultural enterprises, Jews everywhere are urged by their leaders to purchase and use *Totzeret ha-Aretz*.

TOURO, JUDAH (1775–1854)
The first prominent Jewish philanthropist in America. Born in Newport, Rhode Island, he settled at the age of 21 in New Orleans where he lived for 50 years as a successful and highly regarded merchant. In 1815 he served under General Andrew Jackson as a volunteer in the defense of New Orleans. He was critically wounded and was nursed back to health by Rezin D. Shepard who became his lifelong friend and was later appointed by Touro as an executor of his will. Touro was a pioneer in large scale philanthropy for Jewish and non-Jewish causes for which he spent about half a million dollars. He was one of the principal contributors to the fund for the erection of the Bunker Hill Monument. He gave generously for

Judah Touro, outstanding American philanthropist, whose generosity was extended to a wide variety of institutions, was also a patriot who, during the War of 1812, fought in the Battle of New Orleans under Andrew Jackson.

practically every important Jewish charity in the United States, including gifts for the erection of a synagogue and a hospital in New Orleans; the enclosing of the Jewish cemetery in Newport; and also the building of almshouses in Jerusalem. Both Newport and New Orleans have streets named after him, and the "Touro Synagogue" in Newport has been made a national shrine.

TOWER OF BABEL see Babel, Tower of.

TRANSJORDANIA see Palestine.

TREE OF KNOWLEDGE see Gan Eden.

TREE OF LIFE see Gan Eden.

TREES, NEW YEAR OF see Tu Bi-Shevat.

TRIBES, LOST TEN

Those Israelite tribes which, after the fall of the northern Kingdom of Israel, were carried away by the king of Assyria and placed, according to the Bible, "in Halah, and in Habor, on the river of Gozan and in the cities of the Medes." These places have not been identified, but popular fancy has always attempted to locate the *Ten Lost Tribes* in different countries, and some Jewish travelers (Eldad Ha-Dani and David Reubeni, for instance) claimed to have had contact with them. A popular reference places these tribes near the legendary river *Sambatyon*. Other accounts claimed that the Japanese, the British, or the American Indians, were descendants of these tribes.

The prophet Ezekiel who lived during the Babylonian exile speaks of the ultimate reunion of the House of Israel and the House of Judah. Some scholars maintain that the Israelites who were exiled by Assyria remained relatively intact as a separate community, and that 150 years later, at the time of the Babylonian captivity, the two groups of Jews may have recognized their mutual kinship and reunited. Passages from some of the post-

exilic prophets and from rabbinic and later medieval literature would seem to substantiate the supposition that the so-called Ten Lost Tribes were not lost at all, and that the world Jewish community consists, therefore, of the descendants of all the original tribes.

TRIBES, THE TWELVE see Twelve Tribes.

TROPE

Term used for the special signs for cantillation (accents, musical notes) placed either above or under every word of the Hebrew Bible. The *Trope* is used in the reading of Scripture, and also has a grammatical significance. In Hebrew the Trope is called *Teamim* or *Neginot*.

TRUMPELDOR, JOSEPH (1880–1920)

Socialist Zionist leader, founder of the *Halutz* (Pioneer) movement, and hero. Born in Caucasia, Russia, he enlisted during the Russo-Japanese war (1904), during which he lost his left arm. He refused to be discharged, and was finally taken prisoner when the Russians capitulated to the Japanese. Upon his return to Russia he was promoted in rank, and became the first Jewish officer in the Tsarist army. While a prisoner of war, Trumpeldor began his lifelong work for the cause of socialist Zionism by organizing a group of pioneers for the purpose of establishing a workers settlement in Palestine. In 1912 he left for Palestine with a group of pioneers, and became a farm worker in the oldest workers' cooperative settlement. After the outbreak of World War I, he organized, together with Vladimir Jabotinsky, the Zion Mule Corps, an auxiliary troop in the British army. Trumpeldor's British commander expressed the highest praise for his valor and bravery. He later went with Jabotinsky to London where they organized the Jewish Legion, which distinguished itself in the war of Palestine's lib-

In the celebration of Tu Bi-Shevat, designated in the Talmud as the "New Year of the Trees," Israeli children holding tree cuttings in their hands eagerly await their turn to plant them in the Holy Land.

eration from the Turks. After the war Trumpeldor organized the colonists of Metullah, Tel Hai, and Kfar Giladi in Upper Galilee for their defense against rebel Arab bands. In a savage attack by the Arabs on Tel Hai, Trumpeldor met a heroic death. His last words were: "It does not matter, it is good to die for our country." Trumpeldor's name and his heroic life became a symbol of the pioneering spirit in Palestine. His grave in Tel Hai has become a shrine for many Zionist pilgrims to visit.

TU BI-SHEVAT

Hebrew for "the 15th day of the month of Shevat," or *Hamishah Asar Bi-Shevat*, which is celebrated as Arbor Day in Israel. In the *Mishnah* it is called the "New Year of the Trees." In Israel, because of its warmer climate, the day is set aside for the planting of trees, especially by school children. In the diaspora Jewish children celebrate this day in special assemblies; they partake of the fruits growing in Israel, such as figs, dates, almonds, and "bokser" (carob); and make contributions to the

487

A poor Jewish boy who lives in the Tunis ghetto where most Tunisian Jews are forced to reside.

19th-century silver plaque from Palestine shows the emblems of the Twelve Tribes of Israel in bas-relief. Each tribe is named on the separate leaves of the tree in the center of the plaque.

Jewish National Fund for the purchase of trees to be planted in Israel.

TUDELA, BENJAMIN OF see Benjamin of Tudela.

TUNISIA

Formerly under Turkish rule, Tunisia became a French protectorate in 1881. Jews settled in Tunisia in the era of the Second Commonwealth. During the 7th century, Tunisia was conquered by Arabs and the condition of the Jews continued to be good. However, during the Middle Ages the Jews were exposed to persecution and to forced conversion to Islam. Life under severe restrictions continued until the end of the 19th century, but with the beginning of French rule, the status of the 50,-000 Jews then living in Tunisia improved. The Jews of Tunisia have their own ritual, dress like Orientals, follow Oriental customs, speak Arabic, and have a distinctive pronunciation of Hebrew. Unrest among the Arabs of North Africa during the 1950's and their clashes with French authorities made the position of the Jews insecure, and many sought refuge in the State of Israel. In 1957 Tunisia became independent and was declared a republic. In 1960 the Jewish population was about 80,000, of whom the majority lived in Tunis, the capital.

TURKEY

In 1960 there were about 60,000 Jews living in the republic of Turkey, including its Asiatic regions. Jews have lived in the Ottoman Empire, which extended over Asiatic and North African areas, from early times. When Constantinople was captured by the Turks in the 15th century the Jewish community began a period of growth and development. The Sultans generally looked favorably upon the Jews and encouraged new immigrations, and autonomous Jewish cultural and religious life. About 100,000 persecuted

Jews, expelled from Spain and Portugal, found asylum in Constantinople, Smyrna and Salonica which became important Jewish centers of life and learning. During the 17th and the 18th centuries, the Jews of Turkey, although living under certain restrictions, led a peaceful existence as compared to the fate of Jewish communities elsewhere. Following the revolution in 1908, the Jews were granted equal rights, but after the World War I period, conditions changed for the worse, and thousands of Jews emigrated to other countries.

TWELVE TRIBES

In ancient Israel, according to tradition, especially during the period of the Judges and the early kings, the Jewish people consisted of twelve tribes, named after the twelve sons of Jacob, each occupying a separate territory (excepting the tribe of Levi) in the land of Israel. The Twelve Tribes as recorded in Biblical narrative were: Reuben, Simeon, Levi, Judah, Issachar, Zebulun, Dan, Naphtali, Gad, Asher, Joseph (Ephraim and Manasseh), and Benjamin.

TYRE

Ancient capital of Phoenicia, mentioned in the Bible, especially in connection with its King Hiram who had provided Solomon with building materials for the erection of the Temple in Jerusalem. Tyre was then famous as a world trade center. In modern times Tyre became a small port in Lebanon, now known as Sur, and having but a few thousand inhabitants.

TZADDIK

A righteous man. In Ḥasidism the disciples of a leader call him *Tzaddik*. See *Ḥasidism; Lamed-Vav Tzaddikim*.

TZADE (Tzaddik) (צ)

The eighteenth letter of the Hebrew alphabet, sounded TZ. Its numerical value is 90.

TZEDAKAH see Charity.

TZEENAH U-REENAH

Hebrew title of the "Women's Bible" in Yiddish written by the Talmudist Jacob ben Isaac Ashkenazi in 1590. This book, widely read by the people who could not read Hebrew (especially women), is neither a translation of the Bible, nor a commentary on it, but a free Yiddish rendering of parts of the Bible with an admixture of *Midrashim* and various folk tales retold and adapted to the circumstances and national backgrounds of those for whom it was intended.

TZITZIT see Arba Kanfot; Tallit.

TZOM GEDALYAH see Fast Days.

U

UNLEAVENED BREAD

Behold, this is the bread of affliction

Our fathers ate in the land of Egypt.

Let all who hunger enter and eat;

Let all who are in need come celebrate the Passover

with us.

PASSOVER HAGGADAH

UGANDA

A stretch of land in East Africa which the British Government proposed in 1903 to the World Zionist Organization as a suitable territory for the establishment of a temporary autonomous Jewish settlement. The Uganda project was brought before the Zionist Congress, and was looked favorably upon by Theodor Herzl and some other Zionist leaders, but received strong opposition from the east European Zionist leaders. After the death of Herzl in 1904 the project was championed by Israel Zangwill, but was finally rejected at the 7th Zionist Congress in 1905.

UGARIT DOCUMENTS see Archeology.

U-NETANNEH TOKEF

A hymn recited on Rosh Hashanah and Yom Kippur, written by Rabbi Amnon of Mayence, a martyr at the time of the Crusades. The hymn glorifies God and the Day of Judgment, when man is able by means of repentance, prayer and charity "to avert the evil decree." Tradition recounts that Rabbi Amnon, author of the *U-Netanneh Tokef*, permitted his hands and feet to be removed by the archbishop of Mayence rather than accept conversion to Christianity. Carried to the synagogue on the day of Rosh Hashanah, the martyred rabbi recited the U-Netanneh Tokef, which came to him through inspiration.

UNION OF AMERICAN HEBREW CONGREGATIONS

An association of Jewish reform congregations in the United States and Canada, with its headquarters in New York City. The major objectives of the Union, founded by Rabbi Isaac Mayer Wise in 1873, were: to establish a seminary for rabbis; to stimulate popular Jewish education; and to organize new congregations. Starting with a membership of 38 congregations, the Union has grown to a membership in 1960 of approximately 600 congregations, having a total membership of over 1,000,000. Its auxiliary groups are: National Federation of Temple Sisterhoods (1913); National Federation of Temple Brotherhoods (1923); National Federation of Temple Youth (1939); National Federation of Temple Secretaries (1943); and National Association of Temple Educators (1955). The Union is a member of the World Union for Progressive Judaism.

The Union sponsored its first major institution in 1875, the Hebrew Union College in Cincinnati, the graduates of which have since served as rabbis and educational leaders in the United States and elsewhere. Another important function of the Union was the organization and maintenance of Jewish religious schools, the publication of school texts, and literature for children and youth. It co-sponsors a commission on Jewish education, which has published many volumes on Jewish history, literature, religion, Hebrew, and other educational materials, including *The Jewish Teacher*, a pedagogic quarterly for the one-day a week religious school teachers.

UNION OF ORTHODOX JEWISH CONGREGATIONS OF AMERICA

An organization established in 1898 in New York City for the purpose of advancing the interests of "Biblical, Rabbinical, traditional and historical Judaism." In 1960 the Union had a membership of over 500 synagogues and "represented and served about 3,200 orthodox synagogues in the United States and Canada." It sponsors approximately 240 elementary and secondary orthodox day schools of Jewish education and about 15 large *Yeshivot*; publishes literature on various phases of traditional Judaism; and sponsors a national program for the supervision of *Kashrut* (dietary laws). The Union's major auxiliary organization is the Women's Branch, organized in 1924, composed of synagogue sisterhoods. The Women's Branch organized a Hebrew Teachers Training School for Girls, and other religious cultural clubs and groups. The symbol ⓤ is a mark of the Union's approval of the Kashrut of the article.

UNION OF ORTHODOX RABBIS

Known in Hebrew as "Agudat ha-Rabbanim" (Agudas Horabbonim), it is an organization of orthodox rabbis of the United States and Canada founded in 1902. In the main it is composed of European trained rabbis.

UNION OF SEPHARDIC CONGREGATIONS

An organization founded in New York in 1929 to serve the interests of the Spanish and Portuguese and other Sephardi groups in the United States and elsewhere. In order to maintain the traditional Sephardi ritual, the Union publishes Sephardi Hebrew prayer books, and helps provide Sephardi congregations and groups with Hazzanim, teachers, and other leadership.

UNITED ARAB REPUBLIC see Egypt; Syria.

UNITED HIAS SERVICE

Formed in 1954 by the consolidation of the Hebrew Sheltering and Immigrant Aid Society (HIAS), the United Service for New Americans (USNA), and the overseas migration services of the American Jewish Joint Distribution Committee (AJDC). The oldest single unit of this organization dates back to 1884, and has been commonly known as HIAS. Outstanding among its many activities, this agency sponsors the migration of Jews to various countries throughout the world, provides maximum opportunities for their permanent resettlement in a new land, and reunites families separated by war and other disasters.

The United Hias Service, whose central office is in New York City, maintains affiliated offices in the world's major cities.

UNITED ISRAEL APPEAL

Formerly known as the United Palestine Appeal, an American fund-raising agency for the Palestine Foundation Fund (Keren Ha-Yesod). Established in 1925 and reorganized in 1935, it became an affiliate of the United Jewish Appeal in 1939. In addition to its proportionate share of the funds raised by the United Jewish Appeal, the United Israel Appeal receives contributions from the collections of the Jewish National Fund. The United Israel Appeal conducts a program of educational activities designed to promote understanding of *Keren Kayemet* and *Keren Ha-Yesod* and their importance in the rebuilding of the Jewish homeland.

UNITED JEWISH APPEAL

Established in 1939 as a single fund-raising body in behalf of the American Jewish Joint Distribution Committee, the United Palestine Appeal, and the National Refugee Service. Since its founding, the United Jewish Appeal raised a total of over a billion dollars for overseas relief, Israel, and refugee aid, thus becoming the most forceful expression of the solidarity of American Jewry and its continuing sense of responsibility in facing the needs and problems of Jewish life the world over.

UNITED STATES

The year 1954 marked three hundred years of Jewish settlement in the United States. In 1654 the first group of 23 Jewish immigrants from Recife, Brazil, landed in New Amsterdam, now known as New York. Despite initial unfriendly reception given to the Jewish immigrants, Jewish communities were soon organized in Rhode Island (1658), Connecticut, New Jersey

"The Steerage," Alfred Stieglitz's fine 1907 photograph, shows immigration at its high tide.

The replica of a Union flag given to President Abraham Lincoln in 1860 by his friend Abraham Kohn.

Immigrants of 1921 debark at Ellis Island, then chief port of entry for those coming to America.

Taken in Cleveland in 1858, this is the oldest extant photograph of Jewish shops in the United States. Note the wooden sidewalks and the open display of the clothing for sale hanging outside of the store.

Rabbi Nelson Glueck asks God's blessing for U.S. President John F. Kennedy at the 1961 Presidential Inaugural. Outgoing President Eisenhower and many other dignitaries surround the new President.

and Pennsylvania (1660), North and South Carolina (1669), and Georgia (1733). The first immigrants were mainly of Spanish and Portuguese origin, with an admixture of immigrants from England and Holland. Until the period of the American Revolution, Jews in the American colonies at best enjoyed toleration, but not equality. They were active in the economic development of the colonies, and engaged mainly in domestic and foreign trade. There were about 2,000 Jews in the colonies at the time of the Revolution, the majority of whom allied themselves with the revolutionary cause. Haym Salomon, the "financier of the Revolution" was the symbol of American-Jewish patriotism.

The growth of the Jewish community in the United States took place during the 19th century. Economic and political disabilities of the Jews in Europe brought two significant waves of Jewish immigration to the United States. The first, extending from 1820 to 1870, was the influx of immigrants from Germany; the second and largest wave of immigrants, from eastern Europe, especially from Russia, Poland and Rumania, began in 1881, and reached the figure of 100,000 new arrivals in 1908.

The German-Jewish immigrants, most of whom were educated but poor, started as humble peddlers but, keeping pace with the industrial and commercial development of the country, gradually became owners of department stores and manufacturing enterprises. In time these immigrants laid the foundation of many charitable Jewish institutions, created in order to alleviate the misery of thousands of east European immigrants who found themselves crowded in cities in the eastern United States and the Middle West. They brought with them ideas of religious and educational concern, and made outstanding contributions in the field of Jewish education and religious organization.

East European Jews, representing an overwhelming majority of Jewish immigrants, made a great impact on the development of the economic, social, religious and cultural life of the Jews in the United States. Strengthening the ranks of Jewish orthodoxy in this country, they augmented the number of synagogues and congregations, and developed and maintained a system of traditional Jewish education. As a reaction against the assimilationist and anti-nationalist tendencies of the Reform movement, the Conservative movement in Judaism was started, and gained strength through its outstanding leadership. Growth in the numbers and size of congregations and congregational religious schools of all persuasions proceeded steadily.

A large proportion of east European immigrants was concentrated in large cities, especially in New York, and became the backbone of a strong Jewish working class, stimulating the development of the trade-union movement in the country, especially that of the garment industry. Inasmuch as the majority of the east European immigrants spoke Yiddish, their cultural needs were served through the development of an influential Yiddish press and a flourishing Yiddish literature. Their needs for mutual aid in times of stress and other social and cultural needs were met through the organization of *Landsmanschaften* and fraternal orders, such as the Workmen's Circle (Arbeiter Ring, 1900) and the Farband Labor Zionist Order (formerly the Jewish National Workers' Alliance, 1912). The oldest and largest fraternal organizations, which served the expanding Jewish middle class and which are still active are B'nai B'rith (1843), Free Sons of Israel (1849), and Brith Abraham (1887).

The orthodox, conservative and reform groups in the American Jewish community have each endeavored to sustain themselves and to insure the religious and cultural continuity and development of Jewish life. In addition to their efforts at maintaining Jewish elementary and secondary schools, they established institutions of higher learning for the training of rabbis, scholars, teachers, and other cultural and social leadership. The most important of such institutions are: Yeshiva University (orthodox), The Jewish Theological Seminary (conservative), Hebrew Union College–Jewish Institute of Religion (reform), and Dropsie College for Hebrew and Cognate Learning.

Probably the most significant and unique contribution of the Jewish community in the United States was in the area of philanthropy. World War I gave the greatest impetus for organized relief work in behalf of stricken Jewish people abroad. Separate relief societies, first organized by several groups, united in establishing the Joint Distribution Committee, which Committee is still engaged in collecting and distributing funds for overseas Jewish needs. Two critical events in the history of the Jewish people, namely, the annihilation of most of the Jewish communities in Europe under the Hitler regime and World War II on the one hand, and the establishment of the State of Israel on the other, placed upon the Jewish community in the United States the unprecedented responsibility for the reconstruction of Jewish life and existence in Europe and elsewhere, and particularly for the building of the State of Israel, which became a haven for hundreds of thousands of displaced Jews. This historic challenge has been vigorously met by the United Jewish Appeal and the various Zionist groups, such as the Zionist Organization of America, Labor Zionists, Mizrachi, Hadassah, and Pioneer Women.

The over five million Jews living in the

Dutch woodcut from Utrecht, 1657, shows the preparation and the making of Passover Matzot.

United States continued to hold prominent positions in the cultural, economic, industrial, and political life of the country. Enjoying the freedom of the American democratic society, they are steadily strengthening Jewish communal and institutional life and assuming at the same time ever greater responsibilities for the continued existence and security of the Jewish people the world over.

UNITED SYNAGOGUE OF AMERICA

National organization of the conservative congregations in the United States, founded in 1913 on the initiative of Solomon Schechter. The United Synagogue advocates: loyalty to Torah; observance of Sabbath and dietary laws; building of the Jewish homeland; maintenance of the traditional Hebrew liturgy with some slight modification; encouragement of Jewish religious life in the home; and establishment of religious schools with Hebrew, Bible, Jewish history and practices as the basic curriculum.

The United Synagogue encourages the

establishment of new conservative congregations, which numbered about 650 in 1960, as well as the organization of sisterhoods, men's clubs and young people's organizations. The Women's League of the United Synagogue, organized in 1917, establishes student houses, fosters activities for Jewish students on the campuses of many colleges in the United States, and provides educational programs and speakers for sisterhood meetings.

The United Synagogue Commission on Jewish Education publishes textbooks, curricula, teachers' manuals and other educational materials for pupils and teachers of the conservative religious schools.

UNIVERSITY, HEBREW see Hebrew University of Jerusalem.

UNLEAVENED BREAD

Called *Matzah* in Hebrew and eaten by Jews during the festival of Passover. It is made only of flour and water, in the form of thin perforated cakes, so that baking may be quick in order to prevent fermentation. The Bible calls the Matzah "the bread of affliction," a symbol of the poverty and suffering of the Israelites when they were slaves in Egypt. The dough of which the Matzah is made is not allowed to ferment, a symbol of the haste with which the Israelites left Egypt when freed by Moses. The partaking of Matzah on Passover is one of the most universally observed commandments. Its symbolism has enriched Jewish life through the ages.

URIEL

One of the archangels. Others are Gabriel, Michael, and Raphael.

URIEL DA COSTA see Acosta, Uriel.

URIM AND TUMMIM

Two objects mentioned in the Bible as parts of the breastplate of the High Priest. They were said to possess the mysterious

The "Urim and Tummim" from the Biblical breastplate adopted as Yale University's seal.

power of an oracle giving answers to questions placed before them, expressing the will of God, especially in times of national danger and crisis.

UR OF THE CHALDEES

Known in Hebrew as *Ur Kasdim*, mentioned in the Bible as the Babylonian city where Abraham lived before he migrated, together with his father, to *Haran*. Through archeological excavations during the 1920s, British and American scholars located Ur around Mugheir in Southern Babylonia, and discovered Sumerian relics there. See *Archeology*.

URUGUAY

One of the smallest and most prosperous republics in South America where there were about 50,000 Jews in 1960 in a total population of two and one-half million. The Jewish community in Uruguay was very small until after World War I. The first Jewish settlers were of Sephardi origin, then new arrivals came from Russia and Rumania, and after 1933 from Ger-

many. The liberal government of Uruguay encouraged the settlement of refugees from Nazi dominated countries, and courageously opposed anti-Semitism agitated by German agents. The majority of the Jews live in the capital, Montevideo. They are affiliated with congregations, sponsor Jewish schools, mostly in the Yiddish language, and maintain Yiddish daily newspapers, as well as a Yiddish theatre and a Yiddish radio hour. The Jewish community also operates several cooperatives.

USSISHKIN, MENAHEM MENDEL (1863–1941)

Zionist leader and long time president of the Jewish National Fund. Born in Russia, he associated early in life with the *Hovevei Zion* movement, and later joined the select group of Zionist idealists called *Bene Mosheh*, under the leadership of Ahad Ha-Am. Ussishkin became one of the ardent supporters of Theodor Herzl, and was a delegate to the first Zionist Congress held at Basle in 1897. However, when the British government proposed the *Uganda Project* for the colonization of Jews in East Africa, Ussishkin led the opposition to this plan though it was favored by Herzl. Ussishkin became a close associate of Chaim Weizmann.

In 1920 Ussishkin settled in Palestine, and two years later became president of the Jewish National Fund, which under his devoted leadership purchased large stretches of land for Jewish colonization. Ussishkin also served as a member of the Zionist Executive and his 70th birthday was celebrated by Jews the world over. The settlement *Kfar Menahem Ussishkin* was established in Israel in his honor.

Menahem Mendel Ussishkin, ardent Zionist and delegate to the first Zionist Congress, later became head of the Jewish National Fund. He rejected Britain's plan for Jewish colonies in African Uganda, and insisted on planning for the practical Jewish colonization of Palestine.

VIDDUI

But in Thy love Thou hast given us this day of fasting, this day of atonement, a boundary, for pardon and forgiveness for our sins, that our hands may cease from wickedness, that we may turn again to Thee and perform the laws of Thy will with all our heart. And Thou, in Thy great mercy, will be merciful to us, for Thy desire is not to destroy the earth.

PRAYER BOOK

VAAD ARBA ARATZOT see Council of the Four Lands.

VAAD HA-LASHON HA-IVRIT

Hebrew name of the academy of the Hebrew language, organized in Jerusalem in 1890 by Eliezer ben Yehudah, "father of modern Hebrew," its first president. As Hebrew became the spoken language as well as the language of general studies in the schools of Palestine, the *Vaad Ha-Lashon* undertook the coining of new Hebrew words and also the stimulation of the use of grammatically correct Hebrew. The Vaad Ha-Lashon has published many bulletins, books, periodicals and dictionaries dealing with questions of Hebrew philology and offering Hebrew terms for everyday use and for every need such as food, clothing, furniture, electricity, telephone, carpentry, shoemaking, manufacture, the building trade, mathematics, physics, chemistry, music, art, radio, theatre, the army, navy, aviation, etc. The thousands of words coined by the Vaad Ha-Lashon have become an integral aspect of Hebrew conversation and writing in modern times.

VAAD LEUMI

Hebrew name of the National Council of the Jews in Palestine, which existed during the period of the British Mandate as the official representative of Palestine Jewry in local affairs. The *Vaad Leumi* is to be distinguished from the *Jewish Agency for Palestine*, which represented world Jewry, and which is still functioning in that sphere.

VASHTI

The Persian queen who, as is written in the *Book of Esther*, refused to attend the banquet given by her husband, King Ahasuerus. According to tradition, she was punished for this disobedience by death. See *Esther, Scroll of*.

VAV (ו)

The sixth letter of the Hebrew alphabet. When a consonant, it is sounded like the English *v*. However, a dot placed above it makes it a vowel, and in the Israeli pronunciation it is sounded like the English *aw* in "law"; otherwise it is sounded in any of several ways, like the long ō in "most"; or like *oy* in "boy"; or like *ow* in "how"; or like *ay* in "bay."

With a dot to the left center, the Vav is also used as a vowel and is then pronounced $\overline{oo}$ as in room.

The numerical value of Vav is 6, and its meaning is "hook." Undoubtedly a distinction was drawn in early days between the differing sounds of *Vav* and *Vet*. See *Vowels; Bet*.

VAYIKRA see Leviticus.

VE-ADAR see Adar.

VENEZUELA

Jews of Italian origin settled in Venezuela at the end of the 17th century. In the 19th century, other settlers of Sephardi origin settled in Caracas, the capital of the republic. Under pressure of World War II, the former small community of about 800 Jews had increased to 8,000 by 1960, mostly through the influx of European refugees, and has contributed to the city's growing prosperity.

VIDDUI

Hebrew term for "confession of sin," referring in particular to the prayers *Ashamnu* and *Al Het* recited on Yom Kippur. In Jewish tradition there were other occasions when the *Viddui* was recited. Some pious Jews recite the Viddui every night before retiring, others twice a week (Monday and Thursday) or on the day before Rosh Hodesh (called on that account *Yom Kippur Katan*). The reciting of Viddui on the deathbed is a custom among many Jews.

Vilna, the "Jerusalem of Lithuania," was an important center of Jewish culture and piety. Above, a group of Jewish musicians of Vilna who performed at local weddings and at various other special festivities.

VILNA

Capital of Lithuania which before World War II had 80,000 Jews among its 200,000 inhabitants. Jews first settled in Vilna in the 14th century, and in the course of the succeeding centuries Vilna became one of the important Jewish centers in Europe. It was at first under Polish rule, then passed to Russia, and later back to Poland. In 1939 it became part of Lithuania. Despite the anti-Jewish legislation and persecutions which were characteristic of the Jewish history of Vilna, the city has long been a center of Jewish culture and learning known as "Jerusalem of Lithuania." Vilna was the residence of the great Talmud authority, Elijah ben Solomon, the "Gaon of Vilna." It was at one and the same time the heart of Jewish piety, and a center of the *Haskalah* movement. It was known for its Romm Publishing House where famous editions of the *Talmud*, *Mishnah*, and *Midrash* were printed. Before World War II it was also the seat of the *Yiddish Scientific Institute* ("Yivo"); it had several Yiddish and Hebrew newspapers and periodicals, as well as a successful system of Hebrew and Yiddish schools. Under the Nazi occupation during World War II, the Jewish community in Vilna was almost completely destroyed.

VILNA GAON see Gaon of Vilna.

VITAL, ḤAYIM (1543–1620)

Kabbalist and author. Born in Safed, Palestine, he became one of the most promi-

VLADECK, B. CHARNEY

B. Charney Vladeck, Yiddish writer and labor leader, was general manager of the "Forward," and a popular Socialist Alderman in New York.

nent disciples of R. Isaac Luria when the latter settled in Safed. After Luria's death he became the leader of the Kabbalists and proclaimed himself the "Messiah ben Joseph." In 1594 he settled in Damascus, Syria, where he lived for the rest of his life, and where he wrote his famous work *Etz Hayim* ("Tree of Life"), which was an exposition of the "Lurian" Kabbalah. See *Luria, Isaac*.

VLADECK, B. CHARNEY (1886–1938)

Jewish labor leader and socialist. Born in Russia, he was the brother of Samuel Niger, Yiddish literary critic, and Daniel Charney, also a Yiddish writer. In his youth he was active as a revolutionary in Tsarist Russia, and assumed the name of "Vladeck" to hide his identity. In 1908 he went to the United States where he became active in the Jewish socialist movement. In 1917 he was elected member of the Board of Aldermen in New York on the Socialist ticket. He later became the

general manager of the Yiddish daily newspaper, the *Forward*. Popular with the Jewish workers, he was sent abroad several times on important missions. In 1937 he became a member of the New York City Council, and an advocate of public housing projects. For his distinctive work in this field, a public housing project in New York was named after him.

VOV see Vav.

VOWELS, HEBREW

All the letters of the Hebrew alphabet are consonants; and essentially to this day the Hebrew language is written almost entirely without vowels. The Scroll of the Torah is written without punctuation marks and without vowels. Only Bibles, prayer books, poetry and beginners' books are printed with vowels. The popular use of vowels (points) began as late as the 8th century, largely through the influence of the *Karaite* sect which led to intensive study and research in the proper reading of the Biblical texts. The system of Hebrew vowels in use now comes from the so-called Tiberian system, as distinguished from the Babylonian system.

There are ten vowels in Hebrew, five *long* and five *short*. The vowel signs are written above, below and in the center of the letters which they affect. The five long vowels are: 1) *Kamatz Gadol*, written ᴛ below the letter. In the Sephardi pronunciation it has the sound of *a* as in "father"; its Ashkenazi pronunciation is either that of *a* in "ball" or ō̄o in "moon"; 2) *Tzereh*, written as two dots side by side ·· under the letter and pronounced in Ashkenazi like *a* in "gate," or like *i* in "site." Its Sephardi pronunciation is either like *a* in "gate" or like *e* in "met"; 3) *Hirik Gadol*, written as a single dot under the letter, which is followed by a "Yod" ᾽ ͓ and is pronounced *ee* as in "seen"; 4) *Holam*, written either as a "Vav" with a dot over it $\daleth$, or as a single dot over the left top corner of the letter. Its standard Israeli pronunciation is that of *o* as in "honey"; otherwise it is sounded in any of several ways, like the English long ō as in "most," or *ow* as in "how," or *oy* as in "boy," or *ay* as in "bay"; 5) *Shuruk*, written as the letter "Vav" with a dot in the center $\daleth$ and pronounced like *oo* in "boot." In the Ashkenazi it may also be sounded as a *Hirik*.

The five short vowels are: 1) *Pattaḥ*, written as a dash — under the letter and pronounced *a* as in "what"; 2) *Seggol*, written as three dots in the form of an inverted triangle ∵ under the letter and pronounced *e* as in "get"; 3) *Hirik Katan*, written as a single dot · under the letter and pronounced *i* as in "big"; 4) *Kamatz Katan*, written ⊤ under the letter and pronounced *o* as in "honey"; 5) *Kubbutz*, written in the form of three dots slanted diagonally ⸪ under the letter and pronounced *u* as in "put." In the Ashkenazi it may also be sounded like Hirik.

In addition to the five long and the five short vowels, there are five *half-vowels:* 1) *Sheva Na*, written as two dots, one above the other : under the letter, and pronounced like the English *a* in "alone"; 2) *Sheva Naḥ*, written like the Sheva Na, but not pronounced. It indicates the end of a syllable; 3) *Hataf Pattaḥ*, written as a combination of the Sheva and the Pattaḥ —: under the letter and pronounced like the Pattaḥ but somewhat shorter; 4) *Hataf Kamatz*, written as a combination of the Sheva and the Kamatz ⊤: under the letter,

is pronounced like a Kamatz Katan; 5) *Hataf Seggol*, written as a combination of the Sheva and the Seggol ∵: under the letter, and pronounced like Seggol but somewhat shorter.

In general the Hebrew language in Israel is spoken with a modified Sefardi pronunciation. However, European and American Jews usually speak in the Ashkenazi pronunciation. Within each of these two pronunciations, especially the Ashkenazi, there are numerous variations. These variations in the manner of speech may be frequently traced to the influence of the language spoken in a specific locality.

VOWS

The Hebrew term *Neder* (pl. *Nedarim*) is applied to a voluntary obligation which one takes upon oneself in the form of an oath or vow. Laws concerning vows are recorded in the Bible and are treated in detail in a special tractate of the Talmud called *Nedarim*. There are two kinds of vows, affirmative and negative. The former is undertaken by a person as an obligation to do something voluntarily which is not prescribed by law. The latter is a person's resolution to abstain from something, or to deprive himself of certain pleasures which are otherwise permitted. Jewish law provides that under certain conditions vows in the form of promises to God which cannot be carried out, may be nullified by a proper authority. No vow made to another person may be dissolved without the free consent of that person. See *Kol Nidre*.

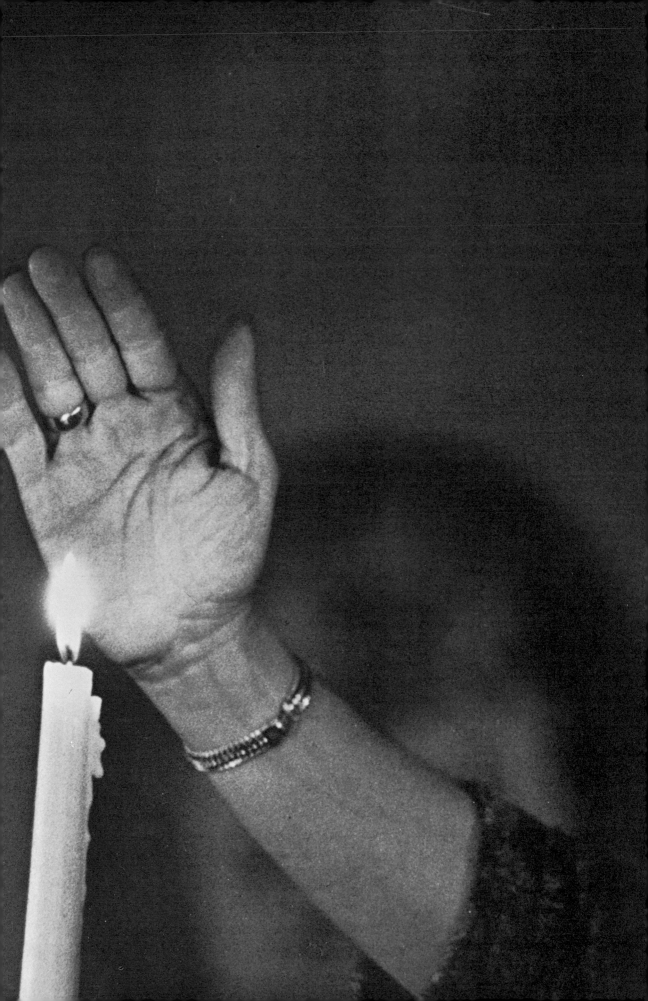

WOMEN

A woman of valour who can find?

For her price is far above rubies.

The heart of her husband doth safely trust in her,

And he hath no lack of gain.

She doeth him good and not evil

All the days of her life.

PROVERBS

WAHL, SAUL

According to legend, was Jewish king of Poland for one day in 1586. He was the son of Rabbi Samuel Judah Katzenellenbogen of Padua, and a brilliant student in a *Yeshivah* in Poland. Wahl became a protégé of Prince Nicholas Radziwill, and when on the death of King Stephen Bathory there arose many claimants to the throne, he was supposedly chosen king at the suggestion of the Prince. Tradition claims descent from Wahl of some branches of contemporary Jewish families such as Ginsberg and Wolk. Wahl's son Meir founded the Council of Lithuania.

WAILING WALL

Known in Hebrew as *Kotel Maaravi*, the "Western Wall" of the Temple in Jerusalem, and the only remnant of the ancient sanctuary. Throughout the centuries it was a place of "wailing" and of religious pilgrimages. The *Wailing Wall*, about 160 feet long and about sixty feet high, is now part of a larger wall surrounding the area of *Haram esh Sherif*, an important Moslem holy place. Despite the fact that the Wailing Wall came under the protection of the British during their administration in Palestine, there arose frequent disputes between the Arabs and the Jews regarding its use by the latter as a place of worship. After the Arab riots in 1929, the League of Nations guaranteed the Jews access to the Wailing Wall under British protection. Following the establishment of the State of Israel and the War of Liberation in 1948, the Old City of Jerusalem became a part of the Jordan territory. Contrary to the provisions of the armistice between the State of Israel and Jordan for free access to the Wailing Wall, the approach to it was forbidden to Jews.

WALD, LILLIAN (1867–1940)

American social worker and pioneer in public health. Born in Cincinnati, Ohio, she graduated from the New York Training School for Nursing and, moved by the deplorable sanitary and health conditions in the slums of New York, she established a nursing and sanitation service for the underprivileged. In 1885 she established the Henry Street Settlement House with the help of Jacob H. Schiff, prominent philanthropist. In addition to visiting nurse service, the Settlement provided social activities, education and advice to young and old of the immigrant population.

Miss Wald sponsored the idea of the Federal Children's Bureau, and it was established in 1908. As an authority in public welfare, she attended international conferences, and became a well-known figure in movements for social betterment, peace and woman's suffrage. She was honored nationally on her 70th birthday, and after her death a playground and a public housing project in New York's East Side were named after her.

WANDERING JEW

A legend widely circulated in European literature about a Jerusalem shoemaker named Ahasuerus who was cursed to wander eternally as a punishment for taunting Jesus of Nazareth while on his way to the crucifixion. Claims to the effect that the "Immortal Jew" had been seen in different places have been made since the 13th century. The story of the endlessly wandering Jew became a popular folk tale and a favorite theme for writers and artists. The best known novel based on this legend is "The Wandering Jew" by Eugene Sue.

The outer portion of the Wailing Wall, remnant of the ancient external Western wall of Herod's Temple. Here, in the old city of Jerusalem, Jews from all over the world come to lament the loss of their Temple and their national homeland. Note huge blocks of stone used in building.

Felix M. Warburg, banker, philanthropist and Jewish community leader, has been a generous supporter of many civic causes, among them Hebrew Union College, and The Jewish Theological Seminary.

WAR OF LIBERATION

The 1948 war between the newly established State of Israel and the Arab nations which invaded and attempted to destroy it.

WARBURG FAMILY

A distinguished Jewish family of bankers, scholars, Jewish communal leaders, and philanthropists. The family, with branches in Germany, Scandinavia, England and the United States, derived its name from Warburg, Westphalia, from which it had originated. Four of the fifteen prominent members of the Warburg family are:

Warburg, Felix M. (1871-1937): Banker, philanthropist, and Jewish communal leader. Born in Hamburg, Germany, he married Frieda Schiff, the only daughter of Jacob H. Schiff, and settled in New York in 1895. He became a partner of Kuhn Loeb and Co. Interested in public welfare and education, he supported the Educational Alliance and the Henry Street Settlement in New York City, and served as commissioner of the New York Board of Education (1902-1905). He was also a generous supporter of the Hebrew Union College in Cincinnati, and especially of The Jewish Theological Seminary of America, of which latter institution he was a member of the Board. Of his many services to the Jewish community in the United States may be mentioned his work in behalf of the Joint Distribution Committee, his active support of the Federation of Jewish Philanthropies in New York, and his initiative in the founding of the Graduate School for Jewish Social Work in New York (1925). Although a non-Zionist, he contributed generously to the Hebrew University in Jerusalem, was one of the founders of the Palestine Economic Corporation, and fought vigorously against restrictions on immigration to Palestine which were imposed by the British Mandatory Government.

512

Warburg, Max M. (1867-1946): Banker, Jewish communal leader and philanthropist. Born in Hamburg, Germany he became a partner in the banking firm Warburg & Co., and served as its head until 1938, one year before he settled in the United States. He had expert knowledge of financial affairs, and served the German government in many commercial and industrial enterprises. He was given an honorary Ph.D. degree by the Hamburg University. He was important in the Jewish community, and a large contributor to numerous Jewish institutions. After the Nazi rise to power, he assisted many refugees to flee Germany and settle in other countries. Soon after his arrival in the U.S. in 1939, he became active in American Jewish affairs, especially those connected with the American Jewish Committee and the Joint Distribution Committee.

Warburg, Otto (1859-1938): Botanist, and Zionist leader. Born in Hamburg, Germany, he devoted himself to the study of tropical plants, and became professor of botany at the University of Berlin. From 1900 he was active in colonization and agricultural projects in Palestine, and from 1911 to 1920 he served as president of the World Zionist Organization.

Warburg, Paul M. (1868-1932): Banker and philanthropist. Born in Hamburg, Germany, he settled in New York in 1902 and became a partner of Kuhn Loeb & Co. In recognition of his outstanding record of public service and his expert knowledge of financial matters, President Wilson appointed him a member of the Federal Reserve Board. He liberally supported both Jewish and non-Jewish charitable and cultural institutions.

WARSAW

Capital of Poland, in which 370,000 Jews lived before the Nazi occupation in 1939, about 30 per cent of the total population.

Jews settled in Warsaw as early as the 14th century, and for several centuries lived under restrictions and even suffered expulsions. A rapid growth of the Jewish community began in the 18th century following expulsions of Jews from other Russian cities. About the middle of the 19th century Warsaw became one of the most influential Jewish centers in the diaspora. It became known for its *Yeshivot* (Talmudical academies); rabbinical and teachers' seminaries; Yiddish and Hebrew periodicals and dailies; Jewish publishing houses; and Zionist and Jewish socialist political parties. The tragic decline of the Jewish community in Warsaw began with the Nazi occupation in 1939. The last heroic stand of the Warsaw Jews against the Nazi hordes took place during the revolt of the Warsaw Ghetto in April 1943, when the remnants of the Jewish community perished as martyrs.

WARSHAWSKY, MARK (1848–1907)

Yiddish poet, author of popular Yiddish folk songs. Born in Russia, he practiced law, but devoted much of his time to the writing of Yiddish lyrics and melodies. Encouraged by his friends, and especially by Sholem Aleichem, he published his first collection of songs entitled "Yiddishe Folkslieder." His songs had an immediate and phenomenal success among the Jewish masses the world over. To this day his well-known "Oifen Pripetchuk" is among the most popular of Yiddish songs. His songs, like Yiddish folk songs in general, depict the intellectual life and the joys and sorrows of the Jews in the diaspora and reflect optimism and faith in a better future for the oppressed Jewish masses.

WAW

The sixth letter of the Hebrew alphabet is sometimes spelled in this manner. Its usual spelling is Vav. See *Vav*.

WEEKLY PORTION see Parashah.

WEEKS, FEAST OF see Shavuot.

WEISS, ISAAC HIRSCH (1815–1905)

Talmudist and literary historian. Born in Moravia, he moved to Vienna in 1858, where he subsequently became a lecturer at the *Bet ha-Midrash*. He is best known for his five-volume "History of Jewish Tradition" known in Hebrew as *Dor Dor Ve-Doreshav*, a history of the development of the *Oral Law* from Biblical times to the end of the Middle Ages. The book is known for its interesting style and for numerous biographies of leading rabbis of the Talmud. Despite the criticism leveled against its novel approach, it is nevertheless regarded as a good presentation of the growth and structure of the Oral Law.

WEIZMANN, CHAIM (1874–1952)

Leader of world Zionism, first president of the State of Israel and distinguished chemist. Born in Poland, he was educated in Germany, and became lecturer in biological chemistry at the University of Manchester, England in 1903. He became interested in Zionism early in life, was active in the *Hovevei Zion* (Lovers of Zion) movement in Russia, and later became one of the followers of Theodor Herzl. An advocate of Hebrew culture and of democratic procedure, Weizmann formed the first Zionist party, the "Democratic Faction," which advocated a synthesis of Hebrew cultural activities and political Zionism. After Herzl's death Weizmann became the spokesman for those Zionists who wanted to combine practical work in Palestine with diplomatic and political Zionist activity. His valuable dis-

Harry S. Truman, president of the United States, holds a Torah given him by Chaim Weizmann, the first president of the State of Israel. This presentation took place shortly after Truman granted recognition to the newly born state.

coveries in chemistry and his services to the British government during World War I made him many friends among British statesmen. His prestige and influence, and those of other leading Jews, were instrumental in securing the Balfour Declaration, issued by the British government in 1917, guaranteeing the establishment of a "Jewish National Homeland" in Palestine. In 1920 he was elected president of the World Zionist Organization, an office which he held until 1931, and again from 1935 until 1948. In accordance with the provisions of the British mandate, Weizmann enlarged the Jewish Agency for Palestine by enlisting non-Zionist Jewish leaders in support of work which had to be undertaken in the Jewish homeland.

Weizmann constantly sought collaboration with the Mandatory Power, having faith that Britain would keep its pledge to help in the establishment of the Jewish homeland. However, when the Passfield White Paper was issued in 1930, limiting Jewish immigration into Palestine, he resigned as head of the Jewish Agency in protest. In the ensuing years Weizmann became known as the "ambassador" of the Zionist movement, working unremittingly for the creation of a better political climate for the aspirations of Zionism. He visited the United States almost annually in behalf of the Zionist cause. At the end of World War II he appeared before the United Nations, pleading for the establishment of a Jewish state in part of Palestine to provide a home for the remnants of the annihilated Jewish communities of Europe, and for the fulfillment of the Jewish dream of national restoration. With the establishment of the State of Israel in 1948, Weizmann became its first president. The Daniel Sieff Research Institute, founded by him in Rehovot, Israel, of which he was the director for many years, is now the Weizmann Research Institute.

WESSELY, NAPHTALI HERZ (1725–1805)

Hebrew poet, and champion of the *Haskalah* movement in Germany and Austria. Born in Hamburg, he wrote a Hebrew philological work *Gan Naul* in 1756, and after moving to Berlin became a close friend of Moses Mendelssohn whom he helped spread the "enlightenment" movement in Germany. For this purpose he wrote a widely read book *Divre Shalom Ve-Emet* (Words of Peace and Truth), in which he urged the Jews of Austria to use the opportunity given to them through the *Edict of Toleration* by Emperor Joseph II, and embark upon a program of modern education and the study of languages and sciences. Another of his works was *Shire Tiferet*, a heroic Hebrew poem in five parts about the Biblical Exodus, in which he expressed the ideas and aspirations of the German Haskalah. His Hebrew works later served as a model for other Hebrew writers.

WESTERN WALL see Wailing Wall.

WIERNICK, PETER (1865–1936)

Pioneer in Yiddish journalism in America, historian and literary critic. Born in Vilna, Lithuania, he settled in the United States in 1885, and six years later became the editor of the *Jewish Morning Journal*, the first Yiddish orthodox daily newspaper in the United States. Wiernick wrote in Yiddish, Hebrew and English, and for over three decades he continued to make a lasting contribution to Yiddish journalism. He wrote in English a *History of the Jews in America* (1912), and also edited *Der Amerikaner*, a Yiddish weekly.

WIG see Sheitel.

Isaac Mayer Wise, American rabbi, author and college president, founder of "The American Israelite," the oldest Jewish weekly in America, the Hebrew Union College, and the Union of American Hebrew Congregations. He was the country's leading proponent of reform Judaism.

WILNO see Vilna.

WISDOM LITERATURE

Ancient Hebrew literature, including the Biblical books of *Proverbs*, *Job*, and *Ecclesiastes*, and non-canonical books *Sirach*, *Wisdom of Solomon*, and *IV Maccabees*. Each example of this type of religious literature, besides having an artistic aim of its own, is known for its careful examination of human conduct and values, such as education, honesty, prudence, industry and friendship.

WISE, ISAAC MAYER (1819–1900)

One of the pioneers of reform Judaism in America. Born in Bohemia, he emigrated to the United States in 1846 and served for two years as rabbi in Albany, New York, and thereafter in Cincinnati, Ohio. Rabbi Wise distinguished himself as an outstanding Jewish personality, and his activities in behalf of the reform movement were manifold. From his pulpit and through his popular lectures and the weekly newspaper the "American Israelite," which he edited, he discussed the point of view of reform Judaism and many other subjects of Jewish interest. In 1873 he organized the Union of American Hebrew Congregations; in 1875 he founded the Hebrew Union College in Cincinnati, of which he was president until his death; and in 1889 he organized the Central Conference of American Rabbis. Rabbi Wise advocated the introduction of new practices in matters of religion. He wrote a reform prayer book, *Minhag America*, which was replaced in 1894 by the *Union Prayer Book*. Among his many books on theological and historical subjects were: *Judaism, Its Doctrines and Duties* (1872); *History of the Hebrew's Second Commonwealth* (1880); *Judaism and Christianity, Their Agreements and Disagreements* (1883); *Defense of Judaism* (1889).

WISE, STEPHEN SAMUEL (1874–1949)

American reform rabbi, communal and Zionist leader. Born in Budapest, Hungary, he was brought to the United States at the age of one. He received his Ph.D. at Columbia University, and became rabbi at Portland, Oregon. An advocate of absolute freedom of expression from the pulpit, he founded the Free Synagogue in New York City in 1907 and served there for the rest of his life. Because of his liberal views and his great talent as a preacher and orator, the Free Synagogue became an influential institution in American Jewish life. Wise's interests and activities extended beyond Jewish affairs, and he became known as an advocate of social betterment, woman's suffrage, child labor reforms and international peace. One of his greatest contributions to the Jewish community was his Zionist activities and leadership. He was one of the founders of the Federation of American Zionists, which later became the Zionist Organization of America. He represented Zionist interests at the Versailles Peace Conference, and served as chairman of the United Palestine Appeal. A believer in the principles of democracy, he was one of the founders of the American Jewish Congress. To provide training of liberal rabbis and leaders in Jewish education and social services, he founded the Jewish Institute of Religion in 1922. Rabbi Wise's leadership was especially effective during the years of the Nazi terror in Germany, and during World War II. He devoted all of his time and energy to Jewish and American interests. In recognition of his devoted and unselfish leadership he was given many honors both in the United States and abroad. Wise was the editor of *Opinion*, a monthly journal of Jewish interest, and author of several books.

WIZO

Abbreviated name of the Women's Inter-national Zionist Organization, founded in 1920 for the purpose of promoting vocational and agricultural training for pioneer women in Israel; initiating child welfare programs, and supporting *Keren Ha-Yesod* and *Keren Kayemet*. WIZO has since established agricultural and training schools for girls in Israel; founded domestic science schools, child-care centers, and training programs in useful crafts for the mothers. It maintains infant welfare stations, playgrounds, summer camps and milk centers; conducts evening classes for teachers and office workers, and operates cooperative shops for the production and sale of the products of Israeli home industry. There are WIZO branches in almost every country except the United States, where these activities were taken over by Hadassah.

WOLF, SIMON (1836–1923)

Lawyer and prominent Jewish communal leader. Born in Germany, he settled in the United States in 1848. As a practicing lawyer in Washington, D.C., Wolf came to be known as the "Ambassador of the Jews of the U.S.A. to Washington." Before the organization of the American Jewish Committee (1906), Wolf was the spokesman of American Jewry representing the B'nai B'rith and other Jewish groups. A friend of three Presidents of the United States, he influenced the Government to intervene in behalf of the persecuted Jews of Rumania and Russia, and saved thousands of Jewish immigrants from deportation. Wolf was the first Jew to hold an important diplomatic post in the United States by serving as

Stephen S. Wise, reform rabbi, Zionist leader, noted writer and lecturer. The founder of the Jewish Institute of Religion, the American Jewish Congress and New York's Free Synagogue, Wise also staunchly defended world Jewry, reform Judaism and liberal democratic causes.

Consul General to Egypt. When Jewish patriotism was questioned, Wolf wrote *The American Jew as Patriot, Soldier, and Citizen* (1895), in which he proved on the basis of records of the army and navy that more than 6,000 Jews fought for the Union in the Civil War.

WOLFFSOHN, DAVID (1856–1914)

Zionist leader. Born in Russia, he moved to East Prussia where he became a prominent merchant. He was a close friend of Theodor Herzl, and using his knowledge of financial affairs, he served the Zionist cause in many important capacities. In 1898 he founded the Jewish Colonial Trust in London, a bank which assisted in colonization activities in Palestine. In 1898 the Zionists accepted his suggestion of the blue and white color scheme for the Zionist flag, symbolizing the traditional prayer shawl. After Herzl's death he was elected president of the World Zionist Organization, and continued to serve in that office until 1911.

WOMEN, ROLE OF

The status and role of women in Jewish life might be characterized by the phrase, "What is apparently true is not actually the case." Their ritual obligations are small, but Jewish women have always held an important and respected place in their families and in their communities. Whatever the ritual limitations women had to bow to, their influence could be felt. Deborah the prophetess, Miriam who was sister to Moses, and Sarah, Rebekah, Rachel and Leah, wives of the Patriarchs, are heroic examples in Jewish history.

Jewish women have a very special place in Jewish life, that of creating the family, of binding it together, of perpetuating its traditions and customs and of teaching the young to carry on the cycle. Long ago, women did not study formally because

they had much else to learn to prepare them for their special role. Women were not bidden to carry out all the commandments because their time was needed in performing their special tasks. The men prayed in the synagogues, and the women brought the ritual to the home.

Today Jewish women, like other women, can and do study, can and do achieve equality with men in the business world. But the Jewish woman still has not lost her special place in Jewish life. In the home, in school groups and community groups, and through increased participation in synagogue activities, Jewish women continue to earn the same respect they have had since earliest Jewish times.

WORKMEN'S CIRCLE (ARBEITER RING)

A fraternal order of the Jewish labor movement in the United States and Canada, chartered in 1900. Organized by Yiddish speaking immigrants from eastern Europe, it provides its members with life insurance and sickness and funeral benefits, as well as with social and cultural activities and projects. The Workmen's Circle has a membership of over 70,000 with branches in all major Jewish communities in the United States and Canada. Its educational activities and institutions include summer camps, lyceums, choruses, orchestras, dramatic groups and forums. It is particularly concerned with promoting Jewish elementary and secondary education, and it maintains throughout the United States and Canada some 150 Yiddish schools, where Yiddish, Jewish history, ceremonies, and current events are taught. The Workmen's Circle is closely affiliated with the trade union movement and it has been particularly active in the promotion of the welfare of the Jewish masses in the United States and elsewhere. It also maintains English speaking branches to serve the needs of the American born. The Workmen's Circle publishes *Der Freind* (The Friend) and the *Workmen's Circle Call*, monthly journals, and its education committee publishes *Kultur un Dertziung* (Culture and Education), as well as Yiddish textbooks, children's literature in Yiddish, and other educational materials for teachers and pupils.

WORLD JEWISH CONGRESS

An association representing Jewish communities and organizations the world over, founded in 1936 for the purpose of defending Jewish rights. The headquarters of the World Jewish Congress is in New York City, with other offices maintained in several capital cities in Europe, South America and Australia.

WORSHIP see Prayer.

WRITTEN LAW

The *Written Law* is the Torah which, tradition tells us, God revealed to Moses on Mount Sinai. It is also called the "Five Books of Moses," or "Pentateuch," comprising the first division of the Bible. The second and third divisions of the Bible also have authority in Jewish life. For example, the minor fast days in the course of the year were instituted by the Prophets (in the second division of the Bible, called *Neviim*); and Purim was instituted by Mordecai and Esther (in the third division of the Bible, called *Ketuvim*). The Hebrew term for Written Law is *Torah Shebikhetav*. See *Oral Law; Torah*.

Y

YAD

. . . and I heard a voice of one that spoke.

And he said unto me,

"Son of man, stand upon thy feet,

And I will speak unto thee."

EZEKIEL

YAD

A Torah ornament usually fashioned out of silver in the form of a hand with a pointed index finger. Because of the reverence in which the Torah Scroll is held, it is considered inappropriate to touch the parchment with one's finger. Instead, a *Yad* (hand) is used to point to the proper place while reading the Torah. Through the centuries there have been *Yadim* made with such skill and beauty that they have been regarded as works of art.

YAD HA-ḤAZAKAH see Maimonides, Moses.

YAHRZEIT see Yortzeit.

YAHVEH (YAHWEH) see Tetragrammaton.

YAMIM NORAIM see Festivals.

YARMULKE see Ceremonial Objects, Jewish.

YAVNEH

Known in Greek as Jamnia, it is the name of an ancient historically important city in Palestine, which became a center of learning shortly before the destruction of the Second Temple. The Talmud tells that the *Tanna* Rabbi Johanan ben Zakkai was given permission by the Romans to preserve a *Yeshivah* at Yavneh, located near the Mediterranean coast between Jaffa and Ashkelon. After the destruction of the Temple, Yavneh became the seat of the *Sanhedrin* (High Court), and the center of Jewish spiritual and intellectual life. In Jewish history Yavneh has become the symbol of Jewish spiritual survival. On the site of the ancient city of Yavneh there exists a small Arab town named Yebna, which is a part of the territory of the State of Israel. In English Bible translation the name is rendered as Jabneh.

YEHOASH (1870–1927)

Pen name of Solomon Bloomgarten, noted Yiddish poet. Born in Lithuania, he settled in the United States in 1891. His poetic works were prolific and universally acclaimed. Together with Dr. C. D. Spivak he compiled a dictionary of the Hebrew elements in Yiddish (1911), considered as a major contribution to the study of the Yiddish language. Yehoash is also remembered for his excellent and authentic Yiddish translation of the Hebrew Bible, to which he devoted the major portion of the last ten years of his life.

YELLOW BADGE see Badge, Jewish.

YEMEN

A Moslem country in the southwest of the Arabian peninsula which before World War II had about 90,000 Jews in a general population of about three million. Tradition recounts that Jews lived in Yemen from the destruction of the First Temple. There seems to be little doubt that during the fifth century there were many Jews in Yemen, and that for a long time some Yemenite rulers were Jews. However, thereafter, from the tenth century, the Yemenite Jews lived under restrictive laws of the Moslem rulers, often exposed to massacres and forced conversions. Because of their bitter suffering Maimonides wrote his famous letter of consolation and advice addressed to the Jews of Yemen. At the end of the 19th century large numbers of Yemenite Jews began to emigrate to Palestine. Following the establishment of the State of Israel in 1948, most Jews of Yemen were saved from increased Arab persecution through mass immigration to Israel. These Jews were taken from a medieval life, ushered on to airplanes and flown to their destination "on the wings of eagles," in the migration referred to as Operation Magic Carpet. Most Yemenite

Yemenite bride before her wedding ceremony in Israel wears traditional headgear which is a fine example of Yemenite handiwork. In 1948, Yemenite Jews were taken to Israel in a mass exodus by air called "Operation Magic Carpet."

Advanced Yeshivah student pores over the "Gemara" and Rabbinic commentaries. For ages, the Yeshivah has been the traditional school of higher learning, Talmud study, and preparation for the rabbinate.

Jews in Israel are manual laborers and porters, and are well adjusted citizens. They are intensely religious, speak Hebrew with a rhythm of their own, and preserve much of their ritual, musical and cultural traditions. In 1960 about 3,500 Jews still remained in Yemen.

YESHIVAH

Hebrew term meaning "Talmudical Academy," or the traditional institution of higher Jewish learning. Talmud academies or *Yeshivot* early became important centers of learning both in Palestine and Babylonia. Centuries later *Yeshivot* (under this or other names) existed in most major Jewish communities in the diaspora, as for example, in France, Italy, Poland, Lithuania, and others. Each lecturer of the Yeshivah was called *Rosh Yeshivah* (Head of

the Yeshivah). In more recent centuries, with Yiddish the language of instruction and social intercourse, the students were called in Yiddish *Yeshivah Bahurim* (Yeshivah students, since the word Yeshivah may mean any group of students sitting and learning rabbinics). Such students were often poor and needed the assistance of scholarships from the community for their food and lodging. When they acquired adequate knowledge, some of them received *Semikhah* (ordination) and entered the practical rabbinate. In the United States the most famous orthodox institution of higher learning is the *Rabbi Isaac Elchanan Theological Seminary* in New York, now one of the affiliates of *Yeshiva University*. Some schools, offering an elementary curriculum, call themselves *Yeshivot Ketannot* (sing. *Yeshivah Ketannah*).

Exterior of Yeshiva University's main building in New York City. Founded as a rabbinical school, Yeshiva has grown to a university of arts and sciences, many faculties, graduate and professional schools.

YESHIVA UNIVERSITY

America's oldest and largest university under Jewish auspices, comprises 17 schools and divisions providing undergraduate, graduate, and professional studies in the arts and sciences and Jewish learning. Situated at six centers in New York City, it offers preparation for careers in the orthodox rabbinate, medicine, education, social work, mathematics, physics, psychology and many other fields. In 1960 Yeshiva University had 5,000 students (men and women), and a faculty of 850. The University also sponsors several community service agencies and a program of research and experimentation; it also publishes scholarly journals and books in various fields. The Yeshiva Eitz Chaim Talmudical Academy was established in 1886 and the Yeshiva R. Isaac Elchanan Theo-

logical Seminary in 1896. In 1915 they merged, in 1928 the name Yeshiva College was adopted and in 1945 Yeshiva University. In 1929 the institution moved from the Lower East Side to its present main center on Amsterdam Avenue. Among the more recently established schools of Yeshiva University are Stern College for Women (1954), Albert Einstein College of Medicine (1955), Sue Golding Graduate Division of Medical Sciences (1957), Graduate School of Education (1957), School of Social Work (1957), and the Graduate School of Mathematical Sciences (1958), which was expanded into the Graduate School of Science in 1960.

YETZER HA-RA

Hebrew term for "evil inclination." According to Jewish tradition man is born with two inclinations, the inclination or the impulse to do the right (*Yetzer ha-Tov*), and the inclination to do wrong (*Yetzer ha-Ra*). Man has the free will to choose between the two opposing inclinations. The rabbis taught that it was the duty of every person to acquire the knowledge and the character for developing the Yetzer ha-Tov. Devotion to the study of Torah was the best way to achieve this goal. However, the significance of the so-called evil inclination was recognized; without it, the rabbis say, there would be no passion, no marrying, no ambition, no building of cities, no civilization. Intrinsically the Yetzer ha-Ra is not necessarily bad. The manner in which a man responds to it determines its ethical value.

YETZER TOV

The "good inclination." See *Yetzer ha-Ra.*

YIDDISH

Second only to Hebrew, the most important of all the languages spoken by Jews the world over. Before Hitler's annihilation of about six million Jews, Yiddish was spoken by about 12 million people. Other names by which Yiddish is known are: *Ivre Teitch* (Hebrew-German), *Mamme-Loshen* (mother tongue). The term "Jewish" as often applied to *Yiddish* by English speaking Jews is a misnomer since it implies that it is the only language of the Jewish people and since also the word "Jewish" covers more than language. Some people called Yiddish "jargon" under the mistaken impression that it was not a language in its own right.

The history of the Yiddish language dates back (according to some authorities) to the 10th or the 11th century when in the German provinces of the Rhineland, Jews speaking the local German dialects intermingled Hebrew expressions for religious and intellectual concepts. Yiddish has since undergone its own development, especially after the migration of the Jews from the German provinces and their subsequent settlement in Poland, the Ukraine, and other east European countries. In addition to the numerous Hebrew elements (about 20 per cent) contained in Yiddish, some other elements from the languages of the countries where Jews lived (mainly Slavic words) were gradually adopted.

Printed and written in Hebrew characters, Yiddish became the vernacular of the Jewish masses. In writing, Yiddish was first used for the making of a popular literature for those who had little knowledge of Hebrew (especially women). In modern times, however, Yiddish became the medium of expression of many outstanding writers who created a great modern Yiddish literature. It has been and still is used as a cultural and educational vehicle for many Jews, especially in North and South America. Despite the decline in the number of Yiddish-speaking Jews, there are still several million Jews the world over who speak Yiddish, read Yiddish newspapers and periodicals, attend Yiddish theatres, and many who send their children to Yiddish elementary and higher schools to study.

During the 19th century, with the revival of Hebrew as a spoken language, many Jews wrote and spoke both Hebrew and Yiddish, and used them in their creative efforts. However, some were afraid that Hebrew would never attain adequate support if Yiddish were continued, and, others were afraid that Yiddish would die if Hebrew gained a permanent foothold among the people. This struggle between Hebraists and Yiddishists was reflected in the early days of the State of Israel when certain restrictive regulations were made with regard to a Yiddish press. Now Hebrew is not only the official language of the State but is also the vernacular of most of the population, and the Hebraists, seeing no danger to Hebrew, have significantly eased off restrictions against Yiddish which they had always loved. The old time Hebraists in the State of Israel had never forgotten Yiddish as their mother tongue. Jews have always been multi-lingual, ever since the Second Commonwealth era when Aramaic began to displace Hebrew in secular life. There is no reason to doubt the future of multi-lingualism, or at least bi-lingualism among the Jews of Israel.

YIDDISH SCIENTIFIC INSTITUTE

Known by its abbreviated Yiddish name YIVO, it was founded in Vilna (1925), and moved to New York City after the outbreak of World War II. The major purpose of YIVO is to collect materials relating to Jewish life, and to carry on research in fields of Yiddish literature, language, history, and economics. It has four major research sections; history, economics and statistics; literature and linguistics; psychology and education. Each section is headed by a research secretary. Although YIVO conducts its research in Yiddish, it has recently published many works in English for non-Yiddish speaking persons. Its major publications are: *Yivo Bleter*, a bimonthly devoted to studies in all fields of research; *Yidishe Shprakh*, on the problems of standard Yiddish; and *Yedies Fun Yivo*, a news bulletin about the activities of YIVO. Other important works published by YIVO are: *A History of the Jewish Labor Movement in the United States; A Thesaurus of the Yiddish Language*, by Nahum Stutchkoff; and *Hitler's Professors*, by Max Weinreich. The library and the archives of the YIVO include tens of thousands of documents, books, leaflets, pamphlets, periodicals, and collections of life histories, private letters, photographs, all bearing on Jewish life and history, especially those relating to the Jewish communities which perished during World War II.

YIGDAL

The opening word of a Hebrew hymn dealing with the thirteen articles of faith, recited or chanted at the beginning of the daily morning prayer by the Ashkenazim, and at the conclusion of services on Sabbaths and festivals, particularly by Sephardim. It is a 15th century composition, probably by Daniel ben Judah Dayan.

YISHUV

Hebrew term meaning "settlement," commonly applied to a Jewish community, especially to the Jewish settlement or the Jewish community in Palestine. Since the establishment of the State of Israel, the term has fallen into disuse.

YIVO see Yiddish Scientific Institute.

YIZKOR

Memorial Service for the dead recited in the synagogue on the eighth day of *Pesaḥ* (Passover), the second day of *Shavuot* (Feast of Weeks), *Yom Kippur* (Day of Atonement), and *Shemini Atzeret* (The Eighth day of Sukkot). The ritual is also called *Hazkarat Neshamot* (remembering the souls).

YMHA

Abbreviated name of Young Men's Hebrew Association. The corresponding organization for women is called YWHA. Most of the "Y" organizations later became known as Jewish Community Centers, although some retained the original names of YMHA and YWHA. See *Center, the Jewish*.

YMHA AND JEWISH COMMUNITY CENTER, WORLD FEDERATION OF

Founded in 1946 as an alliance of the

national associations of YMHAs, Jewish Community Centers and other Jewish youth-serving agencies. In 1960 it had affiliates in 17 countries of North and South America, Europe, Asia and Australia. The Federation maintains headquarters in offices of the National Jewish Welfare Board in New York City, its United States affiliate, which provides most of the Federation's budget. The Federation provides technical and program guidance to its affiliates and fosters the growth of these centers. It also helps maintain the Jerusalem YMHA and YWHA.

YOD (')

The tenth letter of the Hebrew alphabet. As a consonant it is sounded like the English consonantal Y in "yet." When it has no vowel of its own, it has a tendency to lengthen the preceding vowel.

The letter Yod is frequently pronounced *Yood*. Its numerical value is 10. Because it is the first letter of the Tetragrammaton, the sacred name of God, it may form in combination with other letters abbreviations of the Divine Name. Such combinations are avoided; thus instead of writing the number 15 as *Yod-Hé* (10 plus 5), which would have been the expected symbol but which would read YaH (the Holy Name), we subtract one from the Yod and add one to the Hé, and write *Tet-Vav* (9 plus 6) instead. Similarly 16 is written not *Yod-Vav* (10 plus 6), but *Tet-Zayin* (9 plus 7). In Greek, it is called Iota.

YOM HA-ATZMAUT see Israel Independence Day.

YOM KIPPUR

Hebrew for the *Day of Atonement*, the holiest and most solemn day in the Jewish religion. Enjoined in the Bible, where it is described as a "Sabbath of Solemn Rest," it falls on the 10th day of *Tishre* (September-October), and marks the culmination of the *Ten Penitential Days* which begin on Rosh

Youth Aliyah youngsters, in a mandolin band, give performances of classical and folk music.

Hashanah (New Year). Work as well as the taking of food and drink are strictly forbidden on Yom Kippur, which is spent in the synagogue in prayer for forgiveness of sins and reconciliation with both God and fellow man. The fast day begins prior to sunset, and the evening public services commence with the traditional prayer of *Kol Nidre*. The all-day services of Yom Kippur are concluded with the *Neilah* prayer, and the sounding of one blast of the *Shofar*. Yom Kippur is furthermore an important occasion for Jews to give *Tzedakah* (charity) for various causes. This charity is given on the day before the Holy Day. See *Sin*.

YOM TOV

Hebrew term meaning "a good day" used as a general designation for a Jewish holiday or festival. See *Festivals*.

YOOD see Yod.

YORTZEIT

Yiddish term for the anniversary of the death of parents and other close relatives. It is observed yearly on the day of the death by reciting the *Kaddish* in the synagogue and lighting the *Yortzeit Light*.

YOUNG ISRAEL

American organization of orthodox young

people founded in 1912 for the purpose of attracting Jewish youth to orthodox learning, practices and worship. In 1915 Young Israel organized a model synagogue at the Educational Alliance in New York City. The organization has since expanded having branches throughout the United States, and in 1960 it had a constituency of more than 50,000.

The National Council of Young Israel centralizes the various activities of the organization such as synagogue services, adult education, youth clubs, Zionist activities, and fund-raising for orthodox religious institutions.

YOUNG JUDEA

Zionist youth organization founded in 1909 and sponsored by the Zionist Organization of America and Hadassah. Young Judea had a 1960 membership of about 15,000 young people between the ages of ten and eighteen. It conducts educational, religious and physical activities, and it publishes a widely circulated monthly magazine, *The Young Judean.*

YOUTH ALIYAH

Hebrew name applied to the organized mass immigration of Jewish children and youth for settlement in Palestine. This immigration first started in 1934 when the Nazis came to power in Germany and it was necessary to find a place of refuge for Jewish children. The rescue work on a large scale was done under the leadership of Henrietta Szold.

When *Youth Aliyah* from Germany became a mass movement, especially between 1936 and 1939, the *Kibbutzim* in Palestine became the training centers for the young refugees. The early Nazi victories during the Second World War caused havoc and destruction in the Jewish communities of Europe, and groups of Jewish children escaped to Yugoslavia, Siberia, China, Eng-

land, while thousands of others perished in the ghettos. Only a few could find their way to Israel. With financial and technical help from *Hadassah*, the training program of the Youth Aliyah groups continued, and the graduates took over as settlers, as members of the *Haganah* (Israel Defense Army), and as recruits for the Jewish Brigade. In the years following World War II and the establishment of the State of Israel, the great wave of immigration into Israel brought thousands of all types of children to the shores of the new State.

There came children of displaced persons, "underground" children, Jewish children raised by Christians, delinquent children, children who were mentally and physically ill, and lastly, great numbers of Jewish children from the Arab countries.

The present Youth Aliyah program in Israel aims at preparing youth for life in agricultural settlements; training skilled workers and specialists for Israel's growing industry; raising the cultural level of Israel's "melting pot," and preparing them for the defense of the State. By 1960 over 95,000 Jewish children, from 72 countries, had passed through Youth Aliyah. In the same year there were over 12,000 youth in training in 250 Youth Aliyah villages, Kibbutzim, and special schools and centers.

YUGOSLAVIA

Balkan country where 75,000 Jews lived prior to World War II. The Jewish population concentrated in Zagreb, Belgrade and Sarajevo and in other larger cities. Prior to World War II it was one of the few European countries unaffected by anti-Semitism. The occupation of Yugoslavia by the Nazis in 1941 brought an end to the Jewish community. In 1960 there remained of the once flourishing community only about 7,000 Jews.

YURTZEIT see Yortzeit.

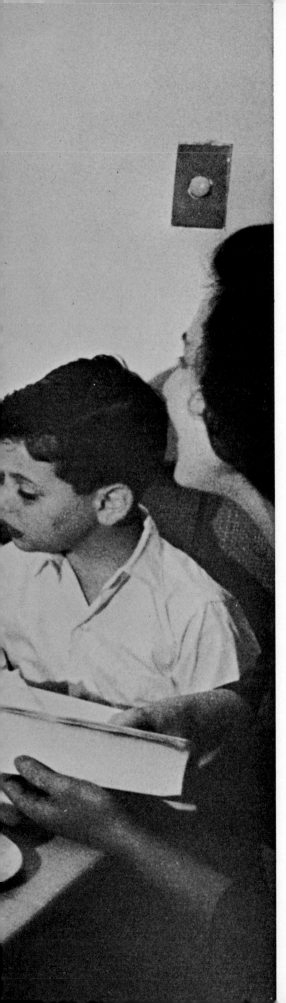

Z

ZEMIROT

. . . and he will turn the heart of the parents to the children and the heart of the children to the parents.

MALACHI

ZADDIK see Ḥasidism.

ZAMENHOF, LUDWIG LAZAR (1859–1917)

Founder of the universal language, Esperanto. Born in Poland, where he studied and practiced medicine, he became internationally famous for his life work devoted to the development of a universal auxiliary language. In 1887 he published his plan and views on the new language based on only 900 root words with a simplified grammar containing only sixteen rules. Zamenhof's pen name "Esperanto" was adopted as the name for the universal language, the acceptance of which was designed to create better international communication and understanding. Well trained in Jewish culture, Zamenhof was fully aware that his aspiration for universal peace was grounded in Hebraic idealism. The idea of Esperanto had a phenomenal success, and following the first international Esperanto Congress held in France in 1905, Zamenhof became the recognized leader of the Esperanto movement in Europe and America despite anti-Semitic attacks on its founder. Many journals and original books in Esperanto have been published, and translations of the best classical literature, including an Esperanto translation of the Bible, were made. The Esperanto movement has millions of followers the world over, and its founder was honored in many countries. In the Esperanto language, the word "Esperanto" itself means "he who hopes."

ZANGWILL, ISRAEL (1864–1926)

Novelist and Jewish leader. Born and reared in the Jewish quarter in London, he carved a literary career for himself as a contributor to the Anglo-Jewish press. From 1888 he became a well-known novelist. Closely associated with the life of east European immigrant Jews, he was commissioned to write a novel for the Jewish

Israel Zangwill, Anglo-Jewish writer, whose work earned him the title of the "Jewish Dickens."

Publication Society of America. He thereupon published *The Children of the Ghetto,* a portrayal of Jewish life in the east end section of London. This novel proved so successful that Zangwill sought further literary expression based on themes of the Jewish environment. Continued success brought Zangwill fame as the "Jewish Dickens." Among his other well-known works of Jewish content were: *Dreamers of the Ghetto, The Voice of Jerusalem, Ghetto Tragedies, King of the Schnorrers,* and *The Melting Pot.*

His literary work, especially that dealing with Jewish life, was accompanied by an intensification of Zangwill's interest in Jewish affairs. He became an active Zionist and one of Herzl's followers. However, he broke away from the Zionist movement in 1905, and became the champion of the territorialist movement and founder and president of the Jewish Territorial Organization (ITO) which functioned until 1925. Through his literary activities, his wit, his Jewish leadership and his great humanitarianism, Zangwill was one of the outstanding Jewish personalities of the first quarter of the 20th century.

ZAYIN (ז)

The seventh letter of the Hebrew alphabet. It is sounded like the English Z, and its numerical value is 7.

ZEALOTS

A name generally applied to devoted Jewish patriots, called in Hebrew *Kannaim,* who zealously defend the honor of God and Israel. Specifically the term applies to the members of an extremist party, which was active for a period of some 100 years before the destruction of the Second Temple by the Romans (70 c.e.). The *Zealots* were bitterly opposed to the Roman rulers in Judea, and occasionally resorted to violence and sometimes even assassination. Because they carried a *Sica* or dagger, the Romans called them *Sicarii.*

ZEBULUN

The sixth son of Jacob and Leah, and ancestor of the Israelite tribe of the same name. This tribe dwelt in the northern part of Israel; tradition speaks of it as a sea-faring tribe. *Zebulun* is mentioned in the song of Deborah as one of the tribes which fought valiantly in the battle which resulted in the defeat of Sisera.

ZECHARIAH

The eleventh of the *Twelve Minor Prophets,* who together with the prophet Haggai preached the rebuilding of the Temple. He flourished during the period following the return from the Babylonian captivity.

ZEMIROT

Hebrew term for the liturgical hymns traditionally chanted during meals on the Sabbath. Some of the *Zemirot* are anonymous compositions; some others were written by known Hebrew poets of the period of the Crusades; and still others, written in Aramaic, date to the 16th century. Of the best known *Zemirot* are *Yah Ribbon Olam* (Lord, the Master of the Universe), *Tzur Mi-shello Akhalnu* (O Rock, from Whose Substance We Have Eaten), and *Yom Zeh Mekhubbad Mikkol Yamim* (This Day of Sabbath is Most Honored of Days).

ZEPHANIAH

One of the *Minor Prophets,* active in the days of Josiah, king of Judah. Living in Jerusalem, and probably of royal descent, Zephaniah denounced the people of Judah for their worship of foreign gods and for the practice of foreign customs. Prophesying God's inevitable punishment of Judah and other sinful nations, he hopefully foresaw Israel's ultimate salvation.

ZERAIM

Hebrew term meaning "seeds," the name of the first division of the *Mishnah.* It contains eleven tractates, most of which deal with the laws and regulations pertaining to charity and agriculture. The first tractate, *Berakhot,* deals with the laws of blessings and prayer.

ZERUBBABEL

Prince of Judah and leader of the Jews who returned from the Babylonian exile. Urged by the prophets Haggai and Zechariah, Zerubbabel took steps for the rebuilding of the Temple in Jerusalem (537 b.c.e.). Acting as governor of Judah, according to tradition, he later returned to Babylon. According to some sources he was to have been proclaimed king of Judah, but was put to death before then by the Persians.

ZHITLOWSKY, CHAIM (1865–1943)

Philosopher of the Yiddish culture movement; advocate of Jewish autonomy in the diaspora, and socialist theoretician. Born in Russia, he was one of the founders of the Russian Socialist Revolutionary Party, and sought a solution to the problems of the Jewish masses in the establishment of a socialist order in the countries where they lived. He opposed the early Zionist movement called *Hibbat Zion*, and advocated the establishment of Jewish national cultural enclaves in the countries of their dispersion, with Yiddish as the Jewish national language. Zhitlowsky became a prominent figure of the Yiddishist and Jewish socialist movements in the United States, where he settled in 1908 and became editor of *Dos Neie Leben* (New Life) and later a literary contributor to *The Day*, a Yiddish daily newspaper. His philosophy and ideas on Jewish survival are embodied in his works, published in twenty-nine volumes. An outstanding lecturer, he appeared before large and eager audiences in almost every sizeable Jewish community in the United States and Canada. His program appears in "Thoughts on the Historic Destiny of the Jews."

ZINBERG, ISRAEL (1873–1943)

Yiddish literary historian. Born in Russia, he settled in St. Petersburg (now Leningrad) where he worked as a chemical engineer. At the same time he was a devoted student of Jewish literature, and became known as a literary critic. He published a history of the Jewish press in Russia and was editor of the section on Hebrew and Yiddish literature in the Jewish Encyclopedia published in the Russian language. Zinberg's literary lifework however, is his *Geschichte fun der Literatur bei Yidn* (History of Jewish Literature), the first volume of which he published in 1929; nine more appeared by 1943.

ZION

Originally the name of one of the hills in Jerusalem, it was subsequently used as a poetical term for the Holy City itself, or for the Land of Israel. From it was derived the term *Zionism*, describing the movement which advocated the return of the Jewish people to its historic land.

ZIONISM

The movement aiming to establish in *Eretz Israel* (the Land of Israel) an autonomous Jewish national home or state. The longing of the Jewish people to return to its historic homeland is as old as the Jewish dispersion, which began after the destruction of Jerusalem by the Romans (70 c.e.). Throughout the centuries the desire to return to *Zion* (poetic name for Palestine) found its expression in the daily prayers of the Jews and in messianic movements headed by *false messiahs*. Throughout the centuries, Jews singly or in small groups, migrated to Palestine.

Not until modern times did these liturgical references to Zion and the visionary plans to return to the "Land of the Fathers" born in times of stress and extreme oppression convert into a realistic and practical program of Jewish colonization in Palestine. In the 18th and the 19th centuries Jewish and even non-Jewish leaders issued pronouncements and formulated projects of Jewish colonization of Palestine and made proposals for the establishment of an autonomous national home. The earliest and most important mass movement of Jewish colonization in Palestine began during the 19th century in England, Germany, Russia and Austria,

Chaim Zhitlowsky, prominent in the Socialist and Yiddishist movements in the U.S., was also one of the founders of the Russian Socialist Revolutionary movement. Against Zionism, he called on Jews to organize their own national cultural enclaves in diaspora for their survival.

In this casino in Basle, Switzerland, the first Zionist Congress, convened by Theodor Herzl in 1897, was held. Here, Zionism as a political movement began, and ultimately led to establishment of Israel.

under the over-all name of *Hibbat Zion* (Love of Zion).

Zionism as a political movement of world Jewry began with the first Zionist Congress held in Basle in 1897, convened by the father of political Zionism, Theodor Herzl. The Congress adopted the "Basle Program" which aimed to create for the Jewish people a home in Palestine secured by public law. The World Zionist Organization attempted to win the approval of the world powers for the political aspirations of Zionism, and in the meantime to initiate colonization projects in Palestine, which until 1918 was under Turkish rule. However, the tireless efforts of Herzl and his followers to persuade the Sultan to grant a charter for a Jewish state in Palestine were unsuccessful, and colonization schemes in territories other than Palestine were rejected by the Zionist leaders representing the Jewish masses in eastern Europe. The first official recognition of

Zionist efforts came with the issuance of the *Balfour Declaration* by the British Government in 1917. This declaration assured the establishment of a national home in Palestine for the Jewish people, and offered to facilitate the achievement of that objective. In 1920 Britain received the League of Nations mandate over Palestine. As a result, a large scale colonization program began through Jewish mass-migrations, the establishment of colonies, cities, schools, and the development of agricultural and industrial projects. Despite the opposition of the Arabs, and the often unfriendly policies of the British administration, the Jewish population in Palestine grew from about 70,000 in 1918 to about 500,000 at the outbreak of World War II. In 1947 the United Nations approved the establishment of a Jewish State in part of Palestine, and in 1948 the British surrendered the mandate. The birth of the State of Israel was proclaimed on the 5th day of

The second Zionist Congress of 1898 in Basle was responsible for the Jewish Colonial Trust, financial organ of Zionism which facilitated the establishment of a national homeland for Jews in Palestine.

the month of Iyar, 5708 (May 14, 1948), and immediately thereafter, seven Arab nations invaded the new State. Israel fought heroically in the War of Liberation, and after the defeat of the invaders, an uneasy armistice was signed. In 1960 Israel had a Jewish population of over two million.

With the establishment of the State of Israel, the political aspirations of Zionism were attained. However, the Zionist movement still had the significant task of assisting Israel in its continuing struggle for economic security, and the additional task of developing a cultural bridge between Israel and the Jewish communities in the diaspora. See *Herzl, Theodor.*

ZIONIST ORGANIZATION

The World Zionist Organization was created by Theodor Herzl in 1897. The members were all persons who identified themselves with the program of Zionism. Local Zionist groups are affiliated with various national federations, such as *General Zionists, Poale Zion* (Labor Zionists), *Mizrachi* (Orthodox Zionists). The members of these federations elect their representatives to the Zionist Congress held each two years. From 1929 the Zionist Organization has worked through the Jewish Agency for Palestine, and the president of the World Zionist Organization is also the president of the Jewish Agency. The Executive of the Zionist Organization is divided into various departments dealing separately with political work, immigration, finance and culture.

ZOHAR

Hebrew title of the fundamental work of Jewish mysticism, known as *Kabbalah.* It was first published in Spain by Moses de Leon (1250-1305), who brought it to the attention of the general public. He ascribed the work to Rabbi Simeon ben Yoḥai, second century c.e., the great

Tanna who was famed for piety and his interest in mysticism. Many scholars believe that the *Zohar*, a compilation of materials based on diverse themes, was drawn from various sources and is not the literary work of any one man.

The Zohar, written partly in Hebrew and partly in Aramaic, is a mystical commentary on the *Pentateuch* (Five Books of Moses). It teaches how God, called by the Kabbalists *En Sof* (the "Endless"), rules the Universe through the *Ten Sefirot* (Ten Spheres). To the Kabbalists the Zohar was as holy as the Bible and the Talmud, and *Israel Baal Shem Tov*, founder of *Hasidism*, was also inspired and deeply affected by its teachings. The first printed edition of the Zohar appeared in 1556, and it has since been translated into a number of other languages, including Hebrew.

Zohar is concerned with interpreting the Bible in mystical and allegorical terms and had had wide influence among Jewish and Christian scholars. See *Kabbalah*.

ZOLA, ÉMILE see Dreyfus Affair.

ZUNZ, LEOPOLD (1794–1886)

Founder of the "Science of Judaism." Born in Germany, he was declared at the age of eleven a "genius in all branches of knowledge." He received his Ph.D. at the University of Berlin, and devoted himself to studies and research in various fields of Jewish knowledge. He and other scholars founded the "Association of Jewish Science and Culture." Zunz's major objective was to reveal to the Jewish and the non-Jewish academic world in a modern and scientific manner the treasures of Jewish literature and religion. His major works, written in German, are: *The Liturgical Poetry of the Middle Ages; Jewish Religious Sermons; On History and Literature; Jewish Names; Rashi;* and *Jewish Statistics*. Zunz was the first Jewish scholar to employ modern techniques of research, and he succeeded in uncovering facts of the past hitherto unknown. Zunz was held in great esteem by scholars in Europe and the United States and was characterized by the great poet, Heinrich Heine, as a "man of word and deed, who created and worked, where others dreamed."

Leopold Zunz, distinguished scholar, was the first to employ modern research techniques in Judaic scholarship. His aim was to reveal the treasures of Jewish literature and religion to the academic world. For this purpose, in 1822 he organized the "Science of Judaism" movement.